## THE WORLD'S CLASSICS

# THE WAY WE LIVE NOW

ANTHONY TROLLOPE (1815–82), the son of a failing London barrister, was brought up an awkward and unhappy youth amidst debt and privation. His mother maintained the family by writing, but Anthony's own first novel did not appear until 1847, when he had at length established a successful Civil Service career in the Post Office, from which he retired in 1867. After a slow start, he achieved fame, with 47 novels and some 16 other books, and sales sometimes topping 100,000. He was acclaimed an unsurpassed portraitist of the lives of the professional and landed classes, especially in his perennially popular *Chronicles of Barsetshire* (1855–67), and his six brilliant Palliser novels (1864–80). His fascinating *Autobiography* (1883) recounts his successes with an enthusiasm which stems from memories of a miserable youth. Throughout the 1870s he developed new styles of fiction, but was losing critical favour by the time of his death.

JOHN SUTHERLAND is Reader in English at University College London, and is the author of a number of books, including *Thackeray at Work* and *Victorian Novelists and Publishers*.

THE WORLD'S CLASSICS

ANTHONY TROLLOPE
# *The Way We Live Now*

*Edited by*
JOHN SUTHERLAND

Oxford New York Toronto Melbourne
OXFORD UNIVERSITY PRESS
1982

*Oxford University Press, Walton Street, Oxford* OX2 6DP
*London Glasgow New York Toronto*
*Delhi Bombay Calcutta Madras Karachi*
*Kuala Lumpur Singapore Hong Kong Tokyo*
*Nairobi Dar es Salaam Cape Town*
*Melbourne Auckland*

*and associate companies in*
*Beirut Berlin Ibadan Mexico City*

*Introduction, Notes and Appendix © John Sutherland 1982*
*Chronology © W. J. McCormack 1982*

*First published by Oxford University Press 1941 in two volumes*
*First issued as a World's Classic paperback with introduction and notes 1982*

*British Library Cataloguing in Publication Data*

*Trollope, Anthony*
*The way we live now.—(The World's classics)*
*I. Title  II. Sutherland, John*
*823'.8[F]  PR5684.T|*
*ISBN 0-19-281576-8*

*Library of Congress Cataloging in Publication Data*

*Trollope, Anthony, 1815–1882.*
*The way we live now. (The World's classics)*
*Originally published: Oxford: Oxford University Press, 1941.*
*I. Sutherland, John, 1903–  II. Title.*
*PR5684.W3 1982  823'.8  81–18729*
*ISBN 0-19-281576-8 (pbk.)  AACR2*

*Printed in Great Britain by*
*Hazell Watson & Viney Limited*
*Aylesbury, Bucks*

# CONTENTS

# INTRODUCTION

## I

In December 1872, Anthony Trollope returned to England. Braced by a year and a half in the colonies, he found the moral stench of London intolerable. Like some enraged father he resolved to horsewhip a generation grown delinquent in his absence. He justified *The Way We Live Now*'s corrective fury in a passage written the following year and published posthumously in his *Autobiography*:

a certain class of dishonesty, dishonesty magnificent in its proportions, and climbing into high places, has become at the same time so rampant and so splendid that there seems to be reason for fearing that men and women will be taught to feel that dishonesty, if it can become splendid, will cease to be abominable. If dishonesty can live in a gorgeous palace with pictures on all its walls, and gems in all its cupboards, with marble and ivory in all its corners, and can give Apician dinners, and get into Parliament, and deal in millions, then dishonesty is not disgraceful, and the man dishonest after such a fashion is not a low scoundrel. Instigated, I say, by some such reflexions as these, I sat down in my new house to write *The Way We Live Now*.* And as I had ventured to take the whip of the satirist into my hand, I went beyond the iniquities of the great speculator who robs everybody, and made an onslaught also on other vices,—on the intrigues of girls who want to get married, on the luxury of young men who prefer to remain single, and on the puffing propensities of authors who desire to cheat the public into buying their volumes.*

Always a ready writer, indignation brought Trollope's creativity to boiling point. The novel was conceived in Spring 1873 and its 425,000 words (it is probably the longest of his works) were composed in two rapid bursts, over the rest of the year.

*The Way We Live Now* was Trollope's 33rd novel and

he was fifty-eight when he wrote it.  He was no longer, as Sadleir puts it, 'the *gros lot* in the lottery of publishing'.* His reputation, after the failure of his political magazine *St Pauls*—and with it his own political career—had suffered.  He was angry and still frighteningly robust. Nowhere in his work do we find less of 'the playfulness of the rhinoceros' than in *The Way We Live Now*.  He had, reluctantly, largely curtailed his favourite recreation; he was no longer to be, in Henry James's sarcasm, 'a novelist who hunted the fox'.  He had given up, too, his house at Waltham Cross where he could play at squires.  Henceforth he was to live in a London which— if we trust this novel—was far from his taste.

In brief, it would seem that the securities and confidence which underpin Trollope's fiction of the 1860s (especially early works in the Barsetshire sequence) are shaken.  The author in *The Way We Live Now* ranges himself frankly with Roger Carbury, the 'old fashioned' and anachronistically 'gentlemanly' squire of Carbury Hall; 'People live now in a way that I don't comprehend' Carbury confesses.  His world ('good in its way', the narrator modestly interjects) has 'passed away'.  'I'm old fashioned, Hetta', Roger admits to the young woman he loves, and whom, typically, he cannot make love him. At thirty-eight (Trollope could decently have made him slightly more ancient) Roger knows he 'will not win the game'.  And finally he retires into merely patriarchal participation, adopting the newly-wed Hetta and Paul Montague—his young rival and the love of his life—as heirs to Carbury.  Much of *The Way We Live Now* could have been written by Roger, especially the reiterated diatribes and bitter asides on 'these days'.  Like Roger Trollope is 'always severe', crusty, self-righteously of another more moral time.  (Compare, for instance, Trollope's comments above about dishonesty with Roger's nearly identical outburst in Chapter LV.)

Trollope admitted, by way of apology, that like most satire *The Way We Live Now* takes too severely a monocular view of things.  All levels of English society are displayed as tainted with the same false values.  Rank

pawns its honour for money. Lord Nidderdale, heir to
a Scottish marquisate, 'trafficks' for the illegitimate and
less than beautiful daughter of the illegitimate and
criminal Melmotte. Aristocracy fawn on 'the Merchant
Prince', and dignify his fraudulent Board as automatically as they bend the knee to the visiting Emperor of
China (a figure who represents, for Trollope as for
Carlyle, the absurdest extreme of the rank system). The
City swallows Melmotte's scrip and prospectuses for
lunatic projects (submarine cables to India, the corner·
ing of all the iron in Britain) as the real thing. Parliament embraces him; the Liberal and Conservative
parties fight for the favour of a foreigner taught in the
political school of the despot, Napoleon III. (Melmotte
graciously chooses the Tories, led by another adventurer,
prudently unnamed in the novel but unmistakably
Disraeli). The Carlton Club—venerable headquarters
of Conservatism—changes its rules to enter him a member. The Protestant and Catholic Churches, no less than
their secular equivalents, solicit Melmotte. The funniest
scene in the novel has Father John Barham intruding on
the supposed convert in his Grosvenor Square Mansion
to be seen off with a volley of curses. Nonetheless the true
church accepts the rebuff in the expectation that Melmotte's money 'will help'. It all proves what Lord
Alfred Grendall tells Melmotte apropos of his imminent
baronetcy, 'there was no knowing what honours might
not be achieved in the present days by money scattered
with a liberal hand'. To such a level is the England of
'present days' descended.

As Roger Carbury observes, Melmotte is 'a sign of
degeneracy' not the cause. 'The Melmotte era' (in fact
it lasts a brief two months) is less a tribute to the financier's omnipotence than clinching proof of the decay of
English standards. 'What are we coming to when such
as he is an honoured guest at our tables?' asks Roger,
with the emphasis on 'we'. 'Our' corruption, as displayed in *The Way We Live Now*'s opening chapters, is so
pervasive as to seem nothing less than epidemic. In the
modern way of the world, heiresses are won like gambling

stakes (Nidderdale jestingly proposes that their cash
value should be posted, to simplify the suitor's life);
princes are bought to dignify balls by the timely redemption from pawn of an important person's diamonds. The
literary world is a racket, run on a system of vendettas,
bribes and—in Lady Carbury's case—something uncomfortably close to carnal prostitution. Just as Melmotte's bubble inflates by what people think it to be, so
literary reputation depends on fooling the reader.
Realising this, Lady Carbury determines to succeed 'not
by producing good books, but by inducing certain people
to say that her books were good'. Similarly, the South
Central Pacific and Mexican railway is not projected to
lay rails across the continent of America, but to make the
speculating public think that rails will be laid.

In the social sphere 'Gentlemen's' clubs like the Beargarden have declined into drinking, smoking and, particularly, gambling dens where debts of honour are converted to paper as worthless as Melmotte's scrip or Mr.
Alf's reviews. Trollope, as it happened, cherished his
cellar, was addicted to his cigar and a rubber at the
Garrick was, for him, 'a daily ceremony'. But he did
not like high stakes, IOUs or the wild gambling which
he saw going on all night in the newer kind of London
club.

Even domestically things have gone to the bad. *The
Way We Live Now* abounds with disobedient and profligate
offspring. Adolphus Longestaffe the younger does not
speak to Adolphus Longestaffe senior: nor does Nidderdale heed the Marquis of Auld Reekie. Marie hatches
'sweet lover-like' plots to rob her father. As for Felix,
this dissolute baronet's relationship with his doting
mother is wonderfully caught in their first exchange,
when he barges into her literary Tuesday evening:

'I wonder whether you can let me have twenty pounds?'
'My dear Felix!'
'Just so, mother;—but how about the twenty pounds?'

It is, as Trollope confesses in the *Autobiography*, an 'exaggerated' portrait of the age. And it upset his by now

routinised 'art of writing novels'. For one thing, he had always ranked himself with the social optimists, maintaining that the world was, on the whole, getting better in spite of modish Carlylean–Ruskinian lamentations. In fact, one can see that this cheerful Trollope breaks through and eventually dominates the second half of *The Way We Live Now*'s narrative. As James Kincaid correctly observes, the novel begins a satire, but ends a comedy with the familiar distribution of good things and a restoration of decent normality.* Melmotte is 'burst up'; the Beargarden is closed down; Fisker, the surviving Melmottes, Vossner, Mrs. Hurtle and Felix are abroad, where they belong; there is a double wedding down in Suffolk and another up in London—'all family feuds are at an end'.

Arguably, however, the organisation of *The Way We Live Now*, both overall and chapter-to-chapter, suffers from its early sections having been written too much at white heat. Trollope over many years had perfected a method which Ruth apRoberts usefully terms 'casuistical';* that is to say one which takes every narrative case in an undogmatic way, without prejudice. In this Trollope is a classic instance of the Victorian 'divided mind'. But the immediate indignations of 1873 seem momentarily to have upset delicate balances in Trollope, to have rigidified a usually flexible morality and unleashed some unattractive irritations of a xenophobic and anti-semitic kind. (Parts of *The Way We Live Now*, especially those dealing with Brehgert in Chapter LX, would, I imagine, be practically unwritable today under the proscriptions of the Race Relations laws). Because of this, the nuclear Trollope novel, which one might provisionally call 'Who will Hetta marry, who will Hetta jilt?', is pushed to the edge of *The Way We Live Now*'s narrative. (Trollope confessed that the Paul, Hetta, Roger love plot is the weakest thing in his novel.)

## II

For whatever reason, *The Way We Live Now*'s 'sour and
pitiless picture of a sordid scene',* is different from anything else in Trollope's vast corpus. This un-Trollopian
quality may account for its unpopularity when it first
appeared—though over-production had made even the
familiar Trollopian article something of a drug on the
market by 1875. A brave-faced Trollope asserts in the
*Autobiography*, 'I by no means look on the book as one of
my failures; nor was it taken as a failure by the public.'
In fact, it was badly and in places savagely reviewed.
(Except, notably, by the *Times*, whose editor, John
Delane, was both friendly with Trollope and of a like
mind as to how the world was going.)* The general dis-
approval is less surprising in view of the opening pages'
assault on the ethics of current reviewing. The Alfs and
Bookers of the literary world would hardly simper at the
portrait given in the first chapters. Nor did the general
reader automatically concede that this was the way *he*
lived now. Subsequently, the novel seems to have incurred a boycott. The British Library has no copy from
1875 (one of the large two volume octavos, made up from
unsold number parts) until the first World's Classic
edition in 1941. *The Warden* whose World's Classic
edition came out in 1918 had meanwhile gone through
dozens of editions. *The Oxford Companion to English Literature* (1932) does not even cite *The Way We Live Now* in its
Trollope entry; nor does the *Encyclopaedia Britannica*'s
eleventh edition (1911) consider it worthy of special
mention. Henry James, in his long and otherwise warm
appreciation written shortly after Trollope's death in
1882, devotes barely a word to this novel. In his pion-
eering *Commentary* Sadleir confirms one's sense that he
was forty years ahead of his time by almost bringing
himself to admit *The Way We Live Now* as Trollope's
finest thing. But on the last page he withdraws the
award in favour of the cheerful Barsetshire novel, *Dr
Thorne*.

With the Trollope revival in the mid-1940s interest in

*The Way We Live Now* picked up. Following the vogue
for 'dark' Dickens, a comparably dark Trollope item
attracted supporters. Leading the field A. O. J. Cockshut saw the novel as a significant stop on Trollope's
'Progress to Pessimism'.* Academic commentators in
learned journals began to sniff out subtle themes and
relevance; Tony Tanner's article on 'the modern signi-
ficance of *The Way We Live Now*' (*Critical Quarterly*, 1967,
pp. 256–71) is symptomatic. The novel's status as a
'classic' was confirmed with the BBC's Forsyte-style
televisation in the 1970s (script by Simon Raven). And
in the glut of monographs brought up by the centenary
of Trollope's death, *The Way We Live Now* emerged as
the most, rather than the least commented on of
Trollope's works. It was also, by and large, the most
admired. To assert in the 1980s that *The Way We Live
Now* is Trollope's masterpiece is to state the critically
obvious.

## III

In notes for the unwritten novel, Trollope reminded
himself that his 'chief character' was to be Lady Carbury,
the 43-year-old coquette, about to embark on a literary
career. Hence the no-nonsense first sentence: 'Let the
reader be introduced to Lady Carbury, upon whose
character and doings much will depend of whatever
interest these pages may have.' Trollope conceived her
a morally tainted woman, 'false from head to foot' but
eventually to be redeemed by a genuine love for her
worthless son. In this same memorandum, the 'hero' is
designated as Roger, with his religious doubts playing an
important part in the plot. With the Lady and Roger
Carbury-centred novel in mind, a literary set of Alfs,
Brounes and Bookers and a clerical set of Yelds and
Barhams are set up early on—later to be left hanging
unemployed for any significant narrative purposes.

In the notes Melmotte is mentioned only in paren-
thesis to his marriageable daughter as 'a great French
swindler'. As Trollope wrote, however, the financier

came increasingly to dominate, and whatever interest there is in the thousand or so pages comes to depend on him. Melmotte barely figures until Chapter IX, nor does he play a main part in the action before Chapter XXII. But 'Melmotte's Glory' is the principal focus of 15 out of the 28 subsequent chapters in the first volume. Those whom Trollope initially intended to star see-saw down accordingly. Lady Carbury can be said to dominate 10 out of the first 21 chapters, and the Carbury–Suffolk set generally no less than 19. Thereafter, they are squeezed into second position, only to come forward again after Melmotte's suicide in Chapter LXXXIII.

It was significant that when he was commissioning designs for the serial cover of the finished novel, Trollope determined one that should feature Melmotte alone. The wheel of fortune motif recalls the title of Lady Carbury's novel. In the centre is the planet, surmounted by a weeping Father Time. Around him, are ten constellated vignettes from Melmotte's glorious six weeks, each framed in a money bag. At the top is his florid, 'arrogant', full face. At the bottom, his corpse, with the acid bottle beside it.

As the intendedly minor figure of Melmotte grew colossal, problems arose for the writer. How, for instance, to dispose of him, by trial, suicide or flight? In his shadowy forethinking of the novel I suspect that Trollope meant to have the ur-Melmotte decamp, like his henchman Cohenlupe and his historical original, Charles Lefevre. A later plan records this indecision (see Appendix). In the event, Trollope bestowed on Melmotte the death by prussic acid of another 'original', John Sadleir.

Melmotte's story, as it is given in the novel, is simply summarised. One of Trollope's new order of men 'without a grandfather', he has no clearly discernible origins. He was born 'in a gutter', we are told; but what nationality of gutter is not clear. He impudently claims to be English—a manifest lie. As the plan suggests, he may be a European Jew (his fat, stupid wife certainly is). After his death it is widely accepted that he was the son of an Irish American forger, one Melmody. Marie, his daughter, was evidently born in New York a Christian bastard; but it is socially convenient for Madame Melmotte to pose as a mother who bore her in Paris in decent wedlock. In passing, we discover that Melmotte was once imprisoned in Hamburg for fraud. His political enemies dig up the fact that he was associated with a dubiously honest Franco–Austrian assurance company. More than this we never know.

It is not precisely stated, but we are to assume that Melmotte came to England from Paris around 1871, a period hardly conducive to business in that capital. He brings with him a moral code of Napoleonic ruthlessness: 'such a man', the American Mrs. Hurtle rhapsodises, 'rises above honesty as a general rises above humanity when he sacrifices an army to conquer a nation'. Mrs. Hurtle's approval is shared by the more advanced spirits in the English community; only old fogies like Roger Carbury find Melmotte's philosophy distasteful.

Chance throws Melmotte together with Hamilton K. Fisker, a little American huckster, spawned, as Trollope says, in some nameless Californian ravine. Fisker has interested himself in grandiose railway speculation (the continental link in America was completed in 1869, an inspiration for all get-rich-quick merchants). In alliance with Paul Montague, one of Trollope's many weak but likeable heroes, a bubble scheme is set going, with Melmotte as its London figurehead. The project is a great South Central Pacific and Mexican railway, to run 2,000 miles from Salt Lake City to Vera Cruz. Trading on the greed and gullibility of the City, Parliament, the Aristocracy, the Church and the Fourth Estate, Melmotte succeeds triumphantly and with dizzying rapidity. He becomes the 'great man' of the day, 'the very navel of the commercial enterprise of the world'. It is Melmotte, Merchant Prince, who is chosen as host to the Royal Family, the Lord Mayor and the Imperial visitor from China. A dinner for 200 and following ball for 1,000 (cost to Melmotte, £10,000) is arranged, to show 'how an English merchant lives'. Competition for tickets

among the like of Sir Damask Monogram is cutthroat.
Swollen by his new grandeur, Melmotte 'scolds Earls
and snubs Dukes' and they meekly submit to the mongrel
upstart.  He is embraced by the Tory Party, currently
under the leadership of that other hateful adventurer,
Disraeli, and selected for the by-election at Westminster.
No sooner is Melmotte at his zenith, however, than the
wheel turns.  His daughter falls in love with the cad
Sir Felix, rather than the more substantial lord bargained
for.  'Confidence' is eroded by malicious newspaper
gossip.  Melmotte is obliged to mortgage property in
Sussex before he has paid for it.  For this purpose, title
deeds need to be forged (Trollope somewhat tripped up
in this plot business, see note to 2.213).  The dinner goes
ahead, but with forty ominously empty Banquo's chairs.
Melmotte sits fuming at the 'right hand of the Brother
of the Sun'.  The Financier is nonetheless elected to
parliament the next day by the new machinery of the
ballot, which Trollope hated and thought would lead to
just such bad choices.  Melmotte is conducted into the
House by his leader, Disraeli—a fine pair, the author
intimates.  But the new member makes a drunken fool
of himself.  Meanwhile tongues have wagged—and the
telegraph has been used.  Above all, Melmotte has contrived to destroy himself by conspicuousness and by sur-
rendering to 'an arrogance, a self-confidence inspired
. . . by the worship of other men which clouded his
intellect'.  The bubble bursts, parasites like the Grendalls fall away.  Melmotte is now cut ruthlessly by those
other men who last week worshipped him.  His daughter,
Marie, obstinately refuses to sign the documents which
will release his emergency £50,000.  There is more
forgery, more disgrace and finally only suicide remains
to him.  The six-week 'Melmotte era' is over.

Although *The Way We Live Now* is clearly set in 1873
Melmotte has no identifiable single original.  Rather he
is a compound of literary and historical antecedents.
The name itself has echoes of Melmoth, the cursed
wanderer of Maturin's Gothic novel: Melmotte, too, is
something of a wanderer.  A nearer literary source is

Dickens's commercial rogue, Merdle. Trollope insisted that he had never read *Little Dorrit* until after writing *The Way We Live Now*. But as Bradford Booth demonstrates, the young Anthony actually offered to review Dickens's novel when it first came out.* Overlooking the small indulgence of professional pride, one may observe that both villains have an ironically 'Roman' death. (At one point Melmotte, while shaving considers 'ending it', Merdle-fashion, with a razor.) Both toy with the idea of buying a baronetcy with their fraudulent wealth; both are 'worshipped' by a degenerate English society. Merdle's interview in his office with Old Dorrit is suspiciously like Melmotte's with Paul Montague. This alleges no culpable plagiarism on Trollope's part; merely that he too was interested in the rich and provocative Victorian theme of how far money could *buy* English society—quite substantially, both novelists seem to have concluded.

Arguably Melmotte and Merdle converge on an historical original. Both fictional characters recall in some detail John Sadleir, banker, MP and suicide. Trollope ended *The New Zealander* (written in 1856, the year of Sadleir's death) with a peroration on 'that wretched man who has lately perished'. Robert Tracy points to other long-notorious commercial villains: the swindler Fauntleroy and the great railway speculator of the 1840s, 'King' Hudson.* Playing the railway manias, Hudson made his millions when Trollope was in his late twenties. Although famously vulgar, the 'Napoleon's' prodigious and sudden wealth enabled him to set up a magnificent establishment at Knightsbridge where he numbered among his acquaintances the Prince Consort and the top drawer of British aristocracy. ('If duchesses condoned it all, did it become her to be prudish?' thinks Lady Carbury, as she argues herself into accepting an invitation to the Melmotte mansion in Grosvenor Square.) Hudson was elected a Conservative MP in 1845. Soon after there was a scandal when the great director was discovered to have increased the authorised issue of shares in his company. After 1849 he lived mainly abroad, a discredited figure. The former colossus died in 1871, a timely reminder for Trollope.

Any survey will show that Trollope had been railing against dishonesty in public life since the 1850s. He associated it, for instance, with Disraeli—Melmotte's political leader. *The Way We Live Now* is not just about dishonesty, however, but the specific 'profligacy' as Trollope calls it, of financiers. In 1873 'financier' was by all accounts a new-sounding word, possibly unfamiliar to a number of Trollope's first readers. The first recorded use of it in the sense of one who profitably manipulates risk capital is given as 1867, in the *Pall Mall Gazette*, a paper with which Trollope had connections and which he guys as the *Evening Pulpit* in the novel. And recent scandal to do with vast misappropriations around the 1870s gave Melmotte, 'the great Financier', a striking topicality. Moreover these scandals emphasise a feature absent in the earlier, home-grown swindlers and sharks, namely that the 'financier' is archetypally 'international', a man without country. Trollope extends the point. All the predators in *The Way We Live Now* are from abroad: Fisker and Mrs. Hurtle, Montague's commercial and sexual tempters, are American; Melmotte is god-knows-what; Vossner, cheating manager of the Beargarden, is German; Alf, the new breed of newspaper proprietor, is probably German-Jewish.

In the creation of Melmotte's Yankee partner, Fisker, Trollope must have had in mind the New York adventurer 'Colonel' Fisk, who was shot to death, by a rival in love, in January 1872. As the *Saturday Review* noted, this 'pedlar's son' was the ruin of a large number of people. He was associated with railway speculation, the fraudulent Erie scheme and Tammany Hall corruption. *The Times*, in an ungenerous obituary, observed that in America 'vast fortunes are built up in a few years by frauds surpassing the wildest dreams of our Old-World criminals' (9 January 1872). With his vast fortune Fisk 'bought' New York society and entered politics. The *Illustrated London News* of the same week took the opportunity of his violent and sordid death to ruminate on

American gun law (Trollope's Mrs. Hurtle, the American 'wild cat', shot a would-be ravisher and once threatened her husband with a gun):

[American] criminal justice is administered in a singular manner . . . a man who had shot a journalist was acquitted in consequence of the pleas that the journalist had seduced his wife. A well known politician a few years ago murdered his wife's lover and was acquitted on a similar plea.

As Mrs. Hurtle observes to her pusillanimous English lover, Paul, America is very different from 'this soft civilization of yours'.

Other newsworthy crimes enriched the conception of Melmotte. In March 1873, as Trollope was winding up to write, there was the trial of four 'smart Yankee swindlers' for a spectacular forgery on the Bank of England which netted a highest-ever criminal haul of £102,000. (Heavily romanced, the escapade reappeared in Stephen Shepherd's bestselling novel of 1979, *The Four Hundred*.) In February 1873, there had been another serious charge of fraud against the sinisterly foreign-sounding merchant, Joseph de Lizardi, who, like Melmotte, mortgaged stock of which he was not the paid-up owner.

About the period 1869–73 British authorities had become seriously alarmed about abuses of international financing operations which, if not actually criminal, made nonsense of traditional business ethics. A Select Committee of the House of Commons was set up, and was investigating loans with foreign states as Trollope wrote. (The report came out simultaneously with the volume issue of his novel, in July 1875: it is just possible that this was by publisher's design.) The principal objects of the Committee's attention were a series of South American schemes for which capital was raised mainly in London and Paris. Most notorious were the Santo Domingo Loan, 1869; the Costa Rica Loan, 1872, the Paraguay Loan, 1871–2; and, above all, the loan for the Interoceanic Railway in Honduras. This last offers the closest resemblance to Melmotte's grand venture. The mastermind behind the Honduras operation was Charles (alias

'Joachim') Lefevre, who may or may not have been a Frenchman. As *The Times* noted in its comments on the Committee's report (31 July 1875): 'the history of the Honduras loan is part of the history of the great Lefevre'.

The great Lefevre (who impudently engaged in correspondence with the paper from his haven in France) was in fact revealed to have a criminal record in Paris. His brain-child, the Honduras Loan, went through a number of fund-raising stages, in 1867, 1869, 1870. But it was not until 1872 that the scheme to complete the Interoceanic Railway was proposed, nor until 1872 that British trustees and British public figures became mixed up in it. In May 1872 the great railway was abandoned with no more than fifty miles laid; there was a furore in the English press, and Honduras loan stock fell through the floor. As with Melmotte, Lefevre might well have continued his swindling way quite happily, had he not over-reached himself with a gigantic transit scheme. But Lefevre came out better. By June 1872, he was safely abroad with a million pounds in his pocket. As *The Times* (2 August 1875) recorded:

by far the larger part [of the loot] remains in the hands of a motley league of men comprising his Excellency the Minister Plenipoteniary of the State of Honduras, some business firms supposed to represent London respectability and an adventurer of criminal antecedents no longer able to attempt at Paris what he had not only with impunity but with unparalleled success accomplished in this city.

Lefevre was aided, as *The Times* sarcastically observed, by a 'respectable' London business firm. Bischoffsheim and Goldschmidt doubtless inspired Todd, Brehgert and Goldsheiner to the novelist. Like Melmotte, Lefevre was also aided by a corrupt MP, Samuel Laing (Cohenlupe in the novel) and entrapped an innocent English gentleman, 'Captain' Bedford Pim (Montague). Pim went to Paris for the redemption of the English loan and was promptly arrested. Although he was released in a couple of days, his disgrace was complete. *The Times* (31 July 1875) concluded:

It appears to be possible for one bold speculator to make a foreign state, its representatives, his own associates, and the public of England and France subservient to his plans and to put in his own pocket almost the entire proceeds of a public loan.

Another likely inspiration for Melmotte is found in the *Illustrated London News* for 15 March 1873. Published some six weeks before he began to write the novel, and as he was about to settle in his new London house, it would surely have caught Trollope's eye:

French News: the trial of the promoters of the notorious 'Transcontinental Memphis–Pacific Railway Company' is exciting great interest in the Paris financial world. This bubble company was launched in 1869, in New York by General Fremont, who profiting by the name and reputation of his son in law, Baron Gauldree Boileau, then Consul General of the French Government in the United States introduced it, with his assistance, upon the Paris Bourse as a most successful speculation. No less than £800,000 were subscribed by over confident French financiers; of which £140,000 were pocketed by Fremont, £100,000 by Parodis, who presided over the starting of the company in Paris, £32,000 by Crampton, another projector and £30,000 by Baron Gauldree Boileau, who appears, however to have been Fremont's tool throughout this transaction. The company collapsed in 1870 . . . Today General Fremont defies French justice from across the Atlantic . . . this fictitious company never laid down a single line of rails.

There are obvious similarities between Melmotte's and Fremont's chimerical Pacific railway schemes: the American connection, the entrapment of respectable dignitaries, the exploitation of social prestige to advance fraud.

One of the most striking features of *The Way We Live Now* is the way in which the originally minor character of Melmotte first grew then complicated in his author's hand. Early references to him in the narrative are accompanied by a reflexive authorial scorn. Trollope's initial attitude is Roger's: 'I look upon him as dirt in the gutter!' In Chapter XXIII, as Melmotte begins to take the novel over, the authorial tone is almost apoplectic:

he is a 'horrid, big, rich scoundrel . . . a bloated swindler
. . . a vile city ruffian'. Gradually a more temperate interest develops. Melmotte even earns a grudging respect.
'Of course he had committed forgery, of course he had
committed robbery' but does he not possess a certain
'manliness' as well? His energy is, at the very least,
preferable to the enervated listlessness of the Beargarden
set; Dolly, for instance, with his 'I'm awfully lazy' or
Nidderdale with his 'it's an awful bore'. Complex cross-
currents are set up around Melmotte in the second half
of the book—even pathos as he is cut by the 'curs' who so
recently fawned on him.

   In the lonely hour of his death Melmotte is almost noble.
The evocations of the death of Caesar are not, like the
earlier sneers against the 'Merchant Prince' or the 'great
man' merely sarcastic. The allusion to the austere
Roman philosopher is finely poised between the ironic
and the heroic, and at the end we could be swept into
accepting at face value the Roman death: 'but he was
Augustus Melmotte, and he must bear his burdens, whatever they were, to the end'. The end itself is communicated by understatement:

at nine o'clock on the following morning the maid-servant
found him dead upon the floor, Drunk as he had been,—
more drunk as he probably became during the night,—still he
was able to deliver himself from the indignities and penalties
to which the law might have subjected him by a dose of prussic
acid.

It is most effective of Trollope to withdraw from the scene
of the death, leaving the suicidal Melmotte secretively
remote, even from the normally omniscient author. The
financial aftermath of the death also perplexes response.
It emerges that Melmotte's business was 'immensely
profitable'. After outstanding debts the estate pays ten
shillings in the pound. To have been, after all, genuinely
prosperous is Melmotte's last double-cross on English
society.

IV

Unravelling some of Melmotte's origins suggests that Trollope took the 'now' in his title seriously. There are other references which cue the reader to the present. Georgiana justifies her outrageous intention to marry Brehgert with the fact that 'one of the greatest judges in the land is a Jew'. The first Jewish judge, was in fact appointed in summer 1873. Trollope notes such changes as the GPO's taking over of the telegraph service (1868), the completion of the American transcontinental railway (1869), the first submarine telegraph (1866). More instrumental to the plot, Melmotte's is the first election to be held by ballot in Westminster: the ballot act was introduced, to Trollope's disgust, in 1872. But the overarching social occasion recorded in the narrative's six months is the State Visit of the Emperor of China. Trollope makes great symbolic play with this ludicrously formal occasion, in which an indifferent potentate, with no word of English, is feted with no less reverence than in his native Orient. The automatic obeisance to this 'brother of the sun' is, of course, ironically analogous to Society's similarly automatic subservience to the Napoleon of commerce, Melmotte. With the Chinese imperial visit, Trollope conflates two big news stories of early 1873. The first was the marriage of the Emperor of China (a fifteen-year-old boy) reported in January. This aroused great curiosity in England. The *Illustrated London News*, for instance, sent an artist to China, and exotic sketches and woodcuts were relayed back throughout all the early part of the year.

Meanwhile, preparations for the state visit of the Shah of Persia were in hand. The Shah, as it happened, was a very different kind of monarch from the Emperor of China: vigorous, intelligent, he was above all concerned to westernise his country. It was intended, therefore, that the King of Kings should see more than the fleet at Spithead and a review of cavalry at Windsor. As the *ILN* (14 June 1873) put it, he was to be exposed to 're-presentative illustrations of the engineering strength, the

manufacturing skill, the industrial organization and the
*commercial enterprise* of the kingdom. Until he has seen
something of these, he can hardly be said to have seen
England as it is' (my italics).

The Shah landed in England in the middle of June, 1873
and to give him some idea of commercial enterprise a ball
in Guildhall was organised by the Lord Mayor, after a
visit to the City. No less than 3,000 guests came to this
'sumptuous entertainment', and there was a dinner for
90 people afterwards. The competition for invitations
was naturally keen; if not as ruthless as for Melmotte's
affair at Grosvenor Square. A number of commentators
were somewhat affronted by the fuss made about the
Shah; *Punch*, for instance, felt that his countrymen were
making themselves 'dirt' before a mere foreign dictator.
Trollope may well have agreed.

Trollope seized on this unorthodox royal visit (the first
mention is in Chapter XXXII, which he was writing in
August 1873, shortly after the Shah had gone). And he
embroidered it with Melmotte's dinner, a function de-
signed to demonstrate that the Merchant Prince was no
less a being than the King of Kings. None of Trollope's
readers, with the headline memories of the Shah's visit
still fresh, would have missed the contemporary reson-
ance.

V

What exactly was Trollope's frame of mind when he wrote
*The Way We Live Now*? He affected to regard it in after-
life as something of an aberration; a loss of normal good
nature in the fever of indignation. Obviously he is to be
believed in this. Lofty Juvenalian motives apart, there is
a strong charge of personal irritability in the novel.
Trollope's star was in the descendant and he had not yet
adjusted; old fellow labourers in fiction, like Dickens,
Lever and Lytton, had recently died. The public was
not so much turning against him, as away from him and
his generation. His ambition to get into Parliament had
failed. His political and social views had consequently
been in flux since 1868, veering from the middle-of-the-

road independent Liberalism which he avowed as a candidate at Beverley, to a crusty Whiggism at one moment and something like radicalism at the next. At this particular period, strange as it now seems, journals like the *Saturday Review* found Trollope something of a firebrand in his hostility to the born aristocracy.

Particularly relevant to *The Way We Live Now* and its gallery of aristocratic and gentrified types is Trollope's long and somewhat vexed quarrel with Carlylism. Trollope enunciated his repudiation of Carlyle's view that the world was going inexorably to the dogs in virtually the same terms at four different phases of his career (he also lampooned Carlyle as 'Pessimist Anticant', in *The Warden*, 1855): in *The New Zealander* (1856), in the essay in *St Paul's* entitled 'Carlylism' (1868), in the section concerning *The Way We Live Now* in the *Autobiography* (1883) and in Chapter LV of the novel itself, where the Bishop of Elmham is made to utter the Trollopian sentiments:

I think that men on the whole do live better lives than they did a hundred years ago. There is a wider spirit of justice abroad, more of mercy from one to another, a more lively charity . . . Taking society as a whole, the big and the little, the rich and the poor, I think that it grows better from year to year.

Critics have conveniently taken this utterance as the moment in *The Way We Live Now* where Trollope's habitual comic perspective takes over from satire.

Nevertheless, Trollope's attitude to Carlyle is inconsistent. And *The Way We Live Now* finds the novelist in large agreement with the sage. Indeed the novel may be thought to return to the fountainhead of Carlylean social criticism, *Past and Present* (1843). This polemic, whose title must surely have inspired Trollope's, contrasts modern Mayfair do-nothingism, City mores and aristocratic dilettantism with old Suffolk feudal virtues; just as *The Way We Live Now* contrasts Roger Carbury and his retainer John Crumb with Sir Felix and Melmotte. (Carlyle, incidentally, sees the insatiably usurious Jew as one cause of the downfall of his feudal Utopia. 'Foreign invasion', by the Normans, is another.) For both authors, Suffolk is a national redoubt; or as Roger observes, 'there is something left among us of old English habits'.

In similar Carlylean vein *The Way We Live Now* renews the Carlylean attack on 'unworking' aristocracy. There is no worthwhile blue-blooded character in the novel, certainly no Plantagenet Palliser. The Longstaffes have 'the name' of being noble, but like the too obviously named Sir Damask Monogram, Dolly and his father are mere ciphers. Nidderdale—heir to the Marquisate of Auld Reekie—has nothing to offer but his prospective title for sale on the marriage market. And he's too bored even to put much effort into that project. The Grendalls, father and son, have become Melmotte's bootjacks. The younger is his secretary, the older the Railway Board's yes-man. The principally satirised drone is, of course, Sir Felix Carbury:

He never read. Thinking was altogether beyond him. And he had never done a day's work in his life. He could lie in bed. He could eat and drink. He could smoke and sit idle. He could play cards; and could amuse himself with women— the lower the culture of the women, the better the amusement.

He has, as the narrator observes with supreme contempt, 'the instincts of a horse, not approaching the higher sympathies of a dog'. Melmotte's parasitism is at least 'splendid' in its scale; Felix's is merely mean; £20 cadged here from his mother, £250 swindled there from Marie who loves him. As he artlessly puts it (he thinks it is thrift): 'I pay for nothing that I can help. I even get my hair cut on credit.' In such company, Melmotte's purloining a Sussex estate on credit appears positively magnanimous.

The Felix we first encounter has just sold out from a fashionable regiment, a branded coward. He has run through the £1,000 a year left by his drunken brute of a father, now he is eating up his mother and sisters' portion. 'It was his business to marry an heiress.' Applying himself, he callously wins the heart of Marie Melmotte, but befuddles himself too comprehensively at the Beargarden to manage the elopement. His more lecherous campaign against the village maid, Ruby Ruggles, brings her to London. But her true love, the flour worker John Crumb (as Henry James notes, Trollope's science of names is not very exact) saves her at seduction's door, and 'baronites' the luckless Sir Felix into the London gutter. Felix ends, less a few teeth, relieving the clergyman entrusted with taking him round the continent of a tenner.

In other less moralistic hands than Trollope's, Felix might have emerged as an amiable rogue, a kind of Victorian Basil Seal. But Trollope's disgust seems not, as with Melmotte, to have undergone any modification. Felix is as odious in Chapter XCIX as he was in Chapter II.

## VI

Emphasis on Carlyle should not imply that in *The Way We Live Now* Trollope is merely confronting the new age with old ideas. In a most useful essay, Asa Briggs has shown how the Palliser sequence, begun in the mid-1860s, is intimately engaged with Walter Bagehot's *The English Constitution* (first published in the late 1860s).* It is possible to extend the comparison. In 1873 Bagehot wrote a paean in praise of English banking, entitled *Lombard Street*. The title, of course, refers to the street in the City running off the Exchange and by the Bank of England. It is surely no coincidence, that Melmotte's office, in Abchurch Lane, is also just by Lombard Street.

Bagehot takes as his starting point the fact that 'England is the greatest moneyed country in the world'. The cause of this vast Victorian prosperity is that 'there never was so much money collected in the world as is now collected in London'. The result was unlimited credit for investment, for schemes both at home and abroad. Central to the deployment of all this credit was the banker/financier. Bagehot's optimism was sustained by the supposed integrity of this *genus*: 'a man of known wealth, known integrity, and known ability is largely entrusted with the money of his neighbours. The confidence is strictly personal.'

For his part, Trollope would seem to have agreed about the oceans of credit swilling around Lombard Street. And one suspects that he must have read and carefully considered Bagehot's book. But he apparently took a more suspicious view about the 'integrity' of those powerful men currently 'entrusted' with the money of others. In Trollope's City, 'Mr. Melmotte's name was worth any money,—though his character was perhaps worth but little.' As with the *English Constitution*, Trollope would seem to accept the large outlines of Bagehot's theory while sceptically rejecting the accompanying moral complacency.

# FURTHER READING

In addition to the books and articles mentioned in the text and notes, the following seem to me to have something particularly useful to say on *The Way We Live Now*.

T. Bareham (ed.), *Anthony Trollope* (London, Vision Press, 1980). See particularly Chapter 9, 'A lesser Thackeray', by Robin Gilmour.

Bradford A. Booth, *Anthony Trollope, Aspects of his Life and Art* (London, Hulton, 1958).

P. D. Edwards, *Anthony Trollope: His Art and Scope* (New York, St Martins, 1978).

G. Harvey, *The Art of Anthony Trollope* (London, Weidenfeld, 1980).

A. Pollard, *Anthony Trollope* (London, Routledge, 1978).

R. C. Terry, *Anthony Trollope: The Artist in Hiding* (London, Macmillan, 1977).

At the time of writing, there is no satisfactory modern biography or edition of the letters, although both are forthcoming from N. John Hall. Still very serviceable, however, are the biographical chapters in Sadleir's *Commentary* and Bradford A. Booth's one volume edition of the letters, published by OUP in 1951.

# A Chronology of Anthony Trollope

Virtually all Trollope's fiction appeared first in serial form, with book production timed to coincide with the final instalment of the serial. In this chronology the titles are dated as on the title-page of the first book edition. On a very few occasions the book edition appeared in December of the year previous to that indicated on the title-page, so as to catch the Christmas sales.

1815 24 Apr.  Born at 6 Keppel Street, Bloomsbury, the fourth son of Thomas and Frances Trollope.

1822  To Harrow as a day-boy.

1825  To a private school at Sunbury.

1827  To Winchester school.

1830  Removed from Winchester and returned to Harrow.

1834  The family move to Bruges.

  Autumn  He accepts a junior clerkship in the General Post Office.

1841 Aug.  Deputy Postal Surveyor at Banagher, King's County, Ireland.

1843 Autumn  Begins work on his first novel, *The Macdermots of Ballycloran*.

1844 11 June  Marries Rose Heseltine.
    Transferred to Clonmel, County Tipperary.

1845  Promoted to the office of Surveyor, and transferred to Mallow, County Cork.

1845–7  Famine and epidemic throughout Ireland, especially the south and west with which Trollope was familiar.

1847  *The Macdermots of Ballycloran* published in 3 vols. (Newbury).

1848  Rebellion in Ireland, concentrated in Cork and Tipperary.
    *The Kellys and the O'Kellys; or Landlords and Tenants* 3 vols. (Colburn).

1850  Writes *The Noble Jilt* (published 1923).

*La Vendee; an Historical Romance* 3 vols. (Colburn).

1851  Transferred to England.

1853  Returns to Ireland; completes *The Warden* (the first of the Barsetshire novels) in Belfast.

1854 Autumn  Leaves Belfast and settles outside Dublin at Donnybrook.

1855  *The Warden* 1 vol. (Longman).

1857  *Barchester Towers* 3 vols. (Longman).

Sept.  Visits his mother in Florence.

1858  *Doctor Thorne* 3 vols. (Chapman & Hall).
   *The Three Clerks* 3 vols. (Bentley).

Feb.  Departs for Egypt on Post Office business.

Mar.  Removes from Egypt to Palestine.

Apr.–May  Returns via Malta, Gibraltar and Spain.

May–July  Visits Scotland and north of England on business.

Aug.–Oct.  At home in Ireland.

Nov.  On Post Office business in the West Indies.

1859  *The Bertrams* 3 vols. (Chapman & Hall).
   *The West Indies and the Spanish Main* 1 vol. (Chapman & Hall).

Sept.  Holiday in the Pyrenees.

Dec.  Leaves Ireland; settles at Waltham Cross.

1860  *Castle Richmond* 3 vols. (Chapman & Hall).

Oct.  With his wife he visits his mother and brother in Florence; makes the acquaintance of Kate Field, a beautiful twenty-year-old American with whom he falls in love.

1861  *Framley Parsonage* 3 vols. (Smith, Elder).
   *Tales of All Countries*—first series, 1 vol. (Chapman & Hall).

Spring  Elected a member of the Garrick Club; some two years later is elected to the committee to fill the vacancy caused by Thackeray's death.

Aug.  To America on official business.

1862  *Orley Farm* 2 vols. (Chapman & Hall).
   *North America* 2 vols. (Chapman & Hall).
   *The Struggles of Brown, Jones and Robinson; by One of the Firm* 1 vol. (New York, Harper—an American piracy).

Spring   Returns home from America.

1863     *Rachel Ray* 2 vols. (Chapman & Hall).
         *Tales of All Countries*—second series 1 vol. (Chapman & Hall).

6 Oct.   Death of his mother, Mrs. Frances Trollope.

Dec.     Death of W. M. Thackeray.

1864     *The Small House at Allington* 2 vols. (Smith, Elder).
         *Can You Forgive Her?* 2 vols. (Chapman & Hall).

Summer   Elected a member of the Athenaeum Club.

1865     *Miss Mackenzie* 1 vol. (Chapman & Hall).
         *Hunting Sketches* 1 vol. (Chapman & Hall).

1866     *The Belton Estate* 3 vols. (Chapman & Hall).
         *Travelling Sketches* 1 vol. (Chapman & Hall).
         *Clergymen of the Church of England* 1 vol. (Chapman & Hall).

1867     *Nina Balatka* 2 vols. (Blackwood).
         *The Last Chronicle of Barset* 2 vols. (Smith, Elder).
         *The Claverings* 2 vols. (Smith, Elder).
         *Lotta Schmidt and Other Stories* 1 vol. (Strahan).

1 Sept.  Resigns from the Civil Service.

1868     *Linda Tressel* 2 vols. (Blackwood).

Mar.     Leaves London for the United States on business involving copyright, in touch again with Kate Field.

July     Returns from America.

Nov.     Stands unsuccessfully as Liberal candidate for Beverley, Yorkshire, losing £2,000 in the enterprise.

1869     *Phineas Finn; the Irish Member* 2 vols. (Virtue & Co.).
         *He Knew He was Right* 2 vols. (Strahan).
         *Did He Steal It? A Comedy in Three Acts* 1 vol.—a version of *The Last Chronicle of Barset* (printed by Virtue & Co.).

1870     *The Vicar of Bullhampton* 1 vol. (Bradbury, Evans).
         *An Editor's Tales* 1 vol. (Strahan).
         *The Commentaries of Caesar* 1 vol. (Blackwood).

1871     *Sir Harry Hotspur of Humblethwaite* 1 vol. (Hurst & Blackett).
         *Ralph the Heir* 3 vols. (Hurst & Blackett).

Apr.     Gives up house at Waltham Cross.

May      Sails to Australia to visit his son.

20 July  Arrives at Melbourne.

1872     *The Golden Lion of Granpère* 1 vol. (Tinsley.
Jan.–Oct.   Travelling in Australia and New Zealand).
Apr.    A dramatised (and pirated) version of *Ralph the Heir* produced by Charles Reade.
Dec.    Returns via the United States, and settles in Montagu Square, London.
1873     *The Eustace Diamonds* 3 vols. (Chapman & Hall).
*Australia and New Zealand* 2 vols. (Chapman & Hall).
Winter    Hunting actively.
1874     *Phineas Redux* 2 vols. (Chapman & Hall).
*Lady Anna* 2 vols. (Chapman & Hall).
*Harry Heathcote of Gangoil; a Tale of Australian Bush Life* 1 vol. (Sampson Low).
1875     *The Way We Live Now* 2 vols. (Chapman & Hall).
Feb.    Travels to Ceylon via Brindisi and the Suez Canal, once again on the way to Australia.
Mar.–Apr.   In Ceylon.
June    Arrives in Australia.
Aug.–Oct.   Sailing homewards.
Oct.    Begins work on his *Autobiography*.
1876     *The Prime Minister* 4 vols. (Chapman & Hall).
1877     *The American Senator* 3 vols. (Chapman & Hall).
*Christmas at Thompson Hall* 1 vol. (New York, Harper).
June    Leaves London for South Africa.
Dec.    Sails for home.
1878     *Is He Popenjoy?* 3 vols. (Chapman & Hall).
*South Africa* 2 vols. (Chapman & Hall).
*How the 'Mastiffs' Went to Iceland* 1 vol. (Virtue & Co.).
June–July   Travels to Iceland in the yacht 'Mastiff'.
1879     *An Eye for an Eye* 2 vols. (Chapman & Hall).
*John Caldigate* 3 vols. (Chapman & Hall).
*Cousin Henry* 2 vols. (Chapman & Hall).
*Thackeray* 1 vol. (Macmillan).
1880     *The Duke's Children* 3 vols. (Chapman & Hall).
July    Settles at Harting Grange, near Petersfield.
1881     *Dr Wortle's School* 2 vols. (Chapman & Hall).
*Ayala's Angel* 3 vols. (Chapman & Hall).
1882     *Why Frau Frohmann Raised Her Prices; and Other Stories* 1 vol. (Isbister).

## Chronology, Topography, and Dialect

The novel's time scheme is very tight. Chapter I opens on 25 February and Chapter C ends the narrative in August of the same year, 1873. The pivotal events—Melmotte's great dinner, his election, his suicide—occur on Monday 8, Tuesday 9 and Friday 18 July. A quarter of the novel, over 100,000 words, is taken up with the events of these 10 days. Forty-five days in June and July occupy no fewer than 66 chapters. Not surprisingly, the intricacy of the chronology requires frequent hopping back, to keep the various plots abreast of each other. (Trollope, incidentally, is not always adroit in this.)

In chapter LXXXIX, Trollope jestingly refers to 'any reader careful as to dates'. Just such a reader turned up when Bert G. Hornback wrote an article on *The Way We Live Now*'s chronology for *Notes and Queries* (December 1963, pp. 454–58). Hornback argues that Trollope eased his labours by having an 1872 calendar on the desk as he wrote. There are, however, some unaccountable errors in weekday and date correlation, from which P. D. Edwards controverted the '1872 calendar on the desk' theory in an answering article (*Notes and Queries*, June 1969, pp. 214–7). Edwards's evidence, from Trollope's working papers, suggests a relatively inexact time chart, drawn up by the novelist himself: 'the identity between the novel's chronology and the calendar of 1872 is sheer coincidence'. My own examination of the working materials suggests that Edwards is right. But the fact that the controversy should take up learned article space in this way at least testifies to the salience of time markers in the novel.

As the chronology of *The Way We Live Now* is tight, so the topography is close. Some 84 of the novel's chapters are set in London, the remainder 'down in Suffolk'. The London settings are very precise and knowledge of the

capital's layout, or an *A to Z*, adds to the work's solidity
of specification.   Many of the main centres of interest
are within close walking distance of each other.   Lady
Carbury's house is in Welbeck Street, just to the north of
Oxford Street.   Melmotte's mansion is in plushier Grosvenor Square, to the south of the thoroughfare.   While
his residence is prepared for the Emperor of China,
Melmotte rents the Longestaffes' town house a few hundred yards to the east, in Bruton Street.   (As a result, the
resentful Longestaffe womenfolk are kept for the season
in hatefully rustic Suffolk.)   Melmotte's Abchurch Lane
business premises are just behind the Exchange and
Lombard Street in the City.

On a pleasant summer morning it is quite feasible for
the Merchant Prince to saunter, as he does on the Tuesday
of his election, from Bruton Street, down to his Committee
Room in Whitehall Place, along Bond Street and
Piccadilly, through Pall Mall, to Charing Cross and the
Carlton Club in St James, thence back to Covent Garden
to give a rousing speech to the electors; after which he
takes a cab to take him further along the river to Abchurch
Lane—rather too far to walk, even in his restless state of
mind.

Awareness of the topography of London gives a
piquancy to Hetta's daring little foray to Mrs. Hurtle.
Having 'studied the geography' Hetta takes the new
Metropolitan underground railway (opened 1863) from
Marylebone along its full length to Farringdon and King's
Cross Road.   From there, she walks into Islington by foot.
The adventure, undertaken alone, confirms her new
independence and her will to fight for possession of Paul
against her American rival (who came, by herself, all the
way from San Francisco).

After fuddling himself at the Beargarden (situated 'in a
little street off St James's Street') on the Wednesday night
he is to elope with Marie, Felix blunders out at four in the
morning, and going wrong at every turn, weaves a route
through Mayfair.   He eventually finds himself in
Marylebone Lane, tantalisingly close to home.   But then,
he remembers he has left his luggage back in the club.

Vaguely conscious of north and south, he staggers across Oxford Street, and back down New Bond Street. There he is stopped by a suspicious policeman who asks him where he lives. Forced to admit Welbeck Street, lest he be taken into custody, he finds himself being escorted back to Oxford Street, and sight of home, by the law. He has no energy left for elopement, and lurches through his mother's front door at between six and seven — decent folks' breakfast time. The walk would take a sober and briskly moving Felix about a quarter of an hour.

Many such itineraries can be reconstructed. It is plausible that Trollope's detailed consciousness of central London is the outcome of his moving there in January 1873, and settling in at Montagu Square (hence Paul Montague, as well), not too far from Welbeck Street. His topography is not always perfect, however. In Chapter XXVI we are told that Paul has comfortable lodgings in Sackville Street, north of Piccadilly, and in Chapter XXXIX that he lodges in Suffolk Street by Pall Mall. There is also some doubt as to exactly where, in Islington, Mrs. Hurtle is lodging. Unless I have missed the reference, Trollope never specifies it. But since Winifred Hurtle is a woman of mystery, this vagueness may be a stroke of art. On the other hand, we can locate, almost to the yard, where about just off Goswell Road and the Angel Felix made his lecherous assault on Ruby, and gets his come-uppance from John Crumb. The music-hall Felix and Ruby patronise near the City Road can be identified as the *Eagle*, famous from 'Pop goes the Weasel'.

The Suffolk settings in the novel are identifiable as to area but masked in some details. There is no Carbury Manor House, Caversham, or Eardly Park. Bungay, where John Crumb is a flour worker, certainly exists, and so does the King's Head, where he proudly holds his wedding party. And Bungay is on the river Waveney, the boundary of Suffolk and Norfolk, which is also close to Roger's estate. The area falls into the ancient Bishopric of Elmham, whose Bishop has a speaking part in the novel. Identifying such places as the small house at Allington is a pleasant Trollopian pastime, and one may

note that Sheep's Acre where the unlovely Ruggles tyran-
nises over Ruby could easily be the 'Shipmeadow' we find
by the Waveney on the map of northern Suffolk, and that
by Shipmeadow there is a 'Manor House' that could
conceivably be the original of Roger's.   The nearby resort of Lowestoft (Trollope calls it 'Lowestoffe', a mental
confusion with Longestaffe, I suspect) was served by train
from both London and Bungay, so the ill-fated meeting
on the sandy beach there is quite plausible.

  Related to the two main locations of the novel, is
Trollope's use of dialect and slang.   The obvious judgement is that while his evocation of the young Beargarden
set's argot is excellent, the Norfolk–Suffolk speech of
Crumb and the Ruggles is abysmal.   (It compares poorly,
for instance, with Dickens's carefully researched East
Anglian in *David Copperfield*.)   At times, John Crumb actually slips into a bastardised Lancashire:

  'Don't know now't about Grandfeyther' [he tells Roger in
Chapter LXXXVII]
  'She'd have made it up wi' me.   Know'd she would when
I'd polish'd t'other 'un off a bit.'

  Trollope's version of Suffolk dialect simply makes
yokels and clowns out of characters who should have at
least an occasional dignity.   (Who can read straight-faced
Crumb's challenge to Felix—'Get up, you wiper!'?)
On the other hand, the smart West End slang of the Beargarden wastrels adds considerably to the novel's sense of
contemporaneity.   In the club, members get 'tight' while
playing 'on tick', since, in general, their 'governors' have
'cut up rough' and won't give them any 'tin'.   Felix, however, knows a 'dodge or two' and determines to 'hook it'
with an heiress but 'comes a cropper' and ends up 'a gone
coon'.   The OED confirms that many of the slang usages
we find in *The Way We Live Now* were spit new when
Trollope wrote and one of the incidental interests of this
work is its lexicon of the modish, ephemeral club-language
of 1873.

Trollope's working calendar for the novel (now kept in the Bodleian Library)* begins with the calculation: 'Carbury novel. 20 numbers. 64 pages each number. 260 words each page. 40 pages a week. To be completed in 32 weeks.' Trollope began writing his 'Carbury novel' on 1 May 1873 and by the end of the month he had completed three numbers, or fifteen chapters (each number in the serial version of the novel has an invariable five chapters). He then broke off to write *Harry Heathcote of Gangoil* which was completely finished by July 1873. The novelist picked up *The Way We Live Now* without a break and between 3 July and 30 July wrote numbers 4–6. Between the end of July and 11 August he took a surely deserved rest. From 11 August to 19 September he wrote numbers 7–14. There followed another short rest until 10 October in which he records 'reading my own manuscript', and presumably correcting it. In the period 11 October to 1 December Trollope polished off the remaining numbers 15–20.

Trollope's rate of work was on average a week to ten days for the early numbers, speeding up to something under a week for numbers 15–17. He took most time (and presumably care—although his life was otherwise very full, moving into his new house) on the last three numbers. At the end of his calendar, Trollope summarises: 'Completed in 34 weeks (instead of 32)—but five weeks were occupied in Harry Heathcote and therefore this novel "The Way We Live Now" has been done in 29 weeks.' Even by Trollope's standards, it was good going for a work of 425,000 words.

*The Way We Live Now* was published by Chapman and Hall. The contract was made on 28 March 1873. It specifies publication in 20 numbers between 1 January 1874 and 1 August 1875. The first half of the work (i.e.

the first volume of the reprint, chapters 1–50) was to be with Chapman and Hall by the end of October 1873, which presumably explains the short break to read manuscript at the beginning of that month.  Trollope, as was habitual with him, made over the copyright entirely (except for Tauchnitz German rights) to the publisher, it being his principle that 'a lump sum' was always preferable to a 'deferred annuity'.  For this, Chapman and Hall engaged to pay Trollope £150 a month, amounting to £3,000 in all.  Given the stage of Trollope's career, it was too high a price and one that he was never to enjoy again.  (For his last full-length novel, published in 1883, Chapman and Hall gave £1,000.)

The decision was made from the start to bring out *The Way We Live Now* in the anachronistic serialisation of 20 monthly numbers, each costing a shilling and containing 32 pages, with a follow up two-volume publication.  This form was associated with the bygone glories of Dickens and Thackeray.  I suspect that in selecting it Trollope and his publishers were influenced by the recent phenomenal success of *Middlemarch* as a serial in eight bi-monthly 'books'.  They miscalculated.  *The Way We Live Now* is the last major English novel to come out on the Dickensian–Thackerayan pattern.  It evidently lost money for the publishers.  After the two-volume issue (whose pages were run off with those of the monthly instalments) the novel was not reprinted.  And Sadleir tells us that there was a surplus unsold stock later disposed of at a knockdown price to Chatto and Windus.

Following the Dickensian–Thackerayan pattern, each monthly number of *The Way We Live Now* carried two full page illustrations.  According to N. John Hall in his *Trollope and his Illustrators* (London, Macmillan, 1980) they represent 'the absolute nadir of illustration in the Trollope canon'.  The artist responsible for this disgrace is not, as was once commonly believed, Luke Fildes (Dickens's illustrator on *Edwin Drood*) but the 'amateur' Lionel Grimshaw Fawkes.  It would seem that having paid Trollope so much, Chapman and Hall made some savings where they could.  It should be noted, however, that the monthly cover illustration described earlier in this introduction is by another and much superior workman.

*The Way We Live Now* came out between February 1874 and September 1875, a month later than agreed. Trollope was careful to end instalments with a 'curtain line', and to pack recapitulated narrative into the first chapters of numbers. He also managed a very effective climax for the end of the first volume, Chapter L (Felix's bungled elopement, Lady Carbury's depth of despair). The two-volume edition came out in July 1875, anticipating the end of the serial run by two months. This was a somewhat unusual arrangement. It may have come about because the publishers wanted to synchronise reviews with press comment on the Foreign Loans Committee which also reported in that month. Or it may just have been that the last numbers were selling so badly that there was no reason to hold back.

In the absence of any known reprint corrected by the author, copy-text for *The Way We Live Now* has to be taken from the two-volume edition. This is the basis of the present World's Classic. Trollope's many inconsistencies as to names (e.g. 'Winifred. . . Winifrid Hurtle,' 'Paul Montagu . . . Montague') have been silently regularised, together with a few other obvious accidental errors in the first edition.

*THE WAY WE LIVE NOW*

# CONTENTS

## Chapter I

### THREE EDITORS

LET the reader be introduced to Lady Carbury, upon whose character and doings much will depend of whatever interest these pages may have, as she sits at her writing-table in her own room in her own house in Welbeck Street. Lady Carbury spent many hours at her desk, and wrote many letters,—wrote also very much beside letters. She spoke of herself in these days as a woman devoted to Literature, always spelling the word with a big L. Something of the nature of her devotion may be learned by the perusal of three letters which on this morning she had written with a quickly running hand. Lady Carbury was rapid in everything, and in nothing more rapid than in the writing of letters. Here is Letter No. 1;—

'Thursday, Welbeck Street.

'DEAR FRIEND,

I have taken care that you shall have the early sheets of my two new volumes to-morrow, or Saturday at latest, so that you may, if so minded, give a poor struggler like myself a lift in your next week's paper. Do give a poor struggler a lift. You and I have so much in common, and I have ventured to flatter myself that we are really friends! I do not flatter you when I say, that not only would aid from you help me more than from any other quarter, but also that praise from you would gratify my vanity more than any other praise. I almost think you will like my 'Criminal Queens.'* The sketch of Semiramis is at any rate spirited, though I had to twist it about a little to bring her in guilty. Cleopatra, of course, I have taken from Shakespeare. What a wench she was! I could not quite make Julia a queen; but it was impossible to pass over so piquant a character. You will recognise in the two or three ladies of the empire how faithfully I have studied my Gibbon. Poor dear old Belisarius! I have

done the best I could with Joanna, but I could not bring
myself to care for her. In our days she would simply have
gone to Broadmore.* I hope you will not think that I
have been too strong in my delineations of Henry VIII.
and his sinful but unfortunate Howard. I don't care a
bit about Anne Boleyne. I am afraid that I have been
tempted into too great length about the Italian
Catherine; but in truth she has been my favourite.
What a woman! What a devil! Pity that a second
Dante could not have constructed for her a special
hell. How one traces the effect of her training in the
life of our Scotch Mary. I trust you will go with me in
my view as to the Queen of Scots. Guilty! guilty always!
Adultery, murder, treason, and all the rest of it. But
recommended to mercy because she was royal. A queen
bred, born and married, and with such other queens
around her, how could she have escaped to be guilty?
Marie Antoinette I have not quite acquitted. It would
be uninteresting;—perhaps untrue. I have accused her
lovingly, and have kissed when I scourged. I trust the
British public will not be angry because I do not white-
wash Caroline,* especially as I go along with them
altogether in abusing her husband.

'But I must not take up your time by sending you
another book, though it gratifies me to think that I am
writing what none but yourself will read. Do it yourself,
like a dear man, and, as you are great, be merciful. Or
rather, as you are a friend, be loving.

'Yours gratefully and faithfully,

'MATILDA CARBURY.'

'After all how few women there are who can raise
themselves above the quagmire of what we call love, and
make themselves anything but playthings for men. Of
almost all these royal and luxurious sinners it was the
chief sin that in some phase of their lives they consented
to be playthings without being wives. I have striven so
hard to be proper; but when girls read everything, why
should not an old woman write anything?'

This letter was addressed to Nicholas Broune, Esq., the

editor of the 'Morning Breakfast Table,'*a daily newspaper of high character; and, as it was the longest, so
was it considered to be the most important of the three.
Mr. Broune was a man powerful in his profession,—and
he was fond of ladies. Lady Carbury in her letter had
called herself an old woman, but she was satisfied to do
so by a conviction that no one else regarded her in that
light. Her age shall be no secret to the reader, though
to her most intimate friends, even to Mr. Broune, it had
never been divulged. She was forty-three, but carried
her years so well, and had received such gifts from nature,
that it was impossible to deny that she was still a beautiful woman. And she used her beauty not only to increase
her influence,—as is natural to women who are well-
favoured,—but also with a well-considered calculation
that she could obtain material assistance in the procuring of bread and cheese, which was very necessary to her,
by a prudent adaptation to her purposes of the good
things with which providence had endowed her. She
did not fall in love, she did not wilfully flirt, she did not
commit herself; but she smiled and whispered, and made
confidences, and looked out of her own eyes into men's
eyes as though there might be some mysterious bond
between her and them—if only mysterious circumstances would permit it. But the end of all was to induce
some one to do something which would cause a publisher
to give her good payment for indifferent writing, or an
editor to be lenient when, upon the merits of the case,
he should have been severe. Among all her literary
friends, Mr. Broune was the one in whom she most
trusted; and Mr. Broune was fond of handsome women.
It may be as well to give a short record of a scene which
had taken place between Lady Carbury and her friend
about a month before the writing of this letter which
has been produced. She had wanted him to take a series
of papers for the 'Morning Breakfast Table,' and to have
them paid for at rate No. 1, whereas she suspected that
he was rather doubtful as to their merit, and knew that,
without special favour, she could not hope for remuneration above rate No. 2, or possibly even No. 3. So she had

looked into his eyes, and had left her soft, plump hand
for a moment in his. A man in such circumstances is so
often awkward, not knowing with any accuracy when to
do one thing and when another! Mr. Broune, in a
moment of enthusiasm, had put his arm round Lady
Carbury's waist and had kissed her. To say that Lady
Carbury was angry, as most women would be angry if so
treated, would be to give an unjust idea of her character.
It was a little accident which really carried with it no
injury, unless it should be the injury of leading to a
rupture between herself and a valuable ally. No feeling
of delicacy was shocked. What did it matter? No unpardonable insult had been offered; no harm had been
done, if only the dear susceptible old donkey could be
made at once to understand that that wasn't the way
to go on!

Without a flutter, and without a blush, she escaped
from his arm, and then made him an excellent little
speech. 'Mr. Broune, how foolish, how wrong, how
mistaken! Is it not so? Surely you do not wish to put
an end to the friendship between us!'

'Put an end to our friendship, Lady Carbury! Oh,
certainly not that.'

'Then why risk it by such an act? Think of my son
and of my daughter,—both grown up. Think of the past
troubles of my life;—so much suffered and so little
deserved. No one knows them so well as you do. Think
of my name, that has been so often slandered but never
disgraced! Say that you are sorry, and it shall be
forgotten.'

When a man has kissed a woman it goes against the
grain with him to say the very next moment that he is
sorry for what he has done. It is as much as to declare
that the kiss had not answered his expectation. Mr.
Broune could not do this, and perhaps Lady Carbury
did not quite expect it. 'You know that for worlds I
would not offend you,' he said. This sufficed. Lady
Carbury again looked into his eyes, and a promise was
given that the articles should be printed—and with
generous remuneration.

When the interview was over Lady Carbury regarded it as having been quite successful. Of course when struggles have to be made and hard work done, there will be little accidents. The lady who uses a street cab must encounter mud and dust which her richer neighbour, who has a private carriage, will escape. She would have preferred not to have been kissed;—but what did it matter? With Mr. Broune the affair was more serious. 'Confound them all,' he said to himself as he left the house; 'no amount of experience enables a man to know them.' As he went away he almost thought that Lady Carbury had intended him to kiss her again, and he was almost angry with himself in that he had not done so. He had seen her three or four times since, but had not repeated the offence.

We will now go on to the other letters, both of which were addressed to the editors of other newspapers. The second was written to Mr. Booker, of the 'Literary Chronicle.' Mr. Booker was a hard-working professor of literature, by no means without talent, by no means without influence, and by no means without a conscience. But, from the nature of the struggles in which he had been engaged, by compromises which had gradually been driven upon him by the encroachment of brother authors on the one side and by the demands on the other of employers who looked only to their profits, he had fallen into a routine of work in which it was very difficult to be scrupulous, and almost impossible to maintain the delicacies of a literary conscience. He was now a bald-headed old man of sixty, with a large family of daughters, one of whom was a widow dependent on him with two little children. He had five hundred a year for editing the 'Literary Chronicle,' which, through his energy, had become a valuable property. He wrote for magazines, and brought out some book of his own almost annually. He kept his head above water, and was regarded by those who knew about him, but did not know him, as a successful man. He always kept up his spirits, and was able in literary circles to show that he could hold his own. But he was driven by the stress of circumstances to take such good things as came in his way, and could hardly afford to be independent. It must be confessed that literary scruple had long departed from his mind. Letter No. 2 was as follows;—

'Welbeck Street, 25th February, 187–.
'DEAR MR. BOOKER,

'I have told Mr. Leadham'—Mr. Leadham was senior partner in the enterprising firm of publishers known as Messrs. Leadham and Loiter—'to send you an early copy of my "Criminal Queens." I have already settled with my friend Mr. Broune that I am to do your "New Tale of a Tub" in the "Breakfast Table." Indeed, I am about it now, and am taking great pains with it. If there is anything you wish to have specially said as to your view of the Protestantism of the time, let me know. I should like you to say a word as to the accuracy of my historical details, which I know you can safely do. Don't put it off, as the sale does so much depend on early notices. I am only getting a royalty,* which does not commence till the first four hundred are sold.

'Yours sincerely,
'MATILDA CARBURY.'
'ALFRED BOOKER, ESQ.,
' "Literary Chronicle" Office, Strand.'

There was nothing in this which shocked Mr. Booker. He laughed inwardly, with a pleasantly reticent chuckle, as he thought of Lady Carbury dealing with his views of Protestantism,—as he thought also of the numerous historical errors into which that clever lady must inevitably fall in writing about matters of which he believed her to know nothing. But he was quite alive to the fact that a favourable notice in the 'Breakfast Table' of his very thoughtful work, called the 'New Tale of a Tub,' would serve him, even though written by the hand of a female literary charlatan, and he would have no compunction as to repaying the service by fulsome praise in the 'Literary Chronicle.' He would not probably say that the book was accurate, but he would be able to

declare that it was delightful reading, that the feminine
characteristics of the queens had been touched with a
masterly hand, and that the work was one which would
certainly make its way into all drawing-rooms. He was
an adept at this sort of work, and knew well how to
review such a book as Lady Carbury's 'Criminal Queens,'
without bestowing much trouble on the reading. He
could almost do it without cutting the book, so that its
value for purposes of after sale might not be injured.
And yet Mr. Booker was an honest man, and had set his
face persistently against many literary malpractices.
Stretched-out type, insufficient lines, and the French
habit of meandering with a few words over an entire
page,* had been rebuked by him with conscientious
strength. He was supposed to be rather an Aristides
among reviewers. But circumstanced as he was he could
not oppose himself altogether to the usages of the time.
'Bad; of course it is bad,' he said to a young friend who
was working with him on his periodical. 'Who doubts
that? How many very bad things are there that we do!
But if we were to attempt to reform all our bad ways at
once, we should never do any good thing. I am not
strong enough to put the world straight, and I doubt if
you are.' Such was Mr. Booker.

Then there was letter No. 3, to Mr. Ferdinand Alf.
Mr. Alf managed, and, as it was supposed, chiefly owned,
the 'Evening Pulpit,' which during the last two years had
become 'quite a property,' as men connected with the
press were in the habit of saying. The 'Evening Pulpit'
was supposed to give daily to its readers all that had been
said and done up to two o'clock in the day by all the leading people in the metropolis, and to prophesy with
wonderful accuracy what would be the sayings and
doings of the twelve following hours. This was effected
with an air of wonderful omniscience, and not unfrequently with an ignorance hardly surpassed by its
arrogance. But the writing was clever. The facts, if
not true, were well invented; the arguments, if not logical,
were seductive. The presiding spirit of the paper had
the gift, at any rate, of knowing what the people for

whom he catered would like to read, and how to get his
subjects handled so that the reading should be pleasant.
Mr. Booker's 'Literary Chronicle' did not presume to
entertain any special political opinions. The 'Breakfast
Table' was decidedly Liberal. The 'Evening Pulpit' was
much given to politics, but held strictly to the motto
which it had assumed;—

'Nullius addictus jurare in verba magistri;'—*

and consequently had at all times the invaluable privilege
of abusing what was being done, whether by one side
or by the other. A newspaper that wishes to make its
fortune should never waste its columns and weary its
readers by praising anything. Eulogy is invariably dull,
—a fact that Mr. Alf had discovered and had utilized.

Mr. Alf had, moreover, discovered another fact.
Abuse from those who occasionally praise is considered
to be personally offensive, and they who give personal
offence will sometimes make the world too hot to hold
them. But censure from those who are always finding
fault is regarded so much as a matter of course that it
ceases to be objectionable. The caricaturist, who draws
only caricatures, is held to be justifiable, let him take
what liberties he may with a man's face and person. It
is his trade, and his business calls upon him to vilify all
that he touches. But were an artist to publish a series of
portraits, in which two out of a dozen were made to be
hideous, he would certainly make two enemies, if not
more. Mr. Alf never made enemies, for he praised no
one, and, as far as the expression of his newspaper went,
was satisfied with nothing.

Personally, Mr. Alf was a remarkable man. No one
knew whence he came or what he had been. He was
supposed to have been born a German Jew; and certain
ladies said that they could distinguish in his tongue the
slightest possible foreign accent. Nevertheless it was conceded to him that he knew England as only an Englishman can know it. During the last year or two he had
'come up' as the phrase goes, and had come up very
thoroughly. He had been blackballed at three or four

clubs, but had effected an entrance at two or three others, and had learned a manner of speaking of those which had rejected him calculated to leave on the minds of hearers a conviction that the societies in question were antiquated, imbecile, and moribund. He was never weary of implying that not to know Mr. Alf, not to be on good terms with Mr. Alf, not to understand that let Mr. Alf have been born where he might and how he might he was always to be recognized as a desirable acquaintance, was to be altogether out in the dark. And that which he so constantly asserted, or implied, men and women around him began at last to believe,—and Mr. Alf became an acknowledged something in the different worlds of politics, letters, and fashion.

He was a good-looking man, about forty years old, but carrying himself as though he was much younger, spare, below the middle height, with dark brown hair which would have shown a tinge of grey but for the dyer's art, with well-cut features, with a smile constantly on his mouth the pleasantness of which was always belied by the sharp severity of his eyes. He dressed with the utmost simplicity, but also with the utmost care. He was unmarried, had a small house of his own close to Berkeley Square at which he gave remarkable dinner parties, kept four or five hunters in Northamptonshire, and was reputed to earn £6,000 a year out of the 'Evening Pulpit' and to spend about half of that income. He also was intimate after his fashion with Lady Carbury, whose diligence in making and fostering useful friendships had been unwearied. Her letter to Mr. Alf was as follows;—

'DEAR MR. ALF,

'Do tell me who wrote the review on Fitzgerald Barker's last poem. Only I know you won't. I remember nothing done so well. I should think the poor wretch will hardly hold his head up again before the autumn. But it was fully deserved. I have no patience with the pretensions of would-be poets who contrive by toadying and underground influences to get their volumes placed on every drawing-room table. I know no one to whom the world has been so good-natured in this way as to Fitzgerald Barker, but I have heard of no one who has extended the good nature to the length of reading his poetry.

'Is it not singular how some men continue to obtain the reputation of popular authorship without adding a word to the literature of their country worthy of note? It is accomplished by unflagging assiduity in the system of puffing. To puff and to get one's self puffed have become different branches of a new profession. Alas, me! I wish I might find a class open in which lessons could be taken by such a poor tyro as myself. Much as I hate the thing from my very soul, and much as I admire the consistency with which the "Pulpit" has opposed it, I myself am so much in want of support for my own little efforts, and am struggling so hard honestly to make for myself a remunerative career, that I think, were the opportunity offered to me, I should pocket my honour, lay aside the high feeling which tells me that praise should be bought neither by money nor friendship, and descend among the low things, in order that I might one day have the pride of feeling that I had succeeded by my own work in providing for the needs of my children.

'But I have not as yet commenced the descent downwards; and therefore I am still bold enough to tell you that I shall look, not with concern but with a deep interest, to anything which may appear in the "Pulpit" respecting my "Criminal Queens." I venture to think that the book,—though I wrote it myself,—has an importance of its own which will secure for it some notice. That my inaccuracy will be laid bare and presumption scourged I do not in the least doubt, but I think your reviewer will be able to certify that the sketches are life-like and the portraits well considered. You will not hear me told, at any rate, that I had better sit at home and darn my stockings, as you said the other day of that poor unfortunate Mrs. Effington Stubbs.

'I have not seen you for the last three weeks. I have a few friends every Tuesday evening;—pray come next

week or the week following. And pray believe that no
amount of editorial or critical severity shall make me
receive you otherwise than with a smile.

'Most sincerely yours,
'MATILDA CARBURY.'

Lady Carbury, having finished her third letter, threw
herself back in her chair, and for a moment or two closed
her eyes, as though about to rest. But she soon remembered that the activity of her life did not admit of such
rest. She therefore seized her pen and began scribbling
further notes.

## Chapter II

### THE CARBURY FAMILY

SOMETHING of herself and condition Lady Carbury
has told the reader in the letters given in the former
chapter, but more must be added. She has declared she
had been cruelly slandered; but she has also shown that
she was not a woman whose words about herself could
be taken with much confidence. If the reader does not
understand so much from her letters to the three editors
they have been written in vain. She has been made to
say that her object in work was to provide for the need
of her children, and that with that noble purpose before
her she was struggling to make for herself a career in
literature. Detestably false as had been her letters to the
editors, absolutely and abominably foul as was the entire
system by which she was endeavouring to achieve success,
far away from honour and honesty as she had been
carried by her ready subserviency to the dirty things
among which she had lately fallen, nevertheless her
statements about herself were substantially true. She had
been ill-treated. She had been slandered. She was true
to her children,—especially devoted to one of them—
and was ready to work her nails off if by doing so she
could advance their interests.

She was the widow of one Sir Patrick Carbury, who
many years since had done great things as a soldier in

India, and had been thereupon created a baronet. He had married a young wife late in life and, having found out when too late that he had made a mistake, had occasionally spoilt his darling and occasionally ill-used her. In doing each he had done it abundantly. Among Lady Carbury's faults had never been that of even incipient, —not even of sentimental—infidelity to her husband. When as a lovely and penniless girl of eighteen she had consented to marry a man of forty-four who had the spending of a large income, she had made up her mind to abandon all hope of that sort of love which poets describe and which young people generally desire to experience. Sir Patrick at the time of his marriage was red-faced, stout, bald, very choleric, generous in money, suspicious in temper, and intelligent. He knew how to govern men. He could read and understand a book. There was nothing mean about him. He had his attractive qualities. He was a man who might be loved;—but he was hardly a man for love. The young Lady Carbury had understood her position and had determined to do her duty. She had resolved before she went to the altar that she would never allow herself to flirt and she had never flirted. For fifteen years things had gone tolerably well with her,—by which it is intended that the reader should understand that they had so gone that she had been able to tolerate them. They had been home in England for three or four years, and then Sir Patrick had returned with some new and higher appointment. For fifteen years, though he had been passionate, imperious, and often cruel, he had never been jealous. A boy and a girl had been born to them, to whom both father and mother had been over indulgent;—but the mother, according to her lights, had endeavoured to do her duty by them. But from the commencement of her life she had been educated in deceit, and her married life had seemed to make the practice of deceit necessary to her. Her mother had run away from her father, and she had been tossed to and fro between this and that protector, sometimes being in danger of wanting any one to care for her, till she had been made sharp, incredulous, and untrustworthy by the difficulties of her position. But she was clever, and had picked up an education and good manners amidst the difficulties of her childhood,—and had been beautiful to look at. To marry and have the command of money, to do her duty correctly, to live in a big house and be respected, had been her ambition,— and during the first fifteen years of her married life she was successful amidst great difficulties. She would smile within five minutes of violent ill-usage. Her husband would even strike her,—and the first effort of her mind would be given to conceal the fact from all the world. In latter years he drank too much, and she struggled hard first to prevent the evil, and then to prevent and to hide the ill effects of the evil. But in doing all this she schemed, and lied, and lived a life of manœuvres. Then, at last, when she felt that she was no longer quite a young woman, she allowed herself to attempt to form friendships for herself, and among her friends was one of the other sex. If fidelity in a wife be compatible with such friendship, if the married state does not exact from a woman the necessity of debarring herself from all friendly intercourse with any man except her lord, Lady Carbury was not faithless. But Sir Carbury became jealous, spoke words which even she could not endure, did things which drove even her beyond the calculations of her prudence,— and she left him. But even this she did in so guarded a way that, as to every step she took, she could prove her inno- cence. Her life at that period is of little moment to our story, except that it is essential that the reader should know in what she had been slandered. For a month or two all hard words had been said against her by her husband's friends, and even by Sir Patrick himself. But gradually the truth was known, and after a year's separation they came again together and she remained the mistress of his house till he died. She brought him home to England, but during the short period left to him of life in his old country he had been a worn-out, dying invalid. But the scandal of her great misfortune had followed her, and some people were never tired of reminding others that in the course of her married life Lady Carbury had run away from her husband, and had been taken back again by the kind-hearted old gentleman.

Sir Patrick had left behind him a moderate fortune, though by no means great wealth. To his son, who was now Sir Felix Carbury, he had left £1,000 a year; and to his widow as much, with a provision that after her death the latter sum should be divided between his son and daughter. It therefore came to pass that the young man, who had already entered the army when his father died, and upon whom devolved no necessity of keeping a house, and who in fact not unfrequently lived in his mother's house, had an income equal to that with which his mother and sister were obliged to maintain a roof over their head. Now Lady Carbury, when she was released from her thraldom at the age of forty, had no idea at all of passing her future life amidst the ordinary penances of widowhood. She had hitherto endeavoured to do her duty, knowing that in accepting her position she was bound to take the good and the bad together. She had certainly encountered hitherto much that was bad. To be scolded, watched, beaten, and sworn at by a choleric old man till she was at last driven out of her house by the violence of his ill-usage; to be taken back as a favour with the assurance that her name would for the remainder of her life be unjustly tarnished; to have her flight constantly thrown in her face; and then at last to become for a year or two the nurse of a dying debauchee, was a high price to pay for such good things as she had hitherto enjoyed. Now at length had come to her a period of relaxation—her reward, her freedom, her chance of happiness. She thought much about herself, and resolved on one or two things. The time for love had gone by, and she would have nothing to do with it. Nor would she marry again for convenience. But she would have friends,—real friends; friends who could help her, —and whom possibly she might help. She would, too, make some career for herself, so that life might not be without an interest to her. She would live in London, and would become somebody at any rate in some circle. Accident at first rather than choice had thrown her among literary people, but that accident had, during the last two years, been supported and corroborated by the desire which had fallen upon her of earning money. She had known from the first that ecomony would be necessary to her,—not chiefly or perhaps not at all from a feeling that she and her daughter could not live comfortably together on a thousand a year,—but on behalf of her son. She wanted no luxury but a house so placed that people might conceive of her that she lived in a proper part of the town. Of her daughter's prudence she was as well convinced as of her own. She could trust Henrietta in everything. But her son, Sir Felix, was not very trustworthy. And yet Sir Felix was the darling of her heart.

At the time of the writing of the three letters, at which our story is supposed to begin, she was driven very hard for money. Sir Felix was then twenty-five, had been in a fashionable regiment for four years, had already sold out,* and, to own the truth at once, had altogether wasted the property which his father had left him. So much the mother knew,—and knew, therefore, that with her limited income she must maintain not only herself and daughter, but also the baronet. She did not know, however, the amount of the baronet's obligations;—nor, indeed, did he, or any one else. A baronet, holding a commission in the Guards, and known to have had a fortune left him by his father, may go very far in getting into debt; and Sir Felix had made full use of all his privileges. His life had been in every way bad. He had become a burden on his mother so heavy,—and on his sister also,—that their life had become one of unavoidable embarrassments. But not for a moment had either of them ever quarrelled with him. Henrietta had been taught by the conduct of both father and mother that every vice might be forgiven in a man and in a son, though every virtue was expected from a woman, and especially from a daughter. The lesson had come to her so early in life that she had learned it without the feeling of any grievance. She lamented her brother's evil conduct as it affected him, but she pardoned it altogether as it affected herself. That all her interests in life should be made subservient to him was natural to her; and when she found that her little comforts were discontinued, and her moderate expenses curtailed, because he, having eaten up all that was his own, was now eating up also all that was his mother's, she never complained. Henrietta had been taught to think that men in that rank of life in which she had been born always did eat up everything.

The mother's feeling was less noble,—or perhaps, it might better be said, more open to censure. The boy, who had been beautiful as a star, had ever been the cynosure of her eyes, the one thing on which her heart had riveted itself. Even during the career of his folly she had hardly ventured to say a word to him with the purport of stopping him on his road to ruin. In everything she had spoilt him as a boy, and in everything she still spoilt him as a man. She was almost proud of his vices, and had taken delight in hearing of doings which if not vicious of themselves had been ruinous from their extravagance. She had so indulged him that even in her own presence he was never ashamed of his own selfishness or apparently conscious of the injustice which he did to others.

From all this it had come to pass that that dabbling in literature which had been commenced partly perhaps from a sense of pleasure in the work, partly as a passport into society, had been converted into hard work by which money if possible might be earned. So that Lady Carbury when she wrote to her friends, the editors, of her struggles was speaking the truth. Tidings had reached her of this and the other man's success, and,—coming near to her still,—of this and that other woman's earnings in literature. And it had seemed to her that, within moderate limits, she might give a wide field to her hopes. Why should she not add a thousand a year to her income, so that Felix might again live like a gentleman and marry that heiress who, in Lady Carbury's look-out into the future, was destined to make all things straight! Who was so handsome as her son? Who could make himself more agreeable? Who had more of that audacity which is the chief thing necessary to the winning of heiresses?

And then he could make his wife Lady Carbury. If only enough money might be earned to tide over the present evil day, all might be well.

The one most essential obstacle to the chance of success in all this was probably Lady Carbury's conviction that her end was to be obtained not by producing good books, but by inducing certain people to say that her books were good. She did work hard at what she wrote,—hard enough at any rate to cover her pages quickly; and was, by nature, a clever woman. She could write after a glib, commonplace, sprightly fashion, and had already acquired the knack of spreading all she knew very thin, so that it might cover a vast surface. She had no ambition to write a good book, but was painfully anxious to write a book that the critics should say was good. Had Mr. Broune, in his closet, told her that her book was absolutely trash, but had undertaken at the same time to have it violently praised in the 'Breakfast Table', it may be doubted whether the critic's own opinion would have even wounded her vanity. The woman was false from head to foot, but there was much of good in her, false though she was.

Whether Sir Felix, her son, had become what he was solely by bad training, or whether he had been born bad, who shall say? It is hardly possible that he should not have been better had he been taken away as an infant and subjected to moral training by moral teachers. And yet again it is hardly possible that any training or want of training should have produced a heart so utterly incapable of feeling for others as was his. He could not even feel his own misfortunes unless they touched the outward comforts of the moment. It seemed that he lacked sufficient imagination to realise future misery though the futurity to be considered was divided from the present but by a single month, a single week,—but by a single night. He liked to be kindly treated, to be praised and petted, to be well fed and caressed; and they who so treated him were his chosen friends. He had in this the instincts of a horse, not approaching the higher sympathies of a dog. But it cannot be said of him that

he had ever loved any one to the extent of denying himself a moment's gratification on that loved one's behalf.
His heart was a stone. But he was beautiful to look at,
ready-witted, and intelligent. He was very dark, with
that soft olive complexion which so generally gives to
young men an appearance of aristocratic breeding. His
hair, which was never allowed to become long, was
nearly black, and was soft and silky without that taint
of grease which is so common with silken-headed darlings.
His eyes were long, brown in colour, and were made
beautiful by the perfect arch of the perfect eyebrow.
But perhaps the glory of the face was due more to the
finished moulding and fine symmetry of the nose and
mouth than to his other features. On his short upper lip
he had a moustache as well formed as his eyebrows, but
he wore no other beard. The form of his chin too was
perfect, but it lacked that sweetness and softness of expression, indicative of softness of heart, which a dimple
conveys. He was about five feet nine in height, and was
as excellent in figure as in face. It was admitted by men
and clamorously asserted by women that no man had
ever been more handsome than Felix Carbury, and it
was admitted also that he never showed consciousness of
his beauty. He had given himself airs on many scores;
—on the score of his money, poor fool, while it lasted;
on the score of his title; on the score of his army standing
till he lost it; and especially on the score of superiority
in fashionable intellect. But he had been clever enough
to dress himself always with simplicity and to avoid the
appearance of thought about his outward man. As yet
the little world of his associates had hardly found out
how callous were his affections,—or rather how devoid
he was of affection. His airs and his appearance, joined
with some cleverness, had carried him through even the
viciousness of his life. In one matter he had marred his
name, and by a moment's weakness had injured his
character among his friends more than he had done by
the folly of three years. There had been a quarrel
between him and a brother officer, in which he had been
the aggressor; and, when the moment came in which a

man's heart should have produced manly conduct, he had first threatened and had then shown the white feather. That was now a year since, and he had partly outlived the evil;—but some men still remembered that Felix Carbury had been cowed, and had cowered.

It was now his business to marry an heiress. He was well aware that it was so, and was quite prepared to face his destiny. But he lacked something in the art of making love. He was beautiful, had the manners of a gentleman, could talk well, lacked nothing of audacity, and had no feeling of repugnance at declaring a passion which he did not feel. But he knew so little of the passion, that he could hardly make even a young girl believe that he felt it. When he talked of love, he not only thought that he was talking nonsense, but showed that he thought so. From this fault he had already failed with one young lady reputed to have £40,000, who had refused him because, as she naïvely said, she knew 'he did not really care.' 'How can I show that I care more than by wishing to make you my wife?' he had asked. 'I don't know that you can, but all the same you don't care,' she said. And so that young lady escaped the pitfall. Now there was another young lady, to whom the reader shall be introduced in time, whom Sir Felix was instigated to pursue with unremitting diligence. Her wealth was not defined, as had been the £40,000 of her predecessor, but was known to be very much greater than that. It was, indeed, generally supposed to be fathomless, bottomless, endless. It was said that in regard to money for ordinary expenditure, money for houses, servants, horses, jewels, and the like, one sum was the same as another to the father of this young lady. He had great concerns;—concerns so great that the payment of ten or twenty thousand pounds upon any trifle was the same thing to him,—as to men who are comfortable in their circumstances it matters little whether they pay sixpence or ninepence for their mutton chops. Such a man may be ruined at any time; but there was no doubt that to any one marrying his daughter during the present season of his outrageous prosperity he could give a very large

fortune indeed. Lady Carbury, who had known the rock
on which her son had been once wrecked, was very
anxious that Sir Felix should at once make a proper use
of the intimacy which he had effected in the house of this
topping Crœsus of the day.

And now there must be a few words said about Henrietta Carbury. Of course she was of infinitely less importance than her brother, who was a baronet, the head
of that branch of the Carburys, and her mother's darling;
and, therefore, a few words should suffice. She also was
very lovely, being like her brother; but somewhat less
dark and with features less absolutely regular. But she
had in her countenance a full measure of that sweetness
of expression which seems to imply that consideration
of self is subordinated to consideration for others. This
sweetness was altogether lacking to her brother. And her
face was a true index of her character. Again, who shall
say why the brother and sister had become so opposite
to each other; whether they would have been thus
different had both been taken away as infants from their
father's and mother's training, or whether the girl's
virtues were owing altogether to the lower place which
she had held in her parent's heart? She, at any rate, had
not been spoilt by a title, by the command of money, and
by the temptations of too early acquaintance with the
world. At the present time she was barely twenty-one
years old, and had not seen much of London society.
Her mother did not frequent balls, and during the last
two years there had grown upon them a necessity for
economy which was inimical to many gloves and costly
dresses. Sir Felix went out of course, but Hetta Carbury
spent most of her time at home with her mother in Welbeck Street. Occasionally the world saw her, and when
the world did see her the world declared that she was a
charming girl. The world was so far right.

But for Henrietta Carbury the romance of life had
already commenced in real earnest. There was another
branch of the Carburys, the head branch, which was
now represented by one Roger Carbury, of Carbury
Hall. Roger Carbury was a gentleman of whom much

will have to be said, but here, at this moment, it need only be told that he was passionately in love with his cousin Henrietta. He was, however, nearly forty years old, and there was one Paul Montague whom Henrietta had seen.

## Chapter III

### THE BEARGARDEN*

LADY CARBURY'S house in Welbeck Street was a modest house enough,—with no pretensions to be a mansion, hardly assuming even to be a residence; but, having some money in her hands when she first took it, she had made it pretty and pleasant, and was still proud to feel that in spite of the hardness of her position she had comfortable belongings around her when her literary friends came to see her on her Tuesday evenings. Here she was now living with her son and daughter. The back drawing-room was divided from the front by doors that were permanently closed, and in this she carried on her great work. Here she wrote her books and contrived her system for the inveigling of editors and critics. Here she was rarely disturbed by her daughter, and admitted no visitors except editors and critics. But her son was controlled by no household laws, and would break in upon her privacy without remorse. She had hardly finished two galloping notes after completing her letter to Mr. Ferdinand Alf, when Felix entered the room with a cigar in his mouth and threw himself upon the sofa.

'My dear boy,' she said, 'pray leave your tobacco below when you come in here.'

'What affectation it is, mother,' he said, throwing, however, the half-smoked cigar into the fire-place. 'Some women swear they like smoke, others say they hate it like the devil. It depends altogether on whether they wish to flatter or snub a fellow.'

'You don't suppose that I wish to snub you?'

'Upon my word I don't know. I wonder whether you can let me have twenty pounds?'

'My dear Felix!'

'Just so, mother;—but how about the twenty pounds?'

'What is it for, Felix?'

'Well;—to tell the truth, to carry on the game for the nonce till something is settled. A fellow can't live without some money in his pocket. I do with as little as most fellows. I pay for nothing that I can help. I even get my hair cut on credit, and as long as it was possible I had a brougham, to save cabs.'

'What is to be the end of it, Felix?'

'I never could see the end of anything, mother. I never could nurse a horse when the hounds were going well in order to be in at the finish. I never could pass a dish that I liked in favour of those that were to follow. What's the use?' The young man did not say 'carpe diem,' but that was the philosophy which he intended to preach.

'Have you been at the Melmottes' to-day?' It was now five o'clock on a winter afternoon, the hour at which ladies are drinking tea, and idle men playing whist at the clubs,—at which young idle men are sometimes allowed to flirt, and at which, as Lady Carbury thought, her son might have been paying his court to Marie Melmotte the great heiress.

'I have just come away.'

'And what do you think of her?'

'To tell the truth, mother, I have thought very little about her. She is not pretty, she is not plain; she is not clever, she is not stupid; she is neither saint nor sinner.'

'The more likely to make a good wife.'

'Perhaps so. I am at any rate quite willing to believe that as wife she would be "good enough for me."'*

'What does the mother say?'

'The mother is a caution. I cannot help speculating whether, if I marry the daughter, I shall ever find out where the mother came from. Dolly Longestaffe says that somebody says that she was a Bohemian Jewess; but I think she's too fat for that.'

'What does it matter, Felix?'

'Not in the least.'

'Is she civil to you?'

'Yes, civil enough.'

'And the father?'

'Well, he does not turn me out, or anything of that sort. Of course there are half-a-dozen after her, and I think the old fellow is bewildered among them all. He's thinking more of getting dukes to dine with him than of his daughter's lovers. Any fellow might pick her up who happened to hit her fancy.'

'And why not you?'

'Why not, mother? I am doing my best, and it's no good flogging a willing horse. Can you let me have the money?'

'Oh, Felix, I think you hardly know how poor we are. You have still got your hunters down at the place!'

'I have got two horses, if you mean that; and I haven't paid a shilling for their keep since the season began. Look here, mother; this is a risky sort of game, I grant, but I am playing it by your advice. If I can marry Miss Melmotte, I suppose all will be right. But I don't think the way to get her would be to throw up everything and let all the world know that I haven't got a copper. To do that kind of thing a man must live a little up to the mark. I've brought my hunting down to a minimum, but if I gave it up altogether there would be lots of fellows to tell them in Grosvenor Square why I had done so.'

There was an apparent truth in this argument which the poor woman was unable to answer. Before the interview was over the money demanded was forthcoming, though at the time it could be but ill afforded, and the youth went away apparently with a light heart, hardly listening to his mother's entreaties that the affair with Marie Melmotte might, if possible, be brought to a speedy conclusion.

Felix, when he left his mother, went down to the only club to which he now belonged. Clubs are pleasant resorts in all respects but one. They require ready money or even worse than that in respect to annual payments, —money in advance; and the young baronet had been absolutely forced to restrict himself. He, as a matter of course, out of those to which he had possessed the right of entrance, chose the worst. It was called the Beargarden, and had been lately opened with the express view of combining parsimony with profligacy. Clubs were ruined, so said certain young parsimonious profligates, by providing comforts for old fogies who paid little or nothing but their subscriptions, and took out by their mere presence three times as much as they gave. This club was not to be opened till three o'clock in the afternoon, before which hour the promoters of the Beargarden thought it improbable that they and their fellows would want a club. There were to be no morning papers taken, no library, no morning-room. Dining-rooms, billiard-rooms, and card-rooms would suffice for the Beargarden. Everything was to be provided by a purveyor, so that the club should be cheated only by one man. Everything was to be luxurious, but the luxuries were to be achieved at first cost. It had been a happy thought, and the club was said to prosper. Herr Vossner, the purveyor, was a jewel, and so carried on affairs that there was no trouble about anything. He would assist even in smoothing little difficulties as to the settling of card accounts, and had behaved with the greatest tenderness to the drawers of cheques whose bankers had harshly declared them to have 'no effects.' Herr Vossner was a jewel, and the Beargarden was a success. Perhaps no young man about town enjoyed the Beargarden more thoroughly than did Sir Felix Carbury. The club was in the close vicinity of other clubs, in a small street turning out of St. James's Street, and piqued itself on its outward quietness and sobriety. Why pay for stone-work for other people to look at;—why lay out money in marble pillars and cornices, seeing that you can neither eat such things, nor drink them, nor gamble with them? But the Beargarden had the best wines,—or thought that it had,—and the easiest chairs, and two billiard-tables than which nothing more perfect had ever been made to stand upon legs. Hither Sir Felix wended on that January afternoon as soon as he had his mother's cheque for £20 in his pocket.

He found his special friend, Dolly Longestaffe, standing on the steps with a cigar in his mouth, and gazing vacantly at the dull brick house opposite. 'Going to dine here, Dolly?' said Sir Felix.

'I suppose I shall, because it's such a lot of trouble to go anywhere else. I'm engaged somewhere, I know; but I'm not up to getting home and dressing. By George! I don't know how fellows do that kind of thing. I can't.'

'Going to hunt to-morrow?'

'Well, yes; but I don't suppose I shall. I was going to hunt every day last week, but my fellow never would get me up in time. I can't tell why it is that things are done in such a beastly way. Why shouldn't fellows begin to hunt at two or three, so that a fellow needn't get up in the middle of the night?'

'Because one can't ride by moonlight, Dolly.'

'It isn't moonlight at three. At any rate I can't get myself to Euston Square by nine. I don't think that fellow of mine likes getting up himself. He says he comes in and wakes me, but I never remember it.'

'How many horses have you got at Leighton, Dolly?'

'How many? There were five, but I think that fellow down there sold one; but then I think he bought another. I know he did something.'

'Who rides them?'

'He does, I suppose. That is, of course, I ride them myself, only I so seldom get down. Somebody told me that Grasslough was riding two of them last week. I don't think I ever told him he might. I think he tipped that fellow of mine; and I call that a low kind of thing to do. I'd ask him, only I know he'd say that I had lent them. Perhaps I did when I was tight, you know.'

'You and Grasslough were never pals.'

'I don't like him a bit. He gives himself airs because he is a lord, and is devilish ill-natured. I don't know why he should want to ride my horses.'

'To save his own.'

'He isn't hard up. Why doesn't he have his own horses? I'll tell you what, Carbury, I've made up my mind to one thing, and, by Jove, I'll stick to it. I never will lend a horse again to anybody. If fellows want horses let them buy them.'

'But some fellows haven't got any money, Dolly.'

'Then they ought to go tick. I don't think I've paid for any of mine I've bought this season. There was somebody here yesterday——'

'What! here at the club?'

'Yes; followed me here to say he wanted to be paid for something! It was horses, I think, because of the fellow's trousers.'

'What did you say?'

'Me! Oh, I didn't say anything.'

'And how did it end?'

'When he'd done talking I offered him a cigar, and while he was biting off the end I went upstairs. I suppose he went away when he was tired of waiting.'

'I'll tell you what, Dolly; I wish you'd let me ride two of yours for a couple of days,—that is, of course, if you don't want them yourself. You ain't tight now, at any rate.'

'No; I ain't tight,' said Dolly, with melancholy acquiescence.

'I mean that I wouldn't like to borrow your horses without your remembering all about it. Nobody knows as well as you do how awfully done up I am. I shall pull through at last, but it's an awful squeeze in the meantime. There's nobody I'd ask such a favour of except you.'

'Well, you may have them;—that is, for two days. I don't know whether that fellow of mine will believe you. He wouldn't believe Grasslough, and told him so. But Grasslough took them out of the stables. That's what somebody told me.'

'You could write a line to your groom.'

'Oh my dear fellow, that is such a bore; I don't think I could do that. My fellow will believe you, because you and I have been pals. I think I'll have a little drop of curaçoa before dinner. Come along and try it. It'll give us an appetite.'

It was then nearly seven o'clock. Nine hours afterwards the same two men, with two others,—of whom young Lord Grasslough, Dolly Longestaffe's peculiar aversion, was one,—were just rising from a card-table in one of the upstairs rooms of the club. For it was understood that, though the Beargarden was not to be open before three o'clock in the afternoon, the accommodation denied during the day was to be given freely during the night. No man could get a breakfast at the Beargarden, but suppers at three o'clock in the morning were quite within the rule. Such a supper, or rather succession of suppering, there had been to-night, various devils and broils and hot toasts having been brought up from time to time first for one and then for another. But there had been no cessation of gambling since the cards had first been opened about ten o'clock. At four in the morning Dolly Longestaffe was certainly in a condition to lend his horses and to remember nothing about it. He was quite affectionate with Lord Grasslough, as he was also with his other companions,—affection being the normal state of his mind when in that condition. He was by no means helplessly drunk, and was, perhaps, hardly more silly than when he was sober; but he was willing to play at any game whether he understood it or not, and for any stakes. When Sir Felix got up and said he would play no more, Dolly also got up, apparently quite contented. When Lord Grasslough, with a dark scowl on his face, expressed his opinion that it was not just the thing for men to break up like that when so much money had been lost, Dolly as willingly sat down again. But Dolly's sitting down was not sufficient. 'I'm going to hunt to-morrow,' said Sir Felix,—meaning that day,—'and I shall play no more. A man must go to bed at some time.'

'I don't see it at all,' said Lord Grasslough. 'It's an understood thing that when a man has won as much as you have he should stay.'

'Stay how long?' said Sir Felix, with an angry look. 'That's nonsense; there must be an end of everything, and there's an end of this for me to-night.'

'Oh, if you choose,' said his lordship.

'I do choose. Good night, Dolly; we'll settle this next time we meet. I've got it all entered.'

The night had been one very serious in its results to Sir Felix. He had sat down to the card-table with the proceeds of his mother's cheque, a poor £20, and now he had,—he didn't at all know how much in his pockets. He also had drunk, but not so as to obscure his mind. He knew that Longestaffe owed him over £300, and he knew also that he had received more than that in ready money and cheques from Lord Grasslough and the other player. Dolly Longestaffe's money, too, would certainly be paid, though Dolly did complain of the importunity of his tradesmen. As he walked up St. James's Street, looking for a cab, he presumed himself to be worth over £700. When begging for a small sum from Lady Carbury, he had said that he could not carry on the game without some ready money, and had considered himself fortunate in fleecing his mother as he had done. Now he was in the possession of wealth,—of wealth that might, at any rate, be sufficient to aid him materially in the object he had in hand. He never for a moment thought of paying his bills. Even the large sum of which he had become so unexpectedly possessed would not have gone far with him in such a quixotic object as that; but he could now look bright, and buy presents, and be seen with money in his hands. It is hard even to make love in these days without something in your purse.

He found no cab, but in his present frame of mind was indifferent to the trouble of walking home. There was something so joyous in the feeling of the possession of all this money that it made the night air pleasant to him. Then, of a sudden, he remembered the low wail with which his mother had spoken of her poverty when he demanded assistance from her. Now he could give her back the £20. But it occurred to him sharply, with an amount of carefulness quite new to him, that it would be foolish to do so. How soon might he want it again? And, moreover, he could not repay the money without explaining to her how he had gotten it. It would be preferable to say nothing about his money. As he let himself into the house and went up to his room he resolved that he would not say anything about it.

On that morning he was at the station at nine, and hunted down in Buckinghamshire, riding two of Dolly Longestaffe's horses,—for the use of which he paid Dolly Longestaffe's 'fellow' thirty shilling.

## Chapter IV

### MADAME MELMOTTE'S BALL

THE next night but one after that of the gambling transaction at the Beargarden, a great ball was given in Grosvenor Square. It was a ball on a scale so magnificent that it had been talked about ever since Parliament met, now about a fortnight since. Some people had expressed an opinion that such a ball as this was intended to be could not be given successfully in February. Others declared that the money which was to be spent,—an amount which would make this affair quite new in the annals of ball-giving,—would give the thing such a character that it would certainly be successful. And much more than money had been expended. Almost incredible efforts had been made to obtain the co-operation of great people, and these efforts had at last been grandly successful. The Duchess of Stevenage had come up from Castle Albury herself to be present at it and to bring her daughters, though it has never been her Grace's wont to be in London at this inclement season. No doubt the persuasion used with the Duchess had been very strong. Her brother, Lord Alfred Grendall, was known to be in great difficulties, which,—so people said, —had been considerably modified by opportune pecuniary assistance. And then it was certain that one of the young Grendalls, Lord Alfred's second son, had been appointed to some mercantile position, for which he received a salary which his most intimate friends thought that he was hardly qualified to earn. It was certainly a fact that he went to Abchurch Lane, in the City, four or five days a week, and that he did not occupy his time in so unaccustomed a manner for nothing. Where the Duchess of Stevenage went all the world would go. And it became known at the last moment, that is to say only, the day before the party, that a prince of the blood royal was to be there. How this had been achieved nobody quite understood; but there were rumours that a certain lady's jewels had been rescued from the pawnbroker's. Everything was done on the same scale. The Prime Minister had indeed declined to allow his name to appear on the list; but one Cabinet Minister and two or three under-secretaries had agreed to come because it was felt that the giver of the ball might before long be the master of considerable parliamentary interest. It was believed that he had an eye to politics, and it is always wise to have great wealth on one's own side. There had at one time been much solicitude about the ball. Many anxious thoughts had been given. When great attempts fail, the failure is disastrous, and may be ruinous. But this ball had now been put beyond the chance of failure.

The giver of the ball was Augustus Melmotte, Esq., the father of the girl whom Sir Felix Carbury desired to marry, and the husband of the lady who was said to have been a Bohemian Jewess. It was thus that the gentleman chose to have himself designated, though within the last two years he had arrived in London from Paris, and had at first been known as M. Melmotte. But he had declared of himself that he had been born in England, and that he was an Englishman. He admitted that his wife was a foreigner,—an admission that was necessary as she spoke very little English. Melmotte himself spoke his 'native' language fluently, but with an accent which betrayed at least a long expatriation. Miss Melmotte,—who a very short time since had been known as Mademoiselle Marie,—spoke English well, but as a foreigner. In regard to her it was acknowledged that she had been born out of England,—some said in New York; but Madame Melmotte, who must have known, had declared that the great event had taken place in Paris.

It was at any rate an established fact that Mr. Melmotte had made his wealth in France. He no doubt had had enormous dealings in other countries, as to which stories were told which must surely have been exaggerated. It was said that he had made a railway across Russia, that he provisioned the Southern army in the American civil war, that he had supplied Austria with arms, and had at one time bought up all the iron in England. He could make or mar any company by buying or selling stock, and could make money dear or cheap as he pleased. All this was said of him in his praise,—but it was also said that he was regarded in Paris as the most gigantic swindler that had ever lived; that he had made that City too hot to hold him; that he had endeavoured to establish himself in Vienna, but had been warned away by the police; and that he had at length found that British freedom would alone allow him to enjoy, without persecution, the fruits of his industry. He was now established privately in Grosvenor Square and officially in Abchurch Lane; and it was known to all the world that a Royal Prince, a Cabinet Minister, and the very cream of duchesses were going to his wife's ball. All this had been done within twelve months.

There was but one child in the family, one heiress for all this wealth. Melmotte himself was a large man, with bushy whiskers and rough thick hair, with heavy eyebrows, and a wonderful look of power about his mouth and chin. This was so strong as to redeem his face from vulgarity; but the countenance and appearance of the man were on the whole unpleasant, and, I may say, untrustworthy. He looked as though he were purse-proud and a bully. She was fat and fair,—unlike in colour to our traditional Jewesses; but she had the Jewish nose and the Jewish contraction of the eyes. There was certainly very little in Madame Melmotte to recommend her, unless it was a readiness to spend money on any object that might be suggested to her by her new acquaintances. It sometimes seemed that she had a commission from her husband to give away presents to any who would accept them. The world had received the man as Augustus Melmotte, Esq. The world so addressed him on the very numerous letters which reached him, and so inscribed him among the directors of three dozen companies to which he belonged. But his wife was still Madame Melmotte. The daughter had been allowed to take her rank with an English title. She was now Miss Melmotte on all occasions.

Marie Melmotte had been accurately described by Felix Carbury to his mother. She was not beautiful, she was not clever, and she was not a saint. But then neither was she plain, nor stupid, nor, especially, a sinner. She was a little thing, hardly over twenty years of age, very unlike her father or mother, having no trace of the Jewess in her countenance, who seemed to be overwhelmed by the sense of her own position. With such people as the Melmottes things go fast, and it was very well known that Miss Melmotte had already had one lover who had been nearly accepted. The affair, however, had gone off. In this 'going off' no one imputed to the young lady blame or even misfortune. It was not supposed that she had either jilted or been jilted. As in royal espousals interests of State regulate their expedience with an acknowledged absence, with even a proclaimed impossibility, of personal predilections, so in this case was money allowed to have the same weight. Such a marriage would or would not be sanctioned in accordance with great pecuniary arrangements. The young Lord Nidderdale, the eldest son of the Marquis of Auld Reekie, had offered to take the girl and make her Marchioness in the process of time for half a million down. Melmotte had not objected to the sum,—so it was said.—but had proposed to tie it up. Nidderdale had desired to have it free in his own grasp, and would not move on any other terms. Melmotte had been anxious to secure the Marquis,—very anxious to secure the Marchioness; for at that time terms had not been made with the Duchess; but at last he had lost his temper, and had asked his lordship's lawyer whether it was likely that he would entrust such a sum of money to such a man. 'You are willing to trust your only child to him,' said the lawyer. Melmotte scowled at the man for a few seconds from under his bushy eyebrows; then told him that his answer had nothing in it, and marched out of the room. So that affair was over. I doubt whether

Lord Nidderdale had ever said a word of love to Marie Melmotte,—or whether the poor girl had expected it. Her destiny had no doubt been explained to her.

Others had tried and had broken down somewhat in the same fashion. Each had treated the girl as an encumbrance he was to undertake,—at a very great price. But as affairs prospered with the Melmottes, as princes and duchesses were obtained by other means,—costly no doubt, but not so ruinously costly,—the immediate disposition of Marie became less necessary, and Melmotte reduced his offers. The girl herself, too, began to have an opinion. It was said that she had absolutely rejected Lord Grasslough, whose father indeed was in a state of bankruptcy, who had no income of his own, who was ugly, vicious, ill-tempered, and without any power of recommending himself to a girl. She had had experience since Lord Nidderdale, with a half laugh, had told her that he might just as well take her for his wife, and was now tempted from time to time to contemplate her own happiness and her own condition. People around were beginning to say that if Sir Felix Carbury managed his affairs well he might be the happy man.

There was a considerable doubt whether Marie was the daughter of that Jewish-looking woman. Enquiries had been made, but not successfully, as to the date of the Melmotte marriage. There was an idea abroad that Melmotte had got his first money with his wife, and had gotten it not very long ago. Then other people said that Marie was not his daughter at all. Altogether the mystery was rather pleasant as the money was certain. Of the certainty of the money in daily use there could be no doubt. There was the house. There was the furniture. There were the carriages, the horses, the servants with the livery coats and powdered heads, and the servants with the black coats and unpowdered heads. There were the gems, and the presents, and all the nice things that money can buy. There were two dinner parties every day, one at two o'clock called lunch, and the other at eight. The tradesmen had learned enough to be quite free of doubt, and in the City Mr. Melmotte's name was worth any money,—though his character was perhaps worth but little.

The large house on the south side of Grosvenor Square was all ablaze by ten o'clock. The broad verandah had been turned into a conservatory, had been covered with boards contrived to look like trellis-work, was heated with hot air and filled with exotics at some fabulous price. A covered way had been made from the door, down across the pathway, to the road, and the police had, I fear, been bribed to frighten foot passengers into a belief that they were bound to go round. The house had been so arranged that it was impossible to know where you were, when once in it. The hall was a paradise. The staircase was fairyland. The lobbies were grottoes rich with ferns. Walls had been knocked away and arches had been constructed. The leads behind had been supported and walled in, and covered and carpeted. The ball had possession of the ground floor and first floor, and the house seemed to be endless. 'It's to cost sixty thousand pounds,' said the Marchioness of Auld Reekie to her old friend the Countess of Mid-Lothian. The Marchioness had come in spite of her son's misfortune when she heard that the Duchess of Stevenage was to be there. 'And worse spent money never was wasted,' said the Countess. 'By all acounts it was as badly come by,' said the Marchioness. Then the two old noblewomen, one after the other, made graciously flattering speeches to the much-worn Bohemian Jewess, who was standing in fairyland to receive her guests, almost fainting under the greatness of the occasion.

The three saloons on the first or drawing-room floor had been prepared for dancing, and here Marie was stationed. The Duchess had however undertaken to see that somebody should set the dancing going, and she had commissioned her nephew Miles Grendall, the young gentleman who now frequented the City, to give directions to the band and to make himself generally useful. Indeed there had sprung up a considerable intimacy betweer the Grendall family,—that is Lord Alfred's branch of the Grendalls,—and the Melmottes; which was as it should be, as each could give much and each receive much. It was known that Lord Alfred had not a shilling; but his brother was a duke and his sister was a duchess, and for the last thirty years there had been one continual anxiety for poor dear Alfred, who had tumbled into an unfortunate marriage without a shilling, had spent his own moderate patrimony, had three sons and three daughters, and had lived now for a very long time entirely on the unwilling contributions of his noble relatives. Melmotte could support the whole family in affluence without feeling the burden;—and why should he not? There had once been an idea that Miles should attempt to win the heiress, but it had soon been found expedient to abandon it. Miles had no title, no position of his own, and was hardly big enough for the place. It was in all respects better that the waters of the fountain should be allowed to irrigate mildly the whole Grendall family;—and so Miles went into the city.

The ball was opened by a quadrille in which Lord Buntingford, the eldest son of the Duchess, stood up with Marie. Various arrangements had been made, and this among them. We may say that it had been a part of the bargain. Lord Buntingford had objected mildly, being a young man devoted to business, fond of his own order, rather shy, and not given to dancing. But he had allowed his mother to prevail. 'Of course they are vulgar,' the Duchess had said,—'so much so as to be no longer distasteful because of the absurdity of the thing. I dare say he hasn't been very honest. When men make so much money, I don't know how they can have been honest. Of course it's done for a purpose. It's all very well saying that it isn't right, but what are we to do about Alfred's children? Miles is to have £500 a-year. And then he is always about the house. And between you and me they have got up those bills of Alfred's, and have said they can lie in their safe till it suits your uncle to pay them.'

'They will lie there a long time,' said Lord Buntingford.

'Of course they expect something in return; do dance

with the girl once.' Lord Buntirgford disapproved—
mildly, and did as his mother asked him.

The affair went off very well. There were three or
four card-tables in one of the lower rooms, and at one of
them sat Lord Alfred Grendall and Mr. Melmotte, with
two or three other players, cutting in and out at the end
of each rubber. Playing whist was Lord Alfred's only
accomplishment, and almost the only occupation of his
life. He began it daily at his club at three o'clock, and
continued playing till two in the morning with an interval
of a couple of hours for his dinner. This he did during
ten months of the year, and during the other two he
frequented some watering-place at which whist prevailed.
He did not gamble, never playing for more than the
club stakes and bets. He gave to the matter his whole
mind, and must have excelled those who were generally
opposed to him. But so obdurate was fortune to Lord
Alfred that he could not make money even of whist.
Melmotte was very anxious to get into Lord Alfred's
club,—The Peripatetics.* It was pleasant to see the grace
with which he lost his money, and the sweet intimacy
with which he called his lordship Alfred. Lord Alfred
had a remnant of feeling left, and would have liked to
kick him. Though Melmotte was by far the bigger man,
and was also the younger, Lord Alfred would not have
lacked the pluck to kick him. Lord Alfred, in spite of
his habitual idleness and vapid uselessness, had still left
about him a dash of vigour, and sometimes thought that
he would kick Melmotte and have done with it. But
there were his poor boys, and those bills in Melmotte's
safe. And then Melmotte lost his points so regularly, and
paid his bets with such absolute good humour! 'Come
and have a glass of champagne, Alfred,' Melmotte said,
as the two cut out together. Lord Alfred liked champagne, and followed his host; but as he went he almost
made up his mind that on some future day he would
kick the man.

Late in the evening Marie Melmotte was waltzing
with Felix Carbury, and Henrietta Carbury was then
standing by talking to one Mr. Paul Montague. Lady

Carbury was also there. She was not well inclined either to balls or to such people as the Melmottes; nor was Henrietta. But Felix had suggested that, bearing in mind his prospects as to the heiress, they had better accept the invitation which he would cause to have sent to them. They did so; and then Paul Montague also got a card, not altogether to Lady Carbury's satisfaction. Lady Carbury was very gracious to Madame Melmotte for two minutes, and then slid into a chair expecting nothing but misery for the evening. She, however, was a woman who could do her duty and endure without complaint.

'It is the first great great ball I ever was at in London,' said Hetta Carbury to Paul Montague.

'And how do you like it?'

'Not at all. How should I like it? I know nobody here. I don't understand how it is that at these parties people do know each other, or whether they all go dancing about without knowing.'

'Just that; I suppose when they are used to it they get introduced backwards and forwards, and then they can know each other as fast as they like. If you would wish to dance why don't you dance with me?'

'I have danced with you,—twice already.'

'Is there any law against dancing three times?'

'But I don't especially want to dance,' said Henrietta. 'I think I'll go and console poor mamma, who has got nobody to speak to her.' Just at this moment, however, Lady Carbury was not in that wretched condition, as an unexpected friend had come to her relief.

Sir Felix and Marie Melmotte had been spinning round and round throughout a long waltz, thoroughly enjoying the excitement of the music and the movement. To give Felix Carbury what little praise might be his due, it is necessary to say that he did not lack physical activity. He would dance, and ride, and shoot eagerly, with an animation that made him happy for the moment. It was an affair not of thought or calculation, but of physical organisation. And Marie Melmotte had been thoroughly happy. She loved dancing with all her heart if she could only dance in a manner pleasant to herself.

She had been warned especially as to some men,—that she should not dance with them. She had been almost thrown into Lord Nidderdale's arms, and had been prepared to take him at her father's bidding. But she had never had the slightest pleasure in his society, and had only not been wretched because she had not as yet recognised that she had an identity of her own in the disposition of which she herself should have a voice. She certainly had never cared to dance with Lord Nidderdale. Lord Grasslough she had absolutely hated, though at first she had hardly dared to say so. One or two others had been obnoxious to her in different ways, but they had passed on, or were passing on, out of her way. There was no one at the present moment whom she had been commanded by her father to accept should an offer be made. But she did like dancing with Sir Felix Carbury.

It was not only that the man was handsome but that he had a power of changing the expression of his countenance, a play of face, which belied altogether his real disposition. He could seem to be hearty and true till the moment came in which he had really to expose his heart,—or to try to expose it. Then he failed, knowing nothing about it. But in the approaches to intimacy with a girl he could be very successful. He had already nearly got beyond this with Marie Melmotte; but Marie was by no means quick in discovering his deficiencies. To her he had seemed like a god. If she might be allowed to be wooed by Sir Felix Carbury, and to give herself to him, she thought that she would be contented.

'How well you dance,' said Sir Felix, as soon as he had breath for speaking.

'Do I?' She spoke with a slightly foreign accent, which gave a little prettiness to her speech. 'I was never told so. But nobody ever told me anything about myself.'

'I should like to tell you everything about yourself, from the begining to the end.'

'Ah,—but you don't know.'

'I would find out. I think I could make some good guesses. I'll tell you what you would like best in all the world.'

'What is that?'

'Somebody that liked you best in all the world.'

'Ah,—yes; if one knew who?'

'How can you know, Miss Melmotte, but by believing?'

'That is not the way to know. If a girl told me that she liked me better than any other girl, I should not know it, just because she said so. I should have to find it out.'

'And if a gentleman told you so?'

'I shouldn't believe him a bit, and I should not care to find out. But I should like to have some girl for a friend whom I could love, oh, ten times better than myself.'

'So should I.'

'Have you no particular friend?'

'I mean a girl whom I could love,—oh, ten times better than myself.'

'Now you are laughing at me, Sir Felix,' said Miss Melmotte.

'I wonder whether that will come to anything?' said Paul Montague to Miss Carbury. They had come back into the drawing-room, and had been watching the approaches to love-making which the baronet was opening.

'You mean Felix and Miss Melmotte. I hate to think of such things, Mr. Montague.'

'It would be a magnificent chance for him.'

'To marry a girl, the daughter of vulgar people, just because she will have a great deal of money? He can't care for her really,—because she is rich.'

'But he wants money so dreadfully! It seems to me that there is no other condition of things under which Felix can face the world, but by being the husband of an heiress.'

'What a dreadful thing to say!'

'But isn't it true? He has beggared himself.'

'Oh, Mr. Montague.'

'And he will beggar you and your mother.'

'I don't care about myself.'

'Others do though.' As he said this he did not look at her, but spoke through his teeth, as if he were angry both with himself and her.

'I did not think you would have spoken so harshly of Felix.'

'I don't speak harshly of him, Miss Carbury. I haven't said that it was his own fault. He seems to be one of those who have been born to spend money; and as this girl will have plenty of money to spend, I think it would be a good thing if he were to marry her. If Felix had £20,000 a year, everybody would think him the finest fellow in the world.' In saying this, however, Mr. Paul Montague showed himself unfit to gauge the opinion of the world. Whether Sir Felix be rich or poor, the world, evil-hearted as it is, will never think him a fine fellow.

Lady Carbury had been seated for nearly half an hour in uncomplaining solitude under a bust, when she was delighted by the appearance of Mr. Ferdinand Alf. 'You here?' she said.

'Why not? Melmotte and I are brother adventurers.'

'I should have thought you would find so little here to amuse you.'

'I have found you; and, in addition to that, duchesses and their daughters without number. They expect Prince George!'

'Do they?'

'And Legge Wilson from the India Office is here already. I spoke to him in some jewelled bower as I made my way here, not five minutes since. It's quite a success. Don't you think it very nice, Lady Carbury?'

'I don't know whether you are joking or in earnest.'

'I never joke. I say it is very nice. These people are spending thousands upon thousands to gratify you and me and others, and all they want in return is a little countenance.'

'Do you mean to give it then?'

'I am giving it them.'

'Ah;—but the countenance of the "Evening Pulpit." Do you mean to give them that?'

'Well; it is not in our line exactly to give a catalogue of names and to record ladies' dresses. Perhaps it may be better for our host himself that he should be kept out of the newspapers.'

'Are you going to be very severe upon poor me, Mr. Alf?' said the lady after a pause.

'We are never severe upon anybody, Lady Carbury. Here's the Prince. What will they do with him now they've caught him! Oh, they're going to make him dance with the heiress. Poor heiress!'

'Poor Prince!' said Lady Carbury.

'Not at all. She's a nice little girl enough, and he'll have nothing to trouble him. But how is she, poor thing, to talk to royal blood?'

Poor thing indeed! The Prince was brought into the big room where Marie was still being talked to by Felix Carbury, and was at once made to understand that she was to stand up and dance with royalty. The introduction was managed in a very business-like manner. Miles Grendall first came in and found the female victim; the Duchess followed with the male victim. Madame Melmotte, who had been on her legs till she was ready to sink, waddled behind, but was not allowed to take any part in the affair. The band were playing a galop, but that was stopped at once, to the great confusion of the dancers. In two minutes Miles Grendall had made up a set. He stood up with his aunt, the Duchess, as vis-à-vis to Marie and the Prince, till, about the middle of the quadrille, Legge Wilson was found and made to take his place. Lord Buntingford had gone away; but then there were still present two daughters of the Duchess who were rapidly caught. Sir Felix Carbury, being good-looking and having a name, was made to dance with one of them, and Lord Grasslough with the other. There were four other couples, all made up of titled people, as it was intended that this special dance should be chronicled, if not in the 'Evening Pulpit,' in some less serious daily journal. A paid reporter was present in the house ready to rush off with the list as soon as the dance should be a realized fact. The Prince himself did not quite understand why he was there, but they who marshalled his life for him had so marshalled it for the present moment. He himself probably knew nothing about the lady's diamonds which had been rescued, or the considerable subscription to St. George's Hospital which had been extracted from Mr. Melmotte as a make-weight. Poor Marie felt as though the burden of the hour would be greater than she could bear, and looked as though she would have fled had flight been possible. But the trouble passed quickly, and was not really severe. The Prince said a word or two between each figure, and did not seem to expect a reply. He made a few words go a long way, and was well trained in the work of easing the burden of his own greatness for those who were for the moment inflicted with it. When the dance was over he was allowed to escape after the ceremony of a single glass of champagne drunk in the presence of the hostess. Considerable skill was shown in keeping the presence of his royal guest a secret from the host himself till the Prince was gone. Melmotte would have desired to pour out that glass of wine with his own hands, to solace his tongue by Royal Highnesses, and would probably have been troublesome and disagreeable. Miles Grendall had understood all this and had managed the affair very well. 'Bless my soul;—his Royal Highness come and gone!' exclaimed Melmotte. 'You and my father were so fast at your whist that it was impossible to get you away,' said Miles. Melmotte was not a fool, and understood it all;—understood not only that it had been thought better that he should not speak to the Prince, but also that it might be better that it should be so. He could not have everything at once. Miles Grendall was very useful to him, and he would not quarrel with Miles, at any rate as yet.

'Have another rubber, Alfred?' he said to Miles's father as the carriages were taking away the guests.

Lord Alfred had taken sundry glasses of champagne, and for a moment forgot the bills in the safe, and the good things which his boys were receiving. 'Damn that kind of nonsense,' he said. 'Call people by their proper names.' Then he left the house without a further word to the master of it. That night before they went to sleep Melmotte required from his weary wife an account of the ball, and especially of Marie's conduct. 'Marie,'

Madame Melmotte said, 'had behaved well, but had
certainly preferred "Sir Carbury" to any other of the
young men.' Hitherto Mr. Melmotte had heard very
little of 'Sir Carbury,' except that he was a baronet.
Though his eyes and ears were always open, though he
attended to everything, and was a man of sharp intelligence, he did not yet quite understand the bearing and
sequence of English titles. He knew that he must get for
his daughter either an eldest son, or one absolutely in
possession himself. Sir Felix, he had learned, was only
a baronet; but then he was in possession. He had discovered also that Sir Felix's son would in course of time
also become Sir Felix. He was not therefore at the
present moment disposed to give any positive orders as
to his daughter's conduct to the young baronet. He did
not, however, conceive that the young baronet had as yet
addressed his girl in such words as Felix had in truth
used when they parted. 'You know who it is,' he
whispered, 'likes you better than any one else in the
world.'

'Nobody does;—don't, Sir Felix.'

'I do,' he said as he held her hand for a minute. He
looked into her face and she thought it very sweet. He
had studied the words as a lesson, and, repeating them
as a lesson, he did it fairly well. He did it well enough
at any rate to send the poor girl to bed with a sweet
conviction that at last a man had spoken to her whom
she could love.

## Chapter V

### AFTER THE BALL

'IT'S weary work,' said Sir Felix as he got into the
brougham with his mother and sister.

'What must it have been to me then, who had nothing
to do?' said his mother.

'It's the having something to do that makes me call it
weary work. By-the-bye, now I think of it, I'll run down

to the club before I go home.' So saying he put his head
out of the brougham, and stopped the driver.

'It is two o'clock, Felix,' said his mother.

'I'm afraid it is, but you see I'm hungry. You had
supper, perhaps; I had none.'

'Are you going down to the club for supper at this time
in the morning?'

'I must go to bed hungry if I don't. Good night.' Then
he jumped out of the brougham, called a cab, and had
himself driven to the Beargarden. He declared to himself that the men there would think it mean of him if he
did not give them their revenge. He had renewed his
play on the preceding night, and had again won. Dolly
Longestaffe owed him now a considerable sum of money,
and Lord Grasslough was also in his debt. He was sure
that Grasslough would go to the club after the ball, and
he was determined that they should not think that he
had submitted to be carried home by his mother and
sister. So he argued with himself; but in truth the devil
of gambling was hot within his bosom; and though he
feared that in losing he might lose real money, and that if
he won it would be long before he was paid, yet he could
not keep himself from the card-table.

Neither mother or daughter said a word till they
reached home and had got upstairs. Then the elder
spoke of the trouble that was nearest to her heart at the
moment. 'Do you think he gambles?'

'He has got no money, mamma.'

'I fear that might not hinder him. And he has money
with him, though, for him and such friends as he has, it
is not much. If he gambles everything is lost.'

'I suppose they all do play,—more or less.'

'I have not known that he played. I am wearied too,
out of all heart, by his want of consideration to me. It is
not that he will not obey me. A mother perhaps should
not expect obedience from a grown-up son. But my
word is nothing to him. He has no respect for me. He
would as soon do what is wrong before me as before the
merest stranger.'

'He has been so long his own master, mamma.'

'Yes,—his own master! And yet I must provide for him as though he were but a child. Hetta, you spent the whole evening talking to Paul Montague.'

'No, mamma;—that is unjust.'

'He was always with you.'

'I knew nobody else. I could not tell him not to speak to me. I danced with him twice.' Her mother was seated, with both her hands up to her forehead, and shook her head. 'If you did not want me to speak to Paul you should not have taken me there.'

'I don't wish to prevent your speaking to him. You know what I want.' Henrietta came up and kissed her, and bade her good night. 'I think I am the unhappiest woman in all London,' she said, sobbing hysterically.

'Is it my fault, mamma?'

'You could save me from much if you would. I work like a horse, and I never spend a shilling that I can help. I want nothing for myself,—nothing for myself. Nobody has suffered as I have. But Felix never thinks of me for a moment.'

'I think of you, mamma.'

'If you did you would accept your cousin's offer. What right have you to refuse him? I believe it is all because of that young man.'

'No, mamma; it is not because of that young man. I like my cousin very much;—but that is all. Good night, mamma.' Lady Carbury just allowed herself to be kissed, and then was left alone.

At eight o'clock the next morning daybreak found four young men who had just risen from a card-table at the Beargarden. The Beargarden was so pleasant a club that there was no rule whatsoever as to its being closed,—the only law being that it should not be opened before three in the afternoon. A sort of sanction had, however, been given to the servants to demur to producing supper or drinks after six in the morning, so that, about eight, un-relieved tobacco began to be too heavy even for juvenile constitutions. The party consisted of Dolly Longestaffe, Lord Grasslough, Miles Grendall, and Felix Carbury, and the four had amused themselves during the last six

hours with various innocent games. They had commenced with whist, and had culminated during the last
half-hour with blind hookey. But during the whole night
Felix had won. Miles Grendall hated him, and there had
been an expressed opinion between Miles and the young
lord that it would be both profitable and proper to relieve Sir Felix of the winnings of the last two nights. The
two men had played with the same object, and being
young had shown their intention,—so that a certain
feeling of hostility had been engendered. The reader is
not to understand that either of them had cheated, or
that the baronet had entertained any suspicion of foul
play. But Felix had felt that Grendall and Grasslough
were his enemies, and had thrown himself on Dolly for
sympathy and friendship. Dolly, however, was very tipsy.

At eight o'clock in the morning there came a sort of
settling, though no money then passed. The ready-money
transactions had not lasted long through the night.
Grasslough was the chief loser, and the figures and scraps
of paper which had been passed over to Carbury, when
counted up, amounted to nearly £2,000. His lordship
contested the fact bitterly, but contested it in vain. There
were his own initials and his own figures, and even Miles
Grendall, who was supposed to be quite wide awake,
could not reduce the amount. Then Grendall had lost
over £400 to Carbury,—an amount, indeed, that mattered little, as Miles could, at present, as easily have
raised £40,000. However, he gave his I.O.U. to his
opponent with an easy air. Grasslough, also, was impecunious; but he had a father,—also impecunious,
indeed; but with them the matter would not be hopeless.
Dolly Longestaffe was so tipsy that he could not even
assist in making up his own account. That was to be left
between him and Carbury for some future occasion.

'I suppose you'll be here to-morrow,—that is to-night,'
said Miles.

'Certainly,—only one thing,' answered Felix.

'What one thing?'

'I think these things should be squared before we play
any more!'

'What do you mean by that?' said Grasslough angrily. 'Do you mean to hint anything?'

'I never hint anything, my Grassy,' said Felix. 'I believe when people play cards, it's intended to be ready-money, that's all. But I'm not going to stand on P's and Q's with you. I'll give you your revenge to-night.'

'That's all right,' said Miles.

'I was speaking to Lord Grasslough,' said Felix. 'He is an old friend, and we know each other. You have been rather rough to-night, Mr. Grendall.'

'Rough;—what the devil do you mean by that?'

'And I think it will be as well that our account should be settled before we begin again.'

'A settlement once a week is the kind of thing I'm used to,' said Grendall.

There was nothing more said; but the young men did not part on good terms. Felix, as he got himself taken home, calculated that if he could realize his spoil, he might begin the campaign again with horses, servants, and all luxuries as before. If all were paid, he would have over £3,000!

## Chapter VI

### ROGER CARBURY AND PAUL MONTAGUE

ROGER CARBURY, of Carbury Hall, the owner of a small property in Suffolk, was the head of the Carbury family. The Carburys had been in Suffolk a great many years,—certainly from the time of the War of the Roses,—and had always held up their heads. But they had never held them very high. It was not known that any had risen ever to the honour of knighthood before Sir Patrick, going higher than that, had been made a baronet. They had, however, been true to their acres and their acres true to them through the perils of civil wars, Reformation, Commonwealth, and Revolution, and the head Carbury of the day had always owned, and had always lived at, Carbury Hall. At the beginning of the present century the squire of Carbury had been a considerable man, if not in his county, at any rate in his part of the county. The income of the estate had sufficed to enable him to live plenteously and hospitably, to drink port wine, to ride a stout hunter, and to keep an old lumbering coach for his wife's use when she went avisiting. He had an old butler who had never lived anywhere else, and a boy from the village who was in a way apprenticed to the butler. There was a cook, not too proud to wash up her own dishes, and a couple of young women; —while the house was kept by Mrs. Carbury herself, who marked and gave out her own linen, made her own preserves, and looked to the curing of her own hams. In the year 1800 the Carbury property was sufficient for the Carbury house. Since that time the Carbury property has considerably increased in value, and the rents have been raised. Even the acreage has been extended by the enclosure of commons. But the income is no longer comfortably adequate to the wants of an English gentleman's household. If a moderate estate in land be left to a man now, there arises the question whether he is not damaged unless an income also be left to him wherewith to keep up the estate. Land is a luxury, and of all luxuries is the most costly. Now the Carburys never had anything but land. Suffolk has not been made rich and great either by coal or iron. No great town had sprung up on the confines of the Carbury property. No eldest son had gone into trade or risen high in a profession so as to add to the Carbury wealth. No great heiress had been married. There had been no ruin,—no misfortune. But in the days of which we write the Squire of Carbury Hall had become a poor man simply through the wealth of others. His estate was supposed to bring him in £2,000 a year. Had he been content to let the Manor House, to live abroad, and to have an agent at home to deal with the tenants, he would undoubtedly have had enough to live luxuriously. But he lived on his own land among his own people, as all the Carburys before him had done, and was poor because he was surrounded by rich neighbours. The Longestaffes of Caversham,—of which family

Dolly Longestaffe was the eldest son and hope,—had the name of great wealth, but the founder of the family had been a Lord Mayor of London and a chandler as lately as in the reign of Queen Anne. The Hepworths, who could boast good blood enough on their own side, had married into new money. The Primeros,—though the goodnature of the country folk had accorded to the head of them the title of Squire Primero,—had been trading Spaniards fifty years ago, and had bought the Bundlesham property from a great duke. The estates of those three gentlemen, with the domain of the Bishop of Elmham, lay all around the Carbury property, and in regard to wealth enabled their owners altogether to overshadow our squire. The superior wealth of a bishop was nothing to him. He desired that bishops should be rich, and was among those who thought that the country had been injured when the territorial possessions of our prelates had been converted into stipends by Act of Parliament. But the grandeur of the Longestaffes and the too apparent wealth of the Primeros did oppress him, though he was a man who would never breathe a word of such oppression into the ear even of his dearest friend. It was his opinion,—which he did not care to declare loudly, but which was fully understood to be his opinion by those with whom he lived intimately,—that a man's standing in the world should not depend at all upon his wealth. The Primeros were undoubtedly beneath him in the social scale, although the young Primeros had three horses apiece, and killed legions of pheasants annually at about 10s. a head. Hepworth of Eardly was a very good fellow, who gave himself no airs and understood his duties as a country gentleman; but he could not be more than on a par with Carbury of Carbury, though he was supposed to enjoy £7,000 a year. The Longestaffes were altogether oppressive. Their footmen, even in the country, had powdered hair. They had a house in town, —a house of their own,—and lived altogether as magnates. The lady was Lady Pomona Longestaffe. The daughters, who certainly were handsome, had been destined to marry peers. The only son, Dolly, had, or

had had, a fortune of his own. They were an oppressive
people in a country neighbourhood. And to make the
matter worse, rich as they were, they never were able to
pay anybody anything that they owed. They continued
to live with all the appurtenances of wealth. The girls
always had horses to ride, both in town and country.
The acquaintance of Dolly the reader has already made.
Dolly, who certainly was a poor creature though good-
natured, had energy in one direction. He would quarrel
perseveringly with his father, who only had a life interest
in the estate. The house at Caversham Park was during
six or seven months of the year full of servants, if not of
guests, and all the tradesmen in the little towns around,
Bungay, Beccles, and Harlestone, were aware that the
Longestaffes were the great people of that country.
Though occasionally much distressed for money, they
would always execute the Longestaffe orders with submissive punctuality, because there was an idea that the
Longestaffe property was sound at the bottom. And,
then, the owner of a property so managed cannot scruti-
nise bills very closely.

Carbury of Carbury had never owed a shilling that he
could not pay, or his father before him. His orders to the
tradesmen at Beccles were not extensive, and care was
used to see that the goods supplied were neither over-
charged nor unnecessary. The tradesmen, consequently,
of Beccles did not care much for Carbury of Carbury;—
though perhaps one or two of the elders among them
entertained some ancient reverence for the family. Roger
Carbury, Esq., was Carbury of Carbury,—a distinction
of itself, which, from its nature, could not belong to the
Longestaffes and Primeros, which did not even belong to
the Hepworths of Eardly. The very parish in which
Carbury Hall stood,—or Carbury Manor House, as it
was more properly called,—was Carbury parish. And
there was Carbury Chase, partly in Carbury parish and
partly in Bundlesham,—but belonging, unfortunately, in
its entirety to the Bundlesham estate.

Roger Carbury himself was all alone in the world. His
nearest relatives of the name were Sir Felix and Henrietta,

but they were no more than second cousins. He had
sisters, but they had long since been married and had
gone away into the world with their husbands, one to
India, and another to the far west of the United States.
At present he was not much short of forty years of age,
and was still unmarried. He was a stout, good-looking
man, with a firmly set square face, with features finely
cut, a small mouth, good teeth, and well-formed chin.
His hair was red, curling round his head, which was now
partly bald at the top. He wore no other beard than
small, almost unnoticeable whiskers. His eyes were small,
but bright, and very cheery when his humour was good.
He was about five feet nine in height, having the appearance of great strength and perfect health. A more manly
man to the eye was never seen. And he was one with
whom you would instinctively wish at first sight to be on
good terms,—partly because in looking at him there
would come on you an unconscious conviction that he
would be very stout in holding his own against his oppo-
nents; partly also from a conviction equally strong, that
he would be very pleasant to his friends.

When Sir Patrick had come home from India as an
invalid, Roger Carbury had hurried up to see him in
London, and had proffered him all kindness. Would Sir
Patrick and his wife and children like to go down to the
old place in the country? Sir Patrick did not care a straw
for the old place in the country, and so told his cousin in
almost those very words. There had not, therefore, been
much friendship during Sir Patrick's life. But when the
violent ill-conditioned old man was dead, Roger paid a
second visit, and again offered hospitality to the widow
and her daughter,—and to the young baronet. The
young baronet had just joined his regiment and did not
care to visit his cousin in Suffolk; but Lady Carbury and
Henrietta had spent a month there, and everything had
been done to make them happy. The effort as regarded
Henrietta had been altogether successful. As regarded
the widow, it must be acknowledged that Carbury Hall
had not quite suited her tastes. She had already begun
to sigh for the glories of a literary career. A career of

some kind,—sufficient to repay her for the sufferings
of her early life,—she certainly desired. 'Dear cousin
Roger,' as she called him, had not seemed to her to have
much power of assisting her in these views. She was a
woman who did not care much for country charms. She
had endeavoured to get up some mild excitement with
the bishop, but the bishop had been too plain spoken and
sincere for her. The Primeros had been odious; the
Hepworths stupid; the Longestaffes,—she had endeavoured to make up a little friendship with Lady Pomona,
—insufferably supercilious. She had declared to Henrietta
'that Carbury Hall was very dull.'

But then there had come a circumstance which altogether changed her opinions as to Carbury Hall, and its
proprietor. The proprietor after a few weeks followed
them up to London, and made a most matter-of-fact offer
to the mother for the daughter's hand. He was at that
time thirty-six, and Henrietta was not yet twenty. He
was very cool;—some might have thought him phlegmatic
in his love-making. Henrietta declared to her mother
that she had not in the least expected it. But he was very
urgent, and very persistent. Lady Carbury was eager on
his side. Though the Carbury Manor House did not
exactly suit her, it would do admirably for Henrietta.
And as for age, to her thinking, she being then over forty,
a man of thirty-six was young enough for any girl. But
Henrietta had an opinion of her own. She liked her
cousin, but did not love him. She was amazed, and even
annoyed by the offer. She had praised him and praised
the house so loudly to her mother,—having in her innocence never dreamed of such a proposition as this,—so
that now she found it difficult to give an adequate reason
for her refusal. Yes;—she had undoubtedly said that her
cousin was charming, but she had not meant charming
in that way. She did refuse the offer very plainly, but
still with some apparent lack of persistency. When Roger
suggested that she should take a few months to think of
it, and her mother supported Roger's suggestion, she
could say nothing stronger than that she was afraid that
thinking about it would not do any good. Their first

visit to Carbury had been made in September. In the
following February she went there again,—much against
the grain as far as her own wishes were concerned; and
when there had been cold, constrained, almost dumb in
the presence of her cousin. Before they left the offer was
renewed, but Henrietta declared that she could not do as
they would have her. She could give no reason, only she
did not love her cousin in that way. But Roger declared
that he by no means intended to abandon his suit. In
truth he verily loved the girl, and love with him was a
serious thing. All this happened a full year before the
beginning of our present story.

But something else happened also. While that second
visit was being made at Carbury there came to the hall
a young man of whom Roger Carbury had said much to
his cousins,—one Paul Montague, of whom some short
account shall be given in this chapter. The squire,—
Roger Carbury was always called the squire about his
own place,—had anticipated no evil when he so timed
this second visit of his cousins to his house that they must
of necessity meet Paul Montague there. But great harm
had come of it. Paul Montague had fallen into love with
his cousin's guest, and there had sprung up much unhappiness.

Lady Carbury and Henrietta had been nearly a month
at Carbury, and Paul Montague had been there barely
a week, when Roger Carbury thus spoke to the guest who
had last arrived. 'I've got to tell you something, Paul.'

'Anything serious?'

'Very serious to me. I may say so serious that nothing
in my own life can approach it in importance.' He had
unconsciously assumed that look, which his friend so
thoroughly understood, indicating his resolve to hold to
what he believed to be his own, and to fight if fighting be
necessary. Montague knew him well, and became half
aware that he had done something, he knew not what,
militating against this serious resolve of his friend. He
looked up, but said nothing. 'I have offered my hand in
marriage to my cousin Henrietta,' said Roger, very gravely.

'Miss Carbury?'

'Yes; to Henrietta Carbury. She has not accepted it. She has refused me twice. But I still have hopes of success. Perhaps I have no right to hope, but I do. I tell it you just as it is. Everything in life to me depends upon it. I think I may count upon your sympathy.'

'Why did you not tell me before?' said Paul Montague in a hoarse voice.

Then there had come a sudden and rapid interchange of quick speaking between the men, each of them speaking the truth exactly, each of them declaring himself to be in the right and to be ill-used by the other, each of them equally hot, equally generous, and equally unreasonable. Montague at once asserted that he also loved Henrietta Carbury. He blurted out his assurance in the baldest and most incomplete manner, but still in such words as to leave no doubt. No;—he had not said a word to her. He had intended to consult Roger Carbury himself,—should have done so in a day or two,—perhaps on that very day had not Roger spoken to him. 'You have neither of you a shilling in the world,' said Roger; 'and now you know what my feelings are you must abandon it.' Then Montague declared that he had a right to speak to Miss Carbury. He did not suppose that Miss Carbury cared a straw about him. He had not the least reason to think that she did. It was altogether impossible. But he had a right to his chance. That chance was all the world to him. As to money,—he would not admit that he was a pauper, and, moreover, he might earn an income as well as other men. Had Carbury told him that the young lady had shown the slightest intention to receive his, Carbury's, addresses, he, Paul, would at once have disappeared from the scene. But as it was not so, he would not say that he would abandon his hope.

The scene lasted for above an hour. When it was ended, Paul Montague packed up all his clothes and was driven away to the railway station by Roger himself, without seeing either of the ladies. There had been very hot words between the men, but the last words which Roger spoke to the other on the railway platform were not quarrelsome in their nature. 'God bless you, old

fellow,' he said, pressing Paul's hands. Paul's eyes were
full of tears, and he replied only by returning the pressure.

Paul Montague's father and mother had long been
dead. The father had been a barrister in London, having
perhaps some small fortune of his own. He had, at any
rate, left to this son, who was one among others, a suffi-
ciency with which to begin the world. Paul when he had
come of age had found himself possessed of about £6,000.
He was then at Oxford, and was intended for the bar.
An uncle of his, a younger brother of his father, had
married a Carbury, the younger sister of two, though
older than her brother Roger. This uncle many years
since had taken his wife out to California, and had there
become an American. He had a large tract of land, growing wool, and wheat, and fruit; but whether he prospered
or whether he did not, had not always been plain to the
Montagues and Carburys at home. The intercourse
between the two families had, in the quite early days of
Paul Montague's life, created an affection between him
and Roger, who, as will be understood by those who have
carefully followed the above family history, were not in
any degree related to each other. Roger, when quite a
young man, had had the charge of the boy's education,
and had sent him to Oxford. But the Oxford scheme, to
be followed by the bar, and to end on some one of the
many judicial benches of the country, had not succeeded.
Paul had got into a 'row' at Balliol, and had been rusti-
cated,—had then got into another row, and was sent
down. Indeed he had a talent for rows,—though, as
Roger Carbury always declared, there was nothing really
wrong about any of them. Paul was then twenty-one,
and he took himself and his money out to California, and
joined his uncle. He had perhaps an idea,—based on
very insufficient grounds,—that rows are popular in
California. At the end of three years he found that he
did not like farming life in California,—and he found also
that he did not like his uncle. So he returned to England,
but on returning was altogether unable to get his
£6,000 out of the Californian farm. Indeed he had been
compelled to come away without any of it, with funds

insufficient even to take him home, accepting with much dissatisfaction an assurance from his uncle that an income amounting to ten per cent. upon his capital should be remitted to him with the regularity of clockwork. The clock alluded to must have been one of Sam Slick's.* It had gone very badly. At the end of the first quarter there came the proper remittance;—then half the amount;— then there was a long interval without anything; then some dropping payments now and again;—and then a twelvemonth without anything. At the end of that twelvemonth he paid a second visit to California, having borrowed money from Roger for his journey. He had now again returned, with some little cash in hand, and with the additional security of a deed executed in his favour by one Hamilton K. Fisker, who had gone into partnership with his uncle, and who had added a vast flour-mill to his uncle's concerns. In accordance with this deed he was to get twelve per cent. on his capital, and had enjoyed the gratification of seeing his name put up as one of the firm, which now stood as Fisker, Montague, and Montague. A business declared by the two elder partners to be most promising had been opened at Fiskerville, about two hundred and fifty miles from San Francisco, and the hearts of Fisker and the elder Montague were very high. Paul hated Fisker horribly, did not love his uncle much, and would willingly have got back his £6,000 had he been able. But he was not able, and returned as one of Fisker, Montague, and Montague, not altogether unhappy, as he had succeeded in obtaining enough of his back income to pay what he owed to Roger, and to live for a few months. He was intent on considering how he should bestow himself, consulting daily with Roger on the subject, when suddenly Roger had perceived that the young man was becoming attached to the girl whom he himself loved. What then occurred has been told.

Not a word was said to Lady Carbury or her daughter of the real cause of Paul's sudden disappearance. It had been necessary that he should go to London. Each of the ladies probably guessed something of the truth, but

neither spoke a word to the other on the subject. Before
they left the Manor the squire again pleaded his cause
with Henrietta, but he pleaded it in vain. Henrietta was
colder than ever,—but she made use of one unfortunate
phrase which destroyed all the effect which her coldness
might have had. She said that she was too young to
think of marrying yet. She had meant to imply that the
difference in their ages was too great, but had not known
how to say it. It was easy to tell her that in a twelvemonth she would be older;—but it was impossible to
convince her that any number of twelvemonths would
alter the disparity between her and her cousin. But even
that disparity was not now her strongest reason for feeling
sure that she could not marry Roger Carbury.

Within a week of the departure of Lady Carbury from
the Manor House, Paul Montague returned, and returned
as a still dear friend. He had promised before he went
that he would not see Henrietta again for three months,
but he would promise nothing further. 'If she won't take
you, there is no reason why I shouldn't try.' That had
been his argument. Roger would not accede to the justice
even of this. It seemed to him that Paul was bound to
retire altogether, partly because he had got no income,
partly because of Roger's previous claim,—partly no
doubt in gratitude, but of this last reason Roger never
said a word. If Paul did not see this himself, Paul was
not such a man as his friend had taken him to be.

Paul did see it himself, and had many scruples. But
why should his friend be a dog in the manger? He would
yield at once to Roger Carbury's older claims if Roger
could make anything of them. Indeed he could have no
chance if the girl were disposed to take Roger for her
husband. Roger had all the advantage of Carbury
Manor at his back, whereas he had nothing but his share
in the doubtful business of Fisker, Montague, and Montague, in a wretched little town 250 miles further off than
San Francisco! But if, with all this, Roger could not
prevail, why should he not try? What Roger said about
want of money was mere nonsense. Paul was sure that
his friend would have created no such difficulty had not

he himself been interested. Paul declared to himself that
he had money, though doubtful money, and that he
certainly would not give up Henrietta on that score.

He came up to London at various times in search of
certain employment which had been half promised him,
and, after the expiration of the three months, constantly
saw Lady Carbury and her daughter. But from time to
time he had given renewed promises to Roger Carbury
that he would not declare his passion,—now for two
months, then for six weeks, then for a month. In the
meantime the two men were fast friends,—so fast that
Montague spent by far the greater part of his time as his
friend's guest,—and all this was done with the understanding that Roger Carbury was to blaze up into hostile
wrath should Paul ever receive the privilege to call himself Henrietta Carbury's favoured lover, but that everything was to be smooth between them should Henrietta
be persuaded to become the mistress of Carbury Hall.
So things went on up to the night at which Montague
met Henrietta at Madame Melmotte's ball. The reader
should also be informed that there had been already a
former love affair in the young life of Paul Montague.
There had been, and indeed there still was, a widow, one
Mrs. Hurtle, whom he had been desperately anxious to
marry before his second journey to California;—but the
marriage had been prevented by the interference of
Roger Carbury.

## Chapter VII

### MENTOR

LADY CARBURY'S desire for a union between Roger
and her daughter was greatly increased by her solicitude in respect to her son. Since Roger's offer had first
been made, Felix had gone on from bad to worse, till his
condition had become one of hopeless embarrassment.
If her daughter could but be settled in the world, Lady
Carbury said to herself, she could then devote herself to

the interests of her son. She had no very clear idea of
what that devotion would be. But she did know that she
had paid so much money for him, and would have so
much more extracted from her, that it might well come
to pass that she would be unable to keep a home for her
daughter. In all these troubles she constantly appealed
to Roger Carbury for advice,—which, however, she
never followed. He recommended her to give up her
house in town, to find a home for her daughter elsewhere,
and also for Felix if he would consent to follow her.
Should he not so consent, then let the young man bear
the brunt of his own misdoings. Doubtless, when he
could no longer get bread in London he would find her
out. Roger was always severe when he spoke of the
baronet,—or seemed to Lady Carbury to be severe.

But, in truth, she did not ask for advice in order that
she might follow it. She had plans in her head with which
she knew that Roger would not sympathise. She still
thought that Sir Felix might bloom and burst out into
grandeur, wealth, and fashion, as the husband of a great
heiress, and in spite of her son's vices, was proud of him
in that anticipation. When he succeeded in obtaining
from her money, as in the case of that £20,—when, with
brazen-faced indifference to her remonstrances, he started
off to his club at two in the morning, when with impudent
drollery he almost boasted of the hopelessness of his debts,
a sickness of heart would come upon her, and she would
weep hysterically, and lie the whole night without sleeping. But could he marry Miss Melmotte, and thus conquer all his troubles by means of his own personal beauty,
—then she would be proud of all that had passed. With
such a condition of mind Roger Carbury could have no
sympathy. To him it seemed that a gentleman was disgraced who owed money to a tradesman which he could
not pay. And Lady Carbury's heart was high with other
hopes,—in spite of her hysterics and her fears. The
'Criminal Queens' might be a great literary success. She
almost thought that it would be a success. Messrs. Leadham and Loiter, the publishers, were civil to her. Mr.
Broune had promised. Mr. Booker had said that he

would see what could be done. She had gathered from Mr. Alf's caustic and cautious words that the book would be noticed in the 'Evening Pulpit.' No;—she would not take dear Roger's advice as to leaving London. But she would continue to ask Roger's advice. Men like to have their advice asked. And, if possible, she would arrange the marriage. What country retirement could be so suitable for a Lady Carbury when she wished to retire for awhile,—as Carbury Manor, the seat of her own daughter? And then her mind would fly away into regions of bliss. If only by the end of this season Henrietta could be engaged to her cousin, Felix be the husband of the richest bride in Europe, and she be the acknowledged author of the cleverest book of the year, what a Paradise of triumph might still be open to her after all her troubles! Then the sanguine nature of the woman would bear her up almost to exultation, and for an hour she would be happy, in spite of everything.

A few days after the ball Roger Carbury was up in town, and was closeted with her in her back drawing-room. The declared cause of his coming was the condition of the baronet's affairs and the indispensable necessity,—so Roger thought,—of taking some steps by which at any rate the young man's present expenses might be brought to an end. It was horrible to him that a man who had not a shilling in the world or any prospect of a shilling, who had nothing and never thought of earning anything, should have hunters! He was very much in earnest about it, and quite prepared to speak his mind to the young man himself,—if he could get hold of him. 'Where is he now, Lady Carbury;—at this moment?'

'I think he's out with the Baron.' Being 'out with the Baron' meant that the young man was hunting with the stag hounds some forty miles away from London.

'How does he manage it? Whose horses does he ride? Who pays for them?'

'Don't be angry with me, Roger. What can I do to prevent it?'

'I think you should refuse to have anything to do with him while he continues in such courses.'

'My own son!'

'Yes;—exactly. But what is to be the end of it? Is he to be allowed to ruin you, and Hetta? It can't go on long.'

'You wouldn't have me throw him over.'

'I think he is throwing you over. And then it is so thoroughly dishonest,—so ungentlemanlike! I don't understand how it goes on from day to day. I suppose you don't supply him with ready money?'

'He has had a little.'

Roger frowned angrily. 'I can understand that you should provide him with bed and food, but not that you should pander to his vices by giving him money.' This was very plain speaking, and Lady Carbury winced under it. 'The kind of life that he is leading requires a large income of itself. I understand the thing, and know that with all I have in the world I could not do it myself.'

'You are so different.'

'I am older of course,—very much older. But he is not so young that he should not begin to comprehend. Has he any money beyond what you give him?'

Then Lady Carbury revealed certain suspicions which she had begun to entertain during the last day or two. 'I think he has been playing.'

'That is the way to lose money,—not to get it,' said Roger.

'I suppose somebody wins,—sometimes.'

'They who win are the sharpers. They who lose are the dupes. I would sooner that he were a fool than a knave.'

'O Roger, you are so severe!'

'You say he plays. How would he pay, were he to lose?'

'I know nothing about it. I don't even know that he does play; but I have reason to think that during the last week he has had money at his command. Indeed I have seen it. He comes home at all manner of hours and sleeps late. Yesterday I went into his room about ten and did not wake him. There were notes and gold lying on his table;—ever so much.'

'Why did you not take them?'

'What; rob my own boy?'

'When you tell me that you are absolutely in want of money to pay your own bills, and that he has not hesitated to take yours from you! Why does he not repay you what he has borrowed?'

'Ah, indeed;—why not? He ought to if he has it. And there were papers, there;—I.O.U's, signed by other men.'

'You looked at them.'

'I saw as much as that. It is not that I am curious, but one does feel about one's own son. I think he has bought another horse. A groom came here and said something about it to the servants.'

'Oh dear;—oh dear!'

'If you could only induce him to stop the gambling! Of course it is very bad whether he wins or loses,—though I am sure that Felix would do nothing unfair. Nobody ever said that of him. If he has won money, it would be a great comfort if he would let me have some of it,—for, to tell the truth, I hardly know how to turn. I am sure nobody can say that I spend it on myself.'

Then Roger again repeated his advice. There could be no use in attempting to keep up the present kind of life in Welbeck Street. Welbeck Street might be very well without a penniless spendthrift such as Sir Felix, but must be ruinous under the present conditions. If Lady Carbury felt, as no doubt she did feel, bound to afford a home to her ruined son in spite of all his wickedness and folly, that home should be found far away from London. If he chose to remain in London, let him do so on his own resources. The young man should make up his mind to do something for himself. A career might possibly be opened for him in India. 'If he be a man he would sooner break stones than live on you,' said Roger. Yes, he would see his cousin to-morrow and speak to him;—that is if he could possibly find him. 'Young men who gamble all night, and hunt all day, are not easily found.' But he would come at twelve as Felix generally breakfasted at that hour. Then he gave an assurance to Lady Carbury which to her was not the least comfortable part of the interview. In the event of her son not giving her the money which she at once required he, Roger, would lend her a hundred pounds till her half year's income should be due. After that his voice changed altogether, as he asked a question on another subject, 'Can I see Henrietta to-morrow?'

'Certainly;—why not? She is at home now, I think.'

'I will wait till to-morrow,—when I call to see Felix. I should like her to know that I am coming. Paul Montague was in town the other day. He was here, I suppose?'

'Yes;—he called.'

'Was that all you saw of him?'

'He was at the Melmottes' ball. Felix got a card for him;—and we were there. Has he gone down to Carbury?'

'No;—not to Carbury. I think he had some business about his partners at Liverpool. There is another case of a young man without anything to do. Not that Paul is at all like Sir Felix.' This he was induced to say by the spirit of honesty which was always strong within him.

'Don't be too hard upon poor Felix,' said Lady Carbury. Roger, as he took his leave, thought that it would be impossible to be too hard upon Sir Felix Carbury.

The next morning Lady Carbury was in her son's bedroom before he was up, and with incredible weakness told him that his cousin Roger was coming to lecture him. 'What the devil's the use of it?' said Felix from beneath the bedclothes.

'If you speak to me in that way, Felix, I must leave the room.'

'But what is the use of his coming to me? I know what he has got to say just as if it were said. It's all very well preaching sermons to good people, but nothing ever was got by preaching to people who ain't good.'

'Why shouldn't you be good?'

'I shall do very well, mother, if that fellow will leave me alone. I can play my hand better than he can play it for me. If you'll go now I'll get up.' She had intended to ask him for some of the money which she believed he still possessed, but her courage failed her. If she asked for his money, and took it, she would in some fashion recognise and tacitly approve his gambling. It was not yet eleven, and it was early for him to leave his bed; but he had resolved that he would get out of the house before that horrible bore should be upon him with his sermon. To do this he must be energetic. He was actually eating his breakfast at half-past eleven, and had already contrived in his mind how he would turn the wrong way as soon as he got into the street,—towards Marylebone Road, by which route Roger would certainly not come. He left the house at ten minutes before twelve, cunningly turned away, dodging round by the first corner,—and just as he had turned it encountered his cousin. Roger, anxious in regard to his errand, with time at his command, had come before the hour appointed and had strolled about, thinking not of Felix but of Felix's sister. The baronet felt that he had been caught,—caught unfairly, but by no means abandoned all hope of escape. 'I was going to your mother's house on purpose to see you,' said Roger.

'Were you indeed? I am so sorry. I have an engagement out here with a fellow which I must keep. I could meet you at any other time, you know.'

'You can come back for ten minutes,' said Roger, taking him by the arm.

'Well;—not conveniently at this moment.'

'You must manage it. I am here at your mother's request, and can't afford to remain in town day after day looking for you. I go down to Carbury this afternoon. Your friend can wait. Come along.' His firmness was too much for Felix, who lacked the courage to shake his cousin off violently, and to go his way. But as he returned he fortified himself with the remembrance of all the money in his pocket,—for he still had his winnings,— remembered too certain sweet words which had passed between him and Marie Melmotte since the ball, and resolved that he would not be 'sat upon' by Roger Carbury. The time was coming,—he might almost say that the time had come,—in which he might defy Roger

Carbury. Nevertheless, he dreaded the words which were now to be spoken to him with a craven fear.

'Your mother tells me,' said Roger, 'that you still keep hunters.'

'I don't know what she calls hunters. I have one that I didn't part with when the others went.'

'You have only one horse?'

'Well;—if you want to be exact, I have a hack as well as the horse I ride.'

'And another up here in town?'

'Who told you that? No; I haven't. At least there is one staying at some stables which has been sent for me to look at.'

'Who pays for all these horses?'

'At any rate I shall not ask you to pay for them.'

'No;—you would be afraid to do that. But you have no scruple in asking your mother, though you should force her to come to me or to other friends for assistance. You have squandered every shilling of your own, and now you are ruining her.'

'That isn't true. I have money of my own.'

'Where did you get it?'

'This is all very well, Roger; but I don't know that you have any right to ask me these questions. I have money. If I buy a horse I can pay for it. If I keep one or two I can pay for them. Of course I owe a lot of money, but other people owe me money too. I'm all right, and you needn't frighten yourself.'

'Then why do you beg her last shilling from your mother, and when you have money not pay it back to her?'

'She can have the twenty pounds, if you mean that.'

'I mean that, and a good deal more than that. I suppose you have been gambling.'

'I don't know that I am bound to answer your questions, and I won't do it. If you have nothing else to say, I'll go about my own business.'

'I have something else to say, and I mean to say it.' Felix had walked towards the door, but Roger was before him, and now leaned his back against it.

'I am not going to be kept here against my will,' said Felix.

'You have to listen to me, so you may as well sit still. Do you wish to be looked upon as a blackguard by all the world?'

'Oh,—go on.'

'That is what it will be. You have spent every shilling of your own,—and because your mother is affectionate and weak, you are now spending all that she has, and are bringing her and your sister to beggary.'

'I don't ask them to pay anything for me.'

'Not when you borrow her money?'

'There is the £20. Take it and give it her,' said Felix, counting the notes out of the pocket-book. 'When I asked her for it, I did not think she would make such a row about such a trifle.' Roger took up the notes and thrust them into his pocket. 'Now, have you done?' said Felix.

'Not quite. Do you purpose that your mother should keep you and clothe you for the rest of your life?'

'I hope to be able to keep her before long, and to do it much better than it has ever been done before. The truth is, Roger, you know nothing about it. If you'll leave me to myself, you'll find that I shall do very well.'

'I don't know any young man who ever did worse, or one who had less moral conception of what is right and wrong.'

'Very well. That's your idea. I differ from you. People can't all think alike, you know. Now, if you please, I'll go.'

Roger felt that he hadn't half said what he had to say, but he hardly knew how to get it said. And of what use could it be to talk to a young man who was altogether callous and without feeling? The remedy for the evil ought to be found in the mother's conduct rather than the son's. She, were she not foolishly weak, would make up her mind to divide herself utterly from her son, at any rate for a while, and to leave him to suffer utter penury. That would bring him round. And then when the agony of want had tamed him, he would be content to take bread and meat from her hand and would be humble. At present he had money in his pocket, and would eat and drink of the best, and be free from inconvenience for the moment. While this prosperity remained it would be impossible to touch him. 'You will ruin your sister, and break your mother's heart,' said Roger, firing a last harmless shot after the young reprobate.

When Lady Carbury came into the room, which she did as soon as the front door was closed behind her son, she seemed to think that a great success had been achieved because the £20 had been recovered. 'I knew he would give it me back, if he had it,' she said.

'Why did he not bring it to you of his own accord?'

'I suppose he did not like to talk about it. Has he said that he got it by—playing?'

'No,—he did not speak a word of truth while he was here. You may take it for granted that he did get it by gambling. How else should he have it? And you may take it for granted also that he will lose all that he has got. He talked in the wildest way,—saying that he would soon have a home for you and Hetta.'

'Did he;—dear boy!'

'Had he any meaning?'

'Oh; yes. And it is quite on the cards that it should be so. You have heard of Miss Melmotte.'

'I have heard of the great French swindler who has come over here, and who is buying his way into society.'

'Everybody visits them now, Roger.'

'More shame for everybody. Who knows anything about him,—except that he left Paris with the reputation of a specially prosperous rogue? But what of him?'

'Some people think that Felix will marry his only child. Felix is handsome; isn't he? What young man is there nearly so handsome? They say she'll have half a million of money.'

'That's his game;—is it?'

'Don't you think he is right?'

'No; I think he's wrong. But we shall hardly agree with each other about that. Can I see Henrietta for a few minutes?'

## Chapter VIII

### LOVE-SICK

ROGER CARBURY said well that it was very improbable that he and his cousin, the widow, should
agree in their opinions as to the expedience of fortune-
hunting by marriage. It was impossible that they should
ever understand each other. To Lady Carbury the
prospect of a union between her son and Miss Melmotte
was one of unmixed joy and triumph. Could it have
been possible that Marie Melmotte should be rich and
her father be a man doomed to a deserved sentence in
a penal settlement, there might perhaps be a doubt about
it. The wealth even in that case would certainly carry
the day against the disgrace, and Lady Carbury would
find reasons why 'poor Marie' should not be punished for
her father's sins, even while enjoying the money which
those sins had produced. But how different were the
existing facts? Mr. Melmotte was not at the galleys, but
was entertaining duchesses in Grosvenor Square. People
said that Mr. Melmotte had a reputation throughout
Europe as a gigantic swindler,—as one who in the dishonest and successful pursuit of wealth had stopped at
nothing. People said of him that he had framed and
carried out long premeditated and deeply laid schemes
for the ruin of those who had trusted him, that he had
swallowed up the property of all who had come in contact with him, that he was fed with the blood of widows
and children;—but what was all this to Lady Carbury?
If the duchesses condoned it all, did it become her to be
prudish? People also said that Melmotte would yet get
a fall,—that a man who had risen after such a fashion
never could long keep his head up. But he might keep
his head up long enough to give Marie her fortune. And
then Felix wanted a fortune so badly;—was so exactly
the young man who ought to marry a fortune! To Lady
Carbury there was no second way of looking at the
matter.

And to Roger Carbury also there was no second way of

looking at it. That condonation of antecedents which, in the hurry of the world, is often vouchsafed to success, that growing feeling which induces people to assert to themselves that they are not bound to go outside the general verdict, and that they may shake hands with whomsoever the world shakes hands with, had never reached him. The old-fashioned idea that the touching of pitch will defile still prevailed with him. He was a gentleman;— and would have felt himself disgraced to enter the house of such a one as Augustus Melmotte. Not all the duchesses in the peerage, or all the money in the city, could alter his notions or induce him to modify his conduct. But he knew that it would be useless for him to explain this to Lady Carbury. He trusted, however, that one of the family might be taught to appreciate the difference between honour and dishonour. Henrietta Carbury had, he thought, a higher turn of mind than her mother, and had as yet been kept free from soil. As for Felix,—he had so grovelled in the gutters as to be dirt all over. Nothing short of the prolonged sufferings of half a life could cleanse him.

He found Henrietta alone in the drawing-room. 'Have you seen Felix?' she said, as soon as they had greeted each other.

'Yes. I caught him in the street.'

'We are so unhappy about him.'

'I cannot say but that you have reason. I think, you know, that your mother indulges him foolishly.'

'Poor mamma! She worships the very ground he treads on.'

'Even a mother should not throw her worship away like that. The fact is that your brother will ruin you both if this goes on.'

'What can mamma do?'

'Leave London, and then refuse to pay a shilling on his behalf.'

'What would Felix do in the country?'

'If he did nothing, how much better would that be than what he does in town? You would not like him to become a professional gambler.'

'Oh, Mr. Carbury; you do not mean that he does that!'

'It seems cruel to say such things to you,—but in a matter of such importance one is bound to speak the truth. I have no influence over your mother; but you may have some. She asks my advice, but has not the slightest idea of listening to it. I don't blame her for that; but I am anxious for the sake of——, for the sake of the family.'

'I am sure you are.'

'Especially for your sake. You will never throw him over.'

'You would not ask me to throw him over.'

'But he may drag you into the mud. For his sake you have already been taken into the house of that man Melmotte.'

'I do not think that I shall be injured by anything of that kind,' said Henrietta, drawing herself up.

'Pardon me if I seem to interfere.'

'Oh, no;—it is no interference from you.'

'Pardon me then if I am rough. To me it seems that an injury is done to you if you are made to go to the house of such a one as this man. Why does your mother seek his society? Not because she likes him; not because she has any sympathy with him or his family;—but simply because there is a rich daughter.'

'Everybody goes there, Mr. Carbury.'

'Yes,—that is the excuse which everybody makes. Is that sufficient reason for you to go to a man's house? Is there not another place to which we are told that a great many are going, simply because the road has become thronged and fashionable? Have you no feeling that you ought to choose your friends for certain reasons of your own? I admit there is one reason here. They have a great deal of money, and it is thought possible that he may get some of it by falsely swearing to a girl that he loves her. After what you have heard, are the Melmottes people with whom you would wish to be connected?'

'I don't know.'

'I do. I know very well. They are absolutely disgraceful. A social connection with the first crossing-sweeper

would be less objectionable.' He spoke with a degree of
energy of which he was himself altogether unaware. He
knit his brows, and his eyes flashed, and his nostrils were
extended. Of course she thought of his own offer to herself. Of course her mind at once conceived,—not that the
Melmotte connection could ever really affect him, for she
felt sure that she would never accept his offer,—but that
he might think that he would be so affected. Of course
she resented the feeling which she thus attributed to him.
But, in truth, he was much too simple-minded for any
such complex idea. 'Felix,' he continued, 'has already
descended so far that I cannot pretend to be anxious as
to what houses he may frequent. But I should be sorry
to think that you should often be seen at Mr. Melmotte's.'

'I think, Mr. Carbury, that mamma will take care that
I am not taken where I ought not to be taken.'

'I wish you to have some opinion of your own as to
what is proper for you.'

'I hope I have. I am sorry you should think that I have
not.'

'I am old-fashioned, Hetta.'

'And we belong to a newer and worse sort of world. I
dare say it is so. You have been always very kind, but
I almost doubt whether you can change us now. I have
sometimes thought that you and mamma were hardly fit
for each other.'

'I have thought that you and I were,—or possibly
might be fit for each other.'

'Oh,—as for me, I shall always take mamma's side. If
mamma chooses to go to the Melmottes I shall certainly
go with her. If that is contamination, I suppose I must
be contaminated. I don't see why I'm to consider myself
better than any one else.'

'I have always thought that you were better than any
one else.'

'That was before I went to the Melmottes. I am sure
you have altered your opinion now. Indeed, you have
told me so. I am afraid, Mr. Carbury, you must go your
way, and we must go ours.'

He looked into her face as she spoke, and gradually

began to perceive the working of her mind. He was so
true himself that he did not understand that there should
be with her even that violet-coloured tinge of prevarica-
tion which women assume as an additional charm. Could
she really have thought that he was attending to his own
possible future interests when he warned her as to the
making of new acquaintances?

'For myself,' he said, putting out his hand and making
a slight vain effort to get hold of hers, 'I have only one
wish in the world; and that is, to travel the same road
with you. I do not say that you ought to wish it too; but
you ought to know that I am sincere. When I spoke of
the Melmottes, did you believe that I was thinking of
myself?'

'Oh no;—how should I?'

'I was speaking to you then as to a cousin who might
regard me as an elder brother. No contact with legions
of Melmottes could make you other to me than the woman
on whom my heart has settled. Even were you in truth
disgraced,—could disgrace touch one so pure as you,—it
would be the same. I love you so well that I have already
taken you for better or for worse. I cannot change. My
nature is too stubborn for such changes. Have you a
word to say to comfort me?' She turned away her head,
but did not answer him at once. 'Do you understand
how much I am in need of comfort?'

'You can do very well without comfort from me.'

'No, indeed. I shall live, no doubt; but I shall not do
very well. As it is, I am not doing at all well. I am becoming sour and moody, and ill at ease with my friends.
I would have you believe me, at any rate, when I say I
love you.'

'I suppose you mean something.'

'I mean a great deal, dear. I mean all that a man can
mean. That is it. You hardly understand that I am
serious to the extent of ecstatic joy on the one side, and
utter indifference to the world on the other. I shall never
give it up till I learn that you are to be married to some
one else.'

'What can I say, Mr. Carbury?'

'That you will love me.'

'But if I don't?'

'Say that you will try.'

'No; I will not say that. Love should come without a struggle. I don't know how one person is to try to love another in that way. I like you very much; but being married is such a terrible thing.'

'It would not be terrible to me, dear.'

'Yes;—when you found that I was too young for your tastes.'

'I shall persevere, you know. Will you assure me of this,—that if you promise your hand to another man, you will let me know at once?'

'I suppose I may promise that,' she said, after pausing for a moment.

'There is no one as yet?'

'There is no one. But, Mr. Carbury, you have no right to question me. I don't think it generous. I allow you to say things that nobody else could say because you are a cousin and because mamma trusts you so much. No one but mamma has a right to ask me whether I care for any one.'

'Are you angry with me?'

'No.'

'If I have offended you it is because I love you so dearly.'

'I am not offended, but I don't like to be questioned by a gentleman. I don't think any girl would like it. I am not to tell everybody all that happens.'

'Perhaps when you reflect how much of my happiness depends upon it you will forgive me. Good-bye now.' She put out her hand to him and allowed it to remain in his for a moment. 'When I walk about the old shrubberies at Carbury where we used to be together, I am always asking myself what chance there is of your walking there as the mistress.'

'There is no chance.'

'I am, of course, prepared to hear you say so. Well; good-bye, and may God bless you.'

The man had no poetry about him. He did not even

care for romance. All the outside belongings of love which are so pleasant to many men and which to many women afford the one sweetness in life which they really relish, were nothing to him. There are both men and women to whom even the delays and disappointments of love are charming, even when they exist to the detriment of hope. It is sweet to such persons to be melancholy, sweet to pine, sweet to feel that they are now wretched after a romantic fashion as have been those heroes and heroines of whose sufferings they have read in poetry. But there was nothing of this with Roger Carbury. He had, as he believed, found the woman that he really wanted, who was worthy of his love, and now, having fixed his heart upon her, he longed for her with an amazing longing. He had spoken the simple truth when he declared that life had become indifferent to him without her. No man in England could be less likely to throw himself off the Monument or to blow out his brains. But he felt numbed in all the joints of his mind by this sorrow. He could not make one thing bear upon another, so as to console himself after any fashion. There was but one thing for him;—to persevere till he got her, or till he had finally lost her. And should the latter be his fate, as he began to fear that it would be, then, he would live, but live only, like a crippled man.

He felt almost sure in his heart of hearts that the girl loved that other, younger man. That she had never owned to such love he was quite sure. The man himself and Henrietta also had both assured him on this point, and he was a man easily satisfied by words and prone to believe. But he knew that Paul Montague was attached to her, and that it was Paul's intention to cling to his love. Sorrowfully looking forward through the vista of future years, he thought he saw that Henrietta would become Paul's wife. Were it so, what should he do? Annihilate himself as far as all personal happiness in the world was concerned, and look solely to their happiness, their prosperity, and their joys? Be as it were a beneficent old fairy to them, though the agony of his own disappointment should never depart from him? Should he do this, and be blessed by them,—or should he let Paul Montague know what deep resentment such ingratitude could produce? When had a father been kinder to a son, or a brother to a brother, than he had been to Paul? His home had been the young man's home, and his purse the young man's purse. What right could the young man have to come upon him just as he was perfecting his bliss and rob him of all that he had in the world? He was conscious all the while that there was a something wrong in his argument,—that Paul when he commenced to love the girl knew nothing of his friend's love,—that the girl, though Paul had never come in the way, might probably have been as obdurate as she was now to his entreaties. He knew all this because his mind was clear. But yet the injustice,—at any rate, the misery was so great, that to forgive it and to reward it would be weak, womanly, and foolish. Roger Carbury did not quite believe in the forgiveness of injuries. If you pardon all the evil done to you, you encourage others to do you evil! If you give your cloak to him who steals your coat, how long will it be before your shirt and trousers will go also? Roger Carbury returned that afternoon to Suffolk, and as he thought of it all throughout the journey, he resolved that he would never forgive Paul Montague if Paul Montague should become his cousin's husband.

## Chapter IX

### THE GREAT RAILWAY TO VERA CRUZ

'YOU have been a guest in his house. Then, I guess, the thing's about as good as done.' These words were spoken with a fine, sharp, nasal twang by a brilliantly-dressed American gentleman in one of the smartest private rooms of the great railway hotel at Liverpool, and they were addressed to a young Englishman who was sitting opposite to him. Between them there was a table covered with maps, schedules, and printed programmes. The American was smoking a very large cigar, which he kept constantly turning in his mouth, and half of which was inside his teeth. The Englishman had a short pipe. Mr. Hamilton K. Fisker, of the firm of Fisker, Montague, and Montague, was the American, and the Englishman was our friend Paul, the junior member of that firm.

'But I didn't even speak to him,' said Paul.

'In commercial affairs that matters nothing. It quite justifies you in introducing me. We are not going to ask your friend to do us a favour. We don't want to borrow money.'

'I thought you did.'

'If he'll go in for the thing he'd be one of us, and there would be no borrowing then. He'll join us if he's as clever as they say, because he'll see his way to making a couple of million of dollars out of it. If he'd take the trouble to run over and show himself in San Francisco, he'd make double that. The moneyed men would go in with him at once, because they know that he understands the game and has got the pluck. A man who has done what he has by financing in Europe,—by George! there's no limit to what he might do with us. We're a bigger people than any of you and have more room. We go after bigger things, and don't stand shilly-shally on the brink as you do. But Melmotte pretty nigh beats the best among us. Anyway he should come and try his luck, and he couldn't have a bigger thing or a safer thing than this. He'd see it immediately if I could talk to him for half an hour.'

'Mr. Fisker,' said Paul mysteriously, 'as we are partners, I think I ought to let you know that many people speak very badly of Mr. Melmotte's honesty.'

Mr. Fisker smiled gently, turned his cigar twice round in his mouth, and then closed one eye. 'There is always a want of charity,' he said, 'when a man is successful.'

The scheme in question was the grand proposal for a South Central Pacific and Mexican railway, which was to run from the Salt Lake City, thus branching off from the San Francisco and Chicago line,—and pass down through the fertile lands of New Mexico and Arizona, into the territory of the Mexican Republic, run by the

city of Mexico, and come out on the gulf at the port of
Vera Cruz. Mr. Fisker admitted at once that it was a
great undertaking, acknowledged that the distance might
be perhaps something over 2,000 miles, acknowledged
that no computation had or perhaps could be made as
to the probable cost of the railway; but seemed to think
that questions such as these were beside the mark and
childish. Melmotte, if he would go into the matter at all,
would ask no such questions.

But we must go back a little. Paul Montague had
received a telegram from his partner, Hamilton K. Fisker,
sent on shore at Queenstown from one of the New York
liners, requesting him to meet Fisker at Liverpool immediately. With this request he had felt himself bound to
comply. Personally he had disliked Fisker,—and perhaps
not the less so because when in California he had never
found himself able to resist the man's good humour,
audacity, and cleverness combined. He had found himself talked into agreeing with any project which Mr.
Fisker might have in hand. It was altogether against the
grain with him, and yet by his own consent, that the
flour-mill had been opened at Fiskerville. He trembled
for his money and never wished to see Fisker again; but
still, when Fisker came to England, he was proud to
remember that Fisker was his partner, and he obeyed the
order and went down to Liverpool.

If the flour-mill had frightened him, what must the
present project have done! Fisker explained that he had
come with two objects,—first to ask the consent of the
English partner to the proposed change in their business,
and secondly to obtain the co-operation of English capitalists. The proposed change in the business meant simply
the entire sale of the establishment at Fiskerville, and the
absorption of the whole capital in the work of getting up
the railway. 'If you could realise all the money it wouldn't
make a mile of the railway,' said Paul. Mr. Fisker laughed
at him. The object of Fisker, Montague, and Montague
was not to make a railway to Vera Cruz, but to float a
company. Paul thought that Mr. Fisker seemed to be indifferent whether the railway should ever be constructed

or not. It was clearly his idea that fortunes were to be made out of the concern before a spadeful of earth had been moved. If brilliantly printed programmes might avail anything, with gorgeous maps, and beautiful little pictures of trains running into tunnels beneath snowy mountains and coming out of them on the margin of sunlit lakes, Mr. Fisker had certainly done much. But Paul, when he saw all these pretty things, could not keep his mind from thinking whence had come the money to pay for them. Mr. Fisker had declared that he had come over to obtain his partner's consent, but it seemed to that partner that a great deal had been done without any consent. And Paul's fears on this hand were not allayed by finding that on all these beautiful papers he himself was described as one of the agents and general managers of the company. Each document was signed Fisker, Montague, and Montague. References on all matters were to be made to Fisker, Montague, and Montague,—and in one of the documents it was stated that a member of the firm had proceeded to London with the view of attending to British interests in the matter. Fisker had seemed to think that his young partner would express unbounded satisfaction at the greatness which was thus falling upon him. A certain feeling of importance, not altogether unpleasant, was produced, but at the same time there was another conviction forced upon Montague's mind, not altogether pleasant, that his money was being made to disappear without any consent given by him, and that it behoved him to be cautious lest such consent should be extracted from him unawares.

'What has become of the mill?' he asked.

'We have put an agent into it?'

'Is not that dangerous? What check have you on him?'

'He pays us a fixed sum, sir. But, my word! when there is such a thing as this on hand a trumpery mill like that is not worth speaking of.'

'You haven't sold it?'

'Well;—no. But we've arranged a price for a sale.'

'You haven't taken the money for it?'

'Well;—yes; we have. We've raised money on it, you

know. You see you weren't there, and so the two resident partners acted for the firm. But Mr. Montague, you'd better go with us. You had indeed.'

'And about my own income?'

'That's a flea-bite. When we've got a little ahead with this it won't matter, sir, whether you spend twenty thousand or forty thousand dollars a year. We've got the concession from the United States Government through the territories, and we're in correspondence with the President of the Mexican Republic. I've no doubt we've an office open already in Mexico and another at Vera Cruz.'

'Where's the money to come from?'

'Money to come from, sir? Where do you suppose the money comes from in all these undertakings? If we can float the shares, the money'll come in quick enough. We hold three million dollars of the stock ourselves.'

'Six hundred thousand pounds!' said Montague.

'We take them at par, of course,—and as we sell we shall pay for them. But of course we shall only sell at a premium. If we can run them up even to 110,* there would be three hundred thousand dollars. But we'll do better than that. I must try and see Melmotte at once. You had better write a letter now.'

'I don't know the man.'

'Never mind. Look here—I'll write it, and you can sign it.' Whereupon Mr. Fisker did write the following letter:—

'Langham Hotel, London. March 4, 18—.

'DEAR SIR,

'I have the pleasure of informing you that my partner Mr. Fisker,—of Fisker, Montague, and Montague, of San Francisco,—is now in London with the view of allowing British capitalists to assist in carrying out perhaps the greatest work of the age,—namely, the South Central Pacific and Mexican Railway, which is to give direct communication between San Francisco and the Gulf of Mexico. He is very anxious to see you upon his arrival, as he is aware that your co-operation would be desirable.

We feel assured that with your matured judgment in such matters you would see at once the magnificence of the enterprise. If you will name a day and an hour, Mr. Fisker will call upon you.

'I have to thank you and Madame Melmotte for a very pleasant evening spent at your house last week.

'Mr. Fisker proposes returning to New York. I shall remain here, superintending the British interests which may be involved.

> 'I have the honour to be,
> > 'Dear Sir,
> > > 'Most faithfully yours,
> > > > '_____ _____.'

'But I have never said that I would superintend the interests,' said Montague.

'You can say so now. It binds you to nothing. You regular John Bull Englishmen are so full of scruples that you lose as much of life as should serve to make an additional fortune.'

After some further conversation Paul Montague recopied the letter and signed it. He did it with doubt,—almost with dismay. But he told himself that he could do no good by refusing. If this wretched American, with his hat on one side and rings on his fingers, had so far got the upper hand of Paul's uncle as to have been allowed to do what he liked with the funds of the partnership, Paul could not stop it. On the following morning they went up to London together, and in the course of the afternoon Mr. Fisker presented himself in Abchurch Lane. The letter written at Liverpool, but dated from the Langham Hotel, had been posted at the Euston Square Railway Station at the moment of Fisker's arrival. Fisker sent in his card, and was asked to wait. In the course of twenty minutes he was ushered into the great man's presence by no less a person than Miles Grendall.

It has been already said that Mr. Melmotte was a big man with large whiskers, rough hair, and with an expression of mental power on a harsh vulgar face. He was certainly a man to repel you by his presence unless attracted to him by some internal consideration. He was magnificent in his expenditure, powerful in his doings, successful in his business, and the world around him therefore was not repelled. Fisker, on the other hand, was a shining little man,—perhaps about forty years of age, with a well-twisted moustache, greasy brown hair, which was becoming bald at the top, good-looking if his features were analysed, but insignificant in appearance. He was gorgeously dressed, with a silk waistcoat and chains, and he carried a little stick. One would at first be inclined to say that Fisker was not much of a man; but after a little conversation most men would own that there was something in Fisker. He was troubled by no shyness, by no scruples, and by no fears. His mind was not capacious, but such as it was it was his own, and he knew how to use it.

Abchurch Lane is not a grand site for the offices of a merchant prince. Here, at a small corner house, there was a small brass plate on a swing door, bearing the words 'Melmotte & Co.' Of whom the Co. was composed no one knew. In one sense Mr. Melmotte might be said to be in company with all the commercial world, for there was no business to which he would refuse his co-operation on certain terms. But he had never burthened himself with a partner in the usual sense of the term. Here Fisker found three or four clerks seated at desks, and was desired to walk upstairs. The steps were narrow and crooked, and the rooms were small and irregular. Here he stayed for a while in a small dark apartment in which 'The Daily Telegraph' was left for the amusement of its occupant till Miles Grendall announced to him that Mr. Melmotte would see him. The millionaire looked at him for a moment or two, just condescending to touch with his fingers the hand which Fisker had projected.

'I don't seem to remember,' he said, 'the gentleman who has done me the honour of writing to me about you.'

'I dare say not, Mr. Melmotte. When I'm at home in San Francisco, I make acquaintance with a great many gents whom I don't remember afterwards. My partner

I think told me that he went to your house with his friend, Sir Felix Carbury.'

'I know a young man called Sir Felix Carbury.'

'That's it. I could have got any amount of introductions to you if I had thought this would not have sufficed.' Mr. Melmotte bowed. 'Our account here in London is kept with the City and West End Joint Stock. But I have only just arrived, and as my chief object in coming to London is to see you, and as I met my partner, Mr. Montague, in Liverpool, I took a note from him and came on straight.'

'And what can I do for you, Mr. Fisker?'

Then Mr. Fisker began his account of the Great South Central Pacific and Mexican Railway, and exhibited considerable skill by telling it all in comparatively few words. And yet he was gorgeous and florid. In two minutes he had displayed his programme, his maps, and his pictures before Mr. Melmotte's eyes, taking care that Mr. Melmotte should see how often the names of Fisker, Montague, and Montague, reappeared upon them. As Mr. Melmotte read the documents, Fisker from time to time put in a word. But the words had no reference at all to the future profits of the railway, or to the benefit which such means of communication would confer upon the world at large; but applied solely to the appetite for such stock as theirs, which might certainly be produced in the speculating world by a proper manipulation of the affairs.

'You seem to think you couldn't get it taken up in your own country,' said Melmotte.

'There's not a doubt about getting it all taken up there. Our folk, sir, are quick enough at the game; but you don't want me to teach you, Mr. Melmotte, that nothing encourages this kind of thing like competition. When they hear at St. Louis and Chicago that the thing is alive in London, they'll be alive there. And it's the same here, sir. When they know that the stock is running like wildfire in America, they'll make it run here too.'

'How far have you got?'

'What we've gone to work upon is a concession for making the line from the United States Congress. We're to have the land for nothing, of course, and a grant of one thousand acres round every station, the stations to be twenty-five miles apart.'

'And the land is to be made over to you,—when?'

'When we have made the line up to the station.' Fisker understood perfectly that Mr. Melmotte did not ask the question in reference to any value that he might attach to the possession of such lands, but to the attractiveness of such a prospectus in the eyes of the outside world of speculators.

'And what do you want me to do, Mr. Fisker?'

'I want to have your name there,' he said. And he placed his finger down on a spot on which it was indicated that there was, or was to be, a chairman of an English Board of Directors, but with a space for the name, hitherto blank.

'Who are to be your directors here, Mr. Fisker?'

'We should ask you to choose them, sir. Mr. Paul Montague should be one, and perhaps his friend Sir Felix Carbury might be another. We could get probably one of the Directors of the City and West End. But we would leave it all to you,—as also the amount of stock you would like to take yourself. If you gave yourself to it, heart and soul, Mr. Melmotte, it would be the finest thing that there has been out for a long time. There would be such a mass of stock!'

'You have to back that with a certain amount of paid-up capital?'

'We take care, sir, in the West not to cripple commerce too closely by old-fashioned bandages. Look at what we've done already, sir, by having our limbs pretty free. Look at our line, sir, right across the continent, from San Francisco to New York. Look at ——'

'Never mind that, Mr. Fisker. People wanted to go from New York to San Francisco, and I don't know that they do want to go to Vera Cruz. But I will look at it, and you shall hear from me.' The interview was over, and Mr. Fisker was contented with it. Had Mr. Melmotte not intended at least to think of it he would not have given ten minutes to the subject. After all, what was wanted from Mr. Melmotte was little more than his name, for the use of which Mr. Fisker proposed that he should receive from the speculative public two or three hundred thousand pounds.

At the end of a fortnight from the date of Mr. Fisker's arrival in London, the company was fully launched in England, with a body of London directors, of whom Mr. Melmotte was the chairman. Among the directors were Lord Alfred Grendall, Sir Felix Carbury, Samuel Cohenlupe, Esq., Member of Parliament for Staines, a gentleman of the Jewish persuasion, Lord Nidderdale, who was also in Parliament, and Mr. Paul Montague. It may be thought that the directory was not strong, and that but little help could be given to any commercial enterprise by the assistance of Lord Alfred or Sir Felix;—but it was felt that Mr. Melmotte was himself so great a tower of strength that the fortune of the Company,—as a company,—was made.

## Chapter X

### MR. FISKER'S SUCCESS

MR. FISKER was fully satisfied with the progress he had made, but he never quite succeeded in reconciling Paul Montague to the whole transaction. Mr. Melmotte was indeed so great a reality, such a fact in the commercial world of London, that it was no longer possible for such a one as Montague to refuse to believe in the scheme. Melmotte had the telegraph at his command, and had been able to make as close inquiries as though San Francisco and Salt Lake City had been suburbs of London. He was chairman of the British branch of the Company, and had had shares allocated to him,—or, as he said, to the house,—to the extent of two millions of dollars. But still there was a feeling of doubt, and a consciousness that Melmotte, though a tower of strength, was thought by many to have been built upon the sands.

Paul had now of course given his full authority to the

work, much in opposition to the advice of his old friend
Roger Carbury,—and had come up to live in town, that
he might personally attend to the affairs of the great
railway. There was an office just behind the Exchange,
with two or three clerks and a secretary, the latter position
being held by Miles Grendall, Esq. Paul, who had a
conscience in the matter and was keenly alive to the fact
that he was not only a director but was also one of the
firm of Fisker, Montague, and Montague which was
responsible for the whole affair, was grievously anxious to
be really at work, and would attend most inopportunely
at the Company's offices. Fisker, who still lingered in
London, did his best to put a stop to this folly, and on
more than one occasion somewhat snubbed his partner.
'My dear fellow, what's the use of your flurrying yourself? In a thing of this kind, when it has once been set
agoing, there is nothing else to do. You may have to
work your fingers off before you can make it move, and
then fail. But all that has been done for you. If you go
there on the Thursdays that's quite as much as you need
do. You don't suppose that such a man as Melmotte
would put up with any real interference.' Paul endeavoured to assert himself, declaring that as one of the
managers he meant to take a part in the management;—
that his fortune, such as it was, had been embarked in
the matter, and was as important to him as was Mr. Melmotte's fortune to Mr. Melmotte. But Fisker got the
better of him and put him down. 'Fortune! what fortune
had either of us? a few beggarly thousands of dollars not
worth talking of, and barely sufficient to enable a man
to look at an enterprise. And now where are you? look
here, sir;—there's more to be got out of the smashing up
of such an affair as this, if it should smash up, than could
be made by years of hard work out of such fortunes as
yours and mine in the regular way of trade.'

Paul Montague certainly did not love Mr. Fisker personally, nor did he relish his commercial doctrines; but
he allowed himself to be carried away by them. 'When
and how was I to have helped myself?' he wrote to Roger
Carbury. 'The money had been raised and spent before

this man came here at all. It's all very well to say that he
had no right to do it; but he had done it. I couldn't even
have gone to law with him without going over to California, and then I should have got no redress.' Through
it all he disliked Fisker, and yet Fisker had one great
merit which certainly recommended itself warmly to
Montague's appreciation. Though he denied the propriety of Paul's interference in the business, he quite
acknowledged Paul's right to a share in the existing dash
of prosperity. As to the real facts of the money affairs of
the firm he would tell Paul nothing. But he was well
provided with money himself, and took care that his
partner should be in the same position. He paid him all
the arrears of his stipulated income up to the present
moment, and put him nominally into possession of a
large number of shares in the railway,—with, however,
an understanding that he was not to sell them till they
had reached ten per cent. above par, and that in any sale
transacted he was to touch no other money than the
amount of profit which would thus accrue. What Melmotte was to be allowed to do with his shares, he never
heard. As far as Montague could understand, Melmotte
was in truth to be powerful over everything. All this
made the young man unhappy, restless, and extravagant.
He was living in London and had money at command,
but he never could rid himself of the fear that the whole
affair might tumble to pieces beneath his feet and that he
might be stigmatised as one among a gang of swindlers.

We all know how, in such circumstances, by far the
greater proportion of a man's life will be given up to the
enjoyments that are offered to him and the lesser proportion to the cares, sacrifices, and sorrows. Had this
young director been describing to his intimate friend the
condition in which he found himself, he would have declared himself to be distracted by doubts, suspicions, and
fears till his life was a burden to him. And yet they who
were living with him at this time found him to be a very
pleasant fellow, fond of amusement, and disposed to
make the most of all the good things which came in his
way. Under the auspices of Sir Felix Carbury he had

become a member of the Beargarden, at which best of all
possible clubs the mode of entrance was as irregular as
its other proceedings. When any young man desired to
come in who was thought to be unfit for its style of living,
it was shown to him that it would take three years before
his name could be brought up at the usual rate of vacan-
cies; but in regard to desirable companions the committee had a power of putting them at the top of the list
of candidates and bringing them in at once. Paul Montague had suddenly become credited with considerable
commercial wealth and greater commercial influence.
He sat at the same Board with Melmotte and Melmotte's
men; and was on this account elected at the Beargarden
without any of that harassing delay to which other less
fortunate candidates are subjected.

And,—let it be said with regret, for Paul Montague
was at heart honest and well-conditioned,—he took to
living a good deal at the Beargarden. A man must dine
somewhere, and everybody knows that a man dines
cheaper at his club than elsewhere. It was thus he
reasoned with himself. But Paul's dinners at the Beargarden were not cheap. He saw a good deal of his brother
directors, Sir Felix Carbury and Lord Nidderdale, entertained Lord Alfred more than once at the club, and had
twice dined with his great chairman amidst all the magnificence of merchant-princely hospitality in Grosvenor
Square. It had indeed been suggested to him by Mr.
Fisker that he also ought to enter himself for the great
Marie-Melmotte plate. Lord Nidderdale had again declared his intention of running, owing to considerable
pressure put upon him by certain interested tradesmen,
and with this intention had become one of the directors
of the Mexican Railway Company. At the time, however, of which we are now writing, Sir Felix was the
favourite for the race among fashionable circles generally.

The middle of April had come, and Fisker was still in
London. When millions of dollars are at stake,—belonging perhaps to widows and orphans, as Fisker remarked,
—a man was forced to set his own convenience on one
side. But this devotion was not left without reward, for

Mr. Fisker had 'a good time' in London. He also was made free of the Beargarden, as an honorary member, and he also spent a good deal of money. But there is this comfort in great affairs, that whatever you spend on yourself can be no more than a trifle. Champagne and ginger-beer are all the same when you stand to win or lose thousands,—with this only difference, that champagne may have deteriorating results which the more innocent beverage will not produce. The feeling that the greatness of these operations relieved them from the necessity of looking to small expenses operated in the champagne direction, both on Fisker and Montague, and the result was deleterious. The Beargarden, no doubt, was a more lively place than Carbury Manor, but Montague found that he could not wake up on these London mornings with thoughts as satisfactory as those which attended his pillow at the old Manor House.

On Saturday, the 19th of April, Fisker was to leave London on his return to New York, and on the 18th a farewell dinner was to be given to him at the club. Mr. Melmotte was asked to meet him, and on such an occasion all the resources of the club were to be brought forth. Lord Alfred Grendall was also to be a guest, and Mr. Cohenlupe, who went about a good deal with Melmotte. Nidderdale, Carbury, Montague, and Miles Grendall were members of the club, and gave the dinner. No expense was spared. Herr Vossner purveyed the viands and wines,—and paid for them. Lord Nidderdale took the chair, with Fisker on his right hand, and Melmotte on his left, and, for a fast-going young lord, was supposed to have done the thing well. There were only two toasts drunk, to the healths of Mr. Melmotte and Mr. Fisker, and two speeches were of course made by them. Mr. Melmotte may have been held to have clearly proved the genuineness of that English birth which he claimed by the awkwardness and incapacity which he showed on the occasion. He stood with his hands on the table and with his face turned to his plate blurted out his assurance that the floating of this railway company would be one of the greatest and most successful commercial operations ever conducted on either side of the Atlantic. It was a great thing,—a very great thing;—he had no hesitation in saying that it was one of the greatest things out. He didn't believe a greater thing had ever come out. He was happy to give his humble assistance to the furtherance of so great a thing,—and so on. These assertions, not varying much one from the other, he jerked out like so many separate interjections, endeavouring to look his friends in the face at each, and then turning his countenance back to his plate as though seeking for inspiration for the next attempt. He was not eloquent; but the gentlemen who heard him remembered that he was the great Augustus Melmotte, that he might probably make them all rich men, and they cheered him to the echo. Lord Alfred had reconciled himself to be called by his Christian name, since he had been put in the way of raising two or three hundred pounds on the security of shares which were to be allotted to him, but of which in the flesh he had as yet seen nothing. Wonderful are the ways of trade! If one can only get the tip of one's little finger into the right pie, what noble morsels, what rich esculents, will stick to it as it is extracted!

When Melmotte sat down Fisker made his speech, and it was fluent, fast, and florid. Without giving it word for word, which would be tedious, I could not adequately set before the reader's eye the speaker's pleasing picture of world-wide commercial love and harmony which was to be produced by a railway from Salt Lake City to Vera Cruz, nor explain the extent of gratitude from the world at large which might be claimed by, and would finally be accorded to, the great firms of Melmotte & Co. of London, and Fisker, Montague, and Montague of San Francisco. Mr. Fisker's arms were waved gracefully about. His head was turned now this way and now that, but never towards his plate. It was very well done. But there was more faith in one ponderous word from Mr. Melmotte's mouth than in all the American's oratory.

There was not one of them then present who had not after some fashion been given to understand that his fortune was to be made, not by the construction of the railway, but by the floating of the railway shares. They had all whispered to each other their convictions on this head. Even Montague did not beguile himself into an idea that he was really a director in a company to be employed in the making and working of a railway. People out of doors were to be advertised into buying shares, and they who were so to say indoors were to have the privilege of manufacturing the shares thus to be sold. That was to be their work, and they all knew it. But now, as there were eight of them collected together, they talked of humanity at large and of the coming harmony of nations.

After the first cigar, Melmotte withdrew, and Lord Alfred went with him. Lord Alfred would have liked to remain, being a man who enjoyed tobacco and soda-and-brandy,—but momentous days had come upon him, and he thought it well to cling to his Melmotte. Mr. Samuel Cohenlupe also went, not having taken a very distinguished part in the entertainment. Then the young men were left alone, and it was soon proposed that they should adjourn to the cardroom. It had been rather hoped that Fisker would go with the elders. Nidderdale, who did not understand much about the races of mankind, had his doubts whether the American gentleman might not be a 'Heathen Chinee,'*such as he had read of in poetry. But Mr. Fisker liked to have his amusement as well as did the others, and went up resolutely into the cardroom. Here they were joined by Lord Grasslough, and were very quickly at work, having chosen loo as their game. Mr. Fisker made an allusion to poker as a desirable pastime, but Lord Nidderdale, remembering his poetry, shook his head. 'Oh! bother,' he said, 'let's have some game that Christians play.' Mr. Fisker declared himself ready for any game,—irrespective of religious prejudices.

It must be explained that the gambling at the Beargarden had gone on with very little interruption, and that on the whole Sir Felix Carbury kept his luck. There had of course been vicissitudes, but his star had been in the ascendant. For some nights together this had been so continual that Mr. Miles Grendall had suggested to his

friend Lord Grasslough that there must be foul play.
Lord Grasslough, who had not many good gifts, was, at
least, not suspicious, and repudiated the idea. 'We'll
keep an eye on him,' Miles Grendall had said. 'You may
do as you like, but I'm not going to watch any one,'
Grasslough had replied. Miles had watched, and had
watched in vain, and it may as well be said at once that
Sir Felix, with all his faults, was not as yet a blackleg.
Both of them now owed Sir Felix a considerable sum of
money, as did also Dolly Longestaffe, who was not present
on this occasion. Latterly very little ready money had
passed hands,—very little in proportion to the sums
which had been written down on paper,—though Sir
Felix was still so well in funds as to feel himself justified
in repudiating any caution that his mother might give
him.

When I.O.U.'s have for some time passed freely in such
a company as that now assembled the sudden introduction of a stranger is very disagreeable, particularly
when that stranger intends to start for San Francisco on
the following morning. If it could be arranged that the
stranger should certainly lose, no doubt then he would be
regarded as a godsend. Such strangers have ready money
in their pockets, a portion of which would be felt to
descend like a soft shower in a time of drought. When
these dealings in unsecured paper have been going on for
a considerable time real bank notes come to have a loveliness which they never possessed before. But should the
stranger win, then there may arise complications incapable of any comfortable solution. In such a state of
things some Herr Vossner must be called in, whose terms
are apt to be ruinous. On this occasion things did not
arrange themselves comfortably. From the very commencement Fisker won, and quite a budget of little papers
fell into his possession, many of which were passed to him
from the hands of Sir Felix,—bearing, however, a 'G'
intended to stand for Grasslough, or an 'N' for Nidderdale, or a wonderful hieroglyphic which was known at
the Beargarden to mean D. L——, or Dolly Longestaffe,
the fabricator of which was not present on the occasion.

Then there was the M. G. of Miles Grendall, which was
a species of paper peculiarly plentiful and very unattractive on these commercial occasions. Paul Montague
hitherto had never given an I.O.U. at the Beargarden,—
nor of late had our friend Sir Felix. On the present
occasion Montague won, though not heavily. Sir Felix
lost continually, and was almost the only loser. But Mr.
Fisker won nearly all that was lost. He was to start for
Liverpool by train at 8.30 A.M., and at 6 A.M. he counted
up his bits of paper and found himself the winner of
about £600. 'I think that most of them came from you,
Sir Felix,' he said,—handing the bundle across the table.

'I dare say they did, but they are all good against these
other fellows.' Then Fisker, with most perfect good
humour, extracted one from the mass which indicated
Dolly Longestaffe's indebtedness to the amount of £50.
'That's Longestaffe,' said Felix, 'and I'll change that of
course.' Then out of his pocket-book he extracted other
minute documents bearing that M. G. which was so
little esteemed among them,—and so made up the sum.
'You seem to have £150 from Grasslough, £145 from
Nidderdale, and £322 10s. from Grendall,' said the
baronet. Then Sir Felix got up as though he had paid
his score. Fisker, with smiling good humour, arranged
the little bits of paper before him and looked round upon
the company.

'This won't do, you know,' said Nidderdale. 'Mr.
Fisker must have his money before he leaves. You've got
it, Carbury.'

'Of course he has,' said Grasslough.

'As it happens, I have not,' said Sir Felix;—'but what
if I had?'

'Mr. Fisker starts for New York immediately,' said
Lord Nidderdale. 'I suppose we can muster £600 among
us. Ring the bell for Vossner. I think Carbury ought to
pay the money as he lost it, and we didn't expect to have
our I.O.U.'s brought up in this way.'

'Lord Nidderdale,' said Sir Felix, 'I have already said
that I have not got the money about me. Why should I
have it more than you, especially as I knew I had I.O.U.'s

more than sufficient to meet anything I could lose when
I sat down?'

'Mr. Fisker must have his money at any rate,' said
Lord Nidderdale, ringing the bell again.

'It doesn't matter one straw, my lord,' said the Ameri-
can. 'Let it be sent to me to Frisco, in a bill, my lord.'
And so he got up to take his hat, greatly to the delight of
Miles Grendall.

But the two young lords would not agree to this. 'If
you must go this very minute I'll meet you at the train
with the money,' said Nidderdale. Fisker begged that
no such trouble should be taken. Of course he would
wait ten minutes if they wished. But the affair was one
of no consequence. Wasn't the post running every day?
Then Herr Vossner came from his bed, suddenly arrayed
in a dressing-gown, and there was a conference in a
corner between him, the two lords, and Mr. Grendall.
In a very few minutes Herr Vossner wrote a cheque for
the amount due by the lords, but he was afraid that he
had not money at his banker's sufficient for the greater
claim. It was well understood that Herr Vossner would
not advance money to Mr. Grendall unless others would
pledge themselves for the amount.

'I suppose I'd better send you a bill over to America,'
said Miles Grendall, who had taken no part in the matter
as long as he was in the same boat with the lords.

'Just so. My partner, Montague, will tell you the
address.' Then bustling off, taking an affectionate adieu
of Paul, shaking hands with them all round, and looking
as though he cared nothing for the money, he took his
leave. 'One cheer for the South Central Pacific and
Mexican Railway,' he said as he went out of the room.

Not one there had liked Fisker. His manners were not
as their manners; his waistcoat not as their waistcoats.
He smoked his cigar after a fashion different from theirs,
and spat upon the carpet. He said 'my lord' too often, and
grated their prejudices equally whether he treated them
with familiarity or deference. But he had behaved well
about the money, and they felt that they were behaving
badly. Sir Felix was the immediate offender, as he

should have understood that he was not entitled to pay
a stranger with documents which, by tacit contract, were
held to be good among themselves. But there was no use
now in going back to that. Something must be done.

'Vossner must get the money,' said Nidderdale. 'Let's
have him up again.'

'I don't think it's my fault,' said Miles. 'Of course no
one thought he was to be called upon in this sort of way.'

'Why shouldn't you be called upon?' said Carbury.
'You acknowledge that you owe the money.'

'I think Carbury ought to have paid it,' said Grasslough.

'Grassy, my boy,' said the baronet, 'your attempts at
thinking are never worth much. Why was I to suppose
that a stranger would be playing among us? Had you a
lot of ready money with you to pay if you had lost it?
I don't always walk about with six hundred pounds in
my pocket;—nor do you!'

'It's no good jawing,' said Nidderdale; 'let's get the
money.' Then Montague offered to undertake the debt
himself, saying that there were money transactions between him and his partner. But this could not be allowed.
He had only lately come among them, had as yet had no
dealing in I.O.U.'s, and was the last man in the company
who ought to be made responsible for the impecuniosity
of Miles Grendall. He, the impecunious one,—the one
whose impecuniosity extended to the absolute want of
credit,—sat silent, stroking his heavy moustache.

There was a second conference between Herr Vossner
and the two lords in another room, which ended in the
preparation of a document by which Miles Grendall
undertook to pay to Herr Vossner £450 at the end of
three months, and this was endorsed by the two lords, by
Sir Felix, and by Paul Montague; and in return for this
the German produced £322 10s. in notes and gold. This
had taken some considerable time. Then a cup of tea
was prepared and swallowed; after which Nidderdale,
with Montague, started off to meet Fisker at the railway
station. 'It'll only be a trifle over £100 each,' said Nidderdale, in the cab.

'Won't Mr. Grendall pay it?'

'Oh, dear no. How the devil should he?'

'Then he shouldn't play.'

'That'd be hard on him, poor fellow. If you went to his uncle the duke, I suppose you could get it. Or Buntingford might put it right for you. Perhaps he might win, you know, some day, and then he'd make it square. He'd be fair enough if he had it. Poor Miles!'

They found Fisker wonderfully brilliant with bright rugs, and greatcoats with silk linings. 'We've brought you the tin,' said Nidderdale, accosting him on the platform.

'Upon my word, my lord, I'm sorry you have taken so much trouble about such a trifle.'

'A man should always have his money when he wins.'

'We don't think anything about such little matters at Frisco, my lord.'

'You're fine fellows at Frisco, I dare say. Here we pay up,—when we can. Sometimes we can't, and then it is not pleasant.' Fresh adieus were made between the two partners, and between the American and the lord;—and then Fisker was taken off on his way towards Frisco. 'He's not half a bad fellow, but he's not a bit like an Englishman,' said Lord Nidderdale, as he walked out of the station.

## Chapter XI

### LADY CARBURY AT HOME

DURING the last six weeks Lady Carbury had lived a life of very mixed depression and elevation. Her great work had come out,—the 'Criminal Queens',—and had been very widely reviewed. In this matter it had been by no means all pleasure, inasmuch as many very hard words had been said of her. In spite of the dear friendship between herself and Mr. Alf, one of Mr. Alf's most sharp-nailed subordinates had been set upon her book, and had pulled it to pieces with almost rabid malignity. One would have thought that so slight a thing could hardly have been worthy of such protracted attention. Error after error was laid bare with merciless prolixity. No doubt the writer of the article must have had all history at his finger-ends, as in pointing out the various mistakes made he always spoke of the historical facts which had been misquoted, misdated, or misrepresented, as being familiar in all their bearings to every schoolboy of twelve years old. The writer of the criticism never suggested the idea that he himself, having been fully provided with books of reference, and having learned the art of finding in them what he wanted at a moment's notice, had, as he went on with his work, checked off the blunders without any more permanent knowledge of his own than a housekeeper has of coals when she counts so many sacks into the coal-cellar. He spoke of the parentage of one wicked ancient lady, and the dates of the frailties of another, with an assurance intended to show that an exact knowledge of all these details abided with him always. He must have been a man of vast and varied erudition, and his name was Jones. The world knew him not, but his erudition was always there at the command of Mr. Alf,—and his cruelty. The greatness of Mr. Alf consisted in this, that he always had a Mr. Jones or two ready to do his work for him. It was a great business, this of Mr. Alf's, for he had his Jones also for philology, for science, for poetry, for politics, as well as for history, and one special Jones, extraordinarily accurate and very well posted up in his references, entirely devoted to the Elizabethan drama.

There is the review intended to sell a book,—which comes out immediately after the appearance of the book, or sometimes before it; the review which gives reputation, but does not affect the sale, and which comes a little later; the review which snuffs a book out quietly; the review which is to raise or lower the author a single peg, or two pegs, as the case may be; the review which is suddenly to make an author, and the review which is to crush him. An exuberant Jones has been known before now to declare aloud that he would crush a man, and a

self-confident Jones has been known to declare that he
has accomplished the deed. Of all reviews, the crushing
review is the most popular, as being the most readable.
When the rumour goes abroad that some notable man
has been actually crushed,—been positively driven over
by an entire Juggernaut's car of criticism till his literary
body be a mere amorphous mass,—then a real success
has been achieved, and the Alf of the day has done a
great thing; but even the crushing of a poor Lady Carbury, if it be absolute, is effective. Such a review will not
make all the world call for the 'Evening Pulpit', but it
will cause those who do take the paper to be satisfied
with their bargain. Whenever the circulation of such a
paper begins to slacken, the proprietors should, as a matter
of course, admonish their Alf to add a little power to the
crushing department.

Lady Carbury had been crushed by the 'Evening
Pulpit.' We may fancy that it was easy work, and that
Mr. Alf's historical Mr. Jones was not forced to fatigue
himself by the handling of many books of reference. The
errors did lie a little near the surface; and the whole
scheme of the work, with its pandering to bad tastes by
pretended revelations of frequently fabulous crime, was
reprobated in Mr. Jones's very best manner. But the
poor authoress, though utterly crushed, and reduced to
little more than literary pulp for an hour or two, was
not destroyed. On the following morning she went to her
publishers, and was closeted for half an hour with the
senior partner, Mr. Leadham. 'I've got it all in black
and white,' she said, full of the wrong which had been
done her, 'and can prove him to be wrong. It was in
1522 that the man first came to Paris, and he couldn't
have been her lover before that. I got it all out of the
"Biographie Universelle." I'll write to Mr. Alf myself,—
a letter to be published, you know.'

'Pray don't do anything of the kind, Lady Carbury.'

'I can prove that I'm right.'

'And they can prove that you're wrong.'

'I've got all the facts,—and the figures.'

Mr. Leadham did not care a straw for facts or figures,

—had no opinion of his own whether the lady or the reviewer were right; but he knew very well that the 'Evening Pulpit' would surely get the better of any mere author in such a contention. 'Never fight the newspapers, Lady Carbury. Who ever yet got any satisfaction by that kind of thing? It's their business, and you are not used to it.'

'And Mr. Alf is my particular friend! It does seem so hard,' said Lady Carbury, wiping hot tears from her cheeks.

'It won't do us the least harm, Lady Carbury.'

'It'll stop the sale?'

'Not much. A book of that sort couldn't hope to go on very long, you know. The "Breakfast Table" gave it an excellent lift, and came just at the right time. I rather like the notice in the "Pulpit," myself.'

'Like it!' said Lady Carbury, still suffering in every fibre of her self-love from the soreness produced by those Juggernaut's car-wheels.

'Anything is better than indifference, Lady Carbury. A great many people remember simply that the book has been noticed, but carry away nothing as to the purport of the review. It's a very good advertisement.'

'But to be told that I have got to learn the A B C of history,—after working as I have worked!'

'That's a mere form of speech, Lady Carbury.'

'You think the book has done pretty well?'

'Pretty well;—just about what we hoped, you know.'

'There'll be something coming to me, Mr. Leadham?'

Mr. Leadham sent for a ledger, and turned over a few pages and ran up a few figures, and then scratched his head. There would be something, but Lady Carbury was not to imagine that it could be very much. It did not often happen that a great deal could be made by a first book. Nevertheless, Lady Carbury, when she left the publisher's shop, did carry a cheque with her. She was smartly dressed and looked very well, and had smiled on Mr. Leadham. Mr. Leadham, too, was no more than man, and had written—a small cheque.

Mr. Alf certainly had behaved badly to her; but both Mr. Broune of the 'Breakfast Table,' and Mr. Booker of the 'Literary Chronicle,' had been true to her interests. Lady Carbury had, as she promised, 'done' Mr. Booker's 'New Tale of a Tub' in the 'Breakfast Table.' That is, she had been allowed, as a reward for looking into Mr. Broune's eyes, and laying her soft hand on Mr. Broune's sleeve, and suggesting to Mr. Broune that no one understood her so well as he did, to bedaub Mr. Booker's very thoughtful book in a very thoughtless fashion,—and to be paid for her work. What had been said about his work in the 'Breakfast Table' had been very distasteful to poor Mr. Booker. It grieved his inner contemplative intelligence that such rubbish should be thrown upon him; but in his outside experience of life he knew that even the rubbish was valuable, and that he must pay for it in the manner to which he had unfortunately become accustomed. So Mr. Booker himself wrote the article on the 'Criminal Queens' in the 'Literary Chronicle,' knowing that what he wrote would also be rubbish. 'Remarkable vivacity.' 'Power of delineating character.' 'Excellent choice of subject.' 'Considerable intimacy with the historical details of various periods.' 'The literary world would be sure to hear of Lady Carbury again.' The composition of the review, together with the reading of the book, consumed altogether perhaps an hour of Mr. Booker's time. He made no attempt to cut the pages, but here and there read those that were open. He had done this kind of thing so often, that he knew well what he was about. He could have reviewed such a book when he was three parts asleep. When the work was done he threw down his pen and uttered a deep sigh. He felt it to be hard upon him that he should be compelled, by the exigencies of his position, to descend so low in literature; but it did not occur to him to reflect that in fact he was not compelled, and that he was quite at liberty to break stones, or to starve honestly, if no other honest mode of carrying on his career was open to him. 'If I didn't, somebody else would,' he said to himself.

But the review in the 'Morning Breakfast Table' was

the making of Lady Carbury's book, as far as it ever was made. Mr. Broune saw the lady after the receipt of the letter given in the first chapter of this Tale, and was induced to make valuable promises which had been fully performed. Two whole columns had been devoted to the work, and the world had been assured that no more delightful mixture of amusement and instruction had ever been concocted than Lady Carbury's 'Criminal Queens.' It was the very book that had been wanted for years. It was a work of infinite research and brilliant imagination combined. There had been no hesitation in the laying on of the paint. At that last meeting Lady Carbury had been very soft, very handsome, and very winning; Mr. Broune had given the order with good will, and it had been obeyed in the same feeling.

Therefore, though the crushing had been very real, there had also been some elation; and as a net result, Lady Carbury was disposed to think that her literary career might yet be a success. Mr. Leadham's cheque had been for a small amount, but it might probably lead the way to something better. People at any rate were talking about her, and her Tuesday evenings at home were generally full. But her literary life, and her literary successes, her flirtations with Mr. Broune, her business with Mr. Booker, and her crushing by Mr. Alf's Mr. Jones, were after all but adjuncts to that real inner life of hers of which the absorbing interest was her son. And with regard to him too she was partly depressed, and partly elated, allowing her hopes however to dominate her fears. There was very much to frighten her. Even the moderate reform in the young man's expenses which had been effected under dire necessity had been of late abandoned. Though he never told her anything, she became aware that during the last month of the hunting season he had hunted nearly every day. She knew, too, that he had a horse up in town. She never saw him but once in the day, when she visited him in his bed about noon, and was aware that he was always at his club throughout the night. She knew that he was gambling, and she hated gambling as being of all pastimes the most dangerous. But she knew that he had ready money for his immediate purposes, and that two or three tradesmen who were gifted with a peculiar power of annoying their debtors, had ceased to trouble her in Welbeck Street. For the present, therefore, she consoled herself by reflecting that his gambling was successful. But her elation sprang from a higher source than this. From all that she could hear, she thought it likely that Felix would carry off the great prize; and then,—should he do that,—what a blessed son would he have been to her! How constantly in her triumph would she be able to forget all his vices, his debts, his gambling, his late hours, and his cruel treatment of herself! As she thought of it the bliss seemed to be too great for the possibility of realisation. She was taught to understand that £10,000 a year, to begin with, would be the least of it; and that the ultimate wealth might probably be such as to make Sir Felix Carbury the richest commoner in England. In her very heart of hearts she worshipped wealth, but desired it for him rather than for herself. Then her mind ran away to baronies and earldoms, and she was lost in the coming glories of the boy whose faults had already nearly engulfed her in his own ruin.

And she had another ground for elation, which comforted her much, though elation from such a cause was altogether absurd. She had discovered that her son had become a Director of the South Central Pacific and Mexican Railway Company. She must have known,—she certainly did know,—that Felix, such as he was, could not lend assistance by his work to any company or commercial enterprise in the world. She was aware that there was some reason for such a choice hidden from the world, and which comprised and conveyed a falsehood. A ruined baronet of five-and-twenty, every hour of whose life since he had been left to go alone had been loaded with vice and folly,—whose egregious misconduct warranted his friends in regarding him as one incapable of knowing what principle is,—of what service could he be, that he should be made a Director? But Lady Carbury, though she knew that he could be of no service, was not at all shocked. She was now able to speak up a little for her boy, and did not forget to send the news by post to Roger Carbury. And her son sat at the same Board with Mr. Melmotte! What an indication was this of coming triumphs!

Fisker had started, as the reader will perhaps remember, on the morning of Saturday 19th April, leaving Sir Felix at the Club at about seven in the morning. All that day his mother was unable to see him. She found him asleep in his room at noon and again at two; and when she sought him again he had flown. But on the Sunday she caught him. 'I hope,' she said, 'you'll stay at home on Tuesday evening.' Hitherto she had never succeeded in inducing him to grace her evening parties by his presence.

'All your people are coming! You know, mother, it is such an awful bore.'

'Madame Melmotte and her daughter will be here.'

'One looks such a fool carrying on that kind of thing in one's own house. Everybody sees that it has been contrived. And it is such a pokey, stuffy little place!'

Then Lady Carbury spoke out her mind. 'Felix, I think you must be a fool. I have given over ever expecting that you would do anything to please me. I sacrifice everything for you and I do not even hope for a return. But when I am doing everything to advance your own interests, when I am working night and day to rescue you from ruin, I think you might at any rate help a little,— not for me of course, but for yourself.'

'I don't know what you mean by working day and night. I don't want you to work day and night.'

'There is hardly a young man in London that is not thinking of this girl, and you have chances that none of them have. I am told they are going out of town at Whitsuntide, and that she's to meet Lord Nidderdale down in the country.'

'She can't endure Nidderdale. She says so herself.'

'She will do as she is told,—unless she can be made to be downright in love with some one like yourself. Why not ask her at once on Tuesday?'

'If I'm to do it at all I must do it after my own fashion.
I'm not going to be driven.'

'Of course if you will not take the trouble to be here to
see her when she comes to your own house, you cannot
expect her to think that you really love her.'

'Love her! what a bother there is about loving! Well;
—I'll look in. What time do the animals come to feed?'

'There will be no feeding. Felix, you are so heartless
and so cruel that I sometimes think I will make up my
mind to let you go your own way and never to speak to
you again. My friends will be here about ten;—I should
say from ten till twelve. I think you should be here to
receive her, not later than ten.'

'If I can get my dinner out of my throat by that time,
I will come.'

When the Tuesday came, the over-driven young man
did contrive to get his dinner eaten, and his glass of
brandy sipped, and his cigar smoked, and perhaps his
game of billiards played, so as to present himself in his
mother's drawing-room not long after half-past ten.
Madame Melmotte and her daughter were already there,
—and many others, of whom the majority were devoted
to literature. Among them Mr. Alf was in the room, and
was at this very moment discussing Lady Carbury's book
with Mr. Booker. He had been quite graciously received,
as though he had not authorised the crushing. Lady
Carbury had given him her hand with that energy of
affection with which she was wont to welcome her literary
friends, and had simply thrown one glance of appeal into
his eyes as she looked into his face,—as though asking him
how he had found it in his heart to be so cruel to one so
tender, so unprotected, so innocent as herself. 'I cannot
stand this kind of thing,' said Mr. Alf, to Mr. Booker.
'There's a regular system of touting got abroad, and I
mean to trample it down.'

'If you're strong enough,' said Mr. Booker.

'Well, I think I am. I'm strong enough, at any
rate, to show that I'm not afraid to lead the way. I've
the greatest possible regard for our friend here;—but
her book is a bad book, a thoroughly rotten book, an

unblushing compilation from half-a-dozen works of established reputation, in pilfering from which she has almost always managed to misapprehend her facts, and to muddle her dates. Then she writes to me and asks me to do the best I can for her. I have done the best I could.'

Mr. Alf knew very well what Mr. Booker had done, and Mr. Booker was aware of the extent of Mr. Alf's knowledge. 'What you say is all very right,' said Mr. Booker; 'only you want a different kind of world to live in.'

'Just so;—and therefore we must make it different. I wonder how our friend Broune felt when he saw that his critic had declared that the "Criminal Queens" was the greatest historical work of modern days.'

'I didn't see the notice. There isn't much in the book, certainly, as far as I have looked at it. I should have said that violent censure or violent praise would be equally thrown away upon it. One doesn't want to break a butterfly on the wheel;—especially a friendly butterfly.'

'As to the friendship, it should be kept separate. That's my idea,' said Mr. Alf, moving away.

'I'll never forget what you've done for me,—never!' said Lady Carbury, holding Mr. Broune's hand for a moment, as she whispered to him.

'Nothing more than my duty,' said he, smiling.

'I hope you'll learn to know that a woman can really be grateful,' she replied. Then she let go his hand and moved away to some other guest. There was a dash of true sincerity in what she had said. Of enduring gratitude it may be doubtful whether she was capable: but at this moment she did feel that Mr. Broune had done much for her, and that she would willingly make him some return of friendship. Of any feeling of another sort, of any turn at the moment towards flirtation, of any idea of encouragement to a gentleman who had once acted as though he were her lover, she was absolutely innocent. She had forgotten that little absurd episode in their joint lives. She was at any rate too much in earnest at the present moment to think about it. But it was otherwise with Mr. Broune. He could not quite make up his mind whether the lady was or was not in love with him,—or whether, if she were, it was incumbent on him to indulge her;—and if so, in what manner. Then as he looked after her, he told himself that she was certainly very beautiful, that her figure was distinguished, that her income was certain, and her rank considerable. Nevertheless, Mr. Broune knew of himself that he was not a marrying man. He had made up his mind that marriage would not suit his business, and he smiled to himself as he reflected how impossible it was that such a one as Lady Carbury should turn him from his resolution.

'I am so glad that you have come to-night, Mr. Alf,' Lady Carbury said to the high-minded editor of the 'Evening Pulpit.'

'Am I not always glad to come, Lady Carbury?'

'You are very good. But I feared——'

'Feared what, Lady Carbury?'

'That you might perhaps have felt that I should be unwilling to welcome you after,—well, after the compliments of last Thursday.'

'I never allow the two things to join themselves together. You see, Lady Carbury, I don't write all these things myself.'

'No indeed. What a bitter creature you would be if you did.'

'To tell the truth, I never write any of them. Of course we endeavour to get people whose judgments we can trust, and if, as in this case, it should unfortunately happen that the judgment of our critic should be hostile to the literary pretensions of a personal friend of my own, I can only lament the accident, and trust that my friend may have spirit enough to divide me as an individual from that Mr. Alf who has the misfortune to edit a newspaper.'

'It is because you have so trusted me that I am obliged to you,' said Lady Carbury with her sweetest smile. She did not believe a word that Mr. Alf had said to her. She thought, and thought rightly, that Mr. Alf's Mr. Jones had taken direct orders from his editor, as to his treatment of the 'Criminal Queens.' But she remembered that she intended to write another book, and that she might

perhaps conquer even Mr. Alf by spirit and courage
under her present infliction.

It was Lady Carbury's duty on the occasion to say
pretty things to everybody. And she did her duty. But
in the midst of it all she was ever thinking of her son and
Marie Melmotte, and she did at last venture to separate
the girl from her mother. Marie herself was not unwilling
to be talked to by Sir Felix. He had never bullied her,
had never seemed to scorn her; and then, he was so beautiful! She, poor girl, bewildered among various suitors,
utterly confused by the life to which she was introduced,
troubled by fitful attacks of admonition from her father,
who would again, fitfully, leave her unnoticed for a week
at a time; with no trust in her pseudo-mother—for poor
Marie had in truth been born before her father had been
a married man, and had never known what was her own
mother's fate,—with no enjoyment in her present life,
had come solely to this conclusion, that it would be well
for her to be taken away somewhere by somebody. Many
a varied phase of life had already come in her way. She
could just remember the dirty street in the German
portion of New York in which she had been born and
had lived for the first four years of her life, and could
remember too the poor, hardly-treated woman who had
been her mother. She could remember being at sea, and
her sickness,—but could not quite remember whether
that woman had been with her. Then she had run about
the streets of Hamburg, and had sometimes been very
hungry, sometimes in rags,—and she had a dim memory
of some trouble into which her father had fallen, and that
he was away from her for a time. She had up to the
present splendid moment her own convictions about that
absence, but she had never mentioned them to a human
being. Then her father had married her present mother
in Frankfort. That she could remember distinctly, as also
the rooms in which she was then taken to live, and the
fact that she was told that from henceforth she was to be
a Jewess. But there had soon come another change.
They went from Frankfort to Paris, and there they were
all Christians. From that time they had lived in various

apartments in the French capital, but had always lived
well. Sometimes there had been a carriage, sometimes
there had been none. And then there came a time in
which she was grown woman enough to understand that
her father was being much talked about. Her father to
her had always been alternately capricious and indifferent
rather than cross or cruel, but just at this period he was
cruel both to her and to his wife. And Madame Melmotte would weep at times and declare that they were all
ruined. Then, at a moment, they burst out into sudden
splendour at Paris. There was an hotel, with carriages
and horses almost unnumbered;—and then there came
to their rooms a crowd of dark, swarthy, greasy men,
who were entertained sumptuously; but there were few
women. At this time Marie was hardly nineteen, and
young enough in manner and appearance to be taken for
seventeen. Suddenly again she was told that she was to
be taken to London, and the migration had been effected
with magnificence. She was first taken to Brighton,
where the half of an hotel had been hired, and had then
been brought to Grosvenor Square, and at once thrown
into the matrimonial market. No part of her life had
been more disagreeable to her, more frightful, than the
first months in which she had been trafficked for by the
Nidderdales and Grassloughs. She had been too frightened, too much of a coward to object to anything proposed to her, but still had been conscious of a desire to
have some hand in her own future destiny. Luckily for
her, the first attempts at trafficking with the Nidderdales
and Grassloughs had come to nothing; and at length she
was picking up a little courage, and was beginning to feel
that it might be possible to prevent a disposition of herself which did not suit her own tastes. She was also
beginning to think that there might be a disposition of
herself which would suit her own tastes.

Felix Carbury was standing leaning against a wall, and
she was seated on a chair close to him. 'I love you better
than anyone in the world,' he said, speaking plainly
enough for her to hear, perhaps indifferent as to the
hearing of others.

'Oh, Sir Felix, pray do not talk like that.'

'You knew that before. Now I want you to say whether you will be my wife.'

'How can I answer that myself? Papa settles everything.'

'May I go to papa?'

'You may if you like,' she replied in a very low whisper. It was thus that the greatest heiress of the day, the greatest heiress of any day if people spoke truly, gave herself away to a man without a penny.

## Chapter XII

### SIR FELIX IN HIS MOTHER'S HOUSE

WHEN all her friends were gone Lady Carbury looked about for her son,—not expecting to find him, for she knew how punctual was his nightly attendance at the Beargarden, but still with some faint hope that he might have remained on this special occasion to tell her of his fortune. She had watched the whispering, had noticed the cool effrontery with which Felix had spoken,—for without hearing the words she had almost known the very moment in which he was asking,—and had seen the girl's timid face, and eyes turned to the ground, and the nervous twitching of her hands as she replied. As a woman, understanding such things, who had herself been wooed, who had at least dreamed of love, she had greatly disapproved her son's manner. But yet, if it might be successful, if the girl would put up. with love-making so slight as that, and if the great Melmotte would accept in return for his money a title so modest as that of her son, how glorious should her son be to her in spite of his indifference!

'I heard him leave the house before the Melmottes went,' said Henrietta, when the mother spoke of going up to her son's bedroom.

'He might have stayed to-night. Do you think he asked her?'

'How can I say, mamma?'

'I should have thought you would have been anxious about your brother. I feel sure he did,—and that she accepted him.'

'If so I hope he will be good to her. I hope he loves her.'

'Why shouldn't he love her as well as any one else? A girl need not be odious because she has money. There is nothing disagreeable about her.'

'No,—nothing disagreeable. I do not know that she is especially attractive.'

'Who is? I don't see anybody specially attractive. It seems to me you are quite indifferent about Felix.'

'Do not say that, mamma.'

'Yes you are. You don't understand all that he might be with this girl's fortune, and what he must be unless he gets money by marriage. He is eating us both up.'

'I wouldn't let him do that, mamma.'

'It's all very well to say that, but I have some heart. I love him. I could not see him starve. Think what he might be with £20,000 a-year!'

'If he is to marry for that only, I cannot think that they will be happy.'

'You had better go to bed, Henrietta. You never say a word to comfort me in all my troubles.'

Then Henrietta went to bed, and Lady Carbury absolutely sat up the whole night waiting for her son, in order that she might hear his tidings. She went up to her room, disembarrassed herself of her finery, and wrapped herself in a white dressing-gown. As she sat opposite to her glass, relieving her head from its garniture of false hair, she acknowledged to herself that age was coming on her. She could hide the unwelcome approach by art,—hide it more completely than can most women of her age; but, there it was, stealing on her with short grey hairs over her ears and around her temples, with little wrinkles round her eyes easily concealed by objectionable cosmetics, and a look of weariness round the mouth which could only be removed by that self-assertion of herself which practice had made always possible to her in company, though it now so frequently deserted her when she was alone.

But she was not a woman to be unhappy because she was growing old. Her happiness, like that of most of us, was ever in the future,—never reached but always coming. She, however, had not looked for happiness to love and loveliness, and need not therefore be disappointed on that score. She had never really determined what it was that might make her happy,—having some hazy aspiration after social distinction and literary fame, in which was ever commingled solicitude respecting money. But at the present moment her great fears and her great hopes were centred on her son. She would not care how grey might be her hair, or how savage might be Mr. Alf, if her Felix were to marry this heiress. On the other hand, nothing that pearl-powder or the 'Morning Breakfast Table' could do would avail anything, unless he could be extricated from the ruin that now surrounded him. So she went down into the dining-room, that she might be sure to hear the key in the door, even should she sleep, and waited for him with a volume of French memoirs in her hand.

Unfortunate woman! she might have gone to bed and have been duly called about her usual time, for it was past eight and the full staring daylight shone into her room when Felix's cab brought him to the door. The night had been very wretched to her. She had slept, and the fire had sunk nearly to nothing and had refused to become again comfortable. She could not keep her mind to her book, and while she was awake the time seemed to be everlasting. And then it was so terrible to her that he should be gambling at such hours as these! Why should he desire to gamble if this girl's fortune was ready to fall into his hands? Fool, to risk his health, his character, his beauty, the little money which at this moment of time might be so indispensable to his great project, for the chance of winning something which in comparison with Marie Melmotte's money must be despicable! But at last he came! She waited patiently till he had thrown aside his hat and coat, and then she appeared at the dining-room door. She had studied her part for the occasion. She would not say a harsh word, and now she endeavoured to meet him with a smile. 'Mother,' he said, 'you up at this hour!' His face was flushed, and she thought that there was some unsteadiness in his gait. She had never seen him tipsy, and it would be doubly terrible to her if such should be his condition.

'I could not go to bed till I had seen you.'

'Why not? why should you want to see me? I'll go to bed now. There'll be plenty of time by-and-by.'

'Is anything the matter, Felix?'

'Matter;—what should be the matter? There's been a gentle row among the fellows at the club;—that's all. I had to tell Grasslough a bit of my mind, and he didn't like it. I didn't mean that he should.'

'There is not going to be any fighting, Felix?'

'What, duelling; oh no,—nothing so exciting as that. Whether somebody may not have to kick somebody is more than I can say at present. You must let me go to bed now, for I am about used up.'

'What did Marie Melmotte say to you?'

'Nothing particular.' And he stood with his hand on the door as he answered her.

'And what did you say to her?'

'Nothing particular. Good heavens, mother, do you think that a man is in a condition to talk about such stuff as that at eight o'clock in the morning, when he has been up all night?'

'If you knew all that I suffer on your behalf you would speak a word to me,' she said, imploring him, holding him by the arm, and looking into his purple face and bloodshot eyes. She was sure that he had been drinking. She could smell it in his breath.

'I must go to the old fellow, of course.'

'She told you to go to her father?'

'As far as I remember, that was about it. Of course, he means to settle it as he likes. I should say that it's ten to one against me.' Pulling himself away with some little roughness from his mother's hold, he made his way up to his own bedroom, occasionally stumbling against the stairs.

Then the heiress herself had accepted her son! If so, surely the thing might be done. Lady Carbury recalled to mind her old conviction that a daughter may always succeed in beating a hard-hearted parent in a contention about marriage, if she be well in earnest. But then the girl must be really in earnest, and her earnestness will depend on that of her lover. In this case, however, there was as yet no reason for supposing that the great man would object. As far as outward signs went, the great man had shown some partiality for her son. No doubt it was Mr. Melmotte who had made Sir Felix a director of the great American Company. Felix had also been kindly received in Grosvenor Square. And then Sir Felix was Sir Felix,—a real baronet. Mr. Melmotte had no doubt endeavoured to catch this and that lord; but, failing a lord, why should he not content himself with a baronet? Lady Carbury thought that her son wanted nothing but money to make him an acceptable suitor to such a father-in-law as Mr. Melmotte;—not money in the funds,* not a real fortune, not so many thousands a-year that could be settled;—the man's own enormous wealth rendered this unnecessary;—but such a one as Mr. Melmotte would not like outward palpable signs of immediate poverty. There should be means enough for present sleekness and present luxury. He must have a horse to ride, and rings and coats to wear, and bright little canes to carry, and above all the means of making presents. He must not be seen to be poor. Fortunately, most fortunately, Chance had befriended him lately and had given him some ready money. But if he went on gambling Chance would certainly take it all away again. For aught that the poor mother knew, Chance might have done so already. And then again, it was indispensable that he should abandon the habit of play—at any rate for the present, while his prospects depended on the good opinions of Mr. Melmotte. Of course such a one as Mr. Melmotte could not like gambling at a club, however much he might approve of it in the City. Why, with such a preceptor to help him, should not Felix learn to do his gambling on the Exchange, or among the brokers, or in the purlieus of the Bank? Lady Carbury would at any rate instigate him to be diligent in his position as director of the Great Mexican Railway,—which position ought to be the beginning to him of a fortune to be made on his own account. But what hope could there be for him if he should take to drink? Would not all hopes be over with Mr. Melmotte should he ever learn that his daughter's lover reached home and tumbled upstairs to bed between eight and nine o'clock in the morning?

She watched for his appearance on the following day, and began at once on the subject.

'Do you know, Felix, I think I shall go down to your cousin Roger for Whitsuntide.'

'To Carbury Manor!' said he, as he eat some devilled kidneys which the cook had been specially ordered to get for his breakfast. 'I thought you found it so dull that you didn't mean to go there any more.'

'I never said so, Felix. And now I have a great object.'

'What will Hetta do?'

'Go too—why shouldn't she?'

'Oh; I didn't know. I thought that perhaps she mightn't like it.'

'I don't see why she shouldn't like it. Besides, everything can't give way to her.'

'Has Roger asked you?'

'No; but I'm sure he'd be pleased to have us if I proposed that we should all go.'

'Not me, mother!'

'Yes; you especially.'

'Not if I know it, mother. What on earth should I do at Carbury Manor?'

'Madame Melmotte told me last night that they were all going down to Caversham to stay three or four days with the Longestaffes. She spoke of Lady Pomona as quite her particular friend.'

'Oh—h! that explains it all.'

'Explains what, Felix?' said Lady Carbury, who had heard of Dolly Longestaffe, and was not without some fear that this projected visit to Caversham might have some matrimonial purpose in reference to that delightful young heir.

'They say at the club that Melmotte has taken up old Longestaffe's affairs, and means to put them straight. There's an old property in Sussex as well as Caversham, and they say that Melmotte is to have that himself. There's some bother because Dolly, who would do anything for anybody else, won't join his father in selling. So the Melmottes are going to Caversham!'

'Madame Melmotte told me so.'

'And the Longestaffes are the proudest people in England.'

'Of course we ought to be at Carbury Manor while they are there. What can be more natural? Everybody goes out of town at Whitsuntide; and why shouldn't we run down to the family place?'

'All very natural if you can manage it, mother.'

'And you'll come?'

'If Marie Melmotte goes, I'll be there at any rate for one day and night,' said Felix.

His mother thought that, for him, the promise had been graciously made.

## Chapter XIII

### THE LONGESTAFFES

MR. ADOLPHUS LONGESTAFFE, the squire of Caversham in Suffolk, and of Pickering Park in Sussex, was closeted on a certain morning for the best part of an hour with Mr. Melmotte in Abchurch Lane, had there discussed all his private affairs, and was about to leave the room with a very dissatisfied air. There are men,—and old men too, who ought to know the world, —who think that if they can only find the proper Medea to boil the cauldron for them, they can have their ruined fortunes so cooked that they shall come out of the pot fresh and new and unembarrassed.* These great con-

jurors are generally sought for in the City; and in truth
the cauldrons are kept boiling though the result of the
process is seldom absolute rejuvenescence. No greater
Medea than Mr. Melmotte had ever been potent in
money matters, and Mr. Longestaffe had been taught
to believe that if he could get the necromancer even to
look at his affairs everything would be made right for
him. But the necromancer had explained to the squire
that property could not be created by the waving of any
wand or the boiling of any cauldron. He, Mr. Melmotte,
could put Mr. Longestaffe in the way of realising
property without delay, of changing it from one shape
into another, or could find out the real market value of
the property in question; but he could create nothing.
'You have only a life interest, Mr. Longestaffe.'

'No; only a life interest. That is customary with family
estates in this country, Mr. Melmotte.'

'Just so. And therefore you can dispose of nothing
else. Your son, of course, could join you, and then you
could sell either one estate or the other.'

'There is no question of selling Caversham, sir. Lady
Pomona and I reside there.'

'Your son will not join you in selling the other place?'

'I have not directly asked him; but he never does do
anything that I wish. I suppose you would not take
Pickering Park on a lease for my life.'

'I think not, Mr. Longestaffe. My wife would not like
the uncertainty.'

Then Mr. Longestaffe took his leave with a feeling of
outraged aristocratic pride. His own lawyer would
almost have done as much for him, and he need not have
invited his own lawyer as a guest to Caversham,—and
certainly not his own lawyer's wife and daughter. He
had indeed succeeded in borrowing a few thousand
pounds from the great man at a rate of interest which
the great man's head clerk was to arrange, and this
had been effected simply on the security of the lease
of a house in town. There had been an ease in this,
an absence of that delay which generally took place
between the expression of his desire for money and the

acquisition of it,—and this had gratified him. But he was already beginning to think that he might pay too dearly for that gratification. At the present moment, too, Mr. Melmotte was odious to him for another reason. He had condescended to ask Mr. Melmotte to make him a director of the South Central Pacific and Mexican Railway, and he,—Adolphus Longestaffe of Caversham, —had had his request refused! Mr. Longestaffe had condescended very low. 'You have made Lord Alfred Grendall one!' he had said in a complaining tone. Then Mr. Melmotte explained that Lord Alfred possessed peculiar aptitudes for the position. 'I'm sure I could do anything that he does,' said Mr. Longestaffe. Upon this Mr. Melmotte, knitting his brows and speaking with some roughness, replied that the number of directors required was completed. Since he had had two duchesses at his house Mr. Melmotte was beginning to feel that he was entitled to bully any mere commoner, especially a commoner who could ask him for a seat at his board.

Mr. Longestaffe was a tall, heavy man, about fifty, with hair and whiskers carefully dyed, whose clothes were made with great care, though they always seemed to fit him too tightly, and who thought very much of his personal appearance. It was not that he considered himself handsome, but that he was specially proud of his aristocratic bearing. He entertained an idea that all who understood the matter would perceive at a single glance that he was a gentleman of the first water, and a man of fashion. He was intensely proud of his position in life, thinking himself to be immensely superior to all those who earned their bread. There were no doubt gentlemen of different degrees, but the English gentleman of gentlemen was he who had land, and family title-deeds, and an old family place, and family portraits, and family embarrassments, and a family absence of any usual employment. He was beginning even to look down upon peers, since so many men of much less consequence than himself had been made lords; and, having stood and been beaten three or four times for his county, he was of opinion that a seat in the House was rather a mark of bad breeding. He was a silly man, who had no fixed idea that it behoved him to be of use to any one; but, yet, he had compassed a certain nobility of feeling. There was very little that his position called upon him to do, but there was much that it forbad him to do. It was not allowed to him to be close in money matters. He could leave his tradesmen's bills unpaid till the men were clamorous, but he could not question the items in their accounts. He could be tyrannical to his servants, but he could not make inquiry as to the consumption of his wines in the servants' hall. He had no pity for his tenants in regard to game, but he hesitated much as to raising their rent. He had his theory of life and endeavoured to live up to it; but the attempt had hardly brought satisfaction to himself or to his family.

At the present moment, it was the great desire of his heart to sell the smaller of his two properties and disembarrass the other. The debt had not been altogether of his own making, and the arrangement would, he believed, serve his whole family as well as himself. It would also serve his son, who was blessed with a third property of his own which he had already managed to burden with debt. The father could not bear to be refused; and he feared that his son would decline. 'But Adolphus wants money as much as any one,' Lady Pomona had said. He had shaken his head, and pished and pshawed. Women never could understand anything about money. Now he walked down sadly from Mr. Melmotte's office and was taken in his brougham to his lawyer's chambers in Lincoln's Inn. Even for the accommodation of those few thousand pounds he was forced to condescend to tell his lawyers that the title-deeds of his house in town must be given up. Mr. Longestaffe felt that the world in general was very hard on him.

'What on earth are we to do with them?' said Sophia, the eldest Miss Longestaffe, to her mother.

'I do think it's a shame of papa,' said Georgiana, the second daughter. 'I certainly shan't trouble myself to entertain them.'

'Of course you will leave them all on my hands,' said Lady Pomona wearily.

'But what's the use of having them?' urged Sophia. 'I can understand going to a crush at their house in town when everybody else goes. One doesn't speak to them, and need not know them afterwards. As to the girl, I'm sure I shouldn't remember her if I were to see her.'

'It would be a fine thing if Adolphus would marry her,' said Lady Pomona.

'Dolly will never marry anybody,' said Georgiana. 'The idea of his taking the trouble of asking a girl to have him! Besides, he won't come down to Caversham; cart-ropes wouldn't bring him. If that is to be the game, mamma, it is quite hopeless.'

'Why should Dolly marry such a creature as that?' asked Sophia.

'Because everybody wants money,' said Lady Pomona. 'I'm sure I don't know what your papa is to do, or how it is that there never is any money for anything. I don't spend it.'

'I don't think that we do anything out of the way,' said Sophia. 'I haven't the slightest idea what papa's income is; but if we're to live at all, I don't know how we are to make a change.'

'It's always been like this ever since I can remember,' said Georgiana, 'and I don't mean to worry about it any more. I suppose it's just the same with other people, only one doesn't know it.'

'But, my dears—when we are obliged to have such people as these Melmottes!'

'As for that, if we didn't have them somebody else would. I shan't trouble myself about them. I suppose it will only be for two days.'

'My dear, they're coming for a week!'

'Then papa must take them about the country, that's all. I never did hear of anything so absurd. What good can they do papa by being down there?'

'He is wonderfully rich,' said Lady Pomona.

'But I don't suppose he'll give papa his money,' continued Georgiana. 'Of course I don't pretend to understand, but I think there is more fuss about these things than they deserve. If papa hasn't got money to live at home, why doesn't he go abroad for a year? The Sidney Beauchamps did that, and the girls had quite a nice time of it in Florence. It was there that Clara Beauchamp met young Lord Liffey. I shouldn't at all mind that kind of thing, but I think it quite horrible to have these sort of people brought down upon us at Caversham. No one knows who they are, or where they came from, or what they'll turn to.' So spoke Georgiana, who among the Longestaffes was supposed to have the strongest head, and certainly the sharpest tongue.

This conversation took place in the drawing-room of the Longestaffes' family town-house in Bruton Street. It was not by any means a charming house, having but few of those luxuries and elegancies which have been added of late years to newly-built London residences. It was gloomy and inconvenient, with large drawing-rooms, bad bedrooms, and very little accommodation for servants. But it was the old family town-house, having been inhabited by three or four generations of Longe-staffes, and did not savour of that radical newness which prevails, and which was peculiarly distasteful to Mr. Longestaffe. Queen's Gate and the quarters around were, according to Mr. Longestaffe, devoted to opulent trades-men. Even Belgrave Square, though its aristocratic properties must be admitted, still smelt of the mortar. Many of those living there and thereabouts had never possessed in their families real family town-houses. The old streets lying between Piccadilly and Oxford Street, with one or two well-known localities to the south and north of these boundaries, were the proper sites for these habitations. When Lady Pomona, instigated by some friend of high rank but questionable taste, had once suggested a change to Eaton Square, Mr. Longestaffe had at once snubbed his wife. If Bruton Street wasn't good enough for her and the girls then they might remain at Caversham. The threat of remaining at Caversham had been often made, for Mr. Longestaffe, proud as he was of his town-house, was, from year to year, very anxious to save the expense of the annual migration. The girls' dresses and the girls' horses, his wife's carriage and his own brougham, his dull London dinner-parties, and the one ball which it was always necessary that Lady Pomona should give, made him look forward to the end of July, with more dread than to any other period. It was then that he began to know what that year's season would cost him. But he had never yet been able to keep his family in the country during the entire year. The girls, who as yet knew nothing of the Continent beyond Paris, had signified their willingness to be taken about Germany and Italy for twelve months, but had shown by every means in their power that they would mutiny against any intention on their father's part to keep them at Caversham during the London season.

Georgiana had just finished her strong-minded protest against the Melmottes, when her brother strolled into the room. Dolly did not often show himself in Bruton Street. He had rooms of his own, and could seldom even be induced to dine with his family. His mother wrote to him notes without end,—notes every day, pressing invitations of all sorts upon him; would he come and dine; would he take them to the theatre; would he go to this ball; would he go to that evening-party? These Dolly barely read, and never answered. He would open them, thrust them into some pocket, and then forget them. Consequently his mother worshipped him; and even his sisters, who were at any rate superior to him in intellect, treated him with a certain deference. He could do as he liked, and they felt themselves to be slaves, bound down by the dulness of the Longestaffe régime. His freedom was grand to their eyes, and very enviable, although they were aware that he had already so used it as to impoverish himself in the midst of his wealth.

'My dear Adolphus,' said the mother, 'this is so nice of you.'

'I think it is rather nice,' said Dolly, submitting himself to be kissed.

'Oh Dolly, whoever would have thought of seeing you?' said Sophia.

'Give him some tea,' said his mother. Lady Pomona was always having tea from four o'clock till she was taken away to dress for dinner.

'I'd sooner have soda and brandy,' said Dolly.

'My darling boy!'

'I didn't ask for it, and I don't expect to get it; indeed I don't want it. I only said I'd sooner have it than tea. Where's the governor?' They all looked at him with wondering eyes. There must be something going on more than they had dreamed of, when Dolly asked to see his father.

'Papa went out in the brougham immediately after lunch,' said Sophia gravely.

'I'll wait a little for him,' said Dolly, taking out his watch.

'Do stay and dine with us,' said Lady Pomona.

'I could not do that, because I've got to go and dine with some fellow.'

'Some fellow! I believe you don't know where you're going,' said Georgiana.

'My fellow knows. At least he's a fool if he don't.'

'Adolphus,' began Lady Pomona very seriously, 'I've got a plan and I want you to help me.'

'I hope there isn't very much to do in it, mother.'

'We're all going to Caversham, just for Whitsuntide, and we particularly want you to come.'

'By George! no; I couldn't do that.'

'You haven't heard half. Madame Melmotte and her daughter are coming.'

'The d— they are!' ejaculated Dolly.

'Dolly!' said Sophia, 'do remember where you are.'

'Yes I will;—and I'll remember too where I won't be. I won't go to Caversham to meet old mother Melmotte.'

'My dear boy,' continued the mother, 'do you know that Miss Melmotte will have twenty—thousand—a year the day she marries; and that in all probability her husband will some day be the richest man in Europe?'

'Half the fellows in London are after her,' said Dolly.

'Why shouldn't you be one of them?'

'She isn't going to stay in the same house with half the fellows in London,' suggested Georgiana. 'If you've a mind to try it you'll have a chance which nobody else can have just at present.'

'But I haven't any mind to try it. Good gracious me; —oh dear! it isn't at all in my way, mother.'

'I knew he wouldn't,' said Georgiana.

'It would put everything so straight,' said Lady Pomona.

'They'll have to remain crooked if nothing else will put them straight. There's the governor. I heard his voice. Now for a row.' Then Mr. Longestaffe entered the room.

'My dear,' said Lady Pomona, 'here's Adolphus come to see us.' The father nodded his head at his son but said nothing. 'We want him to stay and dine, but he's engaged.'

'Though he doesn't know where,' said Sophia.

'My fellow knows;—he keeps a book. I've got a letter, sir, ever so long, from those fellows in Lincoln's Inn. They want me to come and see you about selling something; so I've come. It's an awful bore, because I don't understand anything about it. Perhaps there isn't anything to be sold. If so I can go away again, you know.'

'You'd better come with me into the study,' said the father. 'We needn't disturb your mother and sisters about business.' Then the squire led the way out of the room, and Dolly followed, making a woful grimace at his sisters. The three ladies sat over their tea for about half-an-hour, waiting,—not the result of the conference, for with that they did not suppose that they would be made acquainted,—but whatever signs of good or evil might be collected from the manner and appearance of the squire when he should return to them. Dolly they did not expect to see again,—probably for a month. He and the squire never did come together without quarrelling, and careless as was the young man in every other respect, he had hitherto been obdurate as to his own rights in any dealings which he had with his father. At the end of the half hour Mr. Longestaffe returned to the drawing-room, and at once pronounced the doom of the family. 'My dear,' he said, 'we shall not return from Caversham to London this year.' He struggled hard to maintain a grand dignified tranquillity as he spoke, but his voice quivered with emotion.

'Papa!' screamed Sophia.

'My dear, you don't mean it,' said Lady Pomona.

'Of course papa doesn't mean it,' said Georgiana, rising to her feet.

'I mean it accurately and certainly,' said Mr. Longestaffe. 'We go to Caversham in about ten days, and we shall not return from Caversham to London this year.'

'Our ball is fixed,' said Lady Pomona.

'Then it must be unfixed.' So saying the master of the house left the drawing-room and descended to his study.

The three ladies, when left to deplore their fate, expressed their opinions as to the sentence which had been pronounced very strongly. But the daughters were louder in their anger than was their mother.

'He can't really mean it,' said Sophia.

'He does,' said Lady Pomona, with tears in her eyes.

'He must unmean it again;—that's all,' said Georgiana. 'Dolly has said something to him very rough, and he resents it upon us. Why did he bring us up at all if he means to take us down before the season has begun?'

'I wonder what Adolphus has said to him. Your papa is always hard upon Adolphus.'

'Dolly can take care of himself,' said Georgiana, 'and always does do so. Dolly does not care for us.'

'Not a bit,' said Sophia.

'I'll tell you what you must do, mamma. You mustn't stir from this at all. You must give up going to Caversham altogether, unless he promises to bring us back. I won't stir,—unless he has me carried out of the house.'

'My dear, I couldn't say that to him.'

'Then I will. To go and be buried down in that place for a whole year with no one near us but the rusty old bishop and Mr. Carbury, who is rustier still. I won't stand it. There are some sort of things that one ought not to stand. If you go down I shall stay up with the Primeros.

Mrs. Primero would have me I know. It wouldn't be nice of course. I don't like the Primeros. I hate the Primeros. Oh yes;—it's quite true; I know that as well as you, Sophia; they are vulgar; but not half so vulgar, mamma, as your friend Madame Melmotte.'

'That's ill-natured, Georgiana. She is not a friend of mine.'

'But you're going to have her down at Caversham. I can't think what made you dream of going to Caversham just now, knowing as you do how hard papa is to manage.'

'Everybody has taken to going out of town at Whitsuntide, my dear.'

'No, mamma; everybody has not. People understand too well the trouble of getting up and down for that. The Primeros aren't going down. I never heard of such a thing in all my life. What does he expect is to become of us? If he wants to save money why doesn't he shut Caversham up altogether and go abroad? Caversham costs a great deal more than is spent in London, and it's the dullest house, I think, in all England.'

The family party in Bruton Street that evening was not very gay. Nothing was being done, and they sat gloomily in each other's company. Whatever mutinous resolutions might be formed and carried out by the ladies of the family, they were not brought forward on that occasion. The two girls were quite silent, and would not speak to their father, and when he addressed them they answered simply by monosyllables. Lady Pomona was ill, and sat in a corner of a sofa, wiping her eyes. To her had been imparted upstairs the purport of the conversation between Dolly and his father. Dolly had refused to consent to the sale of Pickering unless half the produce of the sale were to be given to him at once. When it had been explained to him that the sale would be desirable in order that the Caversham property might be freed from debt, which Caversham property would eventually be his, he replied that he also had an estate of his own which was a little mortgaged and would be the better for money. The result seemed to be that Pickering could not be sold,—and, as a consequence of that, Mr. Longestaffe had determined that there should be no more London expenses that year.

The girls, when they got up to go to bed, bent over him and kissed his head, as was their custom. There was very little show of affection in the kiss. 'You had better remember that what you have to do in town must be done this week,' he said. They heard the words, but marched in stately silence out of the room without deigning to notice them.

## Chapter XIV

### CARBURY MANOR

'I DON'T think it quite nice, mamma; that's all. Of course if you have made up your mind to go, I must go with you.'

'What on earth can be more natural than that you should go to your own cousin's house?'

'You know what I mean, mamma.'

'It's done now, my dear, and I don't think there is anything at all in what you say.'

This little conversation arose from Lady Carbury's announcement to her daughter of her intention of soliciting the hospitality of Carbury Manor for the Whitsun week. It was very grievous to Henrietta that she should be taken to the house of a man who was in love with her, even though he was her cousin. But she had no escape. She could not remain in town by herself, nor could she even allude to her grievance to any one but her mother. Lady Carbury, in order that she might be quite safe from opposition, had posted the following letter to her cousin before she spoke to her daughter:—

'Welbeck Street, 24th April, 18—.
'My dear Roger,

'We know how kind you are and how sincere, and that if what I am going to propose doesn't suit you'll say so at once. I have been working very hard,—too hard indeed, and I feel that nothing will do me so much real good as getting into the country for a day or two. Would you take us for a part of Whitsun week? We would come down on the 20th May and stay over the Sunday if you would keep us. Felix says he would run down though he would not trouble you for so long a time as we talk of staying.

'I'm sure you must have been glad to hear of his being put upon that Great American Railway Board as a Director. It opens a new sphere of life to him, and will enable him to prove that he can make himself useful. I think it was a great confidence to place in one so young.

'Of course you will say so at once if my little proposal interferes with any of your plans, but you have been so very very kind to us that I have no scruple in making it.

'Henrietta joins with me in kind love.

'Your affectionate cousin,
'MATILDA CARBURY.'

There was much in this letter that disturbed and even annoyed Roger Carbury. In the first place he felt that Henrietta should not be brought to his house. Much as he loved her, dear as her presence to him always was, he hardly wished to have her at Carbury unless she would come with a resolution to be its future mistress. In one respect he did Lady Carbury an injustice. He knew that she was anxious to forward his suit, and he thought that Henrietta was being brought to his house with that object. He had not heard that the great heiress was coming into his neighbourhood, and therefore knew nothing of Lady Carbury's scheme in that direction. He was, too, disgusted by the ill-founded pride which the mother expressed at her son's position as a director. Roger Carbury did not believe in the Railway. He did not believe in Fisker, nor in Melmotte, and certainly not in the Board generally. Paul Montague had acted in opposition to his advice in yielding to the seductions of Fisker. The whole thing was to his mind false, fraudulent, and ruinous. Of what nature could be a Company which should have itself directed by such men as Lord Alfred Grendall and Sir Felix Carbury? And then as to their

great Chairman, did not everybody know, in spite of
all the duchesses, that Mr. Melmotte was a gigantic
swindler? Although there was more than one immediate
cause for bitterness between them, Roger loved Paul
Montague well and could not bear with patience the
appearance of his friend's name on such a list. And now
he was asked for warm congratulations because Sir
Felix Carbury was one of the Board! He did not know
which to despise most, Sir Felix for belonging to such a
Board, or the Board for having such a director. 'New
sphere of life!' he said to himself. 'The only proper
sphere for them all would be Newgate!'

And there was another trouble. He had asked Paul
Montague to come to Carbury for this special week, and
Paul had accepted the invitation. With the constancy,
which was perhaps his strongest characteristic, he clung
to his old affection for the man. He could not bear the
idea of a permanent quarrel, though he knew that there
must be a quarrel if the man interfered with his dearest
hopes. He had asked him down to Carbury intending
that the name of Henrietta Carbury should not be mentioned between them;—and now it was proposed to him
that Henrietta Carbury should be at the Manor House
at the very time of Paul's visit! He made up his mind at
once that he must tell Paul not to come.

He wrote his two letters at once. That to Lady Carbury
was very short. He would be delighted to see her and
Henrietta at the time named,—and would be very glad
should it suit Felix to come also. He did not say a word
about the Board, or the young man's probable usefulness
in his new sphere of life. To Montague his letter was
longer. 'It is always best to be open and true,' he said.
'Since you were kind enough to say that you would come
to me, Lady Carbury has proposed to visit me just at the
same time and to bring her daughter. After what has
passed between us I need hardly say that I could not
make you both welcome here together. It is not pleasant
to me to have to ask you to postpone your visit, but I
think you will not accuse me of a want of hospitality
towards you.' Paul wrote back to say that he was sure

that there was no want of hospitality, and that he would
remain in town.

Suffolk is not especially a picturesque county, nor can
it be said that the scenery round Carbury was either
grand or beautiful; but there were little prettinesses
attached to the house itself and the grounds around it
which gave it a charm of its own. The Carbury River,
—so called, though at no place is it so wide but that an
active schoolboy might jump across it,—runs, or rather
creeps into the Waveney, and in its course is robbed by
a moat which surrounds Carbury Manor House. The
moat has been rather a trouble to the proprietors, and
especially so to Roger, as in these days of sanitary considerations it has been felt necessary either to keep it
clean with at any rate moving water in it, or else to fill
it up and abolish it altogether. That plan of abolishing
it had to be thought of and was seriously discussed about
ten years since; but then it was decided that such a proceeding would altogether alter the character of the house,
would destroy the gardens, and would create a waste of
mud all round the place which it would take years to
beautify, or even to make endurable. And then an important question had been asked by an intelligent farmer
who had long been a tenant on the property; 'Fill un
oop;—eh, eh; sooner said than doone, squoire. Where
be the stoof to come from?' The squire, therefore, had
given up that idea, and instead of abolishing his moat
had made it prettier than ever. The high road from
Bungay to Beccles ran close to the house,—so close that
the gable ends of the building were separated from it
only by the breadth of the moat. A short, private road,
not above a hundred yards in length, led to the bridge
which faced the front door. The bridge was old, and
high, with sundry architectural pretensions, and guarded
by iron gates in the centre, which, however, were very
rarely closed. Between the bridge and the front door
there was a sweep of ground just sufficient for the turning of a carriage, and on either side of this the house was
brought close to the water, so that the entrance was in a
recess, or irregular quadrangle, of which the bridge and

moat formed one side. At the back of the house there
were large gardens screened from the road by a wall
ten feet high, in which there were yew trees and cypresses
said to be of wonderful antiquity. The gardens were
partly inside the moat, but chiefly beyond them, and
were joined by two bridges—a foot bridge and one with
a carriage way,—and there was another bridge at the
end of the house furthest from the road, leading from the
back door to the stables and farmyard.

The house itself had been built in the time of Charles
II., when that which we call Tudor architecture was
giving way to a cheaper, less picturesque, though perhaps
more useful form. But Carbury Manor House, through
the whole county, had the reputation of being a Tudor
building. The windows were long, and for the most part
low, made with strong mullions, and still contained small,
old-fashioned panes; for the squire had not as yet gone
to the expense of plate glass. There was one high bow
window, which belonged to the library, and which
looked out on to the gravel sweep, at the left of the front
door as you entered it. All the other chief rooms faced
upon the garden. The house itself was built of a stone
that had become buff, or almost yellow, with years, and
was very pretty. It was still covered with tiles, as were all
the attached buildings. It was only two stories high,
except at the end, where the kitchens were placed and
the offices, which thus rose above the other part of the
edifice. The rooms throughout were low, and for the
most part long and narrow, with large wide fireplaces
and deep wainscotings. Taking it altogether, one would
be inclined to say, that it was picturesque rather than
comfortable. Such as it was its owner was very proud
of it,—with a pride of which he never spoke to any one,
which he endeavoured studiously to conceal, but which
had made itself known to all who knew him well. The
houses of the gentry around him were superior to his in
material comfort and general accommodation, but to none
of them belonged that thoroughly established look of old
county position which belonged to Carbury. Bundlesham, where the Primeros lived, was the finest house in

that part of the county, but it looked as if it had been
built within the last twenty years. It was surrounded by
new shrubs and new lawns, by new walls and new out-
houses, and savoured of trade;—so at least thought Roger
Carbury, though he never said the words. Caversham
was a very large mansion, built in the early part of
George III.'s reign, when men did care that things about
them should be comfortable, but did not care that they
should be picturesque. There was nothing at all to
recommend Caversham but its size. Eardly Park, the
seat of the Hepworths, had, as a park, some pretensions.
Carbury possessed nothing that could be called a park,
the enclosures beyond the gardens being merely so many
home paddocks. But the house of Eardly was ugly and
bad. The Bishop's palace was an excellent gentleman's
residence, but then that too was comparatively modern,
and had no peculiar features of its own. Now Carbury
Manor House was peculiar, and in the eyes of its owner
was pre-eminently beautiful.

It often troubled him to think what would come of the
place when he was gone. He was at present forty years
old, and was perhaps as healthy a man as you could find
in the whole county. Those around who had known him
as he grew into manhood among them, especially the
farmers of the neighbourhood, still regarded him as a
young man. They spoke of him at the county fairs as
the young squire. When in his happiest moods he could
be almost a boy, and he still had something of old-
fashioned boyish reverence for his elders. But of late
there had grown up a great care within his breast,—a
care which  oes not often, perhaps, in these days bear
so heavily on men's hearts as it used to do. He had asked
his cousin to marry him,—having assured himself with
certainty that he did love her better than any other
woman,—and she had declined. She had refused him
more than once, and he believed her implicitly when she
told him that she could not love him. He had a way of
believing people, especially when such belief was opposed
to his own interests, and had none of that self-confidence
which makes a man think that if opportunity be allowed

him he can win a woman even in spite of herself. But if
it were fated that he should not succeed with Henrietta,
then,—so he felt assured,—no marriage would now be
possible to him. In that case he must look out for an heir,
and could regard himself simply as a stop-gap among the
Carburys. In that case he could never enjoy the luxury
of doing the best he could with the property in order
that a son of his own might enjoy it.

Now Sir Felix was the next heir. Roger was hampered
by no entail, and could leave every acre of the property
as he pleased. In one respect the natural succession to
it by Sir Felix would generally be considered fortunate.
It had happened that a title had been won in a lower
branch of the family, and were this succession to take
place the family title and the family property would go
together. No doubt to Sir Felix himself such an arrangement would seem to be the most proper thing in the
world,—as it would also to Lady Carbury were it not
that she looked to Carbury Manor as the future home of
another child. But to all this the present owner of the
property had very strong objections. It was not only that
he thought ill of the baronet himself,—so ill as to feel
thoroughly convinced that no good could come from that
quarter,—but he thought ill also of the baronetcy itself.
Sir Patrick, to his thinking, had been altogether unjustifiable in accepting an enduring title, knowing that he
would leave behind him no property adequate for its
support. A baronet, so thought Roger Carbury, should
be a rich man, rich enough to grace the rank which he
assumed to wear. A title, according to Roger's doctrine
on such subjects, could make no man a gentleman, but,
if improperly worn, might degrade a man who would
otherwise be a gentleman. He thought that a gentleman,
born and bred, acknowledged as such without doubt,
could not be made more than a gentleman by all the
titles which the Queen could give. With these old-
fashioned notions Roger hated the title which had fallen
upon a branch of his family. He certainly would not
leave his property to support the title which Sir Felix
unfortunately possessed. But Sir Felix was the natural

heir, and this man felt himself constrained, almost as by
some divine law, to see that his land went by natural
descent. Though he was in no degree fettered as to its
disposition, he did not presume himself to have more than
a life interest in the estate. It was his duty to see that it
went from Carbury to Carbury as long as there was a
Carbury to hold it, and especially his duty to see that it
should go from his hands, at his death, unimpaired in
extent or value. There was no reason why he should himself die for the next twenty or thirty years,—but were he
to die Sir Felix would undoubtedly dissipate the acres,
and then there would be an end of Carbury. But in such
case he, Roger Carbury, would at any rate have done
his duty. He knew that no human arrangements can be
fixed, let the care in making them be ever so great. To
his thinking it would be better that the estate should be
dissipated by a Carbury than held together by a stranger.
He would stick to the old name while there was one to
bear it, and to the old family while a member of it was
left. So thinking, he had already made his will, leaving
the entire property to the man whom of all others he
most despised, should he himself die without child.

In the afternoon of the day on which Lady Carbury
was expected, he wandered about the place thinking of
all this. How infinitely better it would be that he should
have an heir of his own! How wonderfully beautiful
would the world be to him if at last his cousin would
consent to be his wife! How wearily insipid must it be
if no such consent could be obtained from her! And then
he thought much of her welfare too. In very truth he
did not like Lady Carbury. He saw through her character, judging her with almost absolute accuracy. The
woman was affectionate, seeking good things for others
rather than for herself; but she was essentially worldly,
believing that good could come out of evil, that falsehood might in certain conditions be better than truth,
that shams and pretences might do the work of true
service, that a strong house might be built upon the sand!
It was lamentable to him that the girl he loved should be
subjected to this teaching, and live in an atmosphere so

burdened with falsehood. Would not the touch of pitch
at last defile her? In his heart of hearts he believed that
she loved Paul Montague; and of Paul himself he was
beginning to fear evil. What but a sham could be a man
who consented to pretend to sit as one of a Board of
Directors to manage an enormous enterprise with such
colleagues as Lord Alfred Grendall and Sir Felix Carbury, under the absolute control of such a one as Mr.
Augustus Melmotte? Was not this building a house upon
the sand with a vengeance? What a life it would be for
Henrietta Carbury were she to marry a man striving to
become rich without labour and without capital, and
who might one day be wealthy and the next a beggar,—
a city adventurer, who of all men was to him the vilest
and most dishonest? He strove to think well of Paul
Montague, but such was the life which he feared the
young man was preparing for himself.

Then he went into the house and wandered up through
the rooms which the two ladies were to occupy. As their
host, a host without a wife or mother or sister, it was his
duty to see that things were comfortable, but it may be
doubted whether he would have been so careful had the
mother been coming alone. In the smaller room of the
two the hangings were all white, and the room was
sweet with May flowers; and he brought a white rose
from the hot-house, and placed it in a glass on the
dressing table. Surely she would know who put it there.

Then he stood at the open window, looking down
upon the lawn, gazing vacantly for half an hour, till he
heard the wheels of the carriage before the front door.
During that half-hour he resolved that he would try
again as though there had as yet been no repulse.

## Chapter XV

### 'YOU SHOULD REMEMBER THAT I AM HIS MOTHER'

'THIS is so kind of you,' said Lady Carbury, grasping
her cousin's hand as she got out of the carriage.
'The kindness is on your part,' said Roger.

'I felt so much before I dared to ask you to take us. But I did so long to get into the country, and I do so love Carbury. And—and——'

'Where should a Carbury go to escape from London smoke, but to the old house? I am afraid Henrietta will find it dull.'

'Oh no,' said Hetta smiling. 'You ought to remember that I am never dull in the country.'

'The bishop and Mrs. Yeld are coming here to dine to-morrow,—and the Hepworths.'

'I shall be so glad to meet the bishop once more,' said Lady Carbury.

'I think everybody must be glad to meet him, he is such a dear, good fellow, and his wife is just as good. And there is another gentleman coming whom you have never seen.'

'A new neighbour?'

'Yes,—a new neighbour;—Father John Barham, who has come to Beccles as priest. He has got a little cottage about a mile from here, in this parish, and does duty both at Beccles and Bungay. I used to know something of his family.'

'He is a gentleman then?'

'Certainly he is a gentleman. He took his degree at Oxford, and then became what we call a pervert, and what I suppose they call a convert. He has not got a shilling in the world beyond what they pay him as a priest, which I take it amounts to about as much as the wages of a day labourer. He told me the other day that he was absolutely forced to buy second-hand clothes.'

'How shocking!' said Lady Carbury, holding up her hands.

'He didn't seem to be at all shocked at telling it. We have got to be quite friends.'

'Will the bishop like to meet him?'

'Why should not the bishop like to meet him? I've told the bishop all about him, and the bishop particularly wishes to know him. He won't hurt the bishop. But you and Hetta will find it very dull.'

'I shan't find it dull, Mr. Carbury,' said Henrietta.

'It was to escape from the eternal parties that we came down here,' said Lady Carbury. She had nevertheless been anxious to hear what guests were expected at the Manor House. Sir Felix had promised to come down on Saturday, with the intention of returning on Monday, and Lady Carbury had hoped that some visiting might be arranged between Caversham and the Manor House, so that her son might have the full advantage of his closeness to Marie Melmotte.

'I have asked the Longestaffes for Monday,' said Roger.

'They are down here then?'

'I think they arrived yesterday. There is always a flustering breeze in the air and a perturbation generally through the county when they come or go, and I think I perceived the effects about four in the afternoon. They won't come, I dare say.'

'Why not?'

'They never do. They have probably a house full of guests, and they know that my accommodation is limited. I've no doubt they'll ask us on Tuesday or Wednesday, and if you like we will go.'

'I know they are to have guests,' said Lady Carbury. 'What guests?'

'The Melmottes are coming to them.' Lady Carbury, as she made the announcement, felt that her voice and countenance and self-possession were failing her, and that she could not mention the thing as she would any matter that was indifferent to her.

'The Melmottes coming to Caversham!' said Roger, looking at Henrietta, who blushed with shame as she remembered that she had been brought into her lover's house solely in order that her brother might have an opportunity of seeing Marie Melmotte in the country.

'Oh yes,—Madame Melmotte told me. I take it they are very intimate.'

'Mr. Longestaffe ask the Melmottes to visit him at Caversham!'

'Why not?'

'I should almost as soon have believed that I myself might have been induced to ask them here.'

'I fancy, Roger, that Mr. Longestaffe does want a little pecuniary assistance.'

'And he condescends to get it in this way! I suppose it will make no difference soon whom one knows, and whom one doesn't. Things aren't as they were, of course, and never will be again. Perhaps it's all for the better; —I won't say it isn't. But I should have thought that such a man as Mr. Longestaffe might have kept such another man as Mr. Melmotte out of his wife's drawing-room.' Henrietta became redder than ever. Even Lady Carbury flushed up, as she remembered that Roger Carbury knew that she had taken her daughter to Madame Melmotte's ball. He thought of this himself as soon as the words were spoken, and then tried to make some half apology. 'I don't approve of them in London, you know; but I think they are very much worse in the country.'

Then there was a movement. The ladies were shown into their rooms, and Roger again went out into the garden. He began to feel that he understood it all. Lady Carbury had come down to his house in order that she might be near the Melmottes! There was something in this which he felt it difficult not to resent. It was for no love of him that she was there. He had felt that Henrietta ought not to have been brought to his house; but he could have forgiven that, because her presence there was a charm to him. He could have forgiven that, even while he was thinking that her mother had brought her there with the object of disposing of her. If it were so, the mother's object would be the same as his own, and such a manœuvre he could pardon, though he could not approve. His self-love had to some extent been gratified. But now he saw that he and his house had been simply used in order that a vile project of marrying two vile people to each other might be furthered!

As he was thinking of all this, Lady Carbury came out to him in the garden. She had changed her travelling dress, and made herself pretty, as she well knew how to do. And now she dressed her face in her sweetest smiles. Her mind, also, was full of the Melmottes, and she wished

to explain to her stern, unbending cousin all the good
that might come to her and hers by an alliance with the
heiress. 'I can understand, Roger,' she said, taking his
arm, 'that you should not like those people.'

'What people?'

'The Melmottes.'

'I don't dislike them. How should I dislike people that
I never saw? I dislike those who seek their society simply
because they have the reputation of being rich.'

'Meaning me.'

'No; not meaning you. I don't dislike you, as you
know very well, though I do dislike the fact that you
should run after these people. I was thinking of the
Longestaffes then.'

'Do you suppose, my friend, that I run after them for
my own gratification? Do you think that I go to their
house because I find pleasure in their magnificence; or
that I follow them down here for any good that they will
do me?'

'I would not follow them at all.'

'I will go back if you bid me, but I must first explain
what I mean. You know my son's condition,—better,
I fear, than he does himself.' Roger nodded assent to
this, but said nothing. 'What is he to do? The only
chance for a young man in his position is that he should
marry a girl with money. He is good-looking; you can't
deny that.'

'Nature has done enough for him.'

'We must take him as he is. He was put into the army
very young, and was very young when he came into
possession of his own small fortune. He might have done
better; but how many young men placed in such temptations do well? As it is, he has nothing left.'

'I fear not.'

'And therefore is it not imperative that he should marry
a girl with money?'

'I call that stealing a girl's money, Lady Carbury.'

'Oh, Roger, how hard you are!'

'A man must be hard or soft,—which is best?'

'With women I think that a little softness has the most

effect. I want to make you understand this about the Melmottes. It stands to reason that the girl will not marry Felix unless she loves him.'

'But does he love her?'

'Why should he not? Is a girl to be debarred from being loved because she has money? Of course she looks to be married, and why should she not have Felix if she likes him best? Cannot you sympathize with my anxiety so to place him that he shall not be a disgrace to the name and to the family?'

'We had better not talk about the family, Lady Carbury.'

'But I think so much about it.'

'You will never get me to say that I think the family will be benefited by a marriage with the daughter of Mr. Melmotte. I look upon him as dirt in the gutter. To me, in my old-fashioned way, all his money, if he has it, can make no difference. When there is a question of marriage, people at any rate should know something of each other. Who knows anything of this man? Who can be sure that she is his daughter?'

'He would give her her fortune when she married.'

'Yes; it all comes to that. Men say openly that he is an adventurer and a swindler. No one pretends to think that he is a gentleman. There is a consciousness among all who speak of him that he amasses his money not by honest trade, but by unknown tricks,—as does a card-sharper. He is one whom we would not admit into our kitchens, much less to our tables, on the score of his own merits. But because he has learned the art of making money, we not only put up with him, but settle upon his carcase as so many birds of prey.'

'Do you mean that Felix should not marry the girl, even if they love each other?'

He shook his head in disgust, feeling sure that any idea of love on the part of the young man was a sham and a pretence, not only as regarded him, but also his mother. He could not quite declare this, and yet he desired that she should understand that he thought so. 'I have nothing more to say about it,' he continued. 'Had it gone

on in London I should have said nothing. It is no affair
of mine. When I am told that the girl is in the neighbourhood, at such a house as Caversham, and that Felix
is coming here in order that he may be near to his prey,
and when I am asked to be a party to the thing, I can
only say what I think. Your son would be welcome to
my house, because he is your son and my cousin, little
as I approve his mode of life; but I could have wished
that he had chosen some other place for the work that
he has on hand.'

'If you wish it, Roger, we will return to London. I
shall find it hard to explain to Hetta;—but we will go.'

'No; I certainly do not wish that.'

'But you have said such hard things! How are we to
stay? You speak of Felix as though he were all bad.'
She looked at him hoping to get from him some contradiction of this, some retractation, some kindly word; but
it was what he did think, and he had nothing to say. She
could bear much. She was not delicate as to censure
implied, or even expressed. She had endured rough
usage before, and was prepared to endure more. Had
he found fault with herself, or with Henrietta, she would
have put up with it, for the sake of benefits to come,—
would have forgiven it the more easily because perhaps
it might not have been deserved. But for her son she was
prepared to fight. If she did not defend him, who would?
'I am grieved, Roger, that we should have troubled you
with our visit, but I think that we had better go. You
are very harsh, and it crushes me.'

'I have not meant to be harsh.'

'You say that Felix is seeking for his—prey, and that
he is to be brought here to be near—his prey. What
can be more harsh than that? At any rate, you should
remember that I am his mother.'

She expressed her sense of injury very well. Roger
began to be ashamed of himself, and to think that he had
spoken unkind words. And yet he did not know how to
recall them. 'If I have hurt you, I regret it much.'

'Of course you have hurt me. I think I will go in now.
How very hard the world is! I came here thinking to

find peace and sunshine, and there has come a storm at once.'

'You asked me about the Melmottes, and I was obliged to speak. You cannot think that I meant to offend you.' They walked on in silence till they had reached the door leading from the garden into the house, and here he stopped her. 'If I have been over hot with you, let me beg your pardon,' She smiled and bowed; but her smile was not one of forgiveness; and then she essayed to pass on into the house. 'Pray do not speak of going, Lady Carbury.'

'I think I will go to my room now. My head aches so that I can hardly stand.'

It was late in the afternoon,—about six,—and according to his daily custom he should have gone round to the offices to see his men as they came from their work, but he stood still for a few moments on the spot where Lady Carbury had left him and went slowly across the lawn to the bridge and there seated himself on the parapet. Could it really be that she meant to leave his house in anger and to take her daughter with her? Was it thus that he was to part with the one human being in the world that he loved? He was a man who thought much of the duties of hospitality, feeling that a man in his own house was bound to exercise a courtesy towards his guests sweeter, softer, more gracious than the world required elsewhere. And of all guests those of his own name were the best entitled to such courtesy at Carbury. He held the place in trust for the use of others. But if there were one among all others to whom the house should be a house of refuge from care, not an abode of trouble, on whose behalf, were it possible, he would make the very air softer, and the flowers sweeter than their wont, to whom he would declare, were such words possible to his tongue, that of him and of his house, and of all things there, she was the mistress, whether she would condescend to love him or no,—that one was his cousin Hetta. And now he had been told by his guest that he had been so rough to her that she and her daughter must return to London!

And he could not acquit himself. He knew that he
had been rough. He had said very hard words. It was
true that he could not have expressed his meaning without hard words, nor have repressed his meaning without
self-reproach. But in his present mood he could not
comfort himself by justifying himself. She had told him
that he ought to have remembered that Felix was her
son; and as she spoke she had acted well the part of an
outraged mother. His heart was so soft that though he
knew the woman to be false and the son to be worthless,
he utterly condemned himself. Look where he would
there was no comfort. When he had sat half an hour
upon the bridge he turned towards the house to dress for
dinner,—and to prepare himself for an apology, if any
apology might be accepted. At the door, standing in
the doorway as though waiting for him, he met his
cousin Hetta. She had on her bosom the rose he had
placed in her room, and as he approached her he thought
that there was more in her eyes of graciousness towards
him than he had ever seen there before.

'Mr. Carbury,' she said, 'mamma is so unhappy!'

'I fear that I have offended her.'

'It is not that, but that you should be so—so angry
about Felix.'

'I am vexed with myself that I have vexed her,—more
vexed than I can tell you.'

'She knows how good you are.'

'No, I'm not. I was very bad just now. She was so
offended with me that she talked of going back to London.'
He paused for her to speak, but Hetta had no words
ready for the moment. 'I should be wretched indeed if
you and she were to leave my house in anger.'

'I do not think she will do that.'

'And you?'

'I am not angry. I should never dare to be angry with
you. I only wish that Felix would be better. They say
that young men have to be bad, and that they do get to
be better as they grow older. He is something in the
city now, a director they call him, and mamma thinks
that the work will be of service to him.' Roger could

express no hope in this direction or even look as though
he approved of the directorship. 'I don't see why he
should not try at any rate.'

'Dear Hetta, I only wish he were like you.'

'Girls are so different, you know.'

It was not till late in the evening, long after dinner,
that he made his apology in form to Lady Carbury; but
he did make it, and at last it was accepted. 'I think I
was rough to you, talking about Felix,' he said,—'and
I beg your pardon.'

'You were energetic, that was all.'

'A gentleman should never be rough to a lady, and a
man should never be rough to his own guests. I hope
you will forgive me.' She answered him by putting out
her hand and smiling on him; and so the quarrel was
over.

Lady Carbury understood the full extent of her
triumph, and was enabled by her disposition to use it
thoroughly. Felix might now come down to Carbury,
and go over from thence to Caversham, and prosecute
his wooing, and the master of Carbury could make no
further objection. And Felix, if he would come, would
not now be snubbed. Roger would understand that he
was constrained to courtesy by the former severity of his
language. Such points as these Lady Carbury never
missed. He understood it too, and though he was soft
and gracious in his bearing, endeavouring to make his
house as pleasant as he could to his two guests, he felt
that he had been cheated out of his undoubted right to
disapprove of all connection with the Melmottes. In the
course of the evening there came a note,—or rather a
bundle of notes,—from Caversham. That addressed to
Roger was in the form of a letter. Lady Pomona was
sorry to say that the Longestaffe party were prevented
from having the pleasure of dining at Carbury Hall by
the fact that they had a house full of guests. Lady
Pomona hoped that Mr. Carbury and his relatives, who,
Lady Pomona heard, were with him at the Hall, would
do the Longestaffes the pleasure of dining at Caversham
either on the Monday or Tuesday following, as might

best suit the Carbury plans. That was the purport of
Lady Pomona's letter to Roger Carbury. Then there
were cards of invitation for Lady Carbury and her
daughter, and also for Sir Felix.

Roger, as he read his own note, handed the others
over to Lady Carbury, and then asked her what she
would wish to have done. The tone of his voice, as he
spoke, grated on her ear, as there was something in it
of his former harshness. But she knew how to use her
triumph. 'I should like to go,' she said.

'I certainly shall not go,' he replied; 'but there will
be no difficulty whatever in sending you over. You must
answer at once, because their servant is waiting.'

'Monday will be best,' she said; '—that is, if nobody
is coming here.'

'There will be nobody here.'

'I suppose I had better say that I, and Hetta,—and
Felix will accept their invitation.'

'I can make no suggestion,' said Roger, thinking how
delightful it would be if Henrietta could remain with him;
how objectionable it was that Henrietta should be taken
to Caversham to meet the Melmottes. Poor Hetta herself could say nothing. She certainly did not wish to
meet the Melmottes, nor did she wish to dine, alone,
with her cousin Roger.

'That will be best,' said Lady Carbury after a moment's
thought. 'It is very good of you to let us go, and to send
us.'

'Of course you will do here just as you please,' he
replied. But there was still that tone in his voice which
Lady Carbury feared. A quarter of an hour later the
Caversham servant was on his way home with two letters,
—the one from Roger expressing his regret that he could
not accept Lady Pomona's invitation, and the other
from Lady Carbury declaring that she and her son
and daughter would have great pleasure in dining at
Caversham on the Monday.

## Chapter XVI

### THE BISHOP AND THE PRIEST

THE afternoon on which Lady Carbury arrived at her cousin's house had been very stormy. Roger Carbury had been severe, and Lady Carbury had suffered under his severity,—or had at least so well pretended to suffer as to leave on Roger's mind a strong impression that he had been cruel to her. She had then talked of going back at once to London, and when consenting to remain, had remained with a very bad feminine headache. She had altogether carried her point, but had done so in a storm. The next morning was very calm. That question of meeting the Melmottes had been settled, and there was no need for speaking of them again. Roger went out by himself about the farm, immediately after breakfast, having told the ladies that they could have the waggon-ette when they pleased. 'I'm afraid you'll find it tire-some driving about our lanes,' he said. Lady Carbury assured him that she was never dull when left alone with books. Just as he was starting he went into the garden and plucked a rose which he brought to Henrietta. He only smiled as he gave it her, and then went his way. He had resolved that he would say nothing to her of his suit till Monday. If he could prevail with her then he would ask her to remain with him when her mother and brother would be going out to dine at Caversham. She looked up into his face as she took the rose and thanked him in a whisper. She fully appreciated the truth, and honour, and honesty of his character, and could have loved him so dearly as her cousin if he would have contented him-self with such cousinly love! She was beginning, within her heart, to take his side against her mother and brother, and to feel that he was the safest guide that she could have. But how could she be guided by a lover whom she did not love?

'I am afraid, my dear, we shall have a bad time of it here,' said Lady Carbury.

'Why so, mamma?'

'It will be so dull. Your cousin is the best friend in all the world, and would make as good a husband as could be picked out of all the gentlemen of England; but in his present mood with me he is not a comfortable host. What nonsense he did talk about the Melmottes!'

'I don't suppose, mamma, that Mr. and Mrs. Melmotte can be nice people.'

'Why shouldn't they be as nice as anybody else? Pray, Henrietta, don't let us have any of that nonsense from you. When it comes from the superhuman virtue of poor dear Roger it has to be borne, but I beg that you will not copy him.'

'Mamma, I think that is unkind.'

'And I shall think it very unkind if you take upon yourself to abuse people who are able and willing to set poor Felix on his legs. A word from you might undo all that we are doing.'

'What word?'

'What word? Any word! If you have any influence with your brother you should use it in inducing him to hurry this on. I am sure the girl is willing enough. She did refer him to her father.'

'Then why does he not go to Mr. Melmotte?'

'I suppose he is delicate about it on the score of money. If Roger could only let it be understood that Felix is the heir to this place, and that some day he will be Sir Felix Carbury of Carbury, I don't think there would be any difficulty even with old Melmotte.'

'How could he do that, mamma?'

'If your cousin were to die as he is now, it would be so. Your brother would be his heir.'

'You should not think of such a thing, mamma.'

'Why do you dare to tell me what I am to think? Am I not to think of my own son? Is he not to be dearer to me than any one? And what I say, is so. If Roger were to die to-morrow he would be Sir Felix Carbury of Carbury.'

'But, mamma, he will live and have a family. Why should he not?'

'You say he is so old that you will not look at him.'

'I never said so. When we were joking, I said he was old. You know I did not mean that he was too old to get married. Men a great deal older get married every day.'

'If you don't accept him he will never marry. He is a man of that kind,—so stiff and stubborn and old-fashioned* that nothing will change him. He will go on boodying over it, till he will become an old misanthrope. If you would take him I would be quite contented. You are my child as well as Felix. But if you mean to be obstinate I do wish that the Melmottes should be made to understand that the property and title and name of the place will all go together. It will be so, and why should not Felix have the advantage?'

'Who is to say it?'

'Ah;—that's where it is. Roger is so violent and prejudiced that one cannot get him to speak rationally.'

'Oh, mamma;—you wouldn't suggest it to him;—that this place is to go to—Felix, when he—is dead!'

'It would not kill him a day sooner.'

'You would not dare to do it, mamma.'

'I would dare to do anything for my children. But you need not look like that, Henrietta. I am not going to say anything to him of the kind. He is not quick enough to understand of what infinite service he might be to us without in any way hurting himself.' Henrietta would fain have answered that their cousin was quick enough for anything, but was by far too honest to take part in such a scheme as that proposed. She refrained, however, and was silent. There was no sympathy on the matter between her and her mother. She was beginning to understand the tortuous mazes of manœuvres in which her mother's mind had learned to work, and to dislike and almost to despise them. But she felt it to be her duty to abstain from rebukes.

In the afternoon Lady Carbury, alone, had herself driven into Beccles that she might telegraph to her son. 'You are to dine at Caversham on Monday. Come on Saturday if you can. She is there.' Lady Carbury had many doubts as to the wording of this message. The female in the office might too probably understand who was the 'She,' who was spoken of as being at Caversham, and might understand also the project, and speak of it publicly. But then it was essential that Felix should know how great and certain was the opportunity afforded to him. He had promised to come on Saturday and return on Monday,—and, unless warned, would too probably stick to his plan and throw over the Longestaffes and their dinner-party. Again if he were told to come simply for the Monday, he would throw over the chance of wooing her on the Sunday. It was Lady Carbury's desire to get him down for as long a period as was possible, and nothing surely would so tend to bring him and to keep him, as a knowledge that the heiress was already in the neighbourhood. Then she returned, and shut herself up in her bedroom, and worked for an hour or two at a paper which she was writing for the 'Breakfast Table.' Nobody should ever accuse her justly of idleness. And afterwards, as she walked by herself round and round the garden, she revolved in her mind the scheme of a new book. Whatever might happen she would persevere. If the Carburys were unfortunate their misfortunes should come from no fault of hers. Henrietta passed the whole day alone. She did not see her cousin from breakfast till he appeared in the drawing-room before dinner. But she was thinking of him during every minute of the day,— how good he was, how honest, how thoroughly entitled to demand at any rate kindness at her hand! Her mother had spoken of him as of one who might be regarded as all but dead and buried, simply because of his love for her. Could it be true that his constancy was such that he would never marry unless she would take his hand? She came to think of him with more tenderness than she had ever felt before, but, yet, she would not tell herself she loved him. It might, perhaps, be her duty to give herself to him without loving him,—because he was so good; but she was sure that she did not love him.

In the evening the bishop came, and his wife, Mrs. Yeld, and the Hepworths of Eardly, and Father John Barham, the Beccles priest. The party consisted of eight, which is, perhaps, the best number for a mixed gathering of men and women at a dinner-table,—especially if there be no mistress whose prerogative and duty it is to sit opposite to the master. In this case Mr. Hepworth faced the giver of the feast, the bishop and the priest were opposite to each other, and the ladies graced the four corners. Roger, though he spoke of such things to no one, turned them over much in his mind, believing it to be the duty of a host to administer in all things to the comfort of his guests. In the drawing-room he had been especially courteous to the young priest, introducing him first to the bishop and his wife, and then to his cousins. Henrietta watched him through the whole evening, and told herself that he was a very mirror of courtesy in his own house. She had seen it all before, no doubt; but she had never watched him as she now watched him since her mother had told her that he would die wifeless and childless because she would not be his wife and the mother of his children.

The bishop was a man sixty years of age, very healthy and handsome, with hair just becoming grey, clear eyes, a kindly mouth, and something of a double chin. He was all but six feet high, with a broad chest, large hands, and legs which seemed to have been made for clerical breeches and clerical stockings. He was a man of fortune outside his bishopric; and, as he never went up to London, and had no children on whom to spend his money, he was able to live as a nobleman in the country. He did live as a nobleman, and was very popular. Among the poor around him he was idolized, and by such clergy of his diocese as were not enthusiastic in their theology either on the one side or on the other, he was regarded as a model bishop.* By the very high and the very low,—by those rather who regarded ritualism as being either heavenly or devilish,—he was looked upon as a time-server, because he would not put to sea in either of those boats. He was an unselfish man, who loved his neighbour as himself, and forgave all trespasses, and thanked God for his daily bread from his heart, and prayed heartily to be delivered from temptation. But I doubt whether he was competent to teach a creed,—or even to hold one, if it be necessary that a man should understand and define his creed before he can hold it. Whether he was free from, or whether he was scared by, any inward misgivings, who shall say? If there were such he never whispered a word of them even to the wife of his bosom. From the tone of his voice and the look of his eye, you would say that he was unscathed by that agony which doubt on such a matter would surely bring to a man so placed. And yet it was observed of him that he never spoke of his faith, or entered into arguments with men as to the reasons on which he had based it. He was diligent in preaching,—moral sermons that were short, pithy, and useful. He was never weary in furthering the welfare of his clergymen. His house was open to them and to their wives. The edifice of every church in his diocese was a care to him. He laboured at schools, and was zealous in improving the social comforts of the poor; but he was never known to declare to man or woman that the human soul must live or die for ever according to its faith. Perhaps there was no bishop in England more loved or more useful in his diocese than the Bishop of Elmham.

A man more antagonistic to the bishop than Father John Barham, the lately appointed Roman Catholic priest at Beccles, it would be impossible to conceive;— and yet they were both eminently good men. Father John was not above five feet nine in height, but so thin, so meagre, so wasted in appearance, that, unless when he stooped, he was taken to be tall. He had thick dark brown hair, which was cut short in accordance with the usage of his Church; but which he so constantly ruffled by the action of his hands, that, though short, it seemed to be wild and uncombed. In his younger days, when long locks straggled over his forehead, he had acquired a habit, while talking energetically, of rubbing them back with his finger, which he had not since dropped. In discussions he would constantly push back his hair, and then sit with his hand fixed on the top of his head. He had a high, broad forehead, enormous blue eyes, a thin, long nose, cheeks very thin and hollow, a handsome large mouth, and a strong square chin. He was utterly without worldly means, except those which came to him from the ministry of his church, and which did not suffice to find him food and raiment; but no man ever lived more indifferent to such matters than Father John Barham. He had been the younger son of an English country gentleman of small fortune, had been sent to Oxford that he might hold a family living, and on the eve of his ordination had declared himself a Roman Catholic. His family had resented this bitterly, but had not quarrelled with him till he had drawn a sister with him. When banished from the house he had still striven to achieve the conversion of other sisters by his letters, and was now absolutely an alien from his father's heart and care. But of this he never complained. It was a part of the plan of his life that he should suffer for his faith. Had he been able to change his creed without incurring persecution, worldly degradation, and poverty, his own conversion would not have been to him comfortable and satisfactory as it was. He considered that his father, as a Protestant,—and in his mind Protestant and heathen were all the same,—had been right to quarrel with him. But he loved his father, and was endless in prayer, wearying his saints with supplications, that his father might see the truth and be as he was.

To him it was everything that a man should believe and obey,—that he should abandon his own reason to the care of another or of others, and allow himself to be guided in all things by authority. Faith being sufficient and of itself all in all, moral conduct could be nothing to a man, except as a testimony of faith; for to him, whose belief was true enough to produce obedience, moral conduct would certainly be added. The dogmas of his Church were to Father Barham a real religion, and he would teach them in season and out of season, always ready to commit himself to the task of proving their truth, afraid of no enemy, not even fearing the hostility which his perseverance would create. He had but one duty before him,—to do his part towards bringing over the world to his faith. It might be that with the toil of his whole life he should convert but one; that he should but half convert one; that he should do no more than disturb the thoughts of one so that future conversion might be possible. But even that would be work done. He would sow the seed if it might be so; but if it were not given to him to do that, he would at any rate plough the ground.

He had come to Beccles lately, and Roger Carbury had found out that he was a gentleman by birth and education. Roger had found out also that he was very poor, and had consequently taken him by the hand. The young priest had not hesitated to accept his neighbour's hospitality, having on one occasion laughingly protested that he should be delighted to dine at Carbury, as he was much in want of a dinner. He had accepted presents from the garden and the poultry yard, declaring that he was too poor to refuse anything. The apparent frankness of the man about himself had charmed Roger, and the charm had not been seriously disturbed when Father Barham, on one winter evening in the parlour at Carbury, had tried his hand at converting his host. 'I have the most thorough respect for your religion,' Roger had said; 'but it would not suit me.' The priest had gone on with his logic; if he could not sow the seed he might plough the ground. This had been repeated two or three times, and Roger had begun to feel it to be disagreeable. But the man was in earnest, and such earnestness commanded respect. And Roger was quite sure that though he might be bored, he could not be injured by such teaching. Then it occurred to him one day that he had known the Bishop of Elmham intimately for a dozen years, and had never heard from the bishop's mouth,—except when in the pulpit,—a single word of religious teaching; whereas this man, who was a stranger to him, divided from him by the very fact of his creed, was always talking to him about his faith. Roger Carbury was not a man given to much deep thinking, but he felt that the bishop's manner was the pleasanter of the two.

Lady Carbury at dinner was all smiles and pleasantness. No one looking at her, or listening to her, could

think that her heart was sore with many troubles. She
sat between the bishop and her cousin, and was skilful
enough to talk to each without neglecting the other. She
had known the bishop before, and had on one occasion
spoken to him of her soul. The first tone of the good
man's reply had convinced her of her error, and she never
repeated it. To Mr. Alf she commonly talked of her
mind; to Mr. Broune of her heart; to Mr. Booker of her
body—and its wants. She was quite ready to talk of
her soul on a proper occasion, but she was much too wise
to thrust the subject even on a bishop. Now she was full
of the charms of Carbury and its neighbourhood. 'Yes,
indeed,' said the bishop, 'I think Suffolk is a very nice
county; and as we are only a mile or two from Norfolk,
I'll say as much for Norfolk too. "It's an ill bird that
fouls its own nest."'

'I like a county in which there is something left of
county feeling,' said Lady Carbury. 'Staffordshire and
Warwickshire, Cheshire and Lancashire have become
great towns, and have lost all local distinctions.'

'We still keep our name and reputation,' said the
bishop; 'Silly Suffolk!'*

'But that was never deserved.'

'As much, perhaps, as other general epithets. I think
we are a sleepy people. We've got no coal, you see, and
no iron. We have no beautiful scenery, like the lake
country,—no rivers great for fishing, like Scotland,—no
hunting grounds, like the shires.'

'Partridges!' pleaded Lady Carbury, with pretty
energy.

'Yes; we have partridges, fine churches, and the herring
fishery. We shall do very well if too much is not expected
of us. We can't increase and multiply as they do in the
great cities.'

'I like this part of England so much the best for that
very reason. What is the use of a crowded population?'

'The earth has to be peopled, Lady Carbury.'

'Oh, yes,' said her ladyship, with some little reverence
added to her voice, feeling that the bishop was probably
adverting to a divine arrangement. 'The world must be

peopled; but for myself I like the country better than the town.'

'So do I,' said Roger; 'and I like Suffolk. The people are hearty, and radicalism is not quite so rampant as it is elsewhere. The poor people touch their hats, and the rich people think of the poor. There is something left among us of old English habits.'

'That is so nice,' said Lady Carbury.

'Something left of old English ignorance,' said the bishop. 'All the same I dare say we're improving, like the rest of the world. What beautiful flowers you have here, Mr. Carbury! At any rate, we can grow flowers in Suffolk.'

Mrs. Yeld, the bishop's wife, was sitting next to the priest, and was in truth somewhat afraid of her neighbour. She was, perhaps, a little stauncher than her husband in Protestantism; and though she was willing to admit that Mr. Barham might not have ceased to be a gentleman when he became a Roman Catholic priest, she was not quite sure that it was expedient for her or her husband to have much to do with him. Mr. Carbury had not taken them unawares. Notice had been given that the priest was to be there, and the bishop had declared that he would be very happy to meet the priest. But Mrs. Yeld had had her misgivings. She never ventured to insist on her opinion after the bishop had expressed his; but she had an idea that right was right, and wrong wrong,—and that Roman Catholics were wrong, and therefore ought to be put down. And she thought also that if there were no priests there would be no Roman Catholics. Mr. Barham was, no doubt, a man of good family, which did make a difference.

Mr. Barham always made his approaches very gradually. The taciturn humility with which he commenced his operations was in exact proportion to the enthusiastic volubility of his advanced intimacy. Mrs. Yeld thought that it became her to address to him a few civil words, and he replied to her with a shame-faced modesty that almost overcame her dislike to his profession. She spoke of the poor of Beccles, being very careful to allude only to their material position. There was too much beer drunk, no doubt, and the young women would have finery. Where did they get the money to buy those wonderful bonnets which appeared every Sunday? Mr. Barham was very meek, and agreed to everything that was said. No doubt he had a plan ready formed for inducing Mrs. Yeld to have mass said regularly within her husband's palace, but he did not even begin to bring it about on this occasion. It was not till he made some apparently chance allusion to the superior church-attending qualities of 'our people,' that Mrs. Yeld drew herself up and changed the conversation by observing that there had been a great deal of rain lately.

When the ladies were gone the bishop at once put himself in the way of conversation with the priest, and asked questions as to the morality of Beccles. It was evidently Mr. Barham's opinion that 'his people' were more moral than other people, though very much poorer. 'But the Irish always drink,' said Mr. Hepworth.

'Not so much as the English, I think,' said the priest. 'And you are not to suppose that we are all Irish. Of my flock the greater proportion are English.'

'It is astonishing how little we know of our neighbours,' said the bishop. 'Of course I am aware that there are a certain number of persons of your persuasion round about us. Indeed, I could give the exact number in this diocese. But in my own immediate neighbourhood I could not put my hand upon any families which I know to be Roman Catholic.'

'It is not, my lord, because there are none.'

'Of course not. It is because, as I say, I do not know my neighbours.'

'I think, here in Suffolk, they must be chiefly the poor,' said Mr. Hepworth.

'They were chiefly the poor who at first put their faith in our Saviour,' said the priest.

'I think the analogy is hardly correctly drawn,' said the bishop, with a curious smile. 'We were speaking of those who are still attached to an old creed. Our Saviour was the teacher of a new religion. That the poor in the

simplicity of their hearts should be the first to acknowledge the truth of a new religion is in accordance with our
idea of human nature. But that an old faith should remain with the poor after it has been abandoned by the
rich is not so easily intelligible.'

'The Roman population still believed,' said Carbury,
'when the patricians had learned to regard their gods as
simply useful bugbears.'

'The patricians had not ostensibly abandoned their
religion. The people clung to it thinking that their
masters and rulers clung to it also.'

'The poor have ever been the salt of the earth, my lord,'
said the priest.

'That begs the whole question,' said the bishop, turning to his host, and beginning to talk about a breed of
pigs which had lately been imported into the palace styes.
Father Barham turned to Mr. Hepworth and went on
with his argument, or rather began another. It was a
mistake to suppose that the Catholics in the county were
all poor. There were the A——s and the B——s, and the
C——s and the D——s. He knew all their names and
was proud of their fidelity. To him these faithful ones
were really the salt of the earth, who would some day be
enabled by their fidelity to restore England to her pristine
condition. The bishop had truly said that of many of his
neighbours he did not know to what Church they belonged; but Father Barham, though he had not as yet
been twelve months in the county, knew the name of
nearly every Roman Catholic within its borders.

'Your priest is a very zealous man,' said the bishop
afterwards to Roger Carbury, 'and I do not doubt but
that he is an excellent gentleman; but he is perhaps a
little indiscreet.'

'I like him because he is doing the best he can according to his lights; without any reference to his own worldly
welfare.'

'That is all very grand, and I am perfectly willing to
respect him. But I do not know that I should care to talk
very freely in his company.'

'I am sure he would repeat nothing.'

'Perhaps not; but he would always be thinking that he was going to get the best of me.'

'I don't think it answers,' said Mrs. Yeld to her husband as they went home. 'Of course I don't want to be prejudiced; but Protestants are Protestants, and Roman Catholics are Roman Catholics.'

'You may say the same of Liberals and Conservatives, but you wouldn't have them decline to meet each other.'

'It isn't quite the same, my dear. After all religion is religion.'

'It ought to be,' said the bishop.

'Of course I don't mean to put myself up against you, my dear; but I don't know that I want to meet Mr. Barham again.'

'I don't know that I do, either,' said the bishop; 'but if he comes in my way I hope I shall treat him civilly.'

## Chapter XVII

### MARIE MELMOTTE HEARS A LOVE TALE

ON the following morning there came a telegram from Felix. He was to be expected at Beccles on that afternoon by a certain train; and Roger, at Lady Carbury's request, undertook to send a carriage to the station for him. This was done, but Felix did not arrive. There was still another train by which he might come so as to be just in time for dinner if dinner were postponed for half an hour. Lady Carbury with a tender look, almost without speaking a word, appealed to her cousin on behalf of her son. He knit his brows, as he always did, involuntarily, when displeased; but he assented. Then the carriage had to be sent again. Now carriages and carriage-horses were not numerous at Carbury. The squire kept a waggonette and a pair of horses which, when not wanted for house use, were employed about the farm. He himself would walk home from the train, leaving the luggage to be brought by some cheap conveyance. He had already sent the carriage once on this day,—and now sent it again, Lady Carbury having said a word which showed that she hoped that this would be done. But he did it with deep displeasure. To the mother her son was Sir Felix, the baronet, entitled to special consideration because of his position and rank,—because also of his intention to marry the great heiress of the day. To Roger Carbury, Felix was a vicious young man, peculiarly antipathetic to himself, to whom no respect whatever was due. Nevertheless the dinner was put off, and the waggonette was sent. But the waggonette again came back empty. That evening was spent by Roger, Lady Carbury, and Henrietta, in very much gloom.

About four in the morning the house was roused by the coming of the baronet. Failing to leave town by either of the afternoon trains, he had contrived to catch the evening mail, and had found himself deposited at some distant town from which he had posted to Carbury. Roger came down in his dressing-gown to admit him, and Lady Carbury also left her room. Sir Felix evidently thought that he had been a very fine fellow in going through so much trouble. Roger held a very different opinion, and spoke little or nothing. 'Oh, Felix,' said the mother, 'you have so terrified us!'

'I can tell you I was terrified myself when I found that I had to come fifteen miles across the country with a pair of old jades who could hardly get up a trot.'

'But why didn't you come by the train you named?'

'I couldn't get out of the city,' said the baronet with a ready lie.

'I suppose you were at the Board?' To this Felix made no direct answer. Roger knew that there had been no Board. Mr. Melmotte was in the country and there could be no Board, nor could Sir Felix have had business in the city. It was sheer impudence,—sheer indifference, and, into the bargain, a downright lie. The young man, who was of himself so unwelcome, who had come there on a project which he, Roger, utterly disapproved,—who had now knocked him and his household up at four o'clock in the morning,—had uttered no word of apology. 'Miserable cub!' Roger muttered between his teeth. Then he spoke aloud, 'You had better not keep your mother standing here. I will show you your room.'

'All right, old fellow,' said Sir Felix. 'I'm awfully sorry to disturb you all in this way. I think I'll just take a drop of brandy and soda before I go to bed, though.' This was another blow to Roger.

'I doubt whether we have soda-water in the house, and if we have, I don't know where to get it. I can give you some brandy if you will come with me.' He pronounced the word 'brandy' in a tone which implied that it was a wicked, dissipated beverage. It was a wretched work to Roger. He was forced to go upstairs and fetch a key in order that he might wait upon this cub,—this cur! He did it, however, and the cub drank his brandy-and-water, not in the least disturbed by his host's ill-humour. As he went to bed he suggested the probability of his not showing himself till lunch on the following day, and expressed a wish that he might have breakfast sent to him in bed. 'He is born to be hung,' said Roger to himself as he went to his room,—'and he'll deserve it.'

On the following morning, being Sunday, they all went to church,— except Felix. Lady Carbury always went to church when she was in the country, never when she was at home in London. It was one of those moral habits, like early dinners and long walks, which suited country life. And she fancied that were she not to do so, the bishop would be sure to know it and would be displeased. She liked the bishop. She liked bishops generally; and was aware that it was a woman's duty to sacrifice herself for society. As to the purpose for which people go to church, it had probably never in her life occurred to Lady Carbury to think of it. On their return they found Sir Felix smoking a cigar on the gravel path, close in front of the open drawing-room window.

'Felix,' said his cousin, 'take your cigar a little farther. You are filling the house with tobacco.'

'Oh heavens,—what a prejudice!' said the baronet.

'Let it be so, but still do as I ask you.' Sir Felix chucked the cigar out of his mouth on to the gravel walk, whereupon Roger walked up to the spot and kicked the offending weed away. This was the first greeting of the day between the two men.

After lunch Lady Carbury strolled about with her son, instigating him to go over at once to Caversham. 'How the deuce am I to get there?'

'Your cousin will lend you a horse.'

'He's as cross as a bear with a sore head. He's a deal older than I am, and a cousin and all that, but I'm not going to put up with insolence. If it were anywhere else I should just go into the yard and ask if I could have a horse and saddle as a matter of course.'

'Roger has not a great establishment.'

'I suppose he has a horse and saddle, and a man to get it ready. I don't want anything grand.'

'He is vexed because he sent twice to the station for you yesterday.'

'I hate the kind of fellow who is always thinking of little grievances. Such a man expects you to go like clockwork, and because you are not wound up just as he is, he insults you. I shall ask him for a horse as I would any one else, and if he does not like it, he may lump it.' About half an hour after this he found his cousin. 'Can I have a horse to ride over to Caversham this afternoon?' he said.

'Our horses never go out on Sunday,' said Roger. Then he added, after a pause, 'You can have it. I'll give the order.' Sir Felix would be gone on Tuesday, and it should be his own fault if that odious cousin ever found his way into Carbury House again! So he declared to himself as Felix rode out of the yard; but he soon remembered how probable it was that Felix himself would be the owner of Carbury. And should it ever come to pass, —as still was possible,—that Henrietta should be the mistress of Carbury, he could hardly forbid her to receive her brother. He stood for a while on the bridge watching his cousin as he cantered away upon the road, listening to the horse's feet. The young man was offensive in every possible way. Who does not know that ladies only are allowed to canter their friends' horses upon roads? A gentleman trots his horse, and his friend's horse. Roger Carbury had but one saddle horse,—a favourite old

hunter that he loved as a friend. And now this dear old
friend, whose legs probably were not quite so good as
they once were, was being galloped along the hard road
by that odious cub! 'Soda and brandy!' Roger exclaimed
to himself almost aloud, thinking of the discomfiture of
that early morning. 'He'll die some day of delirium
tremens in a hospital!'

Before the Longestaffes left London to receive their
new friends the Melmottes at Caversham, a treaty had
been made between Mr. Longestaffe, the father, and
Georgiana, the strong-minded daughter. The daughter
on her side undertook that the guests should be treated
with feminine courtesy. This might be called the most-
favoured-nation clause.* The Melmottes were to be
treated exactly as though old Melmotte had been a
gentleman and Madame Melmotte a lady. In return for
this the Longestaffe family were to be allowed to return
to town. But here again the father had carried another
clause. The prolonged sojourn in town was to be only for
six weeks. On the 10th of July the Longestaffes were to
be removed into the country for the remainder of the year.
When the question of a foreign tour was proposed, the
father became absolutely violent in his refusal. 'In God's
name where do you expect the money is to come from?'
When Georgiana urged that other people had money to
go abroad, her father told her that a time was coming in
which she might think it lucky if she had a house over her
head. This, however, she took as having been said with
poetical licence, the same threat having been made more
than once before. The treaty was very clear, and the
parties to it were prepared to carry it out with fair
honesty. The Melmottes were being treated with decent
courtesy, and the house in town was not dismantled.

The idea, hardly ever in truth entertained but which
had been barely suggested from one to another among
the ladies of the family, that Dolly should marry Marie
Melmotte, had been abandoned. Dolly, with all his
vapid folly, had a will of his own, which, among his own
family, was invincible. He was never persuaded to any
course either by his father or mother. Dolly certainly

would not marry Marie Melmotte. Therefore when the Longestaffes heard that Sir Felix was coming to the country, they had no special objection to entertaining him at Caversham. He had been lately talked of in London as the favourite in regard to Marie Melmotte. Georgiana Longestaffe had a grudge of her own against Lord Nidderdale, and was on that account somewhat well inclined towards Sir Felix's prospects. Soon after the Melmottes' arrival she contrived to say a word to Marie respecting Sir Felix. 'There is a friend of yours going to dine here on Monday, Miss Melmotte.' Marie, who was at the moment still abashed by the grandeur and size and general fashionable haughtiness of her new acquaintances, made hardly any answer. 'I think you know Sir Felix Carbury,' continued Georgiana.

'Oh yes, we know Sir Felix Carbury.'

'He is coming down to his cousin's. I suppose it is for your bright eyes, as Carbury Manor would hardly be just what he would like.'

'I don't think he is coming because of me,' said Marie blushing. She had once told him that he might go to her father, which according to her idea had been tantamount to accepting his offer as far as her power of acceptance went. Since that she had seen him, indeed, but he had not said a word to press his suit, nor, as far as she knew, had he said a word to Mr. Melmotte. But she had been very rigorous in declining the attentions of other suitors. She had made up her mind that she was in love with Felix Carbury, and she had resolved on constancy. But she had begun to tremble, fearing his faithlessness.

'We had heard,' said Georgiana, 'that he was a particular friend of yours.' And she laughed aloud, with a vulgarity which Madame Melmotte certainly could not have surpassed.

Sir Felix, on the Sunday afternoon, found all the ladies out on the lawn, and he also found Mr. Melmotte there. At the last moment Lord Alfred Grendall had been asked, —not because he was at all in favour with any of the Longestaffes, but in order that he might be useful in disposing of the great Director. Lord Alfred was used to

him and could talk to him, and might probably know
what he liked to eat and drink. Therefore Lord Alfred
had been asked to Caversham, and Lord Alfred had
come, having all his expenses paid by the great Director.
When Sir Felix arrived, Lord Alfred was earning his
entertainment by talking to Mr. Melmotte in a summer-
house. He had cool drink before him and a box of cigars,
but was probably thinking at the time how hard the
world had been to him. Lady Pomona was languid, but
not uncivil in her reception. She was doing her best to
perform her part of the treaty in reference to Madame
Melmotte. Sophia was walking apart with a certain Mr.
Whitstable, a young squire in the neighbourhood, who
had been asked to Caversham because as Sophia was
now reputed to be twenty-eight,—they who decided the
question might have said thirty-one without falsehood,—
it was considered that Mr. Whitstable was good enough,
or at least as good as could be expected. Sophia was
handsome, but with a big, cold, unalluring handsomeness,
and had not quite succeeded in London. Georgiana had
been more admired, and boasted among her friends of the
offers which she had rejected. Her friends on the other
hand were apt to tell of her many failures. Nevertheless
she held her head up, and had not as yet come down
among the rural Whitstables. At the present moment
her hands were empty, and she was devoting herself
to such a performance of the treaty as should make it
impossible for her father to leave his part of it unfulfilled.

For a few minutes Sir Felix sat on a garden chair
making conversation to Lady Pomona and Madame
Melmotte. 'Beautiful garden,' he said; 'for myself I don't
much care for gardens; but if one is to live in the country,
this is the sort of thing that one would like.'

'Delicious,' said Madame Melmotte, repressing a yawn,
and drawing her shawl higher round her throat. It was
the end of May, and the weather was very warm for the
time of the year; but, in her heart of hearts, Madame
Melmotte did not like sitting out in the garden.

'It isn't a pretty place; but the house is comfortable,
and we make the best of it,' said Lady Pomona.

'Plenty of glass, I see,' said Sir Felix. 'If one is to live in the country, I like that kind of thing. Carbury is a very poor place.'

There was offence in this;—as though the Carbury property and the Carbury position could be compared to the Longestaffe property and the Longestaffe position. Though dreadfully hampered for money, the Longestaffes were great people. 'For a small place,' said Lady Pomona, 'I think Carbury is one of the nicest in the county. Of course it is not extensive.'

'No, by Jove,' said Sir Felix, 'you may say that, Lady Pomona. It's like a prison to me with that moat round it.' Then he jumped up and joined Marie Melmotte and Georgiana. Georgiana, glad to be released for a time from performance of the treaty, was not long before she left them together. She had understood that the two horses now in the running were Lord Nidderdale and Sir Felix; and though she would not probably have done much to aid Sir Felix, she was quite willing to destroy Lord Nidderdale.

Sir Felix had his work to do, and was willing to do it,—as far as such willingness could go with him. The prize was so great, and the comfort of wealth was so sure, that even he was tempted to exert himself. It was this feeling which had brought him into Suffolk, and induced him to travel all night, across dirty roads, in an old cab. For the girl herself he cared not the least. It was not in his power really to care for anybody. He did not dislike her much. He was not given to disliking people strongly, except at the moments in which they offended him. He regarded her simply as the means by which a portion of Mr. Melmotte's wealth might be conveyed to his uses. In regard to feminine beauty he had his own ideas, and his own inclinations. He was by no means indifferent to such attraction. But Marie Melmotte, from that point of view, was nothing to him. Such prettiness as belonged to her came from the brightness of her youth, and from a modest shy demeanour joined to an incipient aspiration for the enjoyment of something in the world which should be her own. There was, too, arising within her bosom a struggle to be something in the world, an idea that she, too, could say something, and have thoughts of her own, if only she had some friend near her whom she need not fear. Though still shy, she was always resolving that she would abandon her shyness, and already had thoughts of her own as to the perfectly open confidence which should exist between two lovers. When alone,—and she was much alone,—she would build castles in the air, which were bright with art and love, rather than with gems and gold. The books she read, poor though they generally were, left something bright on her imagination. She fancied to herself brilliant conversations in which she bore a bright part, though in real life she had hitherto hardly talked to any one since she was a child. Sir Felix Carbury, she knew, had made her an offer. She knew also, or thought that she knew, that she loved the man. And now she was with him alone! Now surely had come the time in which some one of her castles in the air might be found to be built of real materials.

'You know why I have come down here?' he said.

'To see your cousin.'

'No, indeed. I'm not particularly fond of my cousin, who is a methodical stiff-necked old bachelor,—as cross as the mischief.'

'How disagreeable!'

'Yes; he is disagreeable. I didn't come down to see him, I can tell you. But when I heard that you were going to be here with the Longestaffes, I determined to come at once. I wonder whether you are glad to see me?'

'I don't know,' said Marie, who could not at once find that brilliancy of words with which her imagination supplied her readily enough in her solitude.

'Do you remember what you said to me that evening at my mother's?'

'Did I say anything? I don't remember anything particular.'

'Do you not? Then I fear you can't think very much of me.' He paused as though he supposed that she would drop into his mouth like a cherry. 'I thought you told me that you would love me.'

'Did I?'

'Did you not?'

'I don't know what I said. Perhaps if I said that, I didn't mean it.'

'Am I to believe that?'

'Perhaps you didn't mean it, yourself.'

'By George, I did. I was quite in earnest. There never was a fellow more in earnest than I was. I've come down here on purpose to say it again.'

'To say what?'

'Whether you'll accept me?'

'I don't know whether you love me well enough.' She longed to be told by him that he loved her. He had no objection to tell her so, but, without thinking much about it, felt it to be a bore. All that kind of thing was trash and twaddle. He desired her to accept him; and he would have wished, were it possible, that she should have gone to her father for his consent. There was something in the big eyes and heavy jaws of Mr. Melmotte which he almost feared. 'Do you really love me well enough?' she whispered.

'Of course I do. I'm bad at making pretty speeches, and all that, but you know I love you.'

'Do you?'

'By George, yes. I always liked you from the first moment I saw you. I did indeed.'

It was a poor declaration of love, but it sufficed. 'Then I will love you,' she said. 'I will with all my heart.'

'There's a darling!'

'Shall I be your darling? Indeed I will. I may call you Felix now;—mayn't I?'

'Rather.'

'Oh, Felix, I hope you will love me. I will so dote upon you. You know a great many men have asked me to love them.'

'I suppose so.'

'But I have never, never cared for one of them in the least;—not in the least.'

'You do care for me?'

'Oh yes.' She looked up into his beautiful face as she

spoke, and he saw that her eyes were swimming with tears. He thought at the moment that she was very common to look at. As regarded appearance only he would have preferred even Sophia Longestaffe. There was indeed a certain brightness of truth which another man might have read in Marie's mingled smiles and tears, but it was thrown away altogether upon him. They were walking in some shrubbery quite apart from the house, where they were unseen; so, as in duty bound, he put his arm round her waist and kissed her. 'Oh, Felix,' she said, giving her face up to him; 'no one ever did it before.' He did not in the least believe her, nor was the matter one of the slightest importance to him. 'Say that you will be good to me, Felix. I will be so good to you.'

'Of course I will be good to you.'

'Men are not always good to their wives. Papa is often very cross to mamma.'

'I suppose he can be cross?'

'Yes, he can. He does not often scold me. I don't know what he'll say when we tell him about this.'

'But I suppose he intends that you shall be married?'

'He wanted me to marry Lord Nidderdale and Lord Glasslough, but I hated them both. I think he wants me to marry Lord Nidderdale again now. He hasn't said so, but mamma tells me. But I never will;—never!'

'I hope not, Marie.'

'You needn't be a bit afraid. I would not do it if they were to kill me. I hate him,—and I do so love you.' Then she leaned with all her weight upon his arm and looked up again into his beautiful face. 'You will speak to papa; won't you?'

'Will that be the best way?'

'I suppose so. How else?'

'I don't know whether Madame Melmotte ought not——'

'Oh dear no. Nothing would induce her. She is more afraid of him than anybody;—more afraid of him than I am. I thought the gentleman always did that.'

'Of course I'll do it,' said Sir Felix. 'I'm not afraid of

him. Why should I? He and I are very good friends,
you know.'

'I'm glad of that.'

'He made me a Director of one of his companies the
other day.'

'Did he? Perhaps he'll like you for a son-in-law.'

'There's no knowing;—is there?'

'I hope he will. I shall like you for papa's son-in-law.
I hope it isn't wrong to say that. Oh, Felix, say that you
love me.' Then she put her face up towards his again.

'Of course I love you,' he said, not thinking it worth
his while to kiss her. 'It's no good speaking to him here.
I suppose I had better go and see him in the city.'

'He is in a good humour now,' said Marie.

'But I couldn't get him alone. It wouldn't be the thing
to do down here.'

'Wouldn't it?'

'Not in the country,—in another person's house. Shall
you tell Madame Melmotte?'

'Yes, I shall tell mamma; but she won't say anything
to him. Mamma does not care much about me. But I'll
tell you all that another time. Of course I shall tell you
everything now. I never yet had anybody to tell anything to, but I shall never be tired of telling you.' Then
he left her as soon as he could, and escaped to the other
ladies. Mr. Melmotte was still sitting in the summer-
house, and Lord Alfred was still with him, smoking and
drinking brandy and seltzer. As Sir Felix passed in front
of the great man he told himself that it was much better
that the interview should be postponed till they were all
in London. Mr. Melmotte did not look as though he
were in a good humour. Sir Felix said a few words to
Lady Pomona and Madame Melmotte. Yes; he hoped
to have the pleasure of seeing them with his mother and
sister on the following day. He was aware that his cousin
was not coming. He believed that his cousin Roger never
did go anywhere like any one else. No; he had not seen
Mr. Longestaffe. He hoped to have the pleasure of seeing
him to-morrow. Then he escaped, and got on his horse,
and rode away.

'That's going to be the lucky man,' said Georgiana to her mother, that evening.

'In what way lucky?'

'He is going to get the heiress and all the money. What a fool Dolly has been!'

'I don't think it would have suited Dolly,' said Lady Pomona. 'After all, why should not Dolly marry a lady?'

## Chapter XVIII

### RUBY RUGGLES HEARS A LOVE TALE

MISS RUBY RUGGLES, the granddaughter of old Daniel Ruggles, of Sheep's Acre, in the parish of Sheepstone, close to Bungay, received the following letter from the hands of the rural post letter-carrier on that Sunday morning;—'A friend will be somewhere near Sheepstone Birches between four and five o'clock on Sunday afternoon.' There was not another word in the letter, but Miss Ruby Ruggles knew well from whom it came.

Daniel Ruggles was a farmer, who had the reputation of considerable wealth, but who was not very well looked on in the neighbourhood as being somewhat of a curmudgeon and a miser. His wife was dead;—he had quarrelled with his only son, whose wife was also dead, and had banished him from his home;—his daughters were married and away; and the only member of his family who lived with him was his granddaughter Ruby. And this granddaughter was a great trouble to the old man. She was twenty-three years old, and had been engaged to a prosperous young man at Bungay in the meal and pollard line, to whom old Ruggles had promised to give £500 on their marriage. But Ruby had taken it into her foolish young head that she did not like meal and pollard, and now she had received the above very dangerous letter. Though the writer had not dared to ·sign his name she knew well that it came from Sir Felix Carbury,—the most beautiful gentleman she had ever

set her eyes upon. Poor Ruby Ruggles! Living down at
Sheep's Acre, on the Waveney, she had heard both too
much and too little of the great world beyond her ken.
There were, she thought, many glorious things to be seen
which she would never see were she in these her early
years to become the wife of John Crumb, the dealer in
meal and pollard at Bungay. Therefore she was full of
a wild joy, half joy half fear, when she got her letter; and,
therefore, punctually at four o'clock on that Sunday she
was ensconced among the Sheepstone Birches, so that she
might see without much danger of being seen. Poor
Ruby Ruggles, who was left to be so much mistress of
herself at the time of her life in which she most required
the kindness of a controlling hand!

Mr. Ruggles held his land, or the greater part of it, on
what is called a bishop's lease, Sheep's Acre Farm being
a part of the property which did belong to the bishopric
of Elmham, and which was still set apart for its sustenta-
tion;—but he also held a small extent of outlying meadow
which belonged to the Carbury estate, so that he was
one of the tenants of Roger Carbury. Those Sheepstone
Birches, at which Felix made his appointment, belonged
to Roger. On a former occasion, when the feeling between the two cousins was kinder than that which now
existed, Felix had ridden over with the landlord to call
on the old man, and had then first seen Ruby;—and had
heard from Roger something of Ruby's history up to that
date. It had then been just made known that she was to
marry John Crumb. Since that time not a word had
been spoken between the men respecting the girl. Mr.
Carbury had heard, with sorrow, that the marriage was
either postponed or abandoned,—but his growing dislike
to the baronet had made it very improbable that there
should be any conversation between them on the subject.
Sir Felix, however, had probably heard more of Ruby
Ruggles than her grandfather's landlord.

There is, perhaps, no condition of mind more difficult
for the ordinarily well-instructed inhabitant of a city to
realise than that of such a girl as Ruby Ruggles. The
rural day labourer and his wife live on a level surface

which is comparatively open to the eye. Their aspirations, whether for good or evil,—whether for food and drink to be honestly earned for themselves and children, or for drink first, to be come by either honestly or dishonestly,—are, if looked at at all, fairly visible. And with the men of the Ruggles class one can generally find out what they would be at, and in what direction their minds are at work. But the Ruggles woman,—especially the Ruggles young woman,—is better educated, has higher aspirations and a brighter imagination, and is infinitely more cunning than the man. If she be good-looking and relieved from the pressure of want, her thoughts soar into a world which is as unknown to her as heaven is to us, and in regard to which her longings are apt to be infinitely stronger than are ours for heaven. Her education has been much better than that of the man. She can read, whereas he can only spell words from a book. She can write a letter after her fashion, whereas he can barely spell words out on a paper. Her tongue is more glib, and her intellect sharper. But her ignorance as to the reality of things is much more gross than his. By such contact as he has with men in markets, in the streets of the towns he frequents, and even in the fields, he learns something unconsciously of the relative condition of his countrymen, —and, as to that which he does not learn, his imagination is obtuse. But the woman builds castles in the air, and wonders, and longs. To the young farmer the squire's daughter is a superior being very much out of his way. To the farmer's daughter the young squire is an Apollo, whom to look at is a pleasure,—by whom to be looked at is a delight. The danger for the most part is soon over. The girl marries after her kind, and then husband and children put the matter at rest for ever.

A mind more absolutely uninstructed than that of Ruby Ruggles as to the world beyond Suffolk and Norfolk it would be impossible to find. But her thoughts were as wide as they were vague, and as active as they were erroneous. Why should she with all her prettiness, and all her cleverness,—with all her fortune to boot,—marry that dustiest of all men, John Crumb, before she had seen

something of the beauties of the things of which she had
read in the books which came in her way? John Crumb
was not bad-looking. He was a sturdy, honest fellow,
too,—slow of speech but sure of his points when he had
got them within his grip,—fond of his beer but not often
drunk, and the very soul of industry at his work. But
though she had known him all her life she had never
known him otherwise than dusty. The meal had so
gotten within his hair, and skin, and raiment, that it
never came out altogether even on Sundays. His normal
complexion was a healthy pallor, through which indeed
some records of hidden ruddiness would make themselves
visible, but which was so judiciously assimilated to his
hat and coat and waistcoat, that he was more like a stout
ghost than a healthy young man. Nevertheless it was
said of him that he could thrash any man in Bungay, and
carry two hundredweight of flour upon his back. And
Ruby also knew this of him,—that he worshipped the
very ground on which she trod.

But, alas, she thought there might be something better
than such worship; and, therefore, when Felix Carbury
came in her way, with his beautiful oval face, and his rich
brown colour, and his bright hair and lovely moustache,
she was lost in a feeling which she mistook for love; and
when he sneaked over to her a second and a third time,
she thought more of his listless praise than ever she had
thought of John Crumb's honest promises. But, though
she was an utter fool, she was not a fool without a principle. She was miserably ignorant; but she did understand that there was a degradation which it behoved her
to avoid. She thought, as the moths seem to think, that
she might fly into the flame and not burn her wings.
After her fashion she was pretty, with long glossy ringlets,
which those about the farm on week days would see confined in curl-papers, and large round dark eyes, and a
clear dark complexion, in which the blood showed itself
plainly beneath the soft brown skin. She was strong, and
healthy, and tall,—and had a will of her own which gave
infinite trouble to old Daniel Ruggles, her grandfather.

Felix Carbury took himself two miles out of his way in

order that he might return by Sheepstone Birches, which
was a little copse distant not above half a mile from
Sheep's Acre farmhouse. A narrow angle of the little
wood came up to the road, by which there was a gate
leading into a grass meadow, which Sir Felix had remembered when he made his appointment. The road was no
more than a country lane, unfrequented at all times, and
almost sure to be deserted on Sundays. He approached
the gate in a walk, and then stood awhile looking into the
wood. He had not stood long before he saw the girl's
bonnet beneath a tree standing just outside the wood, in
the meadow, but on the bank of the ditch. Thinking for
a moment what he would do about his horse, he rode
him into the field, and then, dismounting, fastened him
to a rail which ran down the side of the copse. Then he
sauntered on till he stood looking down upon Ruby
Ruggles as she sat beneath the tree. 'I like your impudence,' she said, 'in calling yourself a friend.'

'Ain't I a friend, Ruby?'

'A pretty sort of friend, you! When you was going
away, you was to be back at Carbury in a fortnight; and
that is,—oh, ever so long ago now.'

'But I wrote to you, Ruby.'

'What's letters? And the postman to know all as in
'em for anything anybody knows, and grandfather to be
almost sure to see 'em. I don't call letters no good at all,
and I beg you won't write 'em any more.'

'Did he see them?'

'No thanks to you if he didn't. I don't know why you
are come here, Sir Felix,—nor yet I don't know why I
should come and meet you. It's all just folly like.'

'Because I love you;—that's why I come; eh, Ruby?
And you have come because you love me; eh, Ruby? Is
not that about it?' Then he threw himself on the ground
beside her, and got his arm round her waist.

It would boot little to tell here all that they said to
each other. The happiness of Ruby Ruggles for that half-
hour was no doubt complete. She had her London lover
beside her; and though in every word he spoke there was
a tone of contempt, still he talked of love, and made her

promises, and told her that she was pretty. He probably did not enjoy it much; he cared very little about her, and carried on the liaison simply because it was the proper sort of thing for a young man to do. He had begun to think that the odour of patchouli was unpleasant, and that the flies were troublesome, and the ground hard, before the half-hour was over. She felt that she could be content to sit there for ever and to listen to him. This was a realisation of those delights of life of which she had read in the thrice-thumbed old novels which she had gotten from the little circulating library at Bungay.

But what was to come next? She had not dared to ask him to marry her,—had not dared to say those very words; and he had not dared to ask her to be his mistress. There was an animal courage about her, and an amount of strength also, and a fire in her eye, of which he had learned to be aware. Before the half-hour was over I think that he wished himself away;—but when he did go, he made a promise to see her again on the Tuesday morning. Her father would be at Harlestone market, and she would meet him at about noon at the bottom of the kitchen garden belonging to the farm. As he made the promise he resolved that he would not keep it. He would write to her again, and bid her come to him in London, and would send her money for the journey.

'I suppose I am to be his wedded wife,' said Ruby to herself, as she crept away down from the road, away also from her own home;—so that on her return her presence should not be associated with that of the young man, should any one chance to see the young man on the road. 'I'll never be nothing unless I'm that,' she said to herself. Then she allowed her mind to lose itself in expatiating on the difference between John Crumb and Sir Felix Carbury.

## Chapter XIX

### HETTA CARBURY HEARS A LOVE TALE

'I HAVE half a mind to go back to-morrow morning,' Felix said to his mother that Sunday evening after dinner. At that moment Roger was walking round the garden by himself, and Henrietta was in her own room.

'To-morrow morning, Felix! You are engaged to dine with the Longestaffes!'

'You could make any excuse you like about that.'

'It would be the most uncourteous thing in the world. The Longestaffes you know are the leading people in this part of the country. No one knows what may happen. If you should ever be living at Carbury, how sad it would be that you should have quarrelled with them.'

'You forget, mother, that Dolly Longestaffe is about the most intimate friend I have in the world.'

'That does not justify you in being uncivil to the father and mother. And you should remember what you came here for.'

'What did I come for?'

'That you might see Marie Melmotte more at your ease than you can in their London house.'

'That's all settled,' said Sir Felix, in the most indifferent tone that he could assume.

'Settled!'

'As far as the girl is concerned. I can't very well go to the old fellow for his consent down here.'

'Do you mean to say, Felix, that Marie Melmotte has accepted you?'

'I told you that before.'

'My dear Felix. Oh, my boy!' In her joy the mother took her unwilling son in her arms and caressed him. Here was the first step taken not only to success, but to such magnificent splendour as should make her son to be envied by all young men, and herself to be envied by all mothers in England! 'No, you didn't tell me before. But I am so happy. Is she really fond of you? I don't wonder that any girl should be fond of you.'

'I can't say anything about that, but I think she means to stick to it.'

'If she is firm, of course her father will give way at last. Fathers always do give way when the girl is firm. Why should he oppose it?'

'I don't know that he will.'

'You are a man of rank, with a title of your own. I suppose what he wants is a gentleman for his girl. I don't see why he should not be perfectly satisfied. With all his enormous wealth a thousand a year or so can't make any difference. And then he made you one of the Directors at his Board. Oh Felix;—it is almost too good to be true.'

'I ain't quite sure that I care very much about being married, you know.'

'Oh, Felix, pray don't say that. Why shouldn't you like being married? She is a very nice girl, and we shall all be so fond of her! Don't let any feeling of that kind come over you; pray don't. You will be able to do just what you please when once the question of her money is settled. Of course you can hunt as often as you like, and you can have a house in any part of London you please. You must understand by this time how very disagreeable it is to have to get on without an established income.'

'I quite understand that.'

'If this were once done you would never have any more trouble of that kind. There would be plenty of money for everything as long as you live. It would be complete success. I don't know how to say enough to you, or to tell you how dearly I love you, or to make you understand how well I think you have done it all.' Then she caressed him again, and was almost beside herself in an agony of mingled anxiety and joy. If, after all, her beautiful boy, who had lately been her disgrace and her great trouble because of his poverty, should shine forth to the world as a baronet with £20,000 a year, how glorious would it be! She must have known,—she did know,—how poor, how selfish a creature he was. But her gratification at the prospect of his splendour obliterated the sorrow with which the vileness of his character sometimes oppressed her. Were he to win this girl with all her father's money, neither she nor his sister would be the better for it, except in this, that the burden of maintaining him would be taken from her shoulders. But his magnificence would be established. He was her son, and the prospect of his fortune and splendour was sufficient to elate her into a very heaven of beautiful dreams. 'But, Felix,' she continued, 'you really must stay and go to the Longestaffes' to-morrow. It will only be one day.—And now were you to run away——'

'Run away! What nonsense you talk.'

'If you were to start back to London at once I mean, it would be an affront to her, and the very thing to set Melmotte against you. You should lay yourself out to please him;—indeed you should.'

'Oh, bother!' said Sir Felix. But nevertheless he allowed himself to be persuaded to remain. The matter was important even to him, and he consented to endure the almost unendurable nuisance of spending another day at the Manor House. Lady Carbury, almost lost in delight, did not know where to turn for sympathy. If her cousin were not so stiff, so pig-headed, so wonderfully ignorant of the affairs of the world, he would have at any rate consented to rejoice with her. Though he might not like Felix,—who, as his mother admitted to herself, had been rude to her cousin,—he would have rejoiced for the sake of the family. But, as it was, she did not dare to tell him. He would have received her tidings with silent scorn. And even Henrietta would not be enthusiastic. She felt that though she would have delighted to expatiate on this great triumph, she must be silent at present. It should now be her great effort to ingratiate herself with Mr. Melmotte at the dinner party at Caversham.

During the whole of that evening Roger Carbury hardly spoke to his cousin Hetta. There was not much conversation between them till quite late, when Father Barham came in for supper. He had been over at Bungay among his people there, and had walked back, taking Carbury on the way. 'What did you think of our bishop?' Roger asked him, rather imprudently.

'Not much of him as a bishop. I don't doubt that he

makes a very nice lord, and that he does more good
among his neighbours than an average lord. But you
don't put power or responsibility into the hands of any
one sufficient to make him a bishop.'

'Nine-tenths of the clergy in the diocese would be
guided by him in any matter of clerical conduct which
might come before him.'

'Because they know that he has no strong opinion of
his own, and would not therefore desire to dominate
theirs. Take any of your bishops that has an opinion,—
if there be one left,—and see how far your clergy consent
to his teaching!' Roger turned round and took up his
book. He was already becoming tired of his pet priest.
He himself always abstained from saying a word deroga-
tory to his new friend's religion in the man's hearing; but
his new friend did not by any means return the compliment. Perhaps also Roger felt that were he to take up
the cudgels for an argument he might be worsted in the
combat, as in such combats success is won by practised
skill rather than by truth. Henrietta was also reading,
and Felix was smoking elsewhere,—wondering whether
the hours would ever wear themselves away in that castle
of dulness, in which no cards were to be seen, and where,
except at meal-times, there was nothing to drink. But
Lady Carbury was quite willing to allow the priest to
teach her that all appliances for the dissemination of
religion outside his own Church must be naught.

'I suppose our bishops are sincere in their beliefs,' she
said with her sweetest smile.

'I'm sure I hope so. I have no possible reason to doubt
it as to the two or three whom I have seen,—nor indeed
as to all the rest whom I have not seen.'

'They are so much respected everywhere as good and
pious men!'

'I do not doubt it. Nothing tends so much to respect
as a good income. But they may be excellent men without being excellent bishops. I find no fault with them,
but much with the system by which they are controlled.
Is it probable that a man should be fitted to select guides
for other men's souls because he has succeeded by infinite

labour in his vocation in becoming the leader of a majority in the House of Commons?'*

'Indeed, no,' said Lady Carbury, who did not in the least understand the nature of the question put to her.

'And when you've got your bishop, is it likely that a man should be able to do his duty in that capacity who has no power of his own to decide whether a clergyman under him is or is not fit for his duty?'

'Hardly, indeed.'

'The English people, or some of them,—that some being the richest, and, at present, the most powerful,— like to play at having a Church, though there is not sufficient faith in them to submit to the control of a Church.'

'Do you think men should be controlled by clergymen, Mr. Barham?'

'In matters of faith I do; and so, I suppose, do you; at least you make that profession. You declare it to be your duty to submit yourself to your spiritual pastors and masters.'

'That, I thought, was for children,' said Lady Carbury. 'The clergyman, in the catechism, says, "My good child."'

'It is what you were taught as a child before you had made profession of your faith to a bishop, in order that you might know your duty when you had ceased to be a child. I quite agree, however, that the matter, as viewed by your Church, is childish altogether, and intended only for children. As a rule, adults with you want no religion.'

'I am afraid that is true of a great many.'

'It is marvellous to me that, when a man thinks of it, he should not be driven by very fear to the comforts of a safer faith,—unless, indeed, he enjoy the security of absolute infidelity.'

'That is worse than anything,' said Lady Carbury with a sigh and a shudder.

'I don't know that it is worse than a belief which is no belief,' said the priest with energy;—'than a creed which sits so easily on a man that he does not even know what it contains, and never asks himself as he repeats it, whether it be to him credible or incredible.'

'That is very bad,' said Lady Carbury.

'We're getting too deep, I think,' said Roger, putting down the book which he had in vain been trying to read.

'I think it is so pleasant to have a little serious conversation on Sunday evening,' said Lady Carbury. The priest drew himself back into his chair and smiled. He was quite clever enough to understand that Lady Carbury had been talking nonsense, and clever enough also to be aware of the cause of Roger's uneasiness. But Lady Carbury might be all the easier converted because she understood nothing and was fond of ambitious talking; and Roger Carbury might possibly be forced into conviction by the very feeling which at present made him unwilling to hear arguments.

'I don't like hearing my Church ill-spoken of,' said Roger.

'You wouldn't like me if I thought ill of it and spoke well of it,' said the priest.

'And, therefore, the less said the sooner mended,' said Roger, rising from his chair. Upon this Father Barham took his departure and walked away to Beccles. It might be that he had sowed some seed. It might be that he had, at any rate, ploughed some ground. Even the attempt to plough the ground was a good work which would not be forgotten.

The following morning was the time on which Roger had fixed for repeating his suit to Henrietta. He had determined that it should be so, and though the words had been almost on his tongue during that Sunday afternoon, he had repressed them because he would do as he had determined. He was conscious, almost painfully conscious, of a certain increase of tenderness in his cousin's manner towards him. All that pride of independence, which had amounted almost to roughness, when she was in London, seemed to have left her. When he greeted her morning and night, she looked softly into his face. She cherished the flowers which he gave her. He could perceive that if he expressed the

slightest wish in any matter about the house she would
attend to it. There had been a word said about punctuality, and she had become punctual as the hand of the
clock. There was not a glance of her eye, nor a turn of
her hand, that he did not watch, and calculate its effect as
regarded himself. But because she was tender to him and
observant, he did not by any means allow himself to
believe that her heart was growing into love for him. He
thought that he understood the working of her mind.
She could see how great was his disgust at her brother's
doings; how fretted he was by her mother's conduct.
Her grace, and sweetness, and sense, took part with him
against those who were nearer to herself, and therefore,—
in pity,—she was kind to him. It was thus he read it, and
he read it almost with exact accuracy.

'Hetta,' he said after breakfast, 'come out into the
garden awhile.'

'Are not you going to the men?'

'Not yet, at any rate. I do not always go to the men as
you call it.' She put on her hat and tripped out with him,
knowing well that she had been summoned to hear the
old story. She had been sure, as soon as she found the
white rose in her room, that the old story would be repeated again before she left Carbury;—and, up to this
time, she had hardly made up her mind what answer
she would give to it. That she could not take his offer,
she thought she did know. She knew well that she loved
the other man. That other man had never asked her for
her love, but she thought that she knew that he desired it.
But in spite of all this there had in truth grown up in her
bosom a feeling of tenderness towards her cousin so strong
that it almost tempted her to declare to herself that he
ought to have what he wanted, simply because he wanted
it. He was so good, so noble, so generous, so devoted, that
it almost seemed to her that she could not be justified in
refusing him. And she had gone entirely over to his side
in regard to the Melmottes. Her mother had talked to
her of the charm of Mr. Melmotte's money, till her very
heart had been sickened. There was nothing noble there;
but, as contrasted with that, Roger's conduct and bearing

were those of a fine gentleman who knew neither fear nor shame. Should such a one be doomed to pine for ever because a girl could not love him,—a man born to be loved, if nobility and tenderness and truth were lovely!

'Hetta,' he said, 'put your arm here.' She gave him her arm. 'I was a little annoyed last night by that priest. I want to be civil to him, and now he is always turning against me.'

'He doesn't do any harm, I suppose?'

'He does do harm if he teaches you and me to think lightly of those things which we have been brought up to revere.' So, thought Henrietta, it isn't about love this time; it's only about the Church. 'He ought not to say things before my guests as to our way of believing, which I wouldn't under any circumstances say as to his. I didn't quite like your hearing it.'

'I don't think he'll do me any harm. I'm not at all that way given. I suppose they all do it. It's their business.'

'Poor fellow! I brought him here just because I thought it was a pity that a man born and bred like a gentleman should never see the inside of a comfortable house.'

'I liked him;—only I didn't like his saying stupid things about the bishop.'

'And I like him.' Then there was a pause. 'I suppose your brother does not talk to you much about his own affairs.'

'His own affairs, Roger? Do you mean money? He never says a word to me about money.'

'I meant about the Melmottes.'

'No; not to me. Felix hardly ever speaks to me about anything.'

'I wonder whether she has accepted him.'

'I think she very nearly did accept him in London.'

'I can't quite sympathise with your mother in all her feelings about this marriage, because I do not think that I recognise as she does the necessity of money.'

'Felix is so disposed to be extravagant.'

'Well; yes. But I was going to say that though I cannot

bring myself to say anything to encourage her about this heiress, I quite recognise her unselfish devotion to his interests.'

'Mamma thinks more of him than of anything,' said Hetta, not in the least intending to accuse her mother of indifference to herself.

'I know it; and though I happen to think myself that her other child would better repay her devotion,'—this he said, looking up to Hetta and smiling,—'I quite feel how good a mother she is to Felix. You know, when she first came the other day we almost had a quarrel.'

'I felt that there was something unpleasant.'

'And then Felix coming after his time put me out. I am getting old and cross, or I should not mind such things.'

'I think you are so good,—and so kind.' As she said this she leaned upon his arm almost as though she meant to tell him that she loved him.

'I have been angry with myself,' he said, 'and so I am making you my father confessor. Open confession is good for the soul sometimes, and I think that you would understand me better than your mother.'

'I do understand you; but don't think there is any fault to confess.'

'You will not exact any penance?' She only looked at him and smiled. 'I am going to put a penance on myself all the same. I can't congratulate your brother on his wooing over at Caversham, as I know nothing about it, but I will express some civil wish to him about things in general.'

'Will that be a penance?'

'If you could look into my mind you'd find that it would. I'm full of fretful anger against him for half-a-dozen little frivolous things. Didn't he throw his cigar on the path? Didn't he lie in bed on Sunday instead of going to church?'

'But then he was travelling all the Saturday night.'

'Whose fault was that? But don't you see it is the triviality of the offence which makes the penance necessary. Had he knocked me over the head with a pickaxe,

or burned the house down, I should have had a right to
be angry. But I was angry because he wanted a horse
on Sunday;—and therefore I must do penance.'

There was nothing of love in all this. Hetta, however,
did not wish him to talk of love. He was certainly now
treating her as a friend,—as a most intimate friend. If
he would only do that without making love to her, how
happy could she be! But his determination still held
good. 'And now,' said he, altering his tone altogether,
'I must speak about myself.' Immediately the weight of
her hand upon his arm was lessened. Thereupon he put
his left hand round and pressed her arm to his. 'No,' he
said; 'do not make any change towards me while I
speak to you. Whatever comes of it we shall at any rate
be cousins and friends.'

'Always friends!' she said.

'Yes;—always friends. And now listen to me for I
have much to say. I will not tell you again that I love
you. You know it, or else you must think me the vainest
and falsest of men. It is not only that I love you, but I
am so accustomed to concern myself with one thing only,
so constrained by the habits and nature of my life to
confine myself to single interests, that I cannot as it were
escape from my love. I am thinking of it always, often
despising myself because I think of it so much. For, after
all, let a woman be ever so good,—and you to me are all
that is good,—a man should not allow his love to dominate his intellect.'

'Oh, no!'

'I do. I calculate my chances within my own bosom
almost as a man might calculate his chances of heaven.
I should like you to know me just as I am, the weak and
the strong together. I would not win you by a lie if I
could. I think of you more than I ought to do. I am sure,
—quite sure that you are the only possible mistress of this
house during my tenure of it. If I am ever to live as
other men do, and to care about the things which other
men care for, it must be as your husband.'

'Pray,—pray do not say that.'

'Yes; I think that I have a right to say it,—and a right

to expect that you should believe me. I will not ask you
to be my wife if you do not love me. Not that I should
fear aught for myself, but that you should not be pressed
to make a sacrifice of yourself because I am your friend
and cousin. But I think it is quite possible you might
come to love me,—unless your heart be absolutely given
away elsewhere.'

'What am I to say?'

'We each of us know of what the other is thinking. If
Paul Montague has robbed me of my love——?'

'Mr. Montague has never said a word.'

'If he had, I think he would have wronged me. He
met you in my house, and I think must have known what
my feelings were towards you.'

'But he never has.'

'We have been like brothers together,—one brother
being very much older than the other, indeed; or like
father and son. I think he should place his hopes elsewhere.'

'What am I to say? If he have such hope he has not
told me. I think it almost cruel that a girl should be
asked in that way.'

'Hetta, I should not wish to be cruel to you. Of
course I know the way of the world in such matters.
I have no right to ask you about Paul Montague,—no
right to expect an answer. But it is all the world to me.
You can understand that I should think you might learn
to love even me, if you loved no one else.' The tone of
his voice was manly, and at the same time full of entreaty.
His eyes as he looked at her were bright with love and
anxiety. She not only believed him as to the tale which
he now told her; but she believed in him altogether. She
knew that he was a staff on which a woman might safely
lean, trusting to it for comfort and protection in life. In
that moment she all but yielded to him. Had he seized
her in his arms and kissed her then, I think she would
have yielded. She did all but love him. She so regarded
him that had it been some other woman that he craved,
she would have used every art she knew to have backed
his suit, and would have been ready to swear that any

woman was a fool who refused him. She almost hated herself because she was unkind to one who so thoroughly deserved kindness. As it was, she made him no answer, but continued to walk beside him trembling. 'I thought I would tell it you all, because I wish you to know exactly the state of my mind. I would show you if I could all my heart and all my thoughts about yourself as in a glass case. Do not coy your love for me if you can feel it. When you know, dear, that a man's heart is set upon a woman as mine is set on you, so that it is for you to make his life bright or dark, for you to open or to shut the gates of his earthly Paradise, I think you will be above keeping him in darkness for the sake of a girlish scruple.'

'Oh, Roger!'

'If ever there should come a time in which you can say it truly, remember my truth to you and say it boldly. I at least shall never change. Of course if you love another man and give yourself to him, it will be all over. Tell me that boldly also. I have said it all now. God bless you, my own heart's darling. I hope,—I hope I may be strong enough through it all to think more of your happiness than of my own.' Then he parted from her abruptly, taking his way over one of the bridges, and leaving her to find her way into the house alone.

## Chapter XX

### LADY POMONA'S DINNER PARTY

ROGER CARBURY'S half-formed plan of keeping Henrietta at home while Lady Carbury and Sir Felix went to dine at Caversham fell to the ground. It was to be carried out only in the event of Hetta's yielding to his prayer. But he had in fact not made a prayer, and Hetta had certainly yielded nothing. When the evening came, Lady Carbury started with her son and daughter, and Roger was left alone. In the ordinary course of his life he was used to solitude. During the greater part of the year he would eat and drink and live without companionship; so that there was to him nothing peculiarly sad in this desertion. But on the present occasion he could not prevent himself from dwelling on the loneliness of his lot in life. These cousins of his who were his guests cared nothing for him. Lady Carbury had come to his house simply that it might be useful to her; Sir Felix did not pretend to treat him with even ordinary courtesy; and Hetta herself, though she was soft to him and gracious, was soft and gracious through pity rather than love. On this day he had, in truth, asked her for nothing; but he had almost brought himself to think that she might give all that he wanted without asking. And yet, when he told her of the greatness of his love, and of its endurance, she was simply silent. When the carriage taking them to dinner went away down the road, he sat on the parapet of the bridge in front of the house listening to the sound of the horses' feet, and telling himself that there was nothing left for him in life.

If ever one man had been good to another, he had been good to Paul Montague, and now Paul Montague was robbing him of everything he valued in the world. His thoughts were not logical, nor was his mind exact. The more he considered it, the stronger was his inward condemnation of his friend. He had never mentioned to any one the services he had rendered to Montague. In speaking of him to Hetta he had alluded only to the affection which had existed between them. But he felt that because of those services his friend Montague had owed it to him not to fall in love with the girl he loved; and he thought that if, unfortunately, this had happened unawares, Montague should have retired as soon as he learned the truth. He could not bring himself to forgive his friend, even though Hetta had assured him that his friend had never spoken to her of love. He was sore all over, and it was Paul Montague who made him sore. Had there been no such man at Carbury when Hetta came there, Hetta might now have been mistress of the house. He sat there till the servant came to tell him that his dinner was on the table. Then he crept in and ate,—so that the man might not see his sorrow; and, after dinner, he sat with a book in his hand seeming to read. But he read not a word, for his mind was fixed altogether on his cousin Hetta. 'What a poor creature a man is,' he said to himself, 'who is not sufficiently his own master to get over a feeling like this.'

At Caversham there was a very grand party,—as grand almost as a dinner party can be in the country. There were the Earl and Countess of Loddon and Lady Jane Pewet from Loddon Park, and the bishop and his wife, and the Hepworths. These, with the Carburys and the parson's family, and the people staying in the house, made twenty-four at the dinner table. As there were fourteen ladies and only ten men, the banquet can hardly be said to have been very well arranged. But those things cannot be done in the country with the exactness which the appliances of London make easy; and then the Longestaffes, though they were decidedly people of fashion, were not famous for their excellence in arranging such matters. If aught, however, was lacking in exactness, it was made up in grandeur. There were three powdered footmen, and in that part of the country Lady Pomona alone was served after this fashion; and there was a very heavy butler, whose appearance of itself was sufficient to give éclat to a family. The grand saloon in which nobody ever lived was thrown open, and sofas and chairs on which nobody ever sat were uncovered. It was not above once in the year that this kind of thing was done at Caversham; but when it was done, nothing was spared which could contribute to the magnificence of the fête. Lady Pomona and her two tall daughters standing up to receive the little Countess of Loddon and Lady Jane Pewet, who was the image of her mother on a somewhat smaller scale, while Madame Melmotte and Marie stood behind as though ashamed of themselves, was a sight to see. Then the Carburys came, and then Mrs. Yeld with the bishop. The grand room was soon fairly full; but nobody had a word to say. The bishop was generally a man of much conversation, and Lady Loddon, if she were well pleased with her listeners, could

talk by the hour without ceasing. But on this occasion
nobody could utter a word. Lord Loddon pottered
about, making a feeble attempt, in which he was
seconded by no one. Lord Alfred stood, stock-still,
stroking his grey moustache with his hand. That much
greater man, Augustus Melmotte, put his thumbs into
the arm-holes of his waistcoat, and was impassible. The
bishop saw at a glance the hopelessness of the occasion,
and made no attempt. The master of the house shook
hands with each guest as he entered, and then devoted
his mind to expectation of the next comer. Lady Pomona
and her two daughters were grand and handsome, but
weary and dumb. In accordance with the treaty,
Madame Melmotte had been entertained civilly for four
entire days. It could not be expected that the ladies of
Caversham should come forth unwearied after such a
struggle.

When dinner was announced Felix was allowed to take
in Marie Melmotte. There can be no doubt but that
the Caversham ladies did execute their part of the treaty.
They were led to suppose that this arrangement would
be desirable to the Melmottes, and they made it. The
great Augustus himself went in with Lady Carbury,
much to her satisfaction. She also had been dumb in the
drawing-room; but now, if ever, it would be her duty
to exert herself. 'I hope you like Suffolk,' she said.

'Pretty well, I thank you. Oh, yes;—very nice place
for a little fresh air.'

'Yes;—that's just it, Mr. Melmotte. When the summer
comes one does long so to see the flowers.'

'We have better flowers in our balconies than any I see
down here,' said Mr. Melmotte.

'No doubt;—because you can command the floral
tribute of the world at large. What is there that money
will not do? It can turn a London street into a bower of
roses, and give you grottoes in Grosvenor Square.'

'It's a very nice place, is London.'

'If you have got plenty of money, Mr. Melmotte.'

'And if you have not, it's the best place I know to get
it. Do you live in London, ma'am?' He had quite for-

gotten Lady Carbury even if he had seen her at his house, and with the dulness of hearing common to men, had not picked up her name when told to take her out to dinner.

'Oh, yes, I live in London. I have had the honour of being entertained by you there.' This she said with her sweetest smile.

'Oh, indeed. So many do come, that I don't always just remember.'

'How should you,—with all the world flocking round you? I am Lady Carbury, the mother of Sir Felix Carbury, whom I think you will remember.'

'Yes; I know Sir Felix. He's sitting there, next to my daughter.'

'Happy fellow!'

'I don't know much about that. Young men don't get their happiness in that way now. They've got other things to think of.'

'He thinks so much of his business.'

'Oh! I didn't know,' said Mr. Melmotte.

'He sits at the same Board with you, I think, Mr. Melmotte.'

'Oh;—that's his business!' said Mr. Melmotte, with a grim smile.

Lady Carbury was very clever as to many things, and was not ill-informed on matters in general that were going on around her; but she did not know much about the city, and was profoundly ignorant as to the duties of those Directors of whom, from time to time, she saw the names in a catalogue. 'I trust that he is diligent, there,' she said; 'and that he is aware of the great privilege which he enjoys in having the advantage of your counsel and guidance.'

'He don't trouble me much, ma'am, and I don't trouble him much.' After this Lady Carbury said no more as to her son's position in the city. She endeavoured to open various other subjects of conversation; but she found Mr. Melmotte to be heavy on her hands. After a while she had to abandon him in despair, and give herself up to raptures in favour of Protestantism at the bidding of the Caversham parson, who sat on the other side of her, and who had been worked to enthusiasm by some mention of Father Barham's name.

Opposite to her, or nearly so, sat Sir Felix and his love. 'I have told mamma,' Marie had whispered, as she walked in to dinner with him. She was now full of the idea so common to girls who are engaged,—and as natural as it is common,—that she might tell everything to her lover.

'Did she say anything?' he asked. Then Marie had to take her place and arrange her dress before she could reply to him. 'As to her, I suppose it does not matter what she says, does it?'

'She said a great deal. She thinks that papa will think you are not rich enough. Hush! Talk about something else, or people will hear.' So much she had been able to say during the bustle.

Felix was not at all anxious to talk about his love, and changed the subject very willingly. 'Have you been riding?' he asked.

'No; I don't think there are horses here,—not for visitors, that is. How did you get home? Did you have any adventures?'

'None at all,' said Felix, remembering Ruby Ruggles. 'I just rode home quietly. I go to town to-morrow.'

'And we go on Wednesday. Mind you come and see us before long.' This she said bringing her voice down to a whisper.

'Of course I shall. I suppose I'd better go to your father in the city. Does he go every day?'

'Oh yes, every day. He's back always about seven. Sometimes 'ie's good-natured enough when he comes back, but sometimes he's very cross. He's best just after dinner. But it's so hard to get to him then. Lord Alfred is almost always there; and then other people come, and they play cards. I think the city will be best.'

'You'll stick to it?' he asked.

'Oh, yes;—indeed I will. Now that I've once said it nothing will ever turn me. I think papa knows that.' Felix looked at her as she said this, and thought that he saw more in her countenance than he had ever read there before. Perhaps she would consent to run away with him; and, if so, being the only child, she would certainly, —almost certainly,—be forgiven. But if he were to run away with her and marry her, and then find that she were not forgiven, and that Melmotte allowed her to starve without a shilling of fortune, where would he be then? Looking at the matter in all its bearings, considering among other things the trouble and the expense of such a measure, he thought that he could not afford to run away with her.

After dinner he hardly spoke to her; indeed, the room itself,—the same big room in which they had been assembled before the feast,—seemed to be ill-adapted for conversation. Again nobody talked to anybody, and the minutes went very heavily till at last the carriages were there to take them all home. 'They arranged that you should sit next to her,' said Lady Carbury to her son, as they were in the carriage.

'Oh, I suppose that came naturally;—one young man and one young woman, you know.'

'Those things are always arranged, and they would not have done it unless they had thought that it would please Mr. Melmotte. Oh, Felix! if you can bring it about.'

'I shall if I can, mother; you needn't make a fuss about it.'

'No, I won't. You cannot wonder that I should be anxious. You behaved beautifully to her at dinner; I was so happy to see you together. Good night, Felix, and God bless you!' she said again, as they were parting for the night. 'I shall be the happiest and the proudest mother in England if this comes about.'

## Chapter XXI

### EVERYBODY GOES TO THEM

WHEN the Melmottes went from Caversham the house was very desolate. The task of entertaining these people was indeed over, and had the return to

London been fixed for a certain near day, there would
have been comfort at any rate among the ladies of the
family. But this was so far from being the case that the
Thursday and Friday passed without anything being
settled, and dreadful fears began to fill the minds of Lady
Pomona and Sophia Longestaffe. Georgiana was also
impatient, but she asserted boldly that treachery, such as
that which her mother and sister contemplated, was impossible. Their father, she thought, would not dare to
propose it. On each of these days,—three or four times
daily,—hints were given and questions were asked, but
without avail. Mr. Longestaffe would not consent to
have a day fixed till he had received some particular
letter, and would not even listen to the suggestion of a
day. 'I suppose we can go at any rate on Tuesday,'
Georgiana said on the Friday evening. 'I don't know
why you should suppose anything of the kind,' the father
replied. Poor Lady Pomona was urged by her daughters
to compel him to name a day; but Lady Pomona was less
audacious in urging the request than her younger child,
and at the same time less anxious for its completion. On
the Sunday morning before they went to church there
was a great discussion upstairs. The Bishop of Elmham
was going to preach at Caversham church, and the three
ladies were dressed in their best London bonnets. They
were in their mother's room, having just completed the
arrangements of their church-going toilet. It was supposed that the expected letter had arrived. Mr. Longestaffe had certainly received a despatch from his lawyer,
but had not as yet vouchsafed any reference to its contents. He had been more than ordinarily silent at breakfast, and,—so Sophia asserted,—more disagreeable than
ever. The question had now arisen especially in reference
to their bonnets. 'You might as well wear them,' said
Lady Pomona, 'for I am sure you will not be in London
again this year.'

'You don't mean it, mamma,' said Sophia.

'I do, my dear. He looked like it when he put those
papers back into his pocket. I know what his face means
so well.'

'It is not possible,' said Sophia. 'He promised, and he got us to have those horrid people because he promised.'

'Well, my dear, if your father says that we can't go back, I suppose we must take his word for it. It is he must decide of course. What he meant I suppose was, that he would take us back if he could.'

'Mamma!' shouted Georgiana. Was there to be treachery not only on the part of their natural adversary, who, adversary though he was, had bound himself to terms by a treaty, but treachery also in their own camp!

'My dear, what can we do?' said Lady Pomona.

'Do!' Georgiana was now going to speak out plainly. 'Make him understand that we are not going to be sat upon like that. I'll do something, if that's going to be the way of it. If he treats me like that I'll run off with the first man that will take me, let him be who it may.'

'Don't talk like that, Georgiana, unless you wish to kill me.'

'I'll break his heart for him. He does not care about us,—not the least,—whether we are happy or miserable; but he cares very much about the family name. I'll tell him that I'm not going to be a slave. I'll marry a London tradesman before I'll stay down here.' The younger Miss Longestaffe was lost in passion at the prospect before her.

'Oh, Georgey, don't say such horrid things as that,' pleaded her sister.

'It's all very well for you, Sophy. You've got George Whitstable.'

'I haven't got George Whitstable.'

'Yes, you have, and your fish is fried. Dolly does just what he pleases, and spends money as fast as he likes. Of course it makes no difference to you, mamma, where you are.'

'You are very unjust,' said Lady Pomona, wailing, 'and you say horrid things.'

'I ain't unjust at all. It doesn't matter to you. And Sophy is the same as settled. But I'm to be sacrificed! How am I to see anybody down here in this horrid hole? Papa promised and he must keep his word.'

Then there came to them a loud voice calling to them

from the hall. 'Are any of you coming to church, or are
you going to keep the carriage waiting all day?' Of
course they were all going to church. They always did
go to church when they were at Caversham; and would
more especially do so to-day, because of the bishop and
because of the bonnets. They trooped down into the hall
and into the carriage, Lady Pomona leading the way.
Georgiana stalked along, passing her father at the front
door without condescending to look at him. Not a word
was spoken on the way to church, or on the way home.
During the service Mr. Longestaffe stood up in the corner
of his pew, and repeated the responses in a loud voice.
In performing this duty he had been an example to the
parish all his life. The three ladies knelt on their hassocks
in the most becoming fashion, and sat during the sermon
without the slightest sign either of weariness or of attention. They did not collect the meaning of any one combination of sentences. It was nothing to them whether
the bishop had or had not a meaning. Endurance of that
kind was their strength. Had the bishop preached for
forty-five minutes instead of half an hour they would not
have complained. It was the same kind of endurance
which enabled Georgiana to go on from year to year
waiting for a husband of the proper sort. She could put
up with any amount of tedium if only the fair chance of
obtaining ultimate relief were not denied to her. But to
be kept at Caversham all the summer would be as bad as
hearing a bishop preach for ever! After the service they
came back to lunch, and that meal also was eaten in
silence. When it was over the head of the family put
himself into the dining-room arm-chair, evidently meaning to be left alone there. In that case he would have
meditated upon his troubles till he went to sleep, and
would have thus got through the afternoon with comfort.
But this was denied to him. The two daughters remained
steadfast while the things were being removed; and Lady
Pomona, though she made one attempt to leave the
room, returned when she found that her daughters would
not follow her. Georgiana had told her sister that she
meant to 'have it out' with her father, and Sophia had

of course remained in the room in obedience to her
sister's behest. When the last tray had been taken out,
Georgiana began. 'Papa, don't you think you could
settle now when we are to go back to town? Of course
we want to know about engagements and all that. There
is Lady Monogram's party on Wednesday. We promised
to be there ever so long ago.'

'You had better write to Lady Monogram and say you
can't keep your engagement.'

'But why not, papa? We could go up on Wednesday
morning.'

'You can't do anything of the kind.'

'But, my dear, we should all like to have a day fixed,'
said Lady Pomona. Then there was a pause. Even
Georgiana, in her present state of mind, would have
accepted some distant, even some undefined time, as a
compromise.

'Then you can't have a day fixed,' said Mr. Longestaffe.

'How long do you suppose that we shall be kept here?'
said Sophia, in a low constrained voice.

'I do not know what you mean by being kept here.
This is your home, and this is where you may make up
your minds to live.'

'But we are to go back?' demanded Sophia. Georgiana
stood by in silence, listening, resolving, and biding her
time.

'You'll not return to London this season,' said Mr.
Longestaffe, turning himself abruptly to a newspaper
which he held in his hands.

'Do you mean that that is settled?' said Lady Pomona.

'I mean to say that that is settled,' said Mr. Longestaffe.

Was there ever treachery like this! The indignation in
Georgiana's mind approached almost to virtue as she
thought of her father's falseness. She would not have left
town at all but for that promise. She would not have
contaminated herself with the Melmottes but for that
promise. And now she was told that the promise was to
be absolutely broken, when it was no longer possible that
she could get back to London,—even to the house of the

hated Primeros,—without absolutely running away from her father's residence! 'Then, papa,' she said, with affected calmness, 'you have simply and with premeditation broken your word to us.'

'How dare you speak to me in that way, you wicked child!'

'I am not a child, papa, as you know very well. I am my own mistress,——by law.'

'Then go and be your own mistress. You dare to tell me, your father, that I have premeditated a falsehood! If you tell me that again, you shall eat your meals in your own room or not eat them in this house.'

'Did you not promise that we should go back if we would come down and entertain these people?'

'I will not argue with a child, insolent and disobedient as you are. If I have anything to say about it, I will say it to your mother. It should be enough for you that I, your father, tell you that you have to live here. Now go away, and if you choose to be sullen, go and be sullen where I shan't see you.' Georgiana looked round on her mother and sister and then marched majestically out of the room. She still meditated revenge, but she was partly cowed, and did not dare in her father's presence to go on with her reproaches. She stalked off into the room in which they generally lived, and there she stood panting with anger, breathing indignation through her nostrils.

'And you mean to put up with it, mamma?' she said.

'What can we do, my dear?'

'I will do something. I'm not going to be cheated and swindled and have my life thrown away into the bargain. I have always behaved well to him. I have never run up bills without saying anything about them.' This was a cut at her elder sister, who had once got into some little trouble of that kind. 'I have never got myself talked about with anybody. If there is anything to be done I always do it. I have written his letters for him till I have been sick, and when you were ill I never asked him to stay out with us after two or half-past two at the latest. And now he tells me that I am to eat my meals up in **my** bedroom because I remind him that he distinctly promised to take us back to London! Did he not promise, mamma?'

'I understood so, my dear.'

'You know he promised, mamma. If I do anything now he must bear the blame of it. I am not going to keep myself straight for the sake of the family, and then be treated in that way.'

'You do that for your own sake, I suppose,' said her sister.

'It is more than you've been able to do for anybody's sake,' said Georgiana, alluding to a very old affair,—to an ancient flirtation, in the course of which the elder daughter had made a foolish and a futile attempt to run away with an officer of dragoons whose private fortune was very moderate. Ten years had passed since that, and the affair was never alluded to except in moments of great bitterness.

'I've kept myself as straight as you have,' said Sophia. 'It's easy enough to be straight, when a person never cares for anybody, and nobody cares for a person.'

'My dears, if you quarrel what am I to do?' said their mother.

'It is I that have to suffer,' continued Georgiana. 'Does he expect me to find anybody here that I could take? Poor George Whitstable is not much; but there is nobody else at all.'

'You may have him if you like,' said Sophia, with a chuck of her head.

'Thank you, my dear, but I shouldn't like it at all. I haven't come to that quite yet.'

'You were talking of running away with somebody.'

'I shan't run away with George Whitstable; you may be sure of that. I'll tell you what I shall do,—I will write papa a letter. I suppose he'll condescend to read it. If he won't take me up to town himself, he must send me up to the Primeros. What makes me most angry in the whole thing is that we should have condescended to be civil to the Melmottes down in the country. In London one does those things, but to have them here was terrible!'

During that entire afternoon nothing more was said.

Not a word passed between them on any subject beyond those required by the necessities of life. Georgiana had been as hard to her sister as to her father, and Sophia in her quiet way resented the affront. She was now almost reconciled to the sojourn in the country, because it inflicted a fitting punishment on Georgiana, and the presence of Mr. Whitstable at a distance of not more than ten miles did of course make a difference to herself. Lady Pomona complained of a headache, which was always an excuse with her for not speaking;—and Mr. Longestaffe went to sleep. Georgiana during the whole afternoon remained apart, and on the next morning the head of the family found the following letter on his dressing-table;—

'My dear Papa,—

'I don't think you ought to be surprised because we feel that our going up to town is so very important to us. If we are not to be in London at this time of the year we can never see anybody, and of course you know what that must mean for me. If this goes on about Sophia, it does not signify for her, and, though mamma likes London, it is not of real importance. But it is very, very hard upon me. It isn't for pleasure that I want to go up. There isn't so very much pleasure in it. But if I'm to be buried down here at Caversham, I might just as well be dead at once. If you choose to give up both houses for a year, or for two years, and take us all abroad, I should not grumble in the least. There are very nice people to be met abroad, and perhaps things go easier that way than in town. And there would be nothing for horses, and we could dress very cheap and wear our old things. I'm sure I don't want to run up bills. But if you would only think what Caversham must be to me, without any one worth thinking about within twenty miles, you would hardly ask me to stay here.

'You certainly did say that if we would come down here with those Melmottes we should be taken back to town, and you cannot be surprised that we should be disappointed when we are told that we are to be kept

here after that. It makes me feel that life is so hard that
I can't bear it. I see other girls having such chances
when I have none, that sometimes I think I don't know
what will happen to me.' (This was the nearest approach
which she dared to make in writing to that threat which
she had uttered to her mother of running away with
somebody.) 'I suppose that now it is useless for me to
ask you to take us all back this summer,—though it was
promised; but I hope you'll give me money to go up to
the Primeros. It would only be me and my maid. Julia
Primero asked me to stay with them when you first talked
of not going up, and I should not in the least object to
reminding her, only it should be done at once. Their
house in Queen's Gate is very large, and I know they've
a room. They all ride, and I should want a horse; but
there would be nothing else, as they have plenty of
carriages, and the groom who rides with Julia would do
for both of us. Pray answer this at once, papa.

'Your affectionate daughter,<br>
'GEORGIANA LONGESTAFFE.'

Mr. Longestaffe did condescend to read the letter. He,
though he had rebuked his mutinous daughter with stern
severity, was also to some extent afraid of her. At a
sudden burst he could stand upon his authority, and
assume his position with parental dignity; but not the
less did he dread the wearing toil of continued domestic
strife. He thought that upon the whole his daughter
liked a row in the house. If not, there surely would not
be so many rows. He himself thoroughly hated them.
He had not any very lively interest in life. He did not
read much; he did not talk much; he was not specially
fond of eating and drinking; he did not gamble, and he
did not care for the farm. To stand about the door and
hall and public rooms of the clubs to which he belonged
and hear other men talk politics or scandal, was what he
liked better than anything else in the world. But he was
quite willing to give this up for the good of his family.
He would be contented to drag through long listless days
at Caversham, and endeavour to nurse his property, if

only his daughter would allow it. By assuming a certain pomp in his living, which had been altogether unserviceable to himself and family, by besmearing his footmen's heads, and bewigging his coachmen, by aping, though never achieving, the grand ways of grander men than himself, he had run himself into debt. His own ambition had been a peerage, and he had thought that this was the way to get it. A separate property had come to his son from his wife's mother,—some £2,000 or £3,000 a year, magnified by the world into double its amount,—and the knowledge of this had for a time reconciled him to increasing the burdens on the family estates. He had been sure that Adolphus, when of age, would have consented to sell the Sussex property in order that the Suffolk property might be relieved. But Dolly was now in debt himself, and though in other respects the most careless of men, was always on his guard in any dealings with his father. He would not consent to the sale of the Suffolk property unless half of the proceeds were to be at once handed to himself. The father could not bring himself to consent to this, but, while refusing it, found the troubles of the world very hard upon him. Melmotte had done something for him,—but in doing this Melmotte was very hard and tyrannical. Melmotte, when at Caversham, had looked into his affairs, and had told him very plainly that with such an establishment in the country he was not entitled to keep a house in town. Mr. Longestaffe had then said something about his daughters,—something especially about Georgiana,—and Mr. Melmotte had made a suggestion.

Mr. Longestaffe, when he read his daughter's appeal, did feel for her, in spite of his anger. But if there was one man he hated more than another, it was his neighbour Mr. Primero; and if one woman, it was Mrs. Primero. Primero, whom Mr. Longestaffe regarded as quite an upstart, and anything but a gentleman, owed no man anything. He paid his tradesmen punctually, and never met the squire of Caversham without seeming to make a parade of his virtue in that direction. He had spent many thousands for his party in county elections and borough elections, and was now himself member for a metropolitan district. He was a radical, of course, or, according to Mr. Longestaffe's view of his political conduct, acted and voted on the radical side because there was nothing to be got by voting and acting on the other. And now there had come into Suffolk a rumour that Mr. Primero was to have a peerage. To others the rumour was incredible, but Mr. Longestaffe believed it, and to Mr. Longestaffe that belief was an agony. A Baron Bundlesham just at his door, and such a Baron Bundlesham, would be more than Mr. Longestaffe could endure. It was quite impossible that his daughter should be entertained in London by the Primeros.

But another suggestion had been made. Georgiana's letter had been laid on her father's table on the Monday morning. On the following morning, when there could have been no intercourse with London by letter, Lady Pomona called her younger daughter to her, and handed her a note to read. 'Your papa has this moment given it me. Of course you must judge for yourself.' This was the note;—

'MY DEAR MR. LONGESTAFFE,

'As you seem determined not to return to London this season, perhaps one of your young ladies would like to come to us. Mrs. Melmotte would be delighted to have Miss Georgiana for June and July. If so, she need only give Mrs. Melmotte a day's notice.

'Yours truly,
'AUGUSTUS MELMOTTE.'

Georgiana, as soon as her eye had glanced down the one side of note paper on which this invitation was written, looked up for the date. It was without a date, and had, she felt sure, been left in her father's hands to be used as he might think fit. She breathed very hard. Both her father and mother had heard her speak of these Melmottes, and knew what she thought of them. There was an insolence in the very suggestion. But at the first moment she said nothing of that. 'Why shouldn't I go to the Primeros?' she asked.

'Your father will not hear of it. He dislikes them especially.'

'And I dislike the Melmottes. I dislike the Primeros of course, but they are not so bad as the Melmottes. That would be dreadful.'

'You must judge for yourself, Georgiana.'

'It is that,—or staying here?'

'I think so, my dear.'

'If papa chooses I don't know why I am to mind. It will be awfully disagreeable,—absolutely disgusting!'

'She seemed to be very quiet.'

'Pooh, mamma! Quiet! She was quiet here because she was afraid of us. She isn't yet used to be with people like us. She'll get over that if I'm in the house with her. And then she is, oh! so frightfully vulgar! She must have been the very sweeping of the gutters. Did you not see it, mamma? She could not even open her mouth, she was so ashamed of herself. I shouldn't wonder if they turned out to be something quite horrid. They make me shudder. Was there ever anything so dreadful to look at as he is?'

'Everybody goes to them,' said Lady Pomona. 'The Duchess of Stevenage has been there over and over again, and so has Lady Auld Reekie. Everybody goes to their house.'

'But everybody doesn't go and live with them. Oh, mamma,—to have to sit down to breakfast every day for ten weeks with that man and that woman!'

'Perhaps they'll let you have your breakfast upstairs.'

'But to have to go out with them;—walking into the room after her! Only think of it!'

'But you are so anxious to be in London, my dear.'

'Of course I am anxious. What other chance have I, mamma? And, oh dear, I am so tired of it! Pleasure, indeed! Papa talks of pleasure. If papa had to work half as hard as I do, I wonder what he'd think of it. I suppose I must do it. I know it will make me so ill that I shall almost die under it. Horrid, horrid people! And papa to propose it, who has always been so proud of everything, —who used to think so much of being with the right set.'

'Things are changed, Georgiana,' said the anxious mother.

'Indeed they are when papa wants me to go and stay with people like that. Why, mamma, the apothecary in Bungay is a fine gentleman compared with Mr. Melmotte, and his wife is a fine lady compared with Madame Melmotte. But I'll go. If papa chooses me to be seen with such people it is not my fault. There will be no disgracing one's self after that. I don't believe in the least that any decent man would propose to a girl in such a house, and you and papa must not be surprised if I take some horrid creature from the Stock Exchange. Papa has altered his ideas; and so, I suppose, I had better alter mine.'

Georgiana did not speak to her father that night, but Lady Pomona informed Mr. Longestaffe that Mr. Melmotte's invitation was to be accepted. She herself would write a line to Madame Melmotte, and Georgiana would go up on the Friday following. 'I hope she'll like it,' said Mr. Longestaffe. The poor man had no intention of irony. It was not in his nature to be severe after that fashion. But to poor Lady Pomona the words sounded very cruel. How could any one like to live in a house with Mr. and Madame Melmotte!

On the Friday morning there was a little conversation between the two sisters, just before Georgiana's departure to the railway station, which was almost touching. She had endeavoured to hold up her head as usual, but had failed. The thing that she was going to do cowed her even in the presence of her sister. 'Sophy, I do so envy you staying here.'

'But it was you who were so determined to be in London.'

'Yes; I was determined, and am determined. I've got to get myself settled somehow, and that can't be done down here. But you are not going to disgrace yourself.'

'There's no disgrace in it, Georgey.'

'Yes, there is. I believe the man to be a swindler and a thief; and I believe her to be anything low that you can think of. As to their pretensions to be gentlefolk, it is monstrous. The footmen and housemaids would be much better.'

'Then don't go, Georgey.'

'I must go. It's the only chance that is left. If I were to remain down here everybody would say that I was on the shelf. You are going to marry Whitstable, and you'll do very well. It isn't a big place, but there's no debt on it, and Whitstable himself isn't a bad sort of fellow.'

'Is he, now?'

'Of course he hasn't much to say for himself, for he's always at home. But he is a gentleman.'

'That he certainly is.'

'As for me I shall give over caring about gentlemen now. The first man that comes to me with four or five thousand a year, I'll take him, though he'd come out of Newgate or Bedlam. And I shall always say it has been papa's doing.'

And so Georgiana Longestaffe went up to London and stayed with the Melmottes.

## Chapter XXII

### LORD NIDDERDALE'S MORALITY

IT was very generally said in the city about this time that the Great South Central Pacific and Mexican Railway was the very best thing out. It was known that Mr. Melmotte had gone into it with heart and hand. There were many who declared,—with gross injustice to the Great Fisker,—that the railway was Melmotte's own child, that he had invented it, advertised it, agitated it, and floated it; but it was not the less popular on that account. A railway from Salt Lake City to Mexico no doubt had much of the flavour of a castle in Spain. Our far-western American brethren are supposed to be imaginative. Mexico has not a reputation among us for commercial security, or that stability which produces its four, five, or six per cent. with the regularity of clock-work. But there was the Panama railway, a small affair which had paid twenty-five per cent.; and there was the great line across the continent to San Francisco,* in which enormous fortunes had been made. It came to be believed that men with their eyes open might do as well with the Great South Central as had ever been done before with other speculations, and this belief was no doubt founded on Mr. Melmotte's partiality for the enterprise. Mr. Fisker had 'struck 'ile' when he induced his partner, Montague, to give him a note to the great man.

Paul Montague himself, who cannot be said to have been a man having his eyes open, in the city sense of the word, could not learn how the thing was progressing. At the regular meetings of the Board, which never sat for above half an hour, two or three papers were read by Miles Grendall. Melmotte himself would speak a few slow words, intended to be cheery, and always indicative of triumph, and then everybody would agree to everything, somebody would sign something, and the 'Board' for that day would be over. To Paul Montague this was very unsatisfactory. More than once or twice he endeavoured to stay the proceedings, not as disapproving, but 'simply as desirous of being made to understand;' but the silent scorn of his chairman put him out of countenance, and the opposition of his colleagues was a barrier which he was not strong enough to overcome. Lord Alfred Grendall would declare that he 'did not think all that was at all necessary.' Lord Nidderdale, with whom Montague had now become intimate at the Beargarden, would nudge him in the ribs and bid him hold his tongue. Mr. Cohenlupe would make a little speech in fluent but broken English, assuring the Committee that everything was being done after the approved city fashion. Sir Felix, after the first two meetings, was never there. And thus Paul Montague, with a sorely burdened conscience, was carried along as one of the Directors of the Great South Central Pacific and Mexican Railway Company.

I do not know whether the burden was made lighter to him or heavier, by the fact that the immediate pecuniary result was certainly very comfortable. The Company had not yet been in existence quite six weeks,—or at any rate Melmotte had not been connected with it above that time,—and it had already been suggested to him twice that he should sell fifty shares at £112 10s. He did not even yet know how many shares he possessed, but on both occasions he consented to the proposal, and on the following day received a cheque for £625,—that sum representing the profit over and above the original nominal price of £100 a share. The suggestion was made to him by Miles Grendall, and when he asked some questions as to the manner in which the shares had been allocated, he was told that all that would be arranged in accordance with the capital invested and must depend on the final disposition of the Californian property. 'But from what we see, old fellow,' said Miles, 'I don't think you have anything to fear. You seem to be about the best in of them all. Melmotte wouldn't advise you to sell out gradually, if he didn't look upon the thing as a certain income as far as you are concerned.'

Paul Montague understood nothing of all this, and felt that he was standing on ground which might be blown from under his feet at any moment. The uncertainty, and what he feared might be the dishonesty, of the whole thing, made him often very miserable. In those wretched moments his conscience was asserting itself. But again there were times in which he also was almost triumphant, and in which he felt the delight of his wealth. Though he was snubbed at the Board when he wanted explanations, he received very great attention outside the board-room from those connected with the enterprise. Melmotte had asked him to dine two or three times. Mr. Cohenlupe had begged him to go down to his little place at Rickmansworth,—an entreaty with which Montague had not as yet complied. Lord Alfred was always gracious to him, and Nidderdale and Carbury were evidently anxious to make him one of their set at the club. Many other houses became open to him from the same source. Though Melmotte was supposed to be the inventor of the railway, it was known that Fisker, Montague, and Montague were largely concerned in it, and it was known also that Paul Montague was one of the Montagues named in that

firm. People, both in the City and the West End, seemed
to think that he knew all about it, and treated him as
though some of the manna falling from that heaven were
at his disposition. There were results from this which
were not unpleasing to the young man. He only partially
resisted the temptation; and though determined at times
to probe the affair to the bottom, was so determined only
at times. The money was very pleasant to him. The
period would now soon arrive before which he understood himself to be pledged not to make a distinct offer to
Henrietta Carbury; and when that period should have
been passed, it would be delightful to him to know that he
was possessed of property sufficient to enable him to give
a wife a comfortable home. In all his aspirations, and in
all his fears, he was true to Hetta Carbury, and made
her the centre of his hopes. Nevertheless, had Hetta
known everything, it may be feared that she would have
at any rate endeavoured to dismiss him from her heart.

There was considerable uneasiness in the bosoms of
others of the Directors, and a disposition to complain
against the Grand Director, arising from a grievance
altogether different from that which afflicted Montague.
Neither had Sir Felix Carbury nor Lord Nidderdale been
invited to sell shares, and consequently neither of them
had received any remuneration for the use of their names.
They knew well that Montague had sold shares. He was
quite open on the subject, and had told Felix, whom he
hoped some day to regard as his brother-in-law, exactly
what shares he had sold, and for how much;—and the
two men had endeavoured to make the matter intelligible
between themselves. The original price of the shares
being £100 each, and £12 10s. a share having been paid
to Montague as the premium, it was to be supposed that
the original capital was re-invested in other shares. But
each owned to the other that the matter was very complicated to him, and Montague could only write to
Hamilton K. Fisker at San Francisco asking for explanation. As yet he had received no answer. But it was not
the wealth flowing into Montague's hands which embittered Nidderdale and Carbury. They understood that

he had really brought money into the concern, and was therefore entitled to take money out of it. Nor did it occur to them to grudge Melmotte his more noble pickings, for they knew how great a man was Melmotte. Of Cohenlupe's doings they heard nothing; but he was a regular city man, and had probably supplied funds. Cohenlupe was too deep for their inquiry. But they knew that Lord Alfred had sold shares, and had received the profit; and they knew also how utterly impossible it was that Lord Alfred should have produced capital. If Lord Alfred Grendall was entitled to plunder, why were not they? And if their day for plunder had not yet come, why Lord Alfred's? And if there was so much cause to fear Lord Alfred that it was necessary to throw him a bone, why should not they also make themselves feared? Lord Alfred passed all his time with Melmotte,—had, as these young men said, become Melmotte's head valet,— and therefore had to be paid. But that reason did not satisfy the young men.

'You haven't sold any shares;—have you?' This question Sir Felix asked Lord Nidderdale at the club. Nidderdale was constant in his attendance at the Board, and Felix was not a little afraid that he might be jockied also by him.

'Not a share.'

'Nor got any profits?'

'Not a shilling of any kind. As far as money is concerned my only transaction has been my part of the expense of Fisker's dinner.'

'What do you get then, by going into the city?' asked Sir Felix.

'I'm blessed if I know what I get. I suppose something will turn up some day.'

'In the meantime, you know, there are our names. And Grendall is making a fortune out of it.'

'Poor old duffer,' said his lordship. 'If he's doing so well, I think Miles ought to be made to pay up something of what he owes. I think we ought to tell him that we shall expect him to have the money ready when that bill of Vossner's comes round.'

'Yes, by George; let's tell him that. Will you do it?'

'Not that it will be the least good. It would be quite unnatural to him to pay anything.'

'Fellows used to pay their gambling debts,' said Sir Felix, who was still in funds, and who still held a considerable assortment of I.O.U.'s.

'They don't now,—unless they like it. How did a fellow manage before, if he hadn't got it?'

'He went smash,' said Sir Felix, 'and disappeared and was never heard of any more. It was just the same as if he'd been found cheating. I believe a fellow might cheat now and nobody'd say anything!'

'I shouldn't,' said Lord Nidderdale. 'What's the use of being beastly ill-natured? I'm not very good at saying my prayers, but I do think there's something in that bit about forgiving people. Of course cheating isn't very nice: and it isn't very nice for a fellow to play when he knows he can't pay; but I don't know that it's worse than getting drunk like Dolly Longestaffe, or quarrelling with everybody as Glasslough does,—or trying to marry some poor devil of a girl merely because she's got money. I believe in living in glass houses, but I don't believe in throwing stones. Do you ever read the Bible, Carbury?'

'Read the Bible! Well;—yes;—no;—that is, I suppose, I used to do.'

'I often think I shouldn't have been the first to pick up a stone and pitch it at that woman. Live and let live;— that's my motto.'

'But you agree that we ought to do something about these shares?' said Sir Felix, thinking that this doctrine of forgiveness might be carried too far.

'Oh, certainly. I'll let old Grendall live with all my heart; but then he ought to let me live too. Only, who's to bell the cat?'

'What cat?'

'It's no good our going to old Grendall,' said Lord Nidderdale, who had some understanding in the matter, 'nor yet to young Grendall. The one would only grunt and say nothing, and the other would tell every lie that

came into his head. The cat in this matter I take to be
our great master, Augustus Melmotte.'

This little meeting occurred on the day after Felix
Carbury's return from Suffolk, and at a time at which,
as we know, it was the great duty of his life to get the
consent of old Melmotte to his marriage with Marie
Melmotte. In doing that he would have to put one bell
on the cat, and he thought that for the present that was
sufficient. In his heart of hearts he was afraid of Melmotte. But then, as he knew very well, Nidderdale was
intent on the same object. Nidderdale, he thought, was
a very queer fellow. That talking about the Bible, and
the forgiving of trespasses, was very queer; and that
allusion to the marrying of heiresses very queer indeed.
He knew that Nidderdale wanted to marry the heiress,
and Nidderdale must also know that he wanted to marry
her. And yet Nidderdale was indelicate enough to talk
about it! And now the man asked who should bell the
cat! 'You go there oftener than I do, and perhaps you
could do it best,' said Sir Felix.

'Go where?'

'To the Board.'

'But you're always at his house. He'd be civil to me,
perhaps, because I'm a lord: but then, for the same
reason, he'd think I was the bigger fool of the two.'

'I don't see that at all,' said Sir Felix.

'I ain't afraid of him, if you mean that,' continued
Lord Nidderdale. 'He's a wretched old reprobate, and
I don't doubt but he'd skin you and me if he could make
money of our carcases. But as he can't skin me, I'll have
a shy at him. On the whole I think he rather likes me,
because I've always been on the square with him. If it
depended on him, you know, I should have the girl
to-morrow.'

'Would you?' Sir Felix did not at all mean to doubt
his friend's assertion, but felt it hard to answer so very
strange a statement.

'But then she don't want me, and I ain't quite sure
that I want her. Where the devil would a fellow find
himself if the money wasn't all there?' Lord Nidderdale

then sauntered away, leaving the baronet in a deep study of thought as to such a condition of things as that which his lordship had suggested. Where the—mischief would he, Sir Felix Carbury, be, if he were to marry the girl, and then to find that the money was not all there?

On the following Friday, which was the Board day, Nidderdale went to the great man's offices in Abchurch Lane, and so contrived that he walked with the great man to the Board meeting. Melmotte was always very gracious in his manner to Lord Nidderdale, but had never, up to this moment, had any speech with his proposed son-in-law about business. 'I wanted just to ask you something,' said the lord, hanging on the chairman's arm.

'Anything you please, my lord.'

'Don't you think that Carbury and I ought to have some shares to sell?'

'No, I don't,—if you ask me.'

'Oh;—I didn't know. But why shouldn't we as well as the others?'

'Have you and Sir Felix put any money into it?'

'Well, if you come to that, I don't suppose we have. How much has Lord Alfred put into it?'

'*I* have taken shares for Lord Alfred,' said Melmotte, putting very heavy emphasis on the personal pronoun. 'If it suits me to advance money to Lord Alfred Grendall, I suppose I may do so without asking your lordship's consent, or that of Sir Felix Carbury.'

'Oh, certainly. I don't want to make inquiry as' to what you do with your money.'

'I'm sure you don't, and, therefore, we won't say anything more about it. You wait awhile, Lord Nidderdale, and you'll find it will come all right. If you've got a few thousand pounds loose, and will put them into the concern, why, of course you can sell; and, if the shares are up, can sell at a profit. It's presumed just at present that, at some early day, you'll qualify for your directorship by doing so, and till that is done, the shares are allocated to you, but cannot be transferred to you.'

'That's it, is it?' said Lord Nidderdale, pretending to understand all about it.

'If things go on as we hope they will between you and
Marie, you can have pretty nearly any number of shares
that you please;—that is, if your father consents to a
proper settlement.'

'I hope it'll all go smooth, I'm sure,' said Nidderdale.
'Thank you; I'm ever so much obliged to you, and I'll
explain it all to Carbury.'

## Chapter XXIII

### 'YES;—I'M A BARONET'

HOW eager Lady Carbury was that her son should
at once go in form to Marie's father and make his
proposition may be easily understood. 'My dear Felix,'
she said, standing over his bedside a little before noon,
'pray don't put it off; you don't know how many slips
there may be between the cup and the lip.'

'It's everything to get him in a good humour,' pleaded
Sir Felix.

'But the young lady will feel that she is ill-used.'

'There's no fear of that; she's all right. What am I to
say to him about money? That's the question.'

'I shouldn't think of dictating anything, Felix.'

'Nidderdale, when he was on before, stipulated for a
certain sum down; or his father did for him. So much
cash was to be paid over before the ceremony, and it
only went off because Nidderdale wanted the money to
do what he liked with.'

'You wouldn't mind having it settled?'

'No;—I'd consent to that on condition that the money
was paid down, and the income insured to me,—say
£7,000 or £8,000 a year. I wouldn't do it for less,
mother; it wouldn't be worth while.'

'But you have nothing left of your own.'

'I've got a throat that I can cut, and brains that I can
blow out,' said the son, using an argument which he conceived might be efficacious with his mother; though, had
she known him, she might have been sure that no man

lived less likely to cut his own throat or blow out his own brains.

'Oh, Felix! how brutal it is to speak to me in that way.'

'It may be brutal; but you know, mother, business is business. You want me to marry this girl because of her money.'

'You want to marry her yourself.'

'I'm quite a philosopher about it. I want her money; and when one wants money, one should make up one's mind how much or how little one means to take,—and whether one is sure to get it.'

'I don't think there can be any doubt.'

'If I were to marry her, and if the money wasn't there, it would be very like cutting my throat then, mother. If a man plays and loses, he can play again and perhaps win; but when a fellow goes in for an heiress, and gets the wife without the money, he feels a little hampered you know.'

'Of course he'd pay the money first.'

'It's very well to say that. Of course he ought; but it would be rather awkward to refuse to go into church after everything had been arranged because the money hadn't been paid over. He's so clever, that he'd contrive that a man shouldn't know whether the money had been paid or not. You can't carry £10,000 a year about in your pocket, you know. If you'll go, mother, perhaps I might think of getting up.'

Lady Carbury saw the danger, and turned over the affair on every side in her own mind. But she could also see the house in Grosvenor Square, the expenditure without limit, the congregating duchesses, the general acceptation of the people, and the mercantile celebrity of the man. And she could weigh against that the absolute pennilessness of her baronet-son. As he was, his condition was hopeless. Such a one must surely run some risk. The embarrassments of such a man as Lord Nidderdale were only temporary. There were the family estates, and the marquisate, and a golden future for him; but there was nothing coming to Felix in the future.

All the goods he would ever have of his own, he had now; —position, a title, and a handsome face. Surely he could afford to risk something! Even the ruins and wreck of such wealth as that displayed in Grosvenor Square would be better than the baronet's present condition. And then, though it was possible that old Melmotte should be ruined some day, there could be no doubt as to his present means; and would it not be probable that he would make hay while the sun shone by securing his daughter's position? She visited her son again on the next morning, which was Sunday, and again tried to persuade him to the marriage. 'I think you should be content to run a little risk,' she said.

Sir Felix had been unlucky at cards on Saturday night, and had taken, perhaps, a little too much wine. He was at any rate sulky, and in a humour to resent interference. 'I wish you'd leave me alone,' he said, 'to manage my own business.'

'Is it not my business too?'

'No; you haven't got to marry her, and to put up with these people. I shall make up my mind what to do myself, and I don't want anybody to meddle with me.'

'You ungrateful boy!'

'I understand all about that. Of course I'm ungrateful when I don't do everything just as you wish it. You don't do any good. You only set me against it all.'

'How do you expect to live, then? Are you always to be a burden on me and your sister? I wonder that you've no shame. Your cousin Roger is right. I will quit London altogether, and leave you to your own wretchedness.'

'That's what Roger says; is it? I always thought Roger was a fellow of that sort.'

'He is the best friend I have.' What would Roger have thought had he heard this assertion from Lady Carbury?

'He's an ill-tempered, close-fisted, interfering cad, and if he meddles with my affairs again, I shall tell him what I think of him. Upon my word, mother, these little disputes up in my bedroom ain't very pleasant. Of course

it's your house; but if you do allow me a room, I think
you might let me have it to myself.' It was impossible for
Lady Carbury, in her present mood, and in his present
mood, to explain to him that in no other way and at no
other time could she ever find him. If she waited till he
came down to breakfast, he escaped from her in five
minutes, and then he returned no more till some unholy
hour in the morning. She was as good a pelican as ever
allowed the blood to be torn from her own breast to
satisfy the greed of her young, but she felt that she should
have something back for her blood,—some return for her
sacrifices. This chick would take all as long as there was
a drop left, and then resent the fondling of the mother-
bird as interference. Again and again there came upon
her moments in which she thought that Roger Carbury
was right. And yet she knew that when the time came
she would not be able to be severe. She almost hated
herself for the weakness of her own love,—but she
acknowledged it. If he should fall utterly, she must fall
with him. In spite of his cruelty, his callous hardness,
his insolence to herself, his wickedness and ruinous indifference to the future, she must cling to him to the
last. All that she had done, and all that she had borne,—
all that she was doing and bearing,—was it not for his
sake?

Sir Felix had been in Grosvenor Square since his
return from Carbury, and had seen Madame Melmotte
and Marie; but he had seen them together, and not a
word had been said about the engagement. He could not
make much use of the elder woman. She was as gracious
as was usual with her; but then she was never very
gracious. She had told him that Miss Longestaffe was
coming to her, which was a great bore, as the young lady
was 'fatigante.' Upon this Marie had declared that she
intended to like the young lady very much. 'Pooh!'
said Madame Melmotte. 'You never like no person at
all.' At this Marie had looked over to her lover and
smiled. 'Ah, yes; that is all very well,—while it lasts;
but you care for no friend.' From which Felix had
judged that Madame Melmotte at any rate knew of his

offer, and did not absolutely disapprove of it. On the Saturday he had received a note at his club from Marie. 'Come on Sunday at half-past two. You will find papa after lunch.' This was in his possession when his mother visited him in his bedroom, and he had determined to obey the behest. But he would not tell her of his intention, because he had drunk too much wine, and was sulky.

At about three on Sunday he knocked at the door in Grosvenor Square and asked for the ladies. Up to the moment of his knocking,—even after he had knocked, and when the big porter was opening the door,—he intended to ask for Mr. Melmotte; but at the last his courage failed him, and he was shown up into the drawing-room. There he found Madame Melmotte, Marie, Georgiana Longestaffe, and—Lord Nidderdale. Marie looked anxiously into his face, thinking that he had already been with her father. He slid into a chair close to Madame Melmotte, and endeavoured to seem at his ease. Lord Nidderdale continued his flirtation with Miss Longestaffe,—a flirtation which she carried on in a half whisper, wholly indifferent to her hostess or the young lady of the house. 'We know what brings you here,' she said.

'I came on purpose to see you.'

'I'm sure, Lord Nidderdale, you didn't expect to find me here.'

'Lord bless you, I knew all about it, and came on purpose. It's a great institution; isn't it?'

'It's an institution you mean to belong to,—permanently.'

'No, indeed. I did have thoughts about it as fellows do when they talk of going into the army or to the bar; but I couldn't pass. That fellow there is the happy man. I shall go on coming here, because you're here. I don't think you'll like it a bit, you know.'

'I don't suppose I shall, Lord Nidderdale.'

After awhile Marie contrived to be alone with her lover near one of the windows for a few seconds. 'Papa is downstairs in the book-room,' she said. 'Lord Alfred was told when he came that he was out.' It was evident

to Sir Felix that everything was prepared for him. 'You
go down,' she continued, 'and ask the man to show you
into the book-room.'

'Shall I come up again?'

'No; but leave a note for me here under cover to
Madame Didon.' Now Sir Felix was sufficiently at home
in the house to know that Madame Didon was Madame
Melmotte's own woman, commonly called Didon by the
ladies of the family. 'Or send it by post,—under cover to
her. That will be better. Go at once, now.' It certainly
did seem to Sir Felix that the very nature of the girl was
altered. But he went, just shaking hands with Madame
Melmotte, and bowing to Miss Longestaffe.

In a few moments he found himself with Mr. Melmotte
in the chamber which had been dignified with the name
of the book-room. The great financier was accustomed
to spend his Sunday afternoons here, generally with the
company of Lord Alfred Grendall. It may be supposed
that he was meditating on millions, and arranging the
prices of money and funds for the New York, Paris, and
London Exchanges. But on this occasion he was waked
from slumber, which he seemed to have been enjoying
with a cigar in his mouth. 'How do you do, Sir Felix?'
he said. 'I suppose you want the ladies.'

'I've just been in the drawing-room, but I thought
I'd look in on you as I came down.' It immediately
occurred to Melmotte that the baronet had come about
his share of the plunder out of the railway, and he at
once resolved to be stern in his manner, and perhaps
rude also. He believed that he should thrive best by
resenting any interference with him in his capacity as
financier. He thought that he had risen high enough to
venture on such conduct, and experience had told him
that men who were themselves only half-plucked, might
easily be cowed by a savage assumption of superiority.
And he, too, had generally the advantage of understanding the game, while those with whom he was
concerned did not, at any rate, more than half understand it. He could thus trade either on the timidity or
on the ignorance of his colleagues. When neither of

these sufficed to give him undisputed mastery, then he cultivated the cupidity of his friends. He liked young associates because they were more timid and less greedy than their elders. Lord Nidderdale's suggestions had soon been put at rest, and Mr. Melmotte anticipated no greater difficulty with Sir Felix. Lord Alfred he had been obliged to buy.

'I'm very glad to see you, and all that,' said Melmotte, assuming a certain exaltation of the eyebrows, which they who had many dealings with him often found to be very disagreeable; 'but this is hardly a day for business, Sir Felix, nor,—yet a place for business.'

Sir Felix wished himself at the Beargarden. He certainly had come about business,—business of a particular sort; but Marie had told him that of all days Sunday would be the best, and had also told him that her father was more likely to be in a good humour on Sunday than on any other day. Sir Felix felt that he had not been received with good humour. 'I didn't mean to intrude, Mr. Melmotte,' he said.

'I dare say not. I only thought I'd tell you. You might have been going to speak about that railway.'

'Oh dear no.'

'Your mother was saying to me down in the country that she hoped you attended to the business. I told her that there was nothing to attend to.'

'My mother doesn't understand anything at all about it,' said Sir Felix.

'Women never do. Well;—what can I do for you, now that you are here?'

'Mr. Melmotte, I'm come,—I'm come to;—in short, Mr. Melmotte, I want to propose myself as a suitor for your daughter's hand.'

'The d—— you do!'

'Well, yes; and we hope you'll give us your consent.'

'She knows you're coming, then?'

'Yes;—she knows.'

'And my wife;—does she know?'

'I've never spoken to her about it. Perhaps Miss Melmotte has.'

'And how long have you and she understood each other?'

'I've been attached to her ever since I saw her,' said Sir Felix. 'I have indeed. I've spoken to her sometimes. You know how that kind of thing goes on.'

'I'm blessed if I do. I know how it ought to go on. I know that when large sums of money are supposed to be concerned, the young man should speak to the father before he speaks to the girl. He's a fool if he don't, if he wants to get the father's money. So she has given you a promise?'

'I don't know about a promise.'

'Do you consider that she's engaged to you?'

'Not if she's disposed to get out of it,' said Sir Felix, hoping that he might thus ingratiate himself with the father. 'Of course, I should be awfully disappointed.'

'She has consented to your coming to me?'

'Well, yes;—in a sort of a way. Of course she knows that it all depends on you.'

'Not at all. She's of age. If she chooses to marry you, she can marry you. If that's all you want, her consent is enough. You're a baronet, I believe?'

'Oh, yes, I'm a baronet.'

'And therefore you've come to your own property. You haven't to wait for your father to die, and I dare say you are indifferent about money.'

This was a view of things which Sir Felix felt that he was bound to dispel, even at the risk of offending the father. 'Not exactly that,' he said. 'I suppose you will give your daughter a fortune, of course.'

'Then I wonder you didn't come to me before you went to her. If my daughter marries to please me, I shall give her money, no doubt. How much is neither here nor there. If she marries to please herself, without considering me, I shan't give her a farthing.'

'I had hoped that you might consent, Mr. Melmotte.'

'I've said nothing about that. It is possible. You're a man of fashion and have a title of your own,—and no doubt a property. If you'll show me that you've an income fit to maintain her, I'll think about it at any rate. What is your property, Sir Felix?'

What could three or four thousand a year, or even five or six, matter to a man like Melmotte? It was thus that Sir Felix looked at it. When a man can hardly count his millions he ought not to ask questions about trifling sums of money. But the question had been asked, and the asking of such a question was no doubt within the prerogative of a proposed father-in-law. At any rate, it must be answered. For a moment it occurred to Sir Felix that he might conveniently tell the truth. It would be nasty for the moment, but there would be nothing to come after. Were he to do so he could not be dragged down lower and lower into the mire by cross-examinings. There might be an end of all his hopes, but there would at the same time be an end of all his misery. But he lacked the necessary courage. 'It isn't a large property, you know,' he said.

'Not like the Marquis of Westminster's,* I suppose,' said the horrid, big, rich scoundrel.

'No;—not quite like that,' said Sir Felix, with a sickly laugh.

'But you have got enough to support a baronet's title?'

'That depends on how you want to support it,' said Sir Felix, putting off the evil day.

'Where's your family seat?'

'Carbury Manor, down in Suffolk, near the Longe-staffes, is the old family place.'

'That doesn't belong to you,' said Melmotte, very sharply.

'No; not yet. But I'm the heir.'

Perhaps if there is one thing in England more difficult than another to be understood by men born and bred out of England, it is the system under which titles and property descend together, or in various lines. The jurisdiction of our Courts of Law is complex, and so is the business of Parliament. But the rules regulating them, though anomalous, are easy to the memory compared with the mixed anomalies of the peerage and primogeniture. They who are brought up among it,

learn it as children do a language, but strangers who
begin the study in advanced life, seldom make themselves
perfect in it. It was everything to Melmotte that he
should understand the ways of the country which he
had adopted; and when he did not understand, he was
clever at hiding his ignorance. Now he was puzzled.
He knew that Sir Felix was a baronet, and therefore presumed him to be the head of the family. He knew that
Carbury Manor belonged to Roger Carbury, and he
judged by the name it must be an old family property.
And now the baronet declared that he was heir to the
man who was simply an Esquire. 'Oh, the heir are you?
But how did he get it before you? You're the head of
the family?'

'Yes, I am the head of the family, of course,' said Sir
Felix, lying directly. 'But the place won't be mine till
he dies. It would take a long time to explain it all.'

'He's a young man, isn't he?'

'No,—not what you'd call a young man. He isn't very
old.'

'If he were to marry and have children, how would it
be then?'

Sir Felix was beginning to think that he might have
told the truth with discretion. 'I don't quite know how
it would be. I have always understood that I am the
heir. It's not very likely that he will marry.'

'And in the meantime what is your own property?'

'My father left me money in the funds and in railway
stock,—and then I am my mother's heir.'

'You have done me the honour of telling me that you
wish to marry my daughter.'

'Certainly.'

'Would you then object to inform me the amount and
nature of the income on which you intend to support
your establishment as a married man? I fancy that the
position you assume justifies the question on my part.'
The bloated swindler, the vile city ruffian, was certainly
taking a most ungenerous advantage of the young
aspirant for wealth. It was then that Sir Felix felt his
own position. Was he not a baronet, and a gentleman,

and a very handsome fellow, and a man of the world
who had been in a crack regiment? If this surfeited
sponge of speculation, this crammed commercial cor-
morant, wanted more than that for his daughter, why
could he not say so without asking disgusting questions
such as these,—questions which it was quite impossible
that a gentleman should answer? Was it not sufficiently
plain that any gentleman proposing to marry the daughter of such a man as Melmotte, must do so under the
stress of pecuniary embarrassment? Would it not be an
understood bargain that as he provided the rank and
position, she would provide the money? And yet the
vulgar wretch took advantage of his assumed authority
to ask these dreadful questions! Sir Felix stood silent,
trying to look the man in the face, but failing;—wishing
that he was well out of the house, and at the Beargarden. 'You don't seem to be very clear about your
own circumstances, Sir Felix. Perhaps you will get your
lawyer to write to me.'

'Perhaps that will be best,' said the lover.

'Either that, or to give it up. My daughter, no doubt,
will have money; but money expects money.' At this
moment Lord Alfred entered the room. 'You're very
late to-day, Alfred. Why didn't you come as you said
you would?'

'I was here more than an hour ago, and they said
you were out.'

'I haven't been out of this room all day,—except to
lunch. Good morning, Sir Felix. Ring the bell, Alfred,
and we'll have a little soda and brandy.' Sir Felix had
gone through some greeting with his fellow Director,
Lord Alfred, and at last succeeded in getting Melmotte
to shake hands with him before he went. 'Do you know
anything about that young fellow?' Melmotte asked as
soon as the door was closed.

'He's a baronet without a shilling;—was in the army
and had to leave it,' said Lord Alfred as he buried his
face in a big tumbler.

'Without a shilling! I supposed so. But he's heir to a
place down in Suffolk;—eh?'

'Not a bit of it. It's the same name, and that's about all. Mr. Carbury has a small property there, and he might give it to me to-morrow. I wish he would, though there isn't much of it. That young fellow has nothing to do with it whatever.'

'Hasn't he now!' Mr. Melmotte, as he speculated upon it, almost admired the young man's impudence.

## Chapter XXIV

### MILES GRENDALL'S TRIUMPH

SIR FELIX as he walked down to his club felt that he had been checkmated,—and was at the same time full of wrath at the insolence of the man who had so easily beaten him out of the field. As far as he could see, the game was over. No doubt he might marry Marie Melmotte. The father had told him so much himself, and he perfectly believed the truth of that oath which Marie had sworn. He did not doubt but that she'd stick to him close enough. She was in love with him, which was natural; and was a fool,—which was perhaps also natural. But romance was not the game which he was playing. People told him that when girls succeeded in marrying without their parents' consent, fathers were always constrained to forgive them at last. That might be the case with ordinary fathers. But Melmotte was decidedly not an ordinary father. He was,—so Sir Felix declared to himself,—perhaps the greatest brute ever created. Sir Felix could not but remember that elevation of the eyebrows, and the brazen forehead, and the hard mouth. He had found himself quite unable to stand up against Melmotte, and now he cursed and swore at the man as he was carried down to the Beargarden in a cab.

But what should he do? Should he abandon Marie Melmotte altogether, never go to Grosvenor Square again, and drop the whole family, including the Great Mexican Railway? Then an idea occurred to him.

Nidderdale had explained to him the result of his application for shares. 'You see we haven't bought any and
therefore can't sell any. There seems to be something
in that. I shall explain it all to my governor, and get
him to go a thou' or two. If he sees his way to get the
money back, he'd do that and let me have the difference.'
On that Sunday afternoon Sir Felix thought over all
this. 'Why shouldn't he "go a thou," and get the difference?' He made a mental calculation. £12 10s. per
£100! £125 for a thousand! and all paid in ready
money. As far as Sir Felix could understand, directly
the one operation had been perfected the thousand
pounds would be available for another. As he looked
into it with all his intelligence he thought that he began
to perceive that that was the way in which the Melmottes
of the world made their money. There was but one
objection. He had not got the entire thousand pounds.
But luck had been on the whole very good to him. He
had more than the half of it in real money, lying at a
bank in the city at which he had opened an account.
And he had very much more than the remainder in
I.O.U.'s from Dolly Longestaffe and Miles Grendall.
In fact if every man had his own,—and his bosom glowed
with indignation as he reflected on the injustice with
which he was kept out of his own,—he could go into the
city and take up his shares to-morrow, and still have
ready money at his command. If he could do this,
would not such conduct on his part be the best refuta-
tion of that charge of not having any fortune which
Melmotte had brought against him? He would endeavour to work the money out of Dolly Longestaffe;—
and he entertained an idea that though it would be impossible to get cash from Miles Grendall, he might use
his claim against Miles in the city. Miles was Secretary
to the Board, and might perhaps contrive that the money
required for the shares should not be all ready money.
Sir Felix was not very clear about it, but thought that
he might possibly in this way use the indebtedness of
Miles Grendall. 'How I do hate a fellow who does not
pay up,' he said to himself as he sat alone in his club,

waiting for some friend to come in. And he formed in his head Draconic laws which he would fain have executed upon men who lost money at play and did not pay. 'How the deuce fellows can look one in the face, is what I can't understand,' he said to himself.

He thought over this great stroke of exhibiting himself to Melmotte as a capitalist till he gave up his idea of abandoning his suit. So he wrote a note to Marie Melmotte in accordance with her instructions.

'DEAR M.,

'Your father cut up very rough,—about money. Perhaps you had better see him yourself; or would your mother?

'Yours always, F.'

This, as directed, he put under cover to Madame Didon,—Grosvenor Square, and posted at the club. He had put nothing at any rate in the letter which would commit him.

There was generally on Sundays a house dinner, so called, at eight o'clock. Five or six men would sit down, and would always gamble afterwards. On this occasion Dolly Longestaffe sauntered in at about seven in quest of sherry and bitters, and Felix found the opportunity a good one to speak of his money. 'You couldn't cash your I.O.U.'s for me to-morrow;—could you?'

'To-morrow! oh, lord!'

'I'll tell you why. You know I'd tell you anything because I think we are really friends. I'm after that daughter of Melmotte's.'

'I'm told you're to have her.'

'I don't know about that. I mean to try at any rate. I've gone in you know for that Board in the city.'

'I don't know anything about Boards, my boy.'

'Yes, you do, Dolly. You remember that American fellow, Montague's friend, that was here one night and won all our money.'

'The chap that had the waistcoat, and went away in the morning to California. Fancy starting to California after a hard night. I always wondered whether he got there alive.'

'Well;—I can't explain to you all about it, because you hate those kinds of things.'

'And because I am such a fool.'

'I don't think you're a fool at all, but it would take a week. But it's absolutely essential for me to take up a lot of shares in the city to-morrow;—or perhaps Wednesday might do. I'm bound to pay for them, and old Melmotte will think that I'm utterly hard up if I don't. Indeed he said as much, and the only objection about me and this girl of his is as to money. Can't you understand, now, how important it may be?'

'It's always important to have a lot of money. I know that.'

'I shouldn't have gone in for this kind of thing if I hadn't thought I was sure. You know how much you owe me, don't you?'

'Not in the least.'

'It's about eleven hundred pounds!'

'I shouldn't wonder.'

'And Miles Grendall owes me two thousand. Grass-lough and Nidderdale when they lose always pay with Miles's I.O.U.'s.'

'So should I, if I had them.'

'It'll come to that soon that there won't be any other stuff going, and they really ain't worth anything. I don't see what's the use of playing when this rubbish is shoved about the table. As for Grendall himself, he has no feeling about it.'

'Not the least, I should say.'

'You'll try and get me the money, won't you, Dolly?'

'Melmotte has been at me twice. He wants me to agree to sell something. He's an old thief, and of course he means to rob me. You may tell him that if he'll let me have the money in the way I've proposed, you are to have a thousand pounds out of it. I don't know any other way.'

'You could write me that,—in a business sort of way.'

'I couldn't do that, Carbury. What's the use? I never

write any letters. I can't do it. You tell him that; and if the sale comes off, I'll make it straight.'

Miles Grendall also dined there, and after dinner, in the smoking-room, Sir Felix tried to do a little business with the Secretary. He began his operations with unusual courtesy, believing that the man must have some influence with the great distributor of shares. 'I'm going to take up my shares in that company,' said Sir Felix.

'Ah;—indeed.' And Miles enveloped himself from head to foot in smoke.

'I didn't quite understand about it, but Nidderdale saw Melmotte and he has explained it. I think I shall go in for a couple of thousand on Wednesday.'

'Oh;—ah.'

'It will be the proper thing to do;—won't it?'

'Very good—thing to do!' Miles Grendall smoked harder and harder as the suggestions were made to him.

'Is it always ready money?'

'Always ready money,' said Miles shaking his head, as though in reprobation of so abominable an institution.

'I suppose they allow some time to their own Directors, if a deposit, say 50 per cent., is made for the shares?'

'They'll give you half the number, which would come to the same thing.'

Sir Felix turned this over in his mind, but let him look at it as he would, could not see the truth of his companion's remark. 'You know I should want to sell again, —for the rise.'

'Oh; you'll want to sell again.'

'And therefore I must have the full number.'

'You could sell half the number, you know,' said Miles.

'I'm determined to begin with ten shares;—that's £1,000. Well;—I have got the money, but I don't want to draw out so much. Couldn't you manage for me that I should get them on paying 50 per cent. down?'

'Melmotte does all that himself.'

'You could explain, you know, that you are a little short in your own payments to me.' This Sir Felix said, thinking it to be a delicate mode of introducing his claim upon the Secretary.

'That's private,' said Miles frowning.

'Of course it's private; but if you would pay me the money I could buy the shares with it, though they are public.'

'I don't think we could mix the two things together, Carbury.'

'You can't help me?'

'Not in that way.'

'Then, when the deuce will you pay me what you owe me?' Sir Felix was driven to this plain expression of his demand by the impassibility of his debtor. Here was a man who did not pay his debts of honour, who did not even propose any arrangement for paying them, and who yet had the impudence to talk of not mixing up private matters with affairs of business! It made the young baronet very sick. Miles Grendall smoked on in silence. There was a difficulty in answering the question, and he therefore made no answer. 'Do you know how much you owe me?' continued the baronet, determined to persist now that he had commenced the attack. There was a little crowd of other men in the room, and the conversation about the shares had been commenced in an undertone. These two last questions Sir Felix had asked in a whisper, but his countenance showed plainly that he was speaking in anger.

'Of course I know,' said Miles.

'Well?'

'I'm not going to talk about it here.'

'Not going to talk about it here?'

'No. This is a public room.'

'I am going to talk about it,' said Sir Felix, raising his voice.

'Will any fellow come upstairs and play a game of billiards?' said Miles Grendall rising from his chair. Then he walked slowly out of the room, leaving Sir Felix to take what revenge he pleased. For a moment Sir Felix thought that he would expose the transaction to the whole room; but he was afraid, thinking that Miles Grendall was a more popular man than himself.

It was Sunday night; but not the less were the gamblers

assembled in the card-room at about eleven. Dolly
Longestaffe was there, and with him the two lords, and
Sir Felix, and Miles Grendall of course, and, I regret
to say, a much better man than any of them, Paul
Montague. Sir Felix had doubted much as to the propriety of joining the party. What was the use of playing
with a man who seemed by general consent to be
liberated from any obligation to pay? But then if he
did not play with him, where should he find another
gambling table? They began with whist, but soon laid
that aside and devoted themselves to loo.* The least
respected man in that confraternity was Grendall, and
yet it was in compliance with the persistency of his
suggestion that they gave up the nobler game. 'Let's
stick to whist; I like cutting out,' said Grasslough. 'It's
much more jolly having nothing to do now and then;
one can always bet,' said Dolly shortly afterwards. 'I
hate loo,' said Sir Felix in answer to a third application.
'I like whist best,' said Nidderdale, 'but I'll play anything anybody likes;—pitch and toss if you please.' But
Miles Grendall had his way, and loo was the game.

At about two o'clock Grendall was the only winner.
The play had not been very high, but nevertheless he
had won largely. Whenever a large pool had collected
itself he swept it into his garners. The men opposed to
him hardly grudged him this stroke of luck. He had
hitherto been unlucky; and they were able to pay him
with his own paper, which was so valueless that they
parted with it without a pang. Even Dolly Longestaffe
seemed to have a supply of it. The only man there not
so furnished was Montague, and while the sums won
were quite small he was allowed to pay with cash. But
to Sir Felix it was frightful to see ready money going
over to Miles Grendall, as under no circumstances could
it be got back from him. 'Montague,' he said, 'just
change these for the time. I'll take them back, if you
still have them when we've done.' And he handed a lot
of Miles's paper across the table. The result of course
would be that Felix would receive so much real money,
and that Miles would get back more of his own worth-

less paper. To Montague it would make no difference, and he did as he was asked;—or rather was preparing to do so, when Miles interfered. On what principle of justice could Sir Felix come between him and another man? 'I don't understand this kind of thing,' he said. 'When I win from you, Carbury, I'll take my I.O.U.'s, as long as you have any.'

'By George, that's kind.'

'But I won't have them handed about the table to be changed.'

'Pay them yourself, then,' said Sir Felix, laying a handful down on the table.

'Don't let's have a row,' said Lord Nidderdale.

'Carbury is always making a row,' said Grasslough.

'Of course he is,' said Miles Grendall.

'I don't make more row than anybody else; but I do say that as we have such a lot of these things, and as we all know that we don't get cash for them as we want it, Grendall shouldn't take money and walk off with it.'

'Who is walking off?' said Miles.

'And why should you be entitled to Montague's money more than any of us?' asked Grasslough.

The matter was debated, and was thus decided. It was not to be allowed that Miles's paper should be negotiated at the table in the manner that Sir Felix had attempted to adopt. But Mr. Grendall pledged his honour that when they broke up the party he would apply any money that he might have won to the redemption of his I.O.U.'s, paying a regular percentage to the holders of them. The decision made Sir Felix very cross. He knew that their condition at six or seven in the morning would not be favourable to such commercial accuracy, —which indeed would require an accountant to effect it; and he felt sure that Miles, if still a winner, would in truth walk off with the ready money.

For a considerable time he did not speak, and became very moderate in his play, tossing his cards about, almost always losing, but losing a minimum, and watching the board. He was sitting next to Grendall, and he thought that he observed that his neighbour moved his chair

farther and farther away from him, and nearer to Dolly
Longestaffe, who was next to him on the other side. This
went on for an hour, during which Grendall still won,—
and won heavily from Paul Montague. 'I never saw a
fellow have such a run of luck in my life,' said Grasslough. 'You've had two trumps dealt to you every hand
almost since we began!'

'Ever so many hands I haven't played at all,' said
Miles.

'You've always won when I've played,' said Dolly.
'I've been looed every time.'

'You oughtn't to begrudge me one run of luck, when
I've lost so much,' said Miles, who, since he began, had
destroyed paper counters of his own making, supposed
to represent considerably above £1,000, and had also,—
which was of infinitely greater concern to him,—received an amount of ready money which was quite a
godsend to him.

'What's the good of talking about it?' said Nidderdale.
'I hate all this row about winning and losing. Let's go
on, or go to bed.' The idea of going to bed was absurd.
So they went on. Sir Felix, however, hardly spoke at all,
played very little, and watched Miles Grendall without
seeming to watch him. At last he felt certain that he
saw a card go into the man's sleeve, and remembered
at the moment that the winner had owed his success to a
continued run of aces. He was tempted to rush at once
upon the player, and catch the card on his person. But
he feared. Grendall was a big man; and where would
he be if there should be no card there? And then, in the
scramble, there would certainly be at any rate a doubt.
And he knew that the men around him would be most
unwilling to believe such an accusation. Grasslough was
Grendall's friend, and Nidderdale and Dolly Longestaffe
would infinitely rather be cheated than suspect any one
of their own set of cheating them. He feared both the
violence of the man he should accuse, and also the im-
passive good humour of the others. He let that opportunity pass by, again watched, and again saw the card
abstracted. Thrice he saw it, till it was wonderful to

him that others also should not see it. As often as the
deal came round, the man did it. Felix watched more
closely, and was certain that in each round the man had an
ace at least once. It seemed to him that nothing could be
easier. At last he pleaded a headache, got up, and went
away, leaving the others playing. He had lost nearly a
thousand pounds, but it had been all in paper. 'There's
something the matter with that fellow,' said Grasslough.

'There's always something the matter with him, I think,'
said Miles. 'He is so awfully greedy about his money.'
Miles had become somewhat triumphant in his success.

'The less said about that, Grendall, the better,' said
Nidderdale. 'We have put up with a good deal, you
know, and he has put up with as much as anybody.'
Miles was cowed at once, and went on dealing without
manœuvring a card on that hand.

## Chapter XXV

### IN GROSVENOR SQUARE

MARIE MELMOTTE was hardly satisfied with the
note which she received from Didon early on the
Monday morning. With a volubility of French eloquence, Didon declared that she would be turned out
of the house if either Monsieur or Madame were to know
what she was doing. Marie told her that Madame would
certainly never dismiss her. 'Well, perhaps not Madame,'
said Didon, who knew too much about Madame to be
dismissed; 'but Monsieur!' Marie declared that by no
possibility could Monsieur know anything about it. In
that house nobody ever told anything to Monsieur. He
was regarded as the general enemy, against whom the
whole household was always making ambushes, always
firing guns from behind rocks and trees. It is not a
pleasant condition for a master of a house; but in this
house the master at any rate knew how he was placed.
It never occurred to him to trust any one. Of course
his daughter might run away. But who would run away

with her without money? And there could be no money
except from him. He knew himself and his own strength.
He was not the man to forgive a girl, and then bestow
his wealth on the Lothario who had injured him. His
daughter was valuable to him because she might make
him the father-in-law of a Marquis or an Earl; but the
higher that he rose without such assistance, the less need
had he of his daughter's aid. Lord Alfred was certainly
very useful to him. Lord Alfred had whispered into his
ear that by certain conduct and by certain uses of his
money, he himself might be made a baronet. 'But if they
should say that I'm not an Englishman?' suggested Melmotte. Lord Alfred had explained that it was not necessary that he should have been born in England, or even
that he should have an English name. No questions
would be asked. Let him first get into Parliament, and
then spend a little money on the proper side,—by which
Lord Alfred meant the Conservative side,—and be
munificent in his entertainments, and the baronetcy
would be almost a matter of course. Indeed, there was
no knowing what honours might not be achieved in the
present days by money scattered with a liberal hand.
In these conversations, Melmotte would speak of his
money and power of making money as though they were
unlimited,—and Lord Alfred believed him.

Marie was dissatisfied with her letter,—not because it
described her father as 'cutting up rough.' To her who
had known her father all her life that was a matter of
course. But there was no word of love in the note. An
impassioned correspondence carried on through Didon
would be delightful to her. She was quite capable of loving, and she did love the young man. She had, no doubt,
consented to accept the addresses of others whom she
did not love,—but this she had done at the moment
almost of her first introduction to the marvellous world
in which she was now living. As days went on she ceased
to be a child, and her courage grew within her. She
became conscious of an identity of her own, which feeling was produced in great part by the contempt which
accompanied her increasing familiarity with grand

people and grand names and grand things. She was
no longer afraid of saying No to the Nidderdales on
account of any awe of them personally. It might be
that she should acknowledge herself to be obliged to
obey her father, though she was drifting away even from
the sense of that obligation. Had her mind been as it was
now when Lord Nidderdale first came to her, she might
indeed have loved him, who, as a man, was infinitely
better than Sir Felix, and who, had he thought it to be
necessary, would have put some grace into his love-
making. But at that time she had been childish. He,
finding her to be a child, had hardly spoken to her. And
she, child though she was, had resented such usage. But
a few months in London had changed all this, and now
she was a child no longer. She was in love with Sir
Felix, and had told her love. Whatever difficulties there
might be, she intended to be true. If necessary, she
would run away. Sir Felix was her idol, and she abandoned herself to its worship. But she desired that her
idol should be of flesh and blood, and not of wood. She
was at first half-inclined to be angry; but as she sat with
his letter in her hand, she remembered that he did not
know Didon as well as she did, and that he might be
afraid to trust his raptures to such custody. She could
write to him at his club, and having no such fear, she
could write warmly.

‘——, Grosvenor Square. Early Monday Morning.
‘DEAREST, DEAREST FELIX,

　‘I have just got your note;—such a scrap! Of course
papa would talk about money because he never thinks
of anything else. I don't know anything about money,
and I don't care in the least how much you have got.
Papa has got plenty, and I think he would give us some
if we were once married. I have told mamma, but
mamma is always afraid of everything. Papa is very
cross to her sometimes;—more so than to me. I will
try to tell him, though I can't always get at him. I very
often hardly see him all day long.. But I don't mean to
be afraid of him, and will tell him that on my word

and honour I will never marry any one except you. I
don't think he will beat me, but if he does, I'll bear
it,—for your sake. He does beat mamma sometimes,
I know.

'You can write to me quite safely through Didon. I
think if you would call some day and give her something,
it would help, as she is very fond of money. Do write
and tell me that you love me. I love you better than
anything in the world, and I will never,—never give you
up. I suppose you can come and call,—unless papa tells
the man in the hall not to let you in. I'll find that out
from Didon, but I can't do it before sending this letter.
Papa dined out yesterday somewhere with that Lord
Alfred, so I haven't seen him since you were here. I
never see him before he goes into the city in the morning.
Now I am going downstairs to breakfast with mamma
and that Miss Longestaffe. She is a stuck-up thing.
Didn't you think so at Caversham?

'Good-bye. You are my own, own, own darling Felix.

'And I am your own, own affectionate ladylove,

'MARIE.'

Sir Felix when he read this letter at his club in the
afternoon of the Monday, turned up his nose and shook
his head. He thought if there were much of that kind
of thing to be done, he could not go on with it, even
though the marriage were certain, and the money secure.
'What an infernal little ass!' he said to himself as he
crumpled the letter up.

Marie having intrusted her letter to Didon, together
with a little present of gloves and shoes, went down to
breakfast. Her mother was the first there, and Miss
Longestaffe soon followed. That lady, when she found
that she was not expected to breakfast with the master
of the house, abandoned the idea of having her meal
sent to her in her own room. Madame Melmotte she
must endure. With Madame Melmotte she had to go
out in the carriage every day. Indeed she could only
go to those parties to which Madame Melmotte accompanied her. If the London season was to be of any use

at all, she must accustom herself to the companionship
of Madame Melmotte. The man kept himself very
much apart from her. She met him only at dinner, and
that not often. Madame Melmotte was very bad; but she
was silent, and seemed to understand that her guest was
only her guest as a matter of business.

But Miss Longestaffe already perceived that her old
acquaintances were changed in their manner to her. She
had written to her dear friend Lady Monogram, whom
she had known intimately as Miss Triplex, and whose
marriage with Sir Damask Monogram had been splendid
preferment, telling how she had been kept down in
Suffolk at the time of her friend's last party, and how
she had been driven to consent to return to London as
the guest of Madame Melmotte. She hoped her friend
would not throw her off on that account. She had been
very affectionate, with a poor attempt at fun, and rather
humble. Georgiana Longestaffe had never been humble
before; but the Monograms were people so much thought
of and in such an excellent set! She would do anything
rather than lose the Monograms. But it was of no use.
She had been humble in vain, for Lady Monogram had
not even answered her note. 'She never really cared for
anybody but herself,' Georgiana said in her wretched
solitude. Then, too, she had found that Lord Nidderdale's manner to her had been quite changed. She was
not a fool, and could read these signs with sufficient
accuracy. There had been little flirtations between her
and Nidderdale,—meaning nothing, as every one knew
that Nidderdale must marry money; but in none of them
had he spoken to her as he spoke when he met her in
Madame Melmotte's drawing-room. She could see it in
the faces of people as they greeted her in the park,—
especially in the faces of the men. She had always
carried herself with a certain high demeanour, and had
been able to maintain it. All that was now gone from
her, and she knew it. Though the thing was as yet but
a few days old she understood that others understood
that she had degraded herself. 'What's all this about?'
Lord Grasslough had said to her, seeing her come into

a room behind Madame Melmotte. She had simpered, had tried to laugh, and had then turned away her face. 'Impudent scoundrel!' she said to herself, knowing that a fortnight ago he would not have dared to address her in such a tone.

A day or two afterwards an occurrence took place worthy of commemoration. Dolly Longestaffe called on his sister! His mind must have been much stirred when he allowed himself to be moved to such uncommon action. He came too at a very early hour, not much after noon, when it was his custom to be eating his breakfast in bed. He declared at once to the servant that he did not wish to see Madame Melmotte or any of the family. He had called to see his sister. He was therefore shown into a separate room where Georgiana joined him.

'What's all this about?'

She tried to laugh as she tossed her head. 'What brings you here, I wonder? This is quite an unexpected compliment.'

'My being here doesn't matter. I can go anywhere without doing much harm. Why are you staying with these people?'

'Ask papa.'

'I don't suppose he sent you here?'

'That's just what he did do.'

'You needn't have come, I suppose, unless you liked it. Is it because they are none of them coming up?'

'Exactly that, Dolly. What a wonderful young man you are for guessing!'

'Don't you feel ashamed of yourself?'

'No;—not a bit.'

'Then I feel ashamed for you.'

'Everybody comes here.'

'No;—everybody does not come and stay here as you are doing. Everybody doesn't make themselves a part of the family. I have heard of nobody doing it except you. I thought you used to think so much of yourself.'

'I think as much of myself as ever I did,' said Georgiana, hardly able to restrain her tears.

'I can tell you nobody else will think much of you if

you remain here. I could hardly believe it when Nidderdale told me.'

'What did he say, Dolly?'

'He didn't say much to me, but I could see what he
thought. And of course everybody thinks the same. How
you can like the people yourself, is what I can't understand!'

'I don't like them,—I hate them.'

'Then why do you come and live with them?'

'Oh, Dolly, it is impossible to make you understand.
A man is so different. You can go just where you please,
and do what you like. And if you're short of money,
people will give you credit. And you can live by yourself, and all that sort of thing. How should you like to be
shut up down at Caversham all the season?'

'I shouldn't mind it,—only for the governor.'

'You have got a property of your own. Your fortune
is made for you. What is to become of me?'

'You mean about marrying?'

'I mean altogether,' said the poor girl, unable to be
quite as explicit with her brother, as she had been with
her father, and mother, and sister. 'Of course I have to
think of myself.'

'I don't see how the Melmottes are to help you. The
long and the short of it is, you oughtn't to be here. It's
not often I interfere, but when I heard it I thought I'd
come and tell you. I shall write to the governor, and
tell him too. He should have known better.'

'Don't write to papa, Dolly!'

'Yes, I shall. I am not going to see everything going
to the devil without saying a word. Good-bye.'

As soon as he had left he hurried down to some club
that was open,—not the Beargarden, as it was long before
the Beargarden hours,—and actually did write a letter
to his father.

'MY DEAR FATHER,

'I have seen Georgiana at Mr. Melmotte's house. She
ought not to be there. I suppose you don't know it, but
everybody says he's a swindler. For the sake of the family

I hope you will get her home again. It seems to me that Bruton Street is the proper place for the girls at this time of the year.

'Your affectionate son,
'ADOLPHUS LONGESTAFFE.'

This letter fell upon old Mr. Longestaffe at Caversham like a thunderbolt. It was marvellous to him that his son should have been instigated to write a letter. The Melmottes must be very bad indeed,—worse than he had thought,—or their iniquities would not have brought about such energy as this. But the passage which angered him most was that which told him that he ought to have taken his family back to town. This had come from his son, who had refused to do anything to help him in his difficulties.

## Chapter XXVI

### MRS. HURTLE

PAUL MONTAGUE at this time lived in comfortable lodgings in Sackville Street, and ostensibly the world was going well with him. But he had many troubles. His troubles in reference to Fisker, Montague, and Montague,—and also their consolation,—are already known to the reader. He was troubled too about his love, though when he allowed his mind to expatiate on the success of the great railway he would venture to hope that on that side his life might perhaps be blessed. Henrietta had at any rate as yet showed no disposition to accept her cousin's offer. He was troubled too about the gambling, which he disliked, knowing that in that direction there might be speedy ruin, and yet returning to it from day to day in spite of his own conscience. But there was yet another trouble which culminated just at this time. One morning, not long after that Sunday night which had been so wretchedly spent at the Beargarden, he got into a cab in Piccadilly and had himself taken to a certain address in Islington. Here he knocked at a decent, modest

door,—at such a house as men live in with two or three
hundred a year,—and asked for Mrs. Hurtle. Yes;—
Mrs. Hurtle lodged there, and he was shown into the
drawing-room. There he stood by the round table for a
quarter of an hour turning over the lodging-house books
which lay there, and then Mrs. Hurtle entered the room.
Mrs. Hurtle was a widow whom he had once promised
to marry. 'Paul,' she said, with a quick, sharp voice, but
with a voice which could be very pleasant when she
pleased,—taking him by the hand as she spoke, 'Paul,
say that that letter of yours must go for nothing. Say
that it shall be so, and I will forgive everything.'

'I cannot say that,' he replied, laying his hand on hers.

'You cannot say it! What do you mean? Will you
dare to tell me that your promises to me are to go for
nothing?'

'Things are changed,' said Paul hoarsely. He had
come thither at her bidding because he had felt that to
remain away would be cowardly, but the meeting was
inexpressibly painful to him. He did think that he had
sufficient excuse for breaking his troth to this woman, but
the justification of his conduct was founded on reasons
which he hardly knew how to plead to her. He had
heard that of her past life which, had he heard it before,
would have saved him from his present difficulty. But
he had loved her,—did love her in a certain fashion; and
her offences, such as they were, did not debar her from
his sympathies.

'How are they changed? I am two years older, if you
mean that.' As she said this she looked round at the
glass, as though to see whether she was become so haggard
with age as to be unfit to become this man's wife. She
was very lovely, with a kind of beauty which we seldom
see now. In these days men regard the form and outward lines of a woman's face and figure more than either
the colour or the expression, and women fit themselves
to men's eyes. With padding and false hair without
limit a figure may be constructed of almost any dimensions. The sculptors who construct them, male and
female, hairdressers and milliners, are very skilful, and

figures are constructed of noble dimensions, sometimes
with voluptuous expansion, sometimes with classic reticence, sometimes with dishevelled negligence which
becomes very dishevelled indeed when long out of the
sculptor's hands. Colours indeed are added, but not the
colours which we used to love. The taste for flesh and
blood has for the day given place to an appetite for horsehair* and pearl powder. But Mrs. Hurtle was not a
beauty after the present fashion. She was very dark,—
a dark brunette,—with large round blue eyes, that could
indeed be soft, but could also be very severe. Her silken
hair, almost black, hung in a thousand curls all round
her head and neck. Her cheeks and lips and neck were
full, and the blood would come and go, giving a varying
expression to her face with almost every word she spoke.
Her nose also was full, and had something of the pug.
But nevertheless it was a nose which any man who loved
her would swear to be perfect. Her mouth was large,
and she rarely showed her teeth. Her chin was full,
marked by a large dimple, and as it ran down to her
neck was beginning to form a second. Her bust was full
and beautifully shaped; but she invariably dressed as
though she were oblivious, or at any rate neglectful, of
her own charms. Her dress, as Montague had seen her,
was always black,—not a sad weeping widow's garment,
but silk or woollen or cotton as the case might be, always
new, always nice, always well-fitting, and most especially
always simple. She was certainly a most beautiful
woman, and she knew it. She looked as though she
knew it,—but only after that fashion in which a woman
ought to know it. Of her age she had never spoken to
Montague. She was in truth over thirty,—perhaps
almost as near thirty-five as thirty. But she was one of
those whom years hardly seem to touch.

'You are beautiful as ever you were,' he said.

'Psha! Do not tell me of that. I care nothing for my
beauty unless it can bind me to your love. Sit down
there and tell me what it means.' Then she let go his
hand, and seated herself opposite to the chair which she
gave him.

'I told you in my letter.'

'You told me nothing in your letter,—except that it was to be—off. Why is it to be—off? Do you not love me?' Then she threw herself upon her knees, and leaned upon his, and looked up in his face. 'Paul,' she said, 'I have come across the Atlantic on purpose to see you,— after so many months,—and will you not give me one kiss? Even though you should leave me for ever, give me one kiss.' Of course he kissed her, not once, but with a long, warm embrace. How could it have been otherwise? With all his heart he wished that she would have remained away, but while she knelt there at his feet what could he do but embrace her? 'Now tell me everything,' she said, seating herself on a footstool at his feet.

She certainly did not look like a woman whom a man might ill-treat or scorn with impunity. Paul felt, even while she was lavishing her caresses upon him, that she might too probably turn and rend him before he left her. He had known something of her temper before, though he had also known the truth and warmth of her love. He had travelled with her from San Francisco to England, and she had been very good to him in illness, in distress of mind and in poverty,—for he had been almost penniless in New York. When they landed at Liverpool they were engaged as man and wife. He had told her all his affairs, had given her the whole history of his life. This was before his second journey to America, when Hamilton K. Fisker was unknown to him. But she had told him little or nothing of her own life,—but that she was a widow, and that she was travelling to Paris on business. When he left her at the London railway station, from which she started for Dover, he was full of all a lover's ardour. He had offered to go with her, but that she had declined. But when he remembered that he must certainly tell his friend Roger of his engagement, and remembered also how little he knew of the lady to whom he was engaged, he became embarrassed. What were her means he did not know. He did know that she was some years older than himself, and that she had spoken hardly a word to him of her own family. She had indeed said that her husband had been one of the greatest miscreants ever created, and had spoken of her release from him as the one blessing she had known before she had met Paul Montague. But it was only when he thought of all this after she had left him,—only when he reflected how bald was the story which he must tell Roger Carbury,—that he became dismayed. Such had been the woman's cleverness, such her charm, so great her power of adaptation, that he had passed weeks in her daily company, with still progressing intimacy and affection, without feeling that anything had been missing.

He had told his friend, and his friend had declared to him that it was impossible that he should marry a woman whom he had met in a railway train without knowing something about her. Roger did all he could to persuade the lover to forget his love,—and partially succeeded. It is so pleasant and so natural that a young man should enjoy the company of a clever, beautiful woman on a long journey,—so natural that during the journey he should allow himself to think that she may during her whole life be all in all to him as she is at that moment;—and so natural again that he should see his mistake when he has parted from her! But Montague, though he was half false to his widow, was half true to her. He had pledged his word, and that he said ought to bind him. Then he returned to California, and learned, through the instrumentality of Hamilton K. Fisker, that in San Francisco Mrs. Hurtle was regarded as a mystery. Some people did not quite believe that there ever had been a Mr. Hurtle. Others said that there certainly had been a Mr. Hurtle, and that to the best of their belief he still existed. The fact, however, best known of her was, that she had shot a man through the head somewhere in Oregon. She had not been tried for it, as the world of Oregon had considered that the circumstances justified the deed. Everybody knew that she was very clever and very beautiful,—but everybody also thought that she was very dangerous. 'She always had money when she was here,' Hamilton Fisker said, 'but no one knew where it

came from.' Then he wanted to know why Paul inquired.
'I don't think, you know, that I should like to go in for
a life partnership, if you mean that,' said Hamilton K.
Fisker.

Montague had seen her in New York as he passed
through on his second journey to San Francisco, and had
then renewed his promises in spite of his cousin's caution.
He told her that he was going to see what he could make
of his broken fortunes,—for at this time, as the reader
will remember, there was no great railway in existence,
—and she had promised to follow him. Since that, they
had never met till this day. She had not made the promised journey to San Francisco, at any rate before he
had left it. Letters from her had reached him in England,
and these he had answered by explaining to her, or endeavouring to explain, that their engagement must be
at an end. And now she had followed him to London!
'Tell me everything,' she said, leaning upon him and
looking up into his face.

'But you,—when did you arrive here?'

'Here, at this house, I arrived the night before last.
On Tuesday I reached Liverpool. There I found that
you were probably in London, and so I came on. I have
come only to see you. I can understand that you should
have been estranged from me. That journey home is
now so long ago! Our meeting in New York was so
short and wretched. I would not tell you because you
then were poor yourself, but at that moment I was penniless. I have got my own now out from the very teeth of
robbers.' As she said this, she looked as though she
could be very persistent in claiming her own,—or what
she might think to be her own. 'I could not get across
to San Francisco as I said I would, and when I was there
you had quarrelled with your uncle and returned. And
now I am here. I at any rate have been faithful.' As
she said this his arm was again thrown over her, so as to
press her head to his knee. 'And now,' she said, 'tell me
about yourself?'

His position was embarrassing and very odious to himself. Had he done his duty properly, he would gently

have pushed her from him, have sprung to his legs, and
have declared that, however faulty might have been his
previous conduct, he now found himself bound to make
her understand that he did not intend to become her
husband. But he was either too much of a man or too
little of a man for conduct such as that. He did make
the avowal to himself, even at that moment as she sat
there. Let the matter go as it would, she should never
be his wife. He would marry no one unless it was Hetta
Carbury. But he did not at all know how to get this said
with proper emphasis, and yet with properly apolo-
getic courtesy. 'I am engaged here about this railway,'
he said. 'You have heard, I suppose, of our projected
scheme?'

'Heard of it! San Francisco is full of it. Hamilton
Fisker is the great man of the day there, and, when I
left, your uncle was buying a villa for seventy-four
thousand dollars. And yet they say that the best of it all
has been transferred to you Londoners. Many there are
very hard upon Fisker for coming here and doing as he
did.'

'It's doing very well, I believe,' said Paul, with some
feeling of shame, as he thought how very little he knew
about it.

'You are the manager here in England?'

'No,—I am a member of the firm that manages it at
San Francisco; but the real manager here is our chairman, Mr. Melmotte.'

'Ah,—I have heard of him. He is a great man;—a
Frenchman, is he not? There was a talk of inviting him
to California. You know him, of course?'

'Yes;—I know him. I see him once a week.'

'I would sooner see that man than your Queen, or any
of your dukes or lords. They tell me that he holds the
world of commerce in his right hand. What power;—
what grandeur!'

'Grand enough,' said Paul, 'if it all came honestly.'

'Such a man rises above honesty,'*said Mrs. Hurtle,
'as a great general rises above humanity when he sacrifices an army to conquer a nation. Such greatness is

incompatible with small scruples. A pigmy man is stopped by a little ditch, but a giant stalks over the rivers.'

'I prefer to be stopped by the ditches,' said Montague.

'Ah, Paul, you were not born for commerce. And I will grant you this, that commerce is not noble unless it rises to great heights. To live in plenty by sticking to your counter from nine in the morning to nine at night, is not a fine life. But this man with a scratch of his pen can send out or call in millions of dollars. Do they say here that he is not honest?'

'As he is my partner in this affair perhaps I had better say nothing against him.'

'Of course such a man will be abused. People have said that Napoleon was a coward, and Washington a traitor. You must take me where I shall see Melmotte. He is a man whose hand I would kiss; but I would not condescend to speak even a word of reverence to any of your Emperors.'

'I fear you will find that your idol has feet of clay.'

'Ah,—you mean that he is bold in breaking those precepts of yours about coveting worldly wealth. All men and women break that commandment, but they do so in a stealthy fashion, half drawing back the grasping hand, praying to be delivered from temptation while they filch only a little, pretending to despise the only thing that is dear to them in the world. Here is a man who boldly says that he recognises no such law; that wealth is power, and that power is good, and that the more a man has of wealth the greater and the stronger and the nobler he can be. I love a man who can turn the hobgoblins inside out and burn the wooden bogies that he meets.'

Montague had formed his own opinions about Melmotte. Though connected with the man, he believed their Grand Director to be as vile a scoundrel as ever lived. Mrs. Hurtle's enthusiasm was very pretty, and there was something of feminine eloquence in her words. But it was shocking to see them lavished on such a subject. 'Personally, I do not like him,' said Paul.

'I had thought to find that you and he were hand and glove.'

'Oh no.'

'But you are prospering in this business?'

'Yes,—I suppose we are prospering. It is one of those hazardous things in which a man can never tell whether he be really prosperous till he is out of it. I fell into it altogether against my will. I had no alternative.'

'It seems to me to have been a golden chance.'

'As far as immediate results go it has been golden.'

'That at any rate is well, Paul. And now,—now that we have got back into our old way of talking, tell me what all this means. I have talked to no one after this fashion since we parted. Why should our engagement be over? You used to love me, did you not?'

He would willingly have left her question unanswered, but she waited for an answer. 'You know I did,' he said.

'I thought so. This I know, that you were sure and are sure of my love to you. Is it not so? Come, speak openly like a man. Do you doubt me?'

He did not doubt her, and was forced to say so. 'No, indeed.'

'Oh, with what bated, half-mouthed words you speak, —fit for a girl from a nursery! Out with it if you have anything to say against me! You owe me so much at any rate. I have never ill-treated you. I have never lied to you. I have taken nothing from you,—if I have not taken your heart. I have given you all that I can give.' Then she leaped to her feet and stood a little apart from him. 'If you hate me, say so.'

'Winifred,' he said, calling her by her name.

'Winifred! Yes, now for the first time, though I have called you Paul from the moment you entered the room. Well, speak out. Is there another woman that you love?'

At this moment Paul Montague proved that at any rate he was no coward. Knowing the nature of the woman, how ardent, how impetuous she could be, and how full of wrath, he had come at her call intending to tell her the truth which he now spoke. 'There is another,' he said.

She stood silent, looking into his face, thinking how she would commence her attack upon him. She fixed her eyes upon him, standing quite upright, squeezing her own right hand with the fingers of the left. 'Oh,' she said, in a whisper;—'that is the reason why I am told that I am to be—off.'

'That was not the reason.'

'What;—can there be more reason than that,—better reason than that? Unless, indeed, it be that as you have learned to love another so also you have learned to—hate me.'

'Listen to me, Winifred.'

'No, sir; no Winifred now! How did you dare to kiss me, knowing that it was on your tongue to tell me I was to be cast aside? And so you love—some other woman! I am too old to please you, too rough,—too little like the dolls of your own country! What were your—other reasons? Let me hear your—other reasons, that I may tell you that they are lies.'

The reasons were very difficult to tell, though when put forward by Roger Carbury they had been easily pleaded. Paul knew but little about Winifred Hurtle, and nothing at all about the late Mr. Hurtle. His reasons curtly put forward might have been so stated. 'We know too little of each other,' he said.

'What more do you want to know? You can know all for the asking. Did I ever refuse to answer you? As to my knowledge of you and your affairs, if I think it sufficient, need you complain? What is it that you want to know? Ask anything and I will tell you. Is it about my money? You knew when you gave me your word that I had next to none. Now I have ample means of my own. You knew that I was a widow. What more? If you wish to hear of the wretch that was my husband, I will deluge you with stories. I should have thought that a man who loved would not have cared to hear much of one—who perhaps was loved once.'

He knew that his position was perfectly indefensible. It would have been better for him not to have alluded to any reasons, but to have remained firm to his assertion

that he loved another woman. He must have acknowledged himself to be false, perjured, inconstant, and very
base. A fault that may be venial to those who do not
suffer, is damnable, deserving of an eternity of tortures,
in the eyes of the sufferer. He must have submitted to
be told that he was a fiend, and might have had to
endure whatever of punishment a lady in her wrath
could inflict upon him. But he would have been called
upon for no further mental effort. His position would
have been plain. But now he was all at sea. 'I wish to
hear nothing,' he said.

'Then why tell me that we know so little of each other?
That, surely, is a poor excuse to make to a woman,—
after you have been false to her. Why did you not say
that when we were in New York together? Think of it,
Paul. Is not that mean?'

'I do not think that I am mean.'

'No;—a man will lie to a woman, and justify it always.
Who is—this lady?'

He knew that he could not at any rate be warranted
in mentioning Hetta Carbury's name. He had never
even asked her for her love, and certainly had received
no assurance that he was loved. 'I cannot name her.'

'And I, who have come hither from California to see
you, am to return satisfied because you tell me that you
have—changed your affections? That is to be all, and
you think that fair? That suits your own mind, and leaves
no sore spot in your heart? You can do that, and shake
hands with me, and go away,—without a pang, without
a scruple?'

'I did not say so.'

'And you are the man who cannot bear to hear me
praise Augustus Melmotte because you think him dishonest! Are you a liar?'

'I hope not.'

'Did you say you would be my husband? Answer
me, sir.'

'I did say so.'

'Do you now refuse to keep your promise? You shall
answer me.'

'I cannot marry you.'

'Then, sir, are you not a liar?' It would have taken him long to explain to her, even had he been able, that a man may break a promise and yet not tell a lie. He had made up his mind to break his engagement before he had seen Hetta Carbury, and therefore he could not accuse himself of falseness on her account. He had been brought to his resolution by the rumours he had heard of her past life, and as to his uncertainty about her husband. If Mr. Hurtle were alive, certainly then he would not be a liar because he did not marry Mrs. Hurtle. He did not think himself to be a liar, but he was not at once ready with his defence. 'Oh, Paul,' she said, changing at once into softness,—'I am pleading to you for my life. Oh, that I could make you feel that I am pleading for my life. Have you given a promise to this lady also?'

'No,' said he. 'I have given no promise.'

'But she loves you?'

'She has never said so.'

'You have told her of your love?'

'Never.'

'There is nothing, then, between you? And you would put her against me,—some woman who has nothing to suffer, no cause of complaint, who, for aught you know, cares nothing for you. Is that so?'

'I suppose it is,' said Paul.

'Then you may still be mine. Oh, Paul, come back to me. Will any woman love you as I do;—live for you as I do? Think what I have done in coming here, where I have no friend,—not a single friend,—unless you are a friend. Listen to me. I have told the woman here that I am engaged to marry you.'

'You have told the woman of the house?'

'Certainly I have. Was I not justified? Were you not engaged to me? Am I to have you to visit me here, and to risk her insults, perhaps to be told to take myself off and to find accommodation elsewhere, because I am too mealy-mouthed to tell the truth as to the cause of my being here? I am here because you have promised to make me your wife, and, as far as I am concerned, I am not ashamed to have the fact advertised in every news-paper in the town. I told her that I was the promised wife of one Paul Montague, who was joined with Mr. Melmotte in managing the new great American railway, and that Mr. Paul Montague would be with me this morning. She was too far-seeing to doubt me, but had she doubted, I could have shown her your letters. Now go and tell her that what I have said is false,—if you dare.' The woman was not there, and it did not seem to be his immediate duty to leave the room in order that he might denounce a lady whom he certainly had ill-used. The position was one which required thought. After a while he took up his hat to go. 'Do you mean to tell her that my statement is untrue?'

'No,'—he said; 'not to-day.'

'And you will come back to me?'

'Yes;—I will come back.'

'I have no friend here, but you, Paul. Remember that. Remember all your promises. Remember all our love, —and be good to me.' Then she let him go without another word.

## Chapter XXVII

### MRS. HURTLE GOES TO THE PLAY

ON the day after the visit just recorded, Paul Monta-gue received the following letter from Mrs. Hurtle:—

'MY DEAR PAUL,—

'I think that perhaps we hardly made ourselves under-stood to each other yesterday, and I am sure that you do not understand how absolutely my whole life is now at stake. I need only refer you to our journey from San Francisco to London to make you conscious that I really love you. To a woman such love is all important. She cannot throw it from her as a man may do amidst the affairs of the world. Nor, if it has to be thrown from her, can she bear the loss as a man bears it. Her thoughts

have dwelt on it with more constancy than his;—and
then too her devotion has separated her from other
things. My devotion to you has separated me from everything.

'But I scorn to come to you as a suppliant. If you
choose to say after hearing me that you will put me away
from you because you have seen some one fairer than
I am, whatever course I may take in my indignation, I
shall not throw myself at your feet to tell you of my
wrongs. I wish, however, that you should hear me. You
say that there is some one you love better than you love
me, but that you have not committed yourself to her.
Alas, I know too much of the world to be surprised that
a man's constancy should not stand out two years in the
absence of his mistress. A man cannot wrap himself up
and keep himself warm with an absent love as a woman
does. But I think that some remembrance of the past
must come back upon you now that you have seen me
again. I think that you must have owned to yourself
that you did love me, and that you could love me again.
You sin against me to my utter destruction if you leave
me. I have given up every friend I have to follow you.
As regards the other—nameless lady, there can be no
fault; for, as you tell me, she knows nothing of your
passion.

'You hinted that there were other reasons,—that we
know too little of each other. You meant no doubt that
you knew too little of me. Is it not the case that you were
content when you knew only what was to be learned in
those days of our sweet intimacy, but that you have been
made discontented by stories told you by your partners
at San Francisco? If this be so, trouble yourself at any
rate to find out the truth before you allow yourself to
treat a woman as you propose to treat me. I think you
are too good a man to cast aside a woman you have
loved,—like a soiled glove,—because ill-natured words
have been spoken of her by men, or perhaps by women,
who know nothing of her life. My late husband, Caradoc
Hurtle, was Attorney-General in the State of Kansas
when I married him, I being then in possession of a

considerable fortune left to me by my mother. There
his life was infamously bad. He spent what money he
could get of mine, and then left me and the State, and
took himself to Texas;—where he drank himself to death.
I did not follow him, and in his absence I was divorced
from him in accordance with the laws of Kansas State.
I then went to San Francisco about property of my
mother's, which my husband had fraudulently sold to a
countryman of ours now resident in Paris,—having
forged my name. There I met you, and in that short
story I tell you all that there is to be told. It may be
that you do not believe me now; but if so, are you not
bound to go where you can verify your own doubts or
my word?

'I try to write dispassionately, but I am in truth over-
borne by passion. I also have heard in California
rumours about myself, and after much delay I received
your letter. I resolved to follow you to England as soon
as circumstances would permit me. I have been forced
to fight a battle about my property, and I have won it.
I had two reasons for carrying this through by my personal efforts before I saw you. I had begun it and had
determined that I would not be beaten by fraud. And
I was also determined that I would not plead to you as
a pauper. We have talked too freely together in past
days of our mutual money matters for me to feel any
delicacy in alluding to them. When a man and woman
have agreed to be husband and wife there should be no
delicacy of that kind. When we came here together we
were both embarrassed. We both had some property,
but neither of us could enjoy it. Since that I have made
my way through my difficulties. From what I have heard
at San Francisco I suppose that you have done the same.
I at any rate shall be perfectly contented if from this
time our affairs can be made one.

'And now about myself,—immediately. I have come
here all alone. Since I last saw you in New York I have
not had altogether a good time. I have had a great
struggle and have been thrown on my own resources and
have been all alone. Very cruel things have been said of

me. You heard cruel things said, but I presume them to
have been said to you with reference to my late husband.
Since that they have been said to others with reference
to you. I have not now come, as my countrymen do
generally, backed with a trunk full of introductions and
with scores of friends ready to receive me. It was necessary to me that I should see you and hear my fate,—and
here I am. I appeal to you to release me in some degree
from the misery of my solitude. You know,—no one so
well,—that my nature is social and that I am not given
to be melancholy. Let us be cheerful together, as we
once were, if it be only for a day. Let me see you as I
used to see you, and let me be seen as I used to be seen.

'Come to me and take me out with you, and let us
dine together, and take me to one of your theatres. If
you wish it I will promise you not to allude to that
revelation you made to me just now, though of course it
is nearer to my heart than any other matter. Perhaps
some woman's vanity makes me think that if you would
only see me again, and talk to me as you used to talk,
you would think of me as you used to think.

'You need not fear but you will find me at home. I
have no whither to go,—and shall hardly stir from the
house till you come to me. Send me a line, however,
that I may have my hat on if you are minded to do as I
ask you.

'Yours with all my heart,
'WINIFRED HURTLE.'

This letter took her much time to write, though she
was very careful so to write as to make it seem that it
had flown easily from her pen. She copied it from the
first draught, but she copied it rapidly, with one or two
premeditated erasures, so that it should look to have
been done hurriedly. There had been much art in it.
She had at any rate suppressed any show of anger. In
calling him to her she had so written as to make him feel
that if he would come he need not fear the claws of an
offended lioness:—and yet she was angry as a lioness
who had lost her cub. She had almost ignored that

other lady whose name she had not yet heard. She had spoken of her lover's entanglement with that other lady as a light thing which might easily be put aside. She had said much of her own wrongs, but had not said much of the wickedness of the wrong-doer. Invited as she had invited him, surely he could not but come to her! And then, in her reference to money, not descending to the details of dollars and cents, she had studied how to make him feel that he might marry her without imprudence. As she read it over to herself she thought that there was a tone through it of natural feminine uncautious eagerness. She put her letter up in an envelope, stuck a stamp on it and addressed it,—and then threw herself back in her chair to think of her position.

He should marry her,—or there should be something done which should make the name of Winifred Hurtle known to the world! She had no plan of revenge yet formed. She would not talk of revenge,—she told herself that she would not even think of revenge,—till she was quite sure that revenge would be necessary. But she did think of it, and could not keep her thoughts from it for a moment. Could it be possible that she, with all her intellectual gifts as well as those of her outward person, should be thrown over by a man whom well as she loved him,—and she did love him with all her heart,—she regarded as greatly inferior to herself! He had promised to marry her; and he should marry her, or the world should hear the story of his perjury!

Paul Montague felt that he was surrounded by difficulties as soon as he read the letter. That his heart was all the other way he was quite sure; but yet it did seem to him that there was no escape from his troubles open to him. There was not a single word in this woman's letter that he could contradict. He had loved her and had promised to make her his wife,—and had determined to break his word to her because he found that she was enveloped in dangerous mystery. He had so resolved before he had ever seen Hetta Carbury, having been made to believe by Roger Carbury that a marriage with an unknown American woman,—of whom he only did know that she was handsome and clever,—would be a step to ruin. The woman, as Roger said, was an adventuress,—might never have had a husband,—might at this moment have two or three,—might be overwhelmed with debt,—might be anything bad, dangerous, and abominable. All that he had heard at San Francisco had substantiated Roger's views. 'Any scrape is better than that scrape,' Roger had said to him. Paul had believed his Mentor, and had believed with a double faith as soon as he had seen Hetta Carbury.

But what should he do now? It was impossible, after what had passed between them, that he should leave Mrs. Hurtle at her lodgings at Islington without any notice. It was clear enough to him that she would not consent to be so left. Then her present proposal,—though it seemed to be absurd and almost comical in the tragical condition of their present circumstances,—had in it some immediate comfort. To take her out and give her a dinner, and then go with her to some theatre, would be easy and perhaps pleasant. It would be easier, and certainly much pleasanter, because she had pledged herself to abstain from talking of her grievances. Then he remembered some happy evenings, delicious hours, which he had so passed with her, when they were first together at New York. There could be no better companion for such a festival. She could talk,—and she could listen as well as talk. And she could sit silent, conveying to her neighbour the sense of her feminine charms by her simple proximity. He had been very happy when so placed. Had it been possible he would have escaped the danger now, but the reminiscence of past delights in some sort reconciled him to the performance of this perilous duty.

But when the evening should be over, how would he part with her? When the pleasant hour should have passed away and he had brought her back to her door, what should he say to her then? He must make some arrangement as to a future meeting. He knew that he was in a great peril, and he did not know how he might best escape it. He could not now go to Roger Carbury for advice; for was not Roger Carbury his rival? It would be for his friend's interest that he should marry the widow. Roger Carbury, as he knew well, was too honest a man to allow himself to be guided in any advice he might give by such a feeling, but, still, on this matter, he could no longer tell everything to Roger Carbury. He could not say all that he would have to say without speaking of Hetta;—and of his love for Hetta he could not speak to his rival.

He had no other friend in whom he could confide. There was no other human being he could trust, unless it was Hetta herself. He thought for a moment that he would write a stern and true letter to the woman, telling her that as it was impossible that there should ever be marriage between them, he felt himself bound to abstain from her society. But then he remembered her solitude, her picture of herself in London without even an acquaintance except himself, and he convinced himself that it would be impossible that he should leave her without seeing her. So he wrote to her thus:—

'DEAR WINIFRED,

'I will come for you to-morrow at half-past five. We will dine together at the Thespian;—and then I will have a box at the Haymarket. The Thespian is a good sort of place, and lots of ladies dine there. You can dine in your bonnet.

'Yours affectionately,
'P. M.'

Some half-formed idea ran through his brain that P. M. was a safer signature than Paul Montague. Then came a long train of thoughts as to the perils of the whole proceeding. She had told him that she had announced herself to the keeper of the lodging-house as engaged to him, and he had in a manner authorized the statement by declining to contradict it at once. And now, after that announcement, he was assenting to her proposal that they should go out and amuse themselves together. Hitherto she had always seemed to him to be open, candid, and free from intrigue. He had known her to be impulsive, capricious, at times violent, but never deceitful. Perhaps he was unable to read correctly the inner character of a woman whose experience of the world had been much wider than his own. His mind misgave him that it might be so; but still he thought that he knew that she was not treacherous. And yet did not her present acts justify him in thinking that she was carrying on a plot against him? The note, however, was sent, and he prepared for the evening of the play, leaving the dangers of the occasion to adjust themselves. He ordered the dinner and he took the box, and at the hour fixed he was again at her lodgings.

The woman of the house with a smile showed him into Mrs. Hurtle's sitting-room, and he at once perceived that the smile was intended to welcome him as an accepted lover. It was a smile half of congratulation to the lover, half of congratulation to herself as a woman that another man had been caught by the leg and made fast. Who does not know the smile? What man, who has been caught and made sure, has not felt a certain dissatisfaction at being so treated, understanding that the smile is intended to convey to him a sense of his own captivity? It has, however, generally mattered but little to us. If we have felt that something of ridicule was intended, because we have been regarded as cocks with their spurs cut away, then we also have a pride when we have declared to ourselves that upon the whole we have gained more than we have lost. But with Paul Montague at the present moment there was no satisfaction, no pride,— only a feeling of danger which every hour became deeper and stronger, with less chance of escape. He was almost tempted at this moment to detain the woman, and tell her the truth,—and bear the immediate consequences. But there would be treason in doing so, and he would not, could not do it.

He was left hardly a moment to think of this. Almost before the woman had shut the door, Mrs. Hurtle came to him out of her bedroom, with her hat on her head. Nothing could be more simple than her dress, and nothing prettier. It was now June, and the weather was warm, and the lady wore a light gauzy black dress, —there is a fabric which the milliners I think call grena-

dine,—coming close up round her throat. It was very
pretty, and she was prettier even than her dress. And
she had on a hat, black also, small and simple, but very
pretty. There are times at which a man going to a
theatre with a lady wishes her to be bright in her apparel,
—almost gorgeous; in which he will hardly be contented
unless her cloak be scarlet, and her dress white, and her
gloves of some bright hue,—unless she wear roses or
jewels in her hair. It is thus our girls go to the theatre
now, when they go intending that all the world shall
know who they are. But there are times again in which
a man would prefer that his companion should be very
quiet in her dress,—but still pretty; in which he would
choose that she should dress herself for him only. All
this Mrs. Hurtle had understood accurately; and Paul
Montague, who understood nothing of it, was gratified.
'You told me to have a hat, and here I am,—hat and
all.' She gave him her hand, and laughed, and looked
pleasantly at him, as though there was no cause of unhappiness between them. The lodging-house woman saw
them enter the cab, and muttered some little word as
they went off. Paul did not hear the word, but was sure
that it bore some indistinct reference to his expected
marriage.

Neither during the drive, nor at the dinner, nor during
the performance at the theatre, did she say a word in
allusion to her engagement. It was with them, as in
former days it had been at New York. She whispered
pleasant words to him, touching his arm now and again
with her finger as she spoke, seeming ever better inclined'
to listen than to speak. Now and again she referred, after
some slightest fashion, to little circumstances that had
occurred between them, to some joke, some hour of
tedium, some moment of delight; but it was done as one
man might do it to another,—if any man could have
done it so pleasantly. There was a scent which he had
once approved, and now she bore it on her handkerchief. There was a ring which he had once given her,
and she wore it on the finger with which she touched his
sleeve. With his own hands he had once adjusted her

curls, and each curl was as he had placed it. She had a way of shaking her head, that was very pretty,—a way that might, one would think, have been dangerous at her age, as likely to betray those first grey hairs which will come to disturb the last days of youth. He had once told her in sport to be more careful. She now shook her head again, and, as he smiled, she told him that she could still dare to be careless. There are a thousand little silly softnesses which are pretty and endearing between acknowledged lovers, with which no woman would like to dispense, to which even men who are in love submit sometimes with delight; but which in other circumstances would be vulgar,—and to the woman distasteful. There are closenesses and sweet approaches, smiles and nods and pleasant winkings, whispers, innuendoes and hints, little mutual admirations and assurances that there are things known to those two happy ones of which the world beyond is altogether ignorant. Much of this comes of nature, but something of it sometimes comes by art. Of such art as there may be in it Mrs. Hurtle was a perfect master. No allusion was made to their engagement,—not an unpleasant word was spoken; but the art was practised with all its pleasant adjuncts. Paul was flattered to the top of his bent; and, though the sword was hanging over his head, though he knew that the sword must fall,—must partly fall that very night,—still he enjoyed it.

There are men who, of their natures, do not like women, even though they may have wives and legions of daughters, and be surrounded by things feminine in all the affairs of their lives. Others again have their strongest affinities and sympathies with women, and are rarely altogether happy when removed from their influence. Paul Montague was of the latter sort. At this time he was thoroughly in love with Hetta Carbury, and was not in love with Mrs. Hurtle. He would have given much of his golden prospects in the American railway to have had Mrs. Hurtle reconveyed suddenly to San Francisco. And yet he had a delight in her presence. 'The acting isn't very good,' he said when the piece was nearly over.

'What does it signify? What we enjoy or what we suffer depends upon the humour. The acting is not first-rate, but I have listened and laughed and cried, because I have been happy.'

He was bound to tell her that he also had enjoyed the evening, and was bound to say it in no voice of hypocritical constraint. 'It has been very jolly,' he said.

'And one has so little that is really jolly, as you call it. I wonder whether any girl ever did sit and cry like that because her lover talked to another woman. What I find fault with is that the writers and actors are so ignorant of men and women as we see them every day. It's all right that she should cry, but she wouldn't cry there.' The position described was so nearly her own, that he could say nothing to this. She had so spoken on purpose, —fighting her own battle after her own fashion, knowing well that her words would confuse him. 'A woman hides such tears. She may be found crying because she is unable to hide them;—but she does not willingly let the other woman see them. Does she?'

'I suppose not.'

'Medea did not weep when she was introduced to Creusa.'*

'Women are not all Medeas,' he replied.

'There's a dash of the savage princess about most of them. I am quite ready if you like. I never want to see the curtain fall. And I have had no nosegay brought in a wheelbarrow to throw on to the stage. Are you going to see me home?'

'Certainly.'

'You need not. I'm not a bit afraid of a London cab by myself.' But of course he accompanied her to Islington. He owed her at any rate as much as that. She continued to talk during the whole journey. What a wonderful place London was,—so immense, but so dirty! New York of course was not so big, but was, she thought, pleasanter. But Paris was the gem of gems among towns. She did not like Frenchmen, and she liked Englishmen even better than Americans; but she fancied that she could never like English women. 'I do so hate all kinds of buckram. I like good conduct, and law, and religion too if it be not forced down one's throat; but I hate what your women call propriety. I suppose what we have been doing to-night is very improper; but I am quite sure that it has not been in the least wicked.'

'I don't think it has,' said Paul Montague very tamely.

It is a long way from the Haymarket to Islington, but at last the cab reached the lodging-house door. 'Yes, this is it,' she said. 'Even about the houses there is an air of stiff-necked propriety which frightens me.' She was getting out as she spoke, and he had already knocked at the door. 'Come in for one moment,' she said as he paid the cabman. The woman the while was standing with the door in her hand. It was near midnight,—but, when people are engaged, hours do not matter. The woman of the house, who was respectability herself,—a nice kind widow, with five children, named Pipkin,—understood that and smiled again as he followed the lady into the sitting-room. She had already taken off her hat and was flinging it on to the sofa as he entered. 'Shut the door for one moment,' she said; and he shut it. Then she threw herself into his arms, not kissing him but looking up into his face. 'Oh Paul,' she exclaimed, 'my darling! Oh Paul, my love! I will not bear to be separated from you. No, no;—never. I swear it, and you may believe me. There is nothing I cannot do for love of you,—but to lose you.' Then she pushed him from her and looked away from him, clasping her hands together. 'But Paul, I mean to keep my pledge to you to-night. It was to be an island in our troubles, a little holiday in our hard school-time, and I will not destroy it at its close. You will see me again soon,—will you not?' He nodded assent, then took her in his arms and kissed her, and left her without a word.

## Chapter XXVIII

### DOLLY LONGESTAFFE GOES INTO THE CITY

IT has been told how the gambling at the Beargarden went on one Sunday night. On the following Monday

Sir Felix did not go to the club. He had watched Miles
Grendall at play, and was sure that on more than one
or two occasions the man had cheated. Sir Felix did
not quite know what in such circumstances it would be
best for him to do. Reprobate as he was himself, this
work of villainy was new to him and seemed to be very
terrible. What steps ought he to take? He was quite
sure of his facts, and yet he feared that Nidderdale and
Grasslough and Longestaffe would not believe him. He
would have told Montague, but Montague had, he
thought, hardly enough authority at the club to be of
any use to him. On the Tuesday again he did not go to
the club. He felt severely the loss of the excitement to
which he had been accustomed, but the thing was too
important to him to be slurred over. He did not dare
to sit down and play with the man who had cheated him
without saying anything about it. On the Wednesday
afternoon life was becoming unbearable to him and he
sauntered into the building at about five in the afternoon.
There, as a matter of course, he found Dolly Longestaffe
drinking sherry and bitters. 'Where the blessed angels
have you been?' said Dolly. Dolly was at that moment
alert with the sense of a duty performed. He had just
called on his sister and written a sharp letter to his father,
and felt himself to be almost a man of business.

'I've had fish of my own to fry,' said Felix, who had
passed the last two days in unendurable idleness. Then
he referred again to the money which Dolly owed him,
not making any complaint, not indeed asking for immediate payment, but explaining with an air of importance
that if a commercial arrangement could be made, it
might, at this moment, be very serviceable to him. 'I'm
particularly anxious to take up those shares,' said Felix.

'Of course you ought to have your money.'

'I don't say that at all, old fellow. I know very well
that you're all right. You're not like that fellow, Miles
Grendall.'

'Well; no. Poor Miles has got nothing to bless himself with. I suppose I could get it, and so I ought to
pay.'

'That's no excuse for Grendall,' said Sir Felix, shaking his head.

'A chap can't pay if he hasn't got it, Carbury. A chap ought to pay of course. I've had a letter from our lawyer within the last half hour—here it is.' And Dolly pulled a letter out of his pocket which he had opened and read indeed the last hour, but which had been duly delivered at his lodgings early in the morning. 'My governor wants to sell Pickering, and Melmotte wants to buy the place. My governor can't sell without me, and I've asked for half the plunder. I know what's what. My interest in the property is greater than his. It isn't much of a place, and they are talking of £50,000, over and above the debt upon it. £25,000 would pay off what I owe on my own property, and make me very square. From what this fellow says I suppose they're going to give in to my terms.'

'By George, that'll be a grand thing for you, Dolly.'

'Oh yes. Of course I want it. But I don't like the place going. I'm not much of a fellow, I know. I'm awfully lazy and can't get myself to go in for things as I ought to do; but I've a sort of feeling that I don't like the family property going to pieces. A fellow oughtn't to let his family property go to pieces.'

'You never lived at Pickering.'

'No;—and I don't know that it is any good. It gives us 3 per cent. on the money it's worth, while the governor is paying 6 per cent., and I'm paying 25, for the money we've borrowed. I know more about it than you'd think. It ought to be sold, and now I suppose it will be sold. Old Melmotte knows all about it, and if you like I'll go with you to the city to-morrow and make it straight about what I owe you. He'll advance me £1,000, and then you can get the shares. Are you going to dine here?'

Sir Felix said that he would dine at the club, but declared, with considerable mystery in his manner, that he could not stay and play whist afterwards. He acceded willingly to Dolly's plans of visiting Abchurch Lane on the following day, but had some difficulty in inducing his friend to consent to fix on an hour early enough for city purposes. Dolly suggested that they should meet at the club at 4 p.m. Sir Felix had named noon, and promised to call at Dolly's lodgings. They split the difference at last and agreed to start at two. They then dined together, Miles Grendall dining alone at the next table to them. Dolly and Grendall spoke to each other frequently, but in that conversation the young baronet would not join. Nor did Grendall ever address himself to Sir Felix. 'Is there anything up between you and Miles?' said Dolly, when they had adjourned to the smoking-room.

'I can't bear him.'

'There never was any love between you two, I know. But you used to speak, and you've played with him all through.'

'Played with him! I should think I have. Though he did get such a haul last Sunday he owes me more than you do now.'

'Is that the reason you haven't played the last two nights?'

Sir Felix paused a moment. 'No;—that is not the reason. I'll tell you all about it in the cab to-morrow.' Then he left the club, declaring that he would go up to Grosvenor Square and see Marie Melmotte. He did go up to the Square, and when he came to the house he would not go in. What was the good? He could do nothing further till he got old Melmotte's consent, and in no way could he so probably do that as by showing that he had got money wherewith to buy shares in the railway. What he did with himself during the remainder of the evening the reader need not know, but on his return home at some comparatively early hour, he found this note from Marie.

'Wednesday Afternoon.

'Dearest Felix,

'Why don't we see you? Mamma would say nothing if you came. Papa is never in the drawing-room. Miss Longestaffe is here of course, and people always come in in the evening. We are just going to dine out at the Duchess of Stevenage's. Papa, and mamma and I.

Mamma told me that Lord Nidderdale is to be there, but you need not be a bit afraid. I don't like Lord Nidderdale, and I will never take any one but the man I love. You know who that is. Miss Longestaffe is so angry because she can't go with us. What do you think of her telling me that she did not understand being left alone? We are to go afterwards to a musical party at Lady Gamut's. Miss Longestaffe is going with us, but she says she hates music. She is such a set-up thing! I wonder why papa has her here. We don't go anywhere to-morrow evening, so pray come.

'And why haven't you written me something and sent it to Didon? She won't betray us. And if she did, what matters? I mean to be true. If papa were to beat me into a mummy I would stick to you. He told me once to take Lord Nidderdale, and then he told me to refuse him. And now he wants me to take him again. But I won't. I'll take no one but my own darling.

'Yours for ever and ever,<br>'MARIE.'

Now that the young lady had begun to have an interest of her own in life, she was determined to make the most of it. All this was delightful to her, but to Sir Felix it was simply 'a bother.' Sir Felix was quite willing to marry the girl to-morrow,—on condition of course that the money was properly arranged; but he was not willing to go through much work in the way of love-making with Marie Melmotte. In such business he preferred Ruby Ruggles as a companion.

On the following day Felix was with his friend at the appointed time, and was only kept an hour waiting while Dolly ate his breakfast and struggled into his coat and boots. On their way to the city Felix told his dreadful story about Miles Grendall. 'By George!' said Dolly. 'And you think you saw him do it!'

'It's not thinking at all. I'm sure I saw him do it three times. I believe he always had an ace somewhere about him.' Dolly sat quite silent thinking of it. 'What had I better do?' asked Sir Felix.

'By George;—I don't know.'

'What should you do?'

'Nothing at all. I shouldn't believe my own eyes. Or if I did, should take care not to look at him.'

'You wouldn't go on playing with him?'

'Yes I should. It'd be such a bore breaking up.'

'But Dolly,—if you think of it!'

'That's all very fine, my dear fellow, but I shouldn't think of it.'

'And you won't give me your advice.'

'Well;—no; I think I'd rather not. I wish you hadn't told me. Why did you pick me out to tell me? Why didn't you tell Nidderdale?'

'He might have said, why didn't you tell Longestaffe?'

'No, he wouldn't. Nobody would suppose that anybody would pick me out for this kind of thing. If I'd known that you were going to tell me such a story as this I wouldn't have come with you.'

'That's nonsense, Dolly.'

'Very well. I can't bear these kind of things. I feel all in a twitter already.'

'You mean to go on playing just the same?'

'Of course I do. If he won anything very heavy I should begin to think about it, I suppose. Oh; this is Abchurch Lane, is it? Now for the man of money.'

The man of money received them much more graciously than Felix had expected. Of course nothing was said about Marie and no further allusion was made to the painful subject of the baronet's 'property.' Both Dolly and Sir Felix were astonished by the quick way in which the great financer understood their views and the readiness with which he undertook to comply with them. No disagreeable questions were asked as to the nature of the debt between the young men. Dolly was called upon to sign a couple of documents, and Sir Felix to sign one,—and then they were assured that the thing was done. Mr. Adolphus Longestaffe had paid Sir Felix Carbury a thousand pounds, and Sir Felix Carbury's commission had been accepted by Mr. Melmotte for the purchase of railway stock to that amount. Sir Felix

attempted to say a word. He endeavoured to explain
that his object in this commercial transaction was to
make money immediately by reselling the shares,—and
to go on continually making money by buying at a low
price and selling at a high price. He no doubt did believe
that, being a Director, if he could once raise the means
of beginning this game, he could go on with it for an
unlimited period;—buy and sell, buy and sell;—so that
he would have an almost regular income. This, as far
as he could understand, was what Paul Montague was
allowed to do,—simply because he had become a Director
with a little money. Mr. Melmotte was cordiality itself,
but he could not be got to go into particulars. It was all
right. 'You will wish to sell again, of course;—of course.
I'll watch the market for you.' When the young men
left the room all they knew, or thought that they knew,
was, that Dolly Longestaffe had authorized Melmotte to
pay a thousand pounds on his behalf to Sir Felix, and
that Sir Felix had instructed the same great man to buy
shares with the amount. 'But why didn't he give you the
scrip?' said Dolly on his way westwards.

'I suppose it's all right with him,' said Sir Felix.

'Oh yes;—it's all right. Thousands of pounds to him
are only like half-crowns to us fellows. I should say it's
all right. All the same, he's the biggest rogue out, you
know.' Sir Felix already began to be unhappy about his
thousand pounds.

## Chapter XXIX

### MISS MELMOTTE'S COURAGE

LADY CARBURY continued to ask frequent questions as to the prosecution of her son's suit, and Sir
Felix began to think that he was persecuted. 'I have
spoken to her father,' he said crossly.

'And what did Mr. Melmotte say?'

'Say;—what should he say? He wanted to know what
income I had got. After all he's an old screw.'

'Did he forbid you to come there any more?'

'Now, mother, it's no use your cross-examining me. If you'll let me alone I'll do the best I can.'

'She has accepted you, herself?'

'Of course she has. I told you that at Carbury.'

'Then, Felix, if I were you I'd run off with her. I would indeed. It's done every day, and nobody thinks any harm of it when you marry the girl. You could do it now because I know you've got money. From all I can hear she's just the sort of girl that would go with you.' The son sat silent, listening to these maternal councils. He did believe that Marie would go off with him, were he to propose the scheme to her. Her own father had almost alluded to such a proceeding,—had certainly hinted that it was feasible,—but at the same time had very clearly stated that in such case the ardent lover would have to content himself with the lady alone. In any such event as that there would be no fortune. But then, might not that only be a threat? Rich fathers generally do forgive their daughters, and a rich father with only one child would surely forgive her when she returned to him, as she would do in this instance, graced with a title. Sir Felix thought of all this as he sat there silent. His mother read his thoughts as she continued. 'Of course, Felix, there must be some risk.'

'Fancy what it would be to be thrown over at last!' he exclaimed. 'I couldn't bear it. I think I should kill her.'

'Oh no, Felix; you wouldn't do that. But when I say there would be some risk I mean that there would be very little. There would be nothing in it that ought to make him really angry. He has nobody else to give his money to, and it would be much nicer to have his daughter, Lady Carbury, with him, than to be left all alone in the world.'

'I couldn't live with him, you know. I couldn't do it.'

'You needn't live with him, Felix. Of course she would visit her parents. When the money was once settled you need see as little of them as you pleased. Pray do not allow trifles to interfere with you. If this should not succeed, what are you to do? We shall all starve unless something be done. If I were you, Felix, I would take her away at once. They say she is of age.'

'I shouldn't know where to take her,' said Sir Felix, almost stunned into thoughtfulness by the magnitude of the proposition made to him. 'All that about Scotland is done with now.'*

'Of course you would marry her at once.'

'I suppose so,—unless it were better to stay as we were, till the money was settled.'

'Oh no; no! Everybody would be against you. If you take her off in a spirited sort of way and then marry her, everybody will be with you. That's what you want. The father and mother will be sure to come round, if——'

'The mother is nothing.'

'He will come round if people speak up in your favour. I could get Mr. Alf and Mr. Broune to help. I'd try it, Felix; indeed I would. Ten thousand a year is not to be had every year.'

Sir Felix gave no assent to his mother's views. He felt no desire to relieve her anxiety by an assurance of activity in the matter. But the prospect was so grand that it had excited even him. He had money sufficient for carrying out the scheme, and if he delayed the matter now, it might well be that he would never again find himself so circumstanced. He thought that he would ask somebody whither he ought to take her, and what he ought to do with her;—and that he would then make the proposition to herself. Miles Grendall would be the man to tell him, because, with all his faults, Miles did understand things. But he could not ask Miles. He and Nidderdale were good friends; but Nidderdale wanted the girl for himself. Grasslough would be sure to tell Nidderdale. Dolly would be altogether useless. He thought that, perhaps, Herr Vossner would be the man to help him. There would be no difficulty out of which Herr Vossner would not extricate 'a fellow,'—if 'the fellow' paid him.

On Thursday evening he went to Grosvenor Square, as desired by Marie,—but unfortunately found Melmotte

in the drawing-room. Lord Nidderdale was there also,
and his lordship's old father, the Marquis of Auld
Reekie, whom Felix, when he entered the room, did not
know. He was a fierce-looking, gouty old man, with
watery eyes, and very stiff grey hair,—almost white. He
was standing up supporting himself on two sticks when
Sir Felix entered the room. There were also present
Madame Melmotte, Miss Longestaffe, and Marie. As
Felix had entered the hall one huge footman had said
that the ladies were not at home; then there had been
for a moment a whispering behind a door,—in which
he afterwards conceived that Madame Didon had taken
a part;—and upon that a second tall footman had contradicted the first and had ushered him up to the drawing-
room. He felt considerably embarrassed, but shook
hands with the ladies, bowed to Melmotte, who seemed
to take no notice of him, and nodded to Lord Nidderdale.
He had not had time to place himself, when the Marquis
arranged things. 'Suppose we go downstairs,' said the
Marquis.

'Certainly, my lord,' said Melmotte. 'I'll show your
lordship the way.' The Marquis did not speak to his son,
but poked at him with his stick, as though poking him
out of the door. So instigated, Nidderdale followed the
financier, and the gouty old Marquis toddled after them.

Madame Melmotte was beside herself with trepidation. 'You should not have been made to come up at
all,' she said. 'Il faut que vous vous retiriez.'

'I am very sorry,' said Sir Felix, looking quite aghast.

'I think that I had at any rate better retire,' said
Miss Longestaffe, raising herself to her full height and
stalking out of the room.

'Qu'elle est méchante,' said Madame Melmotte. 'Oh,
she is so bad. Sir Felix, you had better go too. Yes,—
indeed.'

'No,' said Marie, running to him, and taking hold of
his arm. 'Why should he go? I want papa to know.'

'Il vous tuera,' said Madame Melmotte. 'My God,
yes.'

'Then he shall,' said Marie, clinging to her lover. 'I

will never marry Lord Nidderdale. If he were to cut me
into bits I wouldn't do it. Felix, you love me;—do you
not?'

'Certainly,' said Sir Felix, slipping his arm round her
waist.

'Mamma,' said Marie, 'I will never have any other
man but him;—never, never, never. Oh, Felix, tell her
that you love me.'

'You know that, don't you, ma'am?' Sir Felix was a
little troubled in his mind as to what he should say, or
what he should do.

'Oh, love! It is a beastliness,' said Madame Melmotte.
'Sir Felix, you had better go. Yes, indeed. Will you be
so obliging?'

'Don't go,' said Marie. 'No, mamma, he shan't go.
What has he to be afraid of? I will walk down among
them into papa's room, and say that I will never marry
that man, and that this is my lover. Felix, will you
come?'

Sir Felix did not quite like the proposition. There had
been a savage ferocity in that Marquis's eye, and there
was habitually a heavy sternness about Melmotte, which
together made him resist the invitation. 'I don't think I
have a right to do that,' he said, 'because it is Mr. Melmotte's own house.'

'I wouldn't mind,' said Marie. 'I told papa to-day that
I wouldn't marry Lord Nidderdale.'

'Was he angry with you?'

'He laughed at me. He manages people till he thinks
that everybody must do exactly what he tells them. He
may kill me, but I will not do it. I have quite made up
my mind. Felix, if you will be true to me, nothing shall
separate us. I will not be ashamed to tell everybody that
I love you.'

Madame Melmotte had now thrown herself into a
chair and was sighing. Sir Felix stood on the rug with
his arm round Marie's waist listening to her protestations, but saying little in answer to them,—when, suddenly, a heavy step was heard ascending the stairs.
'C'est lui,' screamed Madame Melmotte, bustling up

from her seat and hurrying out of the room by a side door. The two lovers were alone for one moment, during which Marie lifted up her face, and Sir Felix kissed her lips. 'Now be brave,' she said, escaping from his arm, 'and I'll be brave.' Mr. Melmotte looked round the room as he entered. 'Where are the others?' he asked.

'Mamma has gone away, and Miss Longestaffe went before mamma.'

'Sir Felix, it is well that I should tell you that my daughter is engaged to marry Lord Nidderdale.'

'Sir Felix, I am not engaged—to—marry Lord Nidderdale,' said Marie. 'It's no good, papa. I won't do it. If you chop me to pieces, I won't do it.'

'She will marry Lord Nidderdale,' continued Mr. Melmotte, addressing himself to Sir Felix. 'As that is arranged, you will perhaps think it better to leave us. I shall be happy to renew my acquaintance with you as soon as the fact is recognized;—or happy to see you in the city at any time.'

'Papa, he is my lover,' said Marie.

'Pooh!'

'It is not pooh. He is. I will never have any other. I hate Lord Nidderdale; and as for that dreadful old man, I could not bear to look at him. Sir Felix is as good a gentleman as he is. If you loved me, papa, you would not want to make me unhappy all my life.'

Her father walked up to her rapidly with his hand raised, and she clung only the closer to her lover's arm. At this moment Sir Felix did not know what he might best do, but he thoroughly wished himself out in the square. 'Jade,' said Melmotte, 'get to your room.'

'Of course I will go to bed, if you tell me, papa.'

'I do tell you. How dare you take hold of him in that way before me! Have you no idea of disgrace?'

'I am not disgraced. It is not more disgraceful to love him than that other man. Oh, papa, don't. You hurt me. I am going.' He took her by the arm and dragged her to the door, and then thrust her out.

'I am very sorry, Mr. Melmotte,' said Sir Felix, 'to have had a hand in causing this disturbance.'

'Go away, and don't come back any more;—that's all. You can't both marry her. All you have got to understand is this. I'm not the man to give my daughter a single shilling if she marries against my consent. By the God that hears me, Sir Felix, she shall not have one shilling. But look you,—if you'll give this up, I shall be proud to co-operate with you in anything you may wish to have done in the city.'

After this Sir Felix left the room, went down the stairs, had the door opened for him, and was ushered into the square. But as he went through the hall a woman managed to shove a note into his hand,—which he read as soon as he found himself under a gas lamp. It was dated that morning, and had therefore no reference to the fray which had just taken place. It ran as follows:—

'I hope you will come to-night. There is something I cannot tell you then, but you ought to know it. When we were in France papa thought it wise to settle a lot of money on me. I don't know how much, but I suppose it was enough to live on if other things went wrong. He never talked to me about it, but I know it was done. And it hasn't been undone, and can't be without my leave. He is very angry about you this morning, for I told him I would never give you up. He says he won't give me anything if I marry without his leave. But I am sure he cannot take it away. I tell you, because I think I ought to tell you everything.

'M.'

Sir Felix as he read this could not but think that he had become engaged to a very enterprising young lady. It was evident that she did not care to what extent she braved her father on behalf of her lover, and now she coolly proposed to rob him. But Sir Felix saw no reason why he should not take advantage of the money made over to the girl's name, if he could lay his hands on it. He did not know much of such transactions, but he knew more than Marie Melmotte, and could understand that a man in Melmotte's position should want to secure a portion of his fortune against accidents, by settling it on his daughter. Whether, having so settled it, he could again resume it without the daughter's assent, Sir Felix did not know. Marie, who had no doubt been regarded as an absolutely passive instrument when the thing was done, was now quite alive to the benefit which she might possibly derive from it. Her proposition, put into plain English, amounted to this: 'Take me and marry me without my father's consent,—and then you and I together can rob my father of the money which, for his own purposes, he has settled upon me.' He had looked upon the lady of his choice as a poor weak thing, without any special character of her own, who was made worthy of consideration only by the fact that she was a rich man's daughter; but now she began to loom before his eyes as something bigger than that. She had had a will of her own when the mother had none. She had not been afraid of her brutal father when he, Sir Felix, had trembled before him. She had offered to be beaten, and killed, and chopped to pieces on behalf of her lover. There could be no doubt about her running away if she were asked.

It seemed to him that within the last month he had gained a great deal of experience, and that things which heretofore had been troublesome to him, or difficult, or perhaps impossible, were now coming easily within his reach. He had won two or three thousand pounds at cards, whereas invariable loss had been the result of the small play in which he had before indulged. He had been set to marry this heiress, having at first no great liking for the attempt, because of its difficulties and the small amount of hope which it offered him. The girl was already willing and anxious to jump into his arms. Then he had detected a man cheating at cards,—an extent of iniquity that was awful to him before he had seen it,— and was already beginning to think that there was not very much in that. If there was not much in it, if such a man as Miles Grendall could cheat at cards and be brought to no punishment, why should not he try it? It was a rapid way of winning, no doubt. He remembered that on one or two occasions he had asked his adversary to cut the cards a second time at whist, because he had observed that there was no honour at the bottom. No feeling of honesty had interfered with him. The little trick had hardly been premeditated, but when successful without detection had not troubled his conscience. Now it seemed to him that much more than that might be done without detection. But nothing had opened his eyes to the ways of the world so widely as the sweet lover-like proposition made by Miss Melmotte for robbing her father. It certainly recommended the girl to him. She had been able at an early age, amidst the circumstances of a very secluded life, to throw off from her altogether those scruples of honesty, those bugbears of the world, which are apt to prevent great enterprises in the minds of men.

What should he do next? This sum of money of which Marie wrote so easily was probably large. It would not have been worth the while of such a man as Mr. Melmotte to make a trifling provision of this nature. It could hardly be less than £50,000,—might probably be very much more. But this was certain to him,—that if he and Marie were to claim this money as man and wife, there could then be no hope of further liberality. It was not probable that such a man as Mr. Melmotte would forgive even an only child such an offence as that. Even if it were obtained, £50,000 would not be very much. And Melmotte might probably have means, even if the robbery were duly perpetrated, of making the possession of the money very uncomfortable. These were deep waters into which Sir Felix was preparing to plunge; and he did not feel himself to be altogether comfortable, although he liked the deep waters.

## Chapter XXX

### MR. MELMOTTE'S PROMISE

ON the following Saturday there appeared in Mr. Alf's paper, the 'Evening Pulpit,' a very remarkable article on the South Central Pacific and Mexican Rail-

way. It was an article that attracted a great deal of
attention and was therefore remarkable, but it was in
nothing more remarkable than in this,—that it left on
the mind of its reader no impression of any decided
opinion about the railway. The Editor would at any
future time be able to refer to his article with equal
pride whether the railway should become a great cosmo-
politan fact, or whether it should collapse amidst the
foul struggles of a horde of swindlers. In utrumque
paratus,* the article was mysterious, suggestive, amusing,
well-informed,—that in the 'Evening Pulpit' was a
matter of course,—and, above all things, ironical. Next
to its omniscience its irony was the strongest weapon
belonging to the 'Evening Pulpit.' There was a little
praise given, no doubt in irony, to the duchesses who
served Mr. Melmotte. There was a little praise, given
of course in irony, to Mr. Melmotte's Board of English
Directors. There was a good deal of praise, but still
alloyed by a dash of irony, bestowed on the idea of
civilizing Mexico by joining it to California. Praise was
bestowed upon England for taking up the matter, but
accompanied by some ironical touches at her incapacity
to believe thoroughly in any enterprise not originated by
herself. Then there was something said of the universa-
lity of Mr. Melmotte's commercial genius, but whether
said in a spirit prophetic of ultimate failure and disgrace,
or of heavenborn success and unequalled commercial
splendour, no one could tell.

It was generally said at the clubs that Mr. Alf had
written this article himself. Old Splinter, who was one
of a body of men possessing an excellent cellar of wine
and calling themselves Paides Pallados,* and who had
written for the heavy quarterlies any time this last forty
years, professed that he saw through the article. The
'Evening Pulpit' had been, he explained, desirous of
going as far as it could in denouncing Mr. Melmotte
without incurring the danger of an action for libel. Mr.
Splinter thought that the thing was clever but mean.
These new publications generally were mean. Mr.
Splinter was constant in that opinion; but, putting the

meanness aside, he thought that the article was well done. According to his view it was intended to expose Mr. Melmotte and the railway. But the Paides Pallados generally did not agree with him. Under such an interpretation, what had been the meaning of that paragraph in which the writer had declared that the work of joining one ocean to another was worthy of the nearest approach to divinity that had been granted to men? Old Splinter chuckled and gabbled as he heard this, and declared that there was not wit enough left now even among the Paides Pallados to understand a shaft of irony. There could be no doubt, however, at the time, that the world did not go with old Splinter, and that the article served to enhance the value of shares in the great railway enterprise.

Lady Carbury was sure that the article was intended to write up the railway, and took great joy in it. She entertained in her brain a somewhat confused notion that if she could only bestir herself in the right direction and could induce her son to open his eyes to his own advantage, very great things might be achieved, so that wealth might become his handmaid and luxury the habit and the right of his life. He was the beloved and the accepted suitor of Marie Melmotte. He was a Director of this great company, sitting at the same board with the great commercial hero. He was the handsomest young man in London. And he was a baronet. Very wild ideas occurred to her. Should she take Mr. Alf into her entire confidence? If Melmotte and Alf could be brought together what might they not do? Alf could write up Melmotte, and Melmotte could shower shares upon Alf. And if Melmotte would come and be smiled upon by herself, be flattered as she thought that she could flatter him, be told that he was a god, and have that passage about the divinity of joining ocean to ocean construed to him as she could construe it, would not the great man become plastic under her hands? And if, while this was a-doing, Felix would run away with Marie, could not forgiveness be made easy? And her creative mind ranged still farther. Mr. Broune might help, and even Mr.

Booker. To such a one as Melmotte, a man doing great things through the force of the confidence placed in him by the world at large, the freely-spoken support of the Press would be everything. Who would not buy shares in a railway as to which Mr. Broune and Mr. Alf would combine in saying that it was managed by 'divinity'? Her thoughts were rather hazy, but from day to day she worked hard to make them clear to herself.

On the Sunday afternoon Mr. Booker called on her and talked to her about the article. She did not say much to Mr. Booker as to her own connection with Mr. Melmotte, telling herself that prudence was essential in the present emergency. But she listened with all her ears. It was Mr. Booker's idea that the man was going 'to make a spoon or spoil a horn.'* 'You think him honest;—don't you?' asked Lady Carbury. Mr. Booker smiled and hesitated. 'Of course, I mean honest as men can be in such very large transactions.'

'Perhaps that is the best way of putting it,' said Mr. Booker.

'If a thing can be made great and beneficent, a boon to humanity, simply by creating a belief in it, does not a man become a benefactor to his race by creating that belief?'

'At the expense of veracity?' suggested Mr. Booker.

'At the expense of anything?' rejoined Lady Carbury with energy. 'One cannot measure such men by the ordinary rule.'

'You would do evil to produce good?' asked Mr. Booker.

'I do not call it doing evil.. You have to destroy a thousand living creatures every time you drink a glass of water, but you do not think of that when you are athirst. You cannot send a ship to sea without endangering lives. You do send ships to sea though men perish yearly. You tell me this man may perhaps ruin hundreds, but then again he may create a new world in which millions will be rich and happy.'

'You are an excellent casuist, Lady Carbury.'

'I am an enthusiastic lover of beneficent audacity,' said

Lady Carbury, picking her words slowly, and showing
herself to be quite satisfied with herself as she picked
them. 'Did I hold your place, Mr. Booker, in the literature of my country,——'

'I hold no place, Lady Carbury.'

'Yes;—and a very distinguished place. Were I circumstanced as you are I should have no hesitation in
lending the whole weight of my periodical, let it be what
it might, to the assistance of so great a man and so great
an object as this.'

'I should be dismissed to-morrow,' said Mr. Booker,
getting up and laughing as he took his departure. Lady
Carbury felt that, as regarded Mr. Booker, she had only
thrown out a chance word that could not do any harm.
She had not expected to effect much through Mr. Booker's
instrumentality. On the Tuesday evening,—her regular
Tuesday as she called it,—all her three editors came to
her drawing-room; but there came also a greater man
than either of them. She had taken the bull by the horns,
and without saying anything to anybody had written to
Mr. Melmotte himself, asking him to honour her poor
house with his presence. She had written a very pretty
note to him, reminding him of their meeting at Caversham, telling him that on a former occasion Madame
Melmotte and his daughter had been so kind as to come
to her, and giving him to understand that of all the
potentates now on earth he was the one to whom she
could bow the knee with the purest satisfaction. He
wrote back,—or Miles Grendall did for him,—a very
plain note, accepting the honour of Lady Carbury's
invitation.

The great man came, and Lady Carbury took him
under her immediate wing with a grace that was all her
own. She said a word about their dear friends at Caversham, expressed her sorrow that her son's engagements
did not admit of his being there, and then with the utmost audacity rushed off to the article in the 'Pulpit.'
Her friend, Mr. Alf, the editor, had thoroughly appreciated the greatness of Mr. Melmotte's character, and
the magnificence of Mr. Melmotte's undertakings. Mr.

Melmotte bowed and muttered something that was inaudible. 'Now I must introduce you to Mr. Alf,' said the lady. The introduction was effected, and Mr. Alf explained that it was hardly necessary, as he had already been entertained as one of Mr. Melmotte's guests.

'There were a great many there I never saw, and probably never shall see,' said Mr. Melmotte.

'I was one of the unfortunates,' said Mr. Alf.

'I'm sorry you were unfortunate. If you had come into the whist room you would have found me.'

'Ah,—if I had but known!' said Mr. Alf. The editor, as was proper, carried about with him samples of the irony which his paper used so effectively, but it was altogether thrown away upon Melmotte.

Lady Carbury, finding that no immediate good results could be expected from this last introduction, tried another. 'Mr. Melmotte,' she said, whispering to him, 'I do so want to make you known to Mr. Broune. Mr. Broune I know you have never met before. A morning paper is a much heavier burden to an editor than one published in the afternoon. Mr. Broune, as of course you know, manages the "Breakfast Table." There is hardly a more influential man in London than Mr. Broune. And they declare, you know,' she said, lowering the tone of her whisper as she communicated the fact, 'that his commercial articles are gospel,—absolutely gospel.' Then the two men were named to each other, and Lady Carbury retreated;—but not out of hearing.

'Getting very hot,' said Mr. Melmotte.

'Very hot indeed,' said Mr. Broune.

'It was over 70 in the city to-day. I call that very hot for June.'

'Very hot indeed,' said Mr. Broune again. Then the conversation was over. Mr. Broune sidled away, and Mr. Melmotte was left standing in the middle of the room. Lady Carbury told herself at the moment that Rome was not built in a day. She would have been better satisfied certainly if she could have laid a few more bricks on this day. Perseverance, however, was the thing wanted.

But Mr. Melmotte himself had a word to say, and before he left the house he said it. 'It was very good of you to ask me, Lady Carbury;—very good.' Lady Carbury intimated her opinion that the goodness was all on the other side. 'And I came,' continued Mr. Melmotte, 'because I had something particular to say. Otherwise I don't go out much to evening parties. Your son has proposed to my daughter.' Lady Carbury looked up into his face with all her eyes;—clasped both her hands together; and then, having unclasped them, put one upon his sleeve. 'My daughter, ma'am, is engaged to another man.'

'You would not enslave her affections, Mr. Melmotte?'

'I won't give her a shilling if she marries any one else; that's all. You reminded me down at Caversham that your son is a Director at our Board.'

'I did;—I did.'

'I have a great respect for your son, ma'am. I don't want to hurt him in any way. If he'll signify to my daughter that he withdraws from this offer of his, because I'm against it, I'll see that he does uncommon well in the city. I'll be the making of him. Good night, ma'am.' Then Mr. Melmotte took his departure without another word.

Here at any rate was an undertaking on the part of the great man that he would be the 'making of Felix,' if Felix would only obey him,—accompanied, or rather preceded, by a most positive assurance that if Felix were to succeed in marrying his daughter he would not give his son-in-law a shilling! There was very much to be considered in this. She did not doubt that Felix might be 'made' by Mr. Melmotte's city influences, but then any perpetuity of such making must depend on qualifications in her son which she feared that he did not possess. The wife without the money would be terrible! That would be absolute ruin! There could be no escape then; no hope. There was an appreciation of real tragedy in her heart while she contemplated the position of Sir Felix married to such a girl as she supposed Marie Melmotte to be, without any means of support for either of

them but what she could supply. It would kill her. And
for those young people there would be nothing before
them, but beggary and the workhouse. As she thought
of this she trembled with true maternal instincts. Her
beautiful boy,—so glorious with his outward gifts, so fit,
as she thought him, for all the graces of the grand world!
Though the ambition was vilely ignoble, the mother's
love was noble and disinterested.

But the girl was an only child. The future honours of
the house of Melmotte could be made to settle on no
other head. No doubt the father would prefer a lord for
a son-in-law; and, having that preference, would of
course do as he was now doing. That he should threaten
to disinherit his daughter if she married contrary to his
wishes was to be expected. But would it not be equally
a matter of course that he should make the best of the
marriage if it were once effected? His daughter would
return to him with a title, though with one of a lower
degree than his ambition desired. To herself personally,
Lady Carbury felt that the great financier had been very
rude. He had taken advantage of her invitation that he
might come to her house and threaten her. But she
would forgive that. She could pass that over altogether
if only anything were to be gained by passing it over.

She looked round the room, longing for a friend, whom
she might consult with a true feeling of genuine womanly
dependence. Her most natural friend was Roger Carbury. But even had he been there she could not have
consulted him on any matter touching the Melmottes.
His advice would have been very clear. He would have
told her to have nothing at all to do with such adventurers. But then dear Roger was old-fashioned, and
knew nothing of people as they are now. He lived in a
world which, though slow, had been good in its way;
but which, whether bad or good, had now passed away.
Then her eye settled on Mr. Broune. She was afraid of
Mr. Alf. She had almost begun to think that Mr. Alf
was too difficult of management to be of use to her. But
Mr. Broune was softer. Mr. Booker was serviceable for
an article, but would not be sympathetic as a friend.

Mr. Broune had been very courteous to her lately;—so much so that on one occasion she had almost feared that the 'susceptible old goose' was going to be a goose again. That would be a bore; but still she might make use of the friendly condition of mind which such susceptibility would produce. When her guests began to leave her, she spoke a word aside to him. She wanted his advice. Would he stay for a few minutes after the rest of the company? He did stay, and when all the others were gone she asked her daughter to leave them. 'Hetta,' she said, 'I have something of business to communicate to Mr. Broune.' And so they were left alone.

'I'm afraid you didn't make much of Mr. Melmotte,' she said smiling. He had seated himself on the end of a sofa, close to the arm-chair which she occupied. In reply, he only shook his head and laughed. 'I saw how it was, and I was sorry for it; for he certainly is a wonderful man.'

'I suppose he is, but he is one of those men whose powers do not lie, I should say, chiefly in conversation. Though, indeed, there is no reason why he should not say the same of me;—for if he said little, I said less.'

'It didn't just come off,' Lady Carbury suggested with her sweetest smile. 'But now I want to tell you something. I think I am justified in regarding you as a real friend.'

'Certainly,' he said, putting out his hand for hers.

She gave it to him for a moment, and then took it back again,—finding that he did not relinquish it of his own accord. 'Stupid old goose!' she said to herself. 'And now to my story. You know my boy, Felix?' The editor nodded his head. 'He is engaged to marry that man's daughter.'

'Engaged to marry Miss Melmotte?' Then Lady Carbury nodded her head. 'Why, she is said to be the greatest heiress that the world has ever produced. I thought she was to marry Lord Nidderdale.'

'She has engaged herself to Felix. She is desperately in love with him,—as is he with her.' She tried to tell her story truly, knowing that no advice can be worth anything that is not based on a true story;—but lying had become her nature. 'Melmotte naturally wants her to marry the lord. He came here to tell me that if his daughter married Felix she would not have a penny.'

'Do you mean that he volunteered that,—as a threat?'

'Just so;—and he told me that he had come here simply with the object of saying so. It was more candid than civil, but we must take it as we get it.'

'He would be sure to make some such threat.'

'Exactly. That is just what I feel. And in these days young people are often kept from marrying simply by a father's fantasy. But I must tell you something else. He told me that if Felix would desist, he would enable him to make a fortune in the city.'

'That's bosh,' said Broune with decision.

'Do you think it must be so;—certainly?'

'Yes, I do. Such an undertaking, if intended by Melmotte, would give me a worse opinion of him than I have ever held.'

'He did make it.'

'Then he did very wrong. He must have spoken with the purpose of deceiving.'

'You know my son is one of the Directors of that great American Railway. It was not just as though the promise were made to a young man who was altogether unconnected with him.'

'Sir Felix's name was put there, in a hurry, merely because he has a title, and because Melmotte thought he, as a young man, would not be likely to interfere with him. It may be that he will be able to sell a few shares at a profit; but, if I understand the matter rightly, he has no capital to go into such a business.'

'No;—he has no capital.'

'Dear Lady Carbury, I would place no dependence at all on such a promise as that.'

'You think he should marry the girl then in spite of the father?'

Mr. Broune hesitated before he replied to this question. But it was to this question that Lady Carbury especially wished for a reply. She wanted some one to support her under the circumstances of an elopement. She rose from her chair, and he rose at the same time. 'Perhaps I should have begun by saying that Felix is all but prepared to take her off. She is quite ready to go. She is devoted to him. Do you think he would be wrong?'

'That is a question very hard to answer.'

'People do it every day. Lionel Goldsheiner ran away the other day with Lady Julia Start, and everybody visits them.'

'Oh yes, people do run away, and it all comes right. It was the gentleman had the money then, and it is said you know that old Lady Catchboy, Lady Julia's mother, had arranged the elopement herself as offering the safest way of securing the rich prize. The young lord didn't like it, so the mother had it done in that fashion.'

'There would be nothing disgraceful.'

'I didn't say there would;—but nevertheless it is one of those things a man hardly ventures to advise. If you ask me whether I think that Melmotte would forgive her, and make her an allowance afterwards,—I think he would.'

'I am so glad to hear you say that.'

'And I feel quite certain that no dependence whatever should be placed on that promise of assistance.'

'I quite agree with you. I am so much obliged to you,' said Lady Carbury, who was now determined that Felix should run off with the girl. 'You have been so very kind.' Then again she gave him her hand, as though to bid him farewell for the night.

'And now,' he said, 'I also have something to say to you.'

## Chapter XXXI

### MR. BROUNE HAS MADE UP HIS MIND

'AND now I have something to say to you.' Mr. Broune as he thus spoke to Lady Carbury rose up to his feet and then sat down again. There was an air of perturbation about him which was very manifest to the lady, and the cause and coming result of which she thought that she understood. 'The susceptible old goose is going to do something highly ridiculous and very disagreeable.' It was thus that she spoke to herself of the scene that she saw was prepared for her, but she did not foresee accurately the shape in which the susceptibility of the 'old goose' would declare itself. 'Lady Carbury,' said Mr. Broune, standing up a second time, 'we are neither of us so young as we used to be.'

'No, indeed;—and therefore it is that we can afford to ourselves the luxury of being friends. Nothing but age enables men and women to know each other intimately.'

This speech was a great impediment to Mr. Broune's progress. It was evidently intended to imply that he at least had reached a time of life at which any allusion to love would be absurd. And yet, as a fact, he was nearer fifty than sixty, was young of his age, could walk his four or five miles pleasantly, could ride his cob in the park with as free an air as any man of forty, and could afterwards work through four or five hours of the night with an easy steadiness which nothing but sound health could produce. Mr. Broune, thinking of himself and his own circumstances, could see no reason why he should not be in love. 'I hope we know each other intimately at any rate,' he said somewhat lamely.

'Oh, yes;—and it is for that reason that I have come to you for advice. Had I been a young woman I should not have dared to ask you.'

'I don't see that. I don't quite understand that. But it has nothing to do with my present purpose. When I said that we were neither of us so young as we once were, I uttered what was a stupid platitude,—a foolish truism.'

'I do not think so,' said Lady Carbury smiling.

'Or would have been, only that I intended something further.' Mr. Broune had got himself into a difficulty and hardly knew how to get out of it. 'I was going on to say that I hoped we were not too old to—love.'

Foolish old darling! What did he mean by making such an ass of himself? This was worse even than the kiss, as being more troublesome and less easily pushed on one side and forgotten. It may serve to explain the condition of Lady Carbury's mind at the time if it be stated that she did not even at this moment suppose that the editor of the 'Morning Breakfast Table' intended to make her an offer of marriage. She knew, or thought she knew, that middle-aged men are fond of prating about love, and getting up sensational scenes. The false-ness of the thing, and the injury which may come of it, did not shock her at all. Had she known that the editor professed to be in love with some lady in the next street, she would have been quite ready to enlist the lady in the next street among her friends that she might thus strengthen her own influence with Mr. Broune. For herself such make-believe of an improper passion would be inconvenient, and therefore to be avoided. But that any man, placed as Mr. Broune was in the world,—blessed with power, with a large income, with influence throughout all the world around him, courted, fêted, feared and almost worshipped,—that he should desire to share her fortunes, her misfortunes, her struggles, her poverty and her obscurity, was not within the scope of her imagination. There was a homage in it, of which she did not believe any man to be capable,—and which to her would be the more wonderful as being paid to herself. She thought so badly of men and women gene-rally, and of Mr. Broune and herself as a man and a woman individually, that she was unable to conceive the possibility of such a sacrifice. 'Mr. Broune,' she said, 'I did not think that you would take advantage of the confi-dence I have placed in you to annoy me in this way.'

'To annoy you, Lady Carbury! The phrase at any rate is singular. After much thought I have determined to ask you to be my wife. That I should be—annoyed, and more than annoyed by your refusal, is a matter of course. That I ought to expect such annoyance is per-haps too true. But you can extricate yourself from the dilemma only too easily.'

The word 'wife' came upon her like a thunder-clap. It at once changed all her feelings towards him. She did not dream of loving him. She felt sure that she never could love him. Had it been on the cards with her to love any man as a lover, it would have been some handsome spendthrift who would have hung from her neck like a nether millstone. This man was a friend to be used,—to be used because he knew the world. And now he gave her this clear testimony that he knew as little of the world as any other man. Mr. Broune of the 'Daily Breakfast Table' asking her to be his wife! But mixed with her other feelings there was a tenderness which brought back some memory of her distant youth, and almost made her weep. That a man,—such a man,—should offer to take half her burdens, and to confer upon her half his blessings! What an idiot! But what a god! She had looked upon the man as all intellect, alloyed perhaps by some passionless remnants of the vices of his youth; and now she found that he not only had a human heart in his bosom, but a heart that she could touch. How wonderfully sweet! How infinitely small!

It was necessary that she should answer him;—and to her it was only natural that she should think what answer would best assist her own views without reference to his. It did not occur to her that she could love him; but it did occur to her that he might lift her out of her difficulties. What a benefit it would be to her to have a father, and such a father, for Felix! How easy would be a literary career to the wife of the editor of the 'Morning Breakfast Table!' And then it passed through her mind that somebody had told her that the man was paid £3,000 a year for his work. Would not the world, or any part of it that was desirable, come to her drawing-room if she were the wife of Mr. Broune? It all passed through her brain at once during that minute of silence which she allowed herself after the declaration was made to her. But other ideas and other feelings were present to her also. Perhaps the truest aspiration of her heart had been the love of freedom which the tyranny of her late husband had engendered. Once she had fled from that tyranny and had been almost crushed by the censure to which she had been subjected. Then her husband's protection and his tyranny had been restored to her.

After that the freedom had come. It had been accompanied by many hopes never as yet fulfilled, and embittered by many sorrows which had been always present to her; but still the hopes were alive and the remembrance of the tyranny was very clear to her. At last the minute was over and she was bound to speak. 'Mr. Broune,' she said, 'you have quite taken away my breath. I never expected anything of this kind.'

And now Mr. Broune's mouth was opened, and his voice was free. 'Lady Carbury,' he said, 'I have lived a long time without marrying, and I have sometimes thought that it would be better for me to go on the same way to the end. I have worked so hard all my life that when I was young I had no time to think of love. And, as I have gone on, my mind has been so fully employed, that I have hardly realized the want which nevertheless I have felt. And so it has been with me till I fancied, not that I was too old for love, but that others would think me so. Then I met you. As I said at first, perhaps with scant gallantry, you also are not as young as you once were. But you keep the beauty of your youth, and the energy, and something of the freshness of a young heart. And I have come to love you. I speak with absolute frankness, risking your anger. I have doubted much before I resolved upon this. It is so hard to know the nature of another person. But I think I understand yours;—and if you can confide your happiness with me, I am prepared to entrust mine to your keeping.' Poor Mr. Broune! Though endowed with gifts peculiarly adapted for the editing of a daily newspaper, he could have had but little capacity for reading a woman's character when he talked of the freshness of Lady Carbury's young mind! And he must have surely been much blinded by love, before convincing himself that he could trust his happiness to such keeping.

'You do me infinite honour. You pay me a great compliment,' ejaculated Lady Carbury.

'Well?'

'How am I to answer you at a moment? I expected nothing of this. As God is to be my judge it has come upon me like a dream. I look upon your position as almost the highest in England,—on your prosperity as the uttermost that can be achieved.'

'That prosperity, such as it is, I desire most anxiously to share with you.'

'You tell me so;—but I can hardly yet believe it. And then how am I to know my own feelings so suddenly? Marriage as I have found it, Mr. Broune, has not been happy. I have suffered much. I have been wounded in every joint, hurt in every nerve,—tortured till I could hardly endure my punishment. At last I got my liberty, and to that I have looked for happiness.'

'Has it made you happy?'

'It has made me less wretched. And there is so much to be considered! I have a son and a daughter, Mr. Broune.'

'Your daughter I can love as my own. I think I prove my devotion to you when I say that I am willing for your sake to encounter the troubles which may attend your son's future career.'

'Mr. Broune, I love him better,—always shall love him better,—than anything in the world.' This was calculated to damp the lover's ardour, but he probably reflected that should he now be successful, time might probably change the feeling which had just been expressed. 'Mr. Broune,' she said, 'I am now so agitated that you had better leave me. And it is very late. The servant is sitting up, and will wonder that you should remain. It is near two o'clock.'

'When may I hope for an answer?'

'You shall not be kept waiting. I will write to you, almost at once. I will write to you,—to-morrow; say the day after to-morrow, on Thursday. I feel that I ought to have been prepared with an answer; but I am so surprised that I have none ready.' He took her hand in his, and kissing it, left her without another word.

As he was about to open the front door to let himself out, a key from the other side raised the latch, and Sir Felix, returning from his club, entered his mother's house. The young man looked up into Mr. Broune's

face with mingled impudence and surprise. 'Halloo, old
fellow,' he said, 'you've been keeping it up late here;
haven't you?' He was nearly drunk, and Mr. Broune,
perceiving his condition, passed him without a word.
Lady Carbury was still standing in the drawing-room,
struck with amazement at the scene which had just
passed, full of doubt as to her future conduct, when she
heard her son tumbling up the stairs. It was impossible
for her not to go out to him. 'Felix,' she said, 'why do
you make so much noise as you come in?'

'Noish! I'm not making any noish. I think I'm very
early. Your people's only just gone. I shaw shat editor
fellow at the door that won't call himself Brown. He'sh
great ass'h, that fellow. All right, mother. Oh, ye'sh,
I'm all right.' And so he tumbled up to bed, and his
mother followed him to see that the candle was at any
rate placed squarely on the table, beyond the reach of
the bed curtains.

Mr. Broune as he walked to his newspaper office
experienced all those pangs of doubt which a man feels
when he has just done that which for days and weeks
past he has almost resolved that he had better leave
undone. That last apparition which he had encountered
at his lady love's door certainly had not tended to re-
assure him. What curse can be much greater than that
inflicted by a drunken, reprobate son? The evil, when
in the course of things it comes upon a man, has to be
borne; but why should a man in middle life unneces-
sarily afflict himself with so terrible a misfortune? The
woman, too, was devoted to the cub! Then thousands
of other thoughts crowded upon him. How would this
new life suit him? He must have a new house, and new
ways; must live under a new dominion, and fit himself
to new pleasures. And what was he to gain by it? Lady
Carbury was a handsome woman, and he liked her
beauty. He regarded her too as a clever woman; and,
because she had flattered him, he had liked her conversation. He had been long enough about town to have
known better,—and as he now walked along the streets,
he almost felt that he ought to have known better. Every

now and again he warmed himself a little with the remembrance of her beauty, and told himself that his new
home would be pleasanter, though it might perhaps be
less free, than the old one. He tried to make the best of
it; but as he did so was always repressed by the memory
of the appearance of that drunken young baronet.

Whether for good or for evil, the step had been taken
and the thing was done. It did not occur to him that
the lady would refuse him. All his experience of the
world was against such refusal. Towns which consider,
always render themselves. Ladies who doubt always
solve their doubts in the one direction. Of course she
would accept him;—and of course he would stand to
his guns. As he went to his work he endeavoured to
bathe himself in self-complacency; but, at the bottom
of it, there was a substratum of melancholy which
leavened his prospects.

Lady Carbury went from the door of her son's room
to her own chamber, and there sat thinking through the
greater part of the night. During these hours she perhaps became a better woman, as being more oblivious
of herself, than she had been for many a year. It could
not be for the good of this man that he should marry her,
—and she did in the midst of her many troubles try to
think of the man's condition. Although in the moments
of her triumph,—and such moments were many,—she
would buoy herself up with assurances that her Felix
would become a rich man, brilliant with wealth and
rank, an honour to her, a personage whose society would
be desired by many, still in her heart of hearts she knew
how great was the peril, and in her imagination she could
foresee the nature of the catastrophe which might come.
He would go utterly to the dogs and would take her with
him. And whithersoever he might go, to what lowest
canine regions he might descend, she knew herself well
enough to be sure that whether married or single she
would go with him. Though her reason might be ever
so strong in bidding her to desert him, her heart, she
knew, would be stronger than her reason. He was the
one thing in the world that overpowered her. In all other

matters she could scheme, and contrive, and pretend; could get the better of her feelings and fight the world with a double face, laughing at illusions and telling herself that passions and preferences were simply weapons to be used. But her love for her son mastered her,—and she knew it. As it was so, could it be fit that she should marry another man?

And then her liberty! Even though Felix should bring her to utter ruin, nevertheless she would be and might remain a free woman. Should the worse come to the worst she thought that she could endure a Bohemian life in which, should all her means have been taken from her, she could live on what she earned. Though Felix was a tyrant after a kind, he was not a tyrant who could bid her do this or that. A repetition of marriage vows did not of itself recommend itself to her. As to loving the man, liking his caresses, and being specially happy because he was near her,—no romance of that kind ever presented itself to her imagination. How would it affect Felix and her together,—and Mr. Broune as connected with her and Felix? If Felix should go to the dogs, then would Mr. Broune not want her. Should Felix go to the stars instead of the dogs, and become one of the gilded ornaments of the metropolis, then would not he and she want Mr. Broune. It was thus that she regarded the matter.

She thought very little of her daughter as she considered all this. There was a home for Hetta, with every comfort, if Hetta would only condescend to accept it. Why did not Hetta marry her cousin Roger Carbury and let there be an end of that trouble? Of course Hetta must live wherever her mother lived till she should marry; but Hetta's life was so much at her own disposal that her mother did not feel herself bound to be guided in the great matter by Hetta's predispositions.

But she must tell Hetta should she ultimately make up her mind to marry the man, and in that case the sooner this was done the better. On that night she did not make up her mind. Ever and again as she declared to herself that she would not marry him, the picture of a comfortable assured home over her head, and the conviction that the editor of the 'Morning Breakfast Table' would be powerful for all things, brought new doubts to her mind. But she could not convince herself, and when at last she went to her bed her mind was still vacillating. The next morning she met Hetta at breakfast, and with assumed nonchalance asked a question about the man who was perhaps about to be her husband. 'Do you like Mr. Broune, Hetta?'

'Yes;—pretty well. I don't care very much about him. What makes you ask, mamma?'

'Because among my acquaintances in London there is no one so truly kind to me as he is.'

'He always seems to me to like to have his own way.'

'Why shouldn't he like it?'

'He has to me that air of selfishness which is so very common with people in London;—as though what he said were all said out of surface politeness.'

'I wonder what you expect, Hetta, when you talk of —London people? Why should not London people be as kind as other people? I think Mr. Broune is as oblig-ing a man as any one I know. But if I like anybody, you always make little of him. The only person you seem to think well of is Mr. Montague.'

'Mamma, that is unfair and unkind. I never mention Mr. Montague's name if I can help it,—and I should not have spoken of Mr. Broune, had you not asked me.'

## Chapter XXXII

### LADY MONOGRAM

GEORGIANA LONGESTAFFE had now been stay-ing with the Melmottes for a fortnight, and her prospects in regard to the London season had not much improved. Her brother had troubled her no further, and her family at Caversham had not, as far as she was aware, taken any notice of Dolly's interference. Twice a week she received a cold, dull letter from her mother, —such letters as she had been accustomed to receive when away from home; and these she had answered, always endeavouring to fill her sheet with some customary description of fashionable doings, with some bit of scandal such as she would have repeated for her mother's amusement,—and her own delectation in the telling of it,—had there been nothing painful in the nature of her sojourn in London. Of the Melmottes she hardly spoke. She did not say that she was taken to the houses in which it was her ambition to be seen. She would have lied directly in saying so. But she did not announce her own disappointment. She had chosen to come up to the Melmottes in preference to remaining at Caversham, and she would not declare her own failure. 'I hope they are kind to you,' Lady Pomona always said. But Georgiana did not tell her mother whether the Melmottes were kind or unkind.

In truth, her 'season' was a very unpleasant season. Her mode of living was altogether different to anything she had already known. The house in Bruton Street had never been very bright, but the appendages of life there had been of a sort which was not known in the gorgeous mansion in Grosvenor Square. It had been full of books and little toys and those thousand trifling household gods which are accumulated in years, and which in their accumulation suit themselves to the taste of their owners. In Grosvenor Square there were no Lares;*—no toys, no books, nothing but gold and grandeur, pomatum, powder and pride. The Longestaffe life had not been an easy, natural, or intellectual life; but the Melmotte life was hardly endurable even by a Longestaffe. She had, however, come prepared to suffer much, and was endowed with considerable power of endurance in pursuit of her own objects. Having willed to come, even to the Melmottes, in preference to remaining at Caversham, she fortified herself to suffer much. Could she have ridden in the park at mid-day in desirable company, and found herself in proper houses at midnight, she would have borne the rest, bad as it might have been. But it was not so. She had her horse, but could with difficulty get any proper companion. She had been in the habit of riding with one of the Primero girls,—and old Primero would accompany them, or perhaps a brother Primero, or occasionally her own father. And then, when once out, she would be surrounded by a cloud of young men,— and though there was but little in it, a walking round and round the same bit of ground with the same companions and with the smallest attempt at conversation, still it had been the proper thing and had satisfied her. Now it was with difficulty that she could get any cavalier such as the laws of society demand. Even Penelope Primero snubbed her,—whom she, Georgiana Longestaffe, had hitherto endured and snubbed. She was just allowed to join them when old Primero rode, and was obliged even to ask for that assistance.

But the nights were still worse. She could only go where Madame Melmotte went, and Madame Melmotte was more prone to receive people at home than to go out. And the people she did receive were antipathetic to Miss Longestaffe. She did not even know who they were, whence they came, or what was their nature. They seemed to be as little akin to her as would have been the shopkeepers in the small town near Caversham. She would sit through long evenings almost speechless, trying to fathom the depth of the vulgarity of her associates. Occasionally she was taken out, and was then, probably, taken to very grand houses. The two duchesses and the Marchioness of Auld Reekie received Madame Melmotte, and the garden parties of royalty were open to her. And some of the most elaborate fêtes of the season,—which indeed were very elaborate on behalf of this and that travelling potentate,—were attained. On these occasions Miss Longestaffe was fully aware of the struggle that was always made for invitations, often unsuccessfully, but sometimes with triumph. Even the bargains, conducted by the hands of Lord Alfred and his mighty sister, were not altogether hidden from her. The Emperor of China was to be in London and it was thought proper that some private person, some untitled individual, should give the Emperor a dinner, so that the Emperor might see how an English merchant lives. Mr. Melmotte

was chosen on condition that he would spend £10,000
on the banquet;—and, as a part of his payment for this
expenditure, was to be admitted with his family, to a
grand entertainment given to the Emperor at Windsor
Park. Of these good things Georgiana Longestaffe would
receive her share. But she went to them as a Melmotte
and not as a Longestaffe,—and when amidst these
gaieties, though she could see her old friends, she was
not with them. She was ever behind Madame Melmotte,
till she hated the make of that lady's garments and the
shape of that lady's back.

She had told both her father and mother very plainly
that it behoved her to be in London at this time of the
year that she might—look for a husband. She had not
hesitated in declaring her purpose; and that purpose,
together with the means of carrying it out, had not
appeared to them to be unreasonable. She wanted to
be settled in life. She had meant, when she first started
on her career, to have a lord;—but lords are scarce.
She was herself not very highly born, not very highly
gifted, not very lovely, not very pleasant, and she had
no fortune. She had long made up her mind that she
could do without a lord, but that she must get a commoner of the proper sort. He must be a man with a
place in the country and sufficient means to bring him
annually to London. He must be a gentleman,—and,
probably, in parliament. And above all things he must
be in the right set. She would rather go on for ever
struggling than take some country Whitstable as her sister
was about to do. But now the men of the right sort never
came near her. The one object for which she had subjected herself to all this ignominy seemed to have vanished
altogether in the distance. When by chance she danced
or exchanged a few words with the Nidderdales and
Grassloughs whom she used to know, they spoke to her
with a want of respect which she felt and tasted but
could hardly analyse. Even Miles Grendall, who had
hitherto been below her notice, attempted to patronize
her in a manner that bewildered her. All this nearly
broke her heart.

And then from time to time little rumours reached her
ears which made her aware that, in the teeth of all Mr.
Melmotte's social successes, a general opinion that he
was a gigantic swindler was rather gaining ground than
otherwise. 'Your host is a wonderful fellow, by George!'
said Lord Nidderdale. 'No one seems to know which way
he'll turn up at last.' 'There's nothing like being a
robber, if you can only rob enough,' said Lord Grasslough,—not exactly naming Melmotte, but very clearly
alluding to him. There was a vacancy for a member of
parliament at Westminster, and Melmotte was about to
come forward as a candidate. 'If he can manage that
I think he'll pull through,' she heard one man say. 'If
money'll do it, it will be done,' said another. She could
understand it all. Mr. Melmotte was admitted into
society, because of some enormous power which was
supposed to lie in his hands; but even by those who thus
admitted him he was regarded as a thief and a scoundrel.
This was the man whose house had been selected by her
father in order that she might make her search for a
husband from beneath his wing!

In her agony she wrote to her old friend Julia Triplex,
now the wife of Sir Damask Monogram. She had been
really intimate with Julia Triplex, and had been sympathetic when a brilliant marriage had been achieved.
Julia had been without fortune, but very pretty. Sir
Damask was a man of great wealth, whose father had
been a contractor. But Sir Damask himself was a sportsman, keeping many horses on which other men often
rode, a yacht in which other men sunned themselves, a
deer forest, a moor, a large machinery for making
pheasants. He shot pigeons at Hurlingham, drove four-
in-hand in the park, had a box at every race-course, and
was the most good-natured fellow known. He had really
conquered the world, had got over the difficulty of being
the grandson of a butcher, and was now as good as though
the Monograms had gone to the crusades. Julia Triplex
was equal to her position, and made the very most of it.
She dispensed champagne and smiles, and made everybody, including herself, believe that she was in love with

her husband. Lady Monogram had climbed to the top of the tree, and in that position had been, of course, invaluable to her old friend. We must give her her due and say that she had been fairly true to friendship while Georgiana—behaved herself. She thought that Georgiana in going to the Melmottes had had—not behaved herself, and therefore she had determined to drop Georgiana. 'Heartless, false, purse-proud creature,' Georgiana said to herself as she wrote the following letter in humiliating agony.

'DEAR LADY MONOGRAM,

'I think you hardly understand my position. Of course you have cut me. Haven't you? And of course I must feel it very much. You did not use to be ill-natured, and I hardly think you can have become so now when you have everything pleasant around you. I do not think that I have done anything that should make an old friend treat me in this way, and therefore I write to ask you to let me see you. Of course it is because I am staying here. You know me well enough to be sure that it can't be my own choice. Papa arranged it all. If there is anything against these people, I suppose papa does not know it. Of course they are not nice. Of course they are not like anything that I have been used to. But when papa told me that the house in Bruton Street was to be shut up and that I was to come here, of course I did as I was bid. I don't think an old friend like you, whom I have always liked more than anybody else, ought to cut me for it. It's not about the parties, but about yourself that I mind. I don't ask you to come here, but if you will see me I can have the carriage and will go to you.

'Yours, as ever,
'GEORGIANA LONGESTAFFE.'

It was a troublesome letter to get written. Lady Monogram was her junior in age and had once been lower than herself in social position. In the early days of their friendship she had sometimes domineered over Julia Triplex, and had been entreated by Julia, in reference

to balls here and routes there. The great Monogram
marriage had been accomplished very suddenly, and had
taken place,—exalting Julia very high,—just as Georgiana was beginning to allow her aspirations to descend.
It was in that very season that she moved her castle in
the air from the Upper to the Lower House. And now
she was absolutely begging for notice, and praying that
she might not be cut! She sent her letter by post and on
the following day received a reply, which was left by a
footman.

'DEAR GEORGIANA,

'Of course I shall be delighted to see you. I don't
know what you mean by cutting. I never cut anybody.
We happen to have got into different sets, but that is
not my fault. Sir Damask won't let me call on the Melmottes. I can't help that. You wouldn't have me go
where he tells me not. I don't know anything about
them myself, except that I did go to their ball. But everybody knows that's different. I shall be at home all to-
morrow till three,—that is to-day I mean, for I'm writing
after coming home from Lady Killarney's ball; but if you
wish to see me alone you had better come before lunch.

'Yours affectionately,

'J. MONOGRAM.'

Georgiana condescended to borrow the carriage and
reached her friend's house a little after noon. The two
ladies kissed each other when they met—of course, and
then Miss Longestaffe at once began. 'Julia, I did think
that you would at any rate have asked me to your second
ball.'

'Of course you would have been asked if you had been
up in Bruton Street. You know that as well as I do. It
would have been a matter of course.'

'What difference does a house make?'

'But the people in a house make a great deal of difference, my dear. I don't want to quarrel with you, my
dear; but I can't know the Melmottes.'

'Who asks you?'

'You are with them.'

'Do you mean to say that you can't ask anybody to your house without asking everybody that lives with that person? It's done every day.'

'Somebody must have brought you.'

'I would have come with the Primeros, Julia.

'I couldn't do it. I asked Damask and he wouldn't have it. When that great affair was going on in February, we didn't know much about the people. I was told that everybody was going and therefore I got Sir Damask to let me go. He says now that he won't let me know them; and after having been at their house I can't ask you out of it, without asking them too.'

'I don't see it at all, Julia.'

'I'm very sorry, my dear, but I can't go against my husband.'

'Everybody goes to their house,' said Georgiana, pleading her cause to the best of her ability. 'The Duchess of Stevenage has dined in Grosvenor Square since I have been there.'

'We all know what that means,' replied Lady Monogram.

'And people are giving their eyes to be asked to the dinner party which he is to give to the Emperor in July; —and even to the reception afterwards.'

'To hear you talk, Georgiana, one would think that you didn't understand anything,' said Lady Monogram. 'People are going to see the Emperor, not to see the Melmottes. I dare say we might have gone,—only I suppose we shan't now because of this row.'

'I don't know what you mean by a row, Julia.'

'Well;—it is a row, and I hate rows. Going there when the Emperor of China is there, or anything of that kind, is no more than going to the play. Somebody chooses to get all London into his house, and all London chooses to go. But it isn't understood that that means acquaintance. I should meet Madame Melmotte in the park afterwards and not think of bowing to her.'

'I should call that rude.'

'Very well. Then we differ. But really it does seem to me that you ought to understand these things as well as anybody. I don't find any fault with you for going to

the Melmottes,—though I was very sorry to hear it; but
when you have done it, I don't think you should complain of people because they won't have the Melmottes
crammed down their throats.'

'Nobody has wanted it,' said Georgiana sobbing. At
this moment the door was opened, and Sir Damask came
in. 'I'm talking to your wife about the Melmottes,' she
continued, determined to take the bull by the horns.
'I'm staying there, and—I think it—unkind that Julia
—hasn't been—to see me. That's all.'

'How'd you do, Miss Longestaffe? She doesn't know
them.' And Sir Damask, folding his hands together,
raising his eyebrows, and standing on the rug, looked as
though he had solved the whole difficulty.

'She knows me, Sir Damask.'

'Oh yes;—she knows you. That's a matter of course.
We're delighted to see you, Miss Longestaffe—I am,
always. Wish we could have had you at Ascot. But——.'
Then he looked as though he had again explained everything.

'I've told her that you don't want me to go to the
Melmottes,' said Lady Monogram.

'Well, no;—not just to go there. Stay and have lunch,
Miss Longestaffe.'

'No, thank you.'

'Now you're here, you'd better,' said Lady Monogram.

'No, thank you. I'm sorry that I have not been able
to make you understand me. I could not allow our very
long friendship to be dropped without a word.'

'Don't say—dropped,' exclaimed the baronet.

'I do say dropped, Sir Damask. I thought we should
have understood each other;—your wife and I. But we
haven't. Wherever she might have gone, I should have
made it my business to see her; but she feels differently.
Good-bye.'

'Good-bye, my dear. If you will quarrel, it isn't my
doing.' Then Sir Damask led Miss Longestaffe out, and
put her into Madame Melmotte's carriage. 'It's the
most absurd thing I ever knew in my life,' said the wife
as soon as her husband had returned to her. 'She hasn't

been able to bear to remain down in the country for one
season, when all the world knows that her father can't
afford to have a house for them in town. Then she
condescends to come and stay with these abominations
and pretends to feel surprised that her old friends don't
run after her. She is old enough to have known better.'

'I suppose she likes parties,' said Sir Damask.

'Likes parties! She'd like to get somebody to take her.
It's twelve years now since Georgiana Longestaffe came
out. I remember being told of the time when I was first
entered myself. Yes, my dear, you know all about it, I
dare say. And there she is still. I can feel for her, and
do feel for her. But if she will let herself down in that way
she can't expect not to be dropped. You remember the
woman;—don't you?'

'What woman?'

'Madame Melmotte?'

'Never saw her in my life.'

'Oh yes, you did. You took me there that night when
Prince —— danced with the girl. Don't you remember
the blowsy fat woman at the top of the stairs;—a regular
horror?'

'Didn't look at her. I was only thinking what a lot of
money it all cost.'

'I remember her, and if Georgiana Longestaffe thinks
I'm going there to make an acquaintance with Madame
Melmotte she is very much mistaken. And if she thinks
that that is the way to get married, I think she is mistaken
again.' Nothing perhaps is so efficacious in preventing
men from marrying as the tone in which married women
speak of the struggles made in that direction by their
unmarried friends.

## Chapter XXXIII

### JOHN CRUMB

SIR FELIX CARBURY made an appointment for
meeting Ruby Ruggles a second time at the bottom
of the kitchen-garden belonging to Sheep's Acre farm,

which appointment he neglected, and had, indeed, made
without any intention of keeping it. But Ruby was there,
and remained hanging about among the cabbages till
her grandfather returned from Harlestone market. An
early hour had been named; but hours may be mistaken,
and Ruby had thought that a fine gentleman, such as
was her lover, used to live among fine people up in
London, might well mistake the afternoon for the morning. If he would come at all she could easily forgive such
a mistake. But he did not come, and late in the afternoon
she was obliged to obey her grandfather's summons as
he called her into the house.

After that for three weeks she heard nothing of her
London lover, but she was always thinking of him;—and
though she could not altogether avoid her country lover,
she was in his company as little as possible. One afternoon her grandfather returned from Bungay and told
her that her country lover was coming to see her. 'John
Crumb be a coming over by-and-by,' said the old man.
'See and have a bit o' supper ready for him.'

'John Crumb coming here, grandfather? He's welcome
to stay away then, for me.'

'That be dommed.' The old man thrust his old hat
on to his head and seated himself in a wooden arm-chair
that stood by the kitchen-fire. Whenever he was angry
he put on his hat, and the custom was well understood
by Ruby. 'Why not welcome, and he all one as your
husband? Look ye here, Ruby, I'm going to have an
eend o' this. John Crumb is to marry you next month,
and the banns is to be said.'

'The parson may say what he pleases, grandfather. I
can't stop his saying of 'em. It isn't likely I shall try,
neither. But no parson among 'em all can marry me
without I'm willing.'

'And why should you no be willing, you contrary
young jade, you?'

'You've been a' drinking, grandfather.'

He turned round at her sharp, and threw his old hat
at her head;—nothing to Ruby's consternation, as it was
a practice to which she was well accustomed. She picked

it up, and returned it to him with a cool indifference which was intended to exasperate him. 'Look ye here, Ruby,' he said, 'out o' this place you go. If you go as John Crumb's wife you'll go with five hun'erd pound, and we'll have a dinner here, and a dance, and all Bungay.'

'Who cares for all Bungay,—a set of beery chaps as knows nothing but swilling and smoking;—and John Crumb the main of 'em all? There never was a chap for beer like John Crumb.'

'Never saw him the worse o' liquor in all my life.' And the old farmer, as he gave this grand assurance, rattled his fist down upon the table.

'It ony just makes him stoopider and stoopider the more he swills. You can't tell me, grandfather, about John Crumb. I knows him.'

'Didn't ye say as how ye'd have him? Didn't ye give him a promise?'

'If I did, I ain't the first girl as has gone back of her word,—and I shan't be the last.'

'You means you won't have him?'

'That's about it, grandfather.'

'Then you'll have to have somebody to fend for ye, and that pretty sharp,—for you won't have me.'

'There ain't no difficulty about that, grandfather.'

'Very well. He's a coming here to-night, and you may settle it along wi' him. Out o' this ye shall go. I know of your doings.'

'What doings! You don't know of no doings. There ain't no doings. You don't know nothing ag'in me.'

'He's a coming here to-night, and if you can make it up wi' him, well and good. There's five hun'erd pound, and ye shall have the dinner and dance and all Bungay. He ain't a going to be put off no longer;—he ain't.'

'Whoever wanted him to be put on? Let him go his own gait.'

'If you can't make it up wi' him——'

'Well, grandfather, I shan't anyways.'

'Let me have my say, will ye, yer jade, you? There's five hun'erd pound! and there ain't ere a farmer in

Suffolk or Norfolk paying rent for a bit of land like this can do as well for his darter as that,—let alone only a granddarter. You never thinks o' that;—you don't. If you don't like to take it,—leave it. But you'll leave Sheep's Acre too.'

'Bother Sheep's Acre. Who wants to stop at Sheep's Acre? It's the stoopidest place in all England.'

'Then find another. Then find another. That's all aboot it. John Crumb's a coming up for a bit o' supper. You tell him your own mind. I'm dommed if I trouble aboot it. On'y you don't stay here. Sheep's Acre ain't good enough for you, and you'd best find another home. Stoopid, is it? You'll have to put up wi' places stoopider nor Sheep's Acre, afore you've done.'

In regard to the hospitality promised to Mr. Crumb, Miss Ruggles went about her work with sufficient alacrity. She was quite willing that the young man should have a supper, and she did understand that, so far as the preparation of the supper went, she owed her service to her grandfather. She therefore went to work herself, and gave directions to the servant girl who assisted her in keeping her grandfather's house. But as she did this, she determined that she would make John Crumb understand that she would never be his wife. Upon that she was now fully resolved. As she went about the kitchen, taking down the ham and cutting the slices that were to be broiled, and as she trussed the fowl that was to be boiled for John Crumb, she made mental comparisons between him and Sir Felix Carbury. She could see, as though present to her at the moment, the mealy, floury head of the one, with hair stiff with perennial dust from his sacks, and the sweet glossy dark well-combed locks of the other, so bright, so seductive, that she was ever longing to twine her fingers among them. And she remembered the heavy, flat, broad honest face of the meal-man, with his mouth slow in motion, and his broad nose looking like a huge white promontory, and his great staring eyes, from the corners of which he was always extracting meal and grit;—and then also she remembered the white teeth, the beautiful soft lips, the perfect eyebrows, and the rich complexion of her London lover. Surely a lease of Paradise with the one, though but for one short year, would be well purchased at the price of a life with the other! 'It's no good going against love,' she said to herself, 'and I won't try. He shall have his supper, and be told all about it, and then go home. He cares more for his supper than he do for me.' And then, with this final resolution firmly made, she popped the fowl into the pot. Her grandfather wanted her to leave Sheep's Acre. Very well. She had a little money of her own, and would take herself off to London. She knew what people would say, but she cared nothing for old women's tales. She would know how to take care of herself, and could always say in her own defence that her grandfather had turned her out of Sheep's Acre.

Seven had been the hour named, and punctually at that hour John Crumb knocked at the back door of Sheep's Acre farm-house. Nor did he come alone. He was accompanied by his friend Joe Mixet, the baker of Bungay, who, as all Bungay knew, was to be his best man at his marriage. John Crumb's character was not without any fine attributes. He could earn money,—and having earned it could spend and keep it in fair proportion. He was afraid of no work, and,—to give him his due,—was afraid of no man. He was honest, and ashamed of nothing that he did. And after his fashion he had chivalrous ideas about women. He was willing to thrash any man that ill-used a woman, and would certainly be a most dangerous antagonist to any man who would misuse a woman belonging to him. But Ruby had told the truth of him in saying that he was slow of speech, and what the world calls stupid in regard to all forms of expression. He knew good meal from bad as well as any man, and the price at which he could buy it so as to leave himself a fair profit at the selling. He knew the value of a clear conscience, and without much argument had discovered for himself that honesty is in truth the best policy. Joe Mixet, who was dapper of person and glib of tongue, had often declared that any one buying John Crumb for a fool would lose his money. Joe Mixet was probably right; but there had been a want of prudence, a lack of worldly sagacity, in the way in which Crumb had allowed his proposed marriage with Ruby Ruggles to become a source of gossip to all Bungay. His love was now an old affair; and, though he never talked much, whenever he did talk, he talked about that. He was proud of Ruby's beauty, and of her fortune, and of his own status as her acknowledged lover,—and he did not hide his light under a bushel. Perhaps the publicity so produced had some effect in prejudicing Ruby against the man whose offer she had certainly once accepted. Now when he came to settle the day,—having heard more than once or twice that there was a difficulty with Ruby,—he brought his friend Mixet with him as though to be present at his triumph. 'If here isn't Joe Mixet,' said Ruby to herself. 'Was there ever such a stoopid as John Crumb? There's no end to his being stoopid.'

The old man had slept off his anger and his beer while Ruby had been preparing the feast, and now roused himself to entertain his guests. 'What, Joe Mixet; is that thou? Thou'rt welcome. Come in, man. Well, John, how is it wi' you? Ruby's stewing o' something for us to eat a bit. Don't 'e smell it?'—John Crumb lifted up his great nose, sniffed and grinned.

'John didn't like going home in the dark like,' said the baker, with his little joke. 'So I just come along to drive away the bogies.'

'The more the merrier;—the more the merrier. Ruby'll have enough for the two o' you, I'll go bail. So John Crumb's afraid of bogies;—is he? The more need he to have some 'un in his house to scart 'em away.'

The lover had seated himself without speaking a word; but now he was instigated to ask a question. 'Where be she, Muster Ruggles?' They were seated in the outside or front kitchen, in which the old man and his granddaughter always lived; while Ruby was at work in the back kitchen. As John Crumb asked this question she could be heard distinctly among the pots and the plates. She now came out, and wiping her hands on her apron, shook hands with the two young men. She had enveloped herself in a big household apron when the cooking was in hand, and had not cared to take it off for the greeting of this lover. 'Grandfather said as how you was a coming out for your supper, so I've been a seeing to it. You'll excuse the apron, Mr. Mixet.'

'You couldn't look nicer, miss, if you was to try ever so. My mother says as it's housifery as recommends a girl to the young men. What do you say, John?'

'I loiks to see her loik o' that,' said John rubbing his hands down the back of his trowsers, and stooping till he had brought his eyes down to a level with those of his sweetheart.

'It looks homely; don't it John?' said Mixet.

'Bother!' said Ruby, turning round sharp, and going back to the other kitchen. John Crumb turned round also, and grinned at his friend, and then grinned at the old man.

'You've got it all afore you,' said the farmer,—leaving the lover to draw what lesson he might from this oracular proposition.

'And I don't care how soon I ha'e it in hond;—that I don't,' said John.

'That's the chat,' said Joe Mixet. 'There ain't nothing wanting in his house;—is there, John? It's all there,—cradle, caudle-cup, and the rest of it. A young woman going to John knows what she'll have to eat when she gets up, and what she'll lie down upon when she goes to bed.' This he declared in a loud voice for the benefit of Ruby in the back kitchen.

'That she do,' said John, grinning again. 'There's a hun'erd and fifty poond o' things in my house forbye what mother left behind her.'

After this there was no more conversation till Ruby reappeared with the boiled fowl, and without her apron. She was followed by the girl with a dish of broiled ham and an enormous pyramid of cabbage. Then the old man got up slowly and opening some private little door of which he kept the key in his breeches pocket, drew a jug of ale and placed it on the table. And from a cupboard of which he also kept the key, he brought out a bottle of gin. Everything being thus prepared, the three men sat round the table, John Crumb looking at his chair again and again before he ventured to occupy it. 'If you'll sit yourself down, I'll give you a bit of something to eat,' said Ruby at last. Then he sank at once into his chair. Ruby cut up the fowl standing, and dispensed the other good things, not even placing a chair for herself at the table,—and apparently not expected to do so, for no one invited her. 'Is it to be spirits or ale, Mr. Crumb?' she said, when the other two men had helped themselves. He turned round and gave her a look of love that might have softened the heart of an Amazon; but instead of speaking he held up his tumbler, and bobbed his head at the beer jug. Then she filled it to the brim, frothing it in the manner in which he loved to have it frothed. He raised it to his mouth slowly, and poured the liquor in as though to a vat. Then she filled it again. He had been her lover, and she would be as kind to him as she knew how,—short of love.

There was a good deal of eating done, for more ham came in, and another mountain of cabbage; but very little or nothing was said. John Crumb ate whatever was given to him of the fowl, sedulously picking the bones, and almost swallowing them; and then finished the second dish of ham, and after that the second instalment of cabbage. He did not ask for more beer, but took it as often as Ruby replenished his glass. When the eating was done, Ruby retired into the back kitchen, and there regaled herself with some bone or merry-thought*of the fowl, which she had with prudence reserved, sharing her spoils however with the other maiden. This she did standing, and then went to work, cleaning the dishes. The men lit their pipes and smoked in silence, while Ruby went through her domestic duties. So matters went on for half an hour; during which Ruby escaped by the back door, went round into the house, got into her own room, and formed the grand resolution of going to bed. She began her operations in fear and trembling, not being sure that her grandfather would bring the man upstairs to her. As she thought of this she stayed her hand, and looked to the door. She knew well that there was no bolt there. It would be terrible to her to be invaded by John Crumb after his fifth or sixth glass of beer. And, she declared to herself, that should he come he would be sure to bring Joe Mixet with him to speak his mind for him. So she paused and listened.

When they had smoked for some half hour the old man called for his granddaughter, but called of course in vain. 'Where the mischief is the jade gone?' he said, slowly making his way into the back kitchen. The maid, as soon as she heard her master moving, escaped into the yard and made no response, while the old man stood bawling at the back door. 'The devil's in them. They're off some gates,' he said aloud. 'She'll make the place hot for her, if she goes on this way.' Then he returned to the two young men. 'She's playing off her games somewheres,' he said. 'Take a glass of sperrits and water, Mr. Crumb, and I'll see after her.'

'I'll just take a drop of y'ell,' said John Crumb, apparently quite unmoved by the absence of his sweetheart.

It was sad work for the old man. He went down the yard and into the garden, hobbling among the cabbages, not daring to call very loud, as he did not wish to have it supposed that the girl was lost; but still anxious, and sore at heart as to the ingratitude shown to him. He was not bound to give the girl a home at all. She was not his own child. And he had offered her £500! 'Domm her,' he said aloud as he made his way back to the house. After much search and considerable loss of time he returned to the kitchen in which the two men were sitting, leading Ruby in his hand. She was not smart in her apparel, for she had half undressed herself, and been then compelled by her grandfather to make herself fit to appear in public. She had acknowledged to herself that she had better go down and tell John Crumb the truth. For she was still determined that she would never be John Crumb's wife. 'You can answer him as well as I, grandfather,' she had said. Then the farmer had cuffed her, and told her that she was an idiot. 'Oh, if it comes to that,' said Ruby, 'I'm not afraid of John Crumb, nor yet of nobody else. Only I didn't think you'd go to strike me, grandfather.' 'I'll knock the life out of thee, if thou goest on this gate,' he had said. But she had consented to come down, and they entered the room together.

'We're a disturbing you a'most too late, miss,' said Mr. Mixet.

'It ain't that at all, Mr. Mixet. If grandfather chooses to have a few friends, I ain't nothing against it. I wish he'd have a few friends a deal oftener than he do. I likes nothing better than to do for 'em;—only when I've done for 'em and they're smoking their pipes and that like, I don't see why I ain't to leave 'em to 'emselves.'

'But we've come here on a hauspicious occasion, Miss Ruby.'

'I don't know nothing about auspicious, Mr. Mixet. If you and Mr. Crumb've come out to Sheep's Acre farm for a bit of supper——'

'Which we ain't,' said John Crumb very loudly;— 'nor yet for beer;—not by no means.'

'We've come for the smiles of beauty,' said Joe Mixet.

Ruby chucked up her head. 'Mr. Mixet, if you'll be so good as to stow that! There ain't no beauty here as I knows of, and if there was it isn't nothing to you.'

'Except in the way of friendship,' said Mixet.

'I'm just as sick of all this as a man can be,' said Mr. Ruggles, who was sitting low in his chair, with his back bent, and his head forward. 'I won't put up with it no more.'

'Who wants you to put up with it?' said Ruby. 'Who wants 'em to come here with their trash? Who brought 'em to-night? I don't know what business Mr. Mixet has interfering along o' me. I never interfere along o' him.'

'John Crumb, have you anything to say?' asked the old man.

Then John Crumb slowly arose from his chair, and stood up at his full height. 'I hove,' said he, swinging his head to one side.

'Then say it.'

'I will,' said he. He was still standing bolt upright with his hands down by his side. Then he stretched out his left to his glass which was half full of beer, and strengthened himself as far as that would strengthen him. Having done this he slowly deposited the pipe which he still held in his right hand.

'Now speak your mind, like a man,' said Mixet.

'I intends it,' said John. But he still stood dumb, looking down upon old Ruggles, who from his crouched position was looking up at him. Ruby was standing with both her hands upon the table and her eyes intent upon the wall over the fire-place.

'You've asked Miss Ruby to be your wife a dozen times;—haven't you, John?' suggested Mixet.

'I hove.'

'And you mean to be as good as your word?'

'I do.'

'And she has promised to have you?'

'She hove.'

'More nor once or twice?' To this proposition Crumb found it only necessary to bob his head. 'You're ready? —and willing?'

'I om.'

'You're wishing to have the banns said without any more delay?'

'There ain't no delay 'bout me;—never was.'

'Everything is ready in your own house?'

'They is.'

'And you will expect Miss Ruby to come to the scratch?'

'I sholl.'

'That's about it, I think,' said Joe Mixet, turning to the grandfather. 'I don't think there was ever anything much more straightforward than that. You know, I know, Miss Ruby knows all about John Crumb. John Crumb didn't come to Bungay yesterday,—nor yet the day before. There's been a talk of five hundred pounds, Mr. Ruggles.' Mr. Ruggles made a slight gesture of assent with his head. 'Five hundred pounds is very comfortable; and added to what John has will make things that snug that things never was snugger. But John Crumb isn't after Miss Ruby along of her fortune.'

'Nohows,' said the lover, shaking his head and still standing upright with his hands by his side.

'Not he;—it isn't his ways, and them as knows him'll never say it of him. John has a heart in his buzsom.'

'I has,' said John, raising his hand a little above his stomach.

'And feelings as a man. It's true love as has brought John Crumb to Sheep's Acre farm this night;—love of that young lady, if she'll let me make so free. He's a proposed to her, and she's a haccepted him, and now it's about time as they was married. That's what John Crumb has to say.'

'That's what I has to say,' repeated John Crumb, 'and I means it.'

'And now, miss,' continued Mixet, addressing himself to Ruby, 'you've heard what John has to say.'

'I've heard you, Mr. Mixet, and I've heard quite enough.'

'You can't have anything to say against it, Miss; can you? There's your grandfather as is willing, and the money as one may say counted out,—and John Crumb is willing, with his house so ready that there isn't a ha'porth to do. All we want is for you to name the day.'

'Say to-morrow, Ruby, and I'll not be agen it,' said John Crumb, slapping his thigh.

'I won't say to-morrow, Mr. Crumb, nor yet the day after to-morrow, nor yet no day at all. I'm not going to have you. I've told you as much before.'

'That was only in fun, loike.'

'Then now I tell you in earnest. There's some folk wants such a deal of telling.'

'You don't mean,—never?'

'I do mean never, Mr. Crumb.'

'Didn't you say as you would, Ruby? Didn't you say so as plain as the nose on my face?' John as he asked these questions could hardly refrain from tears.

'Young women is allowed to change their minds,' said Ruby.

'Brute!' exclaimed old Ruggles. 'Pig! Jade! I'll tell 'ee what, John. She'll go out o' this into the streets;—that's what she wull. I won't keep her here, no longer;—nasty, ungrateful, lying slut.'

'She ain't that;—she ain't that,' said John. 'She ain't that at all. She's no slut. I won't hear her called so;—not by her grandfather. But, oh, she has a mind to put me so abouts, that I'll have to go home and hang myself.'

'Dash it, Miss Ruby, you ain't a going to serve a young man that way,' said the baker.

'If you'll jist keep yourself to yourself, I'll be obliged to you, Mr. Mixet,' said Ruby. 'If you hadn't come here at all things might have been different.'

'Hark at that now,' said John, looking at his friend almost with indignation.

Mr. Mixet, who was fully aware of his rare eloquence and of the absolute necessity there had been for its exercise if any arrangement were to be made at all, could not trust himself to words after this. He put on his hat and walked out through the back kitchen into the yard declaring that his friend would find him there, round by the pigsty wall, whenever he was ready to return to Bungay. As soon as Mixet was gone John looked at his sweetheart out of the corners of his eyes and made a slow motion towards her, putting out his right hand as a feeler. 'He's aff now, Ruby,' said John.

'And you'd better be aff after him,' said the cruel girl.

'And when'll I come back again?'

'Never. It ain't no use. What's the good of more words, Mr. Crumb?'

'Domm her; domm her,' said old Ruggles. 'I'll even it to her. She'll have to be out on the roads this night.'

'She shall have the best bed in my house if she'll come for it,' said John, 'and the old woman to look arter her; and I won't come nigh her till she sends for me.'

'I can find a place for myself, thank ye, Mr. Crumb.' Old Ruggles sat grinding his teeth, and swearing to himself, taking his hat off and putting it on again, and meditating vengeance. 'And now if you please, Mr. Crumb, I'll go upstairs to my own room.'

'You don't go up to any room here, you jade you.'
The old man as he said this got up from his chair as
though to fly at her. And he would have struck her with
his stick but that he was stopped by John Crumb.

'Don't hit the girl, no gate, Mr. Ruggles.'

'Domm her, John; she breaks my heart.' While her
lover held her grandfather Ruby escaped, and seated
herself on the bedside, again afraid to undress, lest she
should be disturbed by her grandfather. 'Ain't it more
nor a man ought to have to bear;—ain't it, Mr. Crumb?'
said the grandfather appealing to the young man.

'It's the ways on 'em, Mr. Ruggles.'

'Ways on 'em! A whipping at the cart-tail ought to
be the ways on her. She's been and seen some young
buck.'

Then John Crumb turned red all over, through the
flour, and sparks of anger flashed from his eyes. 'You
ain't a meaning of it, master?'

'I'm told there's been the squoire's cousin aboot,—
him as they call the baronite.'

'Been along wi' Ruby?' The old man nodded at him.
'By the mortials I'll baronite him;—I wull,' said John,
seizing his hat and stalking off through the back kitchen
after his friend.

## Chapter XXXIV

### RUBY RUGGLES OBEYS HER GRANDFATHER

THE next day there was a great surprise at Sheep's
Acre farm, which communicated itself to the towns
of Bungay and Beccles, and even affected the ordinary
quiet life of Carbury Manor. Ruby Ruggles had gone
away, and at about twelve o'clock in the day the old
farmer became aware of the fact. She had started early,
at about seven in the morning; but Ruggles himself had
been out long before that, and had not condescended to
ask for her when he returned to the house for his breakfast. There had been a bad scene up in the bedroom

overnight, after John Crumb had left the farm. The old
man in his anger had tried to expel the girl; but she had
hung on to the bed-post and would not go; and he had
been frightened, when the maid came up crying and
screaming murder. 'You'll be out o' this to-morrow as
sure as my name's Dannel Ruggles,' said the farmer
panting for breath. But for the gin which he had taken
he would hardly have struck her;—but he had struck
her, and pulled her by the hair, and knocked her about;
—and in the morning she took him at his word and was
away. About twelve he heard from the servant girl that
she had gone. She had packed a box and had started up
the road carrying the box herself. 'Grandfather says I'm
to go, and I'm gone,' she had said to the girl. At the
first cottage she had got a boy to carry her box into
Beccles, and to Beccles she had walked. For an hour or
two Ruggles sat, quiet, within the house, telling himself
that she might do as she pleased with herself,—that he
was well rid of her, and that from henceforth he would
trouble himself no more about her. But by degrees there
came upon him a feeling half of compassion and half of
fear, with perhaps some mixture of love, instigating him
to make search for her. She had been the same to him
as a child, and what would people say of him if he
allowed her to depart from him after this fashion? Then
he remembered his violence the night before, and the
fact that the servant girl had heard if she had not seen
it. He could not drop his responsibility in regard to Ruby,
even if he would. So, as a first step, he sent in a message
to John Crumb, at Bungay, to tell him that Ruby Ruggles
had gone off with a box to Beccles. John Crumb went
open-mouthed with the news to Joe Mixet, and all
Bungay soon knew that Ruby Ruggles had run away.

After sending his message to Crumb the old man still
sat thinking, and at last made up his mind that he would
go to his landlord. He held a part of his farm under
Roger Carbury, and Roger Carbury would tell him what
he ought to do. A great trouble had come upon him.
He would fain have been quiet, but his conscience and
his heart and his terrors all were at work together,—and

he found that he could not eat his dinner. So he had out his cart and horse and drove himself off to Carbury Hall.

It was past four when he started, and he found the squire seated on the terrace after an early dinner, and with him was Father Barham, the priest. The old man was shown at once round into the garden, and was not long in telling his story. There had been words between him and his granddaughter about her lover. Her lover had been accepted and had come to the farm to claim his bride. Ruby had behaved very badly. The old man made the most of Ruby's bad behaviour, and of course as little as possible of his own violence. But he did explain that there had been threats used when Ruby refused to take the man, and that Ruby had, this day, taken herself off.

'I always thought it was settled that they were to be man and wife,' said Roger.

'It was settled, squoire;—and he war to have five hun'erd pound down;—money as I'd saved myself. Drat the jade.'

'Didn't she like him, Daniel?'

'She liked him well enough till she'd seed somebody else.' Then old Daniel paused, and shook his head, and was evidently the owner of a secret. The squire got up and walked round the garden with him,—and then the secret was told. The farmer was of opinion that there was something between the girl and Sir Felix. Sir Felix some weeks since had been seen near the farm and on the same occasion Ruby had been observed at some little distance from the house with her best clothes on.

'He's been so little here, Daniel,' said the squire.

'It goes as tinder and a spark o' fire, that does,' said the farmer. 'Girls like Ruby don't want no time to be wooed by one such as that, though they'll fall-lall with a man like John Crumb for years.'

'I suppose she's gone to London.'

'Don't know nothing of where she's gone, squoire;— only she have gone some'eres. May be it's Lowestoffe. There's lots of quality at Lowestoffe a' washing they-selves in the sea.'

Then they returned to the priest, who might be supposed to be cognizant of the guiles of the world and competent to give advice on such an occasion as this. 'If she was one of our people,' said Father Barham, 'we should have her back quick enough.'

'Would ye now?' said Ruggles, wishing at the moment that he and all his family had been brought up as Roman Catholics.

'I don't see how you would have more chance of catching her than we have,' said Carbury.

'She'd catch herself. Wherever she might be she'd go to the priest, and he wouldn't leave her till he'd seen her put on the way back to her friends.'

'With a flea in her lug,' suggested the farmer.

'Your people never go to a clergyman in their distress. It's the last thing they'd think of. Any one might more probably be regarded as a friend than the parson. But with us the poor know where to look for sympathy.'

'She ain't that poor, neither,' said the grandfather.

'She had money with her?'

'I don't know just what she had; but she ain't been brought up poor. And I don't think as our Ruby'd go of herself to any clergyman. It never was her way.'

'It never is the way with a Protestant,' said the priest.

'We'll say no more about that for the present,' said Roger, who was waxing wroth with the priest. That a man should be fond of his own religion is right; but Roger Carbury was beginning to think that Father Barham was too fond of his religion. 'What had we better do? I suppose we shall hear something of her at the railway. There are not so many people leaving Beccles but that she may be remembered.' So the waggonette was ordered, and they all prepared to go off to the station together.

But before they started John Crumb rode up to the door. He had gone at once to the farm on hearing of Ruby's departure, and had followed the farmer from thence to Carbury. Now he found the squire and the priest and the old man standing around as the horses were being put to the carriage. 'Ye aint a' found her,

Mr. Ruggles, ha' ye?' he asked as he wiped the sweat from his brow.

'Noa;—we ain't a' found no one yet.'

'If it was as she was to come to harm, Mr. Carbury, I'd never forgive myself,—never,' said Crumb.

'As far as I can understand it is no doing of yours, my friend,' said the squire.

'In one way, it ain't; and in one way it is. I was over there last night a bothering of her. She'd a' come round may be, if she'd a' been left alone. She wouldn't a' been off now, only for our going over to Sheep's Acre. But, —oh!'

'What is it, Mr. Crumb?'

'He's a coosin o' yours, squoire; and long as I've known Suffolk, I've never known nothing but good o' you and yourn. But if your baronite has been and done this! Oh, Mr. Carbury! If I was to wring his neck round, you wouldn't say as how I was wrong; would ye, now?' Roger could hardly answer the question. On general grounds the wringing of Sir Felix's neck, let the immediate cause for such a performance have been what it might, would have seemed to him to be a good deed. The world would be better, according to his thinking, with Sir Felix out of it than in it. But still the young man was his cousin and a Carbury, and to such a one as John Crumb he was bound to defend any member of his family as far as he might be defensible. 'They says as how he was groping about Sheep's Acre when he was last here, a hiding himself and skulking behind hedges. Drat 'em all. They've gals enough of their own,—them fellows. Why can't they let a fellow alone? I'll do him a mischief, Master Roger; I wull;—if he's had a hand in this.' Poor John Crumb! When he had his mistress to win he could find no words for himself; but was obliged to take an eloquent baker with him to talk for him. Now in his anger he could talk freely enough.

'But you must first learn that Sir Felix has had anything to do with this, Mr. Crumb.'

'In coorse; in coorse. That's right. That's right. Must l'arn as he did it, afore I does it. But when I have l'arned——!' And John Crumb clenched his fist as though a very short lesson would suffice for him upon this occasion.

They all went to the Beccles Station, and from thence to the Beccles Post-office,—so that Beccles soon knew as much about it as Bungay. At the railway station Ruby was distinctly remembered. She had taken a second-class ticket by the morning train for London, and had gone off without any appearance of secrecy. She had been decently dressed, with a hat and cloak, and her luggage had been such as she might have been expected to carry, had all her friends known that she was going. So much was made clear at the railway station, but nothing more could be learned there. Then a message was sent by telegraph to the station in London, and they all waited, loitering about the Post-office,* for a reply. One of the porters in London remembered seeing such a girl as was described, but the man who was supposed to have carried her box for her to a cab had gone away for the day. It was believed that she had left the station in a four-wheel cab. 'I'll be arter her. I'll be arter her at once,' said John Crumb. But there was no train till night, and Roger Carbury was doubtful whether his going would do any good. It was evidently fixed on Crumb's mind that the first step towards finding Ruby would be the breaking of every bone in the body of Sir Felix Carbury. Now it was not at all apparent to the squire that his cousin had had anything to do with this affair. It had been made quite clear to him that the old man had quarrelled with his granddaughter and had threatened to turn her out of his house, not because she had misbehaved with Sir Felix, but on account of her refusing to marry John Crumb. John Crumb had gone over to the farm expecting to arrange it all, and up to that time there had been no fear about Felix Carbury. Nor was it possible that there should have been communication between Ruby and Felix since the quarrel at the farm. Even if the old man were right in supposing that Ruby and the baronet had been acquainted,—and such acquaintance could not but be prejudicial to the girl,—not on that account would the baronet be responsible for her abduction. John Crumb was thirsting for blood and was not very capable in his present mood of arguing the matter out coolly, and Roger, little as he loved his cousin, was not desirous that all Suffolk should know that Sir Felix Carbury had been thrashed within an inch of his life by John Crumb of Bungay. 'I'll tell you what I'll do,' said he, putting his hand kindly on the old man's shoulder. 'I'll go up myself by the first train to-morrow. I can trace her better than Mr. Crumb can do, and you will both trust me.'

'There's not one in the two counties I'd trust so soon,' said the old man.

'But you'll let us know the very truth,' said John Crumb. Roger Carbury made him an indiscreet promise that he would let him know the truth. So the matter was settled, and the grandfather and lover returned together to Bungay.

## Chapter XXXV

### MELMOTTE'S GLORY

AUGUSTUS MELMOTTE was becoming greater and greater in every direction,—mightier and mightier every day. He was learning to despise mere lords, and to feel that he might almost domineer over a duke. In truth he did recognize it as a fact that he must either domineer over dukes, or else go to the wall. It can hardly be said of him that he had intended to play so high a game, but the game that he had intended to play had become thus high of its own accord. A man cannot always restrain his own doings and keep them within the limits which he had himself planned for them. They will very often fall short of the magnitude to which his ambition has aspired. They will sometimes soar higher than his own imagination. So it had now been with Mr. Melmotte. He had contemplated great things; but the things which he was achieving were beyond his contemplation.

The reader will not have thought much of Fisker on his arrival in England. Fisker was, perhaps, not a man worthy of much thought. He had never read a book. He had never written a line worth reading. He had never said a prayer. He cared nothing for humanity. He had sprung out of some Californian gully, was perhaps ignorant of his own father and mother, and had tumbled up in the world on the strength of his own audacity. But, such as he was, he had sufficed to give the necessary impetus for rolling Augustus Melmotte onwards into almost unprecedented commercial greatness. When Mr. Melmotte took his offices in Abchurch Lane, he was undoubtedly a great man, but nothing so great as when the South Central Pacific and Mexican Railway had become not only an established fact, but a fact established in Abchurch Lane. The great company indeed had an office of its own, where the Board was held; but everything was really managed in Mr. Melmotte's own commercial sanctum. Obeying, no doubt, some inscrutable law of commerce, the grand enterprise,—'perhaps the grandest when you consider the amount of territory manipulated, which has ever opened itself before the eyes of a great commercial people,' as Mr. Fisker with his peculiar eloquence observed through his nose, about this time, to a meeting of shareholders at San Francisco, —had swung itself across from California to London, turning itself to the centre of the commercial world as the needle turns to the pole, till Mr. Fisker almost regretted the deed which himself had done. And Melmotte was not only the head, but the body also, and the feet of it all. The shares seemed to be all in Melmotte's pocket, so that he could distribute them as he would; and it seemed also that when distributed and sold, and when bought again and sold again, they came back to Melmotte's pocket. Men were contented to buy their shares and to pay their money, simply on Melmotte's word. Sir Felix had realized a large portion of his winnings at cards,—with commendable prudence for one so young and extravagant,—and had brought his savings to the great man. The great man had swept the earn-

ings of the Beargarden into his till, and had told Sir
Felix that the shares were his. Sir Felix had been not
only contented, but supremely happy. He could now
do as Paul Montague was doing,—and Lord Alfred
Grendall. He could realize a perennial income, buying
and selling. It was only after the reflection of a day or
two that he found that he had as yet got nothing to sell.
It was not only Sir Felix that was admitted into these
good things after this fashion. Sir Felix was but one
among hundreds. In the meantime the bills in Grosvenor
Square were no doubt paid with punctuality,—and these
bills must have been stupendous. The very servants were
as tall, as gorgeous, almost as numerous, as the servants
of royalty,—and remunerated by much higher wages.
There were four coachmen with egregious wigs, and
eight footmen, not one with a circumference of calf less
than eighteen inches.

And now there appeared a paragraph in the 'Morning
Breakfast Table,' and another appeared in the 'Evening
Pulpit,' telling the world that Mr. Melmotte had bought
Pickering Park, the magnificent Sussex property of
Adolphus Longestaffe, Esq., of Caversham. And it was
so. The father and son, who never had agreed before,
and who now had come to no agreement in the presence
of each other, had each considered that their affairs
would be safe in the hands of so great a man as Mr. Melmotte, and had been brought to terms. The purchase-
money, which was large, was to be divided between
them. The thing was done with the greatest ease,—there
being no longer any delay as is the case when small
people are at work. The magnificence of Mr. Melmotte
affected even the Longestaffe lawyers. Were I to buy a
little property, some humble cottage with a garden,—or
you, O reader, unless you be magnificent,—the money
to the last farthing would be wanted, or security for the
money more than sufficient, before we should be able
to enter in upon our new home. But money was the very
breath of Melmotte's nostrils, and therefore his breath
was taken for money. Pickering was his, and before a
week was over a London builder had collected masons

and carpenters by the dozen down at Chichester, and was at work upon the house to make it fit to be a residence for Madame Melmotte. There were rumours that it was to be made ready for the Goodwood week, and that the Melmotte entertainment during that festival would rival the duke's.*

But there was still much to be done in London before the Goodwood week should come round, in all of which Mr. Melmotte was concerned, and of much of which Mr. Melmotte was the very centre. A member for Westminster had succeeded to a peerage, and thus a seat was vacated.* It was considered to be indispensable to the country that Mr. Melmotte should go into Parliament, and what constituency could such a man as Melmotte so fitly represent as one combining as Westminster does all the essences of the metropolis? There was the popular element, the fashionable element, the legislative element, the legal element, and the commercial element. Melmotte undoubtedly was the man for Westminster. His thorough popularity was evinced by testimony which perhaps was never before given in favour of any candidate for any county or borough. In Westminster there must of course be a contest. A seat for Westminster is a thing not to be abandoned by either political party without a struggle. But, at the beginning of the affair, when each party had to seek the most suitable candidate which the country could supply, each party put its hand upon Melmotte. And when the seat, and the battle for the seat, were suggested to Melmotte, then for the first time was that great man forced to descend from the altitudes on which his mind generally dwelt, and to decide whether he would enter Parliament as a Conservative or a Liberal. He was not long in convincing himself that the conservative element in British Society stood the most in need of that fiscal assistance which it would be in his province to give; and on the next day every hoarding in London declared to the world that Melmotte was the conservative candidate for Westminster. It is needless to say that his committee was made up of peers, bankers, and publicans, with all that absence of class prejudice for which the party has become famous since the ballot was introduced among us.* Some unfortunate Liberal was to be made to run against him, for the sake of the party; but the odds were ten to one on Melmotte.

This no doubt was a great matter,—this affair of the seat; but the dinner to be given to the Emperor of China was much greater. It was the middle of June, and the dinner was to be given on Monday, 8th July, now three weeks hence;—but all London was already talking of it. The great purport proposed was to show to the Emperor by this banquet what an English merchant-citizen of London could do. Of course there was a great amount of scolding and a loud clamour on the occasion. Some men said that Melmotte was not a citizen of London, others that he was not a merchant, others again that he was not an Englishman. But no man could deny that he was both able and willing to spend the necessary money; and as this combination of ability and will was the chief thing necessary, they who opposed the arrangement could only storm and scold. On the 20th of June the tradesmen were at work, throwing up a building behind, knocking down walls, and generally transmuting the house in Grosvenor Square in such a fashion that two hundred guests might be able to sit down to dinner in the dining-room of a British merchant.

But who were to be the two hundred? It used to be the case that when a gentleman gave a dinner he asked his own guests;—but when affairs become great, society can hardly be carried on after that simple fashion. The Emperor of China could not be made to sit at table without English royalty, and English royalty must know whom it has to meet,—must select at any rate some of its comrades. The minister of the day also had his candidates for the dinner,—in which arrangement there was however no private patronage, as the list was confined to the cabinet and their wives. The Prime Minister took some credit to himself in that he would not ask for a single ticket for a private friend. But the Opposition*as a body desired their share of seats. Melmotte had elected to stand for Westminster on the conservative interest, and was advised that he must insist on having as it were a conservative cabinet present, with its conservative wives. He was told that he owed it to his party, and that his party exacted payment of the debt. But the great difficulty lay with the city merchants. This was to be a city merchant's private feast, and it was essential that the Emperor should meet this great merchant's brother merchants at the merchant's board. No doubt the Emperor would see all the merchants at the Guildhall; but that would be a semi-public affair, paid for out of the funds of a corporation. This was to be a private dinner. Now the Lord Mayor had set his face against it, and what was to be done? Meetings were held; a committee was appointed; merchant guests were selected, to the number of fifteen with their fifteen wives;—and subsequently the Lord Mayor was made a baronet on the occasion of receiving the Emperor in the city. The Emperor with his suite was twenty. Royalty had twenty tickets, each ticket for guest and wife. The existing Cabinet was fourteen; but the coming was numbered at about eleven only;—each one for self and wife. Five ambassadors and five ambassadresses were to be asked. There were to be fifteen real merchants out of the city. Ten great peers, —with their peeresses,—were selected by the general committee of management. There were to be three wise men, two poets, three independent members of the House of Commons, two Royal Academicians, three editors of papers, an African traveller who had just come home, and a novelist;—but all these latter gentlemen were expected to come as bachelors. Three tickets were to be kept over for presentation to bores endowed with a power of making themselves absolutely unendurable if not admitted at the last moment,—and ten were left for the giver of the feast and his own family and friends. It is often difficult to make things go smooth,—but almost all roughnesses may be smoothed at last with patience and care, and money, and patronage.

But the dinner was not to be all. Eight hundred additional tickets were to be issued for Madame Melmotte's evening entertainment, and the fight for these

was more internecine than for seats at the dinner. The
dinner-seats, indeed, were handled in so statesmanlike a
fashion that there was not much visible fighting about
them. Royalty manages its affairs quietly. The existing
Cabinet was existing, and though there were two or
three members of it who could not have got themselves
elected at a single unpolitical club in London, they had
a right to their seats at Melmotte's table. What disappointed ambition there might be among conservative
candidates was never known to the public. Those gentlemen do not wash their dirty linen in public. The ambassadors of course were quiet, but we may be sure that
the Minister from the United States was among the
favoured five. The city bankers and bigwigs, as has been
already said, were at first unwilling to be present, and
therefore they who were not chosen could not afterwards express their displeasure. No grumbling was
heard among the peers, and that which came from the
peeresses floated down into the current of the great fight
about the evening entertainment. The poet laureate*was
of course asked, and the second poet was as much a
matter of course. Only two Academicians had in this
year painted royalty, so that there was no ground for
jealousy there. There were three, and only three,
specially insolent and specially disagreeable independent
members of Parliament at that time in the House, and
there was no difficulty in selecting them. The wise men
were chosen by their age. Among editors of newspapers
there was some ill-blood. That Mr. Alf and Mr. Broune
should be selected was almost a matter of course. They
were hated accordingly, but still this was expected. But
why was Mr. Booker there? Was it because he had
praised the Prime Minister's translation of Catullus?*
The African traveller chose himself by living through all
his perils and coming home. A novelist was selected; but
as royalty wanted another ticket at the last moment, the
gentleman was only asked to come in after dinner. His
proud heart, however, resented the treatment, and he
joined amicably with his literary brethren in decrying
the festival altogether.

We should be advancing too rapidly into this portion of our story were we to concern ourselves deeply at the present moment with the feud as it raged before the evening came round, but it may be right to indicate that the desire for tickets at last became a burning passion, and a passion which in the great majority of cases could not be indulged. The value of the privilege was so great that Madame Melmotte thought that she was doing almost more than friendship called for when she informed her guest, Miss Longestaffe, that unfortunately there would be no seat for her at the dinner-table; but that, as payment for her loss, she should receive an evening ticket for herself and a joint ticket for a gentleman and his wife. Georgiana was at first indignant, but she accepted the compromise. What she did with her tickets shall be hereafter told.

From all this I trust it will be understood that the Mr. Melmotte of the present hour was a very different man from that Mr. Melmotte who was introduced to the reader in the early chapters of this chronicle. Royalty was not to be smuggled in and out of his house now without his being allowed to see it. No manœuvres now were necessary to catch a simple duchess. Duchesses were willing enough to come. Lord Alfred when he was called by his Christian name felt no aristocratic twinges. He was only too anxious to make himself more and more necessary to the great man. It is true that all this came as it were by jumps, so that very often a part of the world did not know on what ledge in the world the great man was perched at that moment. Miss Longestaffe who was staying in the house did not at all know how great a man her host was. Lady Monogram when she refused to go to Grosvenor Square, or even to allow any one to come out of the house in Grosvenor Square to her parties, was groping in outer darkness. Madame Melmotte did not know. Marie Melmotte did not know. The great man did not quite know himself where, from time to time, he was standing. But the world at large knew. The world knew that Mr. Melmotte was to be Member for Westminster, that Mr. Melmotte was to entertain the Emperor of China, that Mr. Melmotte carried the South Central Pacific and Mexican Railway in his pocket;—and the world worshipped Mr. Melmotte.

In the meantime Mr. Melmotte was much troubled about his private affairs. He had promised his daughter to Lord Nidderdale, and as he rose in the world had lowered the price which he offered for this marriage,— not so much in the absolute amount of fortune to be ultimately given, as in the manner of giving it. Fifteen thousand a year was to be settled on Marie and on her eldest son, and twenty thousand pounds were to be paid into Nidderdale's hands six months after the marriage. Melmotte gave his reasons for not paying this sum at once. Nidderdale would be more likely to be quiet, if he were kept waiting for that short time. Melmotte was to purchase and furnish for them a house in town. It was, too, almost understood that the young people were to have Pickering Park for themselves, except for a week or so at the end of July. It was absolutely given out in the papers that Pickering was to be theirs. It was said on all sides that Nidderdale was doing very well for himself. The absolute money was not perhaps so great as had been at first asked; but then, at that time, Melmotte was not the strong rock, the impregnable tower of commerce, the very navel of the commercial enterprise of the world,—as all men now regarded him. Nidderdale's father, and Nidderdale himself, were, in the present condition of things, content with a very much less stringent bargain than that which they had endeavoured at first to exact.

But, in the midst of all this, Marie, who had at one time consented at her father's instance to accept the young lord, and who in some speechless fashion had accepted him, told both the young lord and her father, very roundly, that she had changed her mind. Her father scowled at her and told her that her mind in the matter was of no concern. He intended that she should marry Lord Nidderdale, and himself fixed some day in August for the wedding. 'It is no use, father, for I will never have him,' said Marie.

'Is it about that other scamp?' he asked angrily.

'If you mean Sir Felix Carbury, it is about him. He has been to you and told you, and therefore I don't know why I need hold my tongue.'

'You'll both starve, my lady; that's all.' Marie however was not so wedded to the grandeur which she encountered in Grosvenor Square as to be afraid of the starvation which she thought she might have to suffer if married to Sir Felix Carbury. Melmotte had not time for any long discussion. As he left her he took hold of her and shook her. 'By ——,' he said, 'if you run rusty after all I've done for you, I'll make you suffer. You little fool; that man's a beggar. He hasn't the price of a petticoat or a pair of stockings. He's looking only for what you haven't got, and shan't have if you marry him. He wants money, not you, you little fool!'

But after that she was quite settled in her purpose when Nidderdale spoke to her. They had been engaged and then it had been off;—and now the young nobleman, having settled everything with the father, expected no great difficulty in resettling everything with the girl. He was not very skilful at making love,—but he was thoroughly good-humoured, from his nature anxious to please, and averse to give pain. There was hardly any injury which he could not forgive, and hardly any kindness which he would not do,—so that the labour upon himself was not too great. 'Well, Miss Melmotte,' he said, 'governors are stern beings: are they not?'

'Is yours stern, my lord?'

'What I mean is that sons and daughters have to obey them. I think you understand what I mean. I was awfully spoony on you that time before; I was indeed.'

'I hope it didn't hurt you much, Lord Nidderdale.'

'That's so like a woman; that is. You know well enough that you and I can't marry without leave from the governors.'

'Nor with it,' said Marie, holding her head.

'I don't know how that may be. There was some hitch somewhere,—I don't quite know where.'—The hitch had been with himself, as he demanded ready money. 'But 'it's all right now. The old fellows are agreed. Can't we make a match of it, Miss Melmotte?'

'No, Lord Nidderdale; I don't think we can.'

'Do you mean that?'

'I do mean it. When that was going on before I knew nothing about it. I have seen more of things since then.'

'And you've seen somebody you like better than me?'

'I say nothing about that, Lord Nidderdale. I don't think you ought to blame me, my lord.'

'Oh dear no.'

'There was something before, but it was you that was off first. Wasn't it now?'

'The governors were off, I think.'

'The governors have a right to be off, I suppose. But I don't think any governor has a right to make anybody marry any one.'

'I agree with you there;—I do indeed,' said Lord Nidderdale.

'And no governor shall make me marry. I've thought a great deal about it since that other time, and that's what I've come to determine.'

'But I don't know why you shouldn't—just marry me —because you—like me.'

'Only,—just because I don't. Well; I do like you, Lord Nidderdale.'

'Thanks;—so much!'

'I like you ever so,—only marrying a person is different.'

'There's something in that, to be sure.'

'And I don't mind telling you,' said Marie with an almost solemn expression on her countenance, 'because you are good-natured and won't get me into a scrape if you can help it, that I do like somebody else;—oh, so much.'

'I supposed that was it.'

'That is it.'

'It's a deuced pity. The governors had settled everything, and we should have been awfully jolly. I'd have gone in for all the things you go in for; and though your governor was screwing us up a bit, there would have

been plenty of tin to go on with. You couldn't think of
it again?'

'I tell you, my lord, I'm—in love.'

'Oh, ah;—yes. So you were saying. It's an awful bore.
That's all. I shall come to the party all the same if you
send me a ticket.' And so Nidderdale took his dismissal,
and went away,—not however without an idea that the
marriage would still come off. There was always,—so
he thought,—such a bother about things before they
would get themselves fixed. This happened some days
after Mr. Broune's proposal to Lady Carbury, more than
a week since Marie had seen Sir Felix. As soon as Lord
Nidderdale was gone she wrote again to Sir Felix begging
that she might hear from him,—and entrusted her letter
to Didon.

## Chapter XXXVI

### MR. BROUNE'S PERILS

LADY CARBURY had allowed herself two days for
answering Mr. Broune's proposition. It was made
on Tuesday night and she was bound by her promise to
send a reply some time on Thursday. But early on the
Wednesday morning she had made up her mind; and
at noon on that day her letter was written. She had
spoken to Hetta about the man, and she had seen that
Hetta had disliked him. She was not disposed to be
much guided by Hetta's opinion. In regard to her
daughter she was always influenced by a vague idea that
Hetta was an unnecessary trouble. There was an
excellent match ready for her if she would only accept
it. There was no reason why Hetta should continue
to add herself to the family burden. She never said this
even to herself,—but she felt it, and was not therefore
inclined to consult Hetta's comfort on this occasion.
But nevertheless, what her daughter said had its effect.
She had encountered the troubles of one marriage, and
they had been very bad. She did not look upon that

marriage as a mistake,—having even up to this day a
consciousness that it had been the business of her life, as
a portionless girl, to obtain maintenance and position
at the expense of suffering and servility. But that had
been done. The maintenance was, indeed, again doubtful, because of her son's vices; but it might so probably
be again secured,—by means of her son's beauty! Hetta
had said that Mr. Broune liked his own way. Had not
she herself found that all men liked their own way? And
she liked her own way. She liked the comfort of a home
to herself. Personally she did not want the companionship of a husband. And what scenes would there be
between Felix and the man! And added to all this there
was something within her, almost amounting to conscience, which told her that it was not right that she
should burden any one with the responsibility and
inevitable troubles of such a son as her son Felix. What
would she do were her husband to command her to
separate herself from her son? In such circumstances
she would certainly separate herself from her husband.
Having considered these things deeply, she wrote as
follows to Mr. Broune:—

'DEAREST FRIEND,
    'I need not tell you that I have thought much of your
generous and affectionate offer. How could I refuse such
a prospect as you offer me without much thought? I
regard your career as the most noble which a man's
ambition can achieve. And in that career no one is your
superior. I cannot but be proud that such a one as you
should have asked me to be his wife. But, my friend,
life is subject to wounds which are incurable, and my
life has been so wounded. I have not strength left me
to make my heart whole enough to be worthy of your
acceptance. I have been so cut and scotched and lopped
by the sufferings which I have endured that I am best
alone. It cannot all be described;—and yet with you I
would have no reticence. I would put the whole history
before you to read, with all my troubles past and still
present, all my hopes, and all my fears,—with every

circumstance as it has passed by and every expectation that remains, were it not that the poor tale would be too long for your patience. The result of it would be to make you feel that I am no longer fit to enter in upon a new home. I should bring showers instead of sunshine, melancholy in lieu of mirth.

'I will, however, be bold enough to assure you that could I bring myself to be the wife of any man I would now become your wife. But I shall never marry again.

'Nevertheless, I am your most affectionate friend,

'MATILDA CARBURY.'

About six o'clock in the afternoon she sent this letter to Mr. Broune's rooms in Pall Mall East, and then sat for awhile alone,—full of regrets. She had thrown away from her a firm footing which would certainly have served her for her whole life. Even at this moment she was in debt,—and did not know how to pay her debts without mortgaging her life income. She longed for some staff on which she could lean. She was afraid of the future. When she would sit with her paper before her, preparing her future work for the press, copying a bit here and a bit there, inventing historical details, dovetailing her chronicle, her head would sometimes seem to be going round as she remembered the unpaid baker, and her son's horses, and his unmeaning dissipation, and all her doubts about the marriage. As regarded herself, Mr. Broune would have made her secure,—but that now was all over. Poor woman! This at any rate may be said for her,—that had she accepted the man her regrets would have been as deep.

Mr. Broune's feelings were more decided in their tone than those of the lady. He had not made his offer without consideration, and yet from the very moment in which it had been made he repented it. That gently sarcastic appellation by which Lady Carbury had described him to herself when he had kissed her best explained that side of Mr. Broune's character which showed itself in this matter. He was a susceptible old goose. Had she allowed him to kiss her without objection, the kissing

**might** probably have gone on; and, whatever might have come of it, there would have been no offer of marriage. He had believed that her little manœuvres had indicated love on her part, and he had felt himself constrained to reciprocate the passion. She was beautiful in his eyes. She was bright. She wore her clothes like a lady; and,— if it was written in the Book of the Fates that some lady was to sit at the top of his table,—Lady Carbury would look as well there as any other. She had repudiated the kiss, and therefore he had felt himself bound to obtain for himself the right to kiss her.

The offer had no sooner been made than he met her son reeling in, drunk, at the front door. As he made his escape the lad had insulted him. This perhaps helped to open his eyes. When he woke the next morning, or rather late in the next day, after his night's work, he was no longer able to tell himself that the world was all right with him. Who does not know that sudden thoughtfulness at waking, that first matutinal retrospection, and pro-spection, into things as they have been and are to be; and the lowness of heart, the blankness of hope which follows the first remembrance of some folly lately done, some word ill-spoken, some money misspent,—or perhaps a cigar too much, or a glass of brandy and soda-water which he should have left untasted? And when things have gone well, how the waker comforts himself among the bedclothes as he claims for himself to be whole all over, teres atque rotundus,*—so to have managed his little affairs that he has to fear no harm, and to blush inwardly at no error! Mr. Broune, the way of whose life took him among many perils, who in the course of his work had to steer his bark among many rocks, was in the habit of thus auditing his daily account as he shook off sleep about noon,—for such was his lot, that he seldom was in bed before four or five in the morn-ing. On this Wednesday he found that he could not balance his sheet comfortably. He had taken a very great step and he feared that he had not taken it with wisdom. As he drank the cup of tea with which his servant supplied him while he was yet in bed, he could

not say of himself, teres atque rotundus, as he was wont
to do when things were well with him. Everything was
to be changed. As he lit a cigarette he bethought himself that Lady Carbury would not like him to smoke in
her bedroom. Then he remembered other things. 'I'll
be d—— if he shall live in my house,' he said to himself.

And there was no way out of it. It did not occur to the
man that his offer could be refused. During the whole
of that day he went about among his friends in a melancholy fashion, saying little snappish uncivil things at the
club, and at last dining by himself with about fifteen newspapers around him. After dinner he did not speak a
word to any man, but went early to the office of the
newspaper in Trafalgar Square at which he did his
nightly work. Here he was lapped in comforts,—if the
best of chairs, of sofas, of writing tables, and of reading
lamps can make a man comfortable who has to read
nightly thirty columns of a newspaper, or at any rate
to make himself responsible for their contents.

He seated himself to his work like a man, but immediately saw Lady Carbury's letter on the table before
him. It was his custom when he did not dine at home
to have such documents brought to him at his office as
had reached his home during his absence;—and here
was Lady Carbury's letter. He knew her writing well,
and was aware that here was the confirmation of his
fate. It had not been expected, as she had given herself
another day for her answer,—but here it was, beneath
his hand. Surely this was almost unfeminine haste. He
chucked the letter, unopened, a little from him, and
endeavoured to fix his attention on some printed slip*
that was ready for him. For some ten minutes his eyes
went rapidly down the lines, but he found that his
mind did not follow what he was reading. He struggled
again, but still his thoughts were on the letter. He did
not wish to open it, having some vague idea that, till
the letter should have been read, there was a chance of
escape. The letter would not become due to be read till
the next day. It should not have been there now to
tempt his thoughts on this night. But he could do

nothing while it lay there. 'It shall be a part of the bargain that I shall never have to see him,' he said to himself, as he opened it. The second line told him that the danger was over.

When he had read so far he stood up with his back to the fireplace, leaving the letter on the table. Then, after all, the woman wasn't in love with him! But that was a reading of the affair which he could hardly bring himself to look upon as correct. The woman had shown her love by a thousand signs. There was no doubt, however, that she now had her triumph. A woman always has a triumph when she rejects a man,—and more especially when she does so at a certain time of life. Would she publish her triumph? Mr. Broune would not like to have it known about among brother editors, or by the world at large, that he had offered to marry Lady Carbury and that Lady Carbury had refused him. He had escaped; but the sweetness of his present safety was not in proportion to the bitterness of his late fears.

He could not understand why Lady Carbury should have refused him! As he reflected upon it, all memory of her son for the moment passed away from him. Full ten minutes had passed, during which he had still stood upon the rug, before he read the entire letter. ' "Cut and scotched and lopped!" I suppose she has been,' he said to himself. He had heard much of Sir Patrick, and knew well that the old general had been no lamb. 'I shouldn't have cut her, or scotched her, or lopped her.' When he had read the whole letter patiently there crept upon him gradually a feeling of admiration for her, greater than he had ever yet felt,—and, for awhile, he almost thought that he would renew his offer to her. ' "Showers instead of sunshine; melancholy instead of mirth,"' he repeated to himself. 'I should have done the best for her, taking the showers and the melancholy if they were necessary.'

He went to his work in a mixed frame of mind, but certainly without that dragging weight which had oppressed him when he entered the room. Gradually, through the night, he realized the conviction that he had escaped, and threw from him altogether the idea of repeating his offer. Before he left he wrote her a line—

'Be it so. It need not break our friendship.

'N. B.'

This he sent by a special messenger, who returned with a note to his lodgings long before he was up on the following morning.

'No;—no; certainly not. No word of this will ever pass my mouth.

'M. C.'

Mr. Broune thought that he was very well out of the danger, and resolved that Lady Carbury should never want anything that his friendship could do for her.

## Chapter XXXVII

### THE BOARD-ROOM

ON Friday, the 21st June, the Board of the South Central Pacific and Mexican Railway sat in its own room behind the Exchange, as was the Board's custom every Friday. On this occasion all the members were there, as it had been understood that the chairman was to make a special statement. There was the great chairman as a matter of course. In the midst of his numerous and immense concerns he never threw over the railway, or delegated to other less experienced hands those cares which the commercial world had intrusted to his own. Lord Alfred was there, with Mr. Cohenlupe, the Hebrew gentleman, and Paul Montague, and Lord Nidderdale, —and even Sir Felix Carbury. Sir Felix had come, being very anxious to buy and sell, and not as yet having had an opportunity of realizing his golden hopes, although he had actually paid a thousand pounds in hard money into Mr. Melmotte's hands. The secretary, Mr. Miles Grendall, was also present as a matter of course. The Board always met at three, and had generally been dissolved at a quarter past three. Lord Alfred and Mr. Cohenlupe sat at the chairman's right and left hand. Paul Montague generally sat immediately below, with Miles Grendall opposite to him;—but on this occasion the young lord and the young baronet took the next places. It was a nice little family party, the great chairman with his two aspiring sons-in-law, his two particular friends,—the social friend, Lord Alfred, and the commercial friend Mr. Cohenlupe,—and Miles, who was Lord Alfred's son. It would have been complete in its friendliness, but for Paul Montague, who had lately made himself disagreeable to Mr. Melmotte;—and most ungratefully so, for certainly no one had been allowed so free a use of the shares as the younger member of the house of Fisker, Montague, and Montague.

It was understood that Mr. Melmotte was to make a statement. Lord Nidderdale and Sir Felix had conceived that this was to be done as it were out of the great man's heart, of his own wish, so that something of the condition of the company might be made known to the directors of the company. But this was not perhaps exactly the truth. Paul Montague had insisted on giving vent to certain doubts at the last meeting but one, and, having made himself very disagreeable indeed, had forced this trouble on the great chairman. On the intermediate Friday the chairman had made himself very unpleasant to Paul, and this had seemed to be an effort on his part to frighten the inimical director out of his opposition, so that the promise of a statement need not be fulfilled. What nuisance can be so great to a man busied with immense affairs, as to have to explain,—or to attempt to explain,—small details to men incapable of understanding them? But Montague had stood to his guns. He had not intended, he said, to dispute the commercial success of the company. But he felt very strongly, and he thought that his brother directors should feel as strongly, that it was necessary that they should know more than they did know. Lord Alfred had declared that he did not in the least agree with his brother director. 'If anybody don't understand, it's his own fault,' said Mr. Cohenlupe. But Paul would not give way, and it was understood that Mr. Melmotte would make a statement.

The 'Boards' were always commenced by the reading of a certain record of the last meeting out of a book. This was always done by Miles Grendall; and the record was supposed to have been written by him. But Montague had discovered that this statement in the book was always prepared and written by a satellite of Melmotte's from Abchurch Lane who was never present at the meeting. The adverse director had spoken to the secretary,— it will be remembered that they were both members of the Beargarden,—and Miles had given a somewhat evasive reply. 'A cussed deal of trouble and all that, you know! He's used to it, and it's what he's meant for. I'm not going to flurry myself about stuff of that kind.' Montague after this had spoken on the subject both to Nidderdale and Felix Carbury. 'He couldn't do it, if it was ever so,' Nidderdale had said. 'I don't think I'd bully him if I were you. He gets £500 a-year, and if you knew all he owes, and all he hasn't got, you wouldn't try to rob him of it.' With Felix Carbury, Montague had as little success. Sir Felix hated the secretary, had detected him cheating at cards, had resolved to expose him,—and had then been afraid to do so. He had told Dolly Longestaffe, and the reader will perhaps remember with what effect. He had not mentioned the affair again, and had gradually fallen back into the habit of playing at the club. Loo, however, had given way to whist, and Sir Felix had satisfied himself with the change. He still meditated some dreadful punishment for Miles Grendall, but, in the meantime, felt himself unable to oppose him at the Board. Since the day at which the aces had been manipulated at the club he had not spoken to Miles Grendall except in reference to the affairs of the whist-table. The 'Board' was now commenced as usual. Miles read the short record out of the book,—stumbling over every other word, and going through the performance so badly that had there been anything to understand no one could have understood it. 'Gentlemen,' said Mr. Melmotte, in his usual hurried way, 'is it your pleasure

that I shall sign the record?' Paul Montague rose to say
that it was not his pleasure that the record should be
signed. But Melmotte had made his scrawl, and was
deep in conversation with Mr. Cohenlupe before Paul
could get upon his legs.

Melmotte, however, had watched the little struggle.
Melmotte, whatever might be his faults, had eyes to see
and ears to hear. He perceived that Montague had made
a little struggle and had been cowed; and he knew how
hard it is for one man to persevere against five or six, and
for a young man to persevere against his elders. Nidderdale was filliping bits of paper across the table at Carbury.
Miles Grendall was poring over the book which was in
his charge. Lord Alfred sat back in his chair, the picture
of a model director, with his right hand within his waistcoat. He looked aristocratic, respectable, and almost
commercial. In that room he never by any chance
opened his mouth, except when called on to say that
Mr. Melmotte was right, and was considered by the
chairman really to earn his money. Melmotte for a
minute or two went on conversing with Cohenlupe,
having perceived that Montague for the moment was
cowed. Then Paul put both his hands upon the table,
intending to rise and ask some perplexing question.
Melmotte saw this also and was upon his legs before
Montague had risen from his chair. 'Gentlemen,' said
Mr. Melmotte, 'it may perhaps be as well if I take this
occasion of saying a few words to you about the affairs
of the company.' Then, instead of going on with his
statement, he sat down again, and began to turn over
sundry voluminous papers very slowly, whispering a
word or two every now and then to Mr. Cohenlupe.
Lord Alfred never changed his posture and never took
his hand from his breast. Nidderdale and Carbury
filliped their paper pellets backwards and forwards.
Montague sat profoundly listening,—or ready to listen
when anything should be said. As the chairman had
risen from his chair to commence his statement, Paul
felt that he was bound to be silent. When a speaker is
in possession of the floor, he is in possession even though

he be somewhat dilatory in looking to his references, and
whispering to his neighbour. And, when that speaker is
a chairman, of course some additional latitude must be
allowed to him. Montague understood this, and sat
silent. It seemed that Melmotte had much to say to
Cohenlupe, and Cohenlupe much to say to Melmotte.
Since Cohenlupe had sat at the Board he had never
before developed such powers of conversation.

Nidderdale didn't quite understand it. He had been
there twenty minutes, was tired of his present amusement, having been unable to hit Carbury on the nose,
and suddenly remembered that the Beargarden would
now be open. He was no respecter of persons, and had
got over any little feeling of awe with which the big table
and the solemnity of the room may have first inspired
him. 'I suppose that's about all,' he said, looking up at
Melmotte.

'Well;—perhaps as your lordship is in a hurry, and as
my lord here is engaged elsewhere,'—turning round to
Lord Alfred, who had not uttered a syllable or made a
sign since he had been in his seat,—'we had better
adjourn this meeting for another week.'

'I cannot allow that,' said Paul Montague.

'I suppose then we must take the sense of the Board,'
said the Chairman.

'I have been discussing certain circumstances with our
friend and Chairman,' said Cohenlupe, 'and I must say
that it is not expedient just at present to go into matters
too freely.'

'My Lords and Gentlemen,' said Melmotte. 'I hope
that you trust me.'

Lord Alfred bowed down to the table and muttered
something which was intended to convey most absolute
confidence. 'Hear, hear,' said Mr. Cohenlupe. 'All
right,' said Lord Nidderdale; 'go on;' and he fired
another pellet with improved success.

'I trust,' said the Chairman, 'that my young friend,
Sir Felix, doubts neither my discretion nor my ability.'

'Oh dear, no;—not at all,' said the baronet, much
flattered at being addressed in this kindly tone. He had

come there with objects of his own, and was quite prepared to support the Chairman on any matter whatever.

'My Lords and Gentlemen,' continued Melmotte, 'I am delighted to receive this expression of your confidence. If I know anything in the world I know something of commercial matters. I am able to tell you that we are prospering. I do not know that greater prosperity has ever been achieved in a shorter time by a commercial company. I think our friend here, Mr. Montague, should be as feelingly aware of that as any gentleman.'

'What do you mean by that, Mr. Melmotte?' asked Paul.

'What do I mean?—Certainly nothing adverse to your character, sir. Your firm in San Francisco, sir, know very well how the affairs of the Company are being transacted on this side of the water. No doubt you are in correspondence with Mr. Fisker. Ask him. The telegraph wires are open to you, sir, But, my Lords and Gentlemen, I am able to inform you that in affairs of this nature great discretion is necessary. On behalf of the shareholders at large whose interests are in our hands, I think it expedient that any general statement should be postponed for a short time, and I flatter myself that in that opinion I shall carry the majority of this Board with me.' Mr. Melmotte did not make his speech very fluently; but, being accustomed to the place which he occupied, he did manage to get the words spoken in such a way as to make them intelligible to the company. 'I now move that this meeting be adjourned to this day week,' he added.

'I second that motion,' said Lord Alfred, without moving his hand from his breast.

'I understood that we were to have a statement,' said Montague.

'You've had a statement,' said Mr. Cohenlupe.

'I will put my motion to the vote,' said the Chairman.

'I shall move an amendment,' said Paul, determined that he would not be altogether silenced.

'There is nobody to second it,' said Mr. Cohenlupe.

'How do you know till I've made it?' asked the rebel.

'I shall ask Lord Nidderdale to second it, and when he has heard it I think that he will not refuse.'

'Oh, gracious me! why me? No;—don't ask me. I've got to go away. I have indeed.'

'At any rate I claim the right of saying a few words. I do not say whether every affair of this Company should or should not be published to the world.'

'You'd break up everything if you did,' said Cohenlupe.

'Perhaps everything ought to be broken up. But I say nothing about that. What I do say is this. That as we sit here as directors and will be held to be responsible as such by the public, we ought to know what is being done. We ought to know where the shares really are. I for one do not even know what scrip has been issued.'

'You've bought and sold enough to know something about it,' said Melmotte.

Paul Montague became very red in the face. 'I, at any rate, began,' he said, 'by putting what was to me a large sum of money into the affair.'

'That's more than I know,' said Melmotte. 'Whatever shares you have, were issued at San Francisco, and not here.'

'I have taken nothing that I haven't paid for,' said Montague. 'Nor have I yet had allotted to me anything like the number of shares which my capital would represent. But I did not intend to speak of my own concerns.'

'It looks very like it,' said Cohenlupe.

'So far from it that I am prepared to risk the not improbable loss of everything I have in the world. I am determined to know what is being done with the shares, or to make it public to the world at large that I, one of the directors of the Company, do not in truth know anything about it. I cannot, I suppose, absolve myself from further responsibility; but I can at any rate do what is right from this time forward,—and that course I intend to take.'

'The gentleman had better resign his seat at this Board,' said Melmotte. 'There will be no difficulty about that.'

'Bound up as I am with Fisker and Montague in California I fear that there will be difficulty.'

'Not in the least,' continued the Chairman. 'You need only gazette your resignation*and the thing is done. I had intended, gentlemen, to propose an addition to our number. When I name to you a gentleman, personally known to many of you, and generally esteemed throughout England as a man of business, as a man of probity, and as a man of fortune, a man standing deservedly high in all British circles, I mean Mr. Longestaffe of Caversham——'

'Young Dolly, or old?' asked Lord Nidderdale.

'I mean Mr. Adolphus Longestaffe, senior, of Caversham. I am sure that you will all be glad to welcome him among you. I had thought to strengthen our number by this addition. But if Mr. Montague is determined to leave us,—and no one will regret the loss of his services so much as I shall,—it will be my pleasing duty to move that Adolphus Longestaffe, senior, Esquire, of Caversham, be requested to take his place. If on consideration Mr. Montague shall determine to remain with us,—and I for one most sincerely hope that such reconsideration may lead to such determination,—then I shall move that an additional director be added to our number, and that Mr. Longestaffe be requested to take the chair of that additional director.' The latter speech Mr. Melmotte got through very glibly, and then immediately left the chair, so as to show that the business of the Board was closed for that day without any possibility of re-opening it.

Paul went up to him and took him by the sleeve, signifying that he wished to speak to him before they parted. 'Certainly,' said the great man bowing. 'Carbury,' he said, looking round on the young baronet with his blandest smile, 'if you are not in a hurry, wait a moment for me. I have a word or two to say before you go. Now, Mr. Montague, what can I do for you?' Paul began his story, expressing again the opinion which he had already very plainly expressed at the table. But Melmotte stopped him very shortly, and with much less courtesy than he had shown in the speech which he had

made from the chair. 'The thing is about this way, I
take it, Mr. Montague;—you think you know more of
this matter than I do.'

'Not at all, Mr. Melmotte.'

'And I think that I know **more** of it than you do.
Either of us may be right. But as I don't intend to give
way to you, perhaps the less we speak together about it
the better. You can't be in earnest in the threat you
made, because you would be making public things
communicated to you under the seal of privacy,—and
no gentleman would do that. But as long as you are
hostile to me, I can't help you;—and so good afternoon.'
Then, without giving Montague the possibility of a reply,
he escaped into an inner room which had the word
'Private' painted on the door, and which was supposed to
belong to the chairman individually. He shut the door
behind him, and then, after a few moments, put out his
head and beckoned to Sir Felix Carbury. Nidderdale
was gone. Lord Alfred with his son were already on the
stairs. Cohenlupe was engaged with Melmotte's clerk
on the record-book. Paul Montague, finding himself
without support and alone, slowly made his way out into
the court.

Sir Felix had come into the city intending to suggest
to the Chairman that having paid his thousand pounds
he should like to have a few shares to go on with. He was,
indeed, at the present moment very nearly penniless, and
had negotiated, or lost at cards, all the I.O.U.'s which
were in any degree serviceable. He still had a pocket-
book full of those issued by Miles Grendall; but it was
now an understood thing at the Beargarden that no one
was to be called upon to take them except Miles Grendall
himself;—an arrangement which robbed the card-table
of much of its delight. Beyond this, also, he had lately
been forced to issue a little paper himself,—in doing
which he had talked largely of his shares in the railway.
His case certainly was hard. He had actually paid a
thousand pounds down in hard cash, a commercial
transaction which, as performed by himself, he regarded
as stupendous. It was almost incredible to himself that

he should have paid any one a thousand pounds, but he had done it with much difficulty,—having carried Dolly junior with him all the way into the city,—in the belief that he would thus put himself in the way of making a continual and unfailing income. He understood that as a director he would be always entitled to buy shares at par, and, as a matter of course, always able to sell them at the market price. This he understood to range from ten to fifteen and twenty per cent. profit. He would have nothing to do but to buy and sell daily. He was told that Lord Alfred was allowed to do it to a small extent; and that Melmotte was doing it to an enormous extent. But before he could do it he must get something,—he hardly knew what,—out of Melmotte's hands. Melmotte certainly did not seem to shun him, and therefore there could be no difficulty about the shares. As to danger;—who could think of danger in reference to money intrusted to the hands of Augustus Melmotte?

'I am delighted to see you here,' said Melmotte, shaking him cordially by the hand. 'You come regularly, and you'll find that it will be worth your while. There's nothing like attending to business. You should be here every Friday.'

'I will,' said the baronet.

'And let me see you sometimes up at my place in Abchurch Lane. I can put you more in the way of understanding things there than I can here. This is all a mere formal sort of thing. You can see that.'

'Oh yes, I see that.'

'We are obliged to have this kind of thing for men like that fellow Montague. By-the-bye, is he a friend of yours?'

'Not particularly. He is a friend of a cousin of mine; and the women know him at home. He isn't a pal of mine if you mean that.'

'If he makes himself disagreeable, he'll have to go to the wall;—that's all. But never mind him at present. Was your mother speaking to you of what I said to her?'

'No, Mr. Melmotte,' said Sir Felix, staring with all his eyes.

'I was talking to her about you, and I thought that perhaps she might have told you. This is all nonsense, you know, about you and Marie.' Sir Felix looked into the man's face. It was not savage, as he had seen it. But there had suddenly come upon his brow that heavy look of a determined purpose which all who knew the man were wont to mark. Sir Felix had observed it a few minutes since in the Board-room, when the chairman was putting down the rebellious director. 'You understand that; don't you?' Sir Felix still looked at him, but made no reply. 'It's all d—— nonsense. You haven't got a brass farthing, you know. You've no income at all; you're just living on your mother, and I'm afraid she's not very well off. How can you suppose that I shall give my girl to you?' Felix still looked at him but did not dare to contradict a single statement made. Yet when the man told him that he had not a brass farthing he thought of his own thousand pounds which were now in the man's pocket. 'You're a baronet, and that's about all, you know,' continued Melmotte. 'The Carbury property, which is a very small thing, belongs to a distant cousin who may leave it to me if he pleases;—and who isn't very much older than you are yourself.'

'Oh, come, Mr. Melmotte; he's a great deal older than me.'

'It wouldn't matter if he were as old as Adam. The thing is out of the question, and you must drop it.' Then the look on his brow became a little heavier. 'You hear what I say. She is going to marry Lord Nidderdale. She was engaged to him before you ever saw her. What do you expect to get by it?'

Sir Felix had not the courage to say that he expected to get the girl he loved. But as the man waited for an answer he was obliged to say something. 'I suppose it's the old story,' he said.

'Just so;—the old story. You want my money, and she wants you, just because she has been told to take somebody else. You want something to live on;—that's what you want. Come;—out with it. Is not that it?

When we understand each other I'll put you in the way
of making money.'

'Of course I'm not very well off,' said Felix.

'About as badly as any young man that I can hear of.
You give me your written promise that you'll drop this
affair with Marie, and you shan't want for money.'

'A written promise!'

'Yes;—a written promise. I give nothing for nothing.
I'll put you in the way of doing so well with these shares
that you shall be able to marry any other girl you please;
—or to live without marrying, which you'll find to be
better.'

There was something worthy of consideration in Mr.
Melmotte's proposition. Marriage of itself, simply as a
domestic institution, had not specially recommended itself to Sir Felix Carbury. A few horses at Leighton, Ruby
Ruggles or any other beauty, and life at the Beargarden
were much more to his taste. And then he was quite
alive to the fact that it was possible that he might find
himself possessed of the wife without the money. Marie,
indeed, had a grand plan of her own, with reference to
that settled income; but then Marie might be mistaken,
—or she might be lying. If he were sure of making
money in the way Melmotte now suggested, the loss of
Marie would not break his heart. But then also Melmotte
might be—lying. 'By-the-bye, Mr. Melmotte,' said he,
'could you let me have those shares?'

'What shares?' And the heavy brow became still
heavier.

'Don't you know?—I gave you a thousand pounds,
and I was to have ten shares.'

'You must come about that on the proper day, to the
proper place.'

'When is the proper day?'

'It is the twentieth of each month, I think.' Sir Felix
looked very blank at hearing this, knowing that this
present was the twenty-first of the month. 'But what
does that signify? Do you want a little money?'

'Well, I do,' said Sir Felix. 'A lot of fellows owe me
money, but it's so hard to get it.'

'That tells a story of gambling,' said Mr. Melmotte.
'You think I'd give my girl to a gambler?'

'Nidderdale 's in it quite as thick as I am.'

'Nidderdale has a settled property which neither he
nor his father can destroy. But don't you be such a fool
as to argue with me. You won't get anything by it. If
you'll write that letter here now——'

'What;—to Marie?'

'No;—not to Marie at all; but to me. It need never
be known to her. If you'll do that I'll stick to you and
make a man of you. And if you want a couple of hundred
pounds I'll give you a cheque for it before you leave the
room. Mind, I can tell you this. On my word of honour
as a gentleman, if my daughter were to marry you, she'd
never have a single shilling. I should immediately make
a will and leave all my property to St. George's Hospital.
I have quite made up my mind about that.'

'And couldn't you manage that I should have the
shares before the twentieth of next month?'

'I'll see about it. Perhaps I could let you have a few
of my own. At any rate I won't see you short of money.'

The terms were enticing and the letter was of course
written. Melmotte himself dictated the words, which
were not romantic in their nature. The reader shall see
the letter.

'DEAR SIR,

'In consideration of the offers made by you to me, and
on a clear understanding that such a marriage would be
disagreeable to you and to the lady's mother, and would
bring down a father's curse upon your daughter, I hereby
declare and promise that I will not renew my suit to the
young lady, which I hereby altogether renounce.

'I am, Dear Sir,
'Your obedient Servant,
'FELIX CARBURY.

'AUGUSTUS MELMOTTE, Esq.,
'—, Grosvenor Square.'

The letter was dated 21st July,* and bore the printed

address of the offices of the South Central Pacific and Mexican Railway.

'You'll give me that cheque for £200, Mr. Melmotte?' The financier hesitated for a moment, but did give the baronet the cheque as promised. 'And you'll see about letting me have those shares?'

'You can come to me in Abchurch Lane, you know.' Sir Felix said that he would call in Abchurch Lane.

As he went westward towards the Beargarden, the baronet was not happy in his mind. Ignorant as he was as to the duties of a gentleman, indifferent as he was to the feelings of others, still he felt ashamed of himself. He was treating the girl very badly. Even he knew that he was behaving badly. He was so conscious of it that he tried to console himself by reflecting that his writing such a letter as that would not prevent his running away with the girl, should he, on consideration, find it to be worth his while to do so.

That night he was again playing at the Beargarden, and he lost a great part of Mr. Melmotte's money. He did in fact lose much more than the £200; but when he found his ready money going from him he issued paper.

## Chapter XXXVIII

### PAUL MONTAGUE'S TROUBLES

PAUL MONTAGUE had other troubles on his mind beyond this trouble of the Mexican Railway. It was now more than a fortnight since he had taken Mrs. Hurtle to the play, and she was still living in lodgings at Islington. He had seen her twice, once on the following day, when he was allowed to come and go without any special reference to their engagement, and again, three or four days afterwards, when the meeting was by no means so pleasant. She had wept, and after weeping had stormed. She had stood upon what she called her rights, and had dared him to be false to her. Did he mean to deny that he had promised to marry her? Was not his conduct to

her, ever since she had now been in London, a repetition
of that promise? And then again she became soft, and
pleaded with him. But for the storm he might have
given way. At the moment he had felt that any fate in
life would be better than a marriage on compulsion.
Her tears and her pleadings, nevertheless, touched him
very nearly. He had promised her most distinctly. He
had loved her and had won her love. And she was lovely.
The very violence of the storm made the sunshine more
sweet. She would sit down on a stool at his feet, and it
was impossible to drive her away from him. She would
look up in his face and he could not but embrace her.
Then there had come a passionate flood of tears and she
was in his arms. How he had escaped he hardly knew,
but he did know that he had promised to be with her
again before two days should have passed.

On the day named he wrote to her a letter excusing
himself, which was at any rate true in words. He had
been summoned, he said, to Liverpool on business, and
must postpone seeing her till his return. And he explained that the business on which he was called was
connected with the great American railway, and, being
important, demanded his attention. In words this was
true. He had been corresponding with a gentleman at
Liverpool with whom he had become acquainted on his
return home after having involuntarily become a partner
in the house of Fisker, Montague, and Montague. This
man he trusted and had consulted, and the gentleman,
Mr. Ramsbottom by name, had suggested that he should
come to him at Liverpool. He had gone, and his conduct
at the Board had been the result of the advice which he
had received; but it may be doubted whether some
dread of the coming interview with Mrs. Hurtle had not
added strength to Mr. Ramsbottom's invitation.

In Liverpool he had heard tidings of Mrs. Hurtle,
though it can hardly be said that he obtained any trustworthy information. The lady after landing from an
American steamer had been at Mr. Ramsbottom's
office, inquiring for him, Paul; and Mr. Ramsbottom
had thought that the inquiries were made in a manner

indicating danger. He therefore had spoken to a fellow-traveller with Mrs. Hurtle, and the fellow-traveller had opined that Mrs. Hurtle was 'a queer card.' 'On board ship we all gave it up to her that she was about the handsomest woman we had ever seen, but we all said that there was a bit of the wild cat in her breeding.' Then Mr. Ramsbottom had asked whether the lady was a widow. 'There was a man on board from Kansas,' said the fellow-traveller, 'who knew a man named Hurtle at Leavenworth, who was separated from his wife and is still alive. There was, according to him, a queer story about the man and his wife having fought a duel with pistols, and then having separated.' This Mr. Ramsbottom, who in an earlier stage of the affair had heard something of Paul and Mrs. Hurtle together, managed to communicate to the young man. His advice about the railway company was very clear and general, and such as an honest man would certainly give; but it might have been conveyed by letter. The information, such as it was, respecting Mrs. Hurtle, could only be given vivâ voce, and perhaps the invitation to Liverpool had originated in Mr. Ramsbottom's appreciation of this fact. 'As she was asking after you here, perhaps it is well that you should know,' his friend said to him. Paul had only thanked him, not daring on the spur of the moment to speak of his own difficulties.

In all this there had been increased dismay, but there had also been some comfort. It had only been at moments in which he had been subject to her softer influences that Paul had doubted as to his adherence to the letter which he had written to her, breaking off his engagement. When she told him of her wrongs and of her love; of his promise and his former devotion to her; when she assured him that she had given up everything in life for him, and threw her arms round him, looking into his eyes;—then he would almost yield. But when, what the traveller called the breeding of the wild cat, showed itself;—and when, having escaped from her, he thought of Hetta Carbury and of her breeding,—he was fully determined that, let his fate be what it might, it should not be that of

being the husband of Mrs. Hurtle. That he was in a
mass of troubles from which it would be very difficult for
him to extricate himself he was well aware;—but if it were
true that Mr. Hurtle was alive, that fact might help him.
She certainly had declared him to be,—not separated,
or even divorced,—but dead. And if it were true also
that she had fought a duel with one husband, that also
ought to be a reason why a gentleman should object
to become her second husband. These facts would at
any rate justify himself to himself, and would enable
himself to break from his engagement without thinking
himself to be a false traitor.

But he must make up his mind as to some line of
conduct. She must be made to know the truth. If he
meant to reject the lady finally on the score of her being
a wild cat, he must tell her so. He felt very strongly that
he must not flinch from the wild cat's claws. That he
would have to undergo some severe handling, an amount
of clawing which might perhaps go near his life, he could
perceive. Having done what he had done he would have
no right to shrink from such usage. He must tell her to
her face that he was not satisfied with her past life, and
that therefore he would not marry her. Of course he
might write to her;—but when summoned to her presence
he would be unable to excuse himself, even to himself,
for not going. It was his misfortune,—and also his fault,
—that he had submitted to be loved by a wild cat.

But it might be well that before he saw her he should
get hold of information that might have the appearance
of real evidence. He returned from Liverpool to London
on the morning of the Friday on which the Board was
held, and thought even more of all this than he did of the
attack which he was prepared to make on Mr. Melmotte.
If he could come across that traveller he might learn
something. The husband's name had been Caradoc
Carson Hurtle. If Caradoc Carson Hurtle had been seen
in the State of Kansas within the last two years, that
certainly would be sufficient evidence. As to the duel he
felt that it might be very hard to prove that, and that if
proved, it might be hard to found upon the fact any

absolute right on his part to withdraw from the engagement. But there was a rumour also, though not corroborated during his last visit to Liverpool, that she had shot a gentleman in Oregon. Could he get at the truth of that story? If they were all true, surely he could justify himself to himself.

But this detective's work was very distasteful to him. After having had the woman in his arms how could he undertake such inquiries as these? And it would be almost necessary that he should take her in his arms again while he was making them,—unless indeed he made them with her knowledge. Was it not his duty, as a man, to tell everything to herself? To speak to her thus:—'I am told that your life with your last husband was, to say the least of it, eccentric; that you even fought a duel with him. I could not marry a woman who had fought a duel, —certainly not a woman who had fought with her own husband. I am told also that you shot another gentleman in Oregon. It may well be that the gentleman deserved to be shot; but there is something in the deed so repulsive to me,—no doubt irrationally,—that, on that score also, I must decline to marry you. I am told also that Mr. Hurtle has been seen alive quite lately. I had understood from you that he is dead. No doubt you may have been deceived. But as I should not have engaged myself to you had I known the truth, so now I consider myself justified in absolving myself from an engagement which was based on a misconception.' It would no doubt be difficult to get through all these details; but it might be accomplished gradually,—unless in the process of doing so he should incur the fate of the gentleman in Oregon. At any rate he would declare to her as well as he could the ground on which he claimed a right to consider himself free, and would bear the consequences. Such was the resolve which he made on his journey up from Liverpool, and that trouble was also on his mind when he rose up to attack Mr. Melmotte single-handed at the Board.

When the Board was over, he also went down to the Beargarden. Perhaps, with reference to the Board, the

feeling which hurt him most was the conviction that he
was spending money which he would never have had to
spend had there been no Board. He had been twitted
with this at the Board-meeting, and had justified himself by referring to the money which had been invested
in the company of Fisker, Montague, and Montague,
which money was now supposed to have been made over
to the railway. But the money which he was spending
had come to him after a loose fashion, and he knew that
if called upon for an account, he could hardly make out
one which would be square and intelligible to all parties.
Nevertheless he spent much of his time at the Beargarden, dining there when no engagement carried him
elsewhere. On this evening he joined his table with
Nidderdale's, at the young lord's instigation. 'What
made you so savage at old Melmotte to-day?' said the
young lord.

'I didn't mean to be savage, but I think that as we
call ourselves Directors we ought to know something
about it.'

'I suppose we ought. I don't know, you know. I'll
tell you what I've been thinking. I can't make out why
the mischief they made me a Director.'

'Because you're a lord,' said Paul bluntly.

'I suppose there's something in that. But what good
can I do them? Nobody thinks that I know anything
about business. Of course I'm in Parliament, but I don't
often go there unless they want me to vote. Everybody
knows that I'm hard up. I can't understand it. The
Governor said that I was to do it, and so I've done it.'

'They say, you know,—there's something between you
and Melmotte's daughter.'

'But if there is, what has that to do with a railway in
the city? And why should Carbury be there? And,
heaven and earth, why should old Grendall be a Director?
I'm impecunious; but if you were to pick out the two
most hopeless men in London in regard to money, they
would be old Grendall and young Carbury. I've been
thinking a good deal about it, and I can't make it out.'

'I have been thinking about it too,' said Paul.

'I suppose old Melmotte is all right?' asked Nidderdale. This was a question which Montague found it difficult to answer. How could he be justified in whispering suspicions to the man who was known to be at any rate one of the competitors for Marie Melmotte's hand? 'You can speak out to me, you know,' said Nidderdale, nodding his head.

'I've got nothing to speak. People say that he is about the richest man alive.'

'He lives as though he were.'

'I don't see why it shouldn't be all true. Nobody, I take it, knows very much about him.' When his companion had left him, Nidderdale sat down, thinking of it all. It occurred to him that he would 'be coming a cropper rather,' were he to marry Melmotte's daughter for her money, and then find that she had got none.

A little later in the evening he invited Montague to go up to the card-room. 'Carbury, and Grasslough, and Dolly Longestaffe are there waiting,' he said. But Paul declined. He was too full of his troubles for play. 'Poor Miles isn't there, if you're afraid of that,' said Nidderdale.

'Miles Grendall wouldn't hinder me,' said Montague.

'Nor me either. Of course it's a confounded shame. I know that as well as anybody. But, God bless me, I owe a fellow down in Leicestershire heaven knows how much for keeping horses, and that's a shame.'

'You'll pay him some day.'

'I suppose I shall,—if I don't die first. But I should have gone on with the horses just the same if there had never been anything to come;—only they wouldn't nave given me tick, you know. As far as I'm concerned it's just the same. I like to live whether I've got money or not. And I fear I don't have many scruples about paying. But then I like to let live too. There's Carbury always saying nasty things about poor Miles. He's playing himself without a rap to back him. If he were to lose, Vossner wouldn't stand him a £10 note. But because he has won, he goes on as though he were old Melmotte himself. You'd better come up.'

But Montague wouldn't go up. Without any fixed purpose he left the club, and slowly sauntered northwards through the streets till he found himself in Welbeck Street. He hardly knew why he went there, and certainly had not determined to call on Lady Carbury when he left the Beargarden. His mind was full of Mrs. Hurtle. As long as she was present in London,—as long at any rate as he was unable to tell himself that he had finally broken away from her,—he knew himself to be an unfit companion for Henrietta Carbury. And, indeed, he was still under some promise made to Roger Carbury, not that he would avoid Hetta's company, but that for a certain period, as yet unexpired, he would not ask her to be his wife. It had been a foolish promise, made and then repented without much attention to words;—but still it was existing, and Paul knew well that Roger trusted that it would be kept. Nevertheless Paul made his way up to Welbeck Street and almost unconsciously knocked at the door. No;—Lady Carbury was not at home. She was out somewhere with Mr. Roger Carbury. Up to that moment Paul had not heard that Roger was in town; but the reader may remember that he had come up in search of Ruby Ruggles. Miss Carbury was at home, the page went on to say. Would Mr. Montague go up and see Miss Carbury? Without much consideration Mr. Montague said that he would go up and see Miss Carbury. 'Mamma is out with Roger,' said Hetta, endeavouring to save herself from confusion. 'There is a soirée of learned people somewhere, and she made poor Roger take her. The ticket was only for her and her friend, and therefore I could not go.'

'I am so glad to see you. What an age it is since we met.'

'Hardly since the Melmottes' ball,' said Hetta.

'Hardly indeed. I have been here once since that. What has brought Roger up to town?'

'I don't know what it is. Some mystery, I think. Whenever there is a mystery I am always afraid that there is something wrong about Felix. I do get so unhappy about Felix, Mr. Montague.'

'I saw him to-day in the city, at the Railway Board.'

'But Roger says the Railway Board is all a sham,'—Paul could not keep himself from blushing as he heard this,—'and that Felix should not be there. And then there is something going on about that horrid man's daughter.'

'She is to marry Lord Nidderdale, I think.'

'Is she? They are talking of her marrying Felix, and of course it is for her money. And I believe that man is determined to quarrel with them.'

'What man, Miss Carbury?'

'Mr. Melmotte himself. It's all horrid from beginning to end.'

'But I saw them in the city to-day and they seemed to be the greatest friends. When I wanted to see Mr. Melmotte he bolted himself into an inner room, but he took your brother with him. He would not have done that if they had not been friends. When I saw it I almost thought that he had consented to the marriage.'

'Roger has the greatest dislike to Mr. Melmotte.'

'I know he has,' said Paul.

'And Roger is always right. It is always safe to trust him. Don't you think so, Mr. Montague?' Paul did think so, and was by no means disposed to deny to his rival the praise which rightly belonged to him; but still he found the subject difficult. 'Of course I will never go against mamma,' continued Hetta, 'but I always feel that my cousin Roger is a rock of strength, so that if one did whatever he said one would never get wrong. I never found any one else that I thought that of, but I do think it of him.'

'No one has more reason to praise him than I have.'

'I think everybody has reason to praise him that has to do with him. And I'll tell you why I think it is. Whenever he thinks anything he says it;—or, at least, he never says anything that he doesn't think. If he spent a thousand pounds, everybody would know that he'd got it to spend; but other people are not like that.'

'You're thinking of Melmotte.'

'I'm thinking of everybody, Mr. Montague;—of everybody except Roger.'

'Is he the only man you can trust? But it is abominable to me to seem even to contradict you. Roger Carbury has been to me the best friend that any man ever had. I think as much of him as you do.'

'I didn't say he was the only person;—or I didn't mean to say so. But all my friends——'

'Am I among the number, Miss Carbury?'

'Yes;—I suppose so. Of course you are. Why not? Of course you are a friend,—because you are his friend.'

'Look here, Hetta,' he said. 'It is no good going on like this. I love Roger Carbury,—as well as one man can love another. He is all that you say,—and more. You hardly know how he denies himself, and how he thinks of everybody near him. He is a gentleman all round and every inch. He never lies. He never takes what is not his own. I believe he does love his neighbour as himself.'

'Oh, Mr. Montague! I am so glad to hear you speak of him like that.'

'I love him better than any man,—as well as a man can love a man. If you will say that you love him as well as a woman can love a man,—I will leave England at once, and never return to it.'

'There's mamma,' said Henrietta;—for at that moment there was a double knock at the door.

## Chapter XXXIX

### 'I DO LOVE HIM'

SO it was. Lady Carbury had returned home from the soirée of learned people, and had brought Roger Carbury with her. They both came up to the drawing-room and found Paul and Henrietta together. It need hardly be said that they were both surprised. Roger supposed that Montague was still at Liverpool, and, knowing that he was not a frequent visitor in Welbeck

Street, could hardly avoid a feeling that a meeting between the two had now been planned in the mother's absence. The reader knows that it was not so. Roger certainly was a man not liable to suspicion, but the circumstances in this case were suspicious. There would have been nothing to suspect,—no reason why Paul should not have been there,—but from the promise which had been given. There was, indeed, no breach of that promise proved by Paul's presence in Welbeck Street; but Roger felt rather than thought that the two could hardly have spent the evening together without such breach. Whether Paul had broken the promise by what he had already said the reader must be left to decide.

Lady Carbury was the first to speak. 'This is quite an unexpected pleasure, Mr. Montague.' Whether Roger suspected anything or not, she did. The moment she saw Paul the idea occurred to her that the meeting between Hetta and him had been preconcerted.

'Yes,' he said,—making a lame excuse, where no excuse should have been made,—'I had nothing to do, and was lonely, and thought that I would come up and see you.' Lady Carbury disbelieved him altogether, but Roger felt assured that his coming in Lady Carbury's absence had been an accident. The man had said so, and that was enough.

'I thought you were at Liverpool,' said Roger.

'I came back to-day,—to be present at that Board in the city. I have had a good deal to trouble me. I will tell you all about it just now. What has brought you to London?'

'A little business,' said Roger.

Then there was an awkward silence. Lady Carbury was angry, and hardly knew whether she ought not to show her anger. For Henrietta it was very awkward. She, too, could not but feel that she had been caught, though no innocence could be whiter than hers. She knew well her mother's mind, and the way in which her mother's thoughts would run. Silence was frightful to her, and she found herself forced to speak. 'Have you had a pleasant evening, mamma?'

'Have you had a pleasant evening, my dear?' said Lady Carbury, forgetting herself in her desire to punish her daughter.

'Indeed, no,' said Hetta, attempting to laugh, 'I have been trying to work hard at Dante, but one never does any good when one has to try to work. I was just going to bed when Mr. Montague came in. What did you think of the wise men and the wise women, Roger?'

'I was out of my element, of course; but I think your mother liked it.'

'I was very glad indeed to meet Dr. Palmoil. It seems that if we can only open the interior of Africa a little further, we can get everything that is wanted to complete the chemical combination necessary for feeding the human race. Isn't that a grand idea, Roger?'

'A little more elbow grease is the combination that I look to.'

'Surely, Roger, if the Bible is to go for anything, we are to believe that labour is a curse and not a blessing. Adam was not born to labour.'

'But he fell; and I doubt whether Dr. Palmoil will be able to put his descendants back into Eden.'

'Roger, for a religous man, you do say the strangest things! I have quite made up my mind to this;—if ever I can see things so settled here as to enable me to move, I will visit the interior of Africa. It is the garden of the world.'

This scrap of enthusiasm so carried them through their immediate difficulties that the two men were able to take their leave and to get out of the room with fair comfort. As soon as the door was closed behind them Lady Carbury attacked her daughter. 'What brought him here?'

'He brought himself, mamma.'

'Don't answer me in that way, Hetta. Of course he brought himself. That is insolent.'

'Insolent, mamma! How can you say such hard words? I meant that he came of his own accord.'

'How long was he here?'

'Two minutes before you came in. Why do you cross-question me like this? I could not help his coming. I did not desire that he might be shown up.'

'You did not know that he was to come?'

'Mamma, if I am to be suspected, all is over between us.'

'What do you mean by that?'

'If you can think that I would deceive you, you will think so always. If you will not trust me, how am I to live with you as though you did? I knew nothing of his coming.'

'Tell me this, Hetta; are you engaged to marry him?'

'No;—I am not.'

'Has he asked you to marry him?'

Hetta paused a moment, considering, before she answered this question. 'I do not think he ever has.'

'You do not think?'

'I was going on to explain. He never has asked me. But he has said that which makes me know that he wishes me to be his wife.'

'What has he said? When did he say it?'

Again she paused. But again she answered with straightforward simplicity. 'Just before you came in, he said——; I don't know what he said; but it meant that.'

'You told me he had been here but a minute.'

'It was but very little more. If you take me at my word in that way, of course you can make me out to be wrong, mamma. It was almost no time, and yet he said it.'

'He had come prepared to say it.'

'How could he,—expecting to find you?'

'Psha! He expected nothing of the kind.'

'I think you do him wrong, mamma. I am sure you are doing me wrong. I think his coming was an accident, and that what he said was—an accident.'

'An accident!'

'It was not intended,—not then, mamma. I have known it ever so long;—and so have you. It was natural that he should say so when we were alone together.'

'And you;—what did you say?'

'Nothing. You came.'

'I am sorry that my coming should have been so

inopportune. But I must ask one other question, Hetta. What do you intend to say?' Hetta was again silent, and now for a longer space. She put her hand up to her brow and pushed back her hair as she thought whether her mother had a right to continue this cross-examination. She had told her mother everything as it had happened. She had kept back no deed done, no word spoken, either now or at any time. But she was not sure that her mother had a right to know her thoughts, feeling as she did that she had so little sympathy from her mother. 'How do you intend to answer him?' demanded Lady Carbury.

'I do not know that he will ask again.'

'That is prevaricating.'

'No, mamma;—I do not prevaricate. It is unfair to say that to me. I do love him. There. I think it ought to have been enough for you to know that I should never give him encouragement without telling you about it. I do love him, and I shall never love any one else.'

'He is a ruined man. Your cousin says that all this Company in which he is involved will go to pieces.'

Hetta was too clever to allow this argument to pass. She did not doubt that Roger had so spoken of the Railway to her mother, but she did doubt that her mother had believed the story. 'If so,' said she, 'Mr. Melmotte will be a ruined man too, and yet you want Felix to marry Marie Melmotte.'

'It makes me ill to hear you talk,—as if you understood these things. And you think you will marry this man because he is to make a fortune out of the Railway!' Lady Carbury was able to speak with an extremity of scorn in reference to the assumed pursuit by one of her children of an advantageous position which she was doing all in her power to recommend to the other child.

'I have not thought of his fortune. I have not thought of marrying him, mamma. I think you are very cruel to me. You say things so hard, that I cannot bear them.'

'Why will you not marry your cousin?'

'I am not good enough for him.'

'Nonsense!'

'Very well; you say so. But that is what I think. He

is so much above me, that, though I do love him, I cannot think of him in that way. And I have told you that I do love some one else. I have no secret from you now. Good night, mamma,' she said, coming up to her mother and kissing her. 'Do be kind to me; and pray, —pray,—do believe me.' Lady Carbury then allowed herself to be kissed, and allowed her daughter to leave the room.

There was a great deal said that night between Roger Carbury and Paul Montague before they parted. As they walked together to Roger's hotel he said not a word as to Paul's presence in Welbeck Street. Paul had declared his visit in Lady Carbury's absence to have been accidental,—and therefore there was nothing more to be said. Montague then asked as to the cause of Carbury's journey to London. 'I do not wish it to be talked of,' said Roger after a pause,—'and of course I could not speak of it before Hetta. A girl has gone away from our neighbourhood. You remember old Ruggles?'

'You do not mean that Ruby has levanted? She was to have married John Crumb.'

'Just so,—but she has gone off, leaving John Crumb in an unhappy frame of mind. John Crumb is an honest man and almost too good for her.'

'Ruby is very pretty. Has she gone with any one?'

'No;—she went alone. But the horror of it is this. They think down there that Felix has,—well, made love to her, and that she has been taken to London by him.'

'That would be very bad.'

'He certainly has known her. Though he lied, as he always lies, when I first spoke to him, I brought him to admit that he and she had been friends down in Suffolk. Of course we know what such friendship means. But I do not think that she came to London at his instance. Of course he would lie about that. He would lie about anything. If his horse cost him a hundred pounds, he would tell one man that he gave fifty, and another two hundred. But he has not lived long enough yet to be able to lie and tell the truth with the same eye. When he is as old as I am he'll be perfect.'

'He knows nothing about her coming to town?'

'He did not when I first asked him. I am not sure, but I fancy that I was too quick after her. She started last Saturday morning. I followed on the Sunday, and made him out at his club. I think that he knew nothing then of her being in town. He is very clever if he did. Since that he has avoided me. I caught him once but only for half a minute, and then he swore that he had not seen her.'

'You still believed him?'

'No;—he did it very well, but I knew that he was prepared for me. I cannot say how it may have been. To make matters worse old Ruggles has now quarrelled with Crumb, and is no longer anxious to get back his granddaughter. He was frightened at first; but that has gone off, and he is now reconciled to the loss of the girl and the saving of his money.'

After that Paul told all his own story,—the double story, both in regard to Melmotte and to Mrs. Hurtle. As regarded the Railway, Roger could only tell him to follow explicitly the advice of his Liverpool friend. 'I never believed in the thing, you know.'

'Nor did I. But what could I do?'

'I'm not going to blame you. Indeed, knowing you as I do, feeling sure that you intend to be honest, I would not for a moment insist on my own opinion, if it did not seem that Mr. Ramsbottom thinks as I do. In such a matter, when a man does not see his own way clearly, it behoves him to be able to show that he has followed the advice of some man whom the world esteems and recognizes. You have to bind your character to another man's character; and that other man's character, if it be good, will carry you through. From what I hear Mr. Ramsbottom's character is sufficiently good;—but then you must do exactly what he tells you.'

But the Railway business, though it comprised all that Montague had in the world, was not the heaviest of his troubles. What was he to do about Mrs. Hurtle? He had now, for the first time, to tell his friend that Mrs. Hurtle had come to London, and that he had been with her three or four times. There was this great difficulty in the matter, too,—that it was very hard to speak of his engagement with Mrs. Hurtle without in some sort alluding to his love for Henrietta Carbury. Roger knew of both loves;—had been very urgent with his friend to abandon the widow, and at any rate equally urgent with him to give up the other passion. Were he to marry the widow, all danger on the other side would be at an end. And yet, in discussing the question of Mrs Hurtle, he was to do so as though there were no such person existing as Henrietta Carbury. The discussion did take place exactly as though there were no such person as Henrietta Carbury. Paul told it all,—the rumoured duel, the rumoured murder, and the rumour of the existing husband.

'It may be necessary that you should go out to Kansas, —and to Oregon,' said Roger.

'But even if the rumours be untrue I will not marry her,' said Paul. Roger shrugged his shoulders. He was doubtless thinking of Hetta Carbury, but he said nothing. 'And what would she do, remaining here?' continued Paul. Roger admitted that it would be awkward. 'I am determined that under no circumstances will I marry her. I know I have been a fool. I know I have been wrong. But of course, if there be a fair cause for my broken word, I will use it if I can.'

'You will get out of it, honestly if you can; but you will get out of it honestly or—any other way.'

'Did you not advise me to get out of it, Roger;—before we knew as much as we do now?'

'I did,—and I do. If you make a bargain with the Devil, it may be dishonest to cheat him,—and yet I would have you cheat him if you could. As to this woman, I do believe she has deceived you. If I were you, nothing should induce me to marry her;—not though her claws were strong enough to tear me utterly in pieces. I'll tell you what I'll do. I'll go and see her if you like it.'

But Paul would not submit to this. He felt he was bound himself to incur the risk of those claws, and that

no substitute could take his place. They sat long into
the night, and it was at last resolved between them that
on the next morning Paul should go to Islington, should
tell Mrs. Hurtle all the stories which he had heard, and
should end by declaring his resolution that under no
circumstances would he marry her. They both felt how
improbable it was that he should ever be allowed to get
to the end of such a story,—how almost certain it was
that the breeding of the wild cat would show itself before
that time should come. But, still, that was the course to
be pursued as far as circumstances would admit; and
Paul was at any rate to declare, claws or no claws,
husband or no husband,—whether the duel or the
murder was admitted or denied,—that he would never
make Mrs. Hurtle his wife. 'I wish it were over, old
fellow,' said Roger.

'So do I,' said Paul, as he took his leave.

He went to bed like a man condemned to die on the
next morning, and he awoke in the same condition. He
had slept well, but as he shook from him his happy
dream, the wretched reality at once overwhelmed him.
But the man who is to be hung, has no choice. He cannot,
when he wakes, declare that he has changed his mind,
and postpone the hour. It was quite open to Paul
Montague to give himself such instant relief. He put his
hand up to his brow, and almost made himself believe
that his head was aching. This was Saturday. Would it
not be as well that he should think of it further, and put
off his execution till Monday? Monday was so far
distant that he felt that he could go to Islington quite
comfortably on Monday. Was there not some hitherto
forgotten point which it would be well that he should
discuss with his friend Roger before he saw the lady?
Should he not rush down to Liverpool, and ask a few
more questions of Mr. Ramsbottom? Why should he go
forth to execution, seeing that the matter was in his own
hands?

At last he jumped out of bed and into his tub, and
dressed himself as quickly as he could. He worked himself up into a fit of fortitude, and resolved that the thing

should be done before the fit was over. He ate his breakfast about nine, and then asked himself whether he might
not be too early were he to go at once to Islington. But
he remembered that she was always early. In every
respect she was an energetic woman, using her time for
some purpose, either good or bad, not sleeping it away
in bed. If one has to be hung on a given day, would it
not be well to be hung as soon after waking as possible?
I can fancy that the hangman would hardly come early
enough. And if one had to be hung in a given week,
would not one wish to be hung on the first day of the
week, even at the risk of breaking one's last Sabbath day
in this world? Whatever be the misery to be endured,
get it over. The horror of every agony is in its anticipation. Paul had realized something of this when he threw
himself into a Hansom cab, and ordered the man to drive
to Islington.

How quick that cab went! Nothing ever goes so
quick as a Hansom cab when a man starts for a dinner-
party a little too early;—nothing so slow when he starts
too late. Of all cabs this, surely, was the quickest. Paul
was lodging in Suffolk Street, close to Pall Mall,—whence
the way to Islington, across Oxford Street, across Totten-
ham Court Road, across numerous squares north-east of
the Museum, seems to be long. The end of Goswell
Road is the outside of the world in that direction, and
Islington is beyond the end of Goswell Road. And yet
that Hansom cab was there before Paul Montague had
been able to arrange the words with which he would
begin the interview. He had given the street and the
number of the street. It was not till after he had started
that it occurred to him that it might be well that he
should get out at the end of the street, and walk to the
house,—so that he might, as it were, fetch breath before
the interview was commenced. But the cabman dashed
up to the door in a manner purposely devised to make
every inmate of the house aware that a cab had just
arrived before it. There was a little garden before the
house. We all know the garden;—twenty-four feet long,
by twelve broad;—and an iron-grated door, with the

landlady's name on a brass plate. Paul, when he had paid the cabman,—giving the man half-a-crown, and asking for no change in his agony,—pushed in the iron gate and walked very quickly up to the door, rang rather furiously, and before the door was well opened asked for Mrs. Hurtle.

'Mrs. Hurtle is out for the day,' said the girl who opened the door. 'Leastways, she went out yesterday and won't be back till to-night.' Providence had sent him a reprieve! But he almost forgot the reprieve, as he looked at the girl and saw that she was Ruby Ruggles. 'Oh laws, Mr. Montague, is that you?' Ruby Ruggles had often seen Paul down in Suffolk, and recognized him as quickly as he did her. It occurred to her at once that he had come in search of herself. She knew that Roger Carbury was up in town looking for her. So much she had of course learned from Sir Felix,—for at this time she had seen the baronet more than once since her arrival. Montague, she knew, was Roger Carbury's intimate friend, and now she felt that she was caught. In her terror she did not at first remember that the visitor had asked for Mrs. Hurtle.

'Yes, it is I. I was sorry to hear, Miss Ruggles, that you had left your home.'

'I'm all right, Mr. Montague;—I am. Mrs. Pipkin is my aunt, or, leastways, my mother's brother's widow, though grandfather never would speak to her. She's quite respectable, and has five children, and lets lodgings. There's a lady here now, and has gone away with her just for one night down to Southend. They'll be back this evening, and I've the children to mind, with the servant girl. I'm quite respectable here, Mr. Montague, and nobody need be a bit afraid about me.'

'Mrs Hurtle has gone down to Southend?'

'Yes, Mr. Montague; she wasn't quite well, and wanted a breath of air, she said. And aunt didn't like she should go alone, as Mrs. Hurtle is such a stranger. And Mrs. Hurtle said as she didn't mind paying for two, and so they've gone, and the baby with them. Mrs. Pipkin said as the baby shouldn't be no trouble. And Mrs. Hurtle,—

she's most as fond of the baby as aunt. Do you know Mrs. Hurtle, sir?'

'Yes; she's a friend of mine.'

'Oh; I didn't know. I did know as there was some friend as was expected and as didn't come. Be I to say, sir, as you was here?'

Paul thought it might be as well to shift the subject and to ask Ruby a few questions about herself while he made up his mind what message he would leave for Mrs. Hurtle. 'I'm afraid they are very unhappy about you down at Bungay, Miss Ruggles.'

'Then they've got to be unhappy; that's all about it, Mr. Montague. Grandfather is that provoking as a young woman can't live with him, nor yet I won't try never again. He lugged me all about the room by my hair, Mr. Montague. How is a young woman to put up with that? And I did everything for him,—that careful that no one won't do it again;—did his linen, and his victuals, and even cleaned his boots of a Sunday, 'cause he was that mean he wouldn't have anybody about the place only me and the girl who had to milk the cows. There wasn't nobody to do anything, only me. And then he went to drag me about by the hairs of my head. You won't see me again at Sheep's Acre, Mr. Montague;— nor yet won't the Squire.'

'But I thought there was somebody else was to give you a home.'

'John Crumb! Oh yes, there's John Crumb. There's plenty of people to give me a home, Mr. Montague.'

'You were to have been married to John Crumb, I thought.'

'Ladies is to change their minds if they like it, Mr. Montague. I'm sure you've heard that before. Grandfather made me say I'd have him,—but I never cared that for him.'

'I'm afraid, Miss Ruggles, you won't find a better man up here in London.'

'I didn't come here to look for a man, Mr. Montague; I can tell you that. They has to look at me, if they want me. But I am looked after; and that by one as John

Crumb ain't fit to touch.' That told the whole story.
Paul when he heard the little boast was quite sure that
Roger's fear about Felix was well founded. And as for
John Crumb's fitness to touch Sir Felix, Paul felt that the
Bungay mealman might have an opinion of his own on
that matter. 'But there's Betsy a crying upstairs, and I
promised not to leave them children for one minute.'

'I will tell the Squire that I saw you, Miss Ruggles.'

'What does the Squire want o' me? I ain't nothing to
the Squire,—except that I respects him. You can tell if
you please, Mr. Montague, of course. I'm a coming, my
darling.'

Paul made his way into Mrs. Hurtle's sitting-room and
wrote a note for her in pencil. He had come, he said,
immediately on his return from Liverpool, and was sorry
to find that she was away for the day. When should he
call again? If she would make an appointment he would
attend to it. He felt as he wrote this that he might very
safely have himself made an appointment for the morrow;
but he cheated himself into half believing that the
suggestion he now made was the more gracious and civil.
At any rate it would certainly give him another day. Mrs.
Hurtle would not return till late in the evening, and as
the following day was Sunday there would be no delivery
by post. When the note was finished he left it on the
table, and called to Ruby to tell her that he was going.
'Mr. Montague,' she said in a confidential whisper, as
she tripped down the stairs, 'I don't see why you need be
saying anything about me, you know.'

'Mr. Carbury is up in town looking after you.'

'What 'm I to Mr. Carbury?'

'Your grandfather is very anxious about you.'

'Not a bit of it, Mr. Montague. Grandfather knows
very well where I am. There! Grandfather doesn't want
me back, and I ain't a going. Why should the Squire
bother himself about me? I don't bother myself about
him.'

'He's afraid, Miss Ruggles, that you are trusting yourself to a young man who is not trustworthy.'

'I can mind myself very well, Mr. Montague.'

'Tell me this. Have you seen Sir Felix Carbury since you've been in town?' Ruby, whose blushes came very easily, now flushed up to her forehead. 'You may be sure that he means no good to you. What can come of an intimacy between you and such a one as he?'

'I don't see why I shouldn't have my friend, Mr. Montague, as well as you. Howsomever, if you'll not tell, I'll be ever so much obliged.'

'But I must tell Mr. Carbury.'

'Then I ain't obliged to you one bit,' said Ruby, shutting the door.

Paul as he walked away could not help thinking of the justice of Ruby's reproach to him. What business had he to take upon himself to be a Mentor to any one in regard to an affair of love;—he, who had engaged himself to marry Mrs. Hurtle, and who the evening before had for the first time declared his love to Hetta Carbury?

In regard to Mrs. Hurtle he had got a reprieve, as he thought, for two days;—but it did not make him happy or even comfortable. As he walked back to his lodgings he knew it would have been better for him to have had the interview over. But, at any rate, he could now think of Hetta Carbury, and the words he had spoken to her. Had he heard that declaration which she had made to her mother, he would have been able for the hour to have forgotten Mrs. Hurtle.

## Chapter XL

### 'UNANIMITY IS THE VERY SOUL OF THESE THINGS'

THAT evening Montague was surprised to receive at the Beargarden a note from Mr. Melmotte, which had been brought thither by a messenger from the city, —who had expected to have an immediate answer, as though Montague lived at the club.

'DEAR SIR,' said the letter,

'If not inconvenient would you call on me in Grosvenor Square to-morrow, Sunday, at half past eleven. If you

are going to church, perhaps you will make an appointment in the afternoon; if not, the morning will suit best.
I want to have a few words with you in private about the
Company. My messenger will wait for answer if you are
at the club.

> 'Yours truly,
> 'AUGUSTUS MELMOTTE.

'PAUL MONTAGUE, Esq.,
'The Beargarden.'

Paul immediately wrote to say that he would call at
Grosvenor Square at the hour appointed,—abandoning
any intentions which he might have had in reference to
Sunday morning service. But this was not the only letter
he received that evening. On his return to his lodgings,
he found a note, containing only one line, which Mrs.
Hurtle had found the means of sending to him after her
return from Southend. 'I am sorry to have been away.
I will expect you all to-morrow. W. H.' The period of
the reprieve was thus curtailed to less than a day.

On the Sunday morning he breakfasted late and then
walked up to Grosvenor Square, much pondering what
the great man could have to say to him. The great man
had declared himself very plainly in the Board-room,—
especially plainly after the Board had risen. Paul had
understood that war was declared, and had understood
also that he was to fight the battle single-handed, knowing nothing of such strategy as would be required, while
his antagonist was a great master of financial tactics. He
was prepared to go to the wall in reference to his money,
only hoping that in doing so he might save his character
and keep the reputation of an honest man. He was
quite resolved to be guided altogether by Mr. Ramsbottom, and intended to ask Mr. Ramsbottom to draw
up for him such a statement as would be fitting for him
to publish. But it was manifest now that Mr. Melmotte
would make some proposition, and it was impossible
that he should have Mr. Ramsbottom at his elbow to
help him.

He had been in Melmotte's house on the night of the

ball, but had contented himself after that with leaving a
card. He had heard much of the splendour of the place,
but remembered simply the crush and the crowd, and
that he had danced there more than once or twice with
Hetta Carbury. When he was shown into the hall he was
astonished to find that it was not only stripped, but was
full of planks, and ladders, and trussels,* and mortar.
The preparations for the great dinner had been already
commenced. Through all this he made his way to the
stairs, and was taken up to a small room on the second
floor, where the servant told him that Mr. Melmotte
would come to him. Here he waited a quarter of an hour
looking out into the yard at the back. There was not a
book in the room, or even a picture with which he could
amuse himself. He was beginning to think whether his
own personal dignity would not be best consulted by
taking his departure, when Melmotte himself, with
slippers on his feet and enveloped in a magnificent
dressing-gown, bustled into the room. 'My dear sir, I
am so sorry. You are a punctual man, I see. So am I. A
man of business should be punctual. But they ain't
always. Brehgert,—from the house of Todd, Brehgert,
and Goldsheiner, you know,—has just been with me. We
had to settle something about the Moldavian loan.* He
came a quarter late, and of course he went a quarter
late. And how is a man to catch a quarter of an hour?
I never could do it.' Montague assured the great man
that the delay was of no consequence. 'And I am so
sorry to ask you into such a place as this. I had Brehgert
in my room downstairs, and then the house is so knocked
about! We get into a furnished house a little way off in
Bruton Street to-morrow. Longestaffe lets me his house
for a month till this affair of the dinner is over. By-the
by, Montague, if you'd like to come to the dinner, I've
got a ticket I can let you have. You know how they're
run after.' Montague had heard of the dinner, but had
perhaps heard as little of it as any man frequenting a club
at the west end of London. He did not in the least want
to be at the dinner, and certainly did not wish to receive
any extraordinary civility from Mr. Melmotte's hands.

But he was very anxious to know why Mr. Melmotte should offer it. He excused himself saying that he was not particularly fond of big dinners, and that he did not like standing in the way of other people. 'Ah, indeed,' said Melmotte. 'There are ever so many people of title would give anything for a ticket. You'd be astonished at the persons who have asked. We've had to squeeze in a chair on one side for the Master of the Buckhounds, and on the other for the Bishop of ——; I forget what bishop it is, but we had the two archbishops before. They say he must come because he has something to do with getting up the missionaries for Tibet. But I've got the ticket, if you'll have it.' This was the ticket which was to have taken in Georgiana Longestaffe as one of the Melmotte family, had not Melmotte perceived that it might be useful to him as a bribe. But Paul would not take the bribe. 'You're the only man in London, then,' said Melmotte, somewhat offended. 'But at any rate you'll come in the evening, and I'll have one of Madame Melmotte's tickets sent to you.' Paul not knowing how to escape, said that he would come in the evening. 'I am particularly anxious,' continued he, 'to be civil to those who are connected with our great Railway, and of course, in this country, your name stands first,—next to my own.'

Then the great man paused, and Paul began to wonder whether it could be possible that he had been sent for to Grosvenor Square on a Sunday morning in order that he might be asked to dine in the same house a fortnight later. But that was impossible. 'Have you anything special to say about the Railway?' he asked.

'Well, yes. It is so hard to get things said at the Board. Of course there are some there who do not understand matters.'

'I doubt if there be any one there who does understand this matter,' said Paul.

Melmotte affected to laugh. 'Well, well; I am not prepared to go quite so far as that. My friend Cohenlupe has had great experience in these affairs, and of course you are aware that he is in Parliament. And Lord Alfred sees farther into them than perhaps you give him credit for.'

'He may easily do that.'

'Well, well. Perhaps you don't know quite as well as I do.' The scowl began to appear on Mr. Melmotte's brow. Hitherto it had been banished as well as he knew how to banish it. 'What I wanted to say to you was this. We didn't quite agree at the last meeting.'

'No; we did not.'

'I was very sorry for it. Unanimity is everything in the direction of such an undertaking as this. With unanimity we can do—everything.' Mr. Melmotte in the ecstasy of his enthusiasm lifted up both his hands over his head. 'Without unanimity we can do—nothing.' And the two hands fell. 'Unanimity should be printed everywhere about a Board-room. It should, indeed, Mr. Montague.'

'But suppose the directors are not unanimous.'

'They should be unanimous. They should make themselves unanimous. God bless my soul! You don't want to see the thing fall to pieces!'

'Not if it can be carried on honestly.'

'Honestly! Who says that anything is dishonest?' Again the brow became very heavy. 'Look here, Mr. Montague. If you and I quarrel in the Board-room, there is no knowing the amount of evil we may do to every individual shareholder in the Company. I find the responsibility on my shoulders so great that I say the thing must be stopped. Damme, Mr. Montague, it must be stopped. We mustn't ruin widows and children, Mr. Montague. We mustn't let those shares run down 20 below par for a mere chimera. I've known a fine property blasted, Mr. Montague, sent straight to the dogs,—annihilated, sir;—so that it all vanished into thin air, and widows and children past counting were sent out to starve about the streets,—just because one director sat in another director's chair. I did, by G—! What do you think of that, Mr. Montague? Gentlemen who don't know the nature of credit, how strong it is,—as the air,—to buoy you up; how slight it is,—as a mere vapour,—

when roughly touched, can do an amount of mischief of which they themselves don't in the least understand the extent! What is it you want, Mr. Montague?'

'What do I want?' Melmotte's description of the peculiar susceptibility of great mercantile speculations had not been given without some effect on Montague, but this direct appeal to himself almost drove that effect out of his mind. 'I only want justice.'

'But you should know what justice is before you demand it at the expense of other people. Look here, Mr. Montague. I suppose you are like the rest of us, in this matter. You want to make money out of it.'

'For myself, I want interest for my capital; that is all. But I am not thinking of myself.'

'You are getting very good interest. If I understand the matter,'—and here Melmotte pulled out a little book, showing thereby how careful he was in mastering details,—'you had about £6,000 embarked in the business when Fisker joined your firm. You imagine yourself to have that still.'

'I don't know what I've got.'

'I can tell you then. You have that, and you've drawn nearly a thousand pounds since Fisker came over, in one shape or another. That's not bad interest on your money.'

'There was back interest due to me.'

'If so, it's due still. I've nothing to do with that. Look here, Mr. Montague. I am most anxious that you should remain with us. I was about to propose, only for that little rumpus the other day, that, as you're an unmarried man, and have time on your hands, you should go out to California and probably across to Mexico, in order to get necessary information for the Company. Were I of your age, unmarried, and without impediment, it is just the thing I should like. Of course you'd go at the Company's expense. I would see to your own personal interests while you were away;—or you could appoint any one by power of attorney. Your seat at the Board would be kept for you; but, should anything occur amiss, —which it won't, for the thing is as sound as anything I know,—of course you, as absent, would not share the responsibility. That's what I was thinking. It would be a delightful trip;—but if you don't like it, you can of course remain at the Board, and be of the greatest use to me. Indeed, after a bit I could devolve nearly the whole management on you;—and I must do something of the kind, as I really haven't the time for it. But,—if it is to be that way,—do be unanimous. Unanimity is the very soul of these things;—the very soul, Mr. Montague.'

'But if I can't be unanimous?'

'Well;—if you can't, and if you won't take my advice about going out;—which, pray, think about, for you would be most useful. It might be the very making of the railway;—then I can only suggest that you should take your £6,000 and leave us. I, myself, should be greatly distressed; but if you are determined that way I will see that you have your money. I will make myself personally responsible for the payment of it,—some time before the end of the year.'

Paul Montague told the great man that he would consider the whole matter, and see him in Abchurch Lane before the next Board day. 'And now, good-bye,' said Mr. Melmotte, as he bade his young friend adieu in a hurry. 'I'm afraid that I'm keeping Sir Gregory Gribe, the Bank Director, waiting downstairs.'

## Chapter XLI

### ALL PREPARED

DURING all these days Miss Melmotte was by no means contented with her lover's prowess, though she would not allow herself to doubt his sincerity. She had not only assured him of her undying affection in the presence of her father and mother, had not only offered to be chopped in pieces on his behalf, but had also written to him, telling how she had a large sum of her father's money within her power, and how willing she was to make it her own, to throw over her father and mother, and give herself and her fortune to her lover. She felt

that she had been very gracious to her lover, and that
her lover was a little slow in acknowledging the favours
conferred upon him. But, nevertheless, she was true to
her lover, and believed that he was true to her. Didon
had been hitherto faithful. Marie had written various
letters to Sir Felix, and had received two or three very
short notes in reply, containing hardly more than a word
or two each. But now she was told that a day was absolutely fixed for her marriage with Lord Nidderdale, and
that her things were to be got ready. She was to be
married in the middle of August, and here they were,
approaching the end of June. 'You may buy what you
like, mamma,' she said; 'and if papa agrees about Felix,
why then I suppose they'll do. But they'll never be of
any use about Lord Nidderdale. If you were to sew me
up in the things by main force, I wouldn't have him.'
Madame Melmotte groaned, and scolded in English,
French, and German, and wished that she were dead;
she told Marie that she was a pig, and ass, and a toad,
and a dog. And ended, as she always did end, by swearing that Melmotte must manage the matter himself.
'Nobody shall manage this matter for me,' said Marie.
'I know what I'm about now, and I won't marry anybody just because it will suit papa.' 'Que nous étions
encore à Frankfort, ou New York,' said the elder lady,
remembering the humbler but less troubled times of her
earlier life. Marie did not care for Frankfort or New
York; for Paris or for London;—but she did care for Sir
Felix Carbury.

While her father on Sunday morning was transacting
business in his own house with Paul Montague and the
great commercial magnates of the city,—though it may
be doubted whether that very respectable gentleman
Sir Gregory Gribe was really in Grosvenor Square when
his name was mentioned,—Marie was walking inside
the gardens; Didon was also there at some distance from
her; and Sir Felix Carbury was there also close along-
side of her. Marie had the key of the gardens for her own
use; and had already learned that her neighbours in the
square did not much frequent the place during church

time on Sunday morning. Her lover's letter to her father
had of course been shown to her, and she had taxed him
with it immediately. Sir Felix, who had thought much
of the letter as he came from Welbeck Street to keep his
appointment,—having been assured by Didon that the
gate should be left unlocked, and that she would be
there to close it after he had come in,—was of course
ready with a lie. 'It was the only thing to do, Marie;—
it was indeed.'

'But you said you had accepted some offer.'

'You don't suppose I wrote the letter?'

'It was your handwriting, Felix.'

'Of course it was. I copied just what he put down.
He'd have sent you clean away where I couldn't have
got near you if I hadn't written it.'

'And you have accepted nothing?'

'Not at all. As it is, he owes me money. Is not that
odd? I gave him a thousand pounds to buy shares, and
I haven't got anything from him yet.' Sir Felix, no
doubt, forgot the cheque for £200.

'Nobody ever does who gives papa money,' said the
observant daughter.

'Don't they? Dear me! But I just wrote it because I
thought anything better than a downright quarrel.'

'I wouldn't have written it, if it had been ever so.'

'It's no good scolding, Marie. I did it for the best.
What do you think we'd best do now?' Marie looked at
him, almost with scorn. Surely it was for him to propose
and for her to yield. 'I wonder whether you're right
about that money which you say is settled.'

'I'm quite sure. Mamma told me in Paris,—just when
we were coming away,—that it was done so that there
might be something if things went wrong. And papa
told me that he should want me to sign something from
time to time; and of course I said I would. But of course
I won't,—if I should have a husband of my own.' Felix
walked along, pondering the matter, with his hands in
his trousers pockets. He entertained those very fears
which had latterly fallen upon Lord Nidderdale. There
would be no 'cropper' which a man could 'come' so bad

as would be his cropper were he to marry Marie Melmotte, and then find that he was not to have a shilling!
And, were he now to run off with Marie, after having
written that letter, the father would certainly not forgive
him. This assurance of Marie's as to the settled money
was too doubtful! The game to be played was too full of
danger! And in that case he would certainly get neither
his £800, nor the shares. And if he were true to Melmotte, Melmotte would probably supply him with
ready money. But then there was the girl at his elbow,
and he no more dared to tell her to her face that he
meant to give her up, than he dared to tell Melmotte
that he intended to stick to his engagement. Some half
promise would be the only escape for the present. 'What
are you thinking of, Felix?' she asked.

'It's d—— difficult to know what to do.'

'But you do love me?'

'Of course I do. If I didn't love you why should I be
here walking round this stupid place? They talk of your
being married to Nidderdale about the end of August.'

'Some day in August. But that's all nonsense, you
know. They can't take me up and marry me, as they
used to do the girls ever so long ago. I won't marry him.
He don't care a bit for me, and never did. I don't think
you care much, Felix.'

'Yes, I do. A fellow can't go on saying so over and over
again in a beastly place like this. If we were anywhere
jolly together, then I could say it often enough.'

'I wish we were, Felix. I wonder whether we ever
shall be.'

'Upon my word I hardly see my way as yet.'

'You're not going to give it up!'

'Oh no;—not give it up; certainly not. But the bother
is a fellow doesn't know what to do.'

'You've heard of young Mr. Goldsheiner, haven't you?'
suggested Marie.

'He's one of those city chaps.'

'And Lady Julia Start?'

'She's old Lady Catchboy's daughter. Yes; I've heard
of them. They got spliced last winter.'

'Yes,—somewhere in Switzerland, I think. At any rate they went to Switzerland, and now they've got a house close to Albert Gate.'

'How jolly for them! He is awfully rich, isn't he?'

'I don't suppose he's half so rich as papa. They did all they could to prevent her going, but she met him down at Folkestone just as the tidal boat was starting. Didon says that nothing was easier.'

'Oh;—ah. Didon knows all about it.'

'That she does.'

'But she'd lose her place.'

'There are plenty of places. She could come and live with us, and be my maid. If you would give her £50 for herself, she'd arrange it all.'

'And would you come to Folkstone?'

'I think that would be stupid, because Lady Julia did that. We should make it a little different. If you liked I wouldn't mind going to—New York. And then, perhaps, we might—get—married, you know, on board. That's what Didon thinks.'

'And would Didon go too?'

'That's what she proposes. She could go as my aunt, and I'd call myself by her name;—any French name you know. I should go as a French girl. And you could call yourself Smith, and be an American. We wouldn't go together, but we'd get on board just at the last moment. If they wouldn't—marry us on board, they would at New York, instantly.'

'That's Didon's plan?'

'That's what she thinks best,—and she'll do it, if you'll give her £50 for herself, you know. The "Adriatic,"—that's a White Star boat,* goes on Thursday week at noon. There's an early train that would take us down that morning. You had better go and sleep at Liverpool, and take no notice of us at all till we meet on board. We could be back in a month,—and then papa would be obliged to make the best of it.'

Sir Felix at once felt that it would be quite unnecessary for him to go to Herr Vossner or to any other male counsellor for advice as to the best means of carrying off

his love. The young lady had it all at her fingers' ends,
—even to the amount of the fee required by the female
counsellor. But Thursday week was very near, and the
whole thing was taking uncomfortably defined proportions. Where was he to get funds if he were to resolve
that he would do this thing? He had been fool enough
to intrust his ready money to Melmotte, and now he was
told that when Melmotte got hold of ready money he
was not apt to release it. And he had nothing to show;—
no security that he could offer to Vossner. And then,—
this idea of starting to New York with Melmotte's
daughter immediately after he had written to Melmotte
renouncing the girl, frightened him.

> 'There is a tide in the affairs of men,
>  Which taken at the flood leads on to fortune.'*

Sir Felix did not know these lines, but the lesson taught
by them came home to him at this moment. Now was
the tide in his affairs at which he might make himself, or
utterly mar himself. 'It's deuced important,' he said at
last with a groan.

'It's not more important for you than me,' said Marie.

'If you're wrong about the money, and he shouldn't
come round, where should we be then?'

'Nothing venture, nothing have,' said the heiress.

'That's all very well; but one might venture everything and get nothing after all.'

'You'd get me,' said Marie with a pout.

'Yes;—and I'm awfully fond of you. Of course I
should get you! But— '

'Very well then;—if that's your love,' said Marie,
turning back from him.

Sir Felix gave a great sigh, and then announced his
resolution. 'I'll venture it.'

'Oh, Felix, how grand it will be!'

'There's a great deal to do, you know. I don't know
whether it can be Thursday week.' He was putting in
the coward's plea for a reprieve.

'I shall be afraid of Didon if it's delayed long.'

'There's the money to get, and all that.'

'I can get some money. Mamma has money in the house.'

'How much?' asked the baronet eagerly.

'A hundred pounds, perhaps;—perhaps two hundred.'

'That would help certainly. I must go to your father for money. Won't that be a sell? To get it from him, to take you away!'

It was decided that they were to go to New York, on a Thursday,—on Thursday week if possible, but as to that he was to let her know in a day or two. Didon was to pack up the clothes and get them sent out of the house. Didon was to have £50 before she went on board; and as one of the men must know about it, and must assist in having the trunks smuggled out of the house, he was to have £10. All had been settled beforehand, so that Sir Felix really had no need to think about anything. 'And now,' said Marie, 'there's Didon. Nobody's looking and she can open that gate for you. When we're gone, do you creep out. The gate can be left, you know. Then we'll get out on the other side.' Marie Melmotte was certainly a clever girl.

## Chapter XLII

### 'CAN YOU BE READY IN TEN MINUTES?'

AFTER leaving Melmotte's house on Sunday morning Paul Montague went to Roger Carbury's hotel and found his friend just returning from church. He was bound to go to Islington on that day, but had made up his mind that he would defer his visit till the evening. He would dine early and be with Mrs. Hurtle about seven o'clock. But it was necessary that Roger should hear the news about Ruby Ruggles. 'It's not so bad as you thought,' said he, 'as she is living with her aunt.'

'I never heard of such an aunt.'

'She says her grandfather knows where she is, and that he doesn't want her back again.'

'Does she see Felix Carbury?'

'I think she does,' said Paul.

'Then it doesn't matter whether the woman's her aunt or not. I'll go and see her and try to get her back to Bungay.'

'Why not send for John Crumb?'

Roger hesitated for a moment, and then answered, 'He'd give Felix such a thrashing as no man ever had before. My cousin deserves it as well as any man ever deserved a thrashing; but there are reasons why I should not like it. And he could not force her back with him. I don't suppose the girl is all bad,—if she could see the truth.'

'I don't think she's bad at all.'

'At any rate I'll go and see her,' said Roger. 'Perhaps I shall see your widow at the same time.' Paul sighed, but said nothing more about his widow at that moment. 'I'll walk up to Welbeck Street now,' said Roger, taking his hat. 'Perhaps I shall see you to-morrow.' Paul felt that he could not go to Welbeck Street with his friend.

He dined in solitude at the Beargarden, and then again made that journey to Islington in a cab. As he went he thought of the proposal that had been made to him by Melmotte. If he could do it with a clear conscience, if he could really make himself believe in the railway, such an expedition would not be displeasing to him. He had said already more than he had intended to say to Hetta Carbury; and though he was by no means disposed to flatter himself, yet he almost thought that what he had said had been well received. At the moment they had been disturbed, but she, as she heard the sound of her mother coming, had at any rate expressed no anger. He had almost been betrayed into breaking a promise. Were he to start now on this journey, the period of the promise would have passed by before his return. Of course he would take care that she should know that he had gone in the performance of a duty. And then he would escape from Mrs. Hurtle, and would be able to make those inquiries which had been suggested to him. It was possible that Mrs. Hurtle should offer to go with him,—an arrangement which would not at all suit him.

That at any rate must be avoided. But then how could he do this without a belief in the railway generally? And how was it possible that he should have such belief? Mr. Ramsbottom did not believe in it, nor did Roger Carbury. He himself did not in the least believe in Fisker, and Fisker had originated the railway. Then, would it not be best that he should take the Chairman's offer as to his own money? If he could get his £6,000 back and have done with the railway, he would certainly think himself a lucky man. But he did not know how far he could with honesty lay aside his responsibility; and then he doubted whether he could put implicit trust in Melmotte's personal guarantee for the amount. This at any rate was clear to him,—that Melmotte was very anxious to secure his absence from the meetings of the Board.

Now he was again at Mrs. Pipkin's door, and again it was opened by Ruby Ruggles. His heart was in his mouth as he thought of the things he had to say. 'The ladies have come back from Southend, Miss Ruggles?'

'Oh yes, sir, and Mrs. Hurtle is expecting you all the day.' Then she put in a whisper on her own account. 'You didn't tell him as you'd seen me, Mr. Montague?'

'Indeed I did, Miss Ruggles.'

'Then you might as well have left it alone, and not have been ill-natured,—that's all,' said Ruby as she opened the door of Mrs. Hurtle's room.

Mrs. Hurtle got up to receive him with her sweetest smile,—and her smile could be very sweet. She was a witch of a woman, and, as like most witches she could be terrible, so like most witches she could charm. 'Only fancy,' she said, 'that you should have come the only day I have been two hundred yards from the house, except that evening when you took me to the play. I was so sorry.'

'Why should you be sorry? It is easy to come again.'

'Because I don't like to miss you, even for a day. But I wasn't well, and I fancied that the house was stuffy, and Mrs. Pipkin took a bright idea and proposed to carry me off to Southend. She was dying to go herself. She declared that Southend was Paradise.'

'A cockney Paradise.'

'Oh, what a place it is! Do your people really go to Southend and fancy that that is the sea?'

'I believe they do. I never went to Southend myself,—so that you know more about it than I do.'

'How very English it is,—a little yellow river,—and you call it the sea! Ah;—you never were at Newport!'

'But I've been at San Francisco.'

'Yes; you've been at San Francisco, and heard the seals howling. Well; that's better than Southend.'

'I suppose we do have the sea here in England. It's generally supposed we're an island.'

'Of course;—but things are so small. If you choose to go to the west of Ireland, I suppose you'd find the Atlantic. But nobody ever does go there for fear of being murdered.' Paul thought of the gentleman in Oregon, but said nothing;—thought, perhaps, of his own condition, and remembered that a man might be murdered without going either to Oregon or the west of Ireland. 'But we went to Southend, I, and Mrs. Pipkin and the baby, and upon my word I enjoyed it. She was so afraid that the baby would annoy me, and I thought the baby was so much the best of it. And then we ate shrimps, and she was so humble. You must acknowledge that with us nobody would be so humble. Of course I paid. She has got all her children, and nothing but what she can make out of these lodgings. People are just as poor with us;—and other people who happen to be a little better off, pay for them. But nobody is humble to another, as you are here. Of course we like to have money as well as you do, but it doesn't make so much difference.'

'He who wants to receive, all the world over, will make himself as agreeable as he can to him who can give.'

'But Mrs. Pipkin was so humble. However, we got back all right yesterday evening, and then I found that you had been here,—at last.'

'You knew that I had to go to Liverpool.'

'I'm not going to scold. Did you get your business done at Liverpool?'

'Yes;—one generally gets something done, but never

anything very satisfactorily. Of course it's about this railway.'

'I should have thought that that was satisfactory. Everybody talks of it as being the greatest thing ever invented. I wish I was a man that I might be concerned with a really great thing like that. I hate little peddling things. I should like to manage the greatest bank in the world, or to be Captain of the biggest fleet, or to make the largest railway. It would be better even than being President of a Republic, because one would have more of one's own way. What is it that you do in it, Paul?'

'They want me now to go out to Mexico about it,' said he slowly.

'Shall you go?' said she, throwing herself forward and asking the question with manifest anxiety.

'I think not.'

'Why not? Do go. Oh, Paul, I would go with you. Why should you not go? It is just the thing for such a one as you to do. The railway will make Mexico a new country, and then you would be the man who had done it. Why should you throw away such a chance as that? It will never come again. Emperors and kings have tried their hands at Mexico and have been able to do nothing. Emperors and kings never can do anything. Think what it would be to be the regenerator of Mexico!'

'Think what it would be to find one's self there without the means of doing anything, and to feel that one had been sent there merely that one might be out of the way.'

'I would make the means of doing something.'

'Means are money. How can I make that?'

'There is money going. There must be money where there is all this buying and selling of shares. Where does your uncle get the money with which he is living like a prince at San Francisco? Where does Fisker get the money with which he is speculating in New York? Where does Melmotte get the money which makes him the richest man in the world? Why should not you get it as well as the others?'

'If I were anxious to rob on my own account perhaps I might do it.'

'Why should it be robbery? I do not want you to live in a palace and spend millions of dollars on yourself. But I want you to have ambition. Go to Mexico, and chance it. Take San Francisco in your way, and get across the country. I will go every yard with you. Make people there believe that you are in earnest, and there will be no difficulty about the money.'

He felt that he was taking no steps to approach the subject which he should have to discuss before he left her, —or rather the statement which he had resolved that he would make. Indeed every word which he allowed her to say respecting this Mexican project carried him farther away from it. He was giving reasons why the journey should not be made; but was tacitly admitting that if it were to be made she might be one of the travellers. The very offer on her part implied an understanding that his former abnegation of the engagement had been withdrawn, and yet he shrunk from the cruelty of telling her, in a sideway fashion, that he would not submit to her companionship either for the purpose of such a journey or for any other purpose. The thing must be said in a solemn manner, and must be introduced on its own basis. But such preliminary conversation as this made the introduction of it infinitely more difficult.

'You are not in a hurry?' she said.

'Oh no.'

'You're going to spend the evening with me like a good man? Then I'll ask them to let us have tea.' She rang the bell and Ruby came in, and the tea was ordered. 'That young lady tells me that you are an old friend of hers.'

'I've known about her down in the country, and was astonished to find her here yesterday.'

'There's some lover, isn't there;—some would-be husband whom she does not like?'

'And some won't-be husband, I fear, whom she does like.'

'That's quite of course, if the other is true. Miss Ruby isn't the girl to have come to her time of life without a preference. The natural liking of a young woman for a man in a station above her, because he is softer and

cleaner and has better parts of speech,—just as we keep
a pretty dog if we keep a dog at all,—is one of the evils
of the inequality of mankind. The girl is content with
the love without having the love justified, because the
object is more desirable. She can only have her love
justified with an object less desirable. If all men wore
coats of the same fabric, and had to share the soil of the
work of the world equally between them, that evil would
come to an end. A woman here and there might go
wrong from fantasy and diseased passions, but the ever-
existing temptation to go wrong would be at an end.'

'If men were equal to-morrow and all wore the same
coats, they would wear different coats the next day.'

'Slightly different. But there would be no more purple
and fine linen, and no more blue woad. It isn't to be
done in a day of course, nor yet in a century,—nor in a
decade of centuries; but every human being who looks
into it honestly will see that his efforts should be made in
that direction. I remember; you never take sugar; give
me that.'

Neither had he come here to discuss the deeply
interesting questions of women's difficulties and immediate or progressive equality. But having got on to
these rocks,—having, as the reader may perceive, been
taken on to them wilfully by the skill of the woman,—he
did not know how to get his bark out again into clear
waters. But having his own subject before him, with all
its dangers, the wild-cat's claws, and the possible fate of
the gentleman in Oregon, he could not talk freely on
the subjects which she introduced, as had been his wont
in former years. 'Thanks,' he said, changing his cup.
'How well you remember!'

'Do you think I shall ever forget your preferences and
dislikings? Do you recollect telling me about that blue
scarf of mine, that I should never wear blue?'

She stretched herself out towards him, waiting for an
answer, so that he was obliged to speak. 'Of course I do.
Black is your colour;—black and grey; or white,—and
perhaps yellow when you choose to be gorgeous; crimson
possibly. But not blue or green.'

'I never thought much of it before, but I have taken your word for gospel. It is very good to have an eye for such things,—as you have, Paul. But I fancy that taste comes with, or at any rate forebodes, an effete civilization.'

'I am sorry that mine should be effete,' he said smiling.

'You know what I mean, Paul. I speak of nations, not individuals. Civilization was becoming effete, or at any rate men were, in the time of the great painters; but Savonarola and Galileo were individuals. You should throw your lot in with a new people. This railway to Mexico gives you the chance.'

'Are the Mexicans a new people?'

'They who will rule the Mexicans are. All American women I dare say have bad taste in gowns,—and so the vain ones and rich ones send to Paris for their finery; but I think our taste in men is generally good. We like our philosophers; we like our poets; we like our genuine workmen;—but we love our heroes. I would have you a hero, Paul.' He got up from his chair and walked about the room in an agony of despair. To be told that he was expected to be a hero at the very moment in his life in which he felt more devoid of heroism, more thoroughly given up to cowardice than he had ever been before, was not to be endured! And yet, with what utmost stretch of courage,—even though he were willing to devote himself certainly and instantly to the worst fate that he had pictured to himself,—could he immediately rush away from these abstract speculations, encumbered as they were with personal flattery, into his own most unpleasant, most tragic matter! It was the unfitness that deterred him and not the possible tragedy. Nevertheless, through it all, he was sure,—nearly sure,—that she was playing her game, and playing it in direct antagonism to the game which she knew that he wanted to play. Would it not be better that he should go away and write another letter? In a letter he could at any rate say what he had to say;—and having said it he would then strengthen himself to adhere to it. 'What makes you so uneasy?' she asked; still speaking in her most winning way, caressing him with the tones of her voice. 'Do you not like me to say that I would have you be a hero?'

'Winifred,' he said, 'I came here with a purpose, and I had better carry it out.'

'What purpose?' She still leaned forward, but now supported her face on her two hands with her elbows resting on her knees, looking at him intently. But one would have said that there was only love in her eyes;—love which might be disappointed, but still love. The wild cat, if there, was all within, still hidden from sight. Paul stood with his hands on the back of a chair, propping himself up and trying to find fitting words for the occasion. 'Stop, my dear,' she said. 'Must the purpose be told to-night?'

'Why not to-night?'

'Paul, I am not well;—I am weak now. I am a coward. You do not know the delight to me of having a few words of pleasant talk to an old friend after the desolation of the last weeks. Mrs. Pipkin is not very charming. Even her baby cannot supply all the social wants of my life. I had intended that everything should be sweet to-night. Oh, Paul, if it was your purpose to tell me of your love, to assure me that you are still my dear, dear friend, to speak with hope of future days, or with pleasure of those that are past,—then carry out your purpose. But if it be cruel, or harsh, or painful; if you had come to speak daggers;*—then drop your purpose for to-night. Try and think what my solitude must have been to me, and let me have one hour of comfort.'

Of course he was conquered for that night, and could only have that solace which a most injurious reprieve could give him. 'I will not harass you, if you are ill,' he said.

'I am ill. It was because I was afraid that I should be really ill that I went to Southend. The weather is hot, though of course the sun here is not as we have it. But the air is heavy,—what Mrs. Pipkin calls muggy. I was thinking if I were to go somewhere for a week, it would

do me good. Where had I better go?' Paul suggested
Brighton. 'That is full of people; is it not?—a fashionable
place?'

'Not at this time of the year.'

'But it is a big place. I want some little place that
would be pretty. You could take me down; could you
not? Not very far, you know;—not that any place can
be very far from here.' Paul, in his John Bull displeasure,
suggested Penzance, telling her, untruly, that it would
take twenty-four hours. 'Not Penzance then, which I
know is your very Ultima Thule;—not Penzance,
nor yet Orkney. Is there no other place,—except
Southend?'

'There is Cromer in Norfolk,—perhaps ten hours.'

'Is Cromer by the sea?'

'Yes;—what we call the sea.'

'I mean really the sea, Paul?'

'If you start from Cromer right away, a hundred miles
would perhaps take you across to Holland. A ditch of
that kind wouldn't do perhaps.'

'Ah,—now I see you are laughing at me. Is Cromer
pretty?'

'Well, yes;—I think it is. I was there once, but I don't
remember much. There's Ramsgate.'

'Mrs. Pipkin told me of Ramsgate. I don't think I
should like Ramsgate.'

'There's the Isle of Wight. The Isle of Wight is very
pretty.'

'That's the Queen's place.* There would not be room
for her and me too.'

'Or Lowestoffe. Lowestoffe is not so far as Cromer,
and there is a railway all the distance.'

'And sea?'

'Sea enough for anything. If you can't see across it,
and if there are waves, and wind enough to knock you
down, and shipwrecks every other day, I don't see why
a hundred miles isn't as good as a thousand.'

'A hundred miles is just as good as a thousand. But,
Paul, at Southend it isn't a hundred miles across to the
other side of the river. You must admit that. But you

will be a better guide than Mrs. Pipkin. You would not
have taken me to Southend when I expressed a wish for
the ocean;—would you? Let it be Lowestoffe. Is there
an hotel?'

'A small little place.'

'Very small? uncomfortably small? But almost any
place would do for me.'

'They make up, I believe, about a hundred beds; but
in the States it would be very small.'

'Paul,' said she, delighted to have brought him back
to this humour, 'if I were to throw the tea things at you,
it would serve you right. This is all because I did not
lose myself in awe at the sight of the Southend ocean.
It shall be Lowestoffe.' Then she rose up and came to
him, and took his arm. 'You will take me down, will
you not? It is desolate for a woman to go into such a
place all alone. I will not ask you to stay. And I can
return by myself.' She had put both hands on one arm,
and turned herself round, and looked into his face. 'You
will do that for old acquaintance sake?' For a moment
or two he made no answer, and his face was troubled,
and his brow was black. He was endeavouring to think;
—but he was only aware of his danger, and could see no
way through it. 'I don't think you will let me ask in
vain for such a favour as that,' she said.

'No;' he replied. 'I will take you down. When will
you go?' He had cockered himself up with some vain
idea that the railway carriage would be a good place for
the declaration of his purpose, or perhaps the sands at
Lowestoffe.

'When will I go? when will you take me? You have
Boards to attend, and shares to look to, and Mexico to
regenerate. I am a poor woman with nothing on hand
but Mrs. Pipkin's baby. Can you be ready in ten minutes?
—because I could.' Paul shook his head and laughed.
'I've named a time and that doesn't suit. Now, sir, you
name another, and I'll promise it shall suit.' Paul
suggested Saturday, the 29th. He must attend the next
Board, and had promised to see Melmotte before the
Board day. Saturday of course would do for Mrs.

Hurtle. Should she meet him at the railway station? Of course he undertook to come and fetch her.

Then, as he took his leave, she stood close against him, and put her cheek up for him to kiss. There are moments in which a man finds it utterly impossible that he should be prudent,—as to which, when he thought of them afterwards, he could never forgive himself for prudence, let the danger have been what it may. Of course he took her in his arms, and kissed her lips as well as her cheeks.

## Chapter XLIII

### THE CITY ROAD

THE statement made by Ruby as to her connection with Mrs. Pipkin was quite true. Ruby's father had married a Pipkin whose brother had died leaving a widow behind him at Islington. The old man at Sheep's Acre farm had greatly resented this marriage, had never spoken to his daughter-in-law,—or to his son after the marriage, and had steeled himself against the whole Pipkin race. When he undertook the charge of Ruby he had made it matter of agreement that she should have no intercourse with the Pipkins. This agreement Ruby had broken, corresponding on the sly with her uncle's widow at Islington. When therefore she ran away from Suffolk she did the best she could with herself in going to her aunt's house. Mrs. Pipkin was a poor woman, and could not offer a permanent home to Ruby; but she was good-natured, and came to terms. Ruby was to be allowed to stay at any rate for a month, and was to work in the house for her bread. But she made it a part of her bargain that she should be allowed to go out occasionally. Mrs. Pipkin immediately asked after a lover. 'I'm all right,' said Ruby. If the lover was what he ought to be, had he not better come and see her? This was Mrs. Pipkin's suggestion. Mrs. Pipkin thought that scandal might in this way be avoided. 'That's as it may be, by-and-by,' said Ruby.

Then she told all the story of John Crumb;—how she
hated John Crumb; how resolved she was that nothing
should make her marry John Crumb. And she gave
her own account of that night on which John Crumb
and Mr. Mixet ate their supper at the farm, and of the
manner in which her grandfather had treated her
because she would not have John Crumb. Mrs. Pipkin
was a respectable woman in her way, always preferring
respectable lodgers if she could get them;—but bound
to live. She gave Ruby very good advice. Of course if
she was 'dead-set' against John Crumb, that was one
thing! But then there was nothing a young woman
should look to so much as a decent house over her
head,—and victuals. 'What's all the love in the world,
Ruby, if a man can't do for you?' Ruby declared that
she knew somebody who could do for her, and could do
very well for her. She knew what she was about, and
wasn't going to be put off it. Mrs. Pipkin's morals were
good wearing morals, but she was not strait-laced. If
Ruby chose to manage in her own way about her lover
she must. Mrs. Pipkin had an idea that young women
in these days did have, and would have, and must have
more liberty than was allowed when she was young.
The world was being changed very fast. Mrs. Pipkin
knew that as well as others. And therefore when Ruby
went to the theatre once and again,—by herself as far as
Mrs. Pipkin knew, but probably in company with her
lover,—and did not get home till past midnight, Mrs.
Pipkin said very little about it, attributing such novel
circumstances to the altered condition of her country.
She had not been allowed to go to the theatre with a
young man when she had been a girl,—but that had
been in the earlier days of Queen Victoria, fifteen years
ago, before the new dispensation had come. Ruby had
never yet told the name of her lover to Mrs. Pipkin,
having answered all inquiries by saying that she was all
right. Sir Felix's name had never even been mentioned
in Islington till Paul Montague had mentioned it.
She had been managing her own affairs after her
own fashion,—not altogether with satisfaction, but still

without interruption; but now she knew that interference would come. Mr. Montague had found her out, and had told her grandfather's landlord. The Squire would be after her, and then John Crumb would come, accompanied of course by Mr. Mixet,—and after that, as she said to herself on retiring to the couch which she shared with two little Pipkins, 'the fat would be in the fire.'

'Who do you think was at our place yesterday?' said Ruby one evening to her lover. They were sitting together at a music-hall,—half music-hall, half theatre, which pleasantly combined the allurements of the gin-palace, the theatre, and the ball-room, trenching hard on those of other places. Sir Felix was smoking, dressed, as he himself called it, 'incognito,' with a Tom-and-Jerry hat,* and a blue silk cravat, and a green coat. Ruby thought it was charming. Felix entertained an idea that were his West End friends to see him in this attire they would not know him. He was smoking, and had before him a glass of hot brandy and water, which was common to himself and Ruby. He was enjoying life. Poor Ruby! She was half-ashamed of herself, half-frightened, and yet supported by a feeling that it was a grand thing to have got rid of restraints, and be able to be with her young man. Why not? The Miss Longestaffes were allowed to sit and dance and walk about with their young men,—when they had any. Why was she to be given up to a great mass of stupid dust like John Crumb, without seeing anything of the world? But yet, as she sat sipping her lover's brandy and water between eleven and twelve at the music-hall in the City Road, she was not altogether comfortable. She saw things which she did not like to see. And she heard things which she did not like to hear. And her lover, though he was beautiful,—oh, so beautiful!—was not all that a lover should be. She was still a little afraid of him, and did not dare as yet to ask him for the promise which she expected him to make to her. Her mind was set upon—marriage, but the word had hardly passed between them. To have his arm round her waist was heaven to her! Could it be possible that he and John Crumb were of the same order of human beings? But how was this to go on? Even Mrs. Pipkin made disagreeable allusions, and she could not live always with Mrs. Pipkin, coming out at nights to drink brandy and water and hear music with Sir Felix Carbury. She was glad therefore to take the first opportunity of telling her lover that something was going to happen. 'Who do you suppose was at our place yesterday?'

Sir Felix changed colour, thinking of Marie Melmotte, thinking that perhaps some emissary from Marie Melmotte had been there; perhaps Didon herself. He was amusing himself during these last evenings of his in London; but the business of his life was about to take him to New York. That project was still being elaborated. He had had an interview with Didon, and nothing was wanting but the money. Didon had heard of the funds which had been intrusted by him to Melmotte, and had been very urgent with him to recover them. Therefore, though his body was not unfrequently present, late in the night, at the City Road Music-Hall, his mind was ever in Grosvenor Square. 'Who was it, Ruby?'

'A friend of the Squire's, a Mr. Montague. I used to see him about in Bungay and Beccles.'

'Paul Montague!'

'Do you know him, Felix?'

'Well;—rather. He's a member of our club, and I see him constantly in the city—and I know him at home.'

'Is he nice?'

'Well;—that depends on what you call nice. He's a prig of a fellow.'

'He's got a lady friend where I live.'

'The devil he has!' Sir Felix of course had heard of Roger Carbury's suit to his sister, and of the opposition to this suit on the part of Hetta, which was supposed to have been occasioned by her preference for Paul Montague. 'Who is she, Ruby?'

'Well;—she's a Mrs. Hurtle. Such a stunning woman! Aunt says she's an American. She's got lots of money.'

'Is Montague going to marry her?'

'Oh dear yes. It's all arranged. Mr. Montague comes quite regular to see her;—not so regular as he ought, though. When gentlemen are fixed as they're to be married, they never are regular afterwards. I wonder whether it'll be the same with you?'

'Wasn't John Crumb regular, Ruby?'

'Bother John Crumb! That wasn't none of my doings. Oh, he'd been regular enough, if I'd let him; he'd been like clockwork,—only the slowest clock out. But Mr. Montague has been and told the Squire as he saw me. He told me so himself. The Squire's coming about John Crumb. I know that. What am I to tell him, Felix?'

'Tell him to mind his own business. He can't do anything to you.'

'No;—he can't do nothing. I ain't done nothing wrong, and he can't send for the police to have me took back to Sheep's Acre. But he can talk,—and he can look. I ain't one of those, Felix, as don't mind about their characters,—so don't you think it. Shall I tell him as I'm with you?'

'Gracious goodness, no! What would you say that for?'

'I didn't know. I must say something.'

'Tell him you're nothing to him.'

'But aunt will be letting on about my being out late o' nights; I know she will. And who am I with? He'll be asking that.'

'Your aunt does not know?'

'No;—I've told nobody yet. But it won't do to go on like that, you know,—will it? You don't want it to go on always like that;—do you?'

'It's very jolly, I think.'

'It ain't jolly for me. Of course, Felix, I like to be with you. That's jolly. But I have to mind them brats all the day, and to be doing the bedrooms. And that's not the worst of it.'

'What is the worst of it?'

'I'm pretty nigh ashamed of myself. Yes, I am.'
And now Ruby burst out into tears. 'Because I
wouldn't have John Crumb, I didn't mean to be a bad
girl. Nor yet I won't. But what'll I do, if everybody
turns against me? Aunt won't go on for ever in this
way. She said last night that——'

'Bother what she says!' Felix was not at all anxious
to hear what aunt Pipkin might have to say upon such
an occasion.

'She's right too. Of course she knows there's somebody. She ain't such a fool as to think that I'm out at
these hours to sing psalms with a lot of young women.
She says that whoever it is ought to speak out his mind.
There;—that's what she says. And she's right. A
girl has to mind herself, though she's ever so fond of a
young man.'

Sir Felix sucked his cigar and then took a long drink
of brandy and water. Having emptied the beaker
before him, he rapped for the waiter and called for
another. He intended to avoid the necessity of making
any direct reply to Ruby's importunities. He was
going to New York very shortly, and looked on his
journey thither as an horizon in his future beyond
which it was unnecessary to speculate as to any farther
distance. He had not troubled himself to think how it
might be with Ruby when he was gone. He had not
even considered whether he would or would not tell
her that he was going, before he started. It was not
his fault that she had come up to London. She was an
'awfully jolly girl,' and he liked the feeling of the
intrigue better perhaps than the girl herself. But he
assured himself that he wasn't going to give himself
any 'd——d trouble.' The idea of John Crumb
coming up to London in his wrath had never occurred
to him,—or he would probably have hurried on his
journey to New York instead of delaying it, as he was
doing now. 'Let's go in and have a dance,' he said.

Ruby was very fond of dancing,—perhaps liked it
better than anything in the world. It was heaven to

her to be spinning round the big room with her lover's arm tight round her waist, with one hand in his and her other hanging over his back. She loved the music, and loved the motion. Her ear was good, and her strength was great, and she never lacked breath. She could spin along and dance a whole room down, and feel at the time that the world could have nothing to give better worth having than that;—and such moments were too precious to be lost. She went and danced, resolving as she did so that she would have some answer to her question before she left her lover on that night.

'And now I must go,' she said at last. 'You'll see me as far as the Angel, won't you?' Of course he was ready to see her as far as the Angel. 'What am I to say to the Squire?'

'Say nothing.'

'And what am I to say to aunt?'

'Say to her? Just say what you have said all along.'

'I've said nothing all along,—just to oblige you, Felix. I must say something. A girl has got herself to mind. What have you got to say to me, Felix?'

He was silent for about a minute, meditating his answer. 'If you bother me I shall cut it, you know.'

'Cut it!'

'Yes;—cut it. Can't you wait till I am ready to say something?'

'Waiting will be the ruin o' me, if I wait much longer. Where am I to go, if Mrs. Pipkin won't have me no more?'

'I'll find a place for you.'

'You find a place! No; that won't do. I've told you all that before. I'd sooner go into service, or——'

'Go back to John Crumb.'

'John Crumb has more respect for me nor you. He'd make me his wife to-morrow, and only be too happy.'

'I didn't tell you to come away from him,' said Sir Felix.

'Yes, you did. You told me as I was to come up to

London when I saw you at Sheepstone Beeches;—didn't
you? And you told me you loved me;—didn't you?
And that if I wanted anything you'd get it done for
me;—didn't you?'

'So I will. What do you want? I can give you a
couple of sovereigns, if that's what it is.'

'No it isn't;—and I won't have your money. I'd
sooner work my fingers off. I want you to say whether
you mean to marry me. There!'

As to the additional lie which Sir Felix might now
have told, that would have been nothing to him. He
was going to New York, and would be out of the way
of any trouble; and he thought that lies of that kind
to young women never went for anything. Young
women, he thought, didn't believe them, but liked to
be able to believe afterwards that they had been
deceived. It wasn't the lie that stuck in his throat, but
the fact that he was a baronet. It was in his estimation
'confounded impudence' on the part of Ruby Ruggles
to ask to be his wife. He did not care for the lie, but
he did not like to seem to lower himself by telling such
a lie as that at her dictation. 'Marry, Ruby! No, I
don't ever mean to marry. It's the greatest bore out.
I know a trick worth two of that.'

She stopped in the street and looked at him. This
was a state of things of which she had never dreamed.
She could imagine that a man should wish to put it
off, but that he should have the face to declare to his
young woman that he never meant to marry at all, was
a thing that she could not understand. What business
had such a man to go after any young woman? 'And
what do you mean that I'm to do, Sir Felix?' she said.

'Just go easy, and not make yourself a bother.'

'Not make myself a bother! Oh, but I will; I
will. I'm to be carrying on with you, and nothing to
come of it; but for you to tell me that you don't mean
to marry, never at all! Never?'

'Don't you see lots of old bachelors about, Ruby?'

'Of course I does. There's the Squire. But he
don't come asking girls to keep him company.'

'That's more than you know, Ruby.'

'If he did he'd marry her out of hand,—because he's a gentleman. That's what he is, every inch of him. He never said a word to a girl,—not to do her any harm, I'm sure,' and Ruby began to cry. 'You mustn't come no further now, and I'll never see you again—never! I think you're the falsest young man, and the basest, and the lowest-minded that I ever heard tell of. I know there are them as don't keep their words. Things turn up, and they can't. Or they gets to like others better; or there ain't nothing to live on. But for a young man to come after a young woman, and then say, right out, as he never means to marry at all, is the lowest-spirited fellow that ever was. I never read of such a one in none of the books. No, I won't. You go your way, and I'll go mine.' In her passion she was as good as her word, and escaped from him, running all the way to her aunt's door. There was in her mind a feeling of anger against the man, which she did not herself understand, in that he would incur no risk on her behalf. He would not even make a lover's easy promise, in order that the present hour might be made pleasant. Ruby let herself into her aunt's house, and cried herself to sleep with a child on each side of her.

On the next day Roger called. She had begged Mrs. Pipkin to attend the door, and had asked her to declare, should any gentleman ask for Ruby Ruggles, that Ruby Ruggles was out. Mrs. Pipkin had not refused to do so; but, having heard sufficient of Roger Carbury to imagine the cause which might possibly bring him to the house, and having made up her mind that Ruby's present condition of independence was equally unfavourable to the lodging-house and to Ruby herself, she determined that the Squire, if he did come, should see the young lady. When therefore Ruby was called into the little back parlour and found Roger Carbury there, she thought that she had been caught in a trap. She had been very cross all the morning. Though in her rage she had been able on the previous evening to dismiss her titled lover, and to imply that she never meant to see him again, now, when the remembrance of the loss came upon her amidst her daily work,—when she could no longer console herself in her drudgery by thinking of the beautiful things that were in store for her, and by flattering herself that though at this moment she was little better than a maid of all work in a lodging-house, the time was soon coming in which she would bloom forth as a baronet's bride,—now in her solitude she almost regretted the precipitancy of her own conduct. Could it be that she would never see him again;—that she would dance no more in that gilded bright saloon? And might it not be possible that she had pressed him too hard? A baronet of course would not like to be brought to book, as she could bring to book such a one as John Crumb. But yet,—that he should have said never;—that he would never marry! Looking at it in any light, she was very unhappy, and this coming of the Squire did not serve to cure her misery.

Roger was very kind to her, taking her by the hand, and bidding her sit down, and telling her how glad he was to find that she was comfortably settled with her aunt. 'We were all alarmed, of course, when you went away without telling anybody where you were going.'

'Grandfather'd been that cruel to me that I couldn't tell him.'

'He wanted you to keep your word to an old friend of yours.'

'To pull me all about by the hairs of my head wasn't the way to make a girl keep her word;—was it, Mr. Carbury? That's what he did, then;—and Sally Hockett, who is there, heard it. I've been good to grandfather, whatever I may have been to John Crumb; and he shouldn't have treated me like that. No girl'd like to be pulled about the room by the hairs of her head, and she with her things all off, just getting into bed.'

The Squire had no answer to make to this. That old Ruggles should be a violent brute under the influence of gin and water did not surprise him. And the girl, when driven away from her home by such usage, had not done amiss in coming to her aunt. But Roger had already heard a few words from Mrs. Pipkin as to Ruby's late hours, had heard also that there was a lover, and knew very well who that lover was. He also was quite familiar with John Crumb's state of mind. John Crumb was a gallant, loving fellow who might be induced to forgive everything, if Ruby would only go back to him; but would certainly persevere, after some slow fashion of his own, and 'see the matter out,' as he would say himself, if she did not go back. 'As you found yourself obliged to run away,' said Roger, 'I'm glad that you should be here; but you don't mean to stay here always?'

'I don't know,' said Ruby.

'You must think of your future life. You don't want to be always your aunt's maid.'

'Oh dear, no.'

'It would be very odd if you did, when you may be the wife of such a man as Mr. Crumb.'

'Oh, Mr. Crumb! Everybody is going on about Mr. Crumb. I don't like Mr. Crumb, and I never will like him.'

'Now look here, Ruby; I have come to speak to you very seriously, and I expect you to hear me. Nobody can make you marry Mr. Crumb, unless you please.'

'Nobody can't, of course, sir.'

'But I fear you have given him up for somebody else, who certainly won't marry you, and who can only mean to ruin you.'

'Nobody won't ruin me,' said Ruby. 'A girl has to look to herself, and I mean to look to myself.'

'I'm glad to hear you say so, but being out at night with such a one as Sir Felix Carbury is not looking to yourself. That means going to the devil head foremost.'

'I ain't a going to the devil,' said Ruby, sobbing and blushing.

'But you will, if you put yourself into the hands of that young man. He's as bad as bad can be. He's my own cousin, and yet I'm obliged to tell you so. He has no more idea of marrying you than I have; but were he to marry you, he could not support you. He is ruined himself, and would ruin any young woman who trusted him. I'm almost old enough to be your father, and in all my experience I never came across so vile a young man as he is. He would ruin you and cast you from him without a pang of remorse. He has no heart in his bosom;—none.' Ruby had now given way altogether, and was sobbing with her apron to her eyes in one corner of the room. 'That's what Sir Felix Carbury is,' said the Squire, standing up so that he might speak with the more energy, and talk her down more thoroughly. 'And if I understand it rightly,' he continued, 'it is for a vile thing such as he, that you have left a man who is as much above him in character, as the sun is above the earth. You think little of John Crumb because he does not wear a fine coat.'

'I don't care about any man's coat,' said Ruby; 'but John hasn't ever a word to say, was it ever so.'

'Words to say! what do words matter? He loves you. He loves you after that fashion that he wants to make you happy and respectable, not to make you a bye-word and a disgrace.' Ruby struggled hard to make some opposition to the suggestion, but found herself to be incapable of speech at the moment. 'He thinks more of you than of himself, and would give you all that he has. What would that other man give you? If you were once married to John Crumb, would any one then pull you by the hairs of your head? Would there be any want then, or any disgrace?'

'There ain't no disgrace, Mr. Carbury.'

'No disgrace in going about at midnight with such a one as Felix Carbury? You are not a fool, and you know that it is disgraceful. If you are not unfit to be an honest man's wife, go back and beg that man's pardon.'

'John Crumb's pardon! No!'

'Oh, Ruby, if you knew how highly I respect that man, and how lowly I think of the other; how I look

on the one as a noble fellow, and regard the other as
dust beneath my feet, you would perhaps change your
mind a little.'

Her mind was being changed. His words did have
their effect, though the poor girl struggled against the
conviction that was borne in upon her. She had never
expected to hear any one call John Crumb noble.
But she had never respected any one more highly than
Squire Carbury, and he said that John Crumb was
noble. Amidst all her misery and trouble she still
told herself that it was but a dusty, mealy,—and also a
dumb nobility.

'I'll tell you what will take place,' continued Roger.
'Mr. Crumb won't put up with this you know.'

'He can't do nothing to me, sir.'

'That's true enough. Unless it be to take you in his
arms and press you to his heart, he wants to do nothing
to you. Do you think he'd injure you if he could?
You don't know what a man's love really means, Ruby.
But he could do something to somebody else. How do
you think it would be with Felix Carbury, if they two
were in a room together and nobody else by?'

'John's mortial strong, Mr. Carbury.'

'If two men have equal pluck, strength isn't much
needed. One is a brave man, and the other——a
coward. Which do you think is which?'

'He's your own cousin, and I don't know why you
should say everything again him.'

'You know I'm telling you the truth. You know it as
well as I do myself;—and you're throwing yourself
away, and throwing the man who loves you over,—for
such a fellow as that! Go back to him, Ruby, and
beg his pardon.'

'I never will;—never.'

'I've spoken to Mrs. Pipkin, and while you're here
she will see that you don't keep such hours any longer.
You tell me that you're not disgraced, and yet you are
out at midnight with a young blackguard like that!
I've said what I've got to say, and I'm going away.
But I'll let your grandfather know.'

'Grandfather don't want me no more.'

'And I'll come again. If you want money to go home, I will let you have it. Take my advice at least in this;—do not see Sir Felix Carbury any more.' Then he took his leave. If he had failed to impress her with admiration for John Crumb, he had certainly been efficacious in lessening that which she had entertained for Sir Felix.

## Chapter XLIV

### THE COMING ELECTION

THE very greatness of Mr. Melmotte's popularity, the extent of the admiration which was accorded by the public at large to his commercial enterprise and financial sagacity, created a peculiar bitterness in the opposition that was organized against him at Westminster. As the high mountains are intersected by deep valleys, as puritanism in one age begets infidelity in the next, as in many countries the thickness of the winter's ice will be in proportion to the number of the summer musquitoes, so was the keenness of the hostility displayed on this occasion in proportion to the warmth of the support which was manifested. As the great man was praised, so also was he abused. As he was a demi-god to some, so was he a fiend to others. And indeed there was hardly any other way in which it was possible to carry on the contest against him. From the moment in which Mr. Melmotte had declared his purpose of standing for Westminster in the Conservative interest, an attempt was made to drive him down the throats of the electors by clamorous assertions of his unprecedented commercial greatness. It seemed that there was but one virtue in the world, commercial enterprise,—and that Melmotte was its prophet. It seemed, too, that the orators and writers of the day intended all Westminster to believe that Melmotte treated his great affairs in a spirit very different from that which animates the bosoms of merchants in general. He had risen above any feeling of personal

profit. His wealth was so immense that there was no
longer place for anxiety on that score. He already
possessed,—so it was said,—enough to found a dozen
families, and he had but one daughter! But by carrying
on the enormous affairs which he held in his hands, he
would be able to open up new worlds, to afford relief
to the oppressed nationalities of the over-populated old
countries. He had seen how small was the good done
by the Peabodys and the Bairds,* and, resolving to lend
no ear to charities and religions, was intent on projects
for enabling young nations to earn plentiful bread by
the moderate sweat of their brows. He was the head
and front of the railway which was to regenerate
Mexico. It was presumed that the contemplated line
from ocean to ocean across British America would
become a fact in his hands. It was he who was to enter
into terms with the Emperor of China for farming the
tea-fields of that vast country. He was already in treaty
with Russia for a railway from Moscow to Khiva. He
had a fleet,—or soon would have a fleet of emigrant
ships—ready to carry every discontented Irishman out
of Ireland to whatever quarter of the globe the Milesian*
might choose for the exercise of his political principles.
It was known that he had already floated a company
for laying down a submarine wire*from Penzance to
Point de Galle, round the Cape of Good Hope,—so
that, in the event of general wars, England need be
dependent on no other country for its communications
with India. And then there was the philanthropic
scheme for buying the liberty of the Arabian fellahs
from the Khedive of Egypt for thirty millions sterling,*—
the compensation to consist of the concessior of a
territory about four times as big as Great Britain in the
lately annexed country on the great African lakes.*
It may have been the case that some of these things
were as yet only matters of conversation,—speculations
as to which Mr. Melmotte's mind and imagination had
been at work, rather than his pocket or even his credit;
but they were all sufficiently matured to find their
way into the public press, and to be used as strong

arguments why Melmotte should become member of Parliament for Westminster.

All this praise was of course gall to those who found themselves called upon by the demands of their political position to oppose Mr. Melmotte. You can run down a demi-god only by making him out to be a demi-devil. These very persons, the leading Liberals of the leading borough in England as they called themselves, would perhaps have cared little about Melmotte's antecedents had it not become their duty to fight him as a Conservative. Had the great man found at the last moment that his own British politics had been liberal in their nature, these very enemies would have been on his committee. It was their business to secure the seat. And as Melmotte's supporters began the battle with an attempt at what the Liberals called 'bounce,'—to carry the borough with a rush by an overwhelming assertion of their candidate's virtues,—the other party was driven to make some enquiries as to that candidate's antecedents. They quickly warmed to the work, and were not less loud in exposing the Satan of speculation, than had been the Conservatives in declaring the commercial Jove. Emissaries were sent to Paris and Frankfort, and the wires were used to Vienna and New York. It was not difficult to collect stories,—true or false; and some quiet men, who merely looked on at the game, expressed an opinion that Melmotte might have wisely abstained from the glories of Parliament.

Nevertheless there was at first some difficulty in finding a proper Liberal candidate to run against him. The nobleman who had been elevated out of his seat by the death of his father had been a great Whig magnate, whose family was possessed of immense wealth and of popularity equal to its possessions. One of that family might have contested the borough at a much less expense than any other person,—and to them the expense would have mattered but little. But there was no such member of it forthcoming. Lord This and Lord That,—and the Honourable This and the Honourable That, sons of other cognate Lords,—already had seats which

they were unwilling to vacate in the present state of
affairs. There was but one other session for the existing
Parliament; and the odds were held to be very greatly in
Melmotte's favour. Many an outsider was tried, but the
outsiders were either afraid of Melmotte's purse or his
influence. Lord Buntingford was asked, and he and his
family were good old Whigs. But he was nephew to
Lord Alfred Grendall, first cousin to Miles Grendall,
and abstained on behalf of his relatives. An overture
was made to Sir Damask Monogram, who certainly
could afford the contest. But Sir Damask did not see
his way. Melmotte was a working bee, while he was a
drone,—and he did not wish to have the difference
pointed out by Mr. Melmotte's supporters. Moreover,
he preferred his yacht and his four-in-hand.

At last a candidate was selected, whose nomination
and whose consent to occupy the position created very
great surprise in the London world. The press had of
course taken up the matter very strongly. The 'Morning
Breakfast Table' supported Mr. Melmotte with all its
weight. There were people who said that this support
was given by Mr. Broune under the influence of Lady
Carbury, and that Lady Carbury in this way endeavoured to reconcile the great man to a marriage between
his daughter and Sir Felix. But it is more probable
that Mr. Broune saw,—or thought that he saw,—which
way the wind sat, and that he supported the commercial
hero because he felt that the hero would be supported
by the country at large. In praising a book, or putting
foremost the merits of some official or military claimant,
or writing up a charity,—in some small matter of
merely personal interest,—the Editor of the 'Morning
Breakfast Table' might perhaps allow himself to listen
to a lady whom he loved. But he knew his work too
well to jeopardize his paper by such influences in any
matter which might probably become interesting to the
world of his readers. There was a strong belief in
Melmotte. The clubs thought that he would be
returned for Westminster. The dukes and duchesses
fêted him. The city,—even the city was showing a

wavering disposition to come round. Bishops begged
for his name on the list of promoters of their pet
schemes. Royalty without stint was to dine at his
table. Melmotte himself was to sit at the right hand of
the brother of the Sun and of the uncle of the Moon,
and British Royalty was to be arranged opposite, so
that every one might seem to have the place of most
honour. How could a conscientious Editor of a 'Morning
Breakfast Table,' seeing how things were going, do
other than support Mr. Melmotte? In fair justice it
may be well doubted whether Lady Carbury had
exercised any influence in the matter.

But the 'Evening Pulpit' took the other side. Now
this was the more remarkable, the more sure to attract
attention, inasmuch as the 'Evening Pulpit' had never
supported the Liberal interest. As was said in the
first chapter of this work, the motto of that newspaper
implied that it was to be conducted on principles of
absolute independence. Had the 'Evening Pulpit,' like
some of its contemporaries, lived by declaring from day
to day that all Liberal elements were godlike, and
all their opposites satanic, as a matter of course the same
line of argument would have prevailed as to the Westminster election. But as it had not been so, the vigour
of the 'Evening Pulpit' on this occasion was the more
alarming and the more noticeable,—so that the short
articles which appeared almost daily in reference to
Mr. Melmotte were read by everybody. Now they
who are concerned in the manufacture of newspapers
are well aware that censure is infinitely more attractive
than eulogy,—but they are quite as well aware that it is
more dangerous. No proprietor or editor was ever
brought before the courts at the cost of ever so many
hundred pounds,—which if things go badly may rise to
thousands,—because he had attributed all but divinity
to some very poor specimen of mortality. No man was
ever called upon for damages because he had attributed
grand motives. It might be well for politics and
literature and art,—and for truth in general, if it was
possible to do so. But a new law of libel must be

enacted before such salutary proceedings can take place. Censure on the other hand is open to very grave perils. Let the Editor have been ever so conscientious, ever so beneficent,—even ever so true,—let it be ever so clear that what he has written has been written on behalf of virtue, and that he has misstated no fact, exaggerated no fault, never for a moment been allured from public to private matters,—and he may still be in danger of ruin. A very long purse, or else a very high courage is needed for the exposure of such conduct as the 'Evening Pulpit' attributed to Mr. Melmotte. The paper took up this line suddenly. After the second article Mr. Alf sent back to Mr. Miles Grendall, who in the matter was acting as Mr. Melmotte's secretary, the ticket of invitation for the dinner, with a note from Mr. Alf stating that circumstances connected with the forthcoming election for Westminster could not permit him to have the great honour of dining at Mr. Melmotte's table in the presence of the Emperor of China. Miles Grendall showed the note to the dinner committee, and, without consultation with Mr. Melmotte, it was decided that the ticket should be sent to the Editor of a thorough-going Conservative journal. This conduct on the part of the 'Evening Pulpit' astonished the world considerably; but the world was more astonished when it was declared that Mr. Ferdinand Alf himself was going to stand for Westminster on the Liberal interest.

Various suggestions were made. Some said that as Mr. Alf had a large share in the newspaper, and as its success was now an established fact, he himself intended to retire from the laborious position which he filled, and was therefore free to go into Parliament. Others were of opinion that this was the beginning of a new era in literature, of a new order of things, and that from this time forward editors would frequently be found in Parliament, if editors were employed of sufficient influence in the world to find constituencies. Mr. Broune whispered confidentially to Lady Carbury that the man was a fool for his pains, and that he was carried away by pride. 'Very clever,—and dashing,' said Mr.

Broune, 'but he never had ballast.' Lady Carbury shook her head. She did not want to give up Mr. Alf if she could help it. He had never said a civil word of her in his paper;—but still she had an idea that it was well to be on good terms with so great a power. She entertained a mysterious awe for Mr. Alf,—much in excess of any similar feeling excited by Mr. Broune, in regard to whom her awe had been much diminished since he had made her an offer of marriage. Her sympathies as to the election of course were with Mr. Melmotte. She believed in him thoroughly. She still thought that his nod might be the means of making Felix,—or if not his nod, then his money without the nod.

'I suppose he is very rich,' she said, speaking to Mr. Broune respecting Mr. Alf.

'I dare say he has put by something. But this election will cost him £10,000;—and if he goes on as he is doing now, he had better allow another £10,000 for action for libel. They've already declared that they will indict the paper.'

'Do you believe about the Austrian Insurance Company?' This was a matter as to which Mr. Melmotte was supposed to have retired from Paris not with clean hands.

'I don't believe the "Evening Pulpit" can prove it,— and I'm sure that they can't attempt to prove it without an expense of three or four thousand pounds. That's a game in which nobody wins but the lawyers. I wonder at Alf. I should have thought that he would have known how to get all said that he wanted to have said without running with his head into the lion's mouth. He has been so clever up to this! God knows he has been bitter enough, but he has always sailed within the wind.'

Mr. Alf had a powerful committee. By this time an animus in regard to the election had been created strong enough to bring out the men on both sides, and to produce heat, when otherwise there might only have been a warmth or, possibly, frigidity. The Whig

Marquises and the Whig Barons came forward, and
with them the liberal professional men, and the tradesmen who had found that party to answer best, and the
democratical mechanics. If Melmotte's money did not,
at last, utterly demoralise the lower class of voters,
there would still be a good fight. And there was a
strong hope that, under the ballot, Melmotte's money
might be taken without a corresponding effect upon the
voting. It was found upon trial that Mr. Alf was a good
speaker. And though he still conducted the 'Evening
Pulpit', he made time for addressing meetings of the
constituency almost daily. And in his speeches he
never spared Melmotte. No one, he said, had a greater
reverence for mercantile grandeur than himself. But
let them take care that the grandeur was grand. How
great would be the disgrace to such a borough as that
of Westminster if it should find that it had been taken
in by a false spirit of speculation and that it had
surrendered itself to gambling when it had thought to do
honour to honest commerce. This, connected, as of
course it was, with the articles in the paper, was
regarded as very open speaking. And it had its effect.
Some men began to say that Melmotte had not been
known long enough to deserve confidence in his riches,
and the Lord Mayor was already beginning to think that
it might be wise to escape the dinner by some excuse.

Melmotte's committee was also very grand. If Alf was
supported by Marquises and Barons, he was supported
by Dukes and Earls. But his speaking in public did
not of itself inspire much confidence. He had very little
to say when he attempted to explain the political
principles on which he intended to act. After a little he
confined himself to remarks on the personal attacks
made on him by the other side, and even in doing that
was reiterative rather than diffusive. Let them prove
it. He defied them to prove it. Englishmen were too
great, too generous, too honest, too noble,—the men of
Westminster especially were a great deal too high-
minded to pay any attention to such charges as these till
they were proved. Then he began again. Let them

prove it. Such accusations as these were mere lies till
they were proved. He did not say much himself in
public as to actions for libel,—but assurances were made
on his behalf to the electors, especially by Lord Alfred
Grendall and his son, that as soon as the election was
over all speakers and writers would be indicted for
libel, who should be declared by proper legal advice to
have made themselves liable to such action. The
'Evening Pulpit' and Mr. Alf would of course be the
first victims.

The dinner was fixed for Monday, July the 8th. The
election for the borough was to be held on Tuesday the
9th. It was generally thought that the proximity of the
two days had been arranged with the view of enhancing
Melmotte's expected triumph. But such in truth was
not the case. It had been an accident, and an accident
that was distressing to some of the Melmottites. There
was much to be done about the dinner,—which could
not be omitted; and much also as to the election,—
which was imperative. The two Grendalls, father and
son, found themselves to be so driven that the world
seemed for them to be turned topsy-turvy. The
elder had in old days been accustomed to electioneering
in the interest of his own family, and had declared
himself willing to make himself useful on behalf of Mr.
Melmotte. But he found Westminster to be almost too
much for him. He was called here and sent there, till
he was very near rebellion. 'If this goes on much
longer I shall cut it,' he said to his son.

'Think of me, governor,' said the son. 'I have to be
in the city four or five times a week.'

'You've a regular salary.'

'Come, governor; you've done pretty well for that.
What's my salary to the shares you've had? The thing
is;—will it last?'

'How last?'

'There are a good many who say that Melmotte will
burst up.'

'I don't believe it,' said Lord Alfred. 'They don't
know what they're talking about. There are too many

in the same boat to let him burst up. It would be the
bursting up of half London. But I shall tell him after
this that he must make it easier. He wants to know
who's to have every ticket for the dinner, and there's
nobody to tell him except me. And I've got to arrange
all the places, and nobody to help me except that fellow
from the Herald's office. I don't know about people's
rank. Which ought to come first: a director of the
bank or a fellow who writes books?' Miles suggested
that the fellow from the Herald's office would know all
about that, and that his father need not trouble himself
with petty details.

'And you shall come to us for three days,—after it's
over,' said Lady Monogram to Miss Longestaffe; a
proposition to which Miss Longestaffe acceded, willingly
indeed, but not by any means as though a favour had
been conferred upon her. Now the reason why Lady
Monogram had changed her mind as to inviting her old
friend, and thus threw open her hospitality for three
whole days to the poor young lady who had disgraced
herself by staying with the Melmottes, was as follows.
Miss Longestaffe had the disposal of two evening
tickets for Madame Melmotte's grand reception; and so
greatly had the Melmottes risen in general appreciation
that Lady Monogram had found that she was bound, on
behalf of her own position in society, to be present on
that occasion. It would not do that her name should
not be in the printed list of the guests. Therefore she
had made a serviceable bargain with her old friend
Miss Longestaffe. She was to have her two tickets for
the reception, and Miss Longestaffe was to be received
for three days as a guest by Lady Monogram. It had
also been conceded that at any rate on one of these
nights Lady Monogram should take Miss Longestaffe
out with her, and that she should herself receive company
on another. There was perhaps something slightly
painful at the commencement of the negotiation; but
such feelings soon fade away, and Lady Monogram was
quite a woman of the world.

## Chapter XLV

### MR. MELMOTTE IS PRESSED FOR TIME

ABOUT this time, a fortnight or nearly so before the election, Mr. Longestaffe came up to town and saw Mr. Melmotte very frequently. He could not go into his own house, as he had let that for a month to the great financier, nor had he any establishment in town; but he slept at an hotel and lived at the Carlton.* He was quite delighted to find that his new friend was an honest Conservative, and he himself proposed the honest Conservative at the club. There was some idea of electing Mr. Melmotte out of hand, but it was decided that the club could not go beyond its rule, and could only admit Mr. Melmotte out of his regular turn as soon as he should occupy a seat in the House of Commons. Mr. Melmotte, who was becoming somewhat arrogant, was heard to declare that if the club did not take him when he was willing to be taken, it might do without him. If not elected at once, he should withdraw his name. So great was his prestige at this moment with his own party that there were some, Mr. Longestaffe among the number, who pressed the thing on the committee. Mr. Melmotte was not like other men. It was a great thing to have Mr. Melmotte in the party. Mr. Melmotte's financial capabilities would in themselves be a tower of strength. Rules were not made to control the club in a matter of such importance as this. A noble lord, one among seven who had been named as a fit leader of the Upper House on the Conservative side in the next session, was asked to take the matter up; and men thought that the thing might have been done had he complied. But he was old-fashioned, perhaps pig-headed; and the club for the time lost the honour of entertaining Mr. Melmotte.

It may be remembered that Mr. Longestaffe had been anxious to become one of the directors of the Mexican Railway, and that he was rather snubbed than encouraged when he expressed his wish to Mr. Melmotte.

Like other great men, Mr. Melmotte liked to choose his
own time for bestowing favours. Since that request was
made the proper time had come, and he had now
intimated to Mr. Longestaffe that in a somewhat
altered condition of things there would be a place for
him at the Board, and that he and his brother directors
would be delighted to avail themselves of his assistance.
The alliance between Mr. Melmotte and Mr. Longestaffe had become very close. The Melmottes had
visited the Longestaffes at Caversham. Georgiana
Longestaffe was staying with Madame Melmotte in
London. The Melmottes were living in Mr. Longestaffe's town house, having taken it for a month at a
very high rent. Mr. Longestaffe now had a seat at
Mr. Melmotte's board. And Mr. Melmotte had
bought Mr. Longestaffe's estate at Pickering on terms
very favourable to the Longestaffes. It had been
suggested to Mr. Longestaffe by Mr. Melmotte that he
had better qualify for his seat at the Board by taking
shares in the Company to the amount of—perhaps two
or three thousand pounds, and Mr. Longestaffe had of
course consented. There would be no need of any
transaction in absolute cash. The shares could of course
be paid for out of Mr. Longestaffe's half of the purchase
money for Pickering Park, and could remain for the
present in Mr. Melmotte's hands. To this also Mr.
Longestaffe had consented, not quite understanding
why the scrip should not be made over to him at once.

It was a part of the charm of all dealings with this
great man that no ready money seemed ever to be
necessary for anything. Great purchases were made and
great transactions apparently completed without the
signing even of a cheque. Mr. Longestaffe found
himself to be afraid even to give a hint to Mr. Melmotte
about ready money. In speaking of all such matters
Melmotte seemed to imply that everything necessary
had been done, when he had said that it was done.
Pickering had been purchased and the title-deeds made
over to Mr. Melmotte; but the £80,000 had not been
paid,—had not been absolutely paid, though of course

Mr. Melmotte's note assenting to the terms was security sufficient for any reasonable man. The property had been mortgaged, though not heavily, and Mr. Melmotte had no doubt satisfied the mortgagee; but there was still a sum of £50,000 to come, of which Dolly was to have one half and the other was to be employed in paying off Mr. Longestaffe's debts to tradesmen and debts to the bank. It would have been very pleasant to have had this at once,—but Mr. Longestaffe felt the absurdity of pressing such a man as Mr. Melmotte, and was partly conscious of the gradual consummation of a new era in money matters. 'If your banker is pressing you, refer him to me,' Mr. Melmotte had said. As for many years past we have exchanged paper instead of actual money for our commodities, so now it seemed that, under the new Melmotte régime, an exchange of words was to suffice.

But Dolly wanted his money. Dolly, idle as he was, foolish as he was, dissipated as he was and generally indifferent to his debts, liked to have what belonged to him. It had all been arranged. £5,000 would pay off all his tradesmen's debts and leave him comfortably possessed of money in hand, while the other £20,000 would make his own property free. There was a charm in this which awakened even Dolly, and for the time almost reconciled him to his father's society. But now a shade of impatience was coming over him. He had actually gone down to Caversham to arrange the terms with his father,—and had in fact made his own terms. His father had been unable to move him, and had consequently suffered much in spirit. Dolly had been almost triumphant,—thinking that the money would come on the next day, or at any rate during the next week. Now he came to his father early in the morning,— at about two o'clock,—to inquire what was being done. He had not as yet been made blessed with a single ten-pound note in his hand, as the result of the sale.

'Are you going to see Melmotte, sir?' he asked somewhat abruptly.

'Yes;—I'm to be with him to-morrow, and he is to introduce me to the Board.'

'You're going in for that, are you, sir? Do they pay anything?'

'I believe not.'

'Nidderdale and young Carbury belong to it. It's a sort of Beargarden affair.'

'A bear-garden affair, Adolphus. How so?'

'I mean the club. We had them all there for dinner one day, and a jolly dinner we gave them. Miles Grendall and old Alfred belong to it. I don't think they'd go in for it, if there was no money going. I'd make them fork out something if I took the trouble of going all that way.'

'I think that perhaps, Adolphus, you hardly understand these things.'

'No, I don't. I don't understand much about business, I know. What I want to understand is, when Melmotte is going to pay up this money.'

'I suppose he'll arrange it with the banks,' said the father.

' I beg that he won't arrange my money with the banks, sir. You'd better tell him not. A cheque upon his bank which I can pay in to mine is about the best thing going. You'll be in the city to-morrow, and you'd better tell him. If you don't like, you know, I'll get Squercum to do it.' Mr. Squercum was a lawyer whom Dolly had employed of late years much to the annoyance of his parent. Mr. Squercum's name was odious to Mr. Longestaffe.

'I beg you'll do nothing of the kind. It will be very foolish if you do;—perhaps ruinous.'

'Then he'd better pay up, like anybody else,' said Dolly as he left the room. The father knew the son, and was quite sure that Squercum would have his finger in the pie unless the money were paid quickly. When Dolly had taken an idea into his head, no power on earth,—no power at least of which the father could avail himself,—would turn him.

On that same day Melmotte received two visits in

the city from two of his fellow directors. At the time
he was very busy. Though his electioneering speeches
were neither long nor pithy, still he had to think of
them beforehand. Members of his Committee were
always trying to see him. Orders as to the dinner and
the preparation of the house could not be given by
Lord Alfred without some reference to him. And then
those gigantic commercial affairs which were enumerated
in the last chapter could not be adjusted without much
labour on his part. His hands were not empty, but still
he saw each of these young men,—for a few minutes.
'My dear young friend, what can I do for you?' he said
to Sir Felix, not sitting down, so that Sir Felix also
should remain standing.

'About that money, Mr. Melmotte?'

'What money, my dear fellow? You see that a good
many money matters pass through my hands.'

'The thousand pounds I gave you for shares. If you
don't mind, and as the shares seem to be a bother, I'll
take the money back.'

'It was only the other day you had £200,' said
Melmotte, showing that he could apply his memory to
small transactions when he pleased.

'Exactly;—and you might as well let me have the
£800.'

'I've ordered the shares;—gave the order to my
broker the other day.'

'Then I'd better take the shares,' said Sir Felix,
feeling that it might very probably be that day fortnight
before he could start for New York. 'Could I get
them, Mr. Melmotte?'

'My dear fellow, I really think you hardly calculate
the value of my time when you come to me about such
an affair as this.'

'I'd like to have the money or the shares,' said Sir
Felix, who was not specially averse to quarrelling with
Mr. Melmotte now that he had resolved upon taking
that gentleman's daughter to New York in direct
opposition to his written promise. Their quarrel would
be so thoroughly internecine when the departure should

be discovered, that any present anger could hardly increase its bitterness. What Felix thought of now was simply his money, and the best means of getting it out of Melmotte's hands.

'You're a spendthrift,' said Melmotte, apparently relenting, 'and I'm afraid a gambler. I suppose I must give you £200 more on account.'

Sir Felix could not resist the touch of ready money, and consented to take the sum offered. As he pocketed the cheque he asked for the name of the brokers who were employed to buy the shares. But here Melmotte demurred. 'No, my friend,' said Melmotte; 'you are only entitled to shares for £600 pounds now. I will see that the thing is put right.' So Sir Felix departed with £200 only. Marie had said that she could get £200. Perhaps if he bestirred himself and wrote to some of Miles's big relations he could obtain payment of a part of that gentleman's debt to him.

Sir Felix going down the stairs in Abchurch Lane met Paul Montague coming up. Carbury, on the spur of the moment, thought that he would 'take a rise' as he called it out of Montague. 'What's this I hear about a lady at Islington?' he asked.

'Who has told you anything about a lady at Islington?'

'A little bird. There are always little birds about telling of ladies. I'm told that I'm to congratulate you on your coming marriage.'

'Then you've been told an infernal falsehood,' said Montague passing on. He paused a moment and added, 'I don't know who can have told you, but if you hear it again, I'll trouble you to contradict it.' As he was waiting in Melmotte's outer room while the duke's nephew went in to see whether it was the great man's pleasure to see him, he remembered whence Carbury must have heard tidings of Mrs. Hurtle. Of course the rumour had come through Ruby Ruggles.

Miles Grendall brought out word that the great man would see Mr. Montague; but he added a caution. 'He's awfully full of work just now,—you won't forget that;—will you?' Montague assured the duke's nephew that he would be concise, and was shown in.

'I should not have troubled you,' said Paul, 'only that I understood that I was to see you before the Board met.'

'Exactly;—of course. It was quite necessary,—only you see I am a little busy. If this d——d dinner were over I shouldn't mind. It's a deal easier to make a treaty with an Emperor, than to give him a dinner; I can tell you that. Well;—let me see. Oh;—I was proposing that you should go out to Pekin?'

'To Mexico.'

'Yes, yes;—to Mexico. I've so many things running in my head! Well;—if you'll say when you're ready to start, we'll draw up something of instructions. You'd know better, however, than we can tell you, what to do. You'll see Fisker, of course. You and Fisker will manage it. The chief thing will be a cheque for the expenses; eh? We must get that passed at the next Board.'

Mr. Melmotte had been so quick that Montague had been unable to interrupt him. 'There need be no trouble about that, Mr. Melmotte, as I have made up my mind that it would not be fit that I should go.'

'Oh, indeed!'

There had been a shade of doubt on Montague's mind, till the tone in which Melmotte had spoken of the embassy grated on his ears. The reference to the expenses disgusted him altogether. 'No;—even did I see my way to do any good in America my duties here would not be compatible with the undertaking.'

'I don't see that at all. What duties have you got here? What good are you doing the Company? If you do stay, I hope you'll be unanimous; that's all;—or perhaps you intend to go out. If that's it, I'll look to your money. I think I told you that before.'

'That, Mr. Melmotte, is what I should prefer.'

'Very well,—very well. I'll arrange it. Sorry to lose you,—that's all. Miles, isn't Mr. Goldsheiner waiting to see me?'

'You're a little too quick, Mr. Melmotte,' said Paul.

'A man with my business on his hands is bound to be quick, sir.'

'But I must be precise. I cannot tell you as a fact that I shall withdraw from the Board till I receive the advice of a friend with whom I am consulting. I hardly yet know what my duty may be.'

'I'll tell you, sir, what can not be your duty. It cannot be your duty to make known out of that Board-room any of the affairs of the Company which you have learned in that Board-room. It cannot be your duty to divulge the circumstances of the Company or any differences which may exist between Directors of the Company, to any gentleman who is a stranger to the Company. It cannot be your duty——.'

'Thank you, Mr. Melmotte. On matters such as that I think that I can see my own way. I have been in fault in coming in to the Board without understanding what duties I should have to perform——.'

'Very much in fault, I should say,' replied Melmotte, whose arrogance in the midst of his inflated glory was overcoming him.

'But in reference to what I may or may not say to any friend, or how far I should be restricted by the scruples of a gentleman, I do not want advice from you.'

'Very well;—very well. I can't ask you to stay, because a partner from the house of Todd, Brehgert, and Goldsheiner is waiting to see me, about matters which are rather more important than this of yours.' Montague had said what he had to say, and departed.

On the following day, three-quarters of an hour before the meeting of the Board of Directors, old Mr. Longestaffe called in Abchurch Lane. He was received very civilly by Miles Grendall, and asked to sit down. Mr. Melmotte quite expected him, and would walk with him over to the offices of the railway, and introduce him to the Board. Mr. Longestaffe, with some shyness, intimated his desire to have a few moments conversation with the chairman before the Board met. Fearing his son, especially fearing Squercum, he had made up his mind to suggest that the little matter about Pickering

Park should be settled. Miles assured him that the opportunity should be given him, but that at the present moment the chief secretary of the Russian Legation was with Mr. Melmotte. Either the chief secretary was very tedious with his business, or else other big men must have come in, for Mr. Longestaffe was not relieved till he was summoned to walk off to the Board five minutes after the hour at which the Board should have met. He thought that he could explain his views in the street; but on the stairs they were joined by Mr. Cohenlupe, and in three minutes they were in the Board room. Mr. Longestaffe was then presented, and took the chair opposite to Miles Grendall. Montague was not there, but had sent a letter to the secretary explaining that for reasons with which the chairman was acquainted he should absent himself from the present meeting. 'All right,' said Melmotte. 'I know all about it. Go on. I'm not sure but that Mr. Montague's retirement from among us may be an advantage. He could not be made to understand that unanimity in such an enterprise as this is essential. I am confident that the new director whom I have had the pleasure of introducing to you to-day will not sin in the same direction.' Then Mr. Melmotte bowed and smiled very sweetly on Mr. Longestaffe.

Mr. Longestaffe was astonished to find how soon the business was done, and how very little he had been called on to do. Miles Grendall had read something out of a book which he had been unable to follow. Then the chairman had read some figures. Mr. Cohenlupe had declared that their prosperity was unprecedented;—and the Board was over. When Mr. Longestaffe explained to Miles Grendall that he still wished to speak to Mr. Melmotte, Miles explained to him that the chairman had been obliged to run off to a meeting of gentlemen connected with the interior of Africa, which was now being held at the Cannon Street Hotel.

## Chapter XLVI

### ROGER CARBURY AND HIS TWO FRIENDS

ROGER CARBURY, having found Ruby Ruggles, and having ascertained that she was at any rate living in a respectable house with her aunt, returned to Carbury. He had given the girl his advice, and had done so in a manner that was not altogether ineffectual. He had frightened her, and had also frightened Mrs. Pipkin. He had taught Mrs. Pipkin to believe that the new dispensation was not yet so completely established as to clear her from all responsibility as to her niece's conduct. Having done so much, and feeling that there was no more to be done, he returned home. It was out of the question that he should take Ruby with him. In the first place she would not have gone. And then,— had she gone,—he would not have known where to bestow her. For it was now understood throughout Bungay,—and the news had spread to Beccles,—that old Farmer Ruggles had sworn that his granddaughter should never again be received at Sheep's Acre Farm. The squire on his return home heard all the news from his own housekeeper. John Crumb had been at the farm and there had been a fierce quarrel between him and the old man. The old man had called Ruby by every name that is most distasteful to a woman, and John had stormed and had sworn that he would have punched the old man's head but for his age. He wouldn't believe any harm of Ruby,—or if he did he was ready to forgive that harm. But as for the Baro-nite;—the Baro-nite had better look to himself! Old Ruggles had declared that Ruby should never have a shilling of his money;— whereupon Crumb had anathematised old Ruggles and his money too, telling him that he was an old hunx,* and that he had driven the girl away by his cruelty. Roger at once sent over to Bungay for the dealer in meal, who was with him early on the following morning.

'Did ye find her, squoire?'

'Oh, yes, Mr. Crumb, I found her. She's living with her aunt, Mrs. Pipkin, at Islington.'

'Eh, now;—look at that.'

'You knew she had an aunt of that name up in London.'

'Ye-es; I knew'd it, squoire. I a' heard tell of Mrs. Pipkin, but I never see'd her.'

'I wonder it did not occur to you that Ruby would go there.' John Crumb scratched his head, as though acknowledging the shortcoming of his own intellect. 'Of course if she was to go to London it was the proper thing for her to do.'

'I knew she'd do the thing as was right. I said that all along. Darned if I didn't. You ask Mixet, squoire,—him as is baker down Bardsey Lane. I allays guv' it her that she'd do the thing as was right. But how about she and the Baro-nite?'

Roger did not wish to speak of the Baronet just at present. 'I suppose the old man down here did ill-use her?'

'Oh, dreadful;—there ain't no manner of doubt o' that. Dragged her about awful;—as he ought to be took up, only for the rumpus like. D'ye think she's see'd the Baro-nite since she's been in Lon'on, Muster Carbury?'

'I think she's a good girl, if you mean that.'

'I'm sure she be. I don't want none to tell me that, squoire. Tho', squoire, it's better to me nor a ten pun' note to hear you say so. I allays had a leaning to you, squoire; but I'll more nor lean to you, now. I've said all through she was good, and if e'er a man in Bungay said she warn't——; well, I was there, and ready.'

'I hope nobody has said so.'

'You can't stop them women, squoire. There ain't no dropping into them. But, Lord love 'ee, she shall come and be missus of my house to-morrow, and what 'll it matter her then what they say? But, squoire,—did ye hear if the Baro-nite had been a' hanging about that place?'

'About Islington, you mean.'

'He goes a hanging about; he do. He don't come out

straight forrard, and tell a girl as he loves her afore all
the parish. There ain't one in Bungay, nor yet in
Mettingham, nor yet in all the Ilketsals and all the
Elmhams,* as don't know as I'm set on Ruby Ruggles.
Huggery-Muggery is pi'son to me, squoire.'

'We all know that when you've made up your mind,
you have made up your mind.'

'I hove. It's made up ever so as to Ruby. What sort
of a one is her aunt now, squoire?'

'She keeps lodgings;—a very decent sort of a woman I
should say.'

'She won't let the Baro-nite come there?'

'Certainly not,' said Roger, who felt that he was
hardly dealing sincerely with this most sincere of meal-
men. Hitherto he had shuffled off every question that
had been asked him about Felix, though he knew that
Ruby had spent many hours with her fashionable lover.
'Mrs. Pipkin won't let him come there.'

'If I was to give her a ge'own now,—or a blue cloak;—
them lodging-house women is mostly hard put to it;—
or a chest of drawers like, for her best bedroom,
wouldn't that make her more o' my side, squoire?'

'I think she'll try to do her duty without that.'

'They do like things the like o' that; any ways I'll
go up, squoire, arter Sax'nam market, and see how
things is lying.'

'I wouldn't go just yet, Mr. Crumb, if I were you.
She hasn't forgotten the scene at the farm yet.'

'I said nothing as warn't as kind as kind.'

'But her own perversity runs in her own head. If you
had been unkind she could have forgiven that; but as
you were good-natured and she was cross, she can't forgive that.' John Crumb again scratched his head, and
felt that the depths of a woman's character required
more gauging than he had yet given to it. 'And to tell
you the truth, my friend, I think that a little hardship
up at Mrs. Pipkin's will do her good.'

'Don't she have a bellyful o' vittels?' asked John
Crumb, with intense anxiety.

'I don't quite mean that. I dare say she has enough to

eat. But of course she has to work for it with her aunt.
She has three or four children to look after.'

'That moight come in handy by-and-by;—moightn't
it, squoire?' said John Crumb grinning.

'As you say, she'll be learning something that may be
useful to her in another sphere. Of course there is a
good deal to do, and I should not be surprised if she
were to think after a bit that your house in Bungay was
more comfortable than Mrs. Pipkin's kitchen in London.'

'My little back parlour;—eh, squoire! And I've got a
four-poster, most as big as any in Bungay.'

'I am sure you have everything comfortable for her,
and she knows it herself. Let her think about all that,—
and do you go and tell her again in a month's time.
She'll be more willing to settle matters then than she
is now.'

'But,—the Baro-nite!'

'Mrs. Pipkin will allow nothing of that.'

'Girls is so 'cute. Ruby is awful 'cute. It makes me
feel as though I had two hun'erdweight o' meal on my
stomach, lying awake o' nights and thinking as how he
is, may be,——pulling of her about! If I thought that
she'd let him——; oh! I'd swing for it, Muster Carbury.
They'd have to make an eend o' me at Bury, if it was that
way. They would then.'

Roger assured him again and again that he believed
Ruby to be a good girl, and promised that further steps
should be taken to induce Mrs. Pipkin to keep a close
watch upon her niece. John Crumb made no promise
that he would abstain from his journey to London after
Saxmundham fair; but left the squire with a conviction
that his purpose of doing so was shaken. He was still
however resolved to send Mrs. Pipkin the price of a new
blue cloak, and declared his purpose of getting Mixet to
write the letter and enclose the money order. John
Crumb had no delicacy as to declaring his own deficiency
in literary acquirements. He was able to make out a
bill for meal or pollards, but did little beyond that in the
way of writing letters.

This happened on a Saturday morning, and on that

afternoon Roger Carbury rode over to Lowestoffe, to a
meeting there on church matters at which his friend the
bishop presided. After the meeting was over he dined at
the inn with half a dozen clergymen and two or three
neighbouring gentlemen, and then walked down by
himself on to the long strand which has made Lowestoffe
what it is. It was now just the end of June, and the
weather was delightful;—but people were not as yet
flocking to the sea-shore. Every shopkeeper in every
little town through the country now follows the fashion
set by Parliament and abstains from his annual holiday
till August or September. The place therefore was by no
means full. Here and there a few of the townspeople,
who at a bathing place are generally indifferent to the
sea, were strolling about; and another few, indifferent to
fashion, had come out from the lodging-houses and
from the hotel, which had been described as being small
and insignificant,—and making up only a hundred
beds. Roger Carbury, whose house was not many miles
distant from Lowestoffe, was fond of the sea-shore, and
always came to loiter there for a while when any cause
brought him into the town. Now he was walking close
down upon the marge of the tide,—so that the last little
roll of the rising water should touch his feet,—with his
hands joined behind his back, and his face turned down
towards the shore, when he came upon a couple who
were standing with their backs to the land, looking forth
together upon the waves. He was close to them before
he saw them, and before they had seen him. Then he
perceived that the man was his friend Paul Montague.
Leaning on Paul's arm a lady stood, dressed very simply
in black, with a dark straw hat on her head;—very
simple in her attire, but yet a woman whom it would be
impossible to pass without notice. The lady of course was
Mrs. Hurtle.

Paul Montague had been a fool to suggest Lowestoffe,
but his folly had been natural. It was not the first
place he had named; but when fault had been found with
others, he had fallen back upon the sea sands which were
best known to himself. Lowestoffe was just the spot

which Mrs. Hurtle required. When she had been
shown her room, and taken down out of the hotel on to
the strand, she had declared herself to be charmed. She
acknowledged with many smiles that of course she had
had no right to expect that Mrs. Pipkin should understand what sort of place she needed. But Paul would
understand,—and had understood. 'I think the hotel
charming,' she said. 'I don't know what you mean by
your fun about the American hotels, but I think this
quite gorgeous, and the people so civil!' Hotel people
always are civil before the crowds come. Of course it
was impossible that Paul should return to London by the
mail train which started about an hour after his arrival.
He would have reached London at four or five in the
morning, and have been very uncomfortable. The
following day was Sunday, and of course he promised to
stay till Monday. Of course he had said nothing in the
train of those stern things which he had resolved to say.
Of course he was not saying them when Roger Carbury
came upon him; but was indulging in some poetical
nonsense, some probably very trite raptures as to the
expanse of the ocean, and the endless ripples which
connected shore with shore. Mrs. Hurtle, too, as she
leaned with friendly weight upon his arm, indulged also
in moonshine and romance. Though at the back of the
heart of each of them there was a devouring care, still
they enjoyed the hour. We know that the man who is to
be hung likes to have his breakfast well cooked. And
so did Paul like the companionship of Mrs. Hurtle
because her attire, though simple, was becoming;
because the colour glowed in her dark face; because of
the brightness of her eyes, and the happy sharpness of
her words, and the dangerous smile which played upon
her lips. He liked the warmth of her close vicinity, and
the softness of her arm, and the perfume from her hair,—
though he would have given all that he possessed that
she had been removed from him by some impassable
gulf. As he had to be hanged,—and this woman's continued presence would be as bad as death to him,—he
liked to have his meal well dressed.

He certainly had been foolish to bring her to Lowestoffe, and the close neighbourhood of Carbury Manor; —and now he felt his folly. As soon as he saw Roger Carbury he blushed up to his forehead, and then leaving Mrs. Hurtle's arm he came forward, and shook hands with his friend. 'It is Mrs. Hurtle,' he said, 'I must introduce you,' and the introduction was made. Roger took off his hat and bowed, but he did so with the coldest ceremony. Mrs. Hurtle, who was quick enough at gathering the minds of people from their looks, was just as cold in her acknowledgment of the courtesy. In former days she had heard much of Roger Carbury, and surmised that he was no friend to her. 'I did not know that you were thinking of coming to Lowestoffe,' said Roger in a voice that was needlessly severe. But his mind at the present moment was severe, and he could not hide his mind.

'I was not thinking of it. Mrs. Hurtle wished to get to the sea, and as she knew no one else here in England, I brought her.'

'Mr. Montague and I have travelled so many miles together before now,' she said, 'that a few additional will not make much difference.'

'Do you stay long?' asked Roger in the same voice.

'I go back probably on Monday,' said Montague.

'As I shall be here a whole week, and shall not speak a word to any one after he has left me, he has consented to bestow his company on me for two days. Will you join us at dinner, Mr. Carbury, this evening?'

'Thank you, madam;—I have dined.'

'Then, Mr. Montague, I will leave you with your friend. My toilet, though it will be very slight, will take longer than yours. We dine you know in twenty minutes. I wish you could get your friend to join us.' So saying, Mrs. Hurtle tripped back across the sand towards the hotel.

'Is this wise?' demanded Roger in a voice that was almost sepulchral, as soon as the lady was out of hearing.

'You may well ask that, Carbury. Nobody knows the folly of it so thoroughly as I do.'

'Then why do you do it? Do you mean to marry her?'

'No; certainly not.'

'Is it honest then, or like a gentleman, that you should be with her in this way? Does she think that you intend to marry her?'

'I have told her that I would not. I have told her——.' Then he stopped. He was going on to declare that he had told her that he loved another woman, but he felt that he could hardly touch that matter in speaking to Roger Carbury.

'What does she mean then? Has she no regard for her own character?'

'I would explain it to you all, Carbury, if I could. But you would never have the patience to hear me.'

'I am not naturally impatient.'

'But this would drive you mad. I wrote to her assuring her that it must be all over. Then she came here and sent for me. Was I not bound to go to her?'

'Yes;—to go to her and repeat what you had said in your letter.'

'I did do so. I went with that very purpose, and did repeat it.'

'Then you should have left her.'

'Ah; but you do not understand. She begged that I would not desert her in her loneliness. We have been so much together that I could not desert her.'

'I certainly do not understand that, Paul. You have allowed yourself to be entrapped into a promise of marriage; and then, for reasons which we will not go into now but which we both thought to be adequate, you resolved to break your promise, thinking that you would be justified in doing so. But nothing can justify you in living with the lady afterwards on such terms as to induce her to suppose that your old promise holds good.'

'She does not think so. She cannot think so.'

'Then what must she be, to be here with you? And what must you be, to be here, in public, with such a one as she is? I don't know why I should trouble you or myself about it. People live now in a way that I don't comprehend. If this be your way of living, I have no right to complain.'

'For God's sake, Carbury, do not speak in that way. It sounds as though you meant to throw me over.'

'I should have said that you had thrown me over. You come down here to this hotel, where we are both known, with this lady whom you are not going to marry;—and I meet you, just by chance. Had I known it, of course I could have turned the other way. But coming on you by accident, as I did, how am I not to speak to you? And if I speak, what am I to say? Of course I think that the lady will succeed in marrying you.'

'Never.'

'And that such a marriage will be your destruction. Doubtless she is good-looking.'

'Yes, and clever. And you must remember that the manners of her country are not as the manners of this country.'

'Then if I marry at all,' said Roger, with all his prejudice expressed strongly in his voice, 'I trust I may not marry a lady of her country. She does not think that she is to marry you, and yet she comes down here and stays with you. Paul, I don't believe it. I believe you, but I don't believe her. She is here with you in order that she may marry you. She is cunning and strong. You are foolish and weak. Believing as I do that marriage with her would be destruction, I should tell her my mind,—and leave her.' Paul at the moment thought of the gentleman in Oregon, and of certain difficulties in leaving. 'That's what I should do. You must go in now, I suppose, and eat your dinner.'

'I may come to the hall as I go back home?'

'Certainly you may come if you please,' said Roger. Then he bethought himself that his welcome had not been cordial. 'I mean that I shall be delighted to see you,' he added, marching away along the strand. Paul did go into the hotel, and did eat his dinner. In the meantime Roger Carbury marched far away along the strand. In all that he had said to Montague he had spoken the truth, or that which appeared to him to be the truth. He had not been influenced for a moment by any reference to his own affairs. And yet he feared, he almost knew, that this man,—who had promised to marry a strange American woman and who was at this very moment living in close intercourse with the woman after he had told her that he would not keep his promise, —was the chief barrier between himself and the girl that he loved. As he had listened to John Crumb while John spoke of Ruby Ruggles, he had told himself that he and John Crumb were alike. With an honest, true, heartfelt desire they both panted for the companionship of a fellow-creature whom each had chosen. And each was to be thwarted by the make-believe regard of unworthy youth and fatuous good looks! Crumb, by dogged perseverance and indifference to many things, would probably be successful at last. But what chance was there of success for him? Ruby, as soon as want or hardship told upon her, would return to the strong arm that could be trusted to provide her with plenty and comparative ease. But Hetta Carbury, if once her heart had passed from her own dominion into the possession of another, would never change her love. It was possible, no doubt,—nay, how probable,—that her heart was still vacillating. Roger thought that he knew that at any rate she had not as yet declared her love. If she were now to know,—if she could now learn,—of what nature was the love of this other man; if she could be instructed that he was living alone with a lady whom not long since he had promised to marry,—if she could be made to understand this whole story of Mrs. Hurtle, would not that open her eyes? Would she not then see where she could trust her happiness, and where, by so trusting it, she would certainly be shipwrecked!

'Never,' said Roger to himself, hitting at the stones on the beach with his stick. 'Never.' Then he got his horse and rode back to Carbury Manor.

## Chapter XLVII

### MRS. HURTLE AT LOWESTOFFE

WHEN Paul got down into the dining-room Mrs. Hurtle was already there, and the waiter was standing by the side of the table ready to take the cover off the soup. She was radiant with smiles and made herself especially pleasant during dinner, but Paul felt sure that everything was not well with her. Though she smiled, and talked and laughed, there was something forced in her manner. He almost knew that she was only waiting till the man should have left the room to speak in a different strain. And so it was. As soon as the last lingering dish had been removed, and when the door was finally shut behind the retreating waiter, she asked the question which no doubt had been on her mind since she had walked across the strand to the hotel. 'Your friend was hardly civil; was he, Paul?'

'Do you mean that he should have come in? I have no doubt it was true that he had dined.'

'I am quite indifferent about his dinner,—but there are two ways of declining as there are of accepting. I suppose he is on very intimate terms with you?'

'Oh, yes.'

'Then his want of courtesy was the more evidently intended for me. In point of fact he disapproves of me. Is not that it?' To this question Montague did not feel himself called upon to make any immediate answer. 'I can well understand that it should be so. An intimate friend may like or dislike the friend of his friend, without offence. But unless there be strong reason he is bound to be civil to his friend's friend, when accident brings them together. You have told me that Mr. Carbury was your beau ideal of an English gentleman.'

'So he is.'

'Then why didn't he behave as such?' and Mrs. Hurtle again smiled. 'Did not you yourself feel that you were rebuked for coming here with me, when he expressed surprise at your journey? Has he authority over you?'

'Of course he has not. What authority could he have?'

'Nay, I do not know. He may be your guardian. In this safe-going country young men perhaps are not their own masters till they are past thirty. I should have said that he was your guardian, and that he intended to rebuke you for being in bad company. I dare say he did after I had gone.'

This was so true that Montague did not know how to deny it. Nor was he sure that it would be well that he should deny it. The time must come, and why not now as well as at any future moment? He had to make her understand that he could not join his lot with her,—chiefly indeed because his heart was elsewhere, a reason on which he could hardly insist because she could allege that she had a prior right to his heart;—but also because her antecedents had been such as to cause all his friends to warn him against such a marriage. So he plucked up courage for the battle. 'It was nearly that,' he said.

There are many,—and probably the greater portion of my readers will be among the number,—who will declare to themselves that Paul Montague was a poor creature, in that he felt so great a repugnance to face this woman with the truth. His folly in falling at first under the battery of her charms will be forgiven him. His engagement, unwise as it was, and his subsequent determination to break his engagement, will be pardoned. Women, and perhaps some men also, will feel that it was natural that he should have been charmed, natural that he should have expressed his admiration in the form which unmarried ladies expect from unmarried men when any such expression is to be made at all;—natural also that he should endeavour to escape from the dilemma when he found the manifold dangers of the step which he had proposed to take. No woman, I think, will be hard upon him because of his breach of faith to Mrs. Hurtle. But they will be very hard on him on the score of his cowardice,—as, I think, unjustly. In social life we hardly stop to consider how much of that daring spirit which gives mastery comes from hardness of heart

rather than from high purpose, or true courage. The
man who succumbs to his wife, the mother who succumbs
to her daughter, the master who succumbs to his servant,
is as often brought to servility by a continual aversion to
the giving of pain, by a softness which causes the fretful-
ness of others to be an agony to himself,—as by any
actual fear which the firmness of the imperious one may
have produced. There is an inner softness, a thinness
of the mind's skin, an incapability of seeing or even
thinking of the troubles of others with equanimity, which
produces a feeling akin to fear; but which is compatible
not only with courage, but with absolute firmness of
purpose, when the demand for firmness arises so strongly
as to assert itself. With this man it was not really that.
He feared the woman;—or at least such fears did not
prevail upon him to be silent; but he shrank from sub-
jecting her to the blank misery of utter desertion. After
what had passed between them he could hardly bring
himself to tell her that he wanted her no further and to
bid her go. But that was what he had to do. And for
that his answer to her last question prepared the way.
'It was nearly that,' he said.

'Mr. Carbury did take it upon himself to rebuke you
for showing yourself on the sands at Lowestoffe with such
a one as I am?'

'He knew of the letter which I wrote to you.'

'You have canvassed me between you?'

'Of course we have. Is that unnatural? Would you
have had me be silent about you to the oldest and the
best friend I have in the world?'

'No, I would not have had you be silent to your oldest
and best friend. I presume you would declare your
purpose. But I should not have supposed you would
have asked his leave. When I was travelling with you, I
thought you were a man capable of managing your own
actions. I had heard that in your country girls sometimes hold themselves at the disposal of their friends,—
but I did not dream that such could be the case with
a man who had gone out into the world to make his
fortune.'

Paul Montague did not like it. The punishment to be endured was being commenced. 'Of course you can say bitter things,' he replied.

'Is it my nature to say bitter things? Have I usually said bitter things to you? When I have hung round your neck and have sworn that you should be my God upon earth, was that bitter? I am alone and I have to fight my own battles. A woman's weapon is her tongue. Say but one word to me, Paul, as you know how to say it, and there will be soon an end to that bitterness. What shall I care for Mr. Carbury, except to make him the cause of some innocent joke, if you will speak but that one word? And think what it is I am asking. Do you remember how urgent were once your own prayers to me;—how you swore that your happiness could only be secured by one word of mine? Though I loved you, I doubted. There were considerations of money, which have now vanished. But I spoke it,— because I loved you, and because I believed you. Give me that which you swore you had given before I made my gift to you.'

'I cannot say that word.'

'Do you mean that, after all, I am to be thrown off like an old glove? I have had many dealings with men and have found them to be false, cruel, unworthy, and selfish. But I have met nothing like that. No man has ever dared to treat me like that. No man shall dare.'

'I wrote to you.'

'Wrote to me;—yes! And I was to take that as sufficient! No. I think but little of my life and have but little for which to live. But while I do live I will travel over the world's surface to face injustice and to expose it, before I will put up with it. You wrote to me! Heaven and earth;—I can hardly control myself when I hear such impudence!' She clenched her fist upon the knife that lay on the table as she looked at him, and raising it, dropped it again at a further distance. 'Wrote to me! Could any mere letter of your writing break the bond by which we were bound together? Had not the distance between us seemed to have made

you safe would you have dared to write that letter?
The letter must be unwritten. It has already been
contradicted by your conduct to me since I have been in
this country.'

'I am sorry to hear you say that.'

'Am I not justified in saying it?'

'I hope not. When I first saw you I told you everything. If I have been wrong in attending to your wishes
since, I regret it.'

'This comes from your seeing your master for two
minutes on the beach. You are acting now under his
orders. No doubt he came with the purpose. Had you
told him you were to be here?'

'His coming was an accident.'

'It was very opportune at any rate. Well;—what
have you to say to me? Or am I to understand that you
suppose yourself to have said all that is required of you?
Perhaps you would prefer that I should argue the matter
out with your—friend, Mr. Carbury.'

'What has to be said, I believe I can say myself.'

'Say it then. Or are you so ashamed of it, that the
words stick in your throat?'

'There is some truth in that. I am ashamed of it. I
must say that which will be painful, and which would
not have been to be said, had I been fairly careful.'

Then he paused. 'Don't spare me,' she said. 'I know
what it all is as well as though it were already told. I
know the lies with which they have crammed you at
San Francisco. You have heard that up in Oregon—I
shot a man. That is no lie. I did. I brought him down
dead at my feet.' Then she paused, and rose from her
chair, and looked at him. 'Do you wonder that that is
a story that a woman should hesitate to tell? But not
from shame. Do you suppose that the sight of that
dying wretch does not haunt me? that I do not daily
hear his drunken screech, and see him bound from the
earth, and then fall in a heap just below my hand?
But did they tell you also that it was thus alone that I
could save myself,—and that had I spared him, I must
afterwards have destroyed myself? If I were wrong,

why did they not try me for his murder? Why did the
women flock around me and kiss the very hems of my
garments? In this soft civilization of yours you know
nothing of such necessity. A woman here is protected,—
unless it be from lies.'

'It was not that only,' he whispered.

'No; they told you other things,' she continued, still
standing over him. 'They told you of quarrels with my
husband. I know the lies, and who made them, and
why. Did I conceal from you the character of my
former husband? Did I not tell you that he was a
drunkard and a scoundrel? How should I not quarrel
with such a one? Ah, Paul; you can hardly know what
my life has been.'

'They told me that—you fought him.'

'Psha;—fought him! Yes;—I was always fighting
him. What are you to do but to fight cruelty, and fight
falsehood, and fight fraud and treachery,—when they
come upon you and would overwhelm you but for
fighting? You have not been fool enough to believe that
fable about a duel? I did stand once, armed, and
guarded my bedroom door from him, and told him
that he should only enter it over my body. He went
away to the tavern and I did not see him for a week
afterwards. That was the duel. And they have told you
that he is not dead.'

'Yes;—they have told me that.'

'Who has seen him alive? I never said to you that I
had seen him dead. How should I?'

'There would be a certificate.'

'Certificate;—in the back of Texas;—five hundred
miles from Galveston! And what would it matter to
you? I was divorced from him according to the law of
the State of Kansas. Does not the law make a woman
free here to marry again,—and why not with us? I sued
for a divorce on the score of cruelty and drunkenness.
He made no appearance, and the Court granted it me.
Am I disgraced by that?'

'I heard nothing of the divorce.'

'I do not remember. When we were talking of these

old days before, you did not care how short I was in telling my story. You wanted to hear little or nothing then of Caradoc Hurtle. Now you have become more particular. I told you that he was dead,—as I believed myself, and do believe. Whether the other story was told or not I do not know.'

'It was not told.'

'Then it was your own fault,—because you would not listen. And they have made you believe I suppose that I have failed in getting back my property?'

'I have heard nothing about your property but what you yourself have said unasked. I have asked no question about your property.'

'You are welcome. At last I have made it again my own. And now, sir, what else is there? I think I have been open with you. Is it because I protected myself from drunken violence that I am to be rejected? Am I to be cast aside because I saved my life while in the hands of a reprobate husband, and escaped from him by means provided by law;—or because by my own energy I have secured my own property? If I am not to be condemned for these things, then say why am I condemned.'

She had at any rate saved him the trouble of telling the story, but in doing so had left him without a word to say. She had owned to shooting the man. Well; it certainly may be necessary that a woman should shoot a man—especially in Oregon. As to the duel with her husband,—she had half denied and half confessed it. He presumed that she had been armed with a pistol when she refused Mr. Hurtle admittance into the nuptial chamber. As to the question of Hurtle's death,—she had confessed that perhaps he was not dead. But then,—as she had asked,—why should not a divorce for the purpose in hand be considered as good as a death? He could not say that she had not washed herself clean; —and yet, from the story as told by herself, what man would wish to marry her? She had seen so much of drunkenness, had become so handy with pistols, and had done so much of a man's work, that any ordinary man might well hesitate before he assumed to be her master. 'I do not condemn you,' he replied.

'At any rate, Paul, do not lie,' she answered. 'If you tell me that you will not be my husband, you do condemn me. Is it not so?'

'I will not lie if I can help it. I did ask you to be my wife——'

'Well;—rather. How often before I consented?'

'It matters little; at any rate, till you did consent. I have since satisfied myself that such a marriage would be miserable for both of us.'

'You have.'

'I have. Of course, you can speak of me as you please and think of me as you please. I can hardly defend myself.'

'Hardly, I think.'

'But, with whatever result, I know that I shall now be acting for the best in declaring that I will not become— your husband.'

'You will not?' She was still standing, and stretched out her right hand as though again to grasp something.

He also now rose from his chair. 'If I speak with abruptness it is only to avoid a show of indecision. I will not.'

'Oh, God! what have I done that it should be my lot to meet man after man false and cruel as this! You tell me to my face that I am to bear it! Who is the jade that has done it? Has she money?—or rank? Or is it that you are afraid to have by your side a woman who can speak for herself,—and even act for herself if some action be necessary? Perhaps you think that I am— old.' He was looking at her intently as she spoke, and it did seem to him that many years had been added to her face. It was full of lines round the mouth, and the light play of drollery was gone, and the colour was fixed,—and her eyes seemed to be deep in her head. 'Speak, man,—is it that you want a younger wife?'

'You know it is not.'

'Know! How should any one know anything from a liar? From what you tell me I know nothing. I have to gather what I can from your character. I see that you are a coward. It is that man that came to you, and who is your master, that has forced you to this. Between me and him you tremble, and are a thing to be pitied. As for knowing what you would be at, from anything that you would say,—that is impossible. Once again I have come across a mean wretch. Oh, fool!—that men should be so vile, and think themselves masters of the world! My last word to you is, that you are—a liar. Now for the present you can go. Ten minutes since, had I had a weapon in my hand I should have shot another man.'

Paul Montague, as he looked round the room for his hat, could not but think that perhaps Mr. Hurtle might have had some excuse. It seemed at any rate to be her custom to have a pistol with her,—though luckily, for his comfort, she had left it in her bedroom on the present occasion. 'I will say good-bye to you,' he said, when he had found his hat.

'Say no such thing. Tell me that you have triumphed and got rid of me. Pluck up your spirits, if you have any, and show me your joy. Tell me that an Englishman has dared to ill-treat an American woman. You would, —were you not afraid to indulge yourself.' He was now standing in the doorway, and before he escaped she gave him an imperative command. 'I shall not stay here now,' she said—'I shall return on Monday. I must think of what you have said, and must resolve what I myself will do. I shall not bear this without seeking a means of punishing you for your treachery. I shall expect you to come to me on Monday.'

He closed the door as he answered her. 'I do not see that it will serve any purpose.'

'It is for me, sir, to judge of that. I suppose you are not so much a coward that you are afraid to come to me. If so, I shall come to you; and you may be assured that I shall not be too timid to show myself and to tell my story.' He ended by saying that if she desired it he would wait upon her, but that he would not at present fix a day. On his return to town he would write to her.

When he was gone she went to the door and listened awhile. Then she closed it, and turning the lock, stood with her back against the door and with her hands clasped. After a few moments she ran forward, and falling on her knees, buried her face in her hands upon the table. Then she gave way to a flood of tears, and at last lay rolling upon the floor.

Was this to be the end of it? Should she never know rest;—never have one draught of cool water between her lips? Was there to be no end to the storms and turmoils and misery of her life? In almost all that she had said she had spoken the truth, though doubtless not all the truth,—as which among us would in giving the story of his life? She had endured violence, and had been violent. She had been schemed against, and had schemed. She had fitted herself to the life which had befallen her. But in regard to money, she had been honest and she had been loving of heart. With her heart of hearts she had loved this young Englishman;— and now, after all her scheming, all her daring, with all her charms, this was to be the end of it! Oh, what a journey would this be which she must now make back to her own country, all alone!

But the strongest feeling which raged within her bosom was that of disappointed love. Full as had been the vials of wrath which she had poured forth over Montague's head, violent as had been the storm of abuse with which she had assailed him, there had been after all something counterfeited in her indignation. But her love was no counterfeit. At any moment if he would have returned to her and taken her in his arms, she would not only have forgiven him but have blessed him also for his kindness. She was in truth sick at heart of violence and rough living and unfeminine words. When driven by wrongs the old habit came back upon her. But if she could only escape the wrongs, if she could find some niche in the world which would be bearable to her, in which, free from harsh treatment, she could pour forth all the genuine kindness of her woman's nature,—then, she thought she could put away violence and be gentle as a young girl. When she first met this Englishman and found that he took delight in being near her, she had ventured to hope that a haven would at last be open to her. But the reek of the gunpowder from that first pistol shot still clung to her, and she now told herself again, as she had often told herself before, that it would have been better for her to have turned the muzzle against her own bosom.

After receiving his letter she had run over on what she had told herself was a vain chance. Though angry enough when that letter first reached her, she had, with that force of character which marked her, declared to herself that such a resolution on his part was natural. In marrying her he must give up all his old allies, all his old haunts. The whole world must be changed to him. She knew enough of herself, and enough of Englishwomen, to be sure that when her past life should be known, as it would be known, she would be avoided in England. With all the little ridicule she was wont to exercise in speaking of the old country there was ever mixed, as is so often the case in the minds of American men and women, an almost envious admiration of English excellence. To have been allowed to forget the past and to live the life of an English lady would have been heaven to her. But she, who was sometimes scorned and sometimes feared in the eastern cities of her own country, whose name had become almost a proverb for violence out in the far West,—how could she dare to hope that her lot should be so changed for her?

She had reminded Paul that she had required to be asked often before she had consented to be his wife; but she did not tell him that that hesitation had arisen from her own conviction of her own unfitness. But it had been so. Circumstances had made her what she was. Circumstances had been cruel to her. But she could not now alter them. Then gradually, as she came to believe in his love, as she lost herself in love for him, she told herself that she would be changed. She had, however, almost known that it could not be so. But this man had relatives, had business, had property in her own country.

Though she could not be made happy in England,
might not a prosperous life be opened for him in the
far West? Then had risen the offer of that journey to
Mexico with much probability that work of no ordinary
kind might detain him there for years. With what joy
would she have accompanied him as his wife! For that
at any rate she would have been fit.

She was conscious, perhaps too conscious, of her own
beauty. That at any rate, she felt, had not deserted her.
She was hardly aware that time was touching it. And
she knew herself to be clever, capable of causing happiness, and mirth and comfort. She had the qualities of a
good comrade—which are so much in a woman. She
knew all this of herself. If he and she could be together
in some country in which those stories of her past life
would be matter of indifference, could she not make him
happy? But what was she that a man should give up
everything and go away and spend his days in some
half-barbarous country for her alone? She knew it all
and was hardly angry with him in that he had decided
against her. But treated as she had been she must play
her game with such weapons as she possessed. It was
consonant with her old character, it was consonant with
her present plans that she should at any rate seem to
be angry.

Sitting there alone late into the night she made many
plans, but the plan that seemed best to suit the present
frame of her mind was the writing of a letter to Paul
bidding him adieu, sending him her fondest love, and
telling him that he was right. She did write the letter,
but wrote it with a conviction that she would not have
the strength to send it to him. The reader may judge
with what feeling she wrote the following words:—

'DEAR PAUL,—
       'You are right and I am wrong. Our marriage
would not have been fitting. I do not blame you. I
attracted you when we were together; but you have
learned and have learned truly that you should not give
up your life for such attractions. If I have been violent

with you, forgive me. You will acknowledge that I have suffered.

'Always know that there is one woman who will love you better than any one else. I think too that you will love me even when some other woman is by your side. God bless you, and make you happy. Write me the shortest, shortest word of adieu. Not to do so would make you think yourself heartless. But do not come to me.

'For ever,       W. H.'

This she wrote on a small slip of paper, and then having read it twice, she put it into her pocket-book. She told herself that she ought to send it; but told herself as plainly that she could not bring herself to do so. It was early in the morning before she went to bed but she had admitted no one into the room after Montague had left her.

Paul, when he escaped from her presence, roamed out on to the sea-shore, and then took himself to bed, having ordered a conveyance to take him to Carbury Manor early in the morning. At breakfast he presented himself to the squire. 'I have come earlier than you expected,' he said.

'Yes, indeed;—much earlier. Are you going back to Lowestoffe?'

Then he told the whole story. Roger expressed his satisfaction, recalling however the pledge which he had given as to his return. 'Let her follow you, and bear it,' he said. 'Of course you must suffer the effects of your own imprudence.' On that evening Paul Montague returned to London by the mail train, being sure that he would thus avoid a meeting with Mrs. Hurtle in the railway-carriage.

## Chapter XLVIII

### RUBY A PRISONER

RUBY had run away from her lover in great dudgeon after the dance at the Music Hall, and had declared that she never wanted to see him again. But when reflection came with the morning her misery was stronger than her wrath. What would life be to her now without her lover? When she escaped from her grandfather's house she certainly had not intended to become nurse and assistant maid-of-all-work at a London lodging-house. The daily toil she could endure, and the hard life, as long as she was supported by the prospect of some coming delight. A dance with Felix at the Music Hall, though it were three days distant from her, would so occupy her mind that she could wash and dress all the children without complaint. Mrs. Pipkin was forced to own to herself that Ruby did earn her bread. But when she had parted with her lover almost on an understanding that they were never to meet again, things were very different with her. And perhaps she had been wrong. A gentleman like Sir Felix did not of course like to be told about marriage. If she gave him another chance, perhaps he would speak. At any rate she could not live without another dance. And so she wrote him a letter.

Ruby was glib enough with her pen, though what she wrote will hardly bear repeating. She underscored all her loves to him. She underscored the expression of her regret if she had vexed him. She did not want to hurry a gentleman. But she did want to have another dance at the Music Hall. Would he be there next Saturday? Sir Felix sent her a very short reply to say that he would be at the Music Hall on the Tuesday. As at this time he proposed to leave London on the Wednesday on his way to New York, he was proposing to devote his very last night to the companionship of Ruby Ruggles.

Mrs. Pipkin had never interfered with her niece's

letters. It is certainly a part of the new dispensation that
young women shall send and receive letters without
inspection. But since Roger Carbury's visit Mrs. Pipkin
had watched the postman, and had also watched her
niece. For nearly a week Ruby said not a word of going
out at night. She took the children for an airing in a
broken perambulator, nearly as far as Holloway, with
exemplary care, and washed up the cups and saucers as
though her mind was intent upon them. But Mrs.
Pipkin's mind was intent on obeying Mr. Carbury's
behests. She had already hinted something as to which
Ruby had made no answer. It was her purpose to tell
her and to swear to her most solemnly,—should she
find her preparing herself to leave the house after six in
the evening,—that she should be kept out the whole
night, having a purpose equally clear in her own mind
that she would break her oath should she be unsuccessful
in her effort to keep Ruby at home. But on the Tuesday,
when Ruby went up to her room to deck herself, a
bright idea as to a better precaution struck Mrs. Pipkin's
mind. Ruby had been careless,—had left her lover's
scrap of a note in an old pocket when she went out with
the children, and Mrs. Pipkin knew all about it. It was
nine o'clock when Ruby went upstairs,—and then Mrs.
Pipkin locked both the front door and the area gate.
Mrs. Hurtle had come home on the previous day.
'You won't be wanting to go out to-night;—will you,
Mrs. Hurtle?' said Mrs. Pipkin, knocking at her lodger's
door. Mrs. Hurtle declared her purpose of remaining at
home all the evening. 'If you should hear words between
me and my niece, don't you mind, ma'am.'

'I hope there's nothing wrong, Mrs. Pipkin?'

'She'll be wanting to go out, and I won't have it. It
isn't right; is it, ma'am? She's a good girl; but they've
got such a way nowadays of doing just as they pleases,
that one doesn't know what's going to come next.'
Mrs. Pipkin must have feared downright rebellion when
she thus took her lodger into her confidence.

Ruby came down in her silk frock, as she had done
before, and made her usual little speech. 'I'm just going

to step out, aunt, for a little time to-night. I've got the key, and I'll let myself in quite quiet.'

'Indeed, Ruby, you won't,' said Mrs. Pipkin.

'Won't what, aunt?'

'Won't let yourself in, if you go out. If you go out to-night you'll stay out. That's all about it. If you go out to-night you won't come back here any more. I won't have it, and it isn't right that I should. You're going after that young man that they tell me is the greatest scamp in all England.'

'They tell you lies then, Aunt Pipkin.'

'Very well. No girl is going out any more at nights out of my house; so that's all about it. If you had told me you was going before, you needn't have gone up and bedizened yourself. For now it's all to take off again.'

Ruby could hardly believe it. She had expected some opposition,—what she would have called a few words; but she had never imagined that her aunt would threaten to keep her in the streets all night. It seemed to her that she had bought the privilege of amusing herself by hard work. Nor did she believe now that her aunt would be as hard as her threat. 'I've a right to go if I like,' she said.

'That's as you think. You haven't a right to come back again, any way.'

'Yes, I have. I've worked for you a deal harder than the girl downstairs, and I don't want no wages. I've a right to go out, and a right to come back;—and go I shall.'

'You'll be no better than you should be, if you do.'

'Am I to work my very nails off, and push that perambulator about all day till my legs won't carry me,—and then I ain't to go out, not once in a week?'

'Not unless I know more about it, Ruby. I won't have you go and throw yourself into the gutter;—not while you're with me.'

'Who's throwing themselves into the gutter? I've thrown myself into no gutter. I know what I'm about.'

'There's two of us that way, Ruby;—for I know what I'm about.'

'I shall just go then.' And Ruby walked off towards the door.

'You won't get out that way, any way, for the door's locked;—and the area gate. You'd better be said, Ruby, and just take your things off.'

Poor Ruby for the moment was struck dumb with mortification. Mrs. Pipkin had given her credit for more outrageous perseverance than she possessed, and had feared that she would rattle at the front door, or attempt to climb over the area gate. She was a little afraid of Ruby, not feeling herself justified in holding absolute dominion over her as over a servant. And though she was now determined in her conduct,—being fully resolved to surrender neither of the keys which she held in her pocket,—still she feared that she might so far collapse as to fall away into tears, should Ruby be violent. But Ruby was crushed. Her lover would be there to meet her, and the appointment would be broken by her! 'Aunt Pipkin,' she said, 'let me go just this once.'

'No, Ruby;—it ain't proper.'

'You don't know what you're a doing of, aunt; you don't. You'll ruin me,—you will. Dear Aunt Pipkin, do, do! I'll never ask again, if you don't like.'

Mrs. Pipkin had not expected this, and was almost willing to yield. But Mr. Carbury had spoken so very plainly! 'It ain't the thing, Ruby; and I won't do it.'

'And I'm to be——a prisoner! What have I done to be——a prisoner? I don't believe as you've any right to lock me up.'

'I've a right to lock my own doors.'

'Then I shall go away to-morrow.'

'I can't help that, my dear. The door will be open to-morrow, if you choose to go out.'

'Then why not open it to-night? Where's the difference?' But Mrs. Pipkin was stern, and Ruby, in a flood of tears, took herself up to her garret.

Mrs. Pipkin knocked at Mrs. Hurtle's door again. 'She's gone to bed,' she said.

'I'm glad to hear it. There wasn't any noise about it;—was there?'

'Not as I expected, Mrs. Hurtle, certainly. But she was put out a bit. Poor girl! I've been a girl too, and used to like a bit of outing as well as any one,—and a dance too; only it was always when mother knew. She ain't got a mother, poor dear! and as good as no father. And she's got it into her head that she's that pretty that a great gentleman will marry her.'

'She is pretty!'

'But what's beauty, Mrs. Hurtle? It's no more nor skin deep, as the scriptures tell us. And what'd a grand gentleman see in Ruby to marry her? She says she'll leave to-morrow.'

'And where will she go?'

'Just nowhere. After this gentleman,—and you know what that means! You're going to be married yourself, Mrs. Hurtle.'

'We won't mind about that now, Mrs. Pipkin.'

'And this'll be your second, and you know how these things are managed. No gentleman'll marry her because she runs after him. Girls as knows what they're about should let the gentlemen run after them. That's my way of looking at it.'

'Don't you think they should be equal in that respect?'

'Anyways the girls shouldn't let on as they are running after the gentlemen. A gentlemen goes here and he goes there, and he speaks up free, of course. In my time, girls usen't to do that. But then, maybe, I'm old-fashioned,' added Mrs. Pipkin, thinking of the new dispensation.

'I suppose girls do speak for themselves more than they did formerly.'

'A deal more, Mrs. Hurtle; quite different. You hear them talk of spooning with this fellow, and spooning with that fellow,—and that before their very fathers and mothers! When I was young we used to do it, I suppose,—only not like that.'

'You did it on the sly.'

'I think we got married quicker than they do, any

way. When the gentlemen had to take more trouble they thought more about it. But if you wouldn't mind speaking to Ruby to-morrow, Mrs. Hurtle, she'd listen to you when she wouldn't mind a word I said to her. I don't want her to go away from this, out into the street, till she knows where she's to go to, decent. As for going to her young man,—that's just walking the streets.'

Mrs. Hurtle promised that she would speak to Ruby, though when making the promise she could not but think of her unfitness for the task. She knew nothing of the country. She had not a single friend in it, but Paul Montague;—and she had run after him with as little discretion as Ruby Ruggles was showing in running after her lover. Who was she that she should take upon herself to give advice to any female?

She had not sent her letter to Paul, but she still kept it in her pocket-book. At some moments she thought that she would send it; and at others she told herself that she would never surrender this last hope till every stone had been turned. It might still be possible to shame him into a marriage. She had returned from Lowestoffe on the Monday, and had made some trivial excuse to Mrs. Pipkin in her mildest voice. The place had been windy, and too cold for her;—and she had not liked the hotel. Mrs. Pipkin was very glad to see her back again.

## Chapter XLIX

### SIR FELIX MAKES HIMSELF READY

SIR FELIX, when he promised to meet Ruby at the Music Hall on the Tuesday, was under an engagement to start with Marie Melmotte for New York on the Thursday following, and to go down to Liverpool on the Wednesday. There was no reason, he thought, why he should not enjoy himself to the last, and he would say a parting word to poor little Ruby. The details of his

journey were settled between him and Marie, with no
inconsiderable assistance from Didon, in the garden of
Grosvenor Square, on the previous Sunday,—where the
lovers had again met during the hours of morning
service. Sir Felix had been astonished at the completion
of the preparations which had been made. 'Mind you
go by the 5 p.m. train,' Marie said. 'That will take you
into Liverpool at 10.15. There's an hotel at the railway-
station. Didon has got our tickets under the names of
Madame and Mademoiselle Racine. We are to have one
cabin between us. You must get yours to-morrow. She
has found out that there is plenty of room.'

'I'll be all right.'

'Pray don't miss the train that afternoon. Somebody
would be sure to suspect something if we were seen
together in the same train. We leave at 7 a.m. I shan't
go to bed all night, so as to be sure to be in time.
Robert,—he's the man,—will start a little earlier in the
cab with my heavy box. What do you think is in it?'

'Clothes,' suggested Felix.

'Yes, but what clothes?—my wedding dresses. Think
of that! What a job to get them and nobody to know
anything about it except Didon and Madame Craik at
the shop in Mount Street! They haven't come yet, but
I shall be there whether they come or not. And I shall
have all my jewels. I'm not going to leave them behind.
They'll go off in our cab. We can get the things out
behind the house into the mews. Then Didon and I
follow in another cab. Nobody ever is up before near
nine, and I don't think we shall be interrupted.'

'If the servants were to hear.'

'I don't think they'd tell. But if I was to be brought
back again, I should only tell papa that it was no good.
He can't prevent me marrying.'

'Won't your mother find out?'

'She never looks after anything. I don't think she'd
tell if she knew. Papa leads her such a life! Felix! I
hope you won't be like that.'—And she looked up into
his face, and thought that it would be impossible that he
should be.

'I'm all right,' said Felix, feeling very uncomfortable at the time. This great effort of his life was drawing very near. There had been a pleasurable excitement in talking of running away with the great heiress of the day, but now that the deed had to be executed,—and executed after so novel and stupendous a fashion, he almost wished that he had not undertaken it. It must have been much nicer when men ran away with their heiresses only as far as Gretna Green. And even Goldsheiner with Lady Julia had nothing of a job in comparison with this which he was expected to perform. And then if they should be wrong about the girl's fortune! He almost repented. He did repent, but he had not the courage to recede. 'How about money though?' he said hoarsely.

'You have got some?'

'I have just the two hundred pounds which your father paid me, and not a shilling more. I don't see why he should keep my money, and not let me have it back.'

'Look here,' said Marie, and she put her hand into her pocket. 'I told you I thought I could get some. There is a cheque for two hundred and fifty pounds. I had money of my own enough for the tickets.'

'And whose is this?' said Felix, taking the bit of paper with much trepidation.

'It is papa's cheque. Mamma gets ever so many of them to carry on the house and pay for things. But she gets so muddled about it that she doesn't know what she pays and what she doesn't.' Felix looked at the cheque and saw that it was payable to House or Bearer, and that it was signed by Augustus Melmotte. 'If you take it to the bank you'll get the money,' said Marie. 'Or shall I send Didon, and give you the money on board the ship?'

Felix thought over the matter very anxiously. If he did go on the journey he would much prefer to have the money in his own pocket. He liked the feeling of having money in his pocket. Perhaps if Didon were entrusted with the cheque she also would like the feeling. But then might it not be possible that if he presented the cheque himself he might be arrested for stealing Melmotte's money? 'I think Didon had better get the money,' he said, 'and bring it to me to-morrow, at four o'clock in the afternoon, to the club.' If the money did not come he would not go down to Liverpool, nor would he be at the expense of his ticket for New York. 'You see,' he said, 'I'm so much in the City that they might know me at the bank.' To this arrangement Marie assented and took back the cheque. 'And then I'll come on board on Thursday morning,' he said, 'without looking for you.'

'Oh dear, yes;—without looking for us. And don't know us even till we are out at sea. Won't it be fun when we shall be walking about on the deck and not speaking to one another! And, Felix;—what do you think? Didon has found out that there is to be an American clergyman on board. I wonder whether he'd marry us.'

'Of course he will.'

'Won't that be jolly? I wish it was all done. Then, directly it's done, and when we get to New York, we'll telegraph and write to papa, and we'll be ever so penitent and good; won't we? Of course he'll make the best of it.'

'But he's so savage; isn't he?'

'When there's anything to get;—or just at the moment. But I don't think he minds afterwards. He's always for making the best of everything;—misfortunes and all. Things go wrong so often that if he was to go on thinking of them always they'd be too many for anybody. It'll be all right in a month's time. I wonder how Lord Nidderdale will look when he hears that we've gone off. I should so like to see him. He never can say that I've behaved bad to him. We were engaged, but it was he broke it. Do you know, Felix, that though we were engaged to be married, and everybody knew it, he never once kissed me!' Felix at this moment almost wished that he had never done so. As to what the other man had done, he cared nothing at all.

Then they parted with the understanding that they were not to see each other again till they met on board the boat. All arrangements were made. But Felix was determined that he would not stir in the matter unless Didon brought him the full sum of £250; and he almost thought, and indeed hoped, that she would not. Either she would be suspected at the bank and apprehended, or she would run off with the money on her own account when she got it;—or the cheque would have been missed and the payment stopped. Some accident would occur, and then he would be able to recede from his undertaking. He would do nothing till after Monday afternoon.

Should he tell his mother that he was going? His mother had clearly recommended him to run away with the girl, and must therefore approve of the measure. His mother would understand how great would be the expense of such a trip, and might perhaps add something to his stock of money. He determined that he could tell his mother;—that is, if Didon should bring him full change for the cheque.

He walked into the Beargarden exactly at four o'clock on the Monday, and there he found Didon standing in the hall. His heart sank within him as he saw her. Now must he certainly go to New York. She made him a little curtsey, and without a word handed him an envelope, soft and fat with rich enclosures. He bade her wait a moment, and going into a little waiting-room counted the notes. The money was all there;—the full sum of £250. He must certainly go to New York. 'C'est tout en règle?' said Didon in a whisper as he returned to the hall. Sir Felix nodded his head, and Didon took her departure.

Yes; he must go now. He had Melmotte's money in his pocket, and was therefore bound to run away with Melmotte's daughter. It was a great trouble to him as he reflected that Melmotte had more of his money than he had of Melmotte's. And now how should he dispose of his time before he went? Gambling was too dangerous. Even he felt that. Where would he be were he to lose his ready money? He would dine that night at the club, and

in the evening go up to his mother. On the Tuesday he
would take his place for New York in the City, and
would spend the evening with Ruby at the Music
Hall. On the Wednesday, he would start for Liverpool,
—according to his instructions. He felt annoyed that he
had been so fully instructed. But should the affair turn
out well nobody would know that. All the fellows would
give him credit for the audacity with which he had
carried off the heiress to America.

At ten o'clock he found his mother and Hetta in
Welbeck Street—'What; Felix?' exclaimed Lady Carbury.

'You're surprised; are you not?' Then he threw
himself into a chair. 'Mother,' he said, 'would you
mind coming into the other room?' Lady Carbury of
course went with him. 'I've got something to tell you,'
he said.

'Good news?' she asked, clasping her hands together.
From his manner she thought that it was good news.
Money had in some way come into his hands,—or at any
rate a prospect of money.

'That's as may be,' he said, and then he paused.

'Don't keep me in suspense, Felix.'

'The long and the short of it is that I'm going to take
Marie off.'

'Oh, Felix.'

'You said you thought it was the right thing to do;—
and therefore I'm going to do it. The worst of it is that
one wants such a lot of money for this kind of thing.'

'But when?'

'Immediately. I wouldn't tell you till I had arranged
everything. I've had it in my mind for the last fortnight.'

'And how is it to be? Oh, Felix, I hope it may
succeed.'

'It was your own idea, you know. We're going to;—
where do you think?'

'How can I think?—Boulogne.'

'You say that just because Goldsheiner went there.
That wouldn't have done at all for us. We're going to—
New York.'

'To New York! But when will you be married?'

'There will be a clergyman on board. It's all fixed. I wouldn't go without telling you.'

'Oh; I wish you hadn't told me.'

'Come now;—that's kind. You don't mean to say it wasn't you that put me up to it. I've got to get my things ready.'

'Of course, if you tell me that you are going on a journey, I will have your clothes got ready for you. When do you start?'

'Wednesday afternoon.'

'For New York! We must get some things ready-made. Oh, Felix, how will it be if he does not forgive her?' He attempted to laugh. 'When I spoke of such a thing as possible he had not sworn then that he would never give her a shilling.'

'They always say that.'

'You are going to risk it?'

'I am going to take your advice.' This was dreadful to the poor mother. 'There is money settled on her.'

'Settled on whom?'

'On Marie;—money which he can't get back again.'

'How much?'

'She doesn't know;—but a great deal; enough for them all to live upon if things went amiss with them.'

'But that's only a form, Felix. That money can't be her own, to give to her husband.'

'Melmotte will find that it is, unless he comes to terms. That's the pull we've got over him. Marie knows what she's about. She's a great deal sharper than any one would take her to be. What can you do for me about money, mother?'

'I have none, Felix.'

'I thought you'd be sure to help me, as you wanted me so much to do it.'

'That's not true, Felix. I didn't want you to do it. Oh, I am so sorry that that word ever passed my mouth! I have no money. There isn't £20 at the bank altogether.'

'They would let you overdraw for £50 or £60.'

'I will not do it. I will not starve myself and Hetta

You had ever so much money only lately. I will get some things for you, and pay for them as I can if you cannot pay for them after your marriage;—but I have not money to give you.'

'That's a blue look-out,' said he, turning himself in his chair,—'just when £60 or £70 might make a fellow for life! You could borrow it from your friend Broune.'

'I will do no such thing, Felix. £50 or £60 would make very little difference in the expense of such a trip as this. I suppose you have some money?'

'Some;—yes, some. But I'm so short that any little thing would help me.' Before the evening was over she absolutely did give him a cheque for £30, although she had spoken the truth in saying that she had not so much at her banker's.

After this he went back to his club, although he himself understood the danger. He could not bear the idea of going to bed quietly at home at half-past ten. He got into a cab, and was very soon up in the card-room. He found nobody there, and went to the smoking-room, where Dolly, Longestaffe and Miles Grendall were sitting silently together, with pipes in their mouths. 'Here's Carbury,' said Dolly, waking suddenly into life. 'Now we can have a game at three-handed loo.'

'Thank ye; not for me,' said Sir Felix. 'I hate three-handed loo.'

'Dummy,' suggested Dolly.

'I don't think I'll play to-night, old fellow. I hate three fellows sticking down together.' Miles sat silent, smoking his pipe, conscious of the baronet's dislike to play with him. 'By-the-by, Grendall,—look here.' And Sir Felix in his most friendly tone whispered into his enemy's ear a petition that some of the I O U's might be converted into cash.

''Pon my word, I must ask you to wait till next week,' said Miles.

'It's always waiting till next week with you,' said Sir Felix, getting up and standing with his back to the fireplace. There were other men in the room, and this was said so that every one should hear it. 'I wonder whether any fellow would buy these for five shillings in the pound?' And he held up the scraps of paper in his hand. He had been drinking freely before he went up to Welbeck Street, and had taken a glass of brandy on re-entering the club.

'Don't let's have any of that kind of thing down here,' said Dolly. 'If there is to be a row about cards, let it be in the cardroom.'

'Of course,' said Miles. 'I won't say a word about the matter down here. It isn't the proper thing.'

'Come up into the card-room, then,' said Sir Felix, getting up from his chair. 'It seems to me that it makes no difference to you, what room you're in. Come up, now; and Dolly Longestaffe shall come and hear what you say.' But Miles Grendall objected to this arrangement. He was not going up into the card-room that night, as no one was going to play. He would be there to-morrow, and then if Sir Felix Carbury had anything to say, he could say it.

'How I do hate a row!' said Dolly. 'One has to have rows with one's own people, but there ought not to be rows at a club.'

'He likes a row,—Carbury does,' said Miles.

'I should like my money, if I could get it,' said Sir Felix, walking out of the room.

On the next day he went into the City, and changed his mother's cheque. This was done after a little hesitation. The money was given to him, but a gentleman from behind the desks begged him to remind Lady Carbury that she was overdrawing her account. 'Dear, dear;' said Sir Felix, as he pocketed the notes, 'I'm sure she was unaware of it.' Then he paid for his passage from Liverpool to New York under the name of Walter Jones, and felt as he did so that the intrigue was becoming very deep. This was on Tuesday. He dined again at the club, alone, and in the evening went to the Music Hall. There he remained from ten till nearly twelve, very angry at the non-appearance of Ruby Ruggles. As he smoked and drank in solitude, he almost made up his mind that he had intended to tell her of his departure for New York. Of course he would have done no such thing. But now, should she ever complain on that head he would have his answer ready. He had devoted his last night in England to the purpose of telling her, and she had broken her appointment. Everything would now be her fault. Whatever might happen to her she could not blame him.

Having waited till he was sick of the Music Hall,—for a music hall without ladies' society must be somewhat dull,—he went back to his club. He was very cross, as brave as brandy could make him, and well inclined to expose Miles Grendall if he could find an opportunity. Up in the card-room he found all the accustomed men,—with the exception of Miles Grendall. Nidderdale, Grasslough, Dolly, Paul Montague, and one or two others were there. There was, at any rate, comfort in the idea of playing without having to encounter the dead weight of Miles Grendall. Ready money was on the table,—and there was none of the peculiar Beargarden paper flying about. Indeed the men at the Beargarden had become sick of paper, and there had been formed a half-expressed resolution that the play should be somewhat lower, but the payments punctual. The I O U's had been nearly all converted into money,—with the assistance of Herr Vossner,—excepting those of Miles Grendall. The resolution mentioned did not refer back to Grendall's former indebtedness, but was intended to include a clause that he must in future pay ready money. Nidderdale had communicated to him the determination of the committee. 'Bygones are bygones, old fellow; but you really must stump up, you know, after this.' Miles had declared that he would 'stump up.' But on this occasion Miles was absent.

At three o'clock in the morning, Sir Felix had lost over a hundred pounds in ready money. On the following night about one he had lost a further sum of two hundred pounds. The reader will remember that he should at that time have been in the hotel at Liverpool.

But Sir Felix, as he played on in the almost desperate

hope of recovering the money which he so greatly needed, remembered how Fisker had played all night, and how he had gone off from the club to catch the early train for Liverpool, and how he had gone on to New York without delay.

## Chapter L

### THE JOURNEY TO LIVERPOOL

MARIE MELMOTTE, as she had promised, sat up all night, as did also the faithful Didon. I think that to Marie the night was full of pleasure,—or at any rate of pleasurable excitement. With her door locked, she packed and unpacked and repacked her treasures,— having more than once laid out on the bed the dress in which she purposed to be married. She asked Didon her opinion whether that American clergyman of whom they had heard would marry them on board, and whether in that event the dress would be fit for the occasion. Didon thought that the man, if sufficiently paid, would marry them, and that the dress would not much signify. She scolded her young mistress very often during the night for what she called nonsense; but was true to her, and worked hard for her. They determined to go without food in the morning, so that no suspicion should be raised by the use of cups and plates. They could get refreshment at the railway-station.

At six they started. Robert went first with the big boxes, having his ten pounds already in his pocket,— and Marie and Didon with smaller luggage followed in a second cab. No one interfered with them and nothing went wrong. The very civil man at Euston Square gave them their tickets, and even attempted to speak to them in French. They had quite determined that not a word of English was to be spoken by Marie till the ship was out at sea. At the station they got some very bad tea and almost uneatable food,—but Marie's restrained excitement was so great that food was almost unnecessary to her. They took their seats without any impediment,—and then they were off.

During a great part of the journey they were alone, and then Marie gabbled to Didon about her hopes and her future career, and all the things she would do;—how she had hated Lord Nidderdale;—especially when, after she had been awed into accepting him, he had given her no token of love;—'pas un baiser!' Didon suggested that such was the way with English lords. She herself had preferred Lord Nidderdale, but had been willing to join in the present plan,—as she said, from devoted affection to Marie. Marie went on to say that Nidderdale was ugly, and that Sir Felix was as beautiful as the morning. 'Bah!' exclaimed Didon, who was really disgusted that such considerations should prevail. Didon had learned in some indistinct way that Lord Nidderdale would be a marquis and would have a castle, whereas Sir Felix would never be more than Sir Felix, and, of his own, would never have anything at all. She had striven with her mistress, but her mistress liked to have a will of her own. Didon no doubt had thought that New York, with £50 and other perquisites in hand, might offer her a new career. She had therefore yielded, but even now could hardly forbear from expressing disgust at the folly of her mistress. Marie bore it with imperturbable good humour. She was running away,—and was running to a distant continent,—and her lover would be with her! She gave Didon to understand that she cared nothing for marquises.

As they drew near to Liverpool Didon explained that they must still be very careful. It would not do for them to declare at once their destination on the platform,—so that every one about the station should know that they were going on board the packet for New York. They had time enough. They must leisurely look for the big boxes and other things, and need say nothing about the steam packet till they were in a cab. Marie's big box was directed simply 'Madame Racine, Passenger to Liverpool;'—so also was directed a second box, nearly as big, which was Didon's property. Didon declared that her anxiety would not be over till she found the ship moving under her. Marie was sure that all their dangers were over,—if only Sir Felix was safe on board. Poor Marie! Sir Felix was at this moment in Welbeck Street, striving to find temporary oblivion for his distressing situation and loss of money, and some alleviation for his racking temples, beneath the bedclothes.

When the train ran into the station at Liverpool the two women sat for a few moments quite quiet. They would not seek remark by any hurry or noise. The door was opened, and a well-mannered porter offered to take their luggage. Didon handed out the various packages, keeping however the jewel-case in her own hands. She left the carriage first, and then Marie. But Marie had hardly put her foot on the platform, before a gentleman addressed her, touching his hat, 'You, I think, are Miss Melmotte.' Marie was struck dumb, but said nothing. Didon immediately became voluble in French. No; the young lady was not Miss Melmotte; the young lady was Mademoiselle Racine, her niece. She was Madame Racine. Melmotte! What was Melmotte? They knew nothing about Melmottes. Would the gentleman kindly allow them to pass on to their cab?

But the gentleman would by no means kindly allow them to pass on to their cab. With the gentleman was another gentleman,—who did not seem to be quite so much of a gentleman;—and again, not far in the distance Didon quickly espied a policeman, who did not at present connect himself with the affair, but who seemed to have his time very much at command, and to be quite ready if he were wanted. Didon at once gave up the game,—as regarded her mistress.

'I am afraid I must persist in asserting that you are Miss Melmotte,' said the gentleman, 'and that this other—person is your servant, Elise Didon. You speak English, Miss Melmotte.' Marie declared that she spoke French. 'And English too,' said the gentleman. 'I think you had better make up your minds to go back to London. I will accompany you.'

'Ah, Didon, nous sommes perdues!' exclaimed Marie. Didon, plucking up her courage for the moment, asserted the legality of her own position and of that of her mistress. They had both a right to come to Liverpool. They had both a right to get into the cab with their luggage. Nobody had a right to stop them. They had done nothing against the laws. Why were they to be stopped in this way? What was it to anybody whether they called themselves Melmotte or Racine?

The gentleman understood the French oratory, but did not commit himself to reply in the same language. 'You had better trust yourself to me; you had indeed,' said the gentleman.

'But why?' demanded Marie.

Then the gentleman spoke in a very low voice. 'A cheque has been changed which you took from your father's house. No doubt your father will pardon that when you are once with him. But in order that we may bring you back safely we can arrest you on the score of the cheque,—if you force us to do so. We certainly shall not let you go on board. If you will travel back to London with me, you shall be subjected to no inconvenience which can be avoided.'

There was certainly no help to be found anywhere. It may be well doubted whether upon the whole the telegraph has not added more to the annoyances than to the comforts of life, and whether the gentlemen who spent all the public money without authority ought not to have been punished with special severity in that they had injured humanity, rather than pardoned because of the good they had produced. Who is benefited by telegrams? The newspapers are robbed of all their old interest, and the very soul of intrigue is destroyed. Poor Marie, when she heard her fate, would certainly have gladly hanged Mr. Scudamore.*

When the gentleman had made his speech, she offered no further opposition. Looking into Didon's face and bursting into tears, she sat down on one of the boxes.

But Didon became very clamorous on her own behalf,—and her clamour was successful. 'Who was going to stop her? What had she done? Why should not she go where she pleased? Did anybody mean to take her up for stealing anybody's money? If anybody did, that person had better look to himself. She knew the law. She would go where she pleased.' So saying she began to tug the rope of her box as though she intended to drag it by her own force out of the station. The gentleman looked at his telegram,—looked at another document which he now held in his hand, ready prepared, should it be wanted. Elise Didon had been accused of nothing that brought her within the law. The gentleman in imperfect French suggested that Didon had better return with her mistress. But Didon clamoured only the more. No; she would go to New York. She would go wherever she pleased,—all the world over. Nobody should stop her. Then she addressed herself in what little English she could command to half-a-dozen cab-men who were standing round and enjoying the scene. They were to take her trunk at once. She had money and she could pay. She started off to the nearest cab, and no one stopped her. 'But the box in her hand is mine,' said Marie, not forgetting her trinkets in her misery. Didon surrendered the jewel-case, and ensconced herself in the cab without a word of farewell; and her trunk was hoisted on to the roof. Then she was driven away out of the station,—and out of our story. She had a first-class cabin all to herself as far as New York, but what may have been her fate after that it matters not to us to enquire.

Poor Marie! We who know how recreant a knight Sir Felix had proved himself, who are aware that had Miss Melmotte succeeded in getting on board the ship she would have passed an hour of miserable suspense, looking everywhere for her lover, and would then at last have been carried to New York without him, may congratulate her on her escape. And, indeed, we who know his character better than she did, may still hope in her behalf that she may be ultimately saved from so wretched a marriage. But to her her present position was truly miserable. She would have to encounter an enraged father; and when,—when should she see her lover again? Poor, poor Felix! What would be his feelings when he should find himself on his way to New York without his love! But in one matter she made up her mind steadfastly. She would be true to him! They might chop her in pieces! Yes;—she had said it before, and she would say it again. There was, however, doubt in her mind from time to time, whether one course might not be better even than constancy. If she could contrive to throw herself out of the carriage and to be killed,—would not that be the best termination to her present disappointment? Would not that be the best punishment for her father? But how then would it be with poor Felix? 'After all I don't know that he cares for me,' she said to herself, thinking over it all.

The gentleman was very kind to her, not treating her at all as though she were disgraced. As they got near town he ventured to give her a little advice. 'Put a good face on it,' he said, 'and don't be cast down.'

'Oh, I won't,' she answered. 'I don't mean.'

'Your mother will be delighted to have you back again.'

'I don't think that mamma cares. It's papa. I'd do it again to-morrow if I had the chance.' The gentleman looked at her, not having expected so much determination. 'I would. Why is a girl to be made to marry to please any one but herself? I won't. And it's very mean saying that I stole the money. I always take what I want, and papa never says anything about it.'

'Two hundred and fifty pounds is a large sum, Miss Melmotte.'

'It is nothing in our house. It isn't about the money. It's because papa wants me to marry another man;—and I won't. It was downright mean to send and have me taken up before all the people.'

'You wouldn't have come back if he hadn't done that.'

'Of course I wouldn't,' said Marie.

The gentleman had telegraphed up to Grosvenor Square while on the journey, and at Euston Square they were met by one of the Melmotte carriages. Marie was to be taken home in the carriage, and the box was to follow in a cab;—to follow at some interval so that Grosvenor Square might not be aware of what had taken place. Grosvenor Square, of course, very soon knew all about it. 'And are you to come?' Marie asked, speaking to the gentleman. The gentleman replied that he had been requested to see Miss Melmotte home. 'All the people will wonder who you are,' said Marie laughing. Then the gentleman thought that Miss Melmotte would be able to get through her troubles without much suffering.

When she got home she was hurried up at once to her mother's room,—and there she found her father, alone. 'This is your game, is it?' said he, looking down at her.

'Well, papa;—yes. You made me do it.'

'You fool you! You were going to New York,—were you?' To this she vouchsafed no reply. 'As if I hadn't found out all about it. Who was going with you?'

'If you have found out all about it, you know, papa.'

'Of course I know;—but you don't know all about it, you little idiot.'

'No doubt I'm a fool and an idiot. You always say so.'

'Where do you suppose Sir Felix Carbury is now?' Then she opened her eyes and looked at him. 'An hour ago he was in bed at his mother's house in Welbeck Street.'

'I don't believe it, papa.'

'You don't, don't you? You'll find it true. If you had gone to New York, you'd have gone alone. If I'd known at first that he had stayed behind, I think I'd have let you go.'

'I'm sure he didn't stay behind.'

'If you contradict me, I'll box your ears, you jade. He is in London at this moment. What has become of the woman that went with you?'

'She 's gone on board the ship.'

'And where is the money you took from your mother?'
Marie was silent. 'Who got the cheque changed?'

'Didon did.'

'And has she got the money?'

'No, papa.'

'Have you got it?'

'No, papa.'

'Did you give it to Sir Felix Carbury?'

'Yes, papa.'

'Then I'll be hanged if I don't prosecute him for
stealing it.'

'Oh, papa, don't do that;—pray don't do that. He
didn't steal it. I only gave it him to take care of for us.
He'll give it you back again.'

'I shouldn't wonder if he lost it at cards, and therefore
didn't go to Liverpool. Will you give me your word that
you'll never attempt to marry him again if I don't
prosecute him?' Marie considered. 'Unless you do that
I shall go to a magistrate at once.'

'I don't believe you can do anything to him. He
didn't steal it. I gave it to him.'

'Will you promise me?'

'No, papa, I won't. What's the good of promising
when I should only break it. Why can't you let me
have the man I love? What's the good of all the money
if people don't have what they like?'

'All the money!—What do you know about the
money? Look here,' and he took her by the arm.
'I've been very good to you. You've had your share of
everything that has been going;—carriages and horses,
bracelets and brooches, silks and gloves, and every
thing else.' He held her very hard and shook her as
he spoke.

'Let me go, papa; you hurt me. I never asked for such
things. I don't care a straw about bracelets and
brooches.'

'What do you care for?'

'Only for somebody to love me,' said Marie, looking
down.

'You'll soon have nobody to love you, if you go on

this fashion. You've had everything done for you, and if
you don't do something for me in return, by G——, you
shall have a hard time of it. If you weren't such a fool
you'd believe me when I say that I know more than
you do.'

'You can't know better than me what'll make me
happy.'

'Do you think only of yourself? If you'll marry Lord
Nidderdale you'll have a position in the world which
nothing can take from you.'

'Then I won't,' said Marie firmly. Upon this he
shook her till she cried, and calling for Madame Melmotte desired his wife not to let the girl for one minute
out of her presence.

The condition of Sir Felix was I think worse than that
of the lady with whom he was to have run away. He
had played at the Beargarden till four in the morning
and had then left the club, on the breaking-up of the
card-table, intoxicated and almost penniless. During the
last half hour he had made himself very unpleasant at
the club, saying all manner of harsh things of Miles
Grendall;——of whom, indeed, it was almost impossible to
say things too hard, had they been said in a proper
form and at a proper time. He declared that Grendall
would not pay his debts, that he had cheated when
playing loo,——as to which Sir Felix appealed to Dolly
Longestaffe; and he ended by asserting that Grendall
ought to be turned out of the club. They had a desperate
row. Dolly of course had said that he knew nothing
about it, and Lord Grasslough had expressed an opinion
that perhaps more than one person ought to be turned
out. At four o'clock the party was broken up and Sir
Felix wandered forth into the streets, with nothing more
than the change of a ten pound note in his pocket. All
his luggage was lying in the hall of the club, and there
he left it.

There could hardly have been a more miserable
wretch than Sir Felix wandering about the streets of
London that night. Though he was nearly drunk, he
was not drunk enough to forget the condition of his

affairs. There is an intoxication that makes merry in the midst of affliction;—and there is an intoxication that banishes affliction by producing oblivion. But again there is an intoxication which is conscious of itself though it makes the feet unsteady, and the voice thick, and the brain foolish; and which brings neither mirth nor oblivion. Sir Felix trying to make his way to Welbeck Street and losing it at every turn, feeling himself to be an object of ridicule to every wanderer, and of dangerous suspicion to every policeman, got no good at all out of his intoxication. What had he better do with himself? He fumbled in his pocket, and managed to get hold of his ticket for New York. Should he still make the journey? Then he thought of his luggage, and could not remember where it was. At last, as he steadied himself against a letter-post, he was able to call to mind that his portmanteaus were at the club. By this time he had wandered into Marylebone Lane, but did not in the least know where he was. But he made an attempt to get back to his club, and stumbled half down Bond Street. Then a policeman enquired into his purposes, and when he said that he lived in Welbeck Street, walked back with him as far as Oxford Street. Having once mentioned the place where he lived, he had not strength of will left to go back to his purpose of getting his luggage and starting for Liverpool.

Between six and seven he was knocking at the door in Welbeck Street. He had tried his latch-key, but had found it inefficient. As he was supposed to be at Liverpool, the door had in fact been locked. At last it was opened by Lady Carbury herself. He had fallen more than once, and was soiled with the gutter. Most of my readers will not probably know how a man looks when he comes home drunk at six in the morning; but they who have seen the thing will acknowledge that a sorrier sight cannot meet a mother's eye than that of a son in such a condition. 'Oh, Felix!' she exclaimed.

'It'sh all up,' he said, stumbling in.

'What has happened, Felix?'

'Discovered, and be d——— to it! The old shap'sh stopped ush.' Drunk as he was, he was able to lie. At that moment the 'old shap' was fast asleep in Grosvenor Square, altogether ignorant of the plot; and Marie, joyful with excitement, was getting into the cab in the mews. 'Bettersh go to bed.' And so he stumbled upstairs by daylight, the wretched mother helping him. She took off his clothes for him and his boots, and having left him already asleep, she went down to her own room, a miserable woman.

### END OF VOLUME I

## Chapter LI

### WHICH SHALL IT BE?

PAUL MONTAGUE reached London on his return from Suffolk early on the Monday morning, and on the following day he wrote to Mrs. Hurtle. As he sat in his lodgings, thinking of his condition, he almost wished that he had taken Melmotte's offer and gone to Mexico. He might at any rate have endeavoured to promote the railway earnestly, and then have abandoned it if he found the whole thing false. In such case of course he would never have seen Hetta Carbury again; but, as things were, of what use to him was his love,—of what use to him or to her? The kind of life of which he dreamed, such a life in England as was that of Roger Carbury, or, as such life would be, if Roger had a wife whom he loved, seemed to be far beyond his reach. Nobody was like Roger Carbury! Would it not be well that he should go away, and, as he went, write to Hetta and bid her marry the best man that ever lived in the world?

But the journey to Mexico was no longer open to him. He had repudiated the proposition and had quarrelled with Melmotte. It was necessary that he should immediately take some further step in regard to Mrs. Hurtle. Twice lately he had gone to Islington determined that he would see that lady for the last time. Then he had taken her to Lowestoffe, and had been equally firm in his resolution that he would there put an end to his present bonds. Now he had promised to go again to Islington;—and was aware that if he failed to keep his promise, she would come to him. In this way there would never be an end to it.

He would certainly go again, as he had promised,—if she should still require it; but he would first try what a letter would do,—a plain unvarnished tale. Might it still be possible that a plain tale sent by post should have sufficient efficacy? This was his plain tale as he now told it.

'Tuesday, 2nd July, 1873.

'MY DEAR MRS. HURTLE,—

'I promised that I would go to you again in Islington, and so I will, if you still require it. But I think that such a meeting can be of no service to either of us. What is to be gained? I do not for a moment mean to justify my own conduct. It is not to be justified. When I met you on our journey hither from San Francisco, I was charmed with your genius, your beauty, and your character. They are now what I found them to be then. But circumstances have made our lives and temperaments so far different, that I am certain that, were we married, we should not make each other happy. Of course the fault was mine; but it is better to own that fault, and to take all the blame,—and the evil consequences, let them be what they may'—to be shot, for instance, like the gentleman in Oregon,—'than to be married with the consciousness that even at the very moment of the ceremony, such marriage will be a matter of sorrow and repentance. As soon as my mind was made up on this I wrote to you. I can not,—I dare not,—blame you for the step you have since taken. But I can only adhere to the resolution I then expressed.

'The first day I saw you here in London you asked me whether I was attached to another woman. I could answer you only by the truth. But I should not of my own accord have spoken to you of altered affections. It was after I had resolved to break my engagement with you that I first knew this girl. It was not because I had come to love her that I broke it. I have no grounds whatever for hoping that my love will lead to any results.

'I have now told you as exactly as I can the condition of my mind. If it were possible for me in any way to compensate the injury I have done you,—or even to undergo retribution for it,—I would do so. But what compensation can be given, or what retribution can you

exact? I think that our further meeting can avail
nothing. But if, after this, you wish me to come again, I
will come for the last time,—because I have promised.

'Your most sincere friend,
'PAUL MONTAGUE.'

Mrs. Hurtle, as she read this, was torn in two ways.
All that Paul had written was in accordance with the
words written by herself on a scrap of paper which
she still kept in her own pocket. Those words, fairly
transcribed on a sheet of note-paper, would be the most
generous and the fittest answer she could give. And she
longed to be generous. She had all a woman's natural
desire to sacrifice herself. But the sacrifice which would
have been most to her taste would have been of another
kind. Had she found him ruined and penniless she
would have delighted to share with him all that she
possessed. Had she found him a cripple, or blind, or
miserably struck with some disease, she would have
stayed by him and have nursed him and given him
comfort. Even had he been disgraced she would have
fled with him to some far country and have pardoned all
his faults. No sacrifice would have been too much for
her that would have been accompanied by a feeling
that he appreciated all that she was doing for him, and
that she was loved in return. But to sacrifice herself by
going away and never more being heard of, was too
much for her! What woman can endure such sacrifice
as that? To give up not only her love, but her wrath
also;—that was too much for her! The idea of being
tame was terrible to her. Her life had not been very
prosperous, but she was what she was because she had
dared to protect herself by her own spirit. Now, at
last, should she succumb and be trodden on like a
worm? Should she be weaker even than an English
girl? Should she allow him to have amused himself
with her love, to have had 'a good time,' and then to
roam away like a bee, while she was so dreadfully
scorched, so mutilated and punished! Had not her
whole life been opposed to the theory of such passive

endurance? She took out the scrap of paper and read it; and, in spite of all, she felt that there was a feminine softness in it that gratified her.

But no;—she could not send it. She could not even copy the words. And so she gave play to all her strongest feelings on the other side,—being in truth torn in two directions. Then she sat herself down to her desk, and with rapid words, and flashing thoughts, wrote as follows:—

'PAUL MONTAGUE,—

'I have suffered many injuries, but of all injuries this is the worst and most unpardonable,—and the most unmanly. Surely there never was such a coward, never so false a liar. The poor wretch that I destroyed was mad with liquor and was only acting after his kind. Even Caradoc Hurtle never premeditated such wrong as this. What;—you are to bind yourself to me by the most solemn obligation that can join a man and a woman together, and then tell me,—when they have affected my whole life,—that they are to go for nothing, because they do not suit your view of things? On thinking over it, you find that an American wife would not make you so comfortable as some English girl;—and therefore it is all to go for nothing! I have no brother, no man near me;—or you would not dare to do this. You can not but be a coward.

'You talk of compensation! Do you mean money? You do not dare to say so, but you must mean it. It is an insult the more. But as to retribution; yes. You shall suffer retribution. I desire you to come to me,—according to your promise,—and you will find me with a horsewhip in my hand. I will whip you till I have not a breath in my body. And then I will see what you will dare to do;—whether you will drag me into a court of law for the assault.

'Yes; come. You shall come. And now you know the welcome you shall find. I will buy the whip while this is reaching you, and you shall find that I know how to choose such a weapon. I call upon you to come. But should you be afraid and break your promise, I will come to you. I will make London too hot to hold you;—and if I do not find you I will go with my story to every friend you have.

'I have now told you as exactly as I can the condition of my mind.

'WINIFRED HURTLE.'

Having written this she again read the short note, and again gave way to violent tears. But on that day she sent no letter. On the following morning she wrote a third, and sent that. This was the third letter:—

'Yes. Come.
'W. H.'

This letter duly reached Paul Montague at his lodgings. He started immediately for Islington. He had now no desire to delay the meeting. He had at any rate taught her that his gentleness towards her, his going to the play with her, and drinking tea with her at Mrs. Pipkin's, and his journey with her to the sea, were not to be taken as evidence that he was gradually being conquered. He had declared his purpose plainly enough at Lowestoffe,—and plainly enough in his last letter. She had told him, down at the hotel, that had she by chance have been armed at the moment, she would have shot him. She could arm herself now if she pleased; —but his real fear had not lain in that direction. The pang consisted in having to assure her that he was resolved to do her wrong. The worst of that was now over.

The door was opened for him by Ruby, who by no means greeted him with a happy countenance. It was the second morning after the night of her imprisonment; and nothing had occurred to alleviate her woe. At this very moment her lover should have been in Liverpool, but he was, in fact, abed in Welbeck Street. 'Yes, sir; she's at home,' said Ruby, with a baby in her arms and a little child hanging on to her dress. 'Don't pull so, Sally. Please, sir, is Sir Felix still in London?' Ruby had written to Sir Felix the very night of her imprisonment,

but had not as yet received any reply. Paul, whose mind
was altogether intent on his own troubles, declared that
at present he knew nothing about Sir Felix, and was
then shown into Mrs. Hurtle's room.

'So you have come,' she said, without rising from her
chair.

'Of course I came, when you desired it.'

'I don't know why you should. My wishes do not
seem to affect you much. Will you sit down there?' she
said, pointing to a seat at some distance from herself.
'So you think it would be best that you and I should
never see each other again?' She was very calm; but it
seemed to him that the quietness was assumed, and that
at any moment it might be converted into violence. He
thought that there was that in her eye which seemed to
foretell the spring of the wild-cat.

'I did think so certainly. What more can I say?'

'Oh, nothing; clearly nothing.' Her voice was very
low. 'Why should a gentleman trouble himself to say
any more,—than that he has changed his mind? Why
make a fuss about such little things as a woman's life, or a
woman's heart?' Then she paused. 'And having come,
in consequence of my unreasonable request, of course
you are wise to hold your peace.'

'I came because I promised.'

'But you did not promise to speak;—did you?'

'What would you have me say?'

'Ah what! Am I to be so weak as to tell you now
what I would have you say? Suppose you were to say,
"I am a gentleman, and a man of my word, and I
repent me of my intended perfidy," do you not think
you might get your release that way? Might it not be
possible that I should reply that as your heart was
gone from me, your hand might go after it;—that I
scorned to be the wife of a man who did not want
me?' As she asked this she gradually raised her voice,
and half lifted herself in her seat, stretching herself
towards him.

'You might indeed,' he replied, not well knowing what
to say.

'But I should not. I at least will be true. I should take you, Paul,—still take you; with a confidence that I should yet win you to me by my devotion. I have still some kindness of feeling towards you,—none to that woman who is I suppose younger than I, and gentler, and a maid.' She still looked as though she expected a reply, but there was nothing to be said in answer to this. 'Now that you are going to leave me, Paul, is there any advice you can give me, as to what I shall do next? I have given up every friend in the world for you. I have no home. Mrs. Pipkin's room here is more my home than any other spot on the earth. I have all the world to choose from, but no reason whatever for a choice. I have my property. What shall I do with it, Paul? If I could die and be no more heard of, you should be welcome to it.' There was no answer possible to all this. The questions were asked because there was no answer possible. 'You might at any rate advise me. Paul, you are in some degree responsible,—are you not,—for my loneliness?'

'I am. But you know that I cannot answer your questions.'

'You cannot wonder that I should be somewhat in doubt as to my future life. As far as I can see, I had better remain here. I do good at any rate to Mrs. Pipkin. She went into hysterics yesterday when I spoke of leaving her. That woman, Paul, would starve in our country, and I shall be desolate in this.' Then she paused, and there was absolute silence for a minute. 'You thought my letter very short; did you not?'

'It said, I suppose, all you had to say.'

'No, indeed. I did have much more to say. That was the third letter I wrote. Now you shall see the other two. I wrote three, and had to choose which I would send you. I fancy that yours to me was easier written than either one of mine. You had no doubts, you know. I had many doubts. I could not send them all by post, together. But you may see them all now. There is one. You may read that first. While I was writing it, I was determined that that should go.' Then she handed him the sheet of paper which contained the threat of the horsewhip.

'I am glad you did not send that,' he said.

'I meant it.'

'But you have changed your mind?'

'Is there anything in it that seems to you to be unreasonable? Speak out and tell me.'

'I am thinking of you, not of myself.'

'Think of me, then. Is there anything said there which the usage to which I have been subjected does not justify?'

'You ask me questions which I cannot answer. I do not think that under any provocation a woman should use a horsewhip.'

'It is certainly more comfortable for gentlemen,—who amuse themselves,—that women should have that opinion. But, upon my word, I don't know what to say about that. As long as there are men to fight for women, it may be well to leave the fighting to the men. But when a woman has no one to help her, is she to bear everything without turning upon those who ill-use her? Shall a woman be flayed alive because it is unfeminine in her to fight for her own skin? What is the good of being—feminine, as you call it? Have you asked yourself that? That men may be attracted, I should say. But if a woman finds that men only take advantage of her assumed weakness, shall she not throw it off? If she be treated as prey, shall she not fight as a beast of prey? Oh, no;—it is so unfeminine! I also, Paul, had thought of that. The charm of womanly weakness presented itself to my mind in a soft moment,—and then I wrote this other letter. You may as well see them all.' And so she handed him the scrap which had been written at Lowestoffe, and he read that also.

He could hardly finish it, because of the tears which filled his eyes. But, having mastered its contents, he came across the room and threw himself on his knees at her feet, sobbing. 'I have not sent it, you know,' she said. 'I only show it you that you may see how my mind has been at work.'

'It hurts me more than the other,' he replied.

'Nay, I would not hurt you,—not at this moment. Sometimes I feel that I could tear you limb from limb, so great is my disappointment, so ungovernable my rage! Why,—why should I be such a victim? Why should life be an utter blank to me, while you have everything before you? There, you have seen them all. Which will you have?'

'I cannot now take that other as the expression of your mind.'

'But it will be when you have left me;—and was when you were with me at the sea-side. And it was so I felt when I got your first letter in San Francisco. Why should you kneel there? You do not love me. A man should kneel to a woman for love, not for pardon.' But though she spoke thus, she put her hand upon his forehead, and pushed back his hair, and looked into his face. 'I wonder whether that other woman loves you. I do not want an answer, Paul. I suppose you had better go.' She took his hand and pressed it to her breast. 'Tell me one thing. When you spoke of—compensation, did you mean—money?'

'No; indeed no.'

'I hope not;—I hope not that. Well, there;—go. You shall be troubled no more with Winifred Hurtle.' She took the sheet of paper which contained the threat of the horsewhip and tore it into scraps.

'And am I to keep the other?' he asked.

'No. For what purpose would you have it? To prove my weakness? That also shall be destroyed.' But she took it and restored it to her pocket-book.

'Good-bye, my friend,' he said.

'Nay! This parting will not bear a farewell. Go, and let there be no other word spoken.' And so he went.

As soon as the front door was closed behind him she rang the bell and begged Ruby to ask Mrs. Pipkin to come to her. 'Mrs. Pipkin,' she said, as soon as the woman had entered the room; 'everything is over between me and Mr. Montague.' She was standing upright in the middle of the room, and as she spoke there was a smile on her face.

'Lord 'a mercy,' said Mrs. Pipkin, holding up both her hands.

'As I have told you that I was to be married to him, I think it right now to tell you that I'm not going to be married to him.'

'And why not?—and he such a nice young man,—and quiet too.'

'As to the why not, I don't know that I am prepared to speak about that. But it is so. I was engaged to him.'

'I'm well sure of that, Mrs. Hurtle.'

'And now I'm no longer engaged to him. That's all.'

'Dearie me! and you going down to Lowestoffe with him, and all.' Mrs. Pipkin could not bear to think that she should hear no more of such an interesting story.

'We did go down to Lowestoffe together, and we both came back,—not together. And there's an end of it.'

'I'm sure it's not your fault, Mrs. Hurtle. When a marriage is to be, and doesn't come off, it never is the lady's fault.'

'There's an end of it, Mrs. Pipkin. If you please, we won't say anything more about it.'

'And are you going to leave, ma'am?' said Mrs. Pipkin, prepared to have her apron up to her eyes at a moment's notice. Where should she get such another lodger as Mrs. Hurtle,—a lady who not only did not inquire about victuals, but who was always suggesting that the children should eat this pudding or finish that pie, and who had never questioned an item in a bill since she had been in the house!

'We'll say nothing about that yet, Mrs. Pipkin.' Then Mrs. Pipkin gave utterance to so many assurances of sympathy and help that it almost seemed that she was prepared to guarantee to her lodger another lover in lieu of the one who was now dismissed.

## Chapter LII

### THE RESULTS OF LOVE AND WINE

TWO, three, four, and even five o'clock still found
Sir Felix Carbury in bed on that fatal Thursday.
More than once or twice his mother crept up to his
room, but on each occasion he feigned to be fast asleep
and made no reply to her gentle words. But his condition
was one which only admits of short snatches of uneasy
slumber. From head to foot, he was sick and ill and sore,
and could find no comfort anywhere. To lie where he
was, trying by absolute quiescence to soothe the agony
of his brows and to remember that as long as he lay
there he would be safe from attack by the outer world,
was all the solace within his reach. Lady Carbury sent
the page up to him, and to the page he was awake.
The boy brought him tea. He asked for soda and
brandy; but there was none to be had, and in his
present condition he did not dare to hector about it till
it was procured for him.

The world surely was now all over to him. He had
made arrangements for running away with the great
heiress of the day, and had absolutely allowed the young
lady to run away without him. The details of their
arrangement had been such that she absolutely would
start upon her long journey across the ocean before she
could find out that he had failed to keep his appointment. Melmotte's hostility would be incurred by the
attempt, and hers by the failure. Then he had lost all
his money,—and hers. He had induced his poor mother
to assist in raising a fund for him,—and even that was
gone. He was so cowed that he was afraid even of his
mother. And he could remember something, but no
details, of some row at the club,—but still with a conviction on his mind that he had made the row. Ah,—
when would he summon courage to enter the club
again? When could he show himself again anywhere?
All the world would know that Marie Melmotte had
attempted to run off with him, and that at the last

moment he had failed her. What lie could he invent to cover his disgrace? And his clothes! All his things were at the club;—or he thought that they were, not being quite certain whether he had not made some attempt to carry them off to the Railway Station. He had heard of suicide. If ever it could be well that a man should cut his own throat, surely the time had come for him now. But as this idea presented itself to him he simply gathered the clothes around him and tried to sleep. The death of Cato*would hardly have for him persuasive charms.

Between five and six his mother again came up to him, and when he appeared to sleep, stood with her hand upon his shoulder. There must be some end to this. He must at any rate be fed. She, wretched woman, had been sitting all day,—thinking of it. As regarded her son himself, his condition told his story with sufficient accuracy. What might be the fate of the girl she could not stop to inquire. She had not heard all the details of the proposed scheme; but she had known that Felix had proposed to be at Liverpool on the Wednesday night, and to start on Thursday for New York with the young lady; and with the view of aiding him in his object she had helped him with money. She had bought clothes for him, and had been busy with Hetta for two days preparing for his long journey,—having told some lie to her own daughter as to the cause of her brother's intended journey. He had not gone, but had come, drunk and degraded, back to the house. She had searched his pockets with less scruple than she had ever before felt, and had found his ticket for the vessel and the few sovereigns which were left to him. About him she could read the riddle plainly. He had stayed at his club till he was drunk, and had gambled away all his money. When she had first seen him she had asked herself what further lie she should now tell to her daughter. At breakfast there was instant need for some story. 'Mary says that Felix came back this morning, and that he has not gone at all,' Hetta exclaimed. The poor woman could not bring herself to expose the vices of the son to her daughter. She could not say that he had stumbled into the house drunk at six o'clock. Hetta no doubt had her own suspicions. 'Yes; he has come back,' said Lady Carbury, broken-hearted by her troubles. 'It was some plan about the Mexican railway I believe, and has broken through. He is very unhappy and not well. I will see to him.' After that Hetta had said nothing during the whole day. And now, about an hour before dinner, Lady Carbury was standing by her son's bedside, determined that he should speak to her.

'Felix,' she said,—'speak to me, Felix.—I know that you are awake.' He groaned, and turned himself away from her, burying himself further under the bedclothes. 'You must get up for your dinner. It is near six o'clock.'

'All right,' he said at last.

'What is the meaning of this, Felix? You must tell me. It must be told sooner or later. I know you are unhappy. You had better trust your mother.'

'I am so sick, mother.'

'You will be better up. What were you doing last night? What has come of it all? Where are your things?'

'At the club.—You had better leave me now, and let Sam come up to me.' Sam was the page.

'I will leave you presently; but, Felix, you must tell me about this. What has been done?'

'It hasn't come off.'

'But how has it not come off?'

'I didn't get away. What's the good of asking?'

'You said this morning when you came in, that Mr. Melmotte had discovered it.'

'Did I? Then I suppose he has. Oh, mother, I wish I could die. I don't see what's the use of anything. I won't get up to dinner. I'd rather stay here.'

'You must have something to eat, Felix.'

'Sam can bring it me. Do let him get me some brandy and water. I'm so faint and sick with all this that I can hardly bear myself. I can't talk now. If he'll get me a bottle of soda water and some brandy, I'll tell you all about it then.'

'Where is the money, Felix?'

'I paid it for the ticket,' said he, with both his hands up to his head.

Then his mother again left him with the understanding that he was to be allowed to remain in bed till the next morning; but that he was to give her some further explanation when he had been refreshed and invigorated after his own prescription. The boy went out and got him soda water and brandy, and meat was carried up to him, and then he did succeed for a while in finding oblivion from his misery in sleep.

'Is he ill, mamma?' Hetta asked.

'Yes, my dear.'

'Had you not better send for a doctor?'

'No, my dear. He will be better to-morrow.'

'Mamma, I think you would be happier if you would tell me everything.'

'I can't,' said Lady Carbury, bursting out into tears. 'Don't ask. What's the good of asking? It is all misery and wretchedness. There is nothing to tell,—except that I am ruined.'

'Has he done anything, mamma?'

'No. What should he have done? How am I to know what he does? He tells me nothing. Don't talk about it any more. Oh, God,—how much better it would be to be childless!'

'Oh, mamma, do you mean me?' said Hetta, rushing across the room, and throwing herself close to her mother's side on the sofa. 'Mamma, say that you do not mean me.'

'It concerns you as well as me and him. I wish I were childless.'

'Oh, mamma, do not be cruel to me! Am I not good to you? Do I not try to be a comfort to you?'

'Then marry your cousin, Roger Carbury, who is a good man, and who can protect you. You can, at any rate, find a home for yourself, and a friend for us. You are not like Felix. You do not get drunk and gamble,—because you are a woman. But you are stiff-necked, and will not help me in my trouble.'

'Shall I marry him, mamma, without loving him?'

'Love! Have I been able to love? Do you see much of what you call love around you? Why should you not love him? He is a gentleman, and a good man,—soft-hearted, of a sweet nature, whose life would be one effort to make yours happy. You think that Felix is very bad.'

'I have never said so.'

'But ask yourself whether you do not give as much pain, seeing what you could do for us if you would. But it never occurs to you to sacrifice even a fantasy for the advantage of others.'

Hetta retired from her seat on the sofa, and when her mother again went upstairs she turned it all over in her mind. Could it be right that she should marry one man when she loved another? Could it be right that she should marry at all, for the sake of doing good to her family? This man, whom she might marry if she would, —who did in truth worship the ground on which she trod,—was, she well knew, all that her mother had said. And he was more than that. Her mother had spoken of his soft heart, and his sweet nature. But Hetta knew also that he was a man of high honour and a noble courage. In such a condition as was hers now he was the very friend whose advice she could have asked,—had he not been the very lover who was desirous of making her his wife. Hetta felt that she could sacrifice much for her mother. Money, if she had it, she could have given, though she left herself penniless. Her time, her inclinations, her very heart's treasure, and, as she thought, her life, she could give. She could doom herself to poverty, and loneliness, and heart-rending regrets for her mother's sake. But she did not know how she could give herself into the arms of a man she did not love.

'I don't know what there is to explain,' said Felix to his mother. She had asked him why he had not gone to Liverpool, whether he had been interrupted by Melmotte himself, whether news had reached him from Marie that she had been stopped, or whether,—as might have been possible,—Marie had changed her own mind. But he could not bring himself to tell the truth, or any story bordering on the truth. 'It didn't come off,' he said, 'and of course that knocked me off my legs. Well; yes. I did take some champagne when I found how it was. A fellow does get cut up by that kind of thing. Oh, I heard it at the club,—that the whole thing was off. I can't explain anything more. And then I was so mad, I can't tell what I was after. I did get the ticket. There it is. That shows I was in earnest. I spent the £30 in getting it. I suppose the change is there. Don't take it, for I haven't another shilling in the world.' Of course he said nothing of Marie's money, or of that which he had himself received from Melmotte. And as his mother had heard nothing of these sums she could not contradict what he said. She got from him no further statement, but she was sure that there was a story to be told which would reach her ears sooner or later.

That evening, about nine o'clock, Mr. Broune called in Welbeck Street. He very often did call now, coming up in a cab, staying for a cup of tea, and going back in the same cab to the office of his newspaper. Since Lady Carbury had, so devotedly, abstained from accepting his offer, Mr. Broune had become almost sincerely attached to her. There was certainly between them now more of the intimacy of real friendship than had ever existed in earlier days. He spoke to her more freely about his own affairs, and even she would speak to him with some attempt at truth. There was never between them now even a shade of love-making. She did not look into his eyes, nor did he hold her hand. As for kissing her,—he thought no more of it than of kissing the maid-servant. But he spoke to her of the things that worried him,—the unreasonable exactions of proprietors, and the perilous inaccuracy of contributors. He told her of the exceeding weight upon his shoulders, under which an Atlas would have succumbed. And he told her something too of his triumphs;—how he had had this fellow bowled over in punishment for some contradiction, and that man snuffed out for daring to be an enemy. And he expatiated on his own virtues, his justice and clemency. Ah,—if men and women only knew his good nature and his patriotism;—how he had spared the rod here, how he had made the fortune of a man there, how he had saved the country millions by the steadiness of his adherence to some grand truth! Lady Carbury delighted in all this and repaid him by flattery, and little confidences of her own. Under his teaching she had almost made up her mind to give up Mr. Alf. Of nothing was Mr. Broune more certain than that Mr. Alf was making a fool of himself in regard to the Westminster election and those attacks on Melmotte. 'The world of London generally knows what it is about,' said Mr. Broune, 'and the London world believes Mr. Melmotte to be sound. I don't pretend to say that he has never done anything that he ought not to do. I am not going into his antecedents. But he is a man of wealth, power, and genius, and Alf will get the worst of it.' Under such teaching as this, Lady Carbury was almost obliged to give up Mr. Alf.

Sometimes they would sit in the front room with Hetta, to whom also Mr. Broune had become attached; but sometimes Lady Carbury would be in her own sanctum. On this evening she received him there, and at once poured forth all her troubles about Felix. On this occasion she told him everything, and almost told him everything truly. He had already heard the story. 'The young lady went down to Liverpool, and Sir Felix was not there.'

'He could not have been there. He has been in bed in this house all day. Did she go?'

'So I am told;—and was met at the station by the senior officer of the police at Liverpool, who brought her back to London without letting her go down to the ship at all. She must have thought that her lover was on board;—probably thinks so now. I pity her.'

'How much worse it would have been, had she been allowed to start,' said Lady Carbury.

'Yes; that would have been bad. She would have had a sad journey to New York, and a sadder journey back. Has your son told you anything about money?'

'What money?'

'They say that the girl entrusted him with a large sum which she had taken from her father. If that be so he certainly ought to lose no time in restoring it. It might be done through some friend. I would do it, for that matter. If it be so,—to avoid unpleasantness,—it should be sent back at once. It will be for his credit.' This Mr. Broune said with a clear intimation of the importance of his advice.

It was dreadful to Lady Carbury. She had no money to give back, nor, as she was well aware, had her son. She had heard nothing of any money. What did Mr. Broune mean by a large sum? 'That would be dreadful,' she said.

'Had you not better ask him about it?'

Lady Carbury was again in tears. She knew that she could not hope to get a word of truth from her son. 'What do you mean by a large sum?'

'Two or three hundred pounds, perhaps.'

'I have not a shilling in the world, Mr. Broune.' Then it all came out,—the whole story of her poverty, as it had been brought about by her son's misconduct. She told him every detail of her money affairs from the death of her husband, and his will, up to the present moment.

'He is eating you up, Lady Carbury.' Lady Carbury thought that she was nearly eaten up already, but she said nothing. 'You must put a stop to this.'

'But how?'

'You must rid yourself of him. It is dreadful to say so, but it must be done. You must not see your daughter ruined. Find out what money he got from Miss Melmotte and I will see that it is repaid. That must be done;—and we will then try to get him to go abroad. No;—do not contradict me. We can talk of the money another time. I must be off now, as I have stayed too long. Do as I bid you. Make him tell you, and send me word down to the office. If you could do it early to-morrow, that would be best. God bless you.' And so he hurried off.

Early on the following morning a letter from Lady Carbury was put into Mr. Broune's hands, giving the story of the money as far as she had been able to extract it from Sir Felix. Sir Felix declared that Mr. Melmotte had owed him £600, and that he had received £250 out of this from Miss Melmotte,—so that there was still a large balance due to him. Lady Carbury went on to say that her son had at last confessed that he had lost this money at play. The story was fairly true; but Lady Carbury in her letter acknowledged that she was not justified in believing it because it was told to her by her son.

## Chapter LIII

### A DAY IN THE CITY

MELMOTTE had got back his daughter, and was half inclined to let the matter rest there. He would probably have done so had he not known that all his own household were aware that she had gone off to meet Sir Felix Carbury, and had he not also received the condolence of certain friends in the city. It seemed that about two o'clock in the day the matter was known to everybody. Of course Lord Nidderdale would hear of it, and if so all the trouble that he had taken in that direction would have been taken in vain. Stupid fool of a girl to throw away her chance,—nay, to throw away the certainty of a brilliant career, in that way! But his anger against Sir Felix was infinitely more bitter than his anger against his daughter. The man had pledged himself to abstain from any step of this kind,—had given a written pledge,—had renounced under his own signature his intention of marrying Marie! Melmotte had of course learned all the details of the cheque for £250,—how the money had been paid at the bank to Didon, and how Didon had given it to Sir Felix. Marie herself acknowledged that Sir Felix had received the money. If possible he would prosecute the baronet for stealing his money.

Had Melmotte been altogether a prudent man he

would probably have been satisfied with getting back his
daughter and would have allowed the money to go
without further trouble. At this especial point in his
career ready money was very valuable to him, but his
concerns were of such magnitude that £250 could make
but little difference. But there had grown upon the man
during the last few months an arrogance, a self-confidence inspired in him by the worship of other men,
which clouded his intellect, and robbed him of much of
that power of calculation which undoubtedly he naturally possessed. He remembered perfectly his various
little transactions with Sir Felix. Indeed it was one of his
gifts to remember with accuracy all money transactions,
whether great or small, and to keep an account book in
his head, which was always totted up and balanced with
accuracy. He knew exactly how he stood, even with
the crossing-sweeper to whom he had given a penny
last Tuesday, as with the Longestaffes, father and son,
to whom he had not as yet made any payment on
behalf of the purchase of Pickering. But Sir Felix's
money had been consigned into his hands for the
purchase of shares,—and that consignment did not
justify Sir Felix in taking another sum of money from
his daughter. In such a matter he thought that an
English magistrate, and an English jury, would all be
on his side,—especially as he was Augustus Melmotte,
the man about to be chosen for Westminster, the man
about to entertain the Emperor of China!

The next day was Friday,—the day of the Railway
Board. Early in the morning he sent a note to Lord
Nidderdale.

'MY DEAR NIDDERDALE,—
  'Pray come to the Board to-day;—or at any rate come
to me in the city. I specially want to speak to you.
                      'Yours,              'A. M.'

This he wrote, having made up his mind that it would be
wise to make a clear breast of it with his hoped-for son-
in-law. If there was still a chance of keeping the young

lord to his guns that chance would be best supported by
perfect openness on his part. The young lord would of
course know what Marie had done. But the young
lord had for some weeks past been aware that there had
been a difficulty in regard to Sir Felix Carbury, and
had not on that account relaxed his suit. It might be
possible to persuade the young lord that as the young
lady had now tried to elope and tried in vain, his own
chance might on the whole be rather improved than
injured.

Mr. Melmotte on that morning had many visitors,
among whom one of the earliest and most unfortunate
was Mr. Longestaffe. At that time there had been
arranged at the offices in Abchurch Lane a mode of
double ingress and egress,—a front stairs and a back
stairs approach and exit, as is always necessary with
very great men,—in reference to which arrangement
the honour and dignity attached to each is exactly
contrary to that which generally prevails in the world;
the front stairs being intended for everybody, and being
both slow and uncertain, whereas the back stairs are
quick and sure, and are used only for those who are
favoured. Miles Grendall had the command of the
stairs, and found that he had plenty to do in keeping
people in their right courses. Mr. Longestaffe reached
Abchurch Lane before one,—having altogether failed in
getting a moment's private conversation with the big
man on that other Friday, when he had come later. He
fell at once into Miles's hands, and was ushered through
the front stairs passage and into the front stairs waiting-
room, with much external courtesy. Miles Grendall
was very voluble. Did Mr. Longestaffe want to see Mr.
Melmotte? Oh;—Mr. Longestaffe wanted to see Mr.
Melmotte as soon as possible! Of course Mr. Longestaffe should see Mr. Melmotte. He, Miles, knew that
Mr. Melmotte was particularly desirous of seeing Mr.
Longestaffe. Mr. Melmotte had mentioned Mr. Longestaffe's name twice during the last three days. Would
Mr. Longestaffe sit down for a few minutes? Had
Mr. Longestaffe seen the 'Morning Breakfast Table'?

Mr. Melmotte undoubtedly was very much engaged. At
this moment a deputation from the Canadian Government*was with him;—and Sir Gregory Gribe was in the
office waiting for a few words. But Miles thought that
the Canadian Government would not be long,—and as
for Sir Gregory, perhaps his business might be postponed. Miles would do his very best to get an interview
for Mr. Longestaffe,—more especially as Mr. Melmotte
was so very desirous himself of seeing his friend. It was
astonishing that such a one as Miles Grendall should
have learned his business so well and should have made
himself so handy! We will leave Mr. Longestaffe with
the 'Morning Breakfast Table' in his hands, in the front
waiting-room, merely notifying the fact that there he
remained for something over two hours.

In the meantime both Mr. Broune and Lord Nidderdale came to the office, and both were received without
delay. Mr. Broune was the first. Miles knew who he
was, and made no attempt to seat him in the same room
with Mr. Longestaffe. 'I'll just send him a note,' said
Mr. Broune, and he scrawled a few words at the office
counter. 'I'm commissioned to pay you some money
on behalf of Miss Melmotte.' Those were the words,
and they at once procured him admission to the
sanctum. The Canadian Deputation must have taken
its leave, and Sir Gregory could hardly have as yet
arrived. Lord Nidderdale, who had presented himself
almost at the same moment with the Editor, was shown
into a little private room,—which was, indeed, Miles
Grendall's own retreat. 'What's up with the Governor?'
asked the young lord.

'Anything particular do you mean?' said Miles.
'There are always so many things up here.'

'He has sent for me.'

'Yes,—you'll go in directly. There's that fellow who
does the "Breakfast Table" in with him. I don't know
what he's come about. You know what he has sent
for you for?'

Lord Nidderdale answered this question by another.
'I suppose all this about Miss Melmotte is true?'

'She did go off yesterday morning,' said Miles, in a whisper.

'But Carbury wasn't with her.'

'Well, no;—I suppose not. He seems to have mulled* it. He's such a d—— brute, he'd be sure to go wrong whatever he had in hand.'

'You don't like him, of course, Miles. For that matter I've no reason to love him. He couldn't have gone. He staggered out of the club yesterday morning at four o'clock as drunk as Cloe.* He'd lost a pot of money, and had been kicking up a row about you for the last hour.'

'Brute!' exclaimed Miles, with honest indignation.

'I dare say. But though he was able to make a row, I'm sure he couldn't get himself down to Liverpool. And I saw all his things lying about the club hall late last night;—no end of portmanteaux and bags; just what a fellow would take to New York. By George! Fancy taking a girl to New York! It was plucky.'

'It was all her doing,' said Miles, who was of course intimate with Mr. Melmotte's whole establishment, and had had means therefore of hearing the true story.

'What a fiasco!' said the young lord. 'I wonder what the old boy means to say to me about it.' Then there was heard the clear tingle of a little silver bell, and Miles told Lord Nidderdale that his time had come.

Mr. Broune had of late been very serviceable to Mr. Melmotte, and Melmotte was correspondingly gracious. On seeing the Editor he immediately began to make a speech of thanks in respect of the support given by the 'Breakfast Table' to his candidature. But Mr. Broune cut him short. 'I never talk about the "Breakfast Table," ' said he. 'We endeavour to get along as right as we can, and the less said the soonest mended.' Melmotte bowed. 'I have come now about quite another matter, and perhaps, the less said the sooner mended about that also. Sir Felix Carbury on a late occasion received a sum of money in trust from your daughter. Circumstances have prevented its use in the intended manner, and, therefore, as Sir Felix's friend, I have called to return the money to you.' Mr. Broune did not

like calling himself the friend of Sir Felix, but he did
even that for the lady who had been good enough to
him not to marry him.

'Oh, indeed,' said Mr. Melmotte, with a scowl on his
face, which he would have repressed if he could.

'No doubt you understand all about it.'

'Yes;—I understand. D—— scoundrel!'

'We won't discuss that, Mr. Melmotte. I've drawn
a cheque myself, payable to your order,—to make the
matter all straight. The sum was £250, I think.'
And Mr. Broune put a cheque for that amount down
upon the table.

'I dare say it's all right,' said Mr. Melmotte. 'But,
remember, I don't think that this absolves him. He has
been a scoundrel.'

'At any rate he has paid back the money, which
chance put into his hands, to the only person entitled
to receive it on the young lady's behalf. Good morning.'
Mr. Melmotte did put out his hand in token of amity.
Then Mr. Broune departed and Melmotte tinkled his
bell. As Nidderdale was shown in he crumpled up the
cheque, and put it into his pocket. He was at once
clever enough to perceive that any idea which he might
have had of prosecuting Sir Felix must be abandoned.
'Well, my Lord, and how are you?' said he with his
pleasantest smile. Nidderdale declared himself to be
as fresh as paint. 'You don't look down in the mouth,
my Lord.'

Then Lord Nidderdale,—who no doubt felt that it
behoved him to show a good face before his late intended
father-in-law,—sang the refrain of an old song, which
it is trusted my readers may remember.

> 'Cheer up, Sam;
> Don't let your spirits go down.
> There's many a girl that I know well,
> Is waiting for you in the town.'*

'Ha, ha, ha,' laughed Melmotte, 'very good. I've no
doubt there is,—many a one. But you won't let this
stupid nonsense stand in your way with Marie.'

'Upon my word, sir, I don't know about that. Miss

Melmotte has given the most convincing proof of her partiality for another gentleman, and of her indifference to me.'

'A foolish baggage! A silly little romantic baggage! She's been reading novels till she has learned to think she couldn't settle down quietly till she had run off with somebody.'

'She doesn't seem to have succeeded on this occasion, Mr. Melmotte.'

'No;—of course we had her back again from Liverpool.'

'But they say that she got further than the gentleman.'

'He is a dishonest, drunken scoundrel. My girl knows very well what he is now. She'll never try that game again. Of course, my Lord, I'm very sorry. You know that I've been on the square with you always. She's my only child, and sooner or later she must have all that I possess. What she will have at once will make any man wealthy,—that is, if she marries with my sanction; and in a year or two I expect that I shall be able to double what I give her now, without touching my capital. Of course you understand that I desire to see her occupying high rank. I think that, in this country, that is a noble object of ambition. Had she married that sweep I should have broken my heart. Now, my Lord, I want you to say that this shall make no difference to you. I am very honest with you. I do not try to hide anything. The thing of course has been a misfortune. Girls will be romantic. But you may be sure that this little accident will assist rather than impede your views. After this she will not be very fond of Sir Felix Carbury.'

'I dare say not. Though, by Jove, girls will forgive anything.'

'She won't forgive him. By George, she shan't. She shall hear the whole story. You'll come and see her just the same as ever!'

'I don't know about that, Mr. Melmotte.'

'Why not? You're not so weak as to surrender all your settled projects for such a piece of folly as that! He didn't even see her all the time.'

'That wasn't her fault.'

'The money will all be there, Lord Nidderdale.'

'The money's all right, I've no doubt. And there isn't a man in all London would be better pleased to settle down with a good income than I would. But, by Jove, it's a rather strong order when a girl has just run away with another man. Everybody knows it.'

'In three months' time everybody will have forgotten it.'

'To tell you the truth, sir, I think Miss Melmotte has got a will of her own stronger than you give her credit for. She has never given me the slightest encouragement. Ever so long ago, about Christmas, she did once say that she would do as you bade her. But she is very much changed since then. The thing was off.'

'She had nothing to do with that.'

'No;—but she has taken advantage of it, and I have no right to complain.'

'You just come to the house, and ask her again to-morrow. Or come on Sunday morning. Don't let us be done out of all our settled arrangements by the folly of an idle girl. Will you come on Sunday morning about noon?' Lord Nidderdale thought of his position for a few moments and then said that perhaps he would come on Sunday morning. After that Melmotte proposed that they two should go and 'get a bit of lunch' at a certain Conservative club in the City. There would be time before the meeting of the Railway Board. Nidderdale had no objection to the lunch, but expressed a strong opinion that the Board was 'rot'. 'That's all very well for you, young man,' said the chairman, 'but I must go there in order that you may be able to enjoy a splendid fortune.' Then he touched the young man on the shoulder and drew him back as he was passing out by the front stairs. 'Come this way, Nidderdale;—come this way. I must get out without being seen. There are people waiting for me there who think that a man can attend to business from morning to night without ever having a bit in his mouth.' And so they escaped by the back stairs.

At the club, the City Conservative world,—which always lunches well,—welcomed Mr. Melmotte very warmly. The election was coming on, and there was much to be said. He played the part of the big City man to perfection, standing about the room with his hat on, and talking loudly to a dozen men at once. And he was glad to show the club that Lord Nidderdale had come there with him. The club of course knew that Lord Nidderdale was the accepted suitor of the rich man's daughter,—accepted, that is, by the rich man himself,—and the club knew also that the rich man's daughter had tried,—but had failed,—to run away with Sir Felix Carbury. There is nothing like wiping out a misfortune and having done with it. The presence of Lord Nidderdale was almost an assurance to the club that the misfortune had been wiped out, and, as it were, abolished. A little before three Mr. Melmotte returned to Abchurch Lane, intending to regain his room by the back way; while Lord Nidderdale went westward, considering within his own mind whether it was expedient that he should continue to show himself as a suitor for Miss Melmotte's hand. He had an idea that a few years ago a man could not have done such a thing—that he would be held to show a poor spirit should he attempt it; but that now it did not much matter what a man did,—if only he were successful. 'After all, it's only an affair of money,' he said to himself.

Mr. Longestaffe in the meantime had progressed from weariness to impatience, from impatience to ill-humour, and from ill-humour to indignation. More than once he saw Miles Grendall, but Miles Grendall was always ready with an answer. That Canadian Deputation was determined to settle the whole business this morning, and would not take itself away. And Sir Gregory Gribe had been obstinate, beyond the ordinary obstinacy of a bank director. The rate of discount at the bank could not be settled for to-morrow without communication with Mr. Melmotte, and that was a matter on which the details were always most oppressive. At first Mr. Longestaffe was somewhat stunned by the Deputation and Sir Gregory Gribe; but as he waxed wroth the potency of those institutions dwindled away, and as, at last, he waxed hungry, they became as nothing to him. Was he not Mr. Longestaffe of Caversham, a Deputy-Lieutenant of his County, and accustomed to lunch punctually at two o'clock? When he had been in that waiting-room for two hours, it occurred to him that he only wanted his own, and that he would not remain there to be starved for any Mr. Melmotte in Europe. It occurred to him also that that thorn in his side, Squercum, would certainly get a finger into the pie to his infinite annoyance. Then he walked forth, and attempted to see Grendall for the fourth time. But Miles Grendall also liked his lunch, and was therefore declared by one of the junior clerks to be engaged at that moment on most important business with Mr. Melmotte. 'Then say that I can't wait any longer,' said Mr. Longestaffe, stamping out of the room with angry feet.

At the very door he met Mr. Melmotte. 'Ah, Mr. Longestaffe,' said the great financier, seizing him by the hand, 'you are the very man I am desirous of seeing.'

'I have been waiting two hours up in your place,' said the Squire of Caversham.

'Tut, tut, tut;—and they never told me!'

'I spoke to Mr. Grendall half a dozen times.'

'Yes,—yes. And he did put a slip with your name on it on my desk. I do remember. My dear sir, I have so many things on my brain, that I hardly know how to get along with them. You are coming to the Board? It's just the time now.'

'No;'—said Mr. Longestaffe. 'I can stay no longer in the City.' It was cruel that a man so hungry should be asked to go to a Board by a chairman who had just lunched at his club.

'I was carried away to the Bank of England and could not help myself,' said Melmotte. 'And when they get me there I can never get away again.'

'My son is very anxious to have the payments made

about Pickering,' said Mr. Longestaffe, absolutely holding Melmotte by the collar of his coat.

'Payments for Pickering!' said Melmotte, assuming an air of unimportant doubt,—of doubt as though the thing were of no real moment. 'Haven't they been made?'

'Certainly not,' said Mr. Longestaffe, 'unless made this morning.'

'There was something about it, but I cannot just remember what. My second cashier, Mr. Smith, manages all my private affairs, and they go clean out of my head. I'm afraid he's in Grosvenor Square at this moment. Let me see;—Pickering! Wasn't there some question of a mortgage? I'm sure there was something about a mortgage.'

'There was a mortgage, of course;—but that only made three payments necessary instead of two.'

'But there was some unavoidable delay about the papers;—something occasioned by the mortgagee. I know there was. But you shan't be inconvenienced, Mr. Longestaffe.'

'It's my son, Mr. Melmotte. He's got a lawyer of his own.'

'I never knew a young man that wasn't in a hurry for his money,' said Melmotte laughing. 'Oh, yes;—there were three payments to be made; one to you, one to your son, and one to the mortgagee. I will speak to Mr. Smith myself to-morrow—and you may tell your son that he really need not trouble his lawyer. He will only be losing his money, for lawyers are expensive. What! you won't come to the Board? I am sorry for that.' Mr. Longestaffe, having after a fashion said what he had to say, declined to go to the Board. A painful rumour had reached him the day before, which had been communicated to him in a very quiet way by a very old friend,—by a member of a private firm of bankers whom he was accustomed to regard as the wisest and most eminent man of his acquaintance,—that Pickering had been already mortgaged to its full value by its new owner. 'Mind, I know nothing,' said the banker. 'The report has reached me, and if it be true, it shows that Mr. Melmotte must be much pressed for money. It does not concern you at all if you have got your price. But it seems to be rather a quick transaction. I suppose you have, or he wouldn't have the title-deeds.' Mr. Longestaffe thanked his friend, and acknow-ledged that there had been something remiss on his part. Therefore, as he went westward, he was low in spirits. But nevertheless he had been reassured by Melmotte's manner.

Sir Felix Carbury of course did not attend the Board; nor did Paul Montague, for reasons with which the reader has been made acquainted. Lord Nidderdale had declined, having had enough of the City for that day, and Mr. Longestaffe had been banished by hunger. The chairman was therefore supported only by Lord Alfred and Mr. Cohenlupe. But they were such excellent colleagues that the work was got through as well as though those absentees had all attended. When the Board was over Mr. Melmotte and Mr. Cohenlupe retired together.

'I must get that money for Longestaffe,' said Melmotte to his friend.

'What, eighty thousand pounds! You can't do it this week,—nor yet before this day week.'

'It isn't eighty thousand pounds. I've renewed the mortgage, and that makes it only fifty. If I can manage the half of that which goes to the son, I can put the father off.'

'You must raise what you can on the whole property.'

'I've done that already,' said Melmotte hoarsely.

'And where's the money gone?'

'Brehgert has had £40,000. I was obliged to keep it up with them. You can manage £25,000 for me by Monday?' Mr. Cohenlupe said that he would try, but intimated his opinion that there would be considerable difficulty in the operation.

## Chapter LIV

### THE INDIA OFFICE

THE Conservative party at this particular period was putting its shoulder to the wheel,—not to push the coach up any hill, but to prevent its being hurried along at a pace which was not only dangerous, but manifestly destructive. The Conservative party now and then does put its shoulder to the wheel, ostensibly with the great national object above named; but also actuated by a natural desire to keep its own head well above water and be generally doing something, so that other parties may not suppose that it is moribund. There are, no doubt, members of it who really think that when some object has been achieved,—when, for instance, a good old Tory has been squeezed into Parliament for the borough of Porcorum, which for the last three parliaments has been represented by a Liberal,—the coach has been really stopped. To them, in their delightful faith, there comes at these triumphant moments a conviction that after all the people as a people have not been really in earnest in their efforts to take something from the greatness of the great, and to add something to the lowliness of the lowly. The handle of the windlass has been broken, the wheel is turning fast the reverse way, and the rope of Radical progress is running back. Who knows what may not be regained if the Conservative party will only put its shoulder to the wheel and take care that the handle of the windlass be not mended! Sticinthemud, which has ever been a doubtful little borough, has just been carried by a majority of fifteen! A long pull, a strong pull, and a pull altogether,—and the old day will come back again. Venerable patriarchs think of Lord Liverpool and other heroes, and dream dreams of Conservative bishops, Conservative lord-lieutenants, and of a Conservative ministry that shall remain in for a generation.*

Such a time was now present. Porcorum and Sticinthemud had done their duty valiantly,—with much

management. But Westminster! If this special seat for
Westminster could be carried, the country then could
hardly any longer have a doubt on the matter. If only
Mr. Melmotte could be got in for Westminster, it would
be manifest that the people were sound at heart, and
that all the great changes which had been effected during
the last forty years,—from the first reform in Parliament
down to the Ballot,—had been managed by the cunning
and treachery of a few ambitious men. Not, however,
that the Ballot was just now regarded by the party as
an unmitigated evil, though it was the last triumph of
Radical wickedness. The Ballot was on the whole
popular with the party. A short time since, no doubt it
was regarded by the party as being one and the same
as national ruin and national disgrace. But it had
answered well at Porcorum, and with due manipulation
had been found to be favourable at Sticinthemud.
The Ballot might perhaps help the long pull and the
strong pull,—and, in spite of the ruin and disgrace,
was thought by some just now to be a highly Conservative measure. It was considered that the Ballot
might assist Melmotte at Westminster very materially.

Any one reading the Conservative papers of the time,
and hearing the Conservative speeches in the borough,
—any one at least who lived so remote as not to have
learned what these things really mean,—would have
thought that England's welfare depended on Melmotte's
return. In the enthusiasm of the moment, the attacks
made on his character were answered by eulogy as
loud as the censure was bitter. The chief crime laid to
his charge was connected with the ruin of some great
continental assurance company, as to which it was said
that he had so managed it as to leave it utterly stranded,
with an enormous fortune of his own. It was declared
that every shilling which he had brought to England
with him had consisted of plunder stolen from the
shareholders in the company. Now the 'Evening Pulpit,'
in its endeavour to make the facts of this transaction
known, had placed what it called the domicile of this
company in Paris, whereas it was ascertained that its

official head-quarters had in truth been placed at Vienna. Was not such a blunder as this sufficient to show that no merchant of higher honour than Mr. Melmotte had ever adorned the Exchanges of modern capitals? And then two different newspapers of the time, both of them antagonistic to Melmotte, failed to be in accord on a material point. One declared that Mr. Melmotte was not in truth possessed of any wealth. The other said that he had derived his wealth from those unfortunate shareholders. Could anything betray so bad a cause as contradictions such as these? Could anything be so false, so weak, so malignant, so useless, so wicked, so self-condemned,—in fact, so 'Liberal' as a course of action such as this? The belief naturally to be deduced from such statements, nay, the unavoidable conviction on the minds—of, at any rate, the Conservative newspapers—was that Mr. Melmotte had accumulated an immense fortune, and that he had never robbed any shareholder of a shilling.

The friends of Melmotte had moreover a basis of hope, and were enabled to sound premonitory notes of triumph, arising from causes quite external to their party. The 'Breakfast Table' supported Melmotte, but the 'Breakfast Table' was not a Conservative organ. This support was given, not to the great man's political opinions, as to which a well-known writer in that paper suggested that the great man had probably not as yet given very much attention to the party questions which divided the country,—but to his commercial position. It was generally acknowledged that few men living,— perhaps no man alive,—had so acute an insight into the great commercial questions of the age as Mr. Augustus Melmotte. In whatever part of the world he might have acquired his commercial experience,—for it had been said repeatedly that Melmotte was not an Englishman, —he now made London his home and Great Britain his country, and it would be for the welfare of the country that such a man should sit in the British Parliament. Such were the arguments used by the 'Breakfast Table' in supporting Mr. Melmotte. This was, of course, an

assistance;—and not the less so because it was asserted
in other papers that the country would be absolutely
disgraced by his presence in Parliament. The hotter
the opposition the keener will be the support. Honest
good men, men who really loved their country, fine
gentlemen, who had received unsullied names from
great ancestors, shed their money right and left, and
grew hot in personally energetic struggles to have this
man returned to Parliament as the head of the great
Conservative mercantile interests of Great Britain!

There was one man who thoroughly believed that the
thing at the present moment most essentially necessary
to England's glory was the return of Mr. Melmotte for
Westminster. This man was undoubtedly a very ignorant
man. He knew nothing of any one political question
which had vexed England for the last half century,—
nothing whatever of the political history which had
made England what it was at the beginning of that
half century. Of such names as Hampden, Somers, and
Pitt he had hardly ever heard. He had probably never
read a book in his life. He knew nothing of the working
of parliament, nothing of nationality,—had no preference
whatever for one form of government over another,
never having given his mind a moment's trouble on the
subject. He had not even reflected how a despotic
monarch or a federal republic might affect himself, and
possibly did not comprehend the meaning of those
terms. But yet he was fully confident that England did
demand and ought to demand that Mr. Melmotte
should be returned for Westminster. This man was Mr.
Melmotte himself.

In this conjunction of his affairs Mr. Melmotte
certainly lost his head. He had audacity almost sufficient
for the very dangerous game which he was playing;
but, as crisis heaped itself upon crisis, he became
deficient in prudence. He did not hesitate to speak of
himself as the man who ought to represent Westminster,
and of those who opposed him as little malignant beings
who had mean interests of their own to serve. He went
about in his open carriage, with Lord Alfred at his

left hand, with a look on his face which seemed to imply that Westminster was not good enough for him. He even hinted to certain political friends that at the next general election he should try the City.* Six months since he had been a humble man to a Lord,—but now he scolded Earls and snubbed Dukes, and yet did it in a manner which showed how proud he was of connecting himself with their social pre-eminence, and how ignorant of the manner in which such pre-eminence affects English gentlemen generally. The more arrogant he became the more vulgar he was, till even Lord Alfred would almost be tempted to rush away to impecuniosity and freedom. Perhaps there were some with whom this conduct had a salutary effect. No doubt arrogance will produce submission; and there are men who take other men at the price those other men put upon them-selves. Such persons could not refrain from thinking Melmotte to be mighty because he swaggered; and gave their hinder parts to be kicked merely because he put up his toe. We all know men of this calibre,—and how they seem to grow in number. But the net result of his personal demeanour was injurious; and it was debated among some of the warmest of his supporters, whether a hint should not be given him. 'Couldn't Lord Alfred say a word to him?' said the Honourable Beauchamp Beauclerk, who, himself in Parliament, a leading man in his party, thoroughly well acquainted with the borough, wealthy and connected by blood with half the great Conservative families in the kingdom, had been moving heaven and earth on behalf of the great financial king, and working like a slave for his success.

'Alfred's more than half afraid of him,' said Lionel Lupton, a young aristocrat, also in Parliament, who had been inoculated with the idea that the interests of the party demanded Melmotte in Parliament, but who would have given up his Scotch shooting rather than have undergone Melmotte's company for a day.

'Something really must be done, Mr. Beauclerk,' said Mr. Jones, who was the leading member of a very wealthy firm of builders in the borough, who had become a Conservative politician, who had thoughts of the House for himself, but who never forgot his own position. 'He is making a great many personal enemies.'

'He's the finest old turkey cock out,' said Lionel Lupton.

Then it was decided that Mr. Beauclerk should speak a word to Lord Alfred. The rich man and the poor man were cousins, and had always been intimate. 'Alfred,' said the chosen mentor at the club one afternoon, 'I wonder whether you couldn't say something to Melmotte about his manner.' Lord Alfred turned sharp round and looked into his companion's face. 'They tell me he is giving offence. Of course he doesn't mean it. Couldn't he draw it a little milder?'

Lord Alfred made his reply almost in a whisper. 'If you ask me, I don't think he could. If you got him down and trampled on him, you might make him mild. I don't think there's any other way.'

'You couldn't speak to him, then?'

'Not unless I did it with a horsewhip.'

This, coming from Lord Alfred, who was absolutely dependent on the man, was very strong. Lord Alfred had been much afflicted that morning. He had spent some hours with his friend, either going about the borough in the open carriage, or standing just behind him at meetings, or sitting close to him in committee-rooms,—and had been nauseated with Melmotte. When spoken to about his friend he could not restrain himself. Lord Alfred had been born and bred a gentleman, and found the position in which he was now earning his bread to be almost insupportable. It had gone against the grain with him at first, when he was called Alfred; but now that he was told 'just to open the door,' and 'just to give that message,' he almost meditated revenge. Lord Nidderdale, who was quick at observation, had seen something of this in Grosvenor Square, and declared that Lord Alfred had invested part of his recent savings in a cutting whip. Mr. Beau-clerk, when he had got his answer, whistled and with-

drew. But he was true to his party. Melmotte was not
the first vulgar man whom the Conservatives had taken
by the hand, and patted on the back, and told that he
was a god.*

The Emperor of China was now in England, and was
to be entertained one night at the India Office. The
Secretary of State for the second great Asiatic Empire
was to entertain the ruler of the first. This was on
Saturday the 6th of July, and Melmotte's dinner was to
take place on the following Monday. Very great interest
was made by the London world generally to obtain
admission to the India Office,—the making of such
interest consisting in the most abject begging for tickets
of admission, addressed to the Secretary of State, to all
the under secretaries, to assistant secretaries, secretaries
of departments, chief clerks, and to head-messengers
and their wives. If a petitioner could not be admitted
as a guest into the splendour of the reception rooms,
might not he,—or she,—be allowed to stand in some
passage whence the Emperor's back might perhaps be
seen,—so that, if possible, the petitioner's name might
be printed in the list of guests which would be published
on the next morning? Now Mr. Melmotte with his
family was, or course, supplied with tickets. He, who
was to spend a fortune in giving the Emperor a dinner,
was of course entitled to be present at other places to
which the Emperor would be brought to be shown.
Melmotte had already seen the Emperor at a breakfast
in Windsor Park, and at a ball in royal halls. But
hitherto he had not been presented to the Emperor.
Presentations have to be restricted,—if only on the score
of time; and it had been thought that as Mr. Melmotte
would of course have some communication with the
hardworked Emperor at his own house, that would
suffice. But he had felt himself to be ill-used and was
offended. He spoke with bitterness to some of his
supporters of the Royal Family generally, because he
had not been brought to the front rank either at the
breakfast or at the ball,—and now, at the India Office,
was determined to have his due. But he was not on the

list of those whom the Secretary of State intended on this
occasion to present to the Brother of the Sun.

He had dined freely. At this period of his career he
had taken to dining freely,—which was in itself impru-
dent, as he had need at all hours of his best intelligence.
Let it not be understood that he was tipsy. He was a
man whom wine did not often affect after that fashion.
But it made him, who was arrogant before, tower in his
arrogance till he was almost sure to totter. It was
probably at some moment after dinner that Lord Alfred
decided upon buying the cutting whip of which he had
spoken. Melmotte went with his wife and daughter to
the India Office, and soon left them far in the background with a request,—we may say an order,—to
Lord Alfred to take care of them. It may be observed
here that Marie Melmotte was almost as great a
curiosity as the Emperor himself, and was much noticed
as the girl who had attempted to run away to New
York, but had gone without her lover. Melmotte
entertained some foolish idea that as the India Office
was in Westminster, he had a peculiar right to demand
an introduction on this occasion because of his candidature. He did succeed in getting hold of an unfortunate
under secretary of state, a studious and invaluable
young peer, known as Earl De Griffin. He was a shy
man, of enormous wealth, of mediocre intellect, and no
great physical ability, who never amused himself; but
worked hard night and day, and read everything that
anybody could write, and more than any other person
could read, about India. Had Mr. Melmotte wanted
to know the exact dietary of the peasants in Orissa, or
the revenue of the Punjaub, or the amount of crime in
Bombay, Lord De Griffin would have informed him
without a pause. But in this matter of managing the
Emperor, the under secretary had nothing to do, and
would have been the last man to be engaged in such a
service. He was, however, second in command at the
India Office, and of his official rank Melmotte was
unfortunately made aware. 'My Lord,' said he, by no
means hiding his demand in a whisper, 'I am desirous

of being presented to his Imperial Majesty.' Lord De Griffin looked at him in despair, not knowing the great man,—being one of the few men in that room who did not know him.

'This is Mr. Melmotte,' said Lord Alfred, who had deserted the ladies and still stuck to his master. 'Lord De Griffin, let me introduce you to Mr. Melmotte.'

'Oh—oh—oh,' said Lord De Griffin, just putting out his hand. 'I am delighted;—ah, yes,' and pretending to see somebody, he made a weak and quite ineffectual attempt to escape.

Melmotte stood directly in his way, and with unabashed audacity repeated his demand. 'I am desirous of being presented to his Imperial Majesty. Will you do me the honour of making my request known to Mr. Wilson?' Mr. Wilson was the Secretary of State, who was as busy as a Secretary of State is sure to be on such an occasion.

'I hardly know,' said Lord De Griffin. 'I'm afraid it's all arranged. I don't know anything about it myself.'

'You can introduce me to Mr. Wilson.'

'He's up there, Mr. Melmotte; and I couldn't get at him. Really you must excuse me. I'm very sorry. If I see him I'll tell him.' And the poor under secretary again endeavoured to escape.

Mr. Melmotte put up his hand and stopped him. 'I'm not going to stand this kind of thing,' he said. The old Marquis of Auld Reekie was close at hand, the father of Lord Nidderdale, and therefore the proposed father-in-law of Melmotte's daughter, and he poked his thumb heavily into Lord Alfred's ribs. 'It is generally understood, I believe,' continued Melmotte, 'that the Emperor is to do me the honour of dining at my poor house on Monday. He don't dine there unless I'm made acquainted with him before he comes. I mean what I say. I ain't going to entertain even an Emperor unless I'm good enough to be presented to him. Perhaps you'd better let Mr. Wilson know, as a good many people intend to come.'

'Here's a row,' said the old Marquis. 'I wish he'd be as good as his word.'

'He has taken a little wine,' whispered Lord Alfred. 'Melmotte,' he said, still whispering; 'upon my word it isn't the thing. They're only Indian chaps and Eastern swells who are presented here,—not a fellow among 'em all who hasn't been in India or China, or isn't a Secretary of State, or something of that kind.'

'Then they should have done it at Windsor, or at the ball,' said Melmotte, pulling down his waistcoat. 'By George, Alfred! I'm in earnest, and somebody had better look to it. If I'm not presented to his Imperial Majesty to-night, by G——, there shall be no dinner in Grosvenor Square on Monday. I'm master enough of my own house, I suppose, to be able to manage that.'

Here was a row, as the Marquis had said! Lord De Griffin was frightened, and Lord Alfred felt that something ought to be done. 'There's no knowing how far the pig-headed brute may go in his obstinacy,' Lord Alfred said to Mr. Lupton, who was there. It no doubt might have been wise to have allowed the merchant prince to return home with the resolution that his dinner should be abandoned. He would have repented probably before the next morning; and had he continued obdurate it would not have been difficult to explain to Celestial Majesty that something preferable had been found for that particular evening even to a banquet at the house of British commerce. The Government would probably have gained the seat for Westminster, as Melmotte would at once have become very unpopular with the great body of his supporters. But Lord De Griffin was not the man to see this. He did make his way up to Mr. Wilson, and explained to the Amphytrion of the night*the demand which was made on his hospitality. A thoroughly well-established and experienced political Minister of State always feels that if he can make a friend or appease an enemy without paying a heavy price he will be doing a good stroke of business. 'Bring him up,' said Mr. Wilson. 'He's going to do something out in the East, isn't he?' 'Nothing in

India,' said Lord De Griffin. 'The submarine telegraph is quite impossible.' Mr. Wilson, instructing some satellite to find out in what way he might properly connect Mr. Melmotte with China, sent Lord De Griffin away with his commission.

'My dear Alfred, just allow me to manage these things myself,' Mr. Melmotte was saying when the under secretary returned. 'I know my own position and how to keep it. There shall be no dinner. I'll be d——if any of the lot shall dine in Grosvenor Square on Monday.' Lord Alfred was so astounded that he was thinking of making his way to the Prime Minister, a man whom he abhorred and didn't know, and of acquainting him with the terrible calamity which was threatened. But the arrival of the under secretary saved him the trouble.

'If you will come with me,' whispered Lord De Griffin, 'it shall be managed. It isn't just the thing, but as you wish it, it shall be done.'

'I do wish it,' said Melmotte aloud. He was one of those men whom success never mollified, whose enjoyment of a point gained always demanded some hoarse note of triumph from his own trumpet.

'If you will be so kind as to follow me,' said Lord De Griffin. And so the thing was done. Melmotte, as he was taken up to the imperial footstool, was resolved upon making a little speech, forgetful at the moment of interpreters,—of the double interpreters whom the Majesty of China required; but the awful, quiescent solemnity of the celestial one quelled even him, and he shuffled by without saying a word even of his own banquet.

But he had gained his point, and, as he was taken home to poor Mr. Longestaffe's house in Bruton Street, was intolerable. Lord Alfred tried to escape after putting Madame Melmotte and her daughter into the carriage, but Melmotte insisted on his presence. 'You might as well come, Alfred;—there are two or three things I must settle before I go to bed.'

'I'm about knocked up,' said the unfortunate man.

'Knocked up, nonsense! Think what I've been through. I've been all day at the hardest work a man can do.' Had he as usual got in first, leaving his man-of-all-work to follow, the man-of-all-work would have escaped. Melmotte, fearing such defection, put his hand on Lord Alfred's shoulder, and the poor fellow was beaten. As they were taken home a continual sound of cock-crowing was audible, but as the words were not distinguished they required no painful attention; but when the soda water and brandy and cigars made their appearance in Mr. Longestaffe's own back room, then the trumpet was sounded with a full blast. 'I mean to let the fellows know what's what,' said Melmotte, walking about the room. Lord Alfred had thrown himself into an arm-chair, and was consoling himself as best he might with tobacco. 'Give and take is a very good motto. If I scratch their back, I mean them to scratch mine. They won't find many people to spend ten thousand pounds in entertaining a guest of the country's as a private enterprise. I don't know of any other man of business who could do it, or would do it. It's not much any of them can do for me. Thank God, I don't want 'em. But if consideration is to be shown to anybody, I intend to be considered. The Prince treated me very scurvily, Alfred, and I shall take an opportunity of telling him so on Monday. I suppose a man may be allowed to speak to his own guests.'

'You might turn the election against you if you said anything the Prince didn't like.'

'D—— the election, sir. I stand before the electors of Westminster as a man of business, not as a courtier,—as a man who understands commercial enterprise, not as one of the Prince's toadies. Some of you fellows in England don't realize the matter yet; but I can tell you that I think myself quite as great a man as any Prince.' Lord Alfred looked at him, with strong reminiscences of the old ducal home, and shuddered. 'I'll teach them a lesson before long. Didn't I teach 'em a lesson to-night, —eh? They tell me that Lord De Griffin has sixty thousand a-year to spend. What's sixty thousand a year? Didn't I make him go on my business? And didn't I make 'em do as I chose? You want to tell me this and that, but I can tell you that I know more of men and women than some of you fellows do, who think you know a great deal.'

This went on through the whole of a long cigar; and afterwards, as Lord Alfred slowly paced his way back to his lodgings in Mount Street, he thought deeply whether there might not be means of escaping from his present servitude. 'Beast! Brute! Pig!' he said to himself over and over again as he slowly went to Mount Street.

## Chapter LV

### CLERICAL CHARITIES

MELMOTTE'S success, and Melmotte's wealth, and Melmotte's antecedents were much discussed down in Suffolk at this time. He had been seen there in the flesh, and there is no believing like that which comes from sight. He had been staying at Caversham, and many in those parts knew that Miss Longestaffe was now living in his house in London. The purchase of the Pickering estate had also been noticed in all the Suffolk and Norfolk newspapers. Rumours, therefore, of his past frauds, rumour also as to the instability of his presumed fortune, were as current as those which declared him to be by far the richest man in England. Miss Melmotte's little attempt had also been communicated in the papers; and Sir Felix, though he was not recognized as being 'real Suffolk' himself, was so far connected with Suffolk by name as to add something to this feeling of reality respecting the Melmottes generally. Suffolk is very old-fashioned. Suffolk, taken as a whole, did not like the Melmotte fashion. Suffolk, which is, I fear, persistently and irrecoverably Conservative, did not believe in Melmotte as a Conservative Member of Parliament. Suffolk on this occasion was rather ashamed of the Longestaffes, and took occasion to remember that it was barely the other day, as Suffolk counts days, since the original Longestaffe was in trade. This selling of Pickering, and especially the selling of it to Melmotte, was a mean thing. Suffolk, as a whole, thoroughly believed that Melmotte had picked the very bones of every shareholder in that Franco-Austrian Assurance Company.

Mr. Hepworth was over with Roger one morning, and they were talking about him,—or talking rather of the attempted elopement. 'I know nothing about it,' said Roger, 'and I do not intend to ask. Of course I did know when they were down here that he hoped to marry her, and I did believe that she was willing to marry him. But whether the father had consented or not I never inquired.'

'It seems he did not consent.'

'Nothing could have been more unfortunate for either of them than such a marriage. Melmotte will probably be in the "Gazette" before long, and my cousin not only has not a shilling, but could not keep one if he had it.'

'You think Melmotte will turn out a failure.'

'A failure! Of course he's a failure, whether rich or poor;—a miserable imposition, a hollow vulgar fraud from beginning to end,—too insignificant for you and me to talk of, were it not that his position is a sign of the degeneracy of the age. What are we coming to when such as he is an honoured guest at our tables?'

'At just a table here and there,' suggested his friend.

'No;—it is not that. You can keep your house free from him, and so can I mine. But we set no example to the nation at large. They who do set the example go to his feasts, and of course he is seen at theirs in return. And yet these leaders of the fashion know,—at any rate they believe,—that he is what he is because he has been a swindler greater than other swindlers. What follows as a natural consequence? Men reconcile themselves to swindling. Though they themselves mean to be honest, dishonesty of itself is no longer odious to them. Then there comes the jealousy that others should be growing rich with the approval of all the world,—and the natural aptitude to do what all the world approves.

It seems to me that the existence of a Melmotte is not compatible with a wholesome state of things in general.'

Roger dined with the Bishop of Elmham that evening, and the same hero was discussed under a different heading. 'He has given £200,' said the Bishop, 'to the Curates' Aid Society. I don't know that a man could spend his money much better than that.'

'Clap-trap!' said Roger, who in his present mood was very bitter.

'The money is not clap-trap, my friend. I presume that the money is really paid.'

'I don't feel at all sure of that.'

'Our collectors for clerical charities are usually stern men,—very ready to make known defalcations on the part of promising subscribers. I think they would take care to get the money during the election.'

'And you think that money got in that way redounds to his credit?'

'Such a gift shows him to be a useful member of society,—and I am always for encouraging useful men.'

'Even though their own objects may be vile and pernicious?'

'There you beg ever so many questions, Mr. Carbury. Mr. Melmotte wishes to get into Parliament, and if there would vote on the side which you at any rate approve. I do not know that his object in that respect is pernicious. And as a seat in Parliament has been a matter of ambition to the best of our countrymen for centuries, I do not know why we should say that it is vile in this man.' Roger frowned and shook his head. 'Of course Mr. Melmotte is not the sort of gentleman whom you have been accustomed to regard as a fitting member for a Conservative constituency. But the country is changing.'

'It's going to the dogs, I think;—about as fast as it can go.'

'We build churches much faster than we used to do.'

'Do we say our prayers in them when we have built them?' asked the Squire.

'It is very hard to see into the minds of men,' said the

Bishop; 'but we can see the results of their minds' work. I think that men on the whole do live better lives than they did a hundred years ago. There is a wider spirit of justice abroad, more of mercy from one to another, a more lively charity, and if less of religious enthusiasm, less also of superstition. Men will hardly go to heaven, Mr. Carbury, by following forms only because their fathers followed the same forms before them.'

'I suppose men will go to heaven, my Lord, by doing as they would be done by.'

'There can be no safer lesson. But we must hope that some may be saved even if they have not practised at all times that grand self-denial. Who comes up to that teaching? Do you not wish for, nay, almost demand, instant pardon for any trespass that you may commit,— of temper, or manner, for instance? and are you always ready to forgive in that way yourself? Do you not writhe with indignation at being wrongly judged by others who condemn you without knowing your actions or the causes of them; and do you never judge others after that fashion?'

'I do not put myself forward as an example.'

'I apologise for the personal form of my appeal. A clergyman is apt to forget that he is not in the pulpit. Of course I speak of men in general. Taking society as a whole, the big and the little, the rich and the poor, I think that it grows better from year to year, and not worse.* I think, too, that they who grumble at the times, as Horace did, and declare that each age is worse than its forerunner, look only at the small things beneath their eyes, and ignore the course of the world at large.'

'But Roman freedom and Roman manners were going to the dogs when Horace wrote.'

'But Christ was about to be born, and men were already being made fit by wider intelligence for Christ's teaching. And as for freedom, has not freedom grown, almost every year, from that to this?'

'In Rome they were worshipping just such men as this Melmotte. Do you remember the man who sat upon the seats of the knights and scoured the Via Sacra

with his toga, though he had been scourged from pillar
to post for his villainies? I always think of that man
when I hear Melmotte's name mentioned. Hoc, hoc
tribuno militum!* Is this the man to be Conservative
member for Westminster?'

'Do you know of the scourges, as a fact?'

'I think I know that they are deserved.'

'That is hardly doing to others as you would be done
by. If the man is what you say, he will surely be found
out at last, and the day of his punishment will come.
Your friend in the ode probably had a bad time of it,
in spite of his farms and his horses. The world perhaps
is managed more justly than you think, Mr. Carbury.'

'My Lord, I believe you're a Radical at heart,' said
Roger, as he took his leave.

'Very likely,—very likely. Only don't say so to the
Prime Minister, or I shall never get any of the better
things which may be going.'

The Bishop was not hopelessly in love with a young
lady, and was therefore less inclined to take a melancholy
view of things in general than Roger Carbury. To Roger
everything seemed to be out of joint. He had that
morning received a letter from Lady Carbury, reminding
him of the promise of a loan, should a time come to her
of great need. It had come very quickly. Roger Carbury
did not in the least begrudge the hundred pounds which
he had already sent to his cousin; but he did begrudge
any furtherance afforded to the iniquitous schemes of
Sir Felix. He felt all but sure that the foolish mother had
given her son money for his abortive attempt, and that
therefore this appeal had been made to him. He
alluded to no such fear in his letter. He simply enclosed
the cheque, and expressed a hope that the amount might
suffice for the present emergency. But he was disheartened and disgusted by all the circumstances of the
Carbury family. There was Paul Montague, bringing
a woman such as Mrs. Hurtle down to Lowestoffe,
declaring his purpose of continuing his visits to her, and,
as Roger thought, utterly unable to free himself from
his toils,—and yet, on this man's account, Hetta was

cold and hard to him. He was conscious of the honesty of his own love, sure that he could make her happy,— confident, not in himself, but in the fashion and ways of his own life. What would be Hetta's lot if her heart was really given to Paul Montague?

When he got home, he found Father Barham sitting in his library. An accident had lately happened at Father Barham's own establishment. The wind had blown the roof off his cottage; and Roger Carbury, though his affection for the priest was waning, had offered him shelter while the damage was being repaired. Shelter at Carbury Manor was very much more comfortable than the priest's own establishment, even with the roof on, and Father Barham was in clover. Father Barham was reading his own favourite newspaper, 'The Surplice,' when Roger entered the room. 'Have you seen this, Mr. Carbury?' he said.

'What's this? I am not likely to have seen anything that belongs peculiarly to "The Surplice."'

'That's the prejudice of what you are pleased to call the Anglican Church. Mr. Melmotte is a convert to our faith. He is a great man, and will perhaps be one of the greatest known on the face of the globe.'

'Melmotte a convert to Romanism! I'll make you a present of him, and thank you to take him; but I don't believe that we've any such good riddance.'

Then Father Barham read a paragraph out of 'The Surplice.' 'Mr. Augustus Melmotte, the great financier and capitalist, has presented a hundred guineas towards the erection of an altar for the new church of St. Fabricius, in Tothill Fields. The donation was accompanied by a letter from Mr. Melmotte's secretary, which leaves but little doubt that the new member for Westminster will be a member, and no inconsiderable member, of the Catholic party in the House, during the next session.'

'That's another dodge, is it?' said Carbury.

'What do you mean by a dodge, Mr. Carbury? Because money is given for a pious object of which you do not happen to approve, must it be a dodge?'

'But, my dear Father Barham, the day before the same great man gave £200 to the Protestant Curates' Aid Society. I have just left the Bishop exulting in this great act of charity.'

'I don't believe a word of it;—or it may be a parting gift to the Church to which he belonged in his darkness.'

'And you would be really proud of Mr. Melmotte as a convert?'

'I would be proud of the lowest human being that has a soul,' said the priest; 'but of course we are glad to welcome the wealthy and the great.'

'The great! oh dear!'

'A man is great who has made for himself such a position as that of Mr. Melmotte. And when such a one leaves your Church and joins our own, it is a great sign to us that the Truth is prevailing.' Roger Carbury, without another word, took his candle and went to bed.

## Chapter LVI

### FATHER BARHAM VISITS LONDON

IT was considered to be a great thing to catch the Roman Catholic vote in Westminster. For many years it has been considered a great thing both in the House and out of the House to 'catch' Roman Catholic votes. There are two modes of catching these votes. This or that individual Roman Catholic may be promoted to place, so that he personally may be made secure; or the right hand of fellowship may be extended to the people of the Pope generally, so that the people of the Pope may be taught to think that a general step is being made towards the reconversion of the nation. The first measure is the easier, but the effect is but slight and soon passes away. The promoted one, though as far as his prayers go he may remain as good a Catholic as ever, soon ceases to be one of the party to be conciliated, and is apt after a while to be regarded by them as an enemy. But the other mode, if a step be well taken, may be very efficacious. It has now and then

occurred that every Roman Catholic in Ireland and
England has been brought to believe that the nation is
coming round to them;—and in this or that borough
the same conviction has been made to grow. To catch
the Protestant,—that is the peculiarly Protestant,—vote
and the Roman Catholic vote at the same instant is
a feat difficult of accomplishment; but it has been
attempted before, and was attempted now by Mr. Melmotte and his friends. It was perhaps thought by his
friends that the Protestants would not notice the £100
given for the altar to St. Fabricius; but Mr. Alf was wide
awake, and took care that Mr. Melmotte's religious
opinions should be a matter of interest to the world at
large. During all that period of newspaper excitement
there was perhaps no article that created so much
general interest as that which appeared in the 'Evening
Pulpit,' with a special question asked at the head of it,
'For Priest or Parson?' In this article, which was more
than usually delightful as being pungent from the
beginning to the end and as being unalloyed with any
dry didactic wisdom, Mr. Alf's man, who did that
business, declared that it was really important that the
nation at large and especially the electors of Westminster should know what was the nature of Mr.
Melmotte's faith. That he was a man of a highly
religious temperament was most certain by his munificent
charities on behalf of religion. Two noble donations,
which by chance had been made just at this crisis, were
doubtless no more than the regular continuation of his
ordinary flow of Christian benevolence. The 'Evening
Pulpit' by no means insinuated that the gifts were
intended to have any reference to the approaching
election. Far be it from the 'Evening Pulpit' to imagine
that so great a man as Mr. Melmotte looked for any
return in this world from his charitable generosity. But
still, as Protestants naturally desired to be represented
in Parliament by a Protestant member, and as Roman
Catholics as naturally desired to be represented by a
Roman Catholic, perhaps Mr. Melmotte would not
object to declare his creed.

This was biting, and of course did mischief; but Mr. Melmotte and his manager were not foolish enough to allow it to actuate them in any way. He had thrown his bread upon the waters, assisting St. Fabricius with one hand and the Protestant curates with the other, and must leave the results to take care of themselves. If the Protestants chose to believe that he was hyper-protestant, and the Catholics that he was tending towards papacy, so much the better for him. Any enthusiastic religionists wishing to enjoy such convictions would not allow themselves to be enlightened by the manifestly interested malignity of Mr. Alf's newspaper.

It may be doubted whether the donation to the Curates' Aid Society did have much effect. It may perhaps have induced a resolution in some few to go to the poll whose minds were active in regard to religion and torpid as to politics. But the donation to St. Fabricius certainly had results. It was taken up and made much of by the Roman Catholic party generally, till a report got itself spread abroad and almost believed that Mr. Melmotte was going to join the Church of Rome. These manœuvres require most delicate handling, or evil may follow instead of good. On the second afternoon after the question had been asked in the 'Evening Pulpit,' an answer to it appeared, 'For Priest and not for Parson.' Therein various assertions made by Roman Catholic organs and repeated in Roman Catholic speeches were brought together, so as to show that Mr. Melmotte really had at last made up his mind on this important question. All the world knew now, said Mr. Alf's writer, that with that keen sense of honesty which was the Great Financier's peculiar characteristic,—the Great Financier was the name which Mr. Alf had specially invented for Mr. Melmotte, —he had doubted, till the truth was absolutely borne in upon him, whether he could serve the nation best as a Liberal or as a Conservative. He had solved that doubt with wisdom. And now this other doubt had passed through the crucible, and by the aid of fire a golden certainty had been produced. The world of Westminster

at last knew that Mr. Melmotte was a Roman Catholic.
Now nothing was clearer than this,—that though
catching the Catholic vote would greatly help a candidate, no real Roman Catholic could hope to be returned.
This last article vexed Mr. Melmotte, and he proposed
to his friends to send a letter to the 'Breakfast Table'
asserting that he adhered to the Protestant faith of his
ancestors. But, as it was suspected by many, and was
now being whispered to the world at large, that Melmotte had been born a Jew, this assurance would perhaps
have been too strong. 'Do nothing of the kind,' said
Mr. Beauchamp Beauclerk. 'If any one asks you a
question at any meeting, say that you are a Protestant.
But it isn't likely, as we have none but our own people.
Don't go writing letters.'

But unfortunately the gift of an altar to St. Fabricius
was such a godsend that sundry priests about the
country were determined to cling to the good man who
had bestowed his money so well. I think that many of
them did believe that this was a great sign of a beauteous
stirring of people's minds in favour of Rome. The
fervent Romanists have always this point in their
favour, that they are ready to believe. And they have
a desire for the conversion of men which is honest in
an exactly inverse ratio to the dishonesty of the means
which they employ to produce it. Father Barham was
ready to sacrifice anything personal to himself in the
good cause,—his time, his health, his money when he
had any, and his life. Much as he liked the comfort of
Carbury Hall, he would never for a moment condescend
to ensure its continued enjoyment by reticence as to his
religion. Roger Carbury was hard of heart. He could
see that. But the dropping of water might hollow the
stone. If the dropping should be put an end to by
outward circumstances before the stone had been
impressed that would not be his fault. He at any rate
would do his duty. In that fixed resolution Father
Barham was admirable. But he had no scruple whatsoever as to the nature of the arguments he would use,—
or as to the facts which he would proclaim. With the

mingled ignorance of his life and the positiveness of his faith he had at once made up his mind that Melmotte was a great man, and that he might be made a great instrument on behalf of the Pope. He believed in the enormous proportions of the man's wealth,—believed that he was powerful in all quarters of the globe,—and believed, because he was so told by 'The Surplice,' that the man was at heart a Catholic. That a man should be at heart a Catholic, and live in the world professing the Protestant religion, was not to Father Barham either improbable or distressing. Kings who had done so were to him objects of veneration. By such subterfuges and falsehood of life had they been best able to keep alive the spark of heavenly fire. There was a mystery and religious intrigue in this which recommended itself to the young priest's mind. But it was clear to him that this was a peculiar time,—in which it behoved an earnest man to be doing something. He had for some weeks been preparing himself for a trip to London in order that he might spend a week in retreat with kindred souls who from time to time betook themselves to the cells of St. Fabricius. And so, just at this season of the Westminster election, Father Barham made a journey to London.

He had conceived the great idea of having a word or two with Mr. Melmotte himself. He thought that he might be convinced by a word or two as to the man's faith. And he thought, also, that it might be a happiness to him hereafter to have had intercourse with a man who was perhaps destined to be the means of restoring the true faith to his country. On Saturday night,—that Saturday night on which Mr. Melmotte had so successfully exercised his greatness at the India Office,—he took up his quarters in the cloisters of St. Fabricius; he spent a goodly festive Sunday among the various Romanist church services of the metropolis; and on the Monday morning he sallied forth in quest of Mr. Melmotte. Having obtained that address from some circular, he went first to Abchurch Lane. But on this day, and on the next, which would be the day of the election, Mr. Melmotte was not expected in the City, and the priest was referred to his present private residence in Bruton Street. There he was told that the great man might probably be found in Grosvenor Square, and at the house in the square Father Barham was at last successful. Mr. Melmotte was there superintending the arrangements for the entertainment of the Emperor.

The servants, or more probably the workmen, must have been at fault in giving the priest admittance. But in truth the house was in great confusion. The wreaths of flowers and green boughs were being suspended, last daubs of heavy gilding were being given to the wooden capitals of mock pilasters, incense was being burned to kill the smell of the paint, tables were being fixed and chairs were being moved; and an enormous set of open presses were being nailed together for the accommodation of hats and cloaks. The hall was chaos, and poor Father Barham, who had heard a good deal of the Westminster election, but not a word of the intended entertainment of the Emperor, was at a loss to conceive for what purpose these operations were carried on. But through the chaos he made his way, and did soon find himself in the presence of Mr. Melmotte in the banqueting hall.

Mr. Melmotte was attended both by Lord Alfred and his son. He was standing in front of the chair which had been arranged for the Emperor, with his hat on one side of his head, and he was very angry indeed. He had been given to understand when the dinner was first planned, that he was to sit opposite to his august guest;— by which he had conceived that he was to have a seat immediately in face of the Emperor of Emperors, of the Brother of the Sun, of the Celestial One himself. It was now explained to him that this could not be done. In face of the Emperor there must be a wide space, so that his Majesty might be able to look down the hall; and the royal princesses who sat next to the Emperor, and the royal princes who sat next to the princesses, must also be so indulged. And in this way Mr. Melmotte's own seat became really quite obscure. Lord Alfred was having a very bad time of it. 'It's that fellow from "The Herald" office did it, not me,' he said, almost in a passion. 'I don't know how people ought to sit. But that's the reason.'

'I'm d—— if I'm going to be treated in this way in my own house,' were the first words which the priest heard. And as Father Barham walked up the room and came close to the scene of action, unperceived by either of the Grendalls, Mr. Melmotte was trying, but trying in vain, to move his own seat nearer to Imperial Majesty. A bar had been put up of such a nature that Melmotte, sitting in the seat prepared for him, would absolutely be barred out from the centre of his own hall. 'Who the d—— are you?' he asked, when the priest appeared close before his eyes on the inner or more imperial side of the bar. It was not the habit of Father Barham's life to appear in sleek apparel. He was ever clothed in the very rustiest brown black that age can produce. In Beccles where he was known it signified little, but in the halls of the great one in Grosvenor Square, perhaps the stranger's welcome was cut to the measure of his outer man. A comely priest in glossy black might have been received with better grace.

Father Barham stood humbly with his hat off. He was a man of infinite pluck; but outward humility—at any rate at the commencement of an enterprise,—was the rule of his life. 'I am the Rev. Mr. Barham,' said the visitor. 'I am the priest of Beccles in Suffolk. I believe I am speaking to Mr. Melmotte.'

'That's my name, sir. And what may you want? I don't know whether you are aware that you have found your way into my private dining-room without any introduction. Where the mischief are the fellows, Alfred, who ought to have seen about this? I wish you'd look to it, Miles. Can anybody who pleases walk into my hall?'

'I came on a mission which I hope may be pleaded as my excuse,' said the priest. Although he was bold, he found it difficult to explain his mission. Had not Lord Alfred been there he could have done it better, in spite of the very repulsive manner of the great man himself.

'Is it business?' asked Lord Alfred.

'Certainly it is business,' said Father Barham with a smile.

'Then you had better call at the office in Abchurch Lane,—in the City,' said his lordship.

'My business is not of that nature. I am a poor servant of the Cross, who is anxious to know from the lips of Mr. Melmotte himself that his heart is inclined to the true Faith.'

'Some lunatic,' said Melmotte. 'See that there ain't any knives about, Alfred.'

'No otherwise mad, sir, than they have ever been accounted mad who are enthusiastic in their desire for the souls of others.'

'Just get a policeman, Alfred. Or send somebody; you'd better not go away.'

'You will hardly need a policeman, Mr. Melmotte,' continued the priest. 'If I might speak to you alone for a few minutes——'

'Certainly not;—certainly not. I am very busy, and if you will not go away you'll have to be taken away. I wonder whether anybody knows him.'

'Mr. Carbury, of Carbury Hall, is my friend.'

'Carbury! D—— the Carburys! Did any of the Carburys send you here? A set of beggars! Why don't you do something, Alfred, to get rid of him?'

'You'd better go,' said Lord Alfred. 'Don't make a rumpus, there's a good fellow;—but just go.'

'There shall be no rumpus,' said the priest, waxing wrathful. 'I asked for you at the door, and was told to come in by your own servants. Have I been uncivil that you should treat me in this fashion?'

'You're in the way,' said Lord Alfred.

'It's a piece of gross impertinence,' said Melmotte. 'Go away.'

'Will you not tell me before I go whether I shall pray for you as one whose steps in the right path should be made sure and firm; or as one still in error and in darkness?'

'What the mischief does he mean?' asked Melmotte.

'He wants to know whether you're a papist,' said Lord Alfred.

'What the deuce is it to him?' almost screamed Melmotte;—whereupon Father Barham bowed and took his leave.

'That's a remarkable thing,' said Melmotte,—'very remarkable.' Even this poor priest's mad visit added to his inflation. 'I suppose he was in earnest.'

'Mad as a hatter,' said Lord Alfred.

'But why did he come to me in his madness—to me especially? That's what I want to know. I'll tell you what it is. There isn't a man in all England at this moment thought of so much as—your humble servant. I wonder whether the "Morning Pulpit" people sent him here now to find out really what is my religion.'

'Mad as a hatter,' said Lord Alfred again;—'just that and no more.'

'My dear fellow, I don't think you've the gift of seeing very far. The truth is they don't know what to make of me;—and I don't intend that they shall. I'm playing my game, and there isn't one of 'em understands it except myself. It's no good my sitting here, you know. I shan't be able to move. How am I to get at you if I want anything?'

'What can you want? There'll be lots of servants about.'

'I'll have this bar down, at any rate.' And he did succeed in having removed the bar which had been specially put up to prevent his intrusion on his own guests in his own house. 'I look upon that fellow's coming here as a very singular sign of the times,' he went on to say. 'They'll want before long to know where I have my clothes made, and who measures me for my boots!' Perhaps the most remarkable circumstance in the career of this remarkable man was the fact that he came almost to believe in himself.

Father Barham went away certainly disgusted; and yet not altogether disheartened. The man had not declared that he was not a Roman Catholic. He had shown himself to be a brute. He had blasphemed and cursed. He had been outrageously uncivil to a man whom he must have known to be a minister of God. He had manifested himself to this priest, who had been born an English gentleman, as being no gentleman. But, not the less might he be a good Catholic,—or good enough at any rate to be influential on the right side. To his eyes Melmotte, with all his insolent vulgarity, was infinitely a more hopeful man than Roger Carbury. 'He insulted me,' said Father Barham to a brother religionist that evening within the cloisters of St. Fabricius.

'Did he intend to insult you?'

'Certainly he did. But what of that? It is not by the hands of polished men, nor even of the courteous, that this work has to be done. He was preparing for some great festival, and his mind was intent upon that.'

'He entertains the Emperor of China this very day,' said the brother priest, who, as a resident in London, heard from time to time what was being done.

'The Emperor of China! Ah, that accounts for it. I do think that he is on our side, even though he gave me but little encouragement for saying so. Will they vote for him, here at Westminster?'

'Our people will. They think that he is rich and can help them.'

'There is no doubt of his wealth, I suppose,' said Father Barham.

'Some people do doubt;—but others say he is the richest man in the world.'

'He looked like it,—and spoke like it,' said Father Barham. 'Think what such a man might do, if he be really the wealthiest man in the world! And if he had been against us would he not have said so? Though he was uncivil, I am glad that I saw him.' Father Barham, with a simplicity that was singularly mingled with his religious cunning, made himself believe before he returned to Beccles that Mr. Melmotte was certainly a Roman Catholic.

## Chapter LVII

### LORD NIDDERDALE TRIES HIS HAND AGAIN

LORD NIDDERDALE had half consented to renew his suit to Marie Melmotte. He had at any rate half promised to call at Melmotte's house on the Sunday with the object of so doing. As far as that promise had been given it was broken, for on the Sunday he was not seen in Bruton Street. Though not much given to severe thinking, he did feel that on this occasion there was need for thought. His father's property was not very large. His father and his grandfather had both been extravagant men, and he himself had done something towards adding to the family embarrassments. It had been an understood thing, since he had commenced life, that he was to marry an heiress. In such families as his, when such results have been achieved, it is generally understood that matters shall be put right by an heiress. It has become an institution, like primogeniture, and is almost as serviceable for maintaining the proper order of things. Rank squanders money; trade makes it;—and then trade purchases rank by re-gilding its splendour. The arrangement, as it affects the aristocracy generally, is well understood, and was quite approved by the old marquis—so that he had felt himself to be justified in eating up the property, which his son's future marriage would renew as a matter of course. Nidderdale himself had never dissented, had entertained no fanciful theory opposed to this view, had never alarmed his father by any liaison tending towards matrimony with any un-dowered beauty;—but had claimed his right to 'have his fling' before he devoted himself to the redintegration of the family property. His father had felt that it would be wrong and might probably be foolish to oppose so natural a desire. He had regarded all the circumstances of 'the fling' with indulgent eyes. But there arose some little difference as to the duration of the fling, and the father had at last found himself compelled to inform his son that if the fling were carried on much longer it must be done with internecine war between himself and his heir. Nidderdale, whose sense and temper were alike good, saw the thing quite in the proper light. He assured his father that he had no intention of 'cutting up rough,' declared that he was ready for the heiress as soon as the heiress should be put in his way, and set himself honestly about the task imposed on him. This had all been arranged at Auld Reekie Castle during the last winter, and the reader knows the result.

But the affair had assumed abnormal difficulties. Perhaps the Marquis had been wrong in flying at wealth which was reputed to be almost unlimited, but which was not absolutely fixed. A couple of hundred thousand pounds down might have been secured with greater ease. But here there had been a prospect of endless money,—of an inheritance which might not improbably make the Auld Reekie family conspicuous for its wealth even among the most wealthy of the nobility. The old man had fallen into the temptation, and abnormal difficulties had been the result. Some of these the reader knows. Latterly two difficulties had culminated above the others. The young lady preferred another gentleman, and disagreeable stories were afloat, not only as to the way in which the money had been made, but even as to its very existence.

The Marquis, however, was a man who hated to be beaten. As far as he could learn from inquiry, the money would be there,—or, at least, so much money as had been promised. A considerable sum, sufficient to secure the bridegroom from absolute shipwreck,—though by no means enough to make a brilliant marriage,—had in truth been already settled on Marie, and was, indeed, in her possession. As to that, her father had armed himself with a power of attorney for drawing the income,— but had made over the property to his daughter, so that in the event of unforeseen accidents on 'Change, he might retire to obscure comfort, and have the means perhaps of beginning again with whitewashed cleanliness. When doing this, he had doubtless not anticipated the grandeur to which he would soon rise, or the fact that he was about to embark on seas so dangerous that this little harbour of refuge would hardly offer security to his vessel. Marie had been quite correct in her story to her favoured lover. And the Marquis's lawyer had ascertained that if Marie ever married before she herself had restored this money to her father, her husband would be so far safe,—with this as a certainty and the immense remainder in prospect. The Marquis had determined to persevere. Pickering was to be added. Mr. Melmotte had been asked to depone the title-deeds, and had promised to do so as soon as the day of the wedding should have been fixed with the consent of all the parties. The Marquis's lawyer had ventured to express a doubt; but the Marquis had determined to persevere. The reader will, I trust, remember that those dreadful misgivings, which are I trust agitating his own mind, have been borne in upon him by information which had not as yet reached the Marquis in all its details.

But Nidderdale had his doubts. That absurd elopement, which Melmotte declared really to mean nothing, —the romance of a girl who wanted to have one little fling of her own before she settled down for life,—was perhaps his strongest objection. Sir Felix, no doubt, had not gone with her; but then one doesn't wish to have one's intended wife even attempt to run off with any one but oneself. 'She'll be sick of him by this time, I should say,' his father said to him. 'What does it matter, if the money's there?' The Marquis seemed to think that the escapade had simply been the girl's revenge against his son for having made his arrangements so exclusively with Melmotte, instead of devoting himself to her. Nidderdale acknowledged to himself that he had been remiss. He told himself that she was possessed of more spirit than he had thought. By the Sunday evening he had determined that he would try again. He had expected that the plum would fall into his mouth. He would now stretch out his hand to pick it.

On the Monday he went to the house in Bruton Street, at lunch time. Melmotte and the two Grendalls had just come over from their work in the square, and the financier was full of the priest's visit to him. Madame Melmotte was there, and Miss Longestaffe, who was to be sent for by her friend Lady Monogram that afternoon,—and, after they had sat down, Marie came in. Nidderdale got up and shook hands with her,—of course as though nothing had happened. Marie, putting a brave face upon it, struggling hard in the midst of very real difficulties, succeeded in saying an ordinary word or two. Her position was uncomfortable. A girl who has run away with her lover and has been brought back again by her friends, must for a time find it difficult to appear in society with ease. But when a girl has run away without her lover,—has run away expecting her lover to go with her, and has then been brought back, her lover not having stirred, her state of mind must be peculiarly harassing. But Marie's courage was good, and she ate her lunch even though she sat next to Lord Nidderdale.

Melmotte was very gracious to the young lord. 'Did you ever hear anything like that, Nidderdale?' he said, speaking of the priest's visit.

'Mad as a hatter,' said Lord Alfred.

'I don't know much about his madness. I shouldn't wonder if he had been sent by the Archbishop of Westminster. Why don't we have an Archbishop of Westminster when they've got one?* I shall have to see to that when I'm in the House. I suppose there is a bishop, isn't there, Alfred?' Alfred shook his head. 'There's a Dean, I know, for I called on him. He told me flat he wouldn't vote for me. I thought all those parsons were Conservatives. It didn't occur to me that the fellow had come from the Archbishop, or I would have been more civil to him.'

'Mad as a hatter;—nothing else,' said Lord Alfred.

'You should have seen him, Nidderdale. It would have been as good as a play to you.'

'I suppose you didn't ask him to the dinner, sir.'

'D—— the dinner, I'm sick of it,' said Melmotte, frowning. 'We must go back again, Alfred. Those fellows will never get along if they are not looked after.

Come, Miles. Ladies, I shall expect you to be ready at exactly a quarter before eight. His Imperial Majesty is to arrive at eight precisely, and I must be there to receive him. You, Madame, will have to receive your guests in the drawing-room.' The ladies went upstairs, and Lord Nidderdale followed them. Miss Longestaffe took her departure, alleging that she couldn't keep her dear friend Lady Monogram waiting for her. Then there fell upon Madame Melmotte the duty of leaving the young people together, a duty which she found a great difficulty in performing. After all that had happened, she did not know how to get up and go out of the room. As regarded herself, the troubles of these troublous times were becoming almost too much for her. She had no pleasure from her grandeur,—and probably no belief in her husband's achievements. It was her present duty to assist in getting Marie married to this young man, and that duty she could only do by going away. But she did not know how to get out of her chair. She expressed in fluent French her abhorrence of the Emperor, and her wish that she might be allowed to remain in bed during the whole evening. She liked Nidderdale better than any one else who came there, and wondered at Marie's preference for Sir Felix. Lord Nidderdale assured her that nothing was so easy as kings and emperors, because no one was expected to say anything. She sighed and shook her head, and wished again that she might be allowed to go to bed. Marie, who was by degrees plucking up her courage, declared that though kings and emperors were horrors as a rule, she thought an Emperor of China would be good fun. Then Madame Melmotte also plucked up her courage, rose from her chair, and.made straight for the door. 'Mamma, where are you going?' said Marie, also rising. Madame Melmotte, putting her handkerchief up to her face, declared that she was being absolutely destroyed by a toothache. 'I must see if I can't do something for her,' said Marie, hurrying to the door. But Lord Nidderdale was too quick for her, and stood with his back to it. 'That's a shame,' said Marie.

'Your mother has gone on purpose that I may speak to you,' said his lordship. 'Why should you grudge me the opportunity?'

Marie returned to her chair and again seated herself. She also had thought much of her own position since her return from Liverpool. Why had Sir Felix not been there? Why had he not come since her return, and, at any rate, endeavoured to see her? Why had he made no attempt to write to her? Had it been her part to do so, she would have found a hundred ways of getting at him. She absolutely had walked inside the garden of the square on Sunday morning, and had contrived to leave a gate open on each side. But he had made no sign. Her father had told her that he had not gone to Liverpool—and had assured her that he had never intended to go. Melmotte had been very savage with her about the money, and had loudly accused Sir Felix of stealing it. The repayment he never mentioned,—a piece of honesty, indeed, which had showed no virtue on the part of Sir Felix. But even if he had spent the money, why was he not man enough to come and say so? Marie could have forgiven that fault,—could have forgiven even the gambling and the drunkenness which had caused the failure of the enterprise on his side, if he had had the courage to come and confess to her. What she could not forgive was continued indifference,—or the cowardice which forbade him to show himself. She had more than once almost doubted his love, though as a lover he had been better than Nidderdale. But now, as far as she could see, he was ready to consent that the thing should be considered as over between them. No doubt she could write to him. She had more than once almost determined to do so. But then she had reflected that if he really loved her he would come to her. She was quite ready to run away with a lover, if her lover loved her; but she would not fling herself at a man's head. Therefore she had done nothing,—beyond leaving the garden gates open on the Sunday morning.

But what was she to do with herself? She also felt, she knew not why, that the present turmoil of her father's life might be brought to an end by some dreadful convulsion. No girl could be more anxious to be married and taken away from her home. If Sir Felix did not appear again, what should she do? She had seen enough of life to be aware that suitors would come,— would come as long as that convulsion was staved off. She did not suppose that her journey to Liverpool would frighten all the men away. But she had thought that it would put an end to Lord Nidderdale's courtship; and when her father had commanded her, shaking her by the shoulders, to accept Lord Nidderdale when he should come on Sunday, she had replied by expressing her assurance that Lord Nidderdale would never be seen at that house any more. On the Sunday he had not come; but here he was now, standing with his back to the drawing-room door, and cutting off her retreat with the evident intention of renewing his suit. She was determined at any rate that she would speak up. 'I don't know what you should have to say to me, Lord Nidderdale.'

'Why shouldn't I have something to say to you?'

'Because—. Oh, you know why. Besides, I've told you ever so often, my lord. I thought a gentleman would never go on with a lady when the lady has told him that she liked somebody else better.'

'Perhaps I don't believe you when you tell me.'

'Well; that is impudent! You may believe it then. I think I've given you reason to believe it, at any rate.'

'You can't be very fond of him now, I should think.'

'That's all you know about it, my lord. Why shouldn't I be fond of him? Accidents will happen, you know.'

'I don't want to make any allusion to anything that's unpleasant, Miss Melmotte.'

'You may say just what you please. All the world knows about it. Of course I went to Liverpool, and of course papa had me brought back again.'

'Why did not Sir Felix go?'

'I don't think, my lord, that that can be any business of yours.'

'But I think that it is, and I'll tell you why. You

might as well let me say what I've got to say,—out at once.'

'You may say what you like, but it can't make any difference.'

'You knew me before you knew him, you know.'

'What does that matter? If it comes to that, I knew ever so many people before I knew you.'

'And you were engaged to me.'

'You broke it off.'

'Listen to me for a moment or two. I know I did. Or, rather, your father and my father broke it off for us.'

'If we had cared for each other they couldn't have broken it off. Nobody in the world could break me off as long as I felt that he really loved me;—not if they were to cut me in pieces. But you didn't care, not a bit. You did it just because your father told you. And so did I. But I know better than that now. You never cared for me a bit more than for the old woman at the crossing. You thought I didn't understand;—but I did. And now you've come again;—because your father has told you again. And you'd better go away.'

'There's a great deal of truth in what you say.'

'It's all true, my lord. Every word of it.'

'I wish you wouldn't call me my lord.'

'I suppose you are a lord, and therefore I shall call you so. I never called you anything else when they pretended that we were to be married, and you never asked me. I never even knew what your name was till I looked it out in the book after I had consented.'

'There is truth in what you say;—but it isn't true now. How was I to love you when I had seen so little of you? I do love you now.'

'Then you needn't;—for it isn't any good.'

'I do love you now, and I think you'd find that I should be truer to you than that fellow who wouldn't take the trouble to go down to Liverpool with you.'

'You don't know why he didn't go.'

'Well;—perhaps I do. But I did not come here to say anything about that.'

'Why didn't he go, Lord Nidderdale?' She asked the question with an altered tone and an altered face. 'If you really know, you might as well tell me.'

'No, Marie;—that's just what I ought not to do. But he ought to tell you. Do you really in your heart believe that he means to come back to you?'

'I don't know,' she said, sobbing. 'I do love him;—I do indeed. I know that you are good-natured. You are more good-natured than he is. But he did like me. You never did;—no; not a bit. It isn't true. I ain't a fool. I know. No;—go away. I won't let you now. I don't care what he is; I'll be true to him. Go away, Lord Nidderdale. You oughtn't to go on like that because papa and mamma let you come here. I didn't let you come. I don't want you to come. No;—I won't say any kind word to you. I love Sir Felix Carbury better—than any person—in all the world. There! I don't know whether you call that kind, but it's true.'

'Say good-bye to me, Marie.'

'Oh, I don't mind saying good-bye. Good-bye, my lord; and don't come any more.'

'Yes, I shall. Good-bye, Marie. You'll find the difference between me and him yet.' So he took his leave, and as he sauntered away he thought that upon the whole he had prospered, considering the extreme difficulties under which he had laboured in carrying on his suit. 'She's quite a different sort of girl from what I took her to be,' he said to himself. 'Upon my word, she's awfully jolly.'

Marie, when the interview was over, walked about the room almost in dismay. It was borne in upon her by degrees that Sir Felix Carbury was not at all points quite as nice as she had thought him. Of his beauty there was no doubt; but then she could trust him for no other good quality. Why did he not come to her? Why did he not show some pluck? Why did he not tell her the truth? She had quite believed Lord Nidderdale when he said that he knew the cause that had kept Sir Felix from going to Liverpool. And she had believed him, too, when he said that it was not his business to tell her. But the reason, let it be what it might, must, if known, be prejudicial to her love. Lord Nidderdale was, she thought, not at all beautiful. He had a commonplace, rough face, with a turn-up nose, high cheek bones, no especial complexion, sandy-coloured whiskers, and bright laughing eyes,—not at all an Adonis such as her imagination had painted. But if he had only made love at first as he had attempted to do it now, she thought that she would have submitted herself to be cut in pieces for him.

## Chapter LVIII

### MR. SQUERCUM IS EMPLOYED

WHILE these things were being done in Bruton Street and Grosvenor Square horrid rumours were prevailing in the City and spreading from the City westwards to the House of Commons, which was sitting this Monday afternoon with a prospect of an adjournment at seven o'clock in consequence of the banquet to be given to the Emperor. It is difficult to explain the exact nature of this rumour, as it was not thoroughly understood by those who propagated it. But it is certainly the case that the word forgery was whispered by more than one pair of lips.

Many of Melmotte's staunchest supporters thought that he was very wrong not to show himself that day in the City. What good could he do pottering about among the chairs and benches in the banqueting room? There were people to manage that kind of thing. In such an affair it was his business to do simply as he was told, and to pay the bill. It was not as though he were giving a little dinner to a friend, and had to see himself that the wine was brought up in good order. His work was in the City; and at such a time as this and in such a crisis as this, he should have been in the City. Men will whisper forgery behind a man's back who would not dare even to think it before his face.

Of this particular rumour our young friend Dolly

Longestaffe was the parent. With unhesitating resolution, nothing awed by his father, Dolly had gone to his attorney, Mr. Squercum, immediately after that Friday on which Mr. Longestaffe first took his seat at the Railway Board. Dolly was possessed of fine qualities, but it must be owned that veneration was not one of them. 'I don't know why Mr. Melmotte is to be different from anybody else,' he had said to his father. 'When I buy a thing and don't pay for it, it is because I haven't got the tin, and I suppose it's about the same with him. It's all right, no doubt, but I don't see why he should have got hold of the place till the money was paid down.'

'Of course it's all right,' said the father. 'You think you understand everything, when you really understand nothing at all.'

'Of course I'm slow,' said Dolly. 'I don't comprehend these things. But then Squercum does. When a fellow is stupid himself, he ought to have a sharp fellow to look after his business.'

'You'll ruin me and yourself too, if you go to such a man as that. Why can't you trust Mr. Bideawhile? Slow and Bideawhile have been the family lawyers for a century.' Dolly made some remark as to the old family advisers which was by no means pleasing to the father's ears, and went his way. The father knew his boy, and knew that his boy would go to Squercum. All he could himself do was to press Mr. Melmotte for the money with what importunity he could assume. He wrote a timid letter to Mr. Melmotte, which had no result; and then, on the next Friday, again went into the City and there encountered perturbation of spirit and sheer loss of time,—as the reader has already learned.

Squercum was a thorn in the side of all the Bideawhiles. Mr. Slow had been gathered to his fathers, but of the Bideawhiles there were three in the business, a father and two sons, to whom Squercum was a pest and a musquito, a running sore and a skeleton in the cupboard. It was not only in reference to Mr. Longestaffe's affairs that they knew Squercum. The Bideawhiles piqued themselves on the decorous and orderly transaction of their business. It had grown to be a rule in the house that anything done quickly must be done badly. They never were in a hurry for money, and they expected their clients never to be in a hurry for work. Squercum was the very opposite to this. He had established himself, without predecessors and without a partner, and we may add without capital, at a little office in Fetter Lane, and had there made a character for getting things done after a marvellous and new fashion. And it was said of him that he was fairly honest, though it must be owned that among the Bideawhiles of the profession this was not the character which he bore. He did sharp things no doubt, and had no hesitation in supporting the interests of sons against those of their fathers. In more than one case he had computed for a young heir the exact value of his share in a property as compared to that of his father, and had come into hostile contact with many family Bideawhiles. He had been closely watched. There were some who, no doubt, would have liked to crush a man who was at once so clever, and so pestilential. But he had not as yet been crushed, and had become quite in vogue with elder sons. Some three years since his name had been mentioned to Dolly by a friend who had for years been at war with his father, and Squercum had been quite a comfort to Dolly.

He was a mean-looking little man, not yet above forty, who always wore a stiff light-coloured cotton cravat, an old dress coat, a coloured dingy waistcoat, and light trousers of some hue different from his waistcoat. He generally had on dirty shoes and gaiters. He was light-haired, with light whiskers, with putty-formed features, a squat nose, a large mouth, and very bright blue eyes. He looked as unlike the normal Bideawhile of the profession as a man could be; and it must be owned, though an attorney, would hardly have been taken for a gentleman from his personal appearance. He was very quick, and active in his motions, absolutely doing his law work himself, and trusting to his three or four juvenile clerks for little more than scrivener's

labour. He seldom or never came to his office on a
Saturday, and many among his enemies said that he was
a Jew. What evil will not a rival say to stop the flow of
grist to the mill of the hated one? But this report
Squercum rather liked, and assisted. They who knew
the inner life of the little man declared that he kept a
horse and hunted down in Essex on Saturday, doing a
bit of gardening in the summer months;—and they said
also that he made up for this by working hard all
Sunday. Such was Mr. Squercum,—a sign, in his way,
that the old things are being changed.

Squercum sat at a desk, covered with papers in
chaotic confusion, on a chair which moved on a pivot.
His desk was against the wall, and when clients came
to him, he turned himself sharp round, sticking out his
dirty shoes, throwing himself back till his body was an
inclined plane, with his hands thrust into his pockets.
In this attitude he would listen to his client's story, and
would himself speak as little as possible. It was by his
instructions that Dolly had insisted on getting his share
of the purchase money for Pickering into his own hands,
so that the incumbrance on his own property might be
paid off. He now listened as Dolly told him of the delay
in the payment. 'Melmotte's at Pickering?' asked the
attorney. Then Dolly informed him how the tradesmen
of the great financier had already half knocked down
the house. Squercum still listened, and promised to
look to it. He did ask what authority Dolly had given
for the surrender of the title-deeds. Dolly declared that
he had given authority for the sale, but none for the
surrender. His father, some time since, had put before
him, for his signature, a letter, prepared in Mr. Bideawhile's office, which Dolly said that he had refused
even to read, and certainly had not signed. Squercum
again said that he'd look to it, and bowed Dolly out of
his room. 'They've got him to sign something when he
was tight,' said Squercum to himself, knowing something
of the habits of his client. 'I wonder whether his father
did it, or old Bideawhile, or Melmotte himself?' Mr.
Squercum was inclined to think that Bideawhile would

not have done it, that Melmotte could have had no opportunity, and that the father must have been the practitioner. 'It's not the trick of a pompous old fool either,' said Mr. Squercum, in his soliloquy. He went to work, however, making himself detestably odious among the very respectable clerks in Mr. Bideawhile's office,—men who considered themselves to be altogether superior to Squercum himself in professional standing.

And now there came this rumour which was so far particular in its details that it inferred the forgery, of which it accused Mr. Melmotte, to his mode of acquiring the Pickering property. The nature of the forgery was of course described in various ways,—as was also the signature said to have been forged. But there were many who believed, or almost believed, that something wrong had been done,—that some great fraud had been committed; and in connection with this it was ascertained,—by some as a matter of certainty,—that the Pickering estate had been already mortgaged by Melmotte to its full value at an assurance office. In such a transaction there would be nothing dishonest; but as this place had been bought for the great man's own family use, and not as a speculation, even this report of the mortgage tended to injure his credit. And then, as the day went on, other tidings were told as to other properties. Houses in the East-end of London were said to have been bought and sold, without payment of the purchase money as to the buying, and with receipt of the purchase money as to the selling.

It was certainly true that Squercum himself had seen the letter in Mr. Bideawhile's office which conveyed to the father's lawyer the son's sanction for the surrender of the title-deeds, and that that letter, prepared in Mr. Bideawhile's office, purported to have Dolly's signature. Squercum said but little, remembering that his client was not always clear in the morning as to anything he had done on the preceding evening. But the signature, though it was scrawled as Dolly always scrawled it, was not like the scrawl of a drunken man.

The letter was said to have been sent to Mr. Bide-

awhile's office with other letters and papers, direct from
old Mr. Longestaffe. Such was the statement made at
first to Mr. Squercum by the Bidewahile party, who
at that moment had no doubt of the genuineness of
the letter or of the accuracy of their statement. Then
Squercum saw his client again, and returned to the
charge at Bidewahile's office, with the positive assurance
that the signature was a forgery. Dolly, when questioned
by Squercum, quite admitted his propensity to be
'tight'. He had no reticence, no feeling of disgrace on
such matters. But he had signed no letter when he was
tight. 'Never did such a thing in my life, and nothing
could make me,' said Dolly. 'I'm never tight except at
the club, and the letter couldn't have been there. I'll be
drawn and quartered if I ever signed it. That's flat.'
Dolly was intent on going to his father at once, on
going to Melmotte at once, on going to Bidewahile's
at once, and making there 'no end of a row,'—but
Squercum stopped him. 'We'll just ferret this thing out
quietly,' said Squercum, who perhaps thought that
there would be high honour in discovering the peccadillos
of so great a man as Mr. Melmotte. Mr. Longestaffe, the
father, had heard nothing of the matter till the Saturday
after his last interview with Melmotte in the City. He
had then called at Bidewahile's office in Lincoln's Inn
Fields, and had been shown the letter. He declared at
once that he had never sent the letter to Mr. Bidewahile.
He had begged his son to sign the letter and his son
had refused. He did not at that moment distinctly
remember what he had done with the letter unsigned.
He believed he had left it with the other papers; but it
was possible that his son might have taken it away. He
acknowledged that at the time he had been both angry
and unhappy. He didn't think that he could have sent
the letter back unsigned,—but he was not sure. He had
more than once been in his own study in Bruton Street
since Mr. Melmotte had occupied the house,—by that
gentleman's leave,—having left various papers there
under his own lock and key. Indeed it had been matter
of agreement that he should have access to his own study

when he let the house. He thought it probable that he would have kept back the unsigned letter, and have kept it under lock and key, when he sent away the other papers. Then reference was made to Mr. Longestaffe's own letter to the lawyer, and it was found that he had not even alluded to that which his son had been asked to sign; but that he had said, in his own usually pompous style, that Mr. Longestaffe, junior, was still prone to create unsubstantial difficulties. Mr. Bideawhile was obliged to confess that there had been a want of caution among his own people. This allusion to the creation of difficulties by Dolly, accompanied, as it was supposed to have been, by Dolly's letter doing away with all difficulties, should have attracted notice. Dolly's letter must have come in a separate envelope; but such envelope could not be found, and the circumstance was not remembered by the clerk. The clerk who had prepared the letter for Dolly's signature represented himself as having been quite satisfied when the letter came again beneath his notice with Dolly's well-known signature.

Such were the facts as far as they were known at Messrs. Slow and Bideawhile's office,—from whom no slightest rumour emanated; and as they had been in part collected by Squercum, who was probably less prudent. The Bideawhiles were still perfectly sure that Dolly had signed the letter, believing the young man to be quite incapable of knowing on any day what he had done on the day before.

Squercum was quite sure that his client had not signed it. And it must be owned on Dolly's behalf that his manner on this occasion was qualified to convince. 'Yes,' he said to Squercum; 'it's easy saying that I'm lack-a-daisical. But I know when I'm lack-a-daisical and when I'm not. Awake or asleep, drunk or sober, I never signed that letter.' And Mr. Squercum believed him.

It would be hard to say how the rumour first got into the City on this Monday morning. Though the elder Longestaffe had first heard of the matter only on the previous Saturday, Mr. Squercum had been at work for above a week. Mr. Squercum's little matter alone might hardly have attracted the attention which certainly was given on this day to Mr. Melmotte's private affairs;—but other facts coming to light assisted Squercum's views. A great many shares of the South Central Pacific and Mexican Railway had been thrown upon the market, all of which had passed through the hands of Mr. Cohenlupe;—and Mr. Cohenlupe in the City had been all to Mr. Melmotte as Lord Alfred had been at the West End. Then there was the mortgage of this Pickering property, for which the money certainly had not been paid; and there was the traffic with half a street of houses near the Commercial Road, by which a large sum of money had come into Mr. Melmotte's hands. It might, no doubt, all be right. There were many who thought that it would all be right. There were not a few who expressed the most thorough contempt for these rumours. But it was felt to be a pity that Mr. Melmotte was not in the City.

This was the day of the dinner. The Lord Mayor had even made up his mind that he would not go to the dinner. What one of his brother aldermen said to him about leaving others in the lurch might be quite true; but, as his lordship remarked, Melmotte was a commercial man, and as these were commercial transactions it behoved the Lord Mayor of London to be more careful than other men. He had always had his doubts, and he would not go. Others of the chosen few of the City who had been honoured with commands to meet the Emperor resolved upon absenting themselves unless the Lord Mayor went. The affair was very much discussed, and there were no less than six declared City defaulters. At the last moment a seventh was taken ill and sent a note to Miles Grendall excusing himself, which was thrust into the secretary's hands just as the Emperor arrived.

But a reverse worse than this took place;—a defalcation more injurious to the Melmotte interests generally even than that which was caused either by the prudence

or by the cowardice of the City Magnates. The House
of Commons, at its meeting, had heard the tidings in an
exaggerated form. It was whispered about that Melmotte had been detected in forging the deed of conveyance of a large property, and that he had already
been visited by policemen. By some it was believed that
the Great Financier would lie in the hands of the
Philistines while the Emperor of China was being fed
at his house. In the third edition of the 'Evening Pulpit'
came out a mysterious paragraph which nobody could
understand but they who had known all about it before.
'A rumour is prevalent that frauds to an enormous
extent have been committed by a gentleman whose
name we are particularly unwilling to mention. If it be
so it is indeed remarkable that they should have come to
light at the present moment. We cannot trust ourselves
to say more than this.' No one wishes to dine with a
swindler. No one likes even to have dined with a
swindler,—especially to have dined with him at a time
when his swindling was known or suspected. The Emperor of China no doubt was going to dine with this man.
The motions of Emperors are managed with such ponderous care that it was held to be impossible now to save
the country from what would doubtless be felt to be a
disgrace if it should hereafter turn out that a forger had
been solicited to entertain the imperial guest of the
country. Nor was the thing as yet so far certain as to
justify such a charge, were it possible. But many men
were unhappy in their minds. How would the story be
told hereafter if Melmotte should be allowed to play
out his game of host to the Emperor, and be arrested for
forgery as soon as the Eastern Monarch should have left
his house? How would the brother of the Sun like the
remembrance of the banquet which he had been instructed to honour with his presence? How would it tell
in all the foreign newspapers, in New York, in Paris, and
Vienna, that this man who had been cast forth from the
United States, from France, and from Austria had been
selected as the great and honourable type of British
Commerce? There were those in the House who

thought that the absolute consummation of the disgrace might yet be avoided, and who were of opinion that the dinner should be 'postponed.' The leader of the Opposition had a few words on the subject with the Prime Minister. 'It is the merest rumour,' said the Prime Minister. 'I have inquired, and there is nothing to justify me in thinking that the charges can be substantiated.'

'They say that the story is believed in the City.'

'I should not feel myself justified in acting upon such a report. The Prince might probably find it impossible not to go. Where should we be if Mr. Melmotte to-morrow were able to prove the whole to be a calumny, and to show that the thing had been got up with a view of influencing the election at Westminster? The dinner must certainly go on.'

'And you will go yourself?'

'Most assuredly,' said the Prime Minister. 'And I hope that you will keep me in countenance.' His political antagonist declared with a smile that at such a crisis he would not desert his honourable friend;—but he could not answer for his followers. There was, he admitted, a strong feeling among the leaders of the Conservative party of distrust in Melmotte. He considered it probable that among his friends who had been invited there would be some who would be unwilling to meet even the Emperor of China on the existing terms. 'They should remember,' said the Prime Minister, 'that they are also to meet their own Prince, and that empty seats on such an occasion will be a dishonour to him.'

'Just at present I can only answer for myself,' said the leader of the Opposition.—At that moment even the Prime Minister was much disturbed in his mind; but in such emergencies a Prime Minister can only choose the least of two evils. To have taken the Emperor to dine with a swindler would be very bad; but to desert him, and to stop the coming of the Emperor and all the Princes on a false rumour, would be worse.

## Chapter LIX

### THE DINNER

IT does sometimes occur in life that an unambitious man, who is in no degree given to enterprises, who would fain be safe, is driven by the cruelty of circumstances into a position in which he must choose a side, and in which, though he has no certain guide as to which side he should choose, he is aware that he will be disgraced if he should take the wrong side. This was felt as a hardship by many who were quite suddenly forced to make up their mind whether they would go to Melmotte's dinner, or join themselves to the faction of those who had determined to stay away although they had accepted invitations. Some there were not without a suspicion that the story against Melmotte had been got up simply as an electioneering trick,—so that Mr. Alf might carry the borough on the next day. As a dodge for an election this might be very well, but any who might be deterred by such a manœuvre from meeting the Emperor and supporting the Prince would surely be marked men. And none of the wives, when they were consulted, seemed to care a straw whether Melmotte was a swindler or not. Would the Emperor and the Princes and Princesses be there? This was the only question which concerned them. They did not care whether Melmotte was arrested at the dinner or after the dinner, so long as they, with others, could show their diamonds in the presence of eastern and western royalty. But yet,—what a fiasco would it be, if at this very instant of time the host should be apprehended for common forgery! The great thing was to ascertain whether others were going. If a hundred or more out of the two hundred were to be absent how dreadful would be the position of those who were present! And how would the thing go if at the last moment the Emperor should be kept away? The Prime Minister had decided that the Emperor and the Prince should remain altogether in ignorance of the charges

which were preferred against the man; but of that these
doubters were unaware. There was but little time for a
man to go about town and pick up the truth from those
who were really informed; and questions were asked in
an uncomfortable and restless manner. 'Is your Grace
going?' said Lionel Lupton to the Duchess of Stevenage,
—having left the House and gone into the park between
six and seven to pick up some hints among those who
were known to have been invited. The Duchess was Lord
Alfred's sister, and of course she was going. 'I usually
keep engagements when I make them, Mr. Lupton,'
said the Duchess. She had been assured by Lord Alfred
not a quarter of an hour before that everything was as
straight as a die. Lord Alfred had not then even heard
of the rumour. But ultimately both Lionel Lupton and
Beauchamp Beauclerk attended the dinner. They had
received special tickets as supporters of Mr. Melmotte
at the election,—out of the scanty number allotted to
that gentleman himself,—and they thought themselves
bound in honour to be there. But they, with their
leader, and one other influential member of the party,
were all who at last came as the political friends of the
candidate for Westminster. The existing ministers were
bound to attend to the Emperor and the Prince. But
members of the Opposition, by their presence, would
support the man and the politician, and both as a man
and as a politician they were ashamed of him.

When Melmotte arrived at his own door with his wife
and daughter he had heard nothing of the matter.
That a man so vexed with affairs of money, so laden
with cares, encompassed by such dangers, should be
free from suspicion and fear it is impossible to imagine.
That such burdens should be borne at all is a wonder to
those whose shoulders have never been broadened for
such work;—as is the strength of the blacksmith's arm
to men who have never wielded a hammer. Surely his
whole life must have been a life of terrors! But of any
special peril to which he was at that moment subject, or
of any embarrassment which might affect the work of
the evening, he knew nothing. He placed his wife in the

drawing-room and himself in the hall, and arranged his immediate satellites around him,—among whom were included the two Grendalls, young Nidderdale, and Mr. Cohenlupe,—with a feeling of gratified glory. Nidderdale down at the House had heard the rumour, but had determined that he would not as yet fly from his colours. Cohenlupe had also come up from the House, where no one had spoken to him. Though grievously frightened during the last fortnight, he had not dared to be on the wing as yet. And, indeed, to what clime could such a bird as he fly in safety? He had not only heard,—but also knew very much, and was not prepared to enjoy the feast. Since they had been in the hall Miles had spoken dreadful words to his father. 'You've heard about it; haven't you?' whispered Miles. Lord Alfred, remembering his sister's question, became almost pale, but declared that he had heard nothing. 'They're saying all manner of things in the City;—forgery and heaven knows what. The Lord Mayor is not coming.' Lord Alfred made no reply. It was the philosophy of his life that misfortunes when they came should be allowed to settle themselves. But he was unhappy.

The grand arrivals were fairly punctual, and the very grand people all came. The unfortunate Emperor,—we must consider a man to be unfortunate who is compelled to go through such work as this,—with impassible and awful dignity, was marshalled into the room on the ground floor, whence he and other royalties were to be marshalled back into the banqueting hall. Melmotte, bowing to the ground, walked backwards before him, and was probably taken by the Emperor for some Court Master of the Ceremonies especially selected to walk backwards on this occasion. The Princes had all shaken hands with their host, and the Princesses had bowed graciously. Nothing of the rumour had as yet been whispered in royal palaces. Besides royalty the company allowed to enter the room downstairs was very select. The Prime Minister, one archbishop, two duchesses, and an ex-governor of India with whose features the Emperor was supposed to be peculiarly familiar, were alone there. The remainder of the company, under the superintendence of Lord Alfred, were received in the drawing-room above. Everything was going on well, and they who had come and had thought of not coming were proud of their wisdom.

But when the company was seated at dinner the deficiencies were visible enough, and were unfortunate. Who does not know the effect made by the absence of one or two from a table intended for ten or twelve,—how grievous are the empty places, how destructive of the outward harmony and grace which the hostess has endeavoured to preserve are these interstices, how the lady in her wrath declares to herself that those guilty ones shall never have another opportunity of filling a seat at her table? Some twenty, most of whom had been asked to bring their wives, had slunk from their engagements, and the empty spaces were sufficient to declare a united purpose. A week since it had been understood that admission for the evening could not be had for love or money, and that a seat at the dinner-table was as a seat at some banquet of the gods! Now it looked as though the room were but half-filled. There were six absences from the City. Another six of Mr. Melmotte's own political party were away. The archbishops and the bishop were there, because bishops never hear worldly tidings till after other people;—but that very Master of the Buckhounds for whom so much pressure had been made did not come. Two or three peers were absent, and so also was that editor who had been chosen to fill Mr. Alf's place. One poet, two painters, and a philosopher had received timely notice at their clubs, and had gone home. The three independent members of the House of Commons for once agreed in their policy, and would not lend the encouragement of their presence to a man suspected of forgery. Nearly forty places were vacant when the business of the dinner commenced.

Melmotte had insisted that Lord Alfred should sit next to himself at the big table, and having had the objectionable bar removed, and his own chair shoved one step nearer to the centre, had carried his point. With the anxiety natural to such an occasion, he glanced repeatedly round the hall, and of course became aware that many were absent. 'How is it that there are so many places empty?' he said to his faithful Achates.*

'Don't know,' said Achates, shaking his head, steadfastly refusing to look round upon the hall.

Melmotte waited awhile, then looked round again, and asked the question in another shape: 'Hasn't there been some mistake about the numbers? There's room for ever so many more.'

'Don't know,' said Lord Alfred, who was unhappy in his mind, and repenting himself that he had ever seen Mr. Melmotte.

'What the deuce do you mean?' whispered Melmotte. 'You've been at it from the beginning and ought to know. When I wanted to ask Brehgert, you swore that you couldn't squeeze a place.'

'Can't say anything about it,' said Lord Alfred, with his eyes fixed upon his plate.

'I'll be d—— if I don't find out,' said Melmotte. 'There's either some horrible blunder, or else there's been imposition. I don't see quite clearly. Where's Sir Gregory Gribe?'

'Hasn't come, I suppose.'

'And where's the Lord Mayor?' Melmotte, in spite of royalty, was now sitting with his face turned round upon the hall. 'I know all their places, and I know where they were put. Have you seen the Lord Mayor?'

'No; I haven't seen him at all.'

'But he was to come. What's the meaning of it, Alfred?'

'Don't know anything about it.' He shook his head but would not, for even a moment, look round upon the room.

'And where's Mr. Killegrew,—and Sir David Boss?' Mr. Killegrew and Sir David were gentlemen of high standing, and destined for important offices in the Conservative party. 'There are ever so many people not here. Why, there's not above half of them down the room. What's up, Alfred? I must know.'

'I tell you I know nothing. I could not make them come.' Lord Alfred's answers were made not only with a surly voice, but also with a surly heart. He was keenly alive to the failure, and alive also to the feeling that the failure would partly be attached to himself. At the present moment he was anxious to avoid observation, and it seemed to him that Melmotte, by the frequency and impetuosity of his questions, was drawing special attention to him. 'If you go on making a row,' he said, 'I shall go away.' Melmotte looked at him with all his eyes. 'Just sit quiet and let the thing go on. You'll know all about it soon enough.' This was hardly the way to give Mr. Melmotte peace of mind. For a few minutes he did sit quiet. Then he got up and moved down the hall behind the guests.

In the meantime, Imperial Majesty and Royalties of various denominations ate their dinner, without probably observing those Banquo's seats. As the Emperor talked Manchoo only, and as there was no one present who could even interpret Manchoo into English,—the imperial interpreter condescending only to interpret Manchoo into ordinary Chinese which had to be reinterpreted,—it was not within his Imperial Majesty's power to have much conversation with his neighbours. And as his neighbours on each side of him were all cousins and husbands, and brothers and wives, who saw each constantly under, let us presume, more comfortable circumstances, they had not very much to say to each other. Like most of us, they had their duties to do, and, like most of us, probably found their duties irksome. The brothers and sisters and cousins were used to it; but that awful Emperor, solid, solemn, and silent, must, if the spirit of an Eastern Emperor be at all like that of a Western man, have had a weary time of it. He sat there for more than two hours, awful, solid, solemn, and silent, not eating very much,—for this was not his manner of eating; nor drinking very much—for this was not his manner of drinking; but wondering, no doubt, within his own awful bosom, at the changes which were coming when an Emperor of China was forced, by outward circumstances, to sit and hear this buzz of voices and this clatter of knives and forks. 'And this,' he must have said to himself, 'is what they call royalty in the West!' If a prince of our own was forced, for the good of the country, to go among some far-distant outlandish people, and there to be poked in the ribs, and slapped on the back all round, the change to him could hardly be so great.

'Where's Sir Gregory?' said Melmotte, in a hoarse whisper, bending over the chair of a City friend. It was old Todd, the senior partner of Todd, Brehgert, and Goldsheiner. Mr. Todd was a very wealthy man, and had a considerable following in the City.

'Ain't he here?' said Todd,—knowing very well who had come from the City and who had declined.

'No;—and the Lord Mayor's not come;—nor Postlethwaite, nor Bunter. What's the meaning of it?'

Todd looked first at one neighbour and then at another before he answered. 'I'm here, that's all I can say, Mr. Melmotte; and I've had a very good dinner. They who haven't come, have lost a very good dinner.'

There was a weight upon Melmotte's mind of which he could not rid himself. He knew from the old man's manner, and he knew also from Lord Alfred's manner, that there was something which each of them could tell him if he would. But he was unable to make the men open their mouths. And yet it might be so important to him that he should know! 'It's very odd,' he said, 'that gentlemen should promise to come and then stay away. There were hundreds anxious to be present whom I should have been glad to welcome, if I had known that there would be room. I think it is very odd.'

'It is odd,' said Mr. Todd, turning his attention to the plate before him.

Melmotte had lately seen much of Beauchamp Beauclerk, in reference to the coming election. Passing back up the table, he found the gentleman with a vacant seat on one side of him. There were many vacant seats in this part of the room, as the places for the Conservative gentlemen had been set apart together. There Mr. Melmotte seated himself for a minute, thinking that he might get the truth from his new ally. Prudence should have kept him silent. Let the cause of these desertions have been what it might, it ought to have been clear to him that he could apply no remedy to it now. But he was bewildered and dismayed, and his mind within him was changing at every moment. He was now striving to trust to his arrogance and declaring that nothing should cow him. And then again he was so cowed that he was ready to creep to any one for assistance. Personally, Mr. Beauclerk had disliked the man greatly. Among the vulgar, loud upstarts whom he had known, Melmotte was the vulgarest, the loudest, and the most arrogant. But he had taken the business of Melmotte's election in hand, and considered himself bound to stand by Melmotte till that was over; and he was now the guest of the man in his own house, and was therefore constrained to courtesy. His wife was sitting by him, and he at once introduced her to Mr. Melmotte. 'You have a wonderful assemblage here, Mr. Melmotte,' said the lady, looking up at the royal table.

'Yes, ma'am, yes. His Majesty the Emperor has been pleased to intimate that he has been much gratified.'— Had the Emperor in truth said so, no one who looked at him could have believed his imperial word.—'Can you tell me, Mr. Beauchamp, why those other gentlemen are not here? It looks very odd; does it not?'

'Ah; you mean Killegrew.'

'Yes; Mr. Killegrew and Sir David Boss, and the whole lot. I made a particular point of their coming. I said I wouldn't have the dinner at all unless they were to be asked. They were going to make it a Government thing; but I said no. I insisted on the leaders of our own party; and now they're not here. I know the cards were sent;—and, by George, I have their answers, saying they'd come.'

'I suppose some of them are engaged,' said Mr. Beauchamp.

'Engaged! What business has a man to accept one engagement and then take another? And, if so, why shouldn't he write and make his excuses? No, Mr. Beauchamp, that won't go down.'

'I'm here, at any rate,' said Beauchamp, making the very answer that had occurred to Mr. Todd.

'Oh, yes, you're here. You're all right. But what is it, Mr. Beauchamp? There's something up, and you must have heard.' And so it was clear to Mr. Beauchamp that the man knew nothing about it himself. If there was anything wrong, Melmotte was not aware that the wrong had been discovered. 'Is it anything about the election to-morrow?'

'One never can tell what is actuating people,' said Mr. Beauchamp.

'If you know anything about the matter I think you ought to tell me.'

'I know nothing except that the ballot will be taken to-morrow. You and I have got nothing more to do in the matter except to wait the result.'

'Well; I suppose it's all right,' said Melmotte, rising and going back to his seat. But he knew that things were not all right. Had his political friends only been absent, he might have attributed their absence to some political cause which would not have touched him deeply. But the treachery of the Lord Mayor and of Sir Gregory Gribe was a blow. For another hour after he had returned to his place, the Emperor sat solemn in his chair; and then, at some signal given by some one, he was withdrawn. The ladies had already left the room about half an hour. According to the programme arranged for the evening, the royal guests were to return to the smaller room for a cup of coffee, and were then to be paraded upstairs before the multitude who would by that time have arrived, and to remain there long enough to justify the invited ones in saying that they had spent the evening with the Emperor and the Princes and the Princesses. The plan was carried out perfectly. At half-past ten the Emperor was made to walk upstairs, and for half an hour sat awful and com-

posed in an arm-chair that had been prepared for him.
How one would wish to see the inside of the mind of the
Emperor as it worked on that occasion!

Melmotte, when his guests ascended his stairs, went
back into the banqueting-room and through to the
hall, and wandered about till he found Miles Grendall.
'Miles,' he said, 'tell me what the row is.'

'How row?' asked Miles.

'There's something wrong, and you know all about
it. Why didn't the people come?' Miles, looking guilty,
did not even attempt to deny his knowledge. 'Come;
what is it? We might as well know all about it at once.'
Miles looked down on the ground, and grunted something. 'Is it about the election?'

'No, it's not that,' said Miles.

'Then what is it?'

'They got hold of something to-day in the City—about
Pickering.'

'They did, did they? And what were they saying
about Pickering? Come; you might as well out with it.
You don't suppose that I care what lies they tell.'

'They say there's been something—forged. Title-
deeds, I think they say.'

'Title-deeds! that I have forged title-deeds. Well;
that's beginning well. And his lordship has stayed away
from my house after accepting my invitation because he
has heard that story! All right, Miles; that will do.'
And the Great Financier went upstairs into his own
drawing-room.

## Chapter LX

### MISS LONGESTAFFE'S LOVER

A FEW days before that period in our story which
we have now reached, Miss Longestaffe was seated
in Lady Monogram's back drawing-room, discussing
the terms on which the two tickets for Madame Melmotte's grand reception had been transferred to Lady

Monogram,—the place on the cards for the names of
the friends whom Madame Melmotte had the honour of
inviting to meet the Emperor and the Princes, having
been left blank; and the terms also on which Miss
Longestaffe had been asked to spend two or three days
with her dear friend Lady Monogram. Each lady was
disposed to get as much and to give as little as possible,—
in which desire the ladies carried out the ordinary
practice of all parties to a bargain. It had of course been
settled that Lady Monogram was to have the two
tickets,—for herself and her husband,—such tickets at
that moment standing very high in the market. In
payment for these valuable considerations, Lady Monogram was to undertake to chaperon Miss Longestaffe at
the entertainment, to take Miss Longestaffe as a visitor
for three days, and to have one party at her own house
during the time, so that it might be seen that Miss
Longestaffe had other friends in London besides the
Melmottes on whom to depend for her London gaieties.
At this moment Miss Longestaffe felt herself justified in
treating the matter as though she were hardly receiving
a fair equivalent. The Melmotte tickets were certainly
ruling very high. They had just culminated. They fell a
little soon afterwards, and at ten p.m. on the night of
the entertainment were hardly worth anything. At the
moment which we have now in hand, there was a rush
for them. Lady Monogram had already secured the
tickets. They were in her desk. But, as will sometimes
be the case in a bargain, the seller was complaining that
as she had parted with her goods too cheap, some make-
weight should be added to the stipulated price.

'As for that, my dear,' said Miss Longestaffe, who,
since the rise in Melmotte stock generally, had endeavoured to resume something of her old manners, 'I
don't see what you mean at all. You meet Lady Julia
Goldsheiner everywhere, and her father-in-law is Mr.
Brehgert's junior partner.'

'Lady Julia is Lady Julia, my dear, and young Mr.
Goldsheiner has, in some sort of way, got himself in.
He hunts, and Damask says that he is one of the best

shots at Hurlingham. I never met old Mr. Goldsheiner anywhere.'

'I have.'

'Oh, yes, I dare say. Mr. Melmotte, of course, entertains all the City people. I don't think Sir Damask would like me to ask Mr. Brehgert to dine here.' Lady Monogram managed everything herself with reference to her own parties; invited all her own guests, and never troubled Sir Damask,—who, again, on his side, had his own set of friends; but she was very clever in the use which she made of her husband. There were some aspirants who really were taught to think that Sir Damask was very particular as to the guests whom he welcomed to his own house.

'May I speak to Sir Damask about it?' asked Miss Longestaffe, who was very urgent on the occasion.

'Well, my dear, I really don't think you ought to do that. There are little things which a man and his wife must manage together without interference.'

'Nobody can ever say that I interfered in any family. But really, Julia, when you tell me that Sir Damask cannot receive Mr. Brehgert, it does sound odd. As for City people, you know as well as I do, that that kind of thing is all over now. City people are just as good as West End people.'

'A great deal better, I dare say. I'm not arguing about that. I don't make the lines; but there they are; and one gets to know in a sort of way what they are. I don't pretend to be a bit better than my neighbours. I like to see people come here whom other people who come here will like to meet. I'm big enough to hold my own, and so is Sir Damask. But we ain't big enough to introduce new-comers. I don't suppose there's anybody in London understands it better than you do, Georgiana, and therefore it's absurd my pretending to teach you. I go pretty well everywhere, as you are aware; and I shouldn't know Mr. Brehgert if I were to see him.'

'You'll meet him at the Melmottes', and, in spite of all you said once, you're glad enough to go there.'

'Quite true, my dear. I don't think that you are just

the person to throw that in my teeth; but never mind that. There's the butcher round the corner in Bond Street, or the man who comes to do my hair. I don't at all think of asking them to my house. But if they were suddenly to turn out wonderful men, and go everywhere, no doubt I should be glad to have them here. That's the way we live, and you are as well used to it as I am. Mr. Brehgert at present to me is like the butcher round the corner.' Lady Monogram had the tickets safe under lock and key, or I think she would hardly have said this.

'He is not a bit like a butcher,' said Miss Longestaffe, blazing up in real wrath.

'I did not say that he was.'

'Yes, you did; and it was the unkindest thing you could possibly say. It was meant to be unkind. It was monstrous. How would you like it if I said that Sir Damask was like a hair-dresser?'

'You can say so if you please. Sir Damask drives four in hand, rides as though he meant to break his neck every winter, is one of the best shots going, and is supposed to understand a yacht as well as any other gentleman out. And I'm rather afraid that before he was married he used to box with all the prize-fighters, and to be a little too free behind the scenes. If that makes a man like a hair-dresser, well, there he is.'

'How proud you are of his vices.'

'He's very good-natured, my dear, and as he does not interfere with me, I don't interfere with him. I hope you'll do as well. I dare say Mr. Brehgert is good-natured.'

'He's an excellent man of business, and is making a very large fortune.'

'And has five or six grown-up children, who, no doubt, will be a comfort.'

'If I don't mind them, why need you? You have none at all, and you find it lonely enough.'

'Not at all lonely. I have everything that I desire. How hard you are trying to be ill-natured, Georgiana.'

'Why did you say that he was a——butcher?'

'I said nothing of the kind. I didn't even say that he

was like a butcher. What I did say was this,—that I
don't feel inclined to risk my own reputation on the
appearance of new people at my table. Of course, I
go in for what you call fashion. Some people can dare to
ask anybody they meet in the streets. I can't. I've my
own line, and I mean to follow it. It's hard work, I
can tell you; and it would be harder still if I wasn't
particular. If you like Mr. Brehgert to come here on
Tuesday evening, when the rooms will be full, you can
ask him; but as for having him to dinner, I—won't—do
—it.' So the matter was at last settled. Miss Longestaffe
did ask Mr. Brehgert for the Tuesday evening, and the
two ladies were again friends.

Perhaps Lady Monogram, when she illustrated her
position by an allusion to a butcher and a hair-dresser,
had been unaware that Mr. Brehgert had some resemblance to the form which men in that trade are supposed
to bear. Let us at least hope that she was so. He was
a fat, greasy man, good-looking in a certain degree,
about fifty, with hair dyed black, and beard and
moustache dyed a dark purple colour. The charm of his
face consisted in a pair of very bright black eyes, which
were, however, set too near together in his face for the
general delight of Christians. He was stout;—fat all
over rather than corpulent,—and had that look of
command in his face which has become common to
master-butchers, probably by long intercourse with
sheep and oxen. But Mr. Brehgert was considered to be
a very good man of business, and was now regarded
as being, in a commercial point of view, the leading
member of the great financial firm of which he was the
second partner. Mr. Todd's day was nearly done. He
walked about constantly between Lombard Street, the
Exchange, and the Bank, and talked much to merchants;
he had an opinion too of his own on particular cases;
but the business had almost got beyond him, and Mr.
Brehgert was now supposed to be the moving spirit of
the firm. He was a widower, living in a luxurious villa
at Fulham with a family, not indeed grown up, as Lady
Monogram had ill-naturedly said, but which would be

grown up before long, varying from an eldest son of
eighteen, who had just been placed at a desk in the
office, to the youngest girl of twelve, who was at school
at Brighton. He was a man who always asked for what
he wanted; and having made up his mind that he
wanted a second wife, had asked Miss Georgiana Longestaffe to fill that situation. He had met her at the
Melmottes', had entertained her, with Madame Melmotte and Marie, at Beaudesert, as he called his villa,
had then proposed in the square, and two days after had
received an assenting answer in Bruton Street.

Poor Miss Longestaffe! Although she had acknowledged the fact to Lady Monogram in her desire to
pave the way for the reception of herself into society as a
married woman, she had not as yet found courage to tell
her family. The man was absolutely a Jew;—not a
Jew that had been, as to whom there might possibly be a
doubt whether he or his father or his grandfather had
been the last Jew of the family; but a Jew that was. So
was Goldsheiner a Jew, whom Lady Julia Start had
married,—or at any rate had been one a very short time
before he ran away with that lady. She counted up
ever so many instances on her fingers of 'decent people'
who had married Jews or Jewesses. Lord Frederic
Framlinghame had married a girl of the Berrenhoffers;
and Mr. Hart had married a Miss Chute. She did not
know much of Miss Chute, but was certain that she was
a Christian. Lord Frederic's wife and Lady Julia Goldsheiner were seen everywhere. Though she hardly
knew how to explain the matter even to herself, she was
sure that there was at present a general heaving-up of
society on this matter, and a change in progress which
would soon make it a matter of indifference whether
anybody was Jew or Christian. For herself she regarded
the matter not at all, except as far as it might be regarded
by the world in which she wished to live. She was
herself above all personal prejudices of that kind. Jew,
Turk, or infidel was nothing to her. She had seen
enough of the world to be aware that her happiness did
not lie in that direction, and could not depend in the

least on the religion of her husband. Of course she
would go to church herself. She always went to church.
It was the proper thing to do. As to her husband, though
she did not suppose that she could ever get him to
church,—nor perhaps would it be desirable,—she
thought that she might induce him to go nowhere, so
that she might be able to pass him off as a Christian.
She knew that such was the Christianity of young Goldsheiner, of which the Starts were now boasting.

Had she been alone in the world she thought that she
could have looked forward to her destiny with complacency; but she was afraid of her father and mother.
Lady Pomona was distressingly old-fashioned, and had
so often spoken with horror even of the approach of a
Jew,—and had been so loud in denouncing the iniquity
of Christians who allowed such people into their houses!
Unfortunately, too, Georgiana in her earlier days had
re-echoed all her mother's sentiments. And then her
father,—if he had ever earned for himself the right to
be called a Conservative politician by holding a real
opinion of his own,—it had been on that matter of
admitting the Jews into parliament.* When that had
been done he was certain that the glory of England was
sunk for ever. And since that time, whenever creditors
were more than ordinarily importunate, when Slow and
Bideawhile could do nothing for him, he would refer
to that fatal measure as though it was the cause of every
embarrassment which had harassed him. How could
she tell parents such as these that she was engaged to
marry a man who at the present moment went to
synagogue on a Saturday and carried out every other
filthy abomination common to the despised people?

That Mr. Brehgert was a fat, greasy man of fifty,
conspicuous for hair-dye, was in itself distressing:—
but this minor distress was swallowed up in the greater.
Miss Longestaffe was a girl possessing considerable
discrimination, and was able to weigh her own possessions in just scales. She had begun life with very
high aspirations, believing in her own beauty, in her
mother's fashion, and her father's fortune. She had

now been ten years at the work, and was aware that
she had always flown a little too high for her mark at the
time. At nineteen and twenty and twenty-one she had
thought that all the world was before her. With her
commanding figure, regular long features, and bright
complexion, she had regarded herself as one of the
beauties of the day, and had considered herself entitled
to demand wealth and a coronet. At twenty-two,
twenty-three, and twenty-four any young peer, or peer's
eldest son, with a house in town and in the country,
might have sufficed. Twenty-five and six had been the
years for baronets and squires; and even a leading
fashionable lawyer or two had been marked by her as
sufficient since that time. But now she was aware that
hitherto she had always fixed her price a little too high.
On three things she was still determined,—that she
would not be poor, that she would not be banished from
London, and that she would not be an old maid.
'Mamma,' she had often said, 'there's one thing certain.
I shall never do to be poor.' Lady Pomona had expressed
full concurrence with her child. 'And, mamma, to do as
Sophia is doing would kill me. Fancy having to live at
Toodlam all one's life with George Whitstable!' Lady
Pomona had agreed to this also, though she thought that
Toodlam Hall was a very nice home for her elder
daughter. 'And, mamma, I should drive you and papa
mad if I were to stay at home always. And what would
become of me when Dolly was master of everything?'
Lady Pomona, looking forward as well as she was able
to the time at which she should herself have departed,
when her dower and dower-house would have reverted
to Dolly, acknowledged that Georgiana should provide
herself with a home of her own before that time.

And how was this to be done? Lovers with all the
glories and all the graces are supposed to be plentiful as
blackberries by girls of nineteen, but have been proved
to be rare hothouse fruits by girls of twenty-nine.
Brehgert was rich, would live in London, and would
be a husband. People did such odd things now and
'lived them down,' that she could see no reason why she

should not do this and live this down. Courage was the one thing necessary,—that and perseverance. She must teach herself to talk about Brehgert as Lady Monogram did of Sir Damask. She had plucked up so much courage as had enabled her to declare her fate to her old friend,—remembering as she did so how in days long past she and her friend Julia Triplex had scattered their scorn upon some poor girl who had married a man with a Jewish name,—whose grandfather had possibly been a Jew. 'Dear me,' said Lady Monogram. 'Todd, Brehgert, and Goldsheiner! Mr. Todd is—one of us, I suppose.'

'Yes,' said Georgiana boldly, 'and Mr. Brehgert is a Jew. His name is Ezekiel Brehgert, and he is a Jew. You can say what you like about it.'

'I don't say anything about it, my dear.'

'And you can think anything you like. Things are changed since you and I were younger.'

'Very much changed, it appears,' said Lady Monogram. Sir Damask's religion had never been doubted, though except on the occasion of his marriage no acquaintance of his had probably ever seen him in church.

But to tell her father and mother required a higher spirit than she had shown even in her communication to Lady Monogram, and that spirit had not as yet come to her. On the morning before she left the Melmottes in Bruton Street, her lover had been with her. The Melmottes of course knew of the engagement and quite approved of it. Madame Melmotte rather aspired to credit for having had so happy an affair arranged under her auspices. It was some set-off against Marie's unfortunate escapade. Mr. Brehgert, therefore, had been allowed to come and go as he pleased, and on that morning he had pleased to come. They were sitting alone in some back room, and Brehgert was pressing for an early day. 'I don't think we need talk of that yet, Mr. Brehgert,' she said.

'You might as well get over the difficulty and call me Ezekiel at once,' he remarked. Georgiana frowned, and made no soft little attempt at the name as ladies in such circumstances are wont to do. 'Mrs. Brehgert'— he alluded of course to the mother of his children— 'used to call me Ezzy.'

'Perhaps I shall do so some day,' said Miss Longe-staffe, looking at her lover, and asking herself why she should not have been able to have the house and the money and the name of the wife without the troubles appertaining. She did not think it possible that she should ever call him Ezzy.

'And ven shall it be? I should say as early in August as possible.'

'In August!' she almost screamed. It was already July.

'Vy not, my dear? Ve would have our little holiday in Germany,—at Vienna. I have business there, and know many friends.' Then he pressed her hard to fix some day in the next month. It would be expedient that they should be married from the Melmottes' house, and the Melmottes would leave town some time in August. There was truth in this. Unless married from the Melmottes' house, she must go down to Caversham for the occasion,—which would be intoler-able. No;—she must separate herself altogether from father and mother, and become one with the Melmottes and the Brehgerts,—till she could live it down and make a position for herself. If the spending of money could do it, it should be done.

'I must at any rate ask mamma about it,' said Geor-giana. Mr. Brehgert, with the customary good-humour of his people, was satisfied with the answer, and went away promising that he would meet his love at the great Melmotte reception. Then she sat silent, thinking how she should declare the matter to her family. Would it not be better for her to say to them at once that there must be a division among them,—an absolute breaking off of all old ties, so that it should be tacitly acknowledged that she, Georgiana, had gone out from among the Longestaffes altogether, and had become one with the Melmottes, Brehgerts, and Goldsheiners?

## Chapter LXI

### LADY MONOGRAM PREPARES FOR THE PARTY

WHEN the little conversation took place between Lady Monogram and Miss Longestaffe, as recorded in the last chapter, Mr. Melmotte was in all his glory, and tickets for the entertainment were very precious. Gradually their value subsided. Lady Monogram had paid very dear for hers,—especially as the reception of Mr. Brehgert must be considered. But high prices were then being paid. A lady offered to take Marie Melmotte into the country with her for a week; but this was before the elopement. Mr. Cohenlupe was asked out to dinner to meet two peers and a countess. Lord Alfred received various presents. A young lady gave a lock of her hair to Lord Nidderdale, although it was known that he was to marry Marie Melmotte. And Miles Grendall got back an I O U of considerable nominal value from Lord Grasslough, who was anxious to accommodate two country cousins who were in London. Gradually the prices fell;—not at first from any doubt in Melmotte, but through that customary reaction which may be expected on such occasions. But at eight or nine o'clock on the evening of the party the tickets were worth nothing. The rumour had then spread itself through the whole town from Pimlico to Marylebone. Men coming home from clubs had told their wives. Ladies who had been in the park had heard it. Even the hairdressers had it, and ladies' maids had been instructed by the footmen and grooms who had been holding horses and seated on the coach-boxes. It had got into the air, and had floated round dining-rooms and over toilet-tables.

I doubt whether Sir Damask would have said a word about it to his wife as he was dressing for dinner, had he calculated what might be the result to himself. But he came home open-mouthed, and made no calculation. 'Have you heard what's up, Ju?' he said, rushing half-dressed into his wife's room.

'What is up?'

'Haven't you been out?'

'I was shopping, and that kind of thing. I don't want to take that girl into the Park. I've made a mistake in having her here, but I mean to be seen with her as little as I can.'

'Be good-natured, Ju, whatever you are.'

'Oh, bother! I know what I'm about. What is it you mean?'

'They say Melmotte's been found out.'

'Found out!' exclaimed Lady Monogram, stopping her maid in some arrangement which would not need to be continued in the event of her not going to the reception. 'What do you mean by found out?'

'I don't know exactly. There are a dozen stories told. It's something about that place he bought of old Longestaffe.'

'Are the Longestaffes mixed up in it? I won't have her here a day longer if there is anything against them.'

'Don't be an ass, Ju. There's nothing against him except that the poor old fellow hasn't got a shilling of his money.'

'Then he's ruined,—and there's an end of them.'

'Perhaps he will get it now. Some say that Melmotte has forged a receipt, others a letter. Some declare that he has manufactured a whole set of title-deeds. You remember Dolly?'

'Of course I know Dolly Longestaffe,' said Lady Monogram, who had thought at one time that an alliance with Dolly might be convenient.

' They say he has found it all out. There was always something about Dolly more than fellows gave him credit for. At any rate, everybody says that Melmotte will be in quod before long.'

'Not to-night, Damask!'

'Nobody seems to know. Lupton was saying that the policemen would wait about in the room like servants till the Emperor and the Princes had gone away.'

'Is Mr. Lupton going?'

'He was to have been at the dinner, but hadn't made

up his mind whether he'd go or not when I saw him. Nobody seems to be quite certain whether the Emperor will go. Somebody said that a Cabinet Council was to be called to know what to do.'

'A Cabinet Council!'

'Why, you see it's rather an awkward thing, letting the Prince go to dine with a man who perhaps may have been arrested and taken to gaol before dinner-time. That's the worst part of it. Nobody knows.'

Lady Monogram waved her attendant away. She piqued herself upon having a French maid who could not speak a word of English, and was therefore quite careless what she said in the woman's presence. But, of course, everything she did say was repeated downstairs in some language that had become intelligible to the servants generally. Lady Monogram sat motionless for some time, while her husband, retreating to his own domain, finished his operations. 'Damask,' she said, when he reappeared, 'one thing is certain;—we can't go.'

'After you've made such a fuss about it!'

'It is a pity,—having that girl here in the house. You know, don't you, she's going to marry one of these people?'

'I heard about her marriage yesterday. But Brehgert isn't one of Melmotte's set. They tell me that Brehgert isn't a bad fellow. A vulgar cad, and all that, but nothing wrong about him.'

'He's a Jew,—and he's seventy years old, and makes up horribly.'

'What does it matter to you if he's eighty? You are determined, then, you won't go?'

But Lady Monogram had by no means determined that she wouldn't go. She had paid her price, and with that economy which sticks to a woman always in the midst of her extravagances, she could not bear to lose the thing that she had bought. She cared nothing for Melmotte's villainy, as regarded herself. That he was enriching himself by the daily plunder of the innocent she had taken for granted since she had first heard of him. She had but a confused idea of any difference

between commerce and fraud. But it would grieve her
greatly to become known as one of an awkward squad
of people who had driven to the door, and perhaps been
admitted to some wretched gathering of wretched people,
—and not, after all, to have met the Emperor and the
Prince. But then, should she hear on the next morning
that the Emperor and the Princes, that the Princesses,
and the Duchesses, with the Ambassadors, Cabinet
Ministers, and proper sort of world generally, had all
been there,—that the world, in short, had ignored
Melmotte's villainy,—then would her grief be still
greater. She sat down to dinner with her husband and
Miss Longestaffe, and could not talk freely on the
matter. Miss Longestaffe was still a guest of the Melmottes, although she had transferred herself to the
Monograms for a day or two. And a horrible idea
crossed Lady Monogram's mind. What should she do
with her friend Georgiana if the whole Melmotte establishment were suddenly broken up? Of course, Madame
Melmotte would refuse to take the girl back if her
husband were sent to gaol. 'I suppose you'll go,' said
Sir Damask as the ladies left the room.

'Of course we shall,—in about an hour,' said Lady
Monogram as she left the room, looking round at him
and rebuking him for his imprudence.

'Because, you know——' and then he called her back.
'If you want me I'll stay, of course; but if you don't,
I'll go down to the club.'

'How can I say, yet? You needn't mind the club
to-night.'

'All right;—only it's a bore being here alone.'

Then Miss Longestaffe asked what 'was up.' 'Is
there any doubt about our going to-night?'

'I can't say. I'm so harassed that I don't know what
I'm about. There seems to be a report that the Emperor
won't be there.'

'Impossible!'

'It's all very well to say impossible, my dear,' said
Lady Monogram; 'but still that's what people are
saying. You see Mr. Melmotte is a very great man,

but perhaps—something else has turned up, so that he
may be thrown over. Things of that kind do happen.
You had better finish dressing. I shall. But I shan't
make sure of going till I hear that the Emperor is there.'
Then she descended to her husband, whom she found
forlornly consoling himself with a cigar. 'Damask,' she
said, 'you must find out.'

'Find out what?'

'Whether the Prince and the Emperor are there.'

'Send John to ask,' suggested the husband.

'He would be sure to make a blunder about it. If
you'd go yourself you'd learn the truth in a minute.
Have a cab,—just go into the hall and you'll soon know
how it all is;—I'd do it in a minute if I were you.'
Sir Damask was the most good-natured man in the
world, but he did not like the job. 'What can be the
objection?' asked his wife.

'Go to a man's house and find out whether a man's
guests are come before you go yourself! I don't just
see it, Ju.'

'Guests! What nonsense! The Emperor and all the
Royal Family! As if it were like any other party. Such
a thing, probably, never happened before, and never
will happen again. If you don't go, Damask, I must;
and I will.' Sir Damask, after groaning and smoking for
half a minute, said that he would go. He made many
remonstrances. It was a confounded bore. He hated
emperors and he hated princes. He hated the whole box
and dice of that sort of thing! He 'wished to goodness'
that he had dined at his club and sent word up home
that the affair was to be off. But at last he submitted
and allowed his wife to leave the room with the intention of sending for a cab. The cab was sent for and
announced, but Sir Damask would not stir till he had
finished his big cigar.

It was past ten when he left his own house. On
arriving in Grosvenor Square he could at once see that
the party was going on. The house was illuminated.
There was a concourse of servants round the door, and
half the square was already blocked up with carriages.

It was not without delay that he got to the door, and when there he saw the royal liveries. There was no doubt about the party. The Emperor and the Princes and the Princesses were all there. As far as Sir Damask could then perceive, the dinner had been quite a success. But again there was a delay in getting away, and it was nearly eleven before he could reach home. 'It's all right,' said he to his wife. 'They're there, safe enough.'

'You are sure that the Emperor is there.'

'As sure as a man can be without having seen him.'

Miss Longestaffe was present at this moment, and could not but resent what appeared to be a most unseemly slur cast upon her friends. 'I don't understand it at all,' she said. 'Of course the Emperor is there. Everybody has known for the last month that he was coming. What is the meaning of it, Julia?'

'My dear, you must allow me to manage my own little affairs my own way. I dare say I am absurd. But I have my reason. Now, Damask, if the carriage is there we had better start.' The carriage was there, and they did start, and with a delay which seemed unprecedented, even to Lady Monogram, who was accustomed to these things, they reached the door. There was a great crush in the hall, and people were coming downstairs. But at last they made their way into the room above, and found that the Emperor of China and all the Royalties had been there,—but had taken their departure.

Sir Damask put the ladies into the carriage and went at once to his club.

## Chapter LXII

### THE PARTY

LADY MONOGRAM retired from Mr. Melmotte's house in disgust as soon as she was able to escape; but we must return to it for a short time. When the guests were once in the drawing-room the immediate sense of failure passed away. The crowd never became so thick as had been anticipated. They who were knowing in such matters had declared that the people would not be able to get themselves out of the room till three or four o'clock in the morning, and that the carriages would not get themselves out of the Square till breakfast time. With a view to this kind of thing Mr. Melmotte had been told that he must provide a private means of escape for his illustrious guests, and with a considerable sacrifice of walls and general house arrangements this had been done. No such gathering as was expected took place; but still the rooms became fairly full, and Mr. Melmotte was able to console himself with the feeling that nothing certainly fatal had as yet occurred.

There can be no doubt that the greater part of the people assembled did believe that their host had committed some great fraud which might probably bring him under the arm of the law. When such rumours are spread abroad, they are always believed. There is an excitement and a pleasure in believing them. Reasonable hesitation at such a moment is dull and phlegmatic. If the accused one be near enough to ourselves to make the accusation a matter of personal pain, of course we disbelieve. But, if the distance be beyond this, we are almost ready to think that anything may be true of anybody. In this case nobody really loved Melmotte and everybody did believe. It was so probable that such a man should have done something horrible! It was only hoped that the fraud might be great and horrible enough.

Melmotte himself during that part of the evening which was passed upstairs kept himself in the close vicinity of royalty. He behaved certainly very much better than he would have done had he had no weight at his heart. He made few attempts at beginning any conversation, and answered, at any rate with brevity, when he was addressed. With scrupulous care he ticked off on his memory the names of those who had come and whom he knew, thinking that their presence indicated a verdict of acquittal from them on the evidence already before them. Seeing the members of the Government all there, he wished that he had come forward in Westminster as a Liberal. And he freely forgave those omissions of Royalty as to which he had been so angry at the India Office, seeing that not a Prince or Princess was lacking of those who were expected. He could turn his mind to all this, although he knew how great was his danger. Many things occurred to him as he stood, striving to smile as a host should smile. It might be the case that half-a-dozen detectives were already stationed in his own hall,—perhaps one or two, well dressed, in the very presence of royalty,—ready to arrest him as soon as the guests were gone, watching him now lest he should escape. But he bore the burden,—and smiled. He had always lived with the consciousness that such a burden was on him and might crush him at any time. He had known that he had to run these risks. He had told himself a thousand times that when the dangers came, dangers alone should never cow him. He had always endeavoured to go as near the wind as he could, to avoid the heavy hand of the criminal law of whatever country he inhabited. He had studied the criminal laws, so that he might be sure in his reckonings; but he had always felt that he might be carried by circumstances into deeper waters than he intended to enter. As the soldier who leads a forlorn hope, or as the diver who goes down for pearls, or as the searcher for wealth on fever-breeding coasts, knows that as his gains may be great, so are his perils, Melmotte had been aware that in his life, as it opened itself out to him, he might come to terrible destruction. He had not always thought, or even hoped, that he would be as he was now, so exalted as to be allowed to entertain the very biggest ones of the earth; but the greatness had grown upon him,—and so had the danger. He could not now be as exact as he had been. He was prepared himself to bear all mere ignominy with a tranquil mind,—to disregard any shouts of reprobation which might be uttered, and to console himself when the bad quarter of an hour should come with the remembrance that he had garnered up a store sufficient for future wants and placed it beyond the reach of his enemies. But as his intellect opened up to him new schemes, and as his ambition got the better of his prudence, he gradually fell from the security which he had preconceived, and became aware that he might have to bear worse than ignominy.

Perhaps never in his life had he studied his own character and his own conduct more accurately, or made sterner resolves, than he did as he stood there smiling, bowing, and acting without impropriety the part of host to an Emperor. No;—he could not run away. He soon made himself sure of that. He had risen too high to be a successful fugitive, even should he succeed in getting off before hands were laid upon him. He must bide his ground, if only that he might not at once confess his own guilt by flight; and he would do so with courage. Looking back at the hour or two that had just passed he was aware that he had allowed himself not only to be frightened in the dinner-room,—but also to seem to be frightened. The thing had come upon him unawares and he had been untrue to himself. He acknowledged that. He should not have asked those questions of Mr. Todd and Mr. Beauclerk, and should have been more good-humoured than usual with Lord Alfred in discussing those empty seats. But for spilt milk there is no remedy. The blow had come upon him too suddenly, and he had faltered. But he would not falter again. Nothing should cow him,—no touch from a policeman, no warrant from a magistrate, no defalcation of friends, no scorn in the City, no solitude in the West End. He would go down among the electors to-morrow and would stand his ground, as though all with him were right. Men should know at any rate that he had a heart within his bosom. And he confessed also to himself that he had sinned in that matter of arrogance. He could see it now,—as so many of us do see the faults which we have committed, which we strive, but in vain, to discontinue, and which we never confess except to our own bosoms. The task which he had imposed on himself, and to which circumstances had added weight, had been very hard to bear. He should have been good-humoured to these great ones whose society he had gained. He should have bound these people to him by a feeling of kindness as well as by his money. He could see it all now. And he could see too that there was no help for spilt milk. I think he took some pride in his own confidence as to his own courage, as he stood there turning it all over in his mind. Very much might be suspected. Something might be found out. But the task of unravelling it all would not be easy. It is the small vermin and the little birds that are trapped at once. But wolves and vultures can fight hard before they are caught. With the means which would still be at his command, let the worst come to the worst, he could make a strong fight. When a man's frauds have been enormous there is a certain safety in their very diversity and proportions. Might it not be that the fact that these great ones of the earth had been his guests should speak in his favour? A man who had in very truth had the real brother of the Sun dining at his table could hardly be sent into the dock and then sent out of it like a common felon.

Madame Melmotte during the evening stood at the top of her own stairs with a chair behind her on which she could rest herself for a moment when any pause took place in the arrivals. She had of course dined at the table,—or rather sat there;—but had been so placed that no duty had devolved upon her. She had heard no word of the rumours, and would probably be the last person in that house to hear them. It never occurred to her to see whether the places down the table were full or empty. She sat with her large eyes fixed on the Majesty of China and must have wondered at her own destiny at finding herself with an Emperor and Princes to look at. From the dining-room she had gone when she was told to go, up to the drawing-room, and had there performed her task, longing only for the comfort of her bedroom. She, I think, had but small sympathy with her husband in all his work, and but little understanding of the position in which she had been placed. Money she liked, and comfort, and perhaps diamonds and fine dresses, but she can hardly have taken pleasure in duchesses or have enjoyed the company of the Emperor. From the beginning of the Melmotte era it had been an understood thing that no one spoke to Madame Melmotte.

Marie Melmotte had declined a seat at the dinner-table. This at first had been cause of quarrel between her and her father, as he desired to have seen her next to young Lord Nidderdale as being acknowledged to be betrothed to him. But since the journey to Liverpool he had said nothing on the subject. He still pressed the engagement, but thought now that less publicity might be expedient. She was, however, in the drawing-room standing at first by Madame Melmotte, and afterwards retreating among the crowd. To some ladies she was a person of interest as the young woman who had lately run away under such strange circumstances; but no one spoke to her till she saw a girl whom she herself knew, and whom she addressed, plucking up all her courage for the occasion. This was Hetta Carbury who had been brought hither by her mother.

The tickets for Lady Carbury and Hetta had of course been sent before the elopement;—and also, as a matter of course, no reference had been made to them by the Melmotte family after the elopement. Lady Carbury herself was anxious that that affair should not be considered as having given cause for any personal quarrel between herself and Mr. Melmotte, and in her difficulty had consulted Mr. Broune. Mr. Broune was the staff on which she leant at present in all her difficulties. Mr. Broune was going to the dinner. All this of course took place while Melmotte's name was as yet unsullied as snow. Mr. Broune saw no reason why Lady Carbury should not take advantage of her tickets. These invitations were simply tickets to see the Emperor surrounded by the Princes. The young lady's elopement is 'no affair of yours,' Mr. Broune had said. 'I should go, if it were only for the sake of showing that you did not consider yourself to be implicated in the matter.' Lady Carbury did as she was advised, and took her daughter with her. 'Nonsense,' said the mother, when Hetta objected; 'Mr. Broune sees it quite in the right light. This is a grand demonstration in honour of the Emperor, rather than a private party;—and we have done nothing to offend the Melmottes. You know you wish to see the Emperor.' A few minutes before they started from Welbeck Street a note came from Mr. Broune, written in pencil and sent from Melmotte's house by a Commissioner. 'Don't mind what you hear; but come. I am here and as far as I can see it is all right. The E. is beautiful, and P.'s are as thick as blackberries.' Lady Carbury, who had not been in the way of hearing the reports, understood nothing of this; but of course she went. And Hetta went with her.

Hetta was standing alone in a corner, near to her mother, who was talking to Mr. Booker, with her eyes fixed on the awful tranquillity of the Emperor's countenance, when Marie Melmotte timidly crept up to her and asked her how she was. Hetta, probably, was not very cordial to the poor girl, being afraid of her, partly as the daughter of the great Melmotte and partly as the girl with whom her brother had failed to run away; but Marie was not rebuked by this. 'I hope you won't be angry with me for speaking to you.' Hetta smiled more graciously. She could not be angry with the girl for speaking to her, feeling that she was there as the guest of the girl's mother. 'I suppose you know about your brother,' said Marie, whispering with her eyes turned to the ground.

'I have heard about it,' said Hetta. 'He never told me himself.'

'Oh, I do so wish that I knew the truth. I know nothing. Of course, Miss Carbury, I love him. I do love him so dearly! I hope you don't think I would have done it if I hadn't loved him better than anybody in the world. Don't you think that if a girl loves a man,—really loves him,—that ought to go before everything?'

This was a question that Hetta was hardly prepared

to answer. She felt quite certain that under no circumstances would she run away with a man. 'I don't quite know. It is so hard to say,' she replied.

'I do. What's the good of anything if you're to be broken-hearted? I don't care what they say of me, or what they do to me, if he would only be true to me. Why doesn't he—let me know—something about it?' This also was a question difficult to be answered. Since that horrid morning on which Sir Felix had stumbled home drunk,—which was now four days since,—he had not left the house in Welbeck Street till this evening. He had gone out a few minutes before Lady Carbury had started, but up to that time he had almost kept his bed. He would not get up till dinner-time, would come down after some half-dressed fashion, and then get back to his bedroom, where he would smoke and drink brandy-and-water and complain of headache. The theory was that he was ill;—but he was in fact utterly cowed and did not dare to show himself at his usual haunts. He was aware that he had quarrelled at the club, aware that all the world knew of his intended journey to Liverpool, aware that he had tumbled about the streets intoxicated. He had not dared to show himself, and the feeling had grown upon him from day to day. Now, fairly worn out by his confinement, he had crept out intending, if possible, to find consolation with Ruby Ruggles. 'Do tell me. Where is he?' pleaded Marie.

'He has not been very well lately.'

'Is he ill? Oh, Miss Carbury, do tell me. You can understand what it is to love him as I do;—can't you?'

'He has been ill. I think he is better now.'

'Why does he not come to me, or send to me; or let me know something? It is cruel, is it not? Tell me,—you must know,—does he really care for me?'

Hetta was exceedingly perplexed. The real feeling betrayed by the girl recommended her. Hetta could not but sympathize with the affection manifested for her own brother, though she could hardly understand the want of reticence displayed by Marie in thus speaking of her love to one who was almost a stranger. 'Felix hardly ever talks about himself to me,' she said.

'If he doesn't care for me, there shall be an end of it,' Marie said very gravely. 'If I only knew! If I thought that he loved me, I'd go through,—oh,—all the world for him. Nothing that papa could say should stop me. That's my feeling about it. I have never talked to any one but you about it. Isn't that strange? I haven't a person to talk to. That's my feeling, and I'm not a bit ashamed of it. There's no disgrace in being in love. But it's very bad to get married without being in love. That's what I think.'

'It is bad,' said Hetta, thinking of Roger Carbury.

'But if Felix doesn't care for me!' continued Marie, sinking her voice to a low whisper, but still making her words quite audible to her companion. Now Hetta was strongly of opinion that her brother did not in the least 'care for' Marie Melmotte, and that it would be very much for the best that Marie Melmotte should know the truth. But she had not that sort of strength which would have enabled her to tell it. 'Tell me just what you think,' said Marie. Hetta was still silent. 'Ah,—I see. Then I must give him up? Eh?'

'What can I say, Miss Melmotte? Felix never tells me. He is my brother,—and of course I love you for loving him.' This was almost more than Hetta meant; but she felt herself constrained to say some gracious word.

'Do you? Oh! I wish you did. I should so like to be loved by you. Nobody loves me, I think. That man there wants to marry me. Do you know him? He is Lord Nidderdale. He is very nice; but he does not love me any more than he loves you. That's the way with men. It isn't the way with me. I would go with Felix, and slave for him if he were poor. Is it all to be over then? You will give him a message from me?' Hetta, doubting as to the propriety of the promise, promised that she would. 'Just tell him I want to know; that's all. I want to know. You'll understand. I want to know the real truth. I suppose I do know it now. Then I shall

not care what happens to me. It will be all the same.
I suppose I shall marry that young man, though it
will be very bad. I shall just be as if I hadn't any self of
my own at all. But he ought to send me word after all
that has passed. Do not you think he ought to send me
word?'

'Yes, indeed.'

'You tell him, then,' said Marie, nodding her head as
she crept away.

Nidderdale had been observing her while she had
been talking to Miss Carbury. He had heard the
rumour, and of course felt that it behoved him to be on
his guard more specially than any one else. But he had
not believed what he had heard. That men should be
thoroughly immoral, that they should gamble, get
drunk, run into debt, and make love to other men's
wives, was to him a matter of everyday life. Nothing of
that kind shocked him at all. But he was not as yet
quite old enough to believe in swindling. It had been
impossible to convince him that Miles Grendall had
cheated at cards, and the idea that Mr. Melmotte had
forged was as improbable and shocking to him as that
an officer should run away in battle. Common soldiers,
he thought, might do that sort of thing. He had almost
fallen in love with Marie when he saw her last, and was
inclined to feel the more kindly to her now because of
the hard things that were being said about her father.
And yet he knew that he must be careful. If 'he came
a cropper' in this matter, it would be such an awful
cropper! 'How do you like the party?' he said to Marie.

'I don't like it at all, my lord. How do you like it?'

'Very much, indeed. I think the Emperor is the
greatest fun I ever saw. Prince Frederic,'—one of the
German princes who was staying at the time among his
English cousins,—'Prince Frederic says that he's stuffed
with hay, and that he's made up fresh every morning at
a shop in the Haymarket.'

'I've seen him talk.'

'He opens his mouth, of course. There is machinery
as well as hay. I think he's the grandest old buffer

out, and I'm awfully glad that I've dined with him. I couldn't make out whether he really put anything to eat into his jolly old mouth.'

'Of course he did.'

'Have you been thinking about what we were talking about the other day?'

'No, my lord,—I haven't thought about it since. Why should I?'

'Well;—it's a sort of thing that people do think about, you know.'

'You don't think about it.'

'Don't I? I've been thinking about nothing else the last three months.'

'You've been thinking whether you'd get married or not.'

'That's what I mean,' said Lord Nidderdale.

'It isn't what I mean, then.'

'I'll be shot if I can understand you.'

'Perhaps not. And you never will understand me. Oh, goodness;—they're all going, and we must get out of the way. Is that Prince Frederic, who told you about the hay? He is handsome; isn't he? And who is that in the violet dress;—with all the pearls?'

'That's the Princess Dwarza.'

'Dear me;—isn't it odd, having a lot of people in one's own house, and not being able to speak a word to them? I don't think it's at all nice. Good night, my lord. I'm glad you like the Emperor.'

And then the people went, and when they had all gone Melmotte put his wife and daughter into his own carriage, telling them that he would follow them on foot to Bruton Street when he had given some last directions to the people who were putting out the lights, and extinguishing generally the embers of the entertainment. He had looked round for Lord Alfred, taking care to avoid the appearance of searching; but Lord Alfred had gone. Lord Alfred was one of those who knew when to leave a falling house. Melmotte at the moment thought of all that he had done for Lord Alfred, and it was something of the real venom of ingratitude that stung him at

the moment rather than this additional sign of coming
evil. He was more than ordinarily gracious as he put his
wife into the carriage, and remarked that, considering all
things, the party had gone off very well. 'I only wish it
could have been done a little cheaper,' he said laughing.
Then he went back into the house, and up into the
drawing-rooms which were now utterly deserted. Some
of the lights had been put out, but the men were busy in
the rooms below, and he threw himself into the chair in
which the Emperor had sat. It was wonderful that he
should come to such a fate as this;—that he, the boy
out of the gutter, should entertain at his own house, in
London, a Chinese Emperor and English and German
Royalty,—and that he should do so almost with a rope
round his neck. Even if this were to be the end of it all,
men would at any rate remember him. The grand
dinner which he had given before he was put into prison
would live in history. And it would be remembered, too,
that he had been the Conservative candidate for the great
borough of Westminster,—perhaps, even, the elected
member. He, too, in his manner, assured himself that a
great part of him would escape Oblivion. 'Non omnis
moriar,'*in some language of his own, was chanted by
him within his own breast, as he sat there looking out
on his own magnificent suite of rooms from the arm-
chair which had been consecrated by the use of an
Emperor.

No policemen had come to trouble him yet. No hint
that he would be 'wanted' had been made to him. There
was no tangible sign that things were not to go on as
they went before. Things would be exactly as they were
before, but for the absence of those guests from the
dinner-table, and for the words which Miles Grendall
had spoken. Had he not allowed himself to be terrified
by shadows? Of course he had known that there must
be such shadows. His life had been made dark by similar
clouds before now, and he had lived through the storms
which had followed them. He was thoroughly ashamed
of the weakness which had overcome him at the dinner-
table, and of that palsy of fear which he had allowed

himself to exhibit. There should be no more shrinking such as that. When people talked of him they should say that he was at least a man.

As this was passing through his mind a head was pushed in through one of the doors, and immediately withdrawn. It was his Secretary. 'Is that you, Miles?' he said. 'Come in. I'm just going home, and came up here to see how the empty rooms would look after they were all gone. What became of your father?'

'I suppose he went away.'

'I suppose he did,' said Melmotte, unable to hinder himself from throwing a certain tone of scorn into his voice,—as though proclaiming the fate of his own house and the consequent running away of the rat. 'It went off very well, I think.'

'Very well,' said Miles, still standing at the door. There had been a few words of consultation between him and his father,—only a very few words. 'You'd better see it out to-night, as you've had a regular salary, and all that. I shall hook it. I sha'n't go near him to-morrow till I find out how things are going. By G——, I've had about enough of him.' But hardly enough of his money,—or it may be presumed that Lord Alfred would have 'hooked it' sooner.

'Why don't you come in, and not stand there?' said Melmotte. 'There's no Emperor here now for you to be afraid of.'

'I'm afraid of nobody,' said Miles, walking into the middle of the room.

'Nor am I. What's one man that another man should be afraid of him? We've got to die, and there'll be an end of it, I suppose.'

'That's about it,' said Miles, hardly following the working of his master's mind.

'I shouldn't care how soon. When a man has worked as I have done, he gets about tired at my age. I suppose I'd better be down at the committee-room about ten to-morrow?'

'That's the best, I should say.'

'You'll be there by that time?' Miles Grendall

assented slowly, and with imperfect assent. 'And tell your father he might as well be there as early as convenient.'

'All right,' said Miles as he took his departure.

'Curs!' said Melmotte almost aloud. 'They neither of them will be there. If any evil can be done to me by treachery and desertion, they will do it.' Then it occurred to him to think whether the Grendall article had been worth all the money that he had paid for it. 'Curs!' he said again. He walked down into the hall, and through the banqueting-room, and stood at the place where he himself had sat. What a scene it had been, and how frightfully low his heart had sunk within him! It had been the defection of the Lord Mayor that had hit him hardest. 'What cowards they are!' The men went on with their work, not noticing him, and probably not knowing him. The dinner had been done by contract, and the contractor's foreman was there. The care of the house and the alterations had been confided to another contractor, and his foreman was waiting to see the place locked up. A confidential clerk, who had been with Melmotte for years, and who knew his ways, was there also to guard the property. 'Good night, Croll,' he said to the man in German. Croll touched his hat and bade him good night. Melmotte listened anxiously to the tone of the man's voice, trying to catch from it some indication of the mind within. Did Croll know of these rumours, and if so, what did he think of them? Croll had known him in some perilous circumstances before, and had helped him through them. He paused a moment as though he would ask a question, but resolved at last that silence would be safest. 'You'll see everything safe, eh, Croll?' Croll said that he would see everything safe, and Melmotte passed out into the Square.

He had not far to go, round through Berkeley Square into Bruton Street, but he stood for a few moments looking up at the bright stars. If he could be there, in one of those unknown distant worlds, with all his present intellect and none of his present burdens, he would, he thought, do better than he had done here on earth. If he could even now put himself down nameless, fameless, and without possessions in some distant corner of the world, he could, he thought, do better. But he was Augustus Melmotte, and he must bear his burdens, whatever they were, to the end. He could reach no place so distant but that he would be known and traced.

## Chapter LXIII

### MR. MELMOTTE ON THE DAY OF THE ELECTION

NO election of a Member of Parliament by ballot in a borough so large as that of Westminster had as yet been achieved in England since the ballot had been established by law. Men who heretofore had known, or thought that they knew, how elections would go, who counted up promises, told off professed enemies, and weighed the doubtful ones, now confessed themselves to be in the dark. Three days since the odds had been considerably in Melmotte's favour; but this had come from the reputation attached to his name, rather than from any calculation as to the politics of the voters. Then Sunday had intervened. On the Monday Melmotte's name had continued to go down in the betting from morning to evening. Early in the day his supporters had thought little of this, attributing the fall to that vacillation which is customary in such matters; but towards the latter part of the afternoon the tidings from the City had been in everybody's mouth, and Melmotte's committee-room had been almost deserted. At six o'clock there were some who suggested that his name should be withdrawn. No such suggestion, however, was made to him,—perhaps, because no one dared to make it. On the Monday evening all work and strategy for the election, as regarded Melmotte and his party, died away; and the interest of the hour was turned to the dinner.

But Mr. Alf's supporters were very busy. There had been a close consultation among a few of them as to

what should be done by their Committee as to these
charges against the opposite candidate. In the 'Pulpit'
of that evening an allusion had been made to the affair,
which was of course sufficiently intelligible to those
who were immediately concerned in the matter, but
which had given no name and mentioned no details.
Mr. Alf explained that this had been put in by the sub-
editor, and that it only afforded such news as the paper
was bound to give to the public. He himself pointed
out the fact that no note of triumph had been sounded,
and that the rumour had not been connected with the
election.

One old gentleman was of opinion that they were
bound to make the most of it. 'It's no more than we've
all believed all along,' said the old gentleman, 'and why
are we to let a fellow like that get the seat if we can keep
him out?' He was of opinion that everything should be
done to make the rumour with all its exaggerations as
public as possible,—so that there should be no opening
for an indictment for libel; and the clever old gentleman
was full of devices by which this might be effected. But
the Committee generally was averse to fight in this
manner. Public opinion has its Bar as well as the Law
Courts. If, after all, Melmotte had committed no
fraud,—or, as was much more probable, should not be
convicted of fraud,—then it would be said that the
accusation had been forged for purely electioneering
purposes, and there might be a rebound which would
pretty well crush all those who had been concerned.
Individual gentlemen could, of course, say what they
pleased to individual voters; but it was agreed at last
that no overt use should be made of the rumours by
Mr. Alf's Committee. In regard to other matters, they
who worked under the Committee were busy enough.
The dinner to the Emperor was turned into ridicule,
and the electors were asked whether they felt themselves
bound to return a gentleman out of the City to Parliament because he had offered to spend a fortune on
entertaining all the royalties then assembled in London.
There was very much said on placards and published in

newspapers to the discredit of Melmotte, but nothing was
so printed which would not have appeared with equal
venom had the recent rumours never been sent out
from the City. At twelve o'clock at night, when Mr.
Alf's committee-room was being closed, and when
Melmotte was walking home to bed, the general opinion
at the clubs was very much in favour of Mr. Alf.

On the next morning Melmotte was up before eight.
As yet no policeman had called for him, nor had any
official intimation reached him that an accusation was
to be brought against him. On coming down from his
bedroom he at once went into the back-parlour on the
ground floor, which Mr. Longestaffe called his study,
and which Mr. Melmotte had used since he had been
in Mr. Longestaffe's house for the work which he did at
home. He would be there often early in the morning,
and often late at night after Lord Alfred had left him.
There were two heavy desk-tables in the room, furnished with drawers down to the ground. One of these
the owner of the house had kept locked for his own
purposes. When the bargain for the temporary letting
of the house had been made, Mr. Melmotte and Mr.
Longestaffe were close friends. Terms for the purchase
of Pickering had just been made, and no cause for
suspicion had as yet arisen. Everything between the
two gentlemen had been managed with the greatest ease.
Oh dear, yes! Mr. Longestaffe could come whenever
he pleased. He, Melmotte, always left the house at
ten and never returned till six. The ladies would never
enter that room. The servants were to regard Mr.
Longestaffe quite as master of the house as far as that
room was concerned. If Mr. Longestaffe could spare it,
Mr. Melmotte would take the key of one of the tables.
The matter was arranged very pleasantly.

Mr. Melmotte on entering the room bolted the door,
and then, sitting at his own table, took certain papers
out of the drawers,—a bundle of letters and another of
small documents. From these, with very little examination, he took three or four,—two or three perhaps from
each. These he tore into very small fragments and

burned the bits,—holding them over a gas-burner and letting the ashes fall into a large china plate. Then he blew the ashes into the yard through the open window. This he did to all these documents but one. This one he put bit by bit into his mouth, chewing the paper into a pulp till he swallowed it. When he had done this, and had re-locked his own drawers, he walked across to the other table, Mr. Longestaffe's table, and pulled the handle of one of the drawers. It opened;—and then, without touching the contents, he again closed it. He then knelt down and examined the lock, and the hole above into which the bolt of the lock ran. Having done this he again closed the drawer, drew back the bolt of the door, and, seating himself at his own desk, rang the bell which was close to hand. The servant found him writing letters after his usual hurried fashion, and was told that he was ready for breakfast. He always breakfasted alone with a heap of newspapers around him, and so he did on this day. He soon found the paragraph alluding to himself in the 'Pulpit,' and read it without a quiver in his face or the slightest change in his colour. There was no one to see him now,—but he was acting under a resolve that at no moment, either when alone, or in a crowd, or when suddenly called upon for words,— not even when the policemen with their first hints of arrest should come upon him,—would he betray himself by the working of a single muscle, or the loss of a drop of blood from his heart. He would go through it, always armed, without a sign of shrinking. It had to be done, and he would do it.

At ten he walked down to the central committee-room at Whitehall Place. He thought that he would face the world better by walking than if he were taken in his own brougham. He gave orders that the carriage should be at the committee-room at eleven, and wait an hour for him if he was not there. He went along Bond Street and Piccadilly, Regent Street and through Pall Mall to Charing Cross, with the blandly triumphant smile of a man who had successfully entertained the great guest of the day. As he got near the club he met two or three

men whom he knew, and bowed to them. They returned
his bow graciously enough, but not one of them stopped
to speak to him. Of one he knew that he would have
stopped, had it not been for the rumour. Even after the
man had passed on he was careful to show no displeasure
on his face. He would take it all as it would come and
still be the blandly triumphant Merchant Prince,—as
long as the police would allow him. He probably was
not aware how very different was the part he was now
playing from that which he had assumed at the India
Office.

At the committee-room he only found a few understrappers, and was informed that everything was going
on regularly. The electors were balloting; but with the
ballot,—so said the leader of the understrappers,—
there never was any excitement. The men looked half-
frightened,—as though they did not quite know whether
they ought to seize their candidate, and hold him till the
constable came. They certainly had not expected to see
him there. 'Has Lord Alfred been here?' Melmotte
asked, standing in the inner room with his back to the
empty grate. No,—Lord Alfred had not been there.
'Nor Mr. Grendall?' The senior understrapper knew
that Melmotte would have asked for 'his Secretary,' and
not for Mr. Grendall, but for the rumours. It is so hard
not to tumble into Scylla when you are avoiding
Charybdis. Mr. Grendall had not been there. Indeed,
nobody had been there. 'In fact, there is nothing more
to be done, I suppose?' said Mr. Melmotte. The senior
understrapper thought that there was nothing more to
be done. He left word that his brougham should be
sent away, and strolled out again on foot.

He went up into Covent Garden, where there was a
polling booth. The place seemed to him, as one of the
chief centres for a contested election, to be wonderfully
quiet. He was determined to face everybody and everything, and he went close up to the booth. Here he was
recognised by various men, mechanics chiefly, who
came forward and shook hands with him. He remained
there for an hour conversing with people, and at last

made a speech to a little knot around him. He did not
allude to the rumour of yesterday, nor to the paragraph
in the 'Pulpit' to which his name had not been attached;
but he spoke freely enough of the general accusations
that had been brought against him previously. He
wished the electors to understand that nothing which
had been said against him made him ashamed to meet
them here or elsewhere. He was proud of his position,
and proud that the electors of Westminster should
recognise it. He did not, he was glad to say, know
much of the law, but he was told that the law would
protect him from such aspersions as had been unfairly
thrown upon him. He flattered himself that he was too
good an Englishman to regard the ordinary political
attacks to which candidates were, as a matter of course,
subject at elections;—and he could stretch his back to
bear perhaps a little more than these, particularly as he
looked forward to a triumphant return. But things had
been said, and published, which the excitement of an
election could not justify, and as to these things he must
have recourse to the law. Then he made some allusion
to the Princes and the Emperor, and concluded by
observing that it was the proudest boast of his life to be
an Englishman and a Londoner.

It was asserted afterwards that this was the only good
speech he had ever been known to make; and it was
certainly successful, as he was applauded throughout
Covent Garden. A reporter for the 'Breakfast-Table'
who was on duty at the place, looking for paragraphs as
to the conduct of electors, gave an account of the speech
in that paper, and made more of it, perhaps, than it
deserved. It was asserted afterwards, and given as a
great proof of Melmotte's cleverness, that he had planned
the thing and gone to Covent Garden all alone having
considered that in that way could he best regain a step
in reputation; but in truth the affair had not been
preconcerted. It was while in Whitehall Place that he
had first thought of going to Covent Garden, and he
had had no idea of making a speech till the people had
gathered round him.

It was then noon, and he had to determine what he should do next. He was half inclined to go round to all the booths and make speeches. His success at Covent Garden had been very pleasant to him. But he feared that he might not be so successful elsewhere. He had shown that he was not afraid of the electors. Then an idea struck him that he would go boldly into the City,— to his own offices in Abchurch Lane. He had determined to be absent on this day, and would not be expected. But his appearance there could not on that account be taken amiss. Whatever enmities there might be, or whatever perils, he would face them. He got a cab therefore and had himself driven to Abchurch Lane.

The clerks were hanging about doing nothing, as though it were a holiday. The dinner, the election, and the rumour together had altogether demoralized them. But some of them at least were there, and they showed no signs of absolute insubordination. 'Mr. Grendall has not been here?' he asked. No; Mr. Grendall had not been there; but Mr. Cohenlupe was in Mr. Grendall's room. At this moment he hardly desired to see Mr. Cohenlupe. That gentleman was privy to many of his transactions, but was by no means privy to them all. Mr. Cohenlupe knew that the estate at Pickering had been purchased, and knew that it had been mortgaged. He knew also what had become of the money which had so been raised. But he knew nothing of the circumstances of the purchase, although he probably surmised that Melmotte had succeeded in getting the title-deeds on credit, without paying the money. He was afraid that he could hardly see Cohenlupe and hold his tongue, and that he could not speak to him without danger. He and Cohenlupe might have to stand in a dock together; and Cohenlupe had none of his spirit. But the clerks would think, and would talk, were he to leave the office without seeing his old friend. He went therefore into his own room, and called to Cohenlupe as he did so.

'Ve didn't expect you here to-day,' said the member for Staines.

'Nor did I expect to come. But there isn't much to do at Westminster while the ballot is going on; so I came up, just to look at the letters. The dinner went off pretty well yesterday, eh?'

'Uncommon;—nothing better. Vy did the Lord Mayor stay away, Melmotte?'

'Because he's an ass and a cur,' said Mr. Melmotte with an assumed air of indignation. 'Alf and his people had got hold of him. There was ever so much fuss about it at first,—whether he would accept the invitation. I say it was an insult to the City to take it and not to come. I shall be even with him some of these days.'

'Things will go on just the same as usual, Melmotte?'

'Go on. Of course they'll go. What's to hinder them?'

'There's ever so much been said,' whispered Cohenlupe.

'Said;—yes,' ejaculated Melmotte very loudly. 'You're not such a fool, I hope, as to believe every word you hear. You'll have enough to believe, if you do.'

'There's no knowing vat anybody does know, and vat anybody does not know,' said Cohenlupe.

'Look you here, Cohenlupe,'—and now Melmotte also sank his voice to a whisper,—'keep your tongue in your mouth; go about just as usual, and say nothing. It's all right. There has been some heavy pulls upon us.'

'Oh dear, there has indeed!'

'But any paper with my name to it will come right.'

'That's nothing;—nothing at all,' said Cohenlupe.

'And there is nothing;—nothing at all! I've bought some property and have paid for it; and I have bought some, and have not yet paid for it. There's no fraud in that.'

'No, no,—nothing in that.'

'You hold your tongue, and go about your business. I'm going to the bank now.' Cohenlupe had been very low in spirits, and was still low in spirits; but he was somewhat better after the visit of the great man to the City.

Mr. Melmotte was as good as his word and walked straight to the bank. He kept two accounts at different banks, one for his business, and one for his private affairs. The one he now entered was that which kept what we may call his domestic account. He walked straight through, after his old fashion, to the room behind the bank in which sat the manager and the manager's one clerk, and stood upon the rug before the fireplace just as though nothing had happened,— or as nearly as though nothing had happened as was within the compass of his powers. He could not quite do it. In keeping up an appearance intended to be natural he was obliged to be somewhat milder than his wont. The manager did not behave nearly as well as he did, and the clerks manifestly betrayed their emotion. Melmotte saw that it was so;—but he had expected it, and had come there on purpose to 'put it down.'

'We hardly expected to see you in the City to-day, Mr. Melmotte.'

'And I didn't expect to see myself here. But it always happens that when one expects that there's most to be done, there's nothing to be done at all. They're all at work down at Westminster, balloting; but as I can't go on voting for myself, I'm of no use. I've been at Covent Garden this morning, making a stump speech, and if all that they say there is true, I haven't much to be afraid of.'

'And the dinner went off pretty well?' asked the manager.

'Very well, indeed. They say the Emperor liked it better than anything that has been done for him yet.' This was a brilliant flash of imagination. 'For a friend to dine with me every day, you know, I should prefer somebody who had a little more to say for himself. But then, perhaps, you know, if you or I were in China we shouldn't have much to say for ourselves;—eh?' The manager acceded to this proposition. 'We had one awful disappointment. His lordship from over the way didn't come.'

'The Lord Mayor, you mean.'

'The Lord Mayor didn't come! He was frightened at the last moment;—took it into his head that his autho-

rity in the City was somehow compromised. But the
wonder was that the dinner went on without him.'
Then Melmotte referred to the purport of his call there
that day. He would have to draw large cheques for his
private wants. 'You don't give a dinner to an Emperor
of China for nothing, you know.' He had been in the
habit of overdrawing on his private account,—making
arrangements with the manager. But now, in the
manager's presence, he drew a regular cheque on his
business account for a large sum, and then, as a sort of
afterthought, paid in the £250 which he had received
from Mr. Broune on account of the money which Sir
Felix had taken from Marie.

'There don't seem much the matter with him,' said
the manager, when Melmotte had left the room.

'He brazens it out, don't he?' said the senior clerk.
But the feeling of the room after full discussion inclined
to the opinion that the rumours had been a political
manœuvre. Nevertheless, Mr. Melmotte would not
now have been allowed to overdraw at the present
moment.

## Chapter LXIV

### THE ELECTION

MR. ALF'S central committee-room was in Great
George Street, and there the battle was kept alive
all the day. It had been decided, as the reader has been
told, that no direct advantage should be taken of that
loud blast of accusation which had been heard throughout the town on the previous afternoon. There had not
been sufficient time for inquiry as to the truth of that
blast. If there were just ground for the things that had
been said, Mr. Melmotte would no doubt soon be in
gaol, or would be,—wanted. Many had thought that he
would escape as soon as the dinner was over, and had
been disappointed when they heard that he had been
seen walking down towards his own committee-room on
the following morning. Others had been told that at the

last moment his name would be withdrawn,—and a question arose as to whether he had the legal power to withdraw his name after a certain hour on the day before the ballot. An effort was made to convince a portion of the electors that he had withdrawn, or would have withdrawn, or should have withdrawn. When Melmotte was at Covent Garden, a large throng of men went to Whitehall Place with the view of ascertaining the truth. He certainly had made no attempt at withdrawal. They who propagated this report certainly damaged Mr. Alf's cause. A second reaction set in, and there grew a feeling that Mr. Melmotte was being ill-used. Those evil things had been said of him,—many at least so declared,—not from any true motive, but simply to secure Mr. Alf's return. Tidings of the speech in Covent Garden were spread about at the various polling places, and did good service to the so-called Conservative cause. Mr. Alf's friends, hearing all this, instigated him also to make a speech. Something should be said, if only that it might be reported in the newspapers, to show that they had behaved with generosity, instead of having injured their enemy by false attacks. Whatever Mr. Alf might say, he might at any rate be sure of a favourable reporter.

About two o'clock in the day, Mr. Alf did make a speech,—and a very good speech it was, if correctly reported in the 'Evening Pulpit.' Mr. Alf was a clever man, ready at all points, with all his powers immediately at command, and, no doubt, he did make a good speech. But in this speech, in which we may presume that it would be his intention to convince the electors that they ought to return him to Parliament, because, of the two candidates, he was the fittest to represent their views, he did not say a word as to his own political ideas, not, indeed, a word that could be accepted as manifesting his own fitness for the place which it was his ambition to fill. He contented himself with endeavouring to show that the other man was not fit;—and that he and his friends, though solicitous of proving to the electors that Mr. Melmotte was about the most unfit man in the world, had been guilty of nothing shabby in their manner of doing so. 'Mr. Melmotte,' he said, 'comes before you as a Conservative, and has told us, by the mouths of his friends,—for he has not favoured us with many words of his own,—that he is supported by the whole Conservative party. That party is not my party, but I respect it. Where, however, are these Conservative supporters? We have heard, till we are sick of it, of the banquet which Mr. Melmotte gave yesterday. I am told that very few of those whom he calls his Conservative friends could be induced to attend that banquet. It is equally notorious that the leading merchants of the City refused to grace the table of this great commercial prince. I say that the leaders of the Conservative party have at last found their candidate out, have repudiated him;—and are seeking now to free themselves from the individual shame of having supported the candidature of such a man by remaining in their own houses instead of clustering round the polling booths. Go to Mr. Melmotte's committee-room and inquire if those leading Conservatives be there. Look about, and see whether they are walking with him in the streets, or standing with him in public places, or taking the air with him in the parks. I respect the leaders of the Conservative party; but they have made a mistake in this matter, and they know it.' Then he ended by alluding to the rumours of yesterday. 'I scorn,' said he, 'to say anything against the personal character of a political opponent, which I am not in a position to prove. I make no allusion, and have made no allusion, to reports which were circulated yesterday about him, and which I believe were originated in the City. They may be false or they may be true. As I know nothing of the matter, I prefer to regard them as false, and I recommend you to do the same. But I declared to you long before these reports were in men's mouths, that Mr. Melmotte was not entitled by his character to represent you in parliament, and I repeat that assertion. A great British merchant, indeed! How long, do you think, should a man be known in this city before that title be accorded to him? Who knew aught of this man two years since,—unless, indeed, it be some one who had burnt his wings in trafficking with him in some continental city? Ask the character of this great British merchant in Hamburg and Vienna; ask it in Paris;—ask those whose business here has connected them with the assurance companies of foreign countries, and you will be told whether this is a fit man to represent Westminster in the British parliament!' There was much more yet; but such was the tone of the speech which Mr. Alf made with the object of inducing the electors to vote for himself.

At two or three o'clock in the day, nobody knew how the matter was going. It was supposed that the working-classes were in favour of Melmotte, partly from their love of a man who spends a great deal of money, partly from the belief that he was being ill-used,—partly, no doubt, from that occult sympathy which is felt for crime, when the crime committed is injurious to the upper classes. Masses of men will almost feel that a certain amount of injustice ought to be inflicted on their betters, so as to make things even, and will persuade themselves that a criminal should be declared to be innocent, because the crime committed has had a tendency to oppress the rich and pull down the mighty from their seats. Some few years since, the basest calumnies that were ever published in this country, uttered by one of the basest men that ever disgraced the country, levelled, for the most part, at men of whose characters and services the country was proud, were received with a certain amount of sympathy by men not themselves dishonest, because they who were thus slandered had received so many good things from Fortune, that a few evil things were thought to be due to them.* There had not as yet been time for the formation of such a feeling generally, in respect of Mr. Melmotte. But there was a commencement of it. It had been asserted that Melmotte was a public robber. Whom had he robbed? Not the poor. There was not a man in London who caused the payment of a larger sum in weekly wages than Mr. Melmotte.

About three o'clock, the editor of the 'Morning

Breakfast-Table' called on Lady Carbury. 'What is it all about?' she asked, as soon as her friend was seated. There had been no time for him to explain anything at Madame Melmotte's reception, and Lady Carbury had as yet failed in learning any certain news of what was going on.

'I don't know what to make of it,' said Mr. Broune. 'There is a story abroad that Mr. Melmotte has forged some document with reference to a purchase he made,—and hanging on to that story are other stories as to moneys that he has raised. I should say that it was simply an electioneering trick, and a very unfair trick, were it not that all his own side seem to believe it.'

'Do you believe it?'

'Ah,—I could answer almost any question sooner than that.'

'Then he can't be rich at all.'

'Even that would not follow. He has such large concerns in hand that he might be very much pressed for funds, and yet be possessed of immense wealth. Everybody says that he pays all his bills.'

'Will he be returned?' she asked.

'From what we hear, we think not. I shall know more about it in an hour or two. At present I should not like to have to publish an opinion; but were I forced to bet, I would bet against him. Nobody is doing anything for him. There can be no doubt that his own party are ashamed of him. As things used to be, this would have been fatal to him at the day of election; but now, with the ballot, it won't matter so much. If I were a candidate, at present, I think I would go to bed on the last day, and beg all my committee to do the same as soon as they had put in their voting papers.'

'I am glad Felix did not go to Liverpool,' said Lady Carbury.

'It would not have made much difference. She would have been brought back all the same. They say Lord Nidderdale still means to marry her.'

'I saw him talking to her last night.'

'There must be an immense amount of property

somewhere. No one doubts that he was rich when he came to England two years ago, and they say everything has prospered that he has put his hand to since. The Mexican Railway shares had fallen this morning, but they were at £15 premium yesterday morning. He must have made an enormous deal out of that.' But Mr. Broune's eloquence on this occasion was chiefly displayed in regard to the presumption of Mr. Alf. 'I shouldn't think him such a fool if he had announced his resignation of the editorship when he came before the world as a candidate for parliament. But a man must be mad who imagines that he can sit for Westminster and edit a London daily paper at the same time.'

'Has it never been done?'

'Never, I think;—that is, by the editor of such a paper as the "Pulpit". How is a man who sits in parliament himself ever to pretend to discuss the doings of parliament with impartiality? But Alf believes that he can do more than anybody else ever did, and he'll come to the ground. Where's Felix now?'

'Do not ask me,' said the poor mother.

'Is he doing anything?'

'He lies in bed all day, and is out all night.'

'But that wants money.' She only shook her head. 'You do not give him any?'

'I have none to give.'

'I should simply take the key of the house from him,—or bolt the door if he will not give it up.'

'And be in bed, and listen while he knocks,—knowing that he must wander in the streets if I refuse to let him in? A mother cannot do that, Mr. Broune. A child has such a hold upon his mother. When her reason has bade her to condemn him, her heart will not let her carry out the sentence.' Mr. Broune never now thought of kissing Lady Carbury; but when she spoke thus, he got up and took her hand, and she, as she pressed his hand, had no fear that she would be kissed. The feeling between them was changed.

Melmotte dined at home that evening with no company but that of his wife and daughter. Latterly one of the Grendalls had almost always joined their party when they did not dine out. Indeed, it was an understood thing, that Miles Grendall should dine there always, unless he explained his absence by some engagement,—so that his presence there had come to be considered as a part of his duty. Not infrequently 'Alfred' and Miles would both come, as Melmotte's dinners and wines were good, and occasionally the father would take the son's place,—but on this day they were both absent. Madame Melmotte had not as yet said a word to any one indicating her own apprehension of any evil. But not a person had called to-day,—the day after the great party,—and even she, though she was naturally callous in such matters, had begun to think that she was deserted. She had, too, become so used to the presence of the Grendalls, that she now missed their company. She thought that on this day, of all days, when the world was balloting for her husband at Westminster, they would both have been with him to discuss the work of the day. 'Is not Mr. Grendall coming?' she asked, as she took her seat at the table.

'No, he is not,' said Melmotte.

'Nor Lord Alfred?'

'Nor Lord Alfred.' Melmotte had returned home much conforted by the day's proceedings. No one had dared to say a harsh word to his face. Nothing further had reached his ears. After leaving the bank he had gone back to his office, and had written letters,—just as if nothing had happened; and, as far as he could judge, his clerks had plucked up courage. One of them, about five o'clock, came into him with news from the west, and with second editions of the evening papers. The clerk expressed his opinion that the election was going well. Mr. Melmotte, judging from the papers, one of which was supposed to be on his side and the other of course against him, thought that his affairs altogether were looking well. The Westminster election had not the foremost place in his thoughts; but he took what was said on that subject as indicating the minds of men upon the other matter. He read Alf's speech, and

consoled himself with thinking that Mr. Alf had not dared
to make new accusations against him. All that about
Hamburg and Vienna and Paris was as old as the hills,
and availed nothing. His whole candidature had been
carried in the face of that. 'I think we shall do pretty
well,' he said to the clerk. His very presence in Abchurch
Lane of course gave confidence. And thus, when he
came home, something of the old arrogance had come
back upon him, and he could swagger at any rate
before his wife and servants. 'Nor Lord Alfred,' he said
with scorn. Then he added more. 'The father and son
are two d—— curs.' This of course frightened Madame
Melmotte, and she joined this desertion of the Grendalls
to her own solitude all the day.

'Is there anything wrong, Melmotte?' she said afterwards, creeping up to him in the back parlour, and
speaking in French.

'What do you call wrong?'

'I don't know;—but I seem to be afraid of something.'

'I should have thought you were used to that kind of
feeling by this time.'

'Then there is something.'

'Don't be a fool. There is always something. There
is always much. You don't suppose that this kind of
thing can be carried on as smoothly as the life of an old
maid with £400 a year paid quarterly in advance.'

'Shall we have to——move again?' she asked.

'How am I to tell? You haven't much to do when we
move, and may get plenty to eat and drink wherever
you go. Does that girl mean to marry Lord Nidderdale?'
Madame Melmotte shook her head. 'What a poor
creature you must be when you can't talk her out of a
fancy for such a reprobate as young Carbury. If she
throws me over, I'll throw her over. I'll flog her within
an inch of her life if she disobeys me. You tell her that
I say so.'

'Then he may flog me,' said Marie, when so much of
the conversation was repeated to her that evening.
'Papa does not know me if he thinks that I'm to be

made to marry a man by flogging.' No such attempt was at any rate made that night, for the father and husband did not again see his wife or daughter.

Early the next day a report was current that Mr. Alf had been returned. The numbers had not as yet been counted, or the books made up;—but that was the opinion expressed. All the morning newspapers, including the 'Breakfast-Table,' repeated this report,—but each gave it as the general opinion on the matter. The truth would not be known till seven or eight o'clock in the evening. The Conservative papers did not scruple to say that the presumed election of Mr. Alf was owing to a sudden declension in the confidence originally felt in Mr. Melmotte. The 'Breakfast-Table,' which had supported Mr. Melmotte's candidature, gave no reason, and expressed more doubt on the result than the other papers. 'We know not how such an opinion forms itself,' the writer said;—'but it seems to have been formed. As nothing as yet is really known, or can be known, we express no opinion of our own upon the matter.'

Mr. Melmotte again went into the City, and found that things seemed to have returned very much into their usual grooves. The Mexican Railway shares were low, and Mr. Cohenlupe was depressed in spirits and unhappy;—but nothing dreadful had occurred or seemed to be threatened. If nothing dreadful did occur, the railway shares would probably recover, or nearly recover, their position. In the course of the day, Melmotte received a letter from Messrs. Slow and Bideawhile, which, of itself, certainly contained no comfort;—but there was comfort to be drawn even from that letter, by reason of what it did not contain. The letter was unfriendly in its tone and peremptory. It had come evidently from a hostile party. It had none of the feeling which had hitherto prevailed in the intercourse between these two well-known Conservative gentlemen, Mr. Adolphus Longestaffe and Mr. Augustus Melmotte. But there was no allusion in it to forgery; no question of criminal proceedings; no hint at aught beyond the not unnatural desire of Mr. Longestaffe and Mr. Longestaffe's son to be paid for the property at Pickering which Mr. Melmotte had purchased.

'We have to remind you,' said the letter, in continuation of paragraphs which had contained simply demands for the money, 'that the title-deeds were delivered to you on receipt by us of authority to that effect from the Messrs. Longestaffe, father and son, on the understanding that the purchase-money was to be paid to us by you. We are informed that the property has been since mortgaged by you. We do not state this as a fact. But the information, whether true or untrue, forces upon us the necessity of demanding that you should at once pay to us the purchase-money,—£80,000,—or else return to us the title-deeds of the estate.'

This letter, which was signed Slow and Bideawhile, declared positively that the title-deeds had been given up on authority received by them from both the Longestaffes,—father and son. Now the accusation brought against Melmotte, as far as he could as yet understand it, was that he had forged the signature to the young Mr. Longestaffe's letter. Messrs. Slow and Bideawhile were therefore on his side. As to the simple debt, he cared little comparatively about that. Many fine men were walking about London who owed large sums of money which they could not pay.

As he was sitting at his solitary dinner this evening,—for both his wife and daughter had declined to join him, saying that they had dined early,—news was brought to him that he had been elected for Westminster. He had beaten Mr. Alf by something not much less than a thousand votes.

It was very much to be member for Westminster. So much had at any rate been achieved by him who had begun the world without a shilling and without a friend,—almost without education! Much as he loved money, and much as he loved the spending of money, and much as he had made and much as he had spent, no triumph of his life had been so great to him as this.

Brought into the world in a gutter, without father or mother, with no good thing ever done for him, he was now a member of the British Parliament, and member for one of the first cities in the empire. Ignorant as he was he understood the magnitude of the achievement, and dismayed as he was as to his present position, still at this moment he enjoyed keenly a certain amount of elation. Of course he had committed forgery;—of course he had committed robbery. That, indeed, was nothing, for he had been cheating and forging and stealing all his life. Of course he was in danger of almost immediate detection and punishment. He hardly hoped that the evil day would be very much longer protracted, and yet he enjoyed his triumph. Whatever they might do, quick as they might be, they could hardly prevent his taking his seat in the House of Commons. Then if they sent him to penal servitude for life, they would have to say that they had so treated the member for Westminster!

He drank a bottle of claret, and then got some brandy-and-water. In such troubles as were coming upon him now, he would hardly get sufficient support from wine. He knew that he had better not drink;—that is, he had better not drink, supposing the world to be free to him for his own work and his own enjoyment. But if the world were no longer free to him, if he were really coming to penal servitude and annihilation,—then why should he not drink while the time lasted? An hour of triumphant joy might be an eternity to a man, if the man's imagination were strong enough to make him so regard his hour. He therefore took his brandy-and-water freely, and as he took it he was able to throw his fears behind him, and to assure himself that, after all, he might even yet escape from his bondages. No;—he would drink no more. This he said to himself as he filled another beaker. He would work instead. He would put his shoulder to the wheel, and would yet conquer his enemies. It would not be so easy to convict a member for Westminster,—especially if money were spent freely. Was he not the man who,

at his own cost, had entertained the Emperor of China?
Would not that be remembered in his favour? Would
not men be unwilling to punish the man who had
received at his own table all the Princes of the land, and
the Prime Minister, and all the Ministers? To convict
him would be a national disgrace. He fully realized all
this as he lifted the glass to his mouth, and puffed out
the smoke in large volumes through his lips. But money
must be spent! Yes;—money must be had! Cohenlupe
certainly had money. Though he squeezed it out of the
coward's veins he would have it. At any rate, he would
not despair. There was a fight to be fought yet, and he
would fight it to the end. Then he took a deep drink,
and slowly, with careful and almost solemn steps, he
made his way up to his bed.

## Chapter LXV

### MISS LONGESTAFFE WRITES HOME

LADY MONOGRAM, when she left Madame Melmotte's house after that entertainment of Imperial
Majesty which had been to her of so very little avail,
was not in a good humour. Sir Damask, who had
himself affected to laugh at the whole thing, but who
had been in truth as anxious as his wife to see the
Emperor in private society, put her ladyship and Miss
Longestaffe into the carriage without a word, and
rushed off to his club in disgust. The affair from
beginning to end, including the final failure, had been
his wife's doing. He had been made to work like a
slave, and had been taken against his will to Melmotte's house, and had seen no Emperor and shaken
hands with no Prince! 'They may fight it out between
them now like the Kilkenny cats.' That was his idea as
he closed the carriage-door on the two ladies,—thinking
that if a larger remnant were left of one cat than of the
other that larger remnant would belong to his wife.

'What a horrid affair!' said Lady Monogram. 'Did

anybody ever see anything so vulgar?' This was at any rate unreasonable, for whatever vulgarity there may have been, Lady Monogram had seen none of it.

'I don't know why you were so late,' said Georgiana.

'Late! Why it's not yet twelve. I don't suppose it was eleven when we got into the Square. Anywhere else it would have been early.'

'You knew they did not mean to stay long. It was particularly said so. I really think it was your own fault.'

'My own fault. Yes;—I don't doubt that. I know it was my own fault, my dear, to have had anything to do with it. And now I have got to pay for it.'

'What do you mean by paying for it, Julia?'

'You know what I mean very well. Is your friend going to do us the honour of coming to us to-morrow night?' She could not have declared in plainer language how very high she thought the price to be which she had consented to give for those ineffective tickets.

'If you mean Mr. Brehgert, he is coming. You desired me to ask him, and I did so.'

'Desired you! The truth is, Georgiana, when people get into different sets, they'd better stay where they are. It's no good trying to mix things.' Lady Monogram was so angry that she could not control her tongue.

Miss Longestaffe was ready to tear herself with indignation. That she should have been brought to hear insolence such as this from Julia Triplex,—she, the daughter of Adolphus Longestaffe of Caversham and Lady Pomona; she, who was considered to have lived in quite the first London circle! But she could hardly get hold of fit words for a reply. She was almost in tears, and was yet anxious to fight rather than weep. But she was in her friend's carriage, and was being taken to her friend's house, was to be entertained by her friend all the next day, and was to see her lover among her friend's guests. 'I wonder what has made you so ill-natured,' she said at last. 'You didn't use to be like that.'

'It's no good abusing me,' said Lady Monogram.

'Here we are, and I suppose we had better get out,—
unless you want the carriage to take you anywhere
else.' Then Lady Monogram got out and marched into
the house, and taking a candle went direct to her own
room. Miss Longestaffe followed slowly to her own
chamber, and having half undressed herself, dismissed
her maid and prepared to write to her mother.

The letter to her mother must be written. Mr.
Brehgert had twice proposed that he should, in the usual
way, go to Mr. Longestaffe, who had been backwards
and forwards in London, and was there at the present
moment. Of course it was proper that Mr. Brehgert
should see her father,—but, as she had told him, she
preferred that he should postpone his visit for a day or
two. She was now agonized by many doubts. Those
few words about 'various sets' and the 'mixing of things'
had stabbed her to the very heart,—as had been intended. Mr. Brehgert was rich. That was a certainty.
But she already repented of what she had done. If it
were necessary that she should really go down into
another and a much lower world, a world composed
altogether of Brehgerts, Melmottes, and Cohenlupes,
would it avail her much to be the mistress of a gorgeous
house? She had known, and understood, and had
revelled in the exclusiveness of county position. Caversham had been dull, and there had always been there a
dearth of young men of the proper sort; but it had been
a place to talk of, and to feel satisfied with as a home
to be acknowledged before the world. Her mother was
dull, and her father pompous and often cross; but they
were in the right set,—miles removed from the Brehgerts
and Melmottes,—until her father himself had suggested
to her that she should go to the house in Grosvenor
Square. She would write one letter to-night; but
there was a question in her mind whether the letter
should be written to her mother telling her the horrid
truth,—or to Mr. Brehgert begging that the match
should be broken off. I think she would have decided
on the latter had it not been that so many people had
already heard of the match. The Monograms knew it,

and had of course talked far and wide. The Melmottes knew it, and she was aware that Lord Nidderdale had heard it. It was already so far known that it was sure to be public before the end of the season. Each morning lately she had feared that a letter from home would call upon her to explain the meaning of some frightful rumours reaching Caversham, or that her father would come to her and with horror on his face demand to know whether it was indeed true that she had given her sanction to so abominable a report.

And there were other troubles. She had just spoken to Madame Melmotte this evening, having met her late hostess as she entered the drawing-room, and had felt from the manner of her reception that she was not wanted back again. She had told her father that she was going to transfer herself to the Monograms for a time, not mentioning the proposed duration of her visit, and Mr. Longestaffe, in his ambiguous way, had expressed himself glad that she was leaving the Melmottes. She did not think that she could go back to Grosvenor Square, although Mr. Brehgert desired it. Since the expression of Mr. Brehgert's wishes she had perceived that ill-will had grown up between her father and Mr. Melmotte. She must return to Caversham. They could not refuse to take her in, though she had betrothed herself to a Jew!

If she decided that the story should be told to her mother it would be easier to tell it by letter than by spoken words, face to face. But then if she wrote the letter there would be no retreat,—and how should she face her family after such a declaration? She had always given herself credit for courage, and now she wondered at her own cowardice. Even Lady Monogram, her old friend Julia Triplex, had trampled upon her. Was it not the business of her life, in these days, to do the best she could for herself, and would she allow paltry considerations as to the feelings of others to stand in her way and become bugbears to affright her? Who sent her to Melmotte's house? Was it not her own father? Then she sat herself square at the table, and wrote to

her mother,—as follows,—dating her letter for the
following morning:—

'Hill Street, 9th July, 187—.

'MY DEAR MAMMA,

'I am afraid you will be very much astonished by this
letter, and perhaps disappointed. I have engaged
myself to Mr. Brehgert, a member of a very wealthy
firm in the City, called Todd, Brehgert, and Goldsheiner.
I may as well tell you the worst at once. Mr. Brehgert
is a Jew.' This last word she wrote very rapidly, but
largely, determined that there should be no lack of
courage apparent in the letter. 'He is a very wealthy
man, and his business is about banking and what he calls
finance. I understand they are among the most leading
people in the City. He lives at present at a very handsome house at Fulham. I don't know that I ever saw a
place more beautifully fitted up. I have said nothing to
papa, nor has he; but he says he will be willing to satisfy
papa perfectly as to settlements. He has offered to have
a house in London if I like,—and also to keep the villa
at Fulham or else to have a place somewhere in the
country. Or I may have the villa at Fulham and a
house in the country. No man can be more generous
than he is. He has been married before, and has a
family, and now I think I have told you all.

'I suppose you and papa will be very much dissatisfied.
I hope papa won't refuse his consent. It can do no
good. I am not going to remain as I am now all my
life, and there is no use waiting any longer. It was
papa who made me go to the Melmottes, who are not
nearly so well placed as Mr. Brehgert. Everybody knows
that Madame Melmotte is a Jewess, and nobody knows
what Mr. Melmotte is. It is no good going on with the
old thing when everything seems to be upset and at
sixes and sevens. If papa has got to be so poor that he is
obliged to let the house in town, one must of course
expect to be different from what we were.

'I hope you won't mind having me back the day
after to-morrow,—that is to-morrow, Wednesday.

There is a party here to-night, and Mr. Brehgert is coming. But I can't stay longer with Julia, who doesn't make herself nice, and I do not at all want to go back to the Melmottes. I fancy that there is something wrong between papa and Mr. Melmotte.

'Send the carriage to meet me by the 2.30 train from London,—and pray, mamma, don't scold when you see me, or have hysterics, or anything of that sort. Of course it isn't all nice, but things have got so that they never will be nice again. I shall tell Mr. Brehgert to go to papa on Wednesday.

'Your affectionate daughter,

'G.'

When the morning came she desired the servant to take the letter away and have it posted, so that the temptation to stop it might no longer be in her way.

About one o'clock on that day Mr. Longestaffe called at Lady Monogram's. The two ladies had breakfasted upstairs, and had only just met in the drawing-room when he came in. Georgiana trembled at first, but soon perceived that her father had as yet heard nothing of Mr. Brehgert. She immediately told him that she proposed returning home on the following day. 'I am sick of the Melmottes,' she said.

'And so am I,' said Mr. Longestaffe, with a serious countenance.

'We should have been delighted to have had Georgiana to stay with us a little longer,' said Lady Monogram; 'but we have but the one spare bedroom, and another friend is coming.' Georgiana, who knew both these statements to be false, declared that she wouldn't think of such a thing. 'We have a few friends coming to-night, Mr. Longestaffe, and I hope you'll come in and see Georgiana.' Mr. Longestaffe hummed and hawed and muttered something, as old gentlemen always do when they are asked to go out to parties after dinner. 'Mr. Brehgert will be here,' continued Lady Monogram with a peculiar smile.

'Mr. who?' The name was not at first familiar to Mr. Longestaffe.

'Mr. Brehgert.' Lady Monogram looked at her friend. 'I hope I'm not revealing any secret.'

'I don't understand anything about it,' said Mr. Longestaffe. 'Georgiana, who is Mr. Brehgert?' He had understood very much. He had been quite certain from Lady Monogram's manner and words, and also from his daughter's face, that Mr. Brehgert was mentioned as an accepted lover. Lady Monogram had meant that it should be so, and any father would have understood her tone. As she said afterwards to Sir Damask, she was not going to have that Jew there at her house as Georgiana Longestaffe's accepted lover without Mr. Longestaffe's knowledge.

'My dear Georgiana,' she said, 'I supposed your father knew all about it.'

'I know nothing. Georgiana, I hate a mystery. I insist upon knowing. Who is Mr. Brehgert, Lady Monogram?'

'Mr. Brehgert is a—very wealthy gentleman. That is all I know of him. Perhaps, Georgiana, you will be glad to be alone with your father.' And Lady Monogram left the room.

Was there ever cruelty equal to this! But now the poor girl was forced to speak,—though she could not speak as boldly as she had written. 'Papa, I wrote to mamma this morning, and Mr. Brehgert was to come to you to-morrow.'

'Do you mean that you are engaged to marry him?'

'Yes, papa.'

'What Mr. Brehgert is he?'

'He is a merchant.'

'You can't mean the fat Jew whom I've met with Mr. Melmotte;—a man old enough to be your father!' The poor girl's condition now was certainly lamentable. The fat Jew, old enough to be her father, was the very man she did mean. She thought that she would try to brazen it out with her father. But at the present moment she had been so cowed by the manner in which the subject had been introduced that she did not know how to begin to be bold. She only looked at him as though imploring him to spare her. 'Is the man a Jew?' demanded Mr. Longestaffe, with as much thunder as he knew how to throw into his voice.

'Yes, papa,' she said.

'He is that fat man?'

'Yes, papa.'

'And nearly as old as I am?'

'No, papa,—not nearly as old as you are. He is fifty.'

'And a Jew?' He again asked the horrid question, and again threw in the thunder. On this occasion she condescended to make no further reply. 'If you do, you shall do it as an alien from my house. I certainly will never see him. Tell him not to come to me, for I certainly will not speak to him. You are degraded and disgraced; but you shall not degrade and disgrace me and your mother and sister.'

'It was you, papa, who told me to go to the Melmottes.'

'That is not true. I wanted you to stay at Caversham. A Jew! an old fat Jew! Heavens and earth! that it should be possible that you should think of it! You;— my daughter,—that used to take such pride in yourself! Have you written to your mother?'

'I have.'

'It will kill her. It will simply kill her. And you are going home to-morrow?'

'I wrote to say so.'

'And there you must remain. I suppose I had better see the man and explain to him that it is utterly impossible. Heavens on earth;—a Jew! An old fat Jew! My daughter! I will take you down home myself to-morrow. What have I done that I should be punished by my children in this way?' The poor man had had rather a stormy interview with Dolly that morning. 'You had better leave this house to-day, and come to my hotel in Jermyn Street.'

'Oh, papa, I can't do that.'

'Why can't you do it? You can do it, and you shall

do it. I will not have you see him again. I will see
him. If you do not promise me to come, I will send
for Lady Monogram and tell her that I will not permit
you to meet Mr. Brehgert at her house. I do wonder at
her. A Jew! An old fat Jew!' Mr. Longestaffe, putting
up both his hands, walked about the room in despair.

She did consent, knowing that her father and Lady
Monogram between them would be too strong for her.
She had her things packed up, and in the course of the
afternoon allowed herself to be carried away. She said
one word to Lady Monogram before she went. 'Tell
him that I was called away suddenly.'

'I will, my dear. I thought your papa would not like
it.' The poor girl had not spirit sufficient to upbraid her
friend; nor did it suit her now to acerbate an enemy.
For the moment, at least, she must yield to everybody
and everything. She spent a lonely evening with her
father in a dull sitting-room in the hotel, hardly speaking
or spoken to, and the following day she was taken down
to Caversham. She believed that her father had seen
Mr. Brehgert on the morning of that day;—but he
said no word to her, nor did she ask him any question.

That was on the day after Lady Monogram's party.
Early in the evening, just as the gentlemen were coming
up from the dining-room, Mr. Brehgert, apparelled with
much elegance, made his appearance. Lady Monogram
received him with a sweet smile. 'Miss Longestaffe,' she
said, 'has left me and gone to her father.'

'Oh, indeed.'

'Yes,' said Lady Monogram, bowing her head, and
then attending to other persons as they arrived. Nor
did she condescend to speak another word to Mr.
Brehgert, or to introduce him even to her husband. He
stood for about ten minutes inside the drawing-room,
leaning against the wall, and then he departed. No one
had spoken a word to him. But he was an even-tempered,
good-humoured man. When Miss Longestaffe was his
wife things would no doubt be different;—or else she
would probably change her acquaintance.

## Chapter LXVI

### 'SO SHALL BE MY ENMITY'

'YOU shall be troubled no more with Winifred Hurtle.' So Mrs. Hurtle had said, speaking in perfect good faith to the man whom she had come to England with the view of marrying. And then when he had said good-bye to her, putting out his hand to take hers for the last time, she declined that. 'Nay,' she had said; 'this parting will bear no farewell.'

Having left her after that fashion Paul Montague could not return home with very high spirits. Had she insisted on his taking that letter with the threat of the horsewhip as the letter which she intended to write to him,—that letter which she had shown him, owning it to be the ebullition of her uncontrolled passion, and had then destroyed,—he might at any rate have consoled himself with thinking that, however badly he might have behaved, her conduct had been worse than his. He could have made himself warm and comfortable with anger, and could have assured himself that under any circumstances he must be right to escape from the clutches of a wild cat such as that. But at the last moment she had shown that she was no wild cat to him. She had melted, and become soft and womanly. In her softness she had been exquisitely beautiful; and as he returned home he was sad and dissatisfied with himself. He had destroyed her life for her,—or, at least, had created a miserable episode in it which could hardly be obliterated. She had said that she was all alone, and had given up everything to follow him,—and he had believed her. Was he to do nothing for her now? She had allowed him to go, and after her fashion had pardoned him the wrong he had done her. But was that to be sufficient for him,—so that he might now feel inwardly satisfied at leaving her, and make no further inquiry as to her fate? Could he pass on and let her be as the wine that has been drunk,—as the hour that has been enjoyed,— as the day that is past?

But what could he do? He had made good his own escape. He had resolved that, let her be woman or wild cat, he would not marry her, and in that he knew he had been right. Her antecedents, as now declared by herself, unfitted her for such a marriage. Were he to return to her he would be again thrusting his hand into the fire. But his own selfish coldness was hateful to him when he thought that there was nothing to be done but to leave her desolate and lonely in Mrs. Pipkin's lodgings.

During the next three or four days, while the preparations for the dinner and the election were going on, he was busy in respect to the American railway. He again went down to Liverpool, and at Mr. Ramsbottom's advice prepared a letter to the board of directors, in which he resigned his seat, and gave his reasons for resigning it; adding that he should reserve to himself the liberty of publishing his letter, should at any time the circumstances of the railway company seem to him to make such a course desirable. He also wrote a letter to Mr. Fisker, begging that gentleman to come to England, and expressing his own wish to retire altogether from the firm of Fisker, Montague, and Montague upon receiving the balance of money due to him,—a payment which must, he said, be a matter of small moment to his two partners, if, as he had been informed, they had enriched themselves by the success of the railway company in San Francisco. When he wrote these letters at Liverpool the great rumour about Melmotte had not yet sprung up. He returned to London on the day of the festival, and first heard of the report at the Beargarden. There he found that the old set had for the moment broken itself up. Sir Felix Carbury had not been heard of for the last four or five days,—and then the whole story of Miss Melmotte's journey, of which he had read something in the newspapers, was told to him. 'We think that Carbury has drowned himself,' said Lord Grasslough, 'and I haven't heard of anybody being heartbroken about it.' Lord Nidderdale had hardly been seen at the club. 'He's taken up the running with the girl,' said Lord Grasslough. 'What he'll do now, nobody knows. If I was at it, I'd have the money down in hard cash before I went into the church. He was there at the party yesterday, talking to the girl all the night;—a sort of thing he never did before. Nidderdale is the best fellow going, but he was always an ass.' Nor had Miles Grendall been seen in the club for three days. 'We've got into a way of play the poor fellow doesn't like,' said Lord Grasslough; 'and then Melmotte won't let him out of his sight. He has taken to dine there every day.' This was said during the election,— on the very day on which Miles deserted his patron; and on that evening he did dine at the club. Paul Montague also dined there, and would fain have heard something from Grendall as to Melmotte's condition; but the secretary, if not faithful in all things, was faithful at any rate in his silence. Though Grasslough talked openly enough about Melmotte in the smoking-room Miles Grendall said never a word.

On the next day, early in the afternoon, almost without a fixed purpose, Montague strolled up to Welbeck Street, and found Hetta alone. 'Mamma has gone to her publisher's,' she said. 'She is writing so much now that she is always going there. Who has been elected, Mr. Montague?' Paul knew nothing about the election, and cared very little. At that time, however, the election had not been decided. 'I suppose it will make no difference to you whether your chairman be in Parliament or not?' Paul said that Melmotte was no longer a chairman of his. 'Are you out of it altogether, Mr. Montague?' Yes;—as far as it lay within his power to be out of it, he was out of it. He did not like Mr. Melmotte, nor believe in him. Then with considerable warmth he repudiated all connection with the Melmotte party, expressing deep regret that circumstances had driven him for a time into that alliance. 'Then you think that Mr. Melmotte is——?'

'Just a scoundrel;—that's all.'

'You heard about Felix?'

'Of course I heard that he was to marry the girl, and that he tried to run off with her. I don't know much about it. They say that Lord Nidderdale is to marry her now.'

'I think not, Mr. Montague.'

'I hope not, for his sake. At any rate, your brother is well out of it.'

'Do you know that she loves Felix? There is no pretence about that. I do think she is good. The other night at the party she spoke to me.'

'You went to the party, then?'

'Yes;—I could not refuse to go when mamma chose to take me. And when I was there she spoke to me about Felix. I don't think she will marry Lord Nidderdale. Poor girl;—I do pity her. Think what a downfall it will be if anything happens.'

But Paul Montague had certainly not come there with the intention of discussing Melmotte's affairs, nor could he afford to lose the opportunity which chance had given him. He was off with one love, and now he thought that he might be on with the other. 'Hetta,' he said, 'I am thinking more of myself than of her,—or even of Felix.'

'I suppose we all do think more of ourselves than of other people,' said Hetta, who knew from his voice at once what it was in his mind to do.

'Yes;—but I am not thinking of myself only. I am thinking of myself, and you. In all my thoughts of myself I am thinking of you too.'

'I do not know why you should do that.'

'Hetta, you must know that I love you.'

'Do you?' she said. Of course she knew it. And of course she thought that he was equally sure of her love. Had he chosen to read signs that ought to have been plain enough to him, could he have doubted her love after the few words that had been spoken on that night when Lady Carbury had come in with Roger and interrupted them? She could not remember exactly what had been said; but she did remember that he had spoken of leaving England for ever in a certain event, and that she had not rebuked him;—and she remembered also how she had confessed her own love to her mother. He, of course, had known nothing of that confession; but he must have known that he had her heart!

So at least she thought. She had been working some
morsel of lace, as ladies do when ladies wish to be not
quite doing nothing. She had endeavoured to ply her
needle, very idly, while he was speaking to her, but now
she allowed her hands to fall into her lap. She would
have continued to work at the lace had she been able,
but there are times when the eyes will not see clearly,
and when the hands will hardly act mechanically.

'Yes,—I do. Hetta, say a word to me. Can it be so?
Look at me for one moment so as to let me know.' Her
eyes had turned downwards after her work. 'If Roger
is dearer to you than I am, I will go at once.'

'Roger is very dear to me.'

'Do you love him as I would have you love me?'

She paused for a time, knowing that his eyes were fixed
upon her, and then she answered the question in a low
voice, but very clearly. 'No,' she said;—'not like that.'

'Can you love me like that?' He put out both his
arms as though to take her to his breast should the
answer be such as he longed to hear. She raised her
hand towards him, as if to keep him back, and left it
with him when he seized it. 'Is it mine?' he said.

'If you want it.'

Then he was at her feet in a moment, kissing her hands
and her dress, looking up into her face with his eyes
full of tears, ecstatic with joy as though he had really
never ventured to hope for such success. 'Want it!' he
said. 'Hetta, I have never wanted anything but that
with real desire. Oh, Hetta, my own. Since I first
saw you this has been my only dream of happiness.
And now it is my own.'

She was very quiet, but full of joy. Now that she had
told him the truth she did not coy her love. Having
once spoken the word she did not care how often she
repeated it. She did not think that she could ever have
loved anybody but him,—even if he had not been fond
of her. As to Roger,—dear Roger, dearest Roger,—
no; it was not the same thing. 'He is as good as gold,'
she said,—'ever so much better than you are, Paul,'
stroking his hair with her hand and looking into his eyes.

'Better than anybody I have ever known,' said Montague with all his energy.

'I think he is;—but, ah, that is not everything. I suppose we ought to love the best people best; but I don't, Paul.'

'I do,' said he.

'No,—you don't. You must love me best, but I won't be called good. I do not know why it has been so. Do you know, Paul, I have sometimes thought I would do as he would have me, out of sheer gratitude. I did not know how to refuse such a trifling thing to one who ought to have everything that he wants.'

'Where should I have been?'

'Oh, you! Somebody else would have made you happy. But do you know, Paul, I think he will never love any one else. I ought not to say so, because it seems to be making so much of myself. But I feel it. He is not so young a man, and yet I think that he never was in love before. He almost told me so once, and what he says is true. There is an unchanging way with him that is awful to think of. He said that he never could be happy unless I would do as he would have me,—and he made me almost believe even that. He speaks as though every word he says must come true in the end. Oh, Paul, I love you so dearly,—but I almost think that I ought to have obeyed him.' Paul Montague of course had very much to say in answer to this. Among the holy things which did exist to gild this every-day unholy world, love was the holiest. It should be soiled by no falsehood, should know nothing of compromises, should admit no excuses, should make itself subject to no external circumstances. If Fortune had been so kind to him as to give him her heart, poor as his claim might be, she could have no right to refuse him the assurance of her love. And though his rival were an angel, he could have no shadow of a claim upon her,— seeing that he had failed to win her heart. It was very well said,—at least so Hetta thought,—and she made no attempt at argument against him. But what was to be done in reference to poor Roger? She had spoken the

word now, and, whether for good or bad, she had given
herself to Paul Montague. Even though Roger should
have to walk disconsolate to the grave, it could not now
be helped. But would it not be right that it should be
told? 'Do you know I almost feel that he is like a father
to me,' said Hetta, leaning on her lover's shoulder.

Paul thought it over for a few minutes, and then said
that he would himself write to Roger. 'Hetta, do you
know, I doubt whether he will ever speak to me again.'

'I cannot believe that.'

'There is a sternness about him which it is very hard
to understand. He has taught himself to think that as I
met you in his house, and as he then wished you to be
his wife, I should not have ventured to love you. How
could I have known?'

'That would be unreasonable.'

'He is unreasonable—about that. It is not reason
with him. He always goes by his feelings. Had you
been engaged to him——'

'Oh, then, you never could have spoken to me like this.'

'But he will never look at it in that way;—and he will
tell me that I have been untrue to him and ungrateful.'

'If you think, Paul——'

'Nay; listen to me. If it be so I must bear it. It will
be a great sorrow, but it will be as nothing to that other
sorrow, had that come upon me. I will write to him,
and his answer will be all scorn and wrath. Then you
must write to him afterwards. I think he will forgive
you, but he will never forgive me.' Then they parted,
she having promised that she would tell her mother
directly Lady Carbury came home, and Paul undertaking to write to Roger that evening.

And he did, with infinite difficulty, and much
trembling of the spirit. Here is his letter:—

'MY DEAR ROGER,—
'I think it right to tell you at once what has occurred
to-day. I have proposed to Miss Carbury and she has
accepted me. You have long known what my feelings
were, and I have also known yours. I have known, too,

that Miss Carbury has more than once declined to take
your offer. Under these circumstances I cannot think
that I have been untrue to friendship in what I have
done, or that I have proved myself ungrateful for the
affectionate kindness which you have always shown me.
I am authorised by Hetta to say that, had I never
spoken to her, it must have been the same to you.'
This was hardly a fair representation of what had been
said, but the writer, looking back upon his interview
with the lady, thought that it had been implied.

'I should not say so much by way of excusing myself,
but that you once said, that should such a thing occur
there must be a division between us ever after. If I
thought that you would adhere to that threat, I should
be very unhappy and Hetta would be miserable.
Surely, if a man loves he is bound to tell his love, and
to take the chance. You would hardly have thought it
manly in me if I had abstained. Dear friend, take a
day or two before you answer this, and do not banish
us from your heart if you can help it.

'Your affectionate friend,

'PAUL MONTAGUE.'

Roger Carbury did not take a single day,—or a single
hour to answer the letter. He received it at breakfast,
and after rushing out on the terrace and walking there
for a few minutes, he hurried to his desk and wrote his
reply. As he did so, his whole face was red with wrath,
and his eyes were glowing with indignation.

'There is an old French saying that he who makes
excuses is his own accuser. You would not have written
as you have done, had you not felt yourself to be false
and ungrateful. You knew where my heart was, and
there you went and undermined my treasure, and stole
it away. You have destroyed my life, and I will never
forgive you.

'You tell me not to banish you both from my heart.
How dare you join yourself with her in speaking of my
feelings! She will never be banished from my heart.

She will be there morning, noon, and night, and as is and will be my love to her, so shall be my enmity to you.

'ROGER CARBURY.'

It was hardly a letter for a Christian to write; and, yet, in those parts Roger Carbury had the reputation of being a good Christian.

Henrietta told her mother that morning, immediately on her return. 'Mamma, Mr. Paul Montague has been here.'

'He always comes here when I am away,' said Lady Carbury.

'That has been an accident. He could not have known that you were going to Messrs. Leadham and Loiter's.'

'I'm not so sure of that, Hetta.'

'Then, mamma, you must have told him yourself, and I don't think you knew till just before you were going. But, mamma, what does it matter? He has been here, and I have told him——'

'You have not accepted him?'

'Yes, mamma.'

'Without even asking me?'

'Mamma, you knew. I will not marry him without asking you. How was I not to tell him when he asked me whether I—loved him?'

'Marry him! How is it possible you should marry him? Whatever he had got was in that affair of Melmotte's, and that has gone to the dogs. He is a ruined man, and for aught I know may be compromised in all Melmotte's wickedness.'

'Oh, mamma, do not say that!'

'But I do say it. It is hard upon me. I did think that you would try to comfort me after all this trouble with Felix. But you are as bad as he is;—or worse, for you have not been thrown into temptation like that poor boy! And you will break your cousin's heart. Poor Roger! I feel for him;—he that has been so true to us! But you think nothing of that.'

'I think very much of my cousin Roger.'

'And how do you show it;—or your love for me?

There would have been a home for us all. Now we must starve, I suppose. Hetta, you have been worse to me even than Felix.' Then Lady Carbury, in her passion, burst out of the room, and took herself to her own chamber.

## Chapter LXVII

### SIR FELIX PROTECTS HIS SISTER

UP to this period of his life Sir Felix Carbury had probably felt but little of the punishment due to his very numerous shortcomings. He had spent all his fortune; he had lost his commission in the army; he had incurred the contempt of everybody that had known him; he had forfeited the friendship of those who were his natural friends, and had attached to him none others in their place; he had pretty nearly ruined his mother and sister; but, to use his own language, he had always contrived 'to carry on the game.' He had eaten and drunk, had gambled, hunted, and diverted himself generally after the fashion considered to be appropriate to young men about town. He had kept up till now. But now there seemed to him to have come an end to all things. When he was lying in bed in his mother's house he counted up all his wealth. He had a few pounds in ready money, he still had a little roll of Mr. Miles Grendall's notes of hand, amounting perhaps to a couple of hundred pounds,—and Mr. Melmotte owed him £600. But where was he to turn, and what was he to do with himself? Gradually he learned the whole story of the journey to Liverpool,—how Marie had gone there and had been sent back by the police, how Marie's money had been repaid to Mr. Melmotte by Mr. Broune, and how his failure to make the journey to Liverpool had become known. He was ashamed to go to his club. He could not go to Melmotte's house. He was ashamed even to show himself in the streets by day.

He was becoming almost afraid even of his mother. Now that the brilliant marriage had broken down, and seemed to be altogether beyond hope, now that he had to depend on her household for all his comforts, he was no longer able to treat her with absolute scorn,—nor was she willing to yield as she had yielded.

One thing only was clear to him. He must realize his possessions. With this view he wrote both to Miles Grendall and to Melmotte. To the former he said he was going out of town,—probably for some time, and he must really ask for a cheque for the amount due. He went on to remark that he could hardly suppose that a nephew of the Duke of Albury was unable to pay debts of honour to the amount of £200;—but that if such was the case he would have no alternative but to apply to the Duke himself. The reader need hardly be told that to this letter Mr. Grendall vouchsafed no answer whatever. In his letter to Mr. Melmotte he confined himself to one matter of business in hand. He made no allusion whatever to Marie, or to the great man's anger, or to his seat at the board. He simply reminded Mr. Melmotte that there was a sum of £600 still due to him, and requested that a cheque might be sent to him for that amount. Melmotte's answer to this was not altogether unsatisfactory, though it was not exactly what Sir Felix had wished. A clerk from Mr. Melmotte's office called at the house in Welbeck Street, and handed to Felix railway scrip in the South Central Pacific and Mexican Railway to the amount of the sum claimed,—insisting on a full receipt for the money before he parted with the scrip. The clerk went on to explain, on behalf of his employer, that the money had been left in Mr. Melmotte's hands for the purpose of buying these shares. Sir Felix, who was glad to get anything, signed the receipt and took the scrip. This took place on the day after the balloting at Westminster, when the result was not yet known,—and when the shares in the railway were very low indeed. Sir Felix had asked as to the value of the shares at the time. The clerk professed himself unable to quote the price,—but there were the shares if Sir Felix liked to take them. Of course he took them;—and hurrying off into the City found that they might perhaps be worth about half the money due to him. The broker to whom he showed them could not quite answer for anything. Yes;—the scrip had been very high; but there was a panic. They might recover,— or, more probably, they might go to nothing. Sir Felix cursed the Great Financier aloud, and left the scrip for sale. That was the first time that he had been out of the house before dark since his little accident.

But he was chiefly tormented in these days by the want of amusement. He had so spent his life hitherto that he did not know how to get through a day in which no excitement was provided for him. He never read. Thinking was altogether beyond him. And he had never done a day's work in his life. He could lie in bed. He could eat and drink. He could smoke and sit idle. He could play cards; and could amuse himself with women, —the lower the culture of the women, the better the amusement. Beyond these things the world had nothing for him. Therefore he again took himself to the pursuit of Ruby Ruggles.

Poor Ruby had endured a very painful incarceration at her aunt's house. She had been wrathful and had stormed, swearing that she would be free to come and go as she pleased. Free to go, Mrs. Pipkin told her that she was;—but not free to return if she went out otherwise than as she, Mrs. Pipkin, chose. 'Am I to be a slave?' Ruby asked, and almost upset the perambulator which she had just dragged in at the hall door. Then Mrs. Hurtle had taken upon herself to talk to her, and poor Ruby had been quelled by the superior strength of the American lady. But she was very unhappy, finding that it did not suit her to be nursemaid to her aunt. After all John Crumb couldn't have cared for her a bit, or he would have come to look after her. While she was in this condition Sir Felix came to Mrs. Pipkin's house, and asked for her at the door. It happened that Mrs. Pipkin herself had opened the door,—and, in her fright and dismay at the presence of so pernicious a

young man in her own passage, had denied that Ruby
was in the house. But Ruby had heard her lover's voice,
and had rushed up and thrown herself into his arms.
Then there had been a great scene. Ruby had sworn
that she didn't care for her aunt, didn't care for her
grandfather, or for Mrs. Hurtle, or for John Crumb,—
or for any person or anything. She cared only for her
lover. Then Mrs. Hurtle had asked the young man his
intentions. Did he mean to marry Ruby? Sir Felix had
said that he 'supposed he might as well some day.'
'There,' said Ruby, 'there!'—shouting in triumph as
though an offer had been made to her with the com-
pletest ceremony of which such an event admits. Mrs.
Pipkin had been very weak. Instead of calling in the
assistance of her strong-minded lodger, she had allowed
the lovers to remain together for half an hour in the
dining-room. I do not know that Sir Felix in any way
repeated his promise during that time, but Ruby was
probably too blessed with the word that had been
spoken to ask for such renewal. 'There must be an end
of this,' said Mrs. Pipkin, coming in when the half-hour
was over. Then Sir Felix had gone, promising to come
again on the following evening. 'You must not come
here, Sir Felix,' said Mrs. Pipkin, 'unless you puts it in
writing.' To this, of course, Sir Felix made no answer.
As he went home he congratulated himself on the success
of his adventure. Perhaps the best thing he could do
when he had realized the money for the shares would be
to take Ruby for a tour abroad. The money would last
for three or four months,—and three or four months
ahead was almost an eternity.

That afternoon before dinner he found his sister alone
in the drawing-room. Lady Carbury had gone to her
own room after hearing the distressing story of Paul
Montague's love, and had not seen Hetta since. Hetta
was melancholy, thinking of her mother's hard words,—
thinking perhaps of Paul's poverty as declared by her
mother, and of the ages which might have to wear themselves out before she could become his wife; but still
tinting all her thoughts with a rosy hue because of the

love which had been declared to her. She could not
but be happy if he really loved her. And she,—as she
had told him that she loved him,—would be true to
him through everything! In her present mood she
could not speak of herself to her brother, but she took
the opportunity of making good the promise which
Marie Melmotte had extracted from her. She gave him
some short account of the party, and told him that she
had talked with Marie. 'I promised to give you a
message,' she said.

'It's all of no use now,' said Felix.

'But I must tell you what she said. I think, you know,
that she really loves you.'

'But what's the good of it? A man can't marry a girl
when all the policemen in the country are dodging her.'

'She wants you to let her know what,—what you
intend to do. If you mean to give her up, I think you
should tell her.'

'How can I tell her? I don't suppose they would let
her receive a letter.'

'Shall I write to her;—or shall I see her?'

'Just as you like. I don't care.'

'Felix, you are very heartless.'

'I don't suppose I'm much worse than other men;—
or for the matter of that, worse than a great many
women either. You all of you here put me up to marry
her.'

'I never put you up to it.'

'Mother did. And now because it did not go off all
serene, I am to hear nothing but reproaches. Of course I
never cared so very much about her.'

'Oh, Felix, that is so shocking!'

'Awfully shocking, I dare say. You think I am as
black as the very mischief, and that sugar wouldn't
melt in other men's mouths. Other men are just as bad
as I am,—and a good deal worse too. You believe that
there is nobody on earth like Paul Montague.' Hetta
blushed, but said nothing. She was not yet in a condition
to boast of her lover before her brother, but she did, in
very truth, believe that but few young men were as

true-hearted as Paul Montague. 'I suppose you'd be surprised to hear that Master Paul is engaged to marry an American widow living at Islington.'

'Mr. Montague—engaged—to marry—an American widow! I don't believe it.'

'You'd better believe it if it's any concern of yours, for it's true. And it's true too that he travelled about with her for ever so long in the United States, and that he had her down with him at the hotel at Lowestoffe about a fortnight ago. There's no mistake about it.'

'I don't believe it,' repeated Hetta, feeling that to say even as much as that was some relief to her. It could not be true. It was impossible that the man should have come to her with such a lie in his mouth as that. Though the words astounded her, though she felt faint, almost as though she would fall in a swoon, yet in her heart of hearts she did not believe it. Surely it was some horrid joke,—or perhaps some trick to divide her from the man she loved. 'Felix, how dare you say things so wicked as that to me?'

'What is there wicked in it? If you have been fool enough to become fond of the man, it is only right you should be told. He is engaged to marry Mrs. Hurtle, and she is lodging with one Mrs. Pipkin in Islington. I know the house, and could take you there to-morrow, and show you the woman. There,' said he, 'that's where she is;'—and he wrote Mrs. Hurtle's name down on a scrap of paper.

'It is not true,' said Hetta, rising from her seat, and standing upright. 'I am engaged to Mr. Montague, and I am sure he would not treat me in that way.'

'Then, by heaven, he shall answer it to me,' said Felix, jumping up. 'If he has done that, it is time that I should interfere. As true as I stand here, he is engaged to marry a woman called Mrs. Hurtle whom he constantly visits at that place in Islington.'

'I do not believe it,' said Hetta, repeating the only defence for her lover which was applicable at the moment.

'By George, this is beyond a joke. Will you believe it

if Roger Carbury says it's true? I know you'd believe anything fast enough against me, if he told you.'

'Roger Carbury will not say so?'

'Have you the courage to ask him? I say he will say so. He knows all about it,—and has seen the woman.'

'How can you know? Has Roger told you?'

'I do know, and that's enough. I will make this square with Master Paul. By heaven, yes! He shall answer to me. But my mother must manage you. She will not scruple to ask Roger, and she will believe what Roger tells her.'

'I do not believe a word of it,' said Hetta, leaving the room. But when she was alone she was very wretched. There must be some foundation for such a tale. Why should Felix have referred to Roger Carbury? And she did feel that there was something in her brother's manner which forbade her to reject the whole story as being altogether baseless. So she sat upon her bed and cried, and thought of all the tales she had heard of faithless lovers. And yet why should the man have come to her, not only with soft words of love, but asking her hand in marriage, if it really were true that he was in daily communication with another woman whom he had promised to make his wife?

Nothing on the subject was said at dinner. Hetta with difficulty to herself sat at the table, and did not speak. Lady Carbury and her son were nearly as silent. Soon after dinner Felix slunk away to some music hall or theatre in quest probably of some other Ruby Ruggles. Then Lady Carbury, who had now been told as much as her son knew, again attacked her daughter. Very much of the story Felix had learned from Ruby. Ruby had of course learned that Paul was engaged to Mrs. Hurtle. Mrs. Hurtle had at once declared the fact to Mrs. Pipkin, and Mrs. Pipkin had been proud of the position of her lodger. Ruby had herself seen Paul Montague at the house, and had known that he had taken Mrs. Hurtle to Lowestoffe. And it had also become known to the two women, the aunt and her niece, that Mrs. Hurtle had seen Roger Carbury on the

sands at Lowestoffe. Thus the whole story with most of
its details,—not quite with all,—had come round to Lady
Carbury's ears. 'What he has told you, my dear, is true.
Much as I disapprove of Mr. Montague, you do not
suppose that I would deceive you.'

'How can he know, mamma?'

'He does know. I cannot explain to you how. He has
been at the same house.'

'Has he seen her?'

'I do not know that he has, but Roger Carbury has
seen her. If I write to him you will believe what he says?'

'Don't do that, mamma. Don't write to him.'

'But I shall. Why should I not write if he can tell me?
If this other man is a villain am I not bound to protect
you? Of course Felix is not steady. If it came only from
him you might not credit it. And he has not seen her.
If your cousin Roger tells you that it is true,—tells me
that he knows the man is engaged to marry this woman,
then I suppose you will be contented.'

'Contented, mamma!'

'Satisfied that what we tell you is true.'

'I shall never be contented again. If that is true, I
will never believe anything. It can't be true. I suppose
there is something, but it can't be that.'

The story was not altogether displeasing to Lady
Carbury, though it pained her to see the agony which
her daughter suffered. But she had no wish that Paul
Montague should be her son-in-law, and she still thought
that if Roger would persevere he might succeed. On
that very night before she went to bed she wrote to
Roger, and told him the whole story. 'If,' she said, 'you
know that there is such a person as Mrs. Hurtle, and
if you know also that Mr. Montague has promised to
make her his wife, of course you will tell me.' Then she
declared her own wishes, thinking that by doing so she
could induce Roger Carbury to give such real assistance
in this matter that Paul Montague would certainly be
driven away. Who could feel so much interest in doing
this as Roger, or who be so closely acquainted with all
the circumstances of Montague's life? 'You know,' she

said, 'what my wishes are about Hetta, and how utterly opposed I am to Mr. Montague's interference. If it is true, as Felix says, that he is at the present moment entangled with another woman, he is guilty of gross insolence; and if you know all the circumstances you can surely protect us,—and also yourself.'

## Chapter LXVIII

### MISS MELMOTTE DECLARES HER PURPOSE

POOR Hetta passed a very bad night. The story she had heard seemed to be almost too awful to be true,—even about any one else. The man had come to her, and had asked her to be his wife,—and yet at that very moment was living in habits of daily intercourse with another woman whom he had promised to marry! And then, too, his courtship with her had been so graceful, so soft, so modest, and yet so long continued! Though he had been slow in speech, she had known since their first meeting how he regarded her! The whole state of his mind had, she had thought, been visible to her,—had been intelligible, gentle, and affectionate. He had been aware of her friends' feeling, and had therefore hesitated. He had kept himself from her because he had owed so much to friendship. And yet his love had not been the less true, and had not been less dear to poor Hetta. She had waited, sure that it would come,—having absolute confidence in his honour and love. And now she was told that this man had been playing a game so base, and at the same time so foolish, that she could find not only no excuse but no possible cause for it. It was not like any story she had heard before of man's faithlessness. Though she was wretched and sore at heart she swore to herself that she would not believe it. She knew that her mother would write to Roger Carbury,—but she knew also that nothing more would be said about the letter till the answer should

come. Nor could she turn anywhere else for comfort.
She did not dare to appeal to Paul himself. As regarded
him, for the present she could only rely on the assurance,
which she continued to give herself, that she would not
believe a word of the story that had been told her.

But there was other wretchedness besides her own.
She had undertaken to give Marie Melmotte's message
to her brother. She had done so, and she must now let
Marie have her brother's reply. That might be told in
a very few words—'Everything is over!' But it had to
be told.

'I want to call upon Miss Melmotte, if you'll let me,'
she said to her mother at breakfast.

'Why should you want to see Miss Melmotte? I
thought you hated the Melmottes?'

'I don't hate them, mamma. I certainly don't hate
her. I have a message to take to her,—from Felix.'

'A message—from Felix.'

'It is an answer from him. She wanted to know if all
that was over. Of course it is over. Whether he said
so or not, it would be so. They could never be married
now;—could they, mamma?'

The marriage, in Lady Carbury's mind, was no longer
even desirable. She, too, was beginning to disbelieve in
the Melmotte wealth, and did quite disbelieve that that
wealth would come to her son, even should he succeed
in marrying the daughter. It was impossible that Melmotte should forgive such offence as had now been
committed. 'It is out of the question,' she said. 'That,
like everything else with us, has been a wretched
failure. You can go, if you please. Felix is under no
obligation to them, and has taken nothing from them.
I should much doubt whether the girl will get anybody
to take her now. You can't go alone, you know,' Lady
Carbury added. But Hetta said that she did not at all
object to going alone as far as that. It was only just
over Oxford Street.

So she went out and made her way into Grosvenor
Square. She had heard, but at the time remembered
nothing, of the temporary migration of the Melmottes to

Bruton Street. Seeing, as she approached the house, that there was a confusion there of carts and workmen, she hesitated. But she went on, and rang the bell at the door, which was wide open. Within the hall the pilasters and trophies, the wreaths and the banners, which three or four days since had been built up with so much trouble, were now being pulled down and hauled away. And amidst the ruins Melmotte himself was standing. He was now a member of Parliament, and was to take his place that night in the House. Nothing, at any rate, should prevent that. It might be but for a short time;— but it should be written in the history of his life that he had sat in the British House of Commons as member for Westminster. At the present moment he was careful to show himself everywhere. It was now noon, and he had already been into the City. At this moment he was talking to the contractor for the work,—having just propitiated that man by a payment which would hardly have been made so soon but for the necessity which these wretched stories had entailed upon him of keeping up his credit for the possession of money. Hetta timidly asked one of the workmen whether Miss Melmotte was there. 'Do you want my daughter?' said Melmotte coming forward, and just touching his hat. 'She is not living here at present.'

'Oh,—I remember now,' said Hetta.

'May I be allowed to tell her who was asking after her?' At the present moment Melmotte was not unreasonably suspicious about his daughter.

'I am Miss Carbury,' said Hetta in a very low voice.

'Oh, indeed;—Miss Carbury!—the sister of Sir Felix Carbury?' There was something in the tone of the man's voice which grated painfully on Hetta's ears,—but she answered the question. 'Oh;—Sir Felix's sister! May I be permitted to ask whether—you have any business with my daughter?' The story was a hard one to tell, with all the workmen around her, in the midst of the lumber, with the coarse face of the suspicious man looking down upon her; but she did tell it very simply. She had come with a message from her brother. There

had been something between her brother and Miss
Melmotte, and her brother had felt that it would be
best that he should acknowledge that it must be all over.
'I wonder whether that is true,' said Melmotte, looking
at her out of his great coarse eyes, with his eyebrows
knit, with his hat on his head and his hands in his
pockets. Hetta, not knowing how, at the moment, to
repudiate the suspicion expressed, was silent. 'Because,
you know, there has been a deal of falsehood and double
dealing. Sir Felix has behaved infamously; yes,—by
G—, infamously. A day or two before my daughter
started, he gave me a written assurance that the whole
thing was over, and now he sends you here. How am I
to know what you are really after?'

'I have come because I thought I could do some
good,' she said, trembling with anger and fear. 'I was
speaking to your daughter at your party.'

'Oh, you were there;—were you? It may be as you
say, but how is one to tell? When one has been deceived
like that, one is apt to be suspicious, Miss Carbury.'
Here was one who had spent his life in lying to the
world, and who was in his very heart shocked at the
atrocity of a man who had lied to him! 'You are not
plotting another journey to Liverpool;—are you?' To
this Hetta could make no answer. The insult was too
much, but alone, unsupported, she did not know how
to give him back scorn for scorn. At last he proposed to
take her across to Bruton Street himself, and at his
bidding she walked by his side. 'May I hear what you
say to her?' he asked.

'If you suspect me, Mr. Melmotte, I had better not
see her at all. It is only that there may no longer be
any doubt.'

'You can say it all before me.'

'No;—I could not do that. But I have told you, and
you can say it for me. If you please, I think I will go
home now.'

But Melmotte knew that his daughter would not
believe him on such a subject. This girl she probably
would believe. And though Melmotte himself found it

difficult to trust anybody, he thought that there was more possible good than evil to be expected from the proposed interview. 'Oh, you shall see her,' he said. 'I don't suppose she's such a fool as to try that kind of thing again.' Then the door in Bruton Street was opened, and Hetta, repenting her mission, found herself almost pushed into the hall. She was bidden to follow Melmotte upstairs, and was left alone in the drawing-room, as she thought, for a long time. Then the door was slowly opened and Marie crept into the room. 'Miss Carbury,' she said, 'this is so good of you,—so good of you! I do so love you for coming to me! You said you would love me. You will; will you not?' and Marie, sitting down by the stranger, took her hand and encircled her waist.

'Mr. Melmotte has told you why I have come.'

'Yes;—that is, I don't know. I never believe what papa says to me.' To poor Hetta such an announcement as this was horrible. 'We are at daggers drawn. He thinks I ought to do just what he tells me, as though my very soul were not my own. I won't agree to that;— would you?' Hetta had not come there to preach disobedience, but could not fail to remember at the moment that she was not disposed to obey her mother in an affair of the same kind. 'What does he say, dear?'

Hetta's message was to be conveyed in three words, and when those were told, there was nothing more to be said. 'It must all be over, Miss Melmotte.'

'Is that his message, Miss Carbury?' Hetta nodded her head. 'Is that all?'

'What more can I say? The other night you told me to bid him send you word. And I thought he ought to do so. I gave him your message, and I have brought back the answer. My brother, you know, has no income of his own;—nothing at all.'

'But I have,' said Marie with eagerness.

'But your father——'

'It does not depend upon papa. If papa treats me badly, I can give it to my husband. I know I can. If I can venture, cannot he?'

'I think it is impossible.'

'Impossible! Nothing should be impossible. All the people that one hears of that are really true to their loves never find anything impossible. Does he love me, Miss Carbury? It all depends on that. That's what I want to know.' She paused, but Hetta could not answer the question. 'You must know about your brother. Don't you know whether he does love me? If you know I think you ought to tell me.' Hetta was still silent. 'Have you nothing to say?'

'Miss Melmotte——' began poor Hetta very slowly.

'Call me Marie. You said you would love me;—did you not? I don't even know what your name is.'

'My name is——Hetta.'

'Hetta;—that's short for something. But it's very pretty. I have no brother, no sister. And I'll tell you, though you must not tell anybody again;—I have no real mother. Madame Melmotte is not my mamma, though papa chooses that it should be thought so.' All this she whispered, with rapid words, almost into Hetta's ear. 'And papa is so cruel to me! He beats me sometimes.' The new friend, round whom Marie still had her arm, shuddered as she heard this. 'But I never will yield a bit for that. When he boxes and thumps me I always turn and gnash my teeth at him. Can you wonder that I want to have a friend? Can you be surprised that I should be always thinking of my lover? But,—if he doesn't love me, what am I to do then?'

'I don't know what I am to say,' ejaculated Hetta amidst her sobs. Whether the girl was good or bad, to be sought or to be avoided, there was so much tragedy in her position that Hetta's heart was melted with sympathy.

'I wonder whether you love anybody, and whether he loves you,' said Marie. Hetta certainly had not come there to talk of her own affairs, and made no reply to this. 'I suppose you won't tell me about yourself.'

'I wish I could tell you something for your own comfort.'

'He will not try again, you think?'

'I am sure he will not.'

'I wonder what he fears. I should fear nothing,—nothing. Why should not we walk out of the house, and be married any way? Nobody has a right to stop me. Papa could only turn me out of his house. I will venture if he will.'

It seemed to Hetta that even listening to such a proposition amounted to falsehood,—to that guilt of which Mr. Melmotte had dared to suppose that she could be capable. 'I cannot listen to it. Indeed I cannot listen to it. My brother is sure that he cannot—cannot—'

'Cannot love me, Hetta! Say it out, if it is true.'

'It is true,' said Hetta. There came over the face of the other girl a stern hard look, as though she had resolved at the moment to throw away from her all soft womanly things. And she relaxed her hold on Hetta's waist. 'Oh, my dear, I do not mean to be cruel, but you ask me for the truth.'

'Yes; I did.'

'Men are not, I think, like girls.'

'I suppose not,' said Marie slowly. 'What liars they are, what brutes;—what wretches! Why should he tell me lies like that? Why should he break my heart? That other man never said that he loved me. Did he never love me,—once?'

Hetta could hardly say that her brother was incapable of such love as Marie expected, but she knew that it was so. 'It is better that you should think of him no more.'

'Are you like that? If you had loved a man and told him of it, and agreed to be his wife and done as I have, could you bear to be told to think of him no more,—just as though you had got rid of a servant or a horse? I won't love him. No;—I'll hate him. But I must think of him. I'll marry that other man to spite him, and then, when he finds that we are rich, he'll be broken-hearted.'

'You should try to forgive him, Marie.'

'Never. Do not tell him that I forgive him. I command you not to tell him that. Tell him,—tell him,

that I hate him, and that if I ever meet him, I will
look at him so that he shall never forget it. I could,—
oh!—you do not know what I could do. Tell me;—
did he tell you to say that he did not love me?'

'I wish I had not come,' said Hetta.

'I am glad you have come. It was very kind. I don't
hate you. Of course I ought to know. But did he say
that I was to be told that he did not love me?'

'No;—he did not say that.'

'Then how do you know? What did he say?'

'That it was all over.'

'Because he is afraid of papa. Are you sure he does
not love me?'

'I am sure.'

'Then he is a brute. Tell him that I say that he is a
false-hearted liar, and that I trample him under my
foot.' Marie as she said this thrust her foot upon the
ground as though that false one were in truth beneath
it,—and spoke aloud, as though regardless who might
hear her. 'I despise him;—despise him. They are all
bad, but he is the worst of all. Papa beats me, but I can
bear that. Mamma reviles me and I can bear that. He
might have beaten me and reviled me, and I could have
borne it. But to think that he was a liar all the time;—
that I can't bear.' Then she burst into tears. Hetta
kissed her, tried to comfort her, and left her sobbing on
the sofa.

Later in the day, two or three hours after Miss
Carbury had gone, Marie Melmotte, who had not
shown herself at luncheon, walked into Madame Melmotte's room, and thus declared her purpose. 'You can
tell papa that I will marry Lord Nidderdale whenever
he pleases.' She spoke in French and very rapidly.

On hearing this Madame Melmotte expressed herself
to be delighted. 'Your papa,' said she, 'will be very
glad to hear that you have thought better of this at last.
Lord Nidderdale is, I am sure, a very good young man.'

'Yes,' continued Marie, boiling over with passion as
she spoke. 'I'll marry Lord Nidderdale, or that horrid
Mr. Grendall who is worse than all the others, or his old

fool of a father,—or the sweeper at the crossing,—or the black man that waits at table, or anybody else that he chooses to pick up. I don't care who it is the least in the world. But I'll lead him such a life afterwards! I'll make Lord Nidderdale repent the hour he saw me! You may tell papa.' And then, having thus entrusted her message to Madame Melmotte, Marie left the room.

## Chapter LXIX

### MELMOTTE IN PARLIAMENT

MELMOTTE did not return home in time to hear the good news that day,—good news as he would regard it, even though, when told to him, it should be accompanied by all the extraneous additions with which Marie had communicated her purpose to Madame Melmotte. It was nothing to him what the girl thought of the marriage,—if the marriage could now be brought about. He, too, had cause for vexation, if not for anger. If Marie had consented a fortnight since he might have so hurried affairs that Lord Nidderdale might by this time have been secured. Now there might be,—must be, doubt, through the folly of his girl and the villainy of Sir Felix Carbury. Were he once the father-in-law of the eldest son of a marquis, he thought he might almost be safe. Even though something might be all but proved against him,—which might come to certain proof in less august circumstances,—matters would hardly be pressed against a Member for Westminster whose daughter was married to the heir of the Marquis of Auld Reekie! So many persons would then be concerned! Of course his vexation with Marie had been great. Of course his wrath against Sir Felix was unbounded. The seat for Westminster was his. He was to be seen to occupy it before all the world on this very day. But he had not as yet heard that his daughter had yielded in reference to Lord Nidderdale.

There was considerable uneasiness felt in some circles

as to the manner in which Melmotte should take his seat. When he was put forward as the Conservative candidate for the borough a good deal of fuss had been made with him by certain leading politicians. It had been the manifest intention of the party that his return, if he were returned, should be hailed as a great Conservative triumph, and be made much of through the length and the breadth of the land. He was returned,—but the trumpets had not as yet been sounded loudly. On a sudden, within the space of forty-eight hours, the party had become ashamed of their man. And, now, who was to introduce him to the House? But with this feeling of shame on one side, there was already springing up an idea among another class that Melmotte might become as it were a Conservative tribune of the people,—that he might be the realization of that hitherto hazy mixture of Radicalism and old-fogyism, of which we have lately heard from a political master,* whose eloquence has been employed in teaching us that progress can only be expected from those whose declared purpose is to stand still. The new farthing newspaper, 'The Mob,' was already putting Melmotte forward as a political hero, preaching with reference to his commercial transactions the grand doctrine that magnitude in affairs is a valid defence for certain irregularities. A Napoleon, though he may exterminate tribes in carrying out his projects, cannot be judged by the same law as a young lieutenant who may be punished for cruelty to a few negroes. 'The Mob' thought that a good deal should be overlooked in a Melmotte, and that the philanthropy of his great designs should be allowed to cover a multitude of sins. I do not know that the theory was ever so plainly put forward as it was done by the ingenious and courageous writer in 'The Mob'; but in practice it has commanded the assent of many intelligent minds.

Mr. Melmotte, therefore, though he was not where he had been before that wretched Squercum had set afloat the rumours as to the purchase of Pickering, was able to hold his head much higher than on the unfortunate night of the great banquet. He had replied to the letter from Messrs. Slow and Bideawhile, by a note written in the ordinary way in the office, and only signed by himself. In this he merely said that he would lose no time in settling matters as to the purchase of Pickering. Slow and Bideawhile were of course anxious that things should be settled. They wanted no prosecution for forgery. To make themselves clear in the matter, and their client,—and if possible to take some wind out of the sails of the odious Squercum;—this would suit them best. They were prone to hope that for his own sake Melmotte would raise the money. If it were raised there would be no reason why that note purporting to have been signed by Dolly Longestaffe should ever leave their office. They still protested their belief that it did bear Dolly's signature. They had various excuses for themselves. It would have been useless for them to summon Dolly to their office, as they knew from long experience that Dolly would not come. The very letter written by themselves,—as a suggestion,—and given to Dolly's father, had come back to them with Dolly's ordinary signature, sent to them,—as they believed,—with other papers by Dolly's father. What justification could be clearer? But still the money had not been paid. That was the fault of Longestaffe senior. But if the money could be paid, that would set everything right. Squercum evidently thought that the money would not be paid, and was ceaseless in his intercourse with Bideawhile's people. He charged Slow and Bideawhile with having delivered up the title-deeds on the authority of a mere note, and that a note with a forged signature. He demanded that the note should be impounded. On the receipt by Mr. Bideawhile of Melmotte's rather curt reply Mr. Squercum was informed that Mr. Melmotte had promised to pay the money at once, but that a day or two must be allowed. Mr. Squercum replied that on his client's behalf he should open the matter before the Lord Mayor.

But in this way two or three days had passed without any renewal of the accusation before the public, and Melmotte had in a certain degree recovered his position.

The Beauclerks and the Luptons disliked and feared him as much as ever, but they did not quite dare to be so loud and confident in condemnation as they had been. It was pretty well known that Mr. Longestaffe had not received his money,—and that was a condition of things tending greatly to shake the credit of a man living after Melmotte's fashion. But there was no crime in that. No forgery was implied by the publication of any statement to that effect. The Longestaffes, father and son, might probably have been very foolish. Whoever expected anything but folly from either? And Slow and Bide-awhile might have been very remiss in their duty. It was astonishing, some people said, what things attorneys would do in these days! But they who had expected to see Melmotte behind the bars of a prison before this, and had regulated their conduct accordingly, now imagined that they had been deceived.

Had the Westminster triumph been altogether a triumph it would have become the pleasant duty of some popular Conservative to express to Melmotte the pleasure he would have in introducing his new political ally to the House. In such case Melmotte himself would have been walked up the chamber with a pleasurable ovation and the thing would have been done without trouble to him. But now this was not the position of affairs. Though the matter was debated at the Carlton, no such popular Conservative offered his services. 'I don't think we ought to throw him over,' Mr. Beauclerk said. Sir Orlando Drought, quite a leading Conservative, suggested that as Lord Nidderdale was very intimate with Mr. Melmotte he might do it. But Nidderdale was not the man for such a performance. He was a very good fellow and everybody liked him. He belonged to the House because his father had territorial influence in a Scotch county;—but he never did anything there, and his selection for such a duty would be a declaration to the world that nobody else would do it. 'It wouldn't hurt you, Lupton,' said Mr. Beauclerk. 'Not at all,' said Lupton; 'but I also, like Nidderdale, am a young man and of no use,—and a great deal too bashful.'

Melmotte, who knew but little about it, went down to the House at four o'clock, somewhat cowed by want of companionship, but carrying out his resolution that he would be stopped by no phantom fears,—that he would lose nothing by want of personal pluck. He knew that he was a Member, and concluded that if he presented himself he would be able to make his way in and assume his right. But here again fortune befriended him. The very leader of the party, the very founder of that new doctrine of which it was thought that Melmotte might become an apostle and an expounder,—who, as the reader may remember, had undertaken to be present at the banquet when his colleagues were dismayed and untrue to him, and who kept his promise and sat there almost in solitude,—he happened to be entering the House, as his late host was claiming from the door-keeper the fruition of his privilege. 'You had better let me accompany you,' said the Conservative leader, with some-thing of chivalry in his heart. And so Mr. Melmotte was introduced to the House by the head of his party! When this was seen many men supposed that the rumours had been proved to be altogether false. Was not this a guarantee sufficient to guarantee any man's respectability?

Lord Nidderdale saw his father in the lobby of the House of Lords that afternoon and told him what had occurred. The old man had been in a state of great doubt since the day of the dinner party. He was aware of the ruin that would be incurred by a marriage with Melmotte's daughter, if the things which had been said of Melmotte should be proved to be true. But he knew also that if his son should now recede, there must be an end of the match altogether;—and he did not believe the rumours. He was fully determined that the money should be paid down before the marriage was celebrated; but if his son were to secede now, of course no money would be forthcoming. He was prepared to recommend his son to go on with the affair still a little longer. 'Old Cure tells me he doesn't believe a word of it,' said the father. Cure was the family lawyer of the Marquises of Auld Reekie.

'There's some hitch about Dolly Longestaffe's money, sir,' said the son.

'What's that to us if he has our money ready? I suppose it isn't always easy even for a man like that to get a couple of hundred thousand together. I know I've never found it easy to get a thousand. If he has borrowed a trifle from Longestaffe to make up the girl's money, I shan't complain. You stand to your guns. There's no harm done till the parson has said the word.'

'You couldn't let me have a couple of hundred;— could you, sir?' suggested the son.

'No, I couldn't,' replied the father with a very determined aspect.

'I'm awfully hard up.'

'So am I.' Then the old man toddled into his own chamber, and after sitting there ten minutes went away home.

Lord Nidderdale also got quickly through his legislative duties and went to the Beargarden. There he found Grasslough and Miles Grendall dining together, and seated himself at the next table. They were full of news. 'You've heard it, I suppose,' said Miles in an awful whisper.

'Heard what?'

'I believe he doesn't know!' said Lord Grasslough. 'By Jove, Nidderdale, you're in a mess like some others.'

'What's up now?'

'Only fancy that they shouldn't have known down at the House! Vossner has bolted!'

'Bolted!' exclaimed Nidderdale, dropping the spoon with which he was just going to eat his soup.

'Bolted,' repeated Grasslough. Lord Nidderdale looked round the room and became aware of the awful expression of dismay which hung upon the features of all the dining members. 'Bolted, by George! He has sold all our acceptances to a fellow in Great Marlbro' that's called "Flatfleece".'

'I know him,' said Nidderdale shaking his head.

'I should think so,' said Miles ruefully.

'A bottle of champagne!' said Nidderdale, appealing to the waiter in almost a humble voice, feeling that he wanted sustenance in this new trouble that had befallen him. The waiter, beaten almost to the ground by an awful sense of the condition of the club, whispered to him the terrible announcement that there was not a bottle of champagne in the house. 'Good G——,' exclaimed the unfortunate nobleman. Miles Grendall shook his head. Grasslough shook his head.

'It's true,' said another young lord from the table on the other side. Then the waiter, still speaking with suppressed and melancholy voice, suggested that there was some port left. It was now the middle of July.

'Brandy?' suggested Nidderdale. There had been a few bottles of brandy, but they had been already consumed. 'Send out and get some brandy,' said Nidderdale with rapid impetuosity. But the club was so reduced in circumstances that he was obliged to take silver out of his pocket before he could get even such humble comfort as he now demanded.

Then Lord Grasslough told the whole story as far as it was known. Herr Vossner had not been seen since nine o'clock on the preceding evening. The head waiter had known for some weeks that heavy bills were due. It was supposed that three or four thousand pounds were owing to tradesmen, who now professed that the credit had been given, not to Herr Vossner but to the club. And the numerous acceptances for large sums which the accommodating purveyor held from many of the members had all been sold to Mr. Flatfleece. Mr. Flatfleece had spent a considerable portion of the day at the club, and it was now suggested that he and Herr Vossner were in partnership. At this moment Dolly Longestaffe came in. Dolly had been at the club before and had heard the story,—but had gone at once to another club for his dinner when he found that there was not even a bottle of wine to be had. 'Here's a go,' said Dolly. 'One thing atop of another! There'll be nothing left for anybody soon. Is that brandy you're drinking, Nidderdale? There was none here when I left.'

'Had to send round the corner for it, to the public.'

'We shall be sending round the corner for a good many things now. Does anybody know anything of that fellow Melmotte?'

'He's down in the House, as big as life,' said Nidderdale. 'He's all right I think.'

'I wish he'd pay me my money then. That fellow Flatfleece was here, and he showed me notes of mine for about £1,500! I write such a beastly hand that I never know whether I've written it or not. But, by George, a fellow can't eat and drink £1,500 in less than six months!'

'There's no knowing what you can do, Dolly,' said Lord Grasslough.

'He's paid some of your card money, perhaps,' said Nidderdale.

'I don't think he ever did. Carbury had a lot of my I O U's while that was going on, but I got the money for that from old Melmotte. How is a fellow to know? If any fellow writes D. Longestaffe, am I obliged to pay it? Everybody is writing my name! How is any fellow to stand that kind of thing? Do you think Melmotte's all right?' Nidderdale said that he did think so. 'I wish he wouldn't go and write my name then. That's a sort of thing that a man should be left to do for himself. I suppose Vossner is a swindler; but, by Jove, I know a worse than Vossner.' With that he turned on his heels and went into the smoking-room. And, after he was gone, there was silence at the table, for it was known that Lord Nidderdale was to marry Melmotte's daughter.

In the meantime a scene of a different kind was going on in the House of Commons. Melmotte had been seated on one of the back Conservative benches, and there he remained for a considerable time unnoticed and forgotten. The little emotion that had attended his entrance had passed away, and Melmotte was now no more than any one else. At first he had taken his hat off, but, as soon as he observed that the majority of members were covered, he put it on again. Then he sat motionless for an hour, looking round him and wondering. He had never hitherto been even in the gallery of the House. The place was very much smaller than he had thought, and much less tremendous. The Speaker did not strike him with the awe which he had expected, and it seemed to him that they who spoke were talking much like other people in other places. For the first hour he hardly caught the meaning of a sentence that was said, nor did he try to do so. One man got up very quickly after another, some of them barely rising on their legs to say the few words that they uttered. It seemed to him to be a very commonplace affair,—not half so awful as those festive occasions on which he had occasionally been called upon to propose a toast or to return thanks. Then suddenly the manner of the thing was changed, and one gentleman made a long speech. Melmotte by this time, weary of observing, had begun to listen, and words which were familiar to him reached his ears. The gentleman was proposing some little addition to a commercial treaty and was expounding in very strong language the ruinous injustice to which England was exposed by being tempted to use gloves made in a country in which no income tax was levied. Melmotte listened to his eloquence caring nothing about gloves, and very little about England's ruin. But in the course of the debate which followed, a question arose about the value of money, of exchange, and of the conversion of shillings into francs and dollars. About this Melmotte really did know something and he pricked up his ears. It seemed to him that a gentleman whom he knew very well in the city,—and who had maliciously stayed away from his dinner,—one Mr. Brown, who sat just before him on the same side of the House, and who was plodding wearily and slowly along with some pet fiscal theory of his own, understood nothing at all of what he was saying. Here was an opportunity for himself! Here was at his hand the means of revenging himself for the injury done him, and of showing to the world at the same time that he was not afraid of his city enemies! It required some courage

certainly,—this attempt that suggested itself to him of
getting upon his legs a couple of hours after his first
introduction to parliamentary life. But he was full of
the lesson which he was now ever teaching himself.
Nothing should cow him. Whatever was to be done by
brazen-faced audacity he would do. It seemed to be
very easy, and he saw no reason why he should not
put that old fool right. He knew nothing of the forms
of the House;—was more ignorant of them than an
ordinary schoolboy;—but on that very account felt less
trepidation than might another parliamentary novice.
Mr. Brown was tedious and prolix; and Melmotte,
though he thought much of his project and had almost
told himself that he would do the thing, was still doubting, when, suddenly, Mr. Brown sat down. There did
not seem to be any particular end to the speech, nor had
Melmotte followed any general thread of argument.
But a statement had been made and repeated, containing, as Melmotte thought, a fundamental error in
finance; and he longed to set the matter right. At any
rate he desired to show the House that Mr. Brown did
not know what he was talking about,—because Mr.
Brown had not come to his dinner. When Mr. Brown
was seated, nobody at once rose. The subject was not
popular, and they who understood the business of the
House were well aware that the occasion had simply
been one on which two or three commercial gentlemen,
having crazes of their own, should be allowed to ventilate
them. The subject would have dropped;—but on a
sudden the new member was on his legs.

Now it was probably not in the remembrance of any
gentleman there that a member had got up to make a
speech within two or three hours of his first entry into
the House. And this gentleman was one whose recent
election had been of a very peculiar kind. It had been
considered by many of his supporters that his name
should be withdrawn just before the ballot; by others
that he would be deterred by shame from showing himself even if he were elected; and again by another party
that his appearance in Parliament would be prevented

by his disappearance within the walls of Newgate. But here he was, not only in his seat, but on his legs! The favourable grace, the air of courteous attention, which is always shown to a new member when he first speaks, was extended also to Melmotte. There was an excitement in the thing which made gentlemen willing to listen, and a consequent hum, almost of approbation.

As soon as Melmotte was on his legs, and, looking round, found that everybody was silent with the intent of listening to him, a good deal of his courage oozed out of his fingers' ends. The House, which, to his thinking, had by no means been august while Mr. Brown had been toddling through his speech, now became awful. He caught the eyes of great men fixed upon him,—of men who had not seemed to him to be at all great as he had watched them a few minutes before, yawning beneath their hats. Mr. Brown, poor as his speech had been, had, no doubt, prepared it,—and had perhaps made three or four such speeches every year for the last fifteen years. Melmotte had not dreamed of putting two words together. He had thought, as far as he had thought at all, that he could rattle off what he had to say just as he might do it when seated in his chair at the Mexican Railway Board. But there was the Speaker, and those three clerks in their wigs, and the mace,—and worse than all, the eyes of that long row of statesmen opposite to him! His position was felt by him to be dreadful. He had forgotten even the very point on which he had intended to crush Mr. Brown.

But the courage of the man was too high to allow him to be altogether quelled at once. The hum was prolonged; and though he was red in the face, perspiring, and utterly confused, he was determined to make a dash at the matter with the first words which would occur to him. 'Mr. Brown is all wrong,' he said. He had not even taken off his hat as he rose. Mr. Brown turned slowly round and looked up at him. Some one, whom he could not exactly hear, touching him behind, suggested that he should take off his hat. There was a cry of order, which of course he did not understand. 'Yes, you are,' said Melmotte, nodding his head, and frowning angrily at poor Mr. Brown.

'The honourable member,' said the Speaker, with the most good-natured voice which he could assume, 'is not perhaps as yet aware that he should not call another member by his name. He should speak of the gentleman to whom he alluded as the honourable member for Whitechapel. And in speaking he should address, not another honourable member, but the chair.'

'You should take your hat off,' said the good-natured gentleman behind.

In such a position how should any man understand so many and such complicated instructions at once, and at the same time remember the gist of the argument to be produced? He did take off his hat, and was of course made hotter and more confused by doing so. 'What he said was all wrong,' continued Melmotte; 'and I should have thought a man out of the City, like Mr. Brown, ought to have known better.' Then there were repeated calls of order, and a violent ebullition of laughter from both sides of the House. The man stood for a while glaring around him, summoning his own pluck for a renewal of his attack on Mr. Brown, determined that he would be appalled and put down neither by the ridicule of those around him, nor by his want of familiarity with the place; but still utterly unable to find words with which to carry on the combat. 'I ought to know something about it,' said Melmotte sitting down and hiding his indignation and his shame under his hat.

'We are sure that the honourable member for Westminster does understand the subject,' said the leader of the House, 'and we shall be very glad to hear his remarks. The House I am sure will pardon ignorance of its rules in so young a member.'

But Mr. Melmotte would not rise again. He had made a great effort, and had at any rate exhibited his courage. Though they might all say that he had not displayed much eloquence, they would be driven to admit that he had not been ashamed to show himself. He kept his seat till the regular stampede was made for dinner, and then walked out with as stately a demeanour as he could assume.

'Well, that was plucky!' said Cohenlupe, taking his friend's arm in the lobby.

'I don't see any pluck in it. That old fool Brown didn't know what he was talking about, and I wanted to tell them so. They wouldn't let me do it, and there's an end of it. It seems to me to be a stupid sort of a place.'

'Has Longestaffe's money been paid?' said Cohenlupe opening his black eyes while he looked up into his friend's face.

'Don't you trouble your head about Longestaffe, or his money either,' said Melmotte, getting into his brougham; 'do you leave Mr. Longestaffe and his money to me. I hope you are not such a fool as to be scared by what the other fools say. When men play such a game as you and I are concerned in, they ought to know better than to be afraid of every word that is spoken.'

'Oh, dear; yes,' said Cohenlupe apologetically. 'You don't suppose that I am afraid of anything.' But at that moment Mr. Cohenlupe was meditating his own escape from the dangerous shores of England, and was trying to remember what happy country still was left in which an order from the British police would have no power to interfere with the comfort of a retired gentleman such as himself.

That evening Madame Melmotte told her husband that Marie was now willing to marry Lord Nidderdale; —but she did not say anything as to the crossing-sweeper or the black footman, nor did she allude to Marie's threat of the sort of life she would lead her husband.

## Chapter LXX

### SIR FELIX MEDDLES WITH MANY MATTERS

THERE is no duty more certain or fixed in the world than that which calls upon a brother to defend his sister from ill-usage; but, at the same time, in the way we live now, no duty is more difficult, and we may say generally more indistinct. The ill-usage to which men's sisters are most generally exposed is one which hardly admits of either protection or vengeance,—although the duty of protecting and avenging is felt and acknowledged. We are not allowed to fight duels, and that banging about of another man with a stick is always disagreeable and seldom successful. A John Crumb can do it, perhaps, and come out of the affair exulting; but not a Sir Felix Carbury, even if the Sir Felix of the occasion have the requisite courage. There is a feeling, too, when a girl has been jilted,—thrown over, perhaps, is the proper term,—after the gentleman has had the fun of making love to her for an entire season, and has perhaps even been allowed privileges as her promised husband, that the less said the better. The girl does not mean to break her heart for love of the false one, and become the tragic heroine of a tale for three months. It is her purpose again to

—trick her beams, and with new-spangled ore
Flame in the forehead of the morning sky.*

Though this one has been false, as were perhaps two or three before, still the road to success is open. *Uno avulso non deficit alter.** But if all the notoriety of cudgels and cutting whips be given to the late unfortunate affair, the difficulty of finding a substitute will be greatly increased. The brother recognizes his duty, and prepares for vengeance. The injured one probably desires that she may be left to fight her own little battles alone.

'Then, by heaven, he shall answer it to me,' Sir Felix had said very grandly, when his sister had told him that she was engaged to a man who was, as he thought he knew, engaged also to marry another woman. Here, no doubt, was gross ill-usage, and opportunity at any rate for threats. No money was required and no immediate action,—and Sir Felix could act the fine gentleman and the dictatorial brother at very little present expense. But Hetta, who ought perhaps to have known her brother more thoroughly, was fool enough to believe him. On the day but one following, no answer had as yet come from Roger Carbury,—nor could as yet have come. But Hetta's mind was full of her trouble, and she remembered her brother's threat. Felix had forgotten that he had made a threat,—and, indeed, had thought no more of the matter since his interview with his sister.

'Felix,' she said, 'you won't mention that to Mr. Montague!'

'Mention what? Oh! about that woman, Mrs. Hurtle? Indeed I shall. A man who does that kind of thing ought to be crushed;—and, by heavens, if he does it to you, he shall be crushed.'

'I want to tell you, Felix. If it is so, I will see him no more.'

'If it is so! I tell you I know it.'

'Mamma has written to Roger. At least I feel sure she has.'

'What has she written to him for? What has Roger Carbury to do with our affairs?'

'Only you said he knew! If he says so, that is, if you and he both say that he is to marry that woman,—I will not see Mr. Montague again. Pray do not go to him. If such a misfortune does come, it is better to bear it and to be silent. What good can be done?'

'Leave that to me,' said Sir Felix, walking out of the room with much fraternal bluster. Then he went forth, and at once had himself driven to Paul Montague's lodgings. Had Hetta not been foolish enough to remind him of his duty, he would not now have undertaken the task. He too, no doubt, remembered as he went that duels were things of the past, and that even fists and sticks are considered to be out of fashion. 'Montague,' he said, assuming all the dignity of demeanour that his late sorrows had left to him, 'I believe I am right in saying that you are engaged to marry that American lady, Mrs. Hurtle.'

'Then let me tell you that you were never more wrong in your life. What business have you with Mrs. Hurtle?'

'When a man proposes to my sister, I think I've a great deal of business,' said Sir Felix.

'Well;—yes; I admit that fully. If I answered you roughly, I beg your pardon. Now as to the facts. I am not going to marry Mrs. Hurtle. I suppose I know how you have heard her name;—but as you have heard it, I have no hesitation in telling you so much. As you know where she is to be found you can go and ask her if you please. On the other hand, it is the dearest wish of my heart to marry your sister. I trust that will be enough for you.'

'You were engaged to Mrs. Hurtle?'

'My dear Carbury, I don't think I'm bound to tell you all the details of my past life. At any rate, I don't feel inclined to do so in answer to hostile questions. I dare say you have heard enough of Mrs. Hurtle to justify you, as your sister's brother, in asking me whether I am in any way entangled by a connection with her. I tell you that I am not. If you still doubt, I refer you to the lady herself. Beyond that, I do not think I am called on to go; and beyond that I won't go,—at any rate, at present.' Sir Felix still blustered, and made what capital he could out of his position as a brother; but he took no steps towards positive revenge. 'Of course, Carbury,' said the other, 'I wish to regard you as a brother; and if I am rough to you, it is only because you are rough to me.'

Sir Felix was now in that part of town which he had been accustomed to haunt,—for the first time since his misadventure,—and, plucking up his courage, resolved that he would turn into the Beargarden. He would have a glass of sherry, and face the one or two men who would as yet be there, and in this way gradually creep back to his old habits. But when he arrived there, the club was shut up. 'What the deuce is Vossner about?' said he, pulling out his watch. It was nearly five o'clock. He rang the bell, and knocked at the door, feeling that this was an occasion for courage. One of the servants, in what we may call private clothes, after some delay, drew back the bolts, and told him the astounding news;—The club was shut up! 'Do you mean to say I can't come in?' said Sir Felix. The man certainly did mean to tell him so, for he opened the door no more than a foot, and stood in that narrow aperture. Mr. Vossner had gone away. There had been a meeting of the Committee, and the club was shut up. Whatever further information rested in the waiter's bosom he declined to communicate to Sir Felix Carbury.

'By George!' The wrong that was done him filled the young baronet's bosom with indignation. He had intended, he assured himself, to dine at his club, to spend the evening there sportively, to be pleasant among his chosen companions. And now the club was shut up, and Vossner had gone away! What business had the club to be shut up? What right had Vossner to go away? Had he not paid his subscription in advance? Throughout the world, the more wrong a man does, the more indignant is he at wrong done to him. Sir Felix almost thought that he could recover damages from the whole Committee.

He went direct to Mrs. Pipkin's house. When he made that half promise of marriage in Mrs. Pipkin's hearing, he had said that he would come again on the morrow. This he had not done; but of that he thought nothing. Such breaches of faith, when committed by a young man in his position, require not even an apology. He was admitted by Ruby herself, who was of course delighted to see him. 'Who do you think is in town?' she said. 'John Crumb; but though he came here ever so smart, I wouldn't so much as speak to him, except to tell him to go away.' Sir Felix, when he heard the name, felt an uncomfortable sensation creep over him. 'I don't know I'm sure what he should come after me for, and me telling him as plain as the nose on his face that I never want to see him again.'

'He's not of much account,' said the baronet.

'He would marry me out and out immediately, if I'd have him,' continued Ruby, who perhaps thought that her honest old lover should not be spoken of as being altogether of no account. 'And he has everything comfortable in the way of furniture, and all that. And they do say he's ever so much money in the bank. But I detest him,' said Ruby, shaking her pretty head, and inclining herself towards her aristocratic lover's shoulder.

This took place in the back parlour, before Mrs. Pipkin had ascended from the kitchen prepared to disturb so much romantic bliss with wretched references to the cold outer world. 'Well, now, Sir Felix,' she began, 'if things is square, of course you're welcome to see my niece.'

'And what if they're round, Mrs. Pipkin?' said the gallant, careless, sparkling Lothario.

'Well, or round either, so long as they're honest.'

'Ruby and I are both honest;—ain't we, Ruby? I want to take her out to dinner, Mrs. Pipkin. She shall be back before late;—before ten; she shall indeed.' Ruby inclined herself still more closely towards his shoulder. 'Come, Ruby, get your hat and change your dress, and we'll be off. I've ever so many things to tell you.'

Ever so many things to tell her! They must be to fix a day for the marriage, and to let her know where they were to live, and to settle what dress she should wear,—and perhaps to give her the money to go and buy it! Ever so many things to tell her! She looked up into Mrs. Pipkin's face with imploring eyes. Surely on such an occasion as this an aunt would not expect that her niece should be a prisoner and a slave. 'Have it been put in writing, Sir Felix Carbury?' demanded Mrs. Pipkin with cruel gravity. Mrs. Hurtle had given it as her decided opinion that Sir Felix would not really mean to marry Ruby Ruggles unless he showed himself willing to do so with all the formality of a written contract.

'Writing be bothered,' said Sir Felix.

'That's all very well, Sir Felix. Writing do bother,

very often. But when a gentleman has intentions, a bit of writing shows it plainer nor words. Ruby don't go nowhere to dine unless you puts it into writing.'

'Aunt Pipkin!' exclaimed the wretched Ruby.

'What do you think I'm going to do with her?' asked Sir Felix.

'If you want to make her your wife, put it in writing. And if it be as you don't, just say so, and walk away,—free.'

'I shall go,' said Ruby. 'I'm not going to be kept here a prisoner for any one. I can go when I please. You wait, Felix, and I'll be down in a minute.' The girl, with a nimble spring, ran upstairs, and began to change her dress without giving herself a moment for thought.

'She don't come back no more here, Sir Felix,' said Mrs. Pipkin, in her most solemn tones. 'She ain't nothing to me, no more than she was my poor dear husband's sister's child. There ain't no blood between us, and won't be no disgrace. But I'd be loth to see her on the streets.'

'Then why won't you let me bring her back again?'

''Cause that'd be the way to send her there. You don't mean to marry her.' To this Sir Felix said nothing. 'You're not thinking of that. It's just a bit of sport,— and then there she is, an old shoe to be chucked away, just a rag to be swept into the dust-bin. I've seen scores of 'em, and I'd sooner a child of mine should die in a workus', or be starved to death. But it's all nothing to the likes o' you.'

'I haven't done her any harm,' said Sir Felix, almost frightened.

'Then go away, and don't do her any. That's Mrs. Hurtle's door open. You go and speak to her. She can talk a deal better nor me.'

'Mrs. Hurtle hasn't been able to manage her own affairs very well.'

'Mrs. Hurtle's a lady, Sir Felix, and a widow, and one as has seen the world.' As she spoke, Mrs. Hurtle came downstairs, and an introduction, after some rude fashion, was effected between her and Sir Felix. Mrs. Hurtle had heard often of Sir Felix Carbury, and was quite as certain as Mrs. Pipkin that he did not mean to marry Ruby

Ruggles. In a few minutes Felix found himself alone with Mrs. Hurtle in her own room. He had been anxious to see the woman since he had heard of her engagement with Paul Montague, and doubly anxious since he had also heard of Paul's engagement with his sister. It was not an hour since Paul himself had referred him to her for corroboration of his own statement.

'Sir Felix Carbury,' she said, 'I am afraid you are doing that poor girl no good, and are intending to do her none.' It did occur to him very strongly that this could be no affair of Mrs. Hurtle's, and that he, as a man of position in society, was being interfered with in an unjustifiable manner. Aunt Pipkin wasn't even an aunt; but who was Mrs. Hurtle? 'Would it not be better that you should leave her to become the wife of a man who is really fond of her?'

He could already see something in Mrs. Hurtle's eye which prevented his at once bursting into wrath;—but who was Mrs. Hurtle, that she should interfere with him? 'Upon my word, ma'am,' he said, 'I'm very much obliged to you, but I don't quite know to what I owe the honour of your—your——

'Interference you mean.'

'I didn't say so, but perhaps that's about it.'

'I'd interfere to save any woman that God ever made,' said Mrs. Hurtle with energy. 'We're all apt to wait a little too long, because we're ashamed to do any little good that chance puts in our way. You must go and leave her, Sir Felix.'

'I suppose she may do as she pleases about that.'

'Do you mean to make her your wife?' asked Mrs. Hurtle sternly.

'Does Mr. Paul Montague mean to make you his wife?' rejoined Sir Felix with an impudent swagger. He had struck the blow certainly hard enough, and it had gone all the way home. She had not surmised that he would have heard aught of her own concerns. She only barely connected him with that Roger Carbury who, she knew, was Paul's great friend, and she had as yet never heard that Hetta Carbury was the girl whom Paul loved. Had

Paul so talked about her that this young scamp should know all her story?

She thought awhile,—she had to think for a moment, —before she could answer him. 'I do not see,' she said, with a faint attempt at a smile, 'that there is any parallel between the two cases. I, at any rate, am old enough to take care of myself. Should he not marry me, I am as I was before. Will it be so with that poor girl if she allows herself to be taken about the town by you at night?' She had desired in what she said to protect Ruby rather than herself. What could it matter whether this young man was left in a belief that she was, or that she was not, about to be married?

'If you'll answer me, I'll answer you,' said Sir Felix. 'Does Mr. Montague mean to make you his wife?'

'It does not concern you to know,' said she, flashing upon him. 'The question is insolent.'

'It does concern me,—a great deal more than anything about Ruby can concern you. And as you won't answer me, I won't answer you.'

'Then, sir, that girl's fate will be upon your head.'

'I know all about that,' said the baronet.

'And the young man who has followed her up to town will probably know where to find you,' added Mrs. Hurtle.

To such a threat as this, no answer could be made, and Sir Felix left the room. At any rate, John Crumb was not there at present. And were there not policemen in London? And what additional harm would be done to John Crumb, or what increase of danger engendered in that true lover's breast, by one additional evening's amusement? Ruby had danced with him so often at the Music Hall that John Crumb could hardly be made more bellicose by the fact of her dining with him on this evening. When he descended, he found Ruby in the hall, all arrayed. 'You don't come in here again to-night,' said Mrs. Pipkin, thumping the little table which stood in the passage, 'if you goes out of that there door with that there young man.'

'Then I shall,' said Ruby linking herself on to her lover's arm.

'Baggage! Slut!' said Mrs. Pipkin; 'after all I've done for you, just as one as though you were my own flesh and blood.'

'I've worked for it, I suppose;—haven't I?' rejoined Ruby.

'You send for your things to-morrow, for you don't come in here no more. You ain't nothing to me no more nor no other girl. But I'd 've saved you, if you'd but a' let me. As for you,'—and she looked at Sir Felix,— 'only because I've lodgings to let, and because of the lady upstairs, I'd shake you that well, you'd never come here no more after poor girls.' I do not think that she need have feared any remonstrance from Mrs. Hurtle, even had she put her threat into execution.

Sir Felix, thinking that he had had enough of Mrs. Pipkin and her lodger, left the house with Ruby on his arm. For the moment, Ruby had been triumphant, and was happy. She did not stop to consider whether her aunt would or would not open her door when she should return tired, and perhaps repentant. She was on her lover's arm, in her best clothes, and going out to have a dinner given to her. And her lover had told her that he had ever so many things,—ever so many things to say to her! But she would ask no impertinent questions in the first hour of her bliss. It was so pleasant to walk with him up to Pentonville;—so joyous to turn into a gay enclosure, half public-house and half tea-garden; so pleasant to hear him order the good things, which in his company would be so nice! Who cannot understand that even an urban Rosherville*must be an Elysium to those who have lately been eating their meals in all the gloom of a small London underground kitchen? There we will leave Ruby in her bliss.

At about nine that evening John Crumb called at Mrs. Pipkin's, and was told that Ruby had gone out with Sir Felix Carbury. He hit his leg a blow with his fist, and glared out of his eyes. 'He'll have it hot some day,' said John Crumb. He was allowed to remain waiting for Ruby till midnight, and then, with a sorrowful heart, he took his departure.

## Chapter LXXI

### JOHN CRUMB FALLS INTO TROUBLE

IT was on a Friday evening, an inauspicious Friday, that poor Ruby Ruggles had insisted on leaving the security of her Aunt Pipkin's house with her aristocratic and vicious lover, in spite of the positive assurance made to her by Mrs. Pipkin that if she went forth in such company she should not be allowed to return. 'Of course you must let her in,' Mrs. Hurtle had said soon after the girl's departure. Whereupon Mrs. Pipkin had cried. She knew her own softness too well to suppose it to be possible that she could keep the girl out in the streets all night; but yet it was hard upon her, very hard, that she should be so troubled. 'We usen't to have our ways like that when I was young,' she said, sobbing. What was to be the end of it? Was she to be forced by circumstances to keep the girl always there, let the girl's conduct be what it might? Nevertheless she acknowledged that Ruby must be let in when she came back. Then, about nine o'clock, John Crumb came; and the latter part of the evening was more melancholy even than the first. It was impossible to conceal the truth from John Crumb. Mrs. Hurtle saw the poor man and told the story in Mrs. Pipkin's presence.

'She's headstrong, Mr. Crumb,' said Mrs. Hurtle.

'She is that, ma'am. And it was along wi' the baro-nite she went?'

'It was so, Mr. Crumb.'

'Baro-nite! Well;—perhaps I shall catch him some of these days;—went to dinner wi' him, did she? Didn't she have no dinner here?'

Then Mrs. Pipkin spoke up with a keen sense of offence. Ruby Ruggles had had as wholesome a dinner as any young woman in London,—a bullock's heart and pota-toes,—just as much as ever she had pleased to eat of it. Mrs. Pipkin could tell Mr. Crumb that there was 'no starvation nor yet no stint in her house.' John Crumb immediately produced a very thick and admirably useful blue cloth cloak, which he had brought up with him to London from Bungay, as a present to the woman who had been good to his Ruby. He assured her that he did not doubt that her victuals were good and plentiful, and went on to say that he had made bold to bring her a trifle out of respect. It was some little time before Mrs. Pipkin would allow herself to be appeased;—but at last she permitted the garment to be placed on her shoulders. But it was done after a melancholy fashion. There was no smiling consciousness of the bestowal of joy on the countenance of the donor as he gave it, no exuberance of thanks from the recipient as she received it. Mrs. Hurtle, standing by, declared it to be perfect;—but the occasion was one which admitted of no delight. 'It's very good of you, Mr. Crumb, to think of an old woman like me,—particularly when you've such a deal of trouble with a young un'.'

'It's like the smut in the wheat, Mrs. Pipkin, or the d'sease in the 'tatoes;—it has to be put up with, I suppose. Is she very partial, ma'am, to that young baronite?' This question was asked of Mrs. Hurtle.

'Just a fancy for the time, Mr. Crumb,' said the lady.

'They never thinks as how their fancies may wellnigh half kill a man!' Then he was silent for a while, sitting back in his chair, not moving a limb, with his eyes fastened on Mrs. Pipkin's ceiling. Mrs. Hurtle had some work in her hand, and sat watching him. The man was to her an extraordinary being,—so constant, so slow, so unexpressive, so unlike her own countrymen,—willing to endure so much, and at the same time so warm in his affections! 'Sir Felix Carbury!' he said. 'I'll Sir Felix him some of these days. If it was only dinner, wouldn't she be back afore this, ma'am?'

'I suppose they've gone to some place of amusement,' said Mrs. Hurtle.

'Like enough,' said John Crumb in a low voice.

'She's that mad after dancing as never was,' said Mrs. Pipkin.

'And where is it as 'em dances?' asked Crumb, getting up from his chair, and stretching himself. It was evident to both the ladies that he was beginning to think that he would follow Ruby to the music hall. Neither of them answered him, however, and then he sat down again. 'Does 'em dance all night at them places, Mrs. Pipkin?'

'They do pretty nearly all that they oughtn't to do,' said Mrs. Pipkin. John Crumb raised one of his fists, brought it down heavily on the palm of his other hand, and then sat silent for awhile.

'I never knowed as she was fond o' dancing,' he said. 'I'd a had dancing for her down at Bungay,—just as ready as anything. D'ye think, ma'am, it's the dancing she's after, or the baro-nite?' This was another appeal to Mrs. Hurtle.

'I suppose they go together,' said the lady.

Then there was another long pause, at the end of which poor John Crumb burst out with some violence. 'Domn him! Domn him! What 'ad I ever dun to him? Nothing! Did I ever interfere wi' him? Never! But I wull. I wull. I wouldn't wonder but I'll swing for this at Bury!'

'Oh, Mr. Crumb, don't talk like that,' said Mrs. Pipkin.

'Mr. Crumb is a little disturbed, but he'll get over it presently,' said Mrs. Hurtle.

'She's a nasty slut to go and treat a young man as she's treating you,' said Mrs. Pipkin.

'No, ma'am;—she ain't nasty,' said the lover. 'But she's crou'll—horrid crou'll. It's no more use my going down about meal and pollard, nor business, and she up here with that baro-nite,—no, no more nor nothin'! When I handles it I don't know whether its middlings nor nothin' else. If I was to twist his neck, ma'am, would you take it on yourself to say as I was wrong?'

'I'd sooner hear that you had taken the girl away from him,' said Mrs. Hurtle.

'I could pretty well eat him,—that's what I could. Half past eleven; is it? She must come some time, mustn't she?' Mrs. Pipkin, who did not want to burn candles all night long, declared that she could give no assurance on that head. If Ruby did come, she should, on that night, be admitted. But Mrs. Pipkin thought that it would be better to get up and let her in than to sit up for her. Poor Mr. Crumb did not at once take the hint, and remained there for another half-hour, saying little, but waiting with the hope that Ruby might come. But when the clock struck twelve he was told that he must go. Then he slowly collected his limbs and dragged them out of the house.

'That young man is a good fellow,' said Mrs. Hurtle as soon as the door was closed.

'A deal too good for Ruby Ruggles,' said Mrs. Pipkin. 'And he can maintain a wife. Mr. Carbury says as he's as well to do as any tradesman down in them parts.'

Mrs. Hurtle disliked the name of Mr. Carbury, and took this last statement as no evidence in John Crumb's favour. 'I don't know that I think better of the man for having Mr. Carbury's friendship,' she said.

'Mr. Carbury ain't any way like his cousin, Mrs. Hurtle.'

'I don't think much of any of the Carburys, Mrs. Pipkin. It seems to me that everybody here is either too humble or too overbearing. Nobody seems content to stand firm on his own footing and interfere with nobody else.' This was all Greek to poor Mrs. Pipkin. 'I suppose we may as well go to bed now. When that girl comes and knocks, of course we must let her in. If I hear her, I'll go down and open the door for her.'

Mrs. Pipkin made very many apologies to her lodger for the condition of her household. She would remain up herself to answer the door at the first sound, so that Mrs. Hurtle should not be disturbed. She would do her best to prevent any further annoyance. She trusted Mrs. Hurtle would see that she was endeavouring to do her duty by the naughty wicked girl. And then she came round to the point of her discourse. She hoped that Mrs. Hurtle would not be induced to quit the rooms by these disagreeable occurrences. 'I don't mind saying it now, Mrs. Hurtle, but your being here is ever so much to me. I ain't nothing to depend on,—only lodgers, and them as is any good is so hard to get!' The poor woman hardly understood Mrs. Hurtle, who, as a lodger, was certainly peculiar. She cared nothing for disturbances, and rather liked than otherwise the task of endeavouring to assist in the salvation of Ruby. Mrs. Hurtle begged that Mrs. Pipkin would go to bed. She would not be in the least annoyed by the knocking. Another half-hour had thus been passed by the two ladies in the parlour after Crumb's departure. Then Mrs. Hurtle took her candle and had ascended the stairs half way to her own sitting-room, when a loud double knock was heard. She immediately joined Mrs. Pipkin in the passage. The door was opened, and there stood Ruby Ruggles, John Crumb, and two policemen! Ruby rushed in, and casting herself on to one of the stairs began to throw her hands about, and to howl piteously. 'Laws a mercy; what is it?' asked Mrs. Pipkin.

'He's been and murdered him!' screamed Ruby. 'He has! He's been and murdered him!'

'This young woman is living here;—is she?' asked one of the policemen.

'She is living here,' said Mrs. Hurtle. But now we must go back to the adventures of John Crumb after he had left the house.

He had taken a bedroom at a small inn close to the Eastern Counties Railway Station which he was accustomed to frequent when business brought him up to London, and thither he proposed to himself to return. At one time there had come upon him an idea that he would endeavour to seek Ruby and his enemy among the dancing saloons of the metropolis; and he had asked a question with that view. But no answer had been given which seemed to aid him in his project, and his purpose had been abandoned as being too complex and requiring more intelligence than he gave himself credit for possessing. So he had turned down a street with which he was so far acquainted as to know that it would take him to the Islington Angel,—where various roads meet, and whence he would know his way eastwards. He had just passed the Angel, and the end of Goswell Road, and was

standing with his mouth open, looking about, trying to
make certain of himself that he would not go wrong,
thinking that he would ask a policeman whom he saw,
and hesitating because he feared that the man would
want to know his business. Then, of a sudden, he heard
a woman scream, and knew that it was Ruby's voice.
The sound was very near him, but in the glimmer of the
gaslight he could not quite see whence it came. He stood
still, putting his hand up to scratch his head under his
hat,—trying to think what, in such an emergency, it
would be well that he should do. Then he heard the voice
distinctly, 'I won't;—I won't,' and after that a scream.
Then there were further words. 'It's no good—I won't.'
At last he was able to make up his mind. He rushed after
the sound, and turning down a passage to the right
which led back into Goswell Road, saw Ruby struggling
in a man's arms. She had left the dancing establishment
with her lover; and when they had come to the turn of
the passage, there had arisen a question as to her further
destiny for the night. Ruby, though she well remembered Mrs. Pipkin's threats, was minded to try her
chance at her aunt's door. Sir Felix was of opinion that
he could make a preferable arrangement for her; and as
Ruby was not at once amenable to his arguments he had
thought that a little gentle force might avail him. He
had therefore dragged Ruby into the passage. The unfortunate one! That so ill a chance should have come
upon him in the midst of his diversion! He had swallowed
several tumblers of brandy and water, and was therefore
brave with reference to that interference of the police,
the fear of which might otherwise have induced him to
relinquish his hold of Ruby's arm when she first raised
her voice. But what amount of brandy and water would
have enabled him to persevere, could he have dreamed
that John Crumb was near him? On a sudden he found a
hand on his coat, and he was swung violently away, and
brought with his back against the railings so forcibly as
to have the breath almost knocked out of his body. But he
could hear Ruby's exclamation, 'If it isn't John Crumb!'
Then there came upon him a sense of coming destruction,

as though the world for him were all over; and, collapsing throughout his limbs, he slunk down upon the ground.

'Get up, you wiper,' said John Crumb. But the baronet thought it better to cling to the ground. 'You sholl get up,' said John, taking him by the collar of his coat and lifting him. 'Now, Ruby, he's a-going to have it,' said John. Whereupon Ruby screamed at the top of her voice, with a shriek very much louder than that which had at first attracted John Crumb's notice.

'Don't hit a man when he's down,' said the baronet, pleading as though for his life.

'I wunt,' said John;—'but I'll hit a fellow when un's up.' Sir Felix was little more than a child in the man's arms. John Crumb raised him, and catching him round the neck with his left arm,—getting his head into chancery as we used to say when we fought at school,—struck the poor wretch some half-dozen times violently in the face, not knowing or caring exactly where he hit him, but at every blow obliterating a feature. And he would have continued had not Ruby flown at him and rescued Sir Felix from his arms. 'He's about got enough of it,' said John Crumb as he gave over his work. Then Sir Felix fell again to the ground, moaning fearfully. 'I know'd he'd have to have it,' said John Crumb.

Ruby's screams of course brought the police, one arriving from each end of the passage on the scene of action at the same time. And now the cruellest thing of all was that Ruby in the complaints which she made to the policemen said not a word against Sir Felix, but was as bitter as she knew how to be in her denunciations of John Crumb. It was in vain that John endeavoured to make the man understand that the young woman had been crying out for protection when he had interfered. Ruby was very quick of speech and John Crumb was very slow. Ruby swore that nothing so horrible, so cruel, so bloodthirsty had ever been done before. Sir Felix himself when appealed to could say nothing. He could only moan and make futile efforts to wipe away the stream of blood from his face when the men stood him up leaning against the railings. And John, though

he endeavoured to make the policemen comprehend the
extent of the wickedness of the young baronet, would not
say a word against Ruby. He was not even in the least
angered by her denunciations of himself. As he himself
said sometimes afterwards, he had 'dropped into the
baronite' just in time, and, having been successful in
this, felt no wrath against Ruby for having made such
an operation necessary.

There was soon a third policeman on the spot, and a
dozen other persons,—cab-drivers, haunters of the street
by night, and houseless wanderers, casuals who at this
season of the year preferred the pavements to the poor-
house wards. They all took part against John Crumb.
Why had the big man interfered between the young
woman and her young man? Two or three of them
wiped Sir Felix's face, and dabbed his eyes, and proposed
this and the other remedy. Some thought that he had
better be taken straight to an hospital. One lady remarked that he was 'so mashed and mauled' that she was
sure he would never 'come to' again. A precocious youth
remarked that he was 'all one as a dead un'.' A cabman
observed that he had ''ad it awful 'eavy.' To all these
criticisms on his condition Sir Felix himself made no
direct reply, but he intimated his desire to be carried
away somewhere, though he did not much care whither.

At last the policemen among them decided upon a
course of action. They had learned by the united testimony of Ruby and Crumb that Sir Felix was Sir Felix.
He was to be carried in a cab by one constable to
Bartholomew Hospital, who would then take his address
so that he might be produced and bound over to prosecute. Ruby should be even conducted to the address
she gave,—not half a mile from the spot on which they
now stood,—and be left there or not according to the
account which might be given of her. John Crumb
must be undoubtedly locked up in the station-house. He
was the offender;—for aught that any of them yet knew,
the murderer. No one said a good word for him. He
hardly said a good word for himself, and certainly made
no objection to the treatment that had been proposed for

him. But, no doubt, he was buoyed up inwardly by the conviction that he had thoroughly thrashed his enemy.

Thus it came to pass that the two policemen with John Crumb and Ruby came together to Mrs. Pipkin's door. Ruby was still loud with complaints against the ruffian who had beaten her lover,—who, perhaps, had killed her loved one. She threatened the gallows, and handcuffs, and perpetual imprisonment, and an action for damages amidst her lamentations. But from Mrs. Hurtle the policemen did manage to learn something of the truth. Oh yes;—the girl lived there and was—— respectable. This man whom they had arrested was respectable also, and was the girl's proper lover. The other man who had been beaten was undoubtedly the owner of a title; but he was not respectable, and was only the girl's improper lover. And John Crumb's name was given. 'I'm John Crumb of Bungay,' said he, 'and I aint afeared of nothin' nor nobody. And I ain't a been a drinking; no, I ain't. Mauled un'! In course I've mauled un'. And I meaned it. That ere young woman is engaged to be my wife.'

'No, I ain't,' shouted Ruby.

'But she is,' persisted John Crumb.

'Well then, I never will,' rejoined Ruby.

John Crumb turned upon her a look of love, and put his hand on his heart. Whereupon the senior policeman said that he saw at a glance how it all was, but that Mr. Crumb had better come along with him,—just for the present. To this arrangement the unfortunate hero from Bungay made not the slightest objection.

'Miss Ruggles,' said Mrs. Hurtle, 'if that young man doesn't conquer you at last you can't have a heart in your bosom.'

'Indeed and I have then, and I don't mean to give it him if it's ever so. He's been and killed Sir Felix.' Mrs. Hurtle in a whisper to Mrs. Pipkin expressed a wicked wish that it might be so. After that the three women all went to bed.

## Chapter LXXII

### 'ASK HIMSELF'

ROGER CARBURY when he received the letter from Hetta's mother desiring him to tell her all that he knew of Paul Montague's connection with Mrs. Hurtle found himself quite unable to write a reply. He endeavoured to ask himself what he would do in such a case if he himself were not personally concerned. What advice in this emergency would he give to the mother and what to the daughter, were he himself uninterested? He was sure that, as Hetta's cousin and asking as though he were Hetta's brother, he would tell her that Paul Montague's entanglement with that American woman should have forbidden him at any rate for the present to offer his hand to any other lady. He thought that he knew enough of all the circumstances to be sure that such would be his decision. He had seen Mrs. Hurtle with Montague at Lowestoffe, and had known that they were staying together as friends at the same hotel. He knew that she had come to England with the express purpose of enforcing the fulfilment of an engagement which Montague had often acknowledged. He knew that Montague made frequent visits to her in London. He had, indeed, been told by Montague himself that, let the cost be what it might, the engagement should be and in fact had been broken off. He thoroughly believed the man's word, but put no trust whatever in his firmness. And, hitherto, he had no reason whatever for supposing that Mrs. Hurtle had consented to be abandoned. What father, what elder brother would allow a daughter or a sister to become engaged to a man embarrassed by such difficulties? He certainly had counselled Montague to rid himself of the trammels by which he had surrounded himself;—but not on that account could he think that the man in his present condition was fit to engage himself to another woman.

All this was clear to Roger Carbury. But then it had been equally clear to him that he could not, as a man of honour, assist his own cause by telling a tale,—which tale had become known to him as the friend of the man against whom it would have to be told. He had resolved upon that as he left Montague and Mrs. Hurtle together upon the sands at Lowestoffe. But what was he to do now? The girl whom he loved had confessed her love for the other man,—that man, who in seeking the girl's love, had been as he thought so foul a traitor to himself! That he would hold himself as divided from the man by a perpetual and undying hostility he had determined. That his love for the woman would be equally perpetual he was quite sure. Already there were floating across his brain ideas of perpetuating his name in the person of some child of Hetta's,—but with the distinct understanding that he and the child's father should never see each other. No more than twenty-four hours had intervened between the receipt of Paul's letter and that from Lady Carbury,—but during those four-and-twenty hours he had almost forgotten Mrs. Hurtle. The girl was gone from him, and he thought only of his own loss and of Paul's perfidy. Then came the direct question as to which he was called upon for a direct answer. Did he know anything of facts relating to the presence of a certain Mrs. Hurtle in London which were of a nature to make it inexpedient that Hetta should accept Paul Montague as her betrothed lover? Of course he did. The facts were all familiar to him. But how was he to tell the facts? In what words was he to answer such a letter? If he told the truth as he knew it how was he to secure himself against the suspicion of telling a story against his rival in order that he might assist himself, or at any rate, punish the rival?

As he could not trust himself to write an answer to Lady Carbury's letter he determined that he would go to London. If he must tell the story he could tell it better face to face than by any written words. So he made the journey, arrived in town late in the evening, and knocked at the door in Welbeck Street between ten

and eleven on the morning after the unfortunate meeting
which took place between Sir Felix and John Crumb.
The page when he opened the door looked as a page
should look when the family to which he is attached is
suffering from some terrible calamity. 'My lady' had
been summoned to the hospital to see Sir Felix who was,
—as the page reported,—in a very bad way indeed.
The page did not exactly know what had happened,
but supposed that Sir Felix had lost most of his limbs by
this time. Yes; Miss Carbury was upstairs; and would
no doubt see her cousin, though she, too, was in a very
bad condition; and dreadfully put about. That poor
Hetta should be 'put about' with her brother in the
hospital and her lover in the toils of an abominable
American woman was natural enough.

'What's this about Felix?' asked Roger. The new
trouble always has precedence over those which are of
earlier date.

'Oh Roger, I am so glad to see you. Felix did not
come home last night, and this morning there came a
man from the hospital in the city to say that he is there.'

'What has happened to him?'

'Somebody,—somebody has,—beaten him,' said Hetta
whimpering. Then she told the story as far as she knew
it. The messenger from the hospital had declared that
the young man was in no danger and that none of his
bones were broken, but that he was terribly bruised
about the face, that his eyes were in a frightful condition,
sundry of his teeth knocked out, and his lips cut open.
But, the messenger had gone on to say, the house surgeon
had seen no reason why the young gentleman should not
be taken home. 'And mamma has gone to fetch him,'
said Hetta.

'That's John Crumb,' said Roger. Hetta had never
heard of John Crumb, and simply stared into her
cousin's face. 'You have not been told about John
Crumb? No;—you would not hear of him.'

'Why should John Crumb beat Felix like that?'

'They say, Hetta, that women are the cause of most
troubles that occur in the world.' The girl blushed up to

her eyes, as though the whole story of Felix's sin and folly had been told to her. 'If it be as I suppose,' continued Roger, 'John Crumb has considered himself to be aggrieved and has thus avenged himself.'

'Did you—know of him before?'

'Yes indeed;—very well. He is a neighbour of mine and was in love with a girl, with all his heart; and he would have made her his wife and have been good to her. He had a home to offer her, and is an honest man with whom she would have been safe and respected and happy. Your brother saw her and, though he knew the story, though he had been told by myself that this honest fellow had placed his happiness on the girl's love, he thought,—well, I suppose he thought that such a pretty thing as this girl was too good for John Crumb.'

'But Felix has been going to marry Miss Melmotte!'

'You're old-fashioned, Hetta. It used to be the way,— to be off with your old love before you are on with the new; but that seems to be all changed now. Such fine young fellows as there are now can be in love with two at once. That I fear is what Felix has thought;—and now he has been punished.'

'You know all about it then?'

'No;—I don't know. But I think it has been so. I do know that John Crumb had threatened to do this thing, and I felt sure that sooner or later he would be as good as his word. If it has been so, who is to blame him?'

Hetta as she heard the story hardly knew whether her cousin, in his manner of telling the story, was speaking of that other man, of that stranger of whom she had never heard, or of himself. He would have made her his wife and have been good to her. He had a home to offer her. He was an honest man with whom she would have been safe and respected and happy! He had looked at her while speaking as though it were her own case of which he spoke. And then, when he talked of the old-fashioned way, of being off with the old love before you are on with the new, had he not alluded to Paul Montague and this story of the American woman? But, if so, it was not for Hetta to notice it by words. He must speak more plainly than that before she could be supposed to know that he alluded to her own condition. 'It is very shocking,' she said.

'Shocking;—yes. One is shocked at it all. I pity your mother, and I pity you.'

'It seems to me that nothing ever will be happy for us,' said Hetta. She was longing to be told something of Mrs. Hurtle, but she did not as yet dare to ask the question.

'I do not know whether to wait for your mother or not,' said he after a short pause.

'Pray wait for her if you are not very busy.'

'I came up only to see her, but perhaps she would not wish me to be here when she brings Felix back to the house.'

'Indeed she will. She would like you always to be here when there are troubles. Oh, Roger, I wish you could tell me.'

'Tell you what?'

'She has written to you;—has she not?'

'Yes; she has written to me.'

'And about me?'

'Yes;—about you, Hetta. And, Hetta, Mr. Montague has written to me also.'

'He told me that he would,' whispered Hetta.

'Did he tell you my answer?'

'No;—he has told me of no answer. I have not seen him since.'

'You do not think that it can have been very kind, do you? I also have something of the feeling of John Crumb, though I shall not attempt to show it after the same fashion.'

'Did you not say the girl had promised to love that man?'

'I did not say so;—but she had promised. Yes, Hetta; there is a difference. The girl then was fickle and went back from her word. You never have done that. I am not justified in thinking even a hard thought of you. I have never harboured a hard thought of you. It is not you that I reproach. But he,—he has been if possible more false than Felix.'

'Oh, Roger, how has he been false?'

Still he was not wishful to tell her the story of Mrs. Hurtle. The treachery of which he was speaking was that which he had thought had been committed by his friend towards himself. 'He should have left the place and never have come near you,' said Roger, 'when he found how it was likely to be with him. He owed it to me not to take the cup of water from my lips.'

How was she to tell him that the cup of water never could have touched his lips? And yet if this were the only falsehood of which he had to tell, she was bound to let him know that it was so. That horrid story of Mrs. Hurtle;—she would listen to that if she could hear it. She would be all ears for that. But she could not admit that her lover had sinned in loving her. 'But, Roger,' she said—'it would have been the same.'

'You may say so. You may feel it. You may know it. I at any rate will not contradict you when you say that it must have been so. But he didn't feel it. He didn't know it. He was to me as a younger brother,—and he has robbed me of everything. I understand, Hetta, what you mean. I should never have succeeded! My happiness would have been impossible if Paul had never come home from America. I have told myself so a hundred times, but I cannot therefore forgive him. And I won't forgive him, Hetta. Whether you are his wife, or another man's, or whether you are Hetta Carbury on to the end, my feeling to you will be the same. While we both live, you must be to me the dearest creature living. My hatred to him——'

'Oh, Roger, do not say hatred.'

'My hostility to him can make no difference in my feeling to you. I tell you that should you become his wife you will still be my love. As to not coveting,—how is a man to cease to covet that which he has always coveted? But I shall be separated from you. Should I be dying, then I should send for you. You are the very essence of my life. I have no dream of happiness otherwise than as connected with you. He might have my whole property and I would work for my bread, if I could only have a chance of winning you to share my toils with me.'

But still there was no word of Mrs. Hurtle. 'Roger,' she said, 'I have given it all away now. It cannot be given twice.'

'If he were unworthy would your heart never change?'

'I think—never. Roger, is he unworthy?'

'How can you trust me to answer such a question? He is my enemy. He has been ungrateful to me as one man hardly ever is to another. He has turned all my sweetness to gall, all my flowers to bitter weeds; he has choked up all my paths. And now you ask me whether he is unworthy! I cannot tell you.'

'If you thought him worthy you would tell me,' she said, getting up and taking him by the arm.

'No;—I will tell you nothing. Go to some one else, not to me;' and he tried with gentleness but tried ineffectually to disengage himself from her hold.

'Roger, if you knew him to be good you would tell me, because you yourself are so good. Even though you hated him you would say so. It would not be you to leave a false impression even against your enemies. I ask you because, however it may be with you, I know I can trust you. I can be nothing else to you, Roger; but I love you as a sister loves, and I come to you as a sister comes to a brother. He has my heart. Tell me;—is there any reason why he should not also have my hand?'

'Ask himself, Hetta.'

'And you will tell me nothing? You will not try to save me though you know that I am in danger? Who is —Mrs. Hurtle?'

'Have you asked him?'

'I had not heard her name when he parted from me. I did not even know that such a woman lived. Is it true that he has promised to marry her? Felix told me of her, and told me also that you knew. But I cannot trust Felix as I would trust you. And mamma says that it is so;—but mamma also bids me ask you. There is such a woman?'

'There is such a woman certainly.'

'And she has been,—a friend of Paul's?'

'Whatever be the story, Hetta, you shall not hear it

from me. I will say neither evil nor good of the man except in regard to his conduct to myself. Send for him and ask him to tell you the story of Mrs. Hurtle as it concerns himself. I do not think he will lie, but if he lies you will know that he is lying.'

'And that is all?'

'All that I can say, Hetta. You ask me to be your brother;—but I cannot put myself in the place of your brother. I tell you plainly that I am your lover, and shall remain so. Your brother would welcome the man whom you would choose as your husband. I can never welcome any husband of yours. I think if twenty years were to pass over us, and you were still Hetta Carbury, I should still be your lover,—though an old one. What is now to be done about Felix, Hetta?'

'Ah,—what can be done? I think sometimes that it will break mamma's heart.'

'Your mother makes me angry by her continual indulgence.'

'But what can she do? You would not have her turn him into the street?'

'I do not know that I would not. For a time it might serve him perhaps. Here is the cab. Here they are. Yes; you had better go down and let your mother know that I am here. They will perhaps take him up to bed, so that I need not see him.'

Hetta did as she was bid, and met her mother and her brother in the hall. Felix having the full use of his arms and legs was able to descend from the cab, and hurry across the pavement into the house, and then, without speaking a word to his sister, hid himself in the dining-room. His face was strapped up with plaister so that not a feature was visible; and both his eyes were swollen and blue; part of his beard had been cut away, and his physiognomy had altogether been so treated that even the page would hardly have known him. 'Roger is upstairs, mamma,' said Hetta in the hall.

'Has he heard about Felix;—has he come about that?'

'He has heard only what I have told him. He has come

because of your letter. He says that a man named Crumb did it.'

'Then he does know. Who can have told him? He always knows everything. Oh, Hetta, what am I to do? Where shall I go with this wretched boy?'

'Is he hurt, mamma?'

'Hurt;—of course he is hurt; horribly hurt. The brute tried to kill him. They say that he will be dreadfully scarred for ever. But oh, Hetta;—what am I to do with him? What am I to do with myself and you?'

On this occasion Roger was saved from the annoyance of any personal intercourse with his cousin Felix. The unfortunate one was made as comfortable as circumstances would permit in the parlour, and Lady Carbury then went up to her cousin in the drawing-room. She had learned the truth with some fair approach to accuracy, though Sir Felix himself had of course lied as to every detail. There are some circumstances so distressing in themselves as to make lying almost a necessity. When a young man has behaved badly about a woman, when a young man has been beaten without returning a blow, when a young man's pleasant vices are brought directly under a mother's eyes, what can he do but lie? How could Sir Felix tell the truth about that rash encounter? But the policeman who had brought him to the hospital had told all that he knew. The man who had thrashed the baronet had been Crumb, and the thrashing had been given on the score of a young woman called Ruggles. So much was known at the hospital, and so much could not be hidden by any lies which Sir Felix might tell. And when Sir Felix swore that a policeman was holding him while Crumb was beating him, no one believed him. In such cases the liar does not expect to be believed. He knows that his disgrace will be made public, and only hopes to be saved from the ignominy of declaring it with his own words.

'What am I to do with him?' Lady Carbury said to her cousin. 'It is no use telling me to leave him. I can't do that. I know he is bad. I know that I have done much to make him what he is.' As she said this the tears were running down her poor worn cheeks. 'But he is my child. What am I to do with him now?'

This was a question which Roger found it almost impossible to answer. If he had spoken his thoughts he would have declared that Sir Felix had reached an age at which, if a man will go headlong to destruction, he must go headlong to destruction. Thinking as he did of his cousin he could see no possible salvation for him. 'Perhaps I should take him abroad,' he said.

'Would he be better abroad than here?'

'He would have less opportunity for vice, and fewer means of running you into debt.'

Lady Carbury, as she turned this counsel in her mind, thought of all the hopes which she had indulged,—her literary aspirations, her Tuesday evenings, her desire for society, her Brounes, her Alfs, and her Bookers, her pleasant drawing-room, and the determination which she had made that now in the afternoon of her days she would become somebody in the world. Must she give it all up and retire to the dreariness of some French town because it was no longer possible that she should live in London with such a son as hers? There seemed to be a cruelty in this beyond all cruelties that she had hitherto endured. This was harder even than those lies which had been told of her when almost in fear of her life she had run from her husband's house. But yet she must do even this if in no other way she and her son could be together. 'Yes,' she said, 'I suppose it would be so. I only wish that I might die, so that were an end of it.'

'He might go out to one of the Colonies,' said Roger.

'Yes;—be sent away that he might kill himself with drink in the bush, and so be got rid of. I have heard of that before. Wherever he goes I shall go.'

As the reader knows, Roger Carbury had not latterly held this cousin of his in much esteem. He knew her to be worldly and he thought her to be unprincipled. But now, at this moment, her exceeding love for the son whom she could no longer pretend to defend, wiped out all her sins. He forgot the visit made to Carbury under false pretences, and the Melmottes, and all the little tricks which he had detected, in his appreciation of an affection which was pure and beautiful. 'If you like to let your house for a period,' he said, 'mine is open to you.'

'But, Felix?'

'You shall take him there. I am all alone in the world. I can make a home for myself at the cottage. It is empty now. If you think that would save you you can try it for six months.'

'And turn you out of your own house? No, Roger. I cannot do that. And, Roger;—what is to be done about Hetta?' Hetta herself had retreated, leaving Roger and her mother alone together, feeling sure that there would be questions asked and answered in her absence respecting Mrs. Hurtle, which her presence would prevent. She wished it could have been otherwise—that she might have been allowed to hear it all herself—as she was sure that the story coming through her mother would not savour so completely of unalloyed truth as if told to her by her cousin Roger.

'Hetta can be trusted to judge for herself,' he said.

'How can you say that when she has just accepted this young man? Is it not true that he is even now living with an American woman whom he has promised to marry?'

'No;—that is not true.'

'What is true then? Is he not engaged to the woman?'

Roger hesitated a moment. 'I do know that even that is true. When last he spoke to me about it he declared that the engagement was at an end. I have told Hetta to ask himself. Let her tell him that she has heard of this woman from you, and that it behoves her to know the truth. I do not love him, Lady Carbury. He has no longer any place in my friendship. But I think that if Hetta asks him simply what is the nature of his connexion with Mrs. Hurtle, he will tell her the truth.'

Roger did not again see Hetta before he left the house, nor did he see his cousin Felix at all. He had now done all that he could do by his journey up to London, and he returned on that day back to Carbury. Would it not be better for him, in spite of the protestations which he had made, to dismiss the whole family from his mind? There

could be no other love for him. He must be desolate and
alone. But he might then save himself from a world of
cares, and might gradually teach himself to live as though
there were no such woman as Hetta Carbury in the world.
But no! He would not allow himself to believe that this
could be right. The very fact of his love made it a duty
to him,—made it almost the first of his duties,—to watch
over the interests of her he loved and of those who belonged to her.

But among those so belonging he did not recognise
Paul Montague.

## Chapter LXXIII

### MARIE'S FORTUNE

WHEN Marie Melmotte assured Sir Felix Carbury
that her father had already endowed her with a
large fortune which could not be taken from her without
her own consent, she spoke no more than the truth. She
knew of the matter almost as little as it was possible that
she should know. As far as reticence on the subject was
compatible with the object he had in view Melmotte had
kept from her all knowledge of the details of the arrangement. But it had been necessary when the thing was done
to explain, or to pretend to explain, much; and Marie's
memory and also her intelligence had been strong beyond
her father's anticipation. He was deriving a very considerable income from a large sum of money which he had
invested in foreign funds in her name, and had got her to
execute a power of attorney enabling him to draw this
income on her behalf. This he had done fearing ship-
wreck in the course which he meant to run, and resolved
that, let circumstances go as they might, there should
still be left enough to him of the money which he had
realised to enable him to live in comfort and luxury,
should he be doomed to live in obscurity, or even in

infamy. He had sworn to himself solemnly that under no circumstances would he allow this money to go back into the vortex of his speculations, and hitherto he had been true to his oath. Though bankruptcy and apparent ruin might be imminent he would not bolster up his credit by the use of this money even though it might appear at the moment that the money would be sufficient for the purpose. If such a day should come, then, with that certain income, he would make himself happy, if possible, or at any rate luxurious, in whatever city of the world might know least of his antecedents, and give him the warmest welcome on behalf of his wealth. Such had been his scheme of life. But he had failed to consider various circumstances. His daughter might be untrue to him, or in the event of her marriage might fail to release his property,—or it might be that the very money should be required to dower his daughter. Or there might come troubles on him so great that even the certainty of a future income would not enable him to bear them. Now, at this present moment, his mind was tortured by great anxiety. Were he to resume this property it would more than enable him to pay all that was due to the Longestaffes. It would do that and tide him for a time over some other difficulties. Now in regard to the Longestaffes themselves, he certainly had no desire to depart from the rule which he had made for himself, on their behalf. Were it necessary that a crash should come they would be as good creditors as any other. But then he was painfully alive to the fact that something beyond simple indebtedness was involved in that transaction. He had with his own hand traced Dolly Longestaffe's signature on the letter which he had found in old Mr. Longestaffe's drawer.* He had found it in an envelope, addressed by the elder Mr. Longestaffe to Messrs. Slow and Bide-awhile, and he had himself posted this letter in a pillar-box near to his house. In the execution of this manœuvre, circumstances had greatly befriended him. He had become the tenant of Mr. Longestaffe's house, and at the same time had only been the joint tenant of Mr. Longe-staffe's study,—so that Mr. Longestaffe's papers were

almost in his very hands. To pick a lock was with him
an accomplishment long since learned. But his science
in that line did not go so far as to enable him to replace
the bolt in its receptacle. He had picked a lock, had
found the letter prepared by Mr. Bideawhile with its
accompanying envelope, and had then already learned
enough of the domestic circumstances of the Longestaffe
family to feel assured that unless he could assist the
expedition of this hitherto uncompleted letter by his own
skill, the letter would never reach its intended destination. In all this fortune had in some degree befriended
him. The circumstances being as they were it was hardly
possible that the forgery should be discovered. Even
though the young man were to swear that the signature
was not his, even though the old man were to swear that
he had left that drawer properly locked with the unsigned letter in it, still there could be no evidence.
People might think. People might speak. People might
feel sure. And then a crash would come. But there
would still be that ample fortune on which to retire and
eat and drink and make merry for the rest of his days.

Then there came annoying complications in his affairs.
What had been so easy in reference to that letter which
Dolly Longestaffe never would have signed, was less
easy but still feasible in another matter. Under the joint
pressure of immediate need, growing ambition, and increasing audacity it had been done. Then the rumours
that were spread abroad,—which to Melmotte were
serious indeed,—they named, at any rate in reference to
Dolly Longestaffe, the very thing that had been done.
Now if that, or the like of that, were brought actually
home to him, if twelve jurymen could be got to say that
he had done that thing, of what use then would be all
that money? When that fear arose, then there arose also
the question whether it might not be well to use the
money to save him from such ruin, if it might be so used.
No doubt all danger in that Longestaffe affair might be
bought off by payment of the price stipulated for the
Pickering property. Neither would Dolly Longestaffe
nor Squercum, of whom Mr. Melmotte had already heard;

concern himself in this matter if the money claimed were
paid. But then the money would be as good as wasted
by such a payment, if, as he firmly believed, no sufficient
evidence could be produced to prove the thing which
he had done.

But the complications were so many! Perhaps in his
admiration for the country of his adoption Mr. Melmotte
had allowed himself to attach higher privileges to the
British aristocracy than do in truth belong to them. He
did in his heart believe that could he be known to all
the world as the father-in-law of the eldest son of the
Marquis of Auld Reekie he would become, not really
free of the law, but almost safe from its fangs in regard
to such an affair as this. He thought he could so use the
family with which he would be connected as to force from
it that protection which he would need. And then again,
if he could tide over this bad time, how glorious would
it be to have a British Marquis for his son-in-law! Like
many others he had failed altogether to inquire when
the pleasure to himself would come, or what would be
its nature. But he did believe that such a marriage
would add a charm to his life. Now he knew that Lord
Nidderdale could not be got to marry his daughter
without the positive assurance of absolute property, but
he did think that the income which might thus be
transferred with Marie, though it fell short of that which
had been promised, might suffice for the time; and he
had already given proof to the Marquis's lawyer that
his daughter was possessed of the property in question.

And indeed, there was another complication which
had arisen within the last few days and which had
startled Mr. Melmotte very much indeed. On a certain
morning he had sent for Marie to the study and had told
her that he should require her signature in reference to a
deed. She had asked him what deed. He had replied
that it would be a document regarding money and
reminded her that she had signed such a deed once
before, telling her that it was all in the way of business.
It was not necessary that she should ask any more questions as she would be wanted only to sign the paper.

Then Marie astounded him, not merely by showing him that she understood a great deal more of the transaction than he had thought,—but also by a positive refusal to sign anything at all. The reader may understand that there had been many words between them. 'I know, papa. It is that you may have the money to do what you like with. You have been so unkind to me about Sir Felix Carbury that I won't do it. If I ever marry the money will belong to my husband!' His breath almost failed him as he listened to these words. He did not know whether to approach her with threats, with entreaties, or with blows. Before the interview was over he had tried all three. He had told her that he could and would put her in prison for conduct so fraudulent. He besought her not to ruin her parent by such monstrous perversity. And at last he took her by both arms and shook her violently. But Marie was quite firm. He might cut her to pieces; but she would sign nothing. 'I suppose you thought Sir Felix would have had the entire sum,' said the father with deriding scorn.

'And he would;—if he had the spirit to take it,' answered Marie.

This was another reason for sticking to the Nidderdale plan. He would no doubt lose the immediate income, but in doing so he would secure the Marquis. He was therefore induced, on weighing in his nicest-balanced scales the advantages and disadvantages, to leave the Longestaffes unpaid and to let Nidderdale have the money. Not that he could make up his mind to such a course with any conviction that he was doing the best for himself. The dangers on all sides were very great! But at the present moment audacity recommended itself to him, and this was the boldest stroke. Marie had now said that she would accept Nidderdale,—or the sweep at the crossing.

On Monday morning,—it was on the preceding Thursday that he had made his famous speech in Parliament, —one of the Bideawhiles had come to him in the City. He had told Mr. Bideawhile that all the world knew that just at the present moment money was very 'tight' in the

City. 'We are not asking for payment of a commercial debt,' said Mr. Bideawhile, 'but for the price of a considerable property which you have purchased.' Mr. Melmotte had suggested that the characteristics of the money were the same, let the sum in question have become due how it might. Then he offered to make the payment in two bills at three and six months' date, with proper interest allowed. But this offer Mr. Bideawhile scouted with indignation, demanding that the title-deeds might be restored to them.

'You have no right whatever to demand the title-deeds,' said Melmotte. 'You can only claim the sum due, and I have already told you how I propose to pay it.'

Mr. Bideawhile was nearly beside himself with dismay. In the whole course of his business, in all the records of the very respectable firm to which he belonged, there had never been such a thing as this. Of course Mr. Longestaffe had been the person to blame,—so at least all the Bideawhiles declared among themselves. He had been so anxious to have dealings with the man of money that he had insisted that the title-deeds should be given up. But then the title-deeds had not been his to surrender. The Pickering estate had been the joint property of him and his son. The house had been already pulled down, and now the purchaser offered bills in lieu of the purchase money! 'Do you mean to tell me, Mr. Melmotte, that you have not got the money to pay for what you have bought, and that nevertheless the title-deeds have already gone out of your hands?'

'I have property to ten times the value, twenty times the value, thirty times the value,' said Melmotte proudly; 'but you must know I should think by this time that a man engaged in large affairs cannot always realise such a sum as eighty thousand pounds at a day's notice.' Mr. Bideawhile without using language that was absolutely vituperative gave Mr. Melmotte to understand that he thought that he and his client had been robbed, and that he should at once take whatever severest steps the law put in his power. As Mr. Melmotte shrugged his shoulders and made no further reply, Mr. Bideawhile could only take his departure.

The attorney, although he was bound to be staunch to his own client, and to his own house in opposition to Mr. Squercum, nevertheless was becoming doubtful in his own mind as to the genuineness of the letter which Dolly was so persistent in declaring that he had not signed. Mr. Longestaffe himself, who was at any rate an honest man, had given it as his opinion that Dolly had not signed the letter. His son had certainly refused to sign it once, and as far as he knew could have had no opportunity of signing it since. He was all but sure that he had left the letter under lock and key in his own drawer in the room which had latterly become Melmotte's study as well as his own. Then, on entering the room in Melmotte's presence,—their friendship at the time having already ceased,—he found that his drawer was open. This same Mr. Bideawhile was with him at the time. 'Do you mean to say that I have opened your drawer?' said Mr. Melmotte. Mr. Longestaffe had become very red in the face and had replied by saying that he certainly made no such accusation, but as certainly he had not left the drawer unlocked. He knew his own habits and was sure that he had never left that drawer open in his life. 'Then you must have changed the habits of your life on this occasion,' said Mr. Melmotte with spirit. Mr. Longestaffe would trust himself to no other word within the house, but, when they were out in the street together, he assured the lawyer that certainly that drawer had been left locked, and that to the best of his belief the letter unsigned had been left within the drawer. Mr. Bideawhile could only remark that it was the most unfortunate circumstance with which he had ever been concerned.

The marriage with Nidderdale would upon the whole be the best thing, if it could only be accomplished. The reader must understand that though Mr. Melmotte had allowed himself considerable poetical licence in that statement as to property thirty times as great as the price which he ought to have paid for Pickering, still there was property. The man's speculations had been so great and so wide that he did not really know what he owned, or what he owed. But he did know that at the present moment he was driven very hard for large sums. His chief trust for immediate money was in Cohenlupe, in whose hands had really been the manipulation of the shares of the Mexican railway. He had trusted much to Cohenlupe,—more than it had been customary with him to trust to any man. Cohenlupe assured him that nothing could be done with the railway shares at the present moment. They had fallen under the panic almost to nothing. Now in the time of his trouble Melmotte wanted money from the great railway, but just because he wanted money the great railway was worth nothing. Cohenlupe told him that he must tide over the evil hour,—or rather over an evil month. It was at Cohenlupe's instigation that he had offered the two bills to Mr. Bideawhile. 'Offer 'em again,' said Cohenlupe. 'He must take the bills sooner or later.'

On the Monday afternoon Melmotte met Lord Nidderdale in the lobby of the House. 'Have you seen Marie lately?' he said. Nidderdale had been assured that morning, by his father's lawyer, in his father's presence, that if he married Miss Melmotte at present he would undoubtedly become possessed of an income amounting to something over £5,000 a year. He had intended to get more than that,—and was hardly prepared to accept Marie at such a price; but then there probably would be more. No doubt there was a difficulty about Pickering. Melmotte certainly had been raising money. But this might probably be an affair of a few weeks. Melmotte had declared that Pickering should be made over to the young people at the marriage. His father had recommended him to get the girl to name a day. The marriage could be broken off at the last day if the property were not forthcoming.

'I'm going up to your house almost immediately,' said Nidderdale.

'You'll find the women at tea to a certainty between five and six,' said Melmotte.

## Chapter LXXIV

### MELMOTTE MAKES A FRIEND

'HAVE you been thinking any more about it?' Lord
Nidderdale said to the girl as soon as Madame Melmotte had succeeded in leaving them alone together.

'I have thought ever so much more about it,' said
Marie.

'And what's the result?'

'Oh,—I'll have you.'

'That's right,' said Nidderdale, throwing himself on
the sofa close to her, so that he might put his arm round
her waist.

'Wait a moment, Lord Nidderdale,' she said.

'You might as well call me John.'

'Then wait a moment,—John. You think you might
as well marry me, though you don't love me a bit.'

'That's not true, Marie.'

'Yes it is;—it's quite true. And I think just the same,
—that I might as well marry you, though I don't love
you a bit.'

'But you will.'

'I don't know. I don't feel like it just at present. You
had better know the exact truth, you know. I have told
my father that I did not think you'd ever come again,
but that if you did I would accept you. But I'm not going
to tell any stories about it. You know who I've been in
love with.'

'But you can't be in love with him now.'

'Why not? I can't marry him. I know that. And if he
were to come to me, I don't think that I would. He has
behaved bad.'

'Have I behaved bad?'

'Not like him. You never did care, and you never said
you cared.'

'Oh yes,—I have.'

'Not at first. You say it now because you think that

I shall like it. But it makes no difference now. I don't mind about your arm being there if we are to be married, only it's just as well for both of us to look on it as business.'

'How very hard you are, Marie.'

'No, I ain't. I wasn't hard to Sir Felix Carbury, and so I tell you. I did love him.'

'Surely you have found him out now.'

'Yes, I have,' said Marie. 'He's a poor creature.'

'He has just been thrashed, you know, in the streets,— most horribly.' Marie had not been told of this, and started back from her lover's arms. 'You hadn't heard it?'

'Who has thrashed him?'

'I don't want to tell the story against him, but they say he has been cut about in a terrible manner.'

'Why should anybody beat him? Did he do anything?'

'There was a young lady in the question, Marie.'

'A young lady! What young lady? I don't believe it. But it's nothing to me. I don't care about anything, Lord Nidderdale;—not a bit. I suppose you've made up all that out of your own head.'

'Indeed, no. I believe he was beaten, and I believe it was about a young woman. But it signifies nothing to me, and I don't suppose it signifies much to you. Don't you think we might fix a day, Marie?'

'I don't care the least,' said Marie. 'The longer it's put off the better I shall like it;—that's all.'

'Because I'm so detestable?'

'No,—you ain't detestable. I think you are a very good fellow; only you don't care for me. But it is detestable not being able to do what one wants. It's detestable having to quarrel with everybody and never to be good friends with anybody. And it's horribly detestable having nothing on earth to give one any interest.'

'You couldn't take any interest in me?'

'Not the least.'

'Suppose you try. Wouldn't you like to know anything about the place where we live?'

'It's a castle, I know.'

'Yes;—Castle Reekie; ever so many hundred years old.'

'I hate old places. I should like a new house, and a new dress, and a new horse every week,—and a new lover. Your father lives at the castle. I don't suppose we are to go and live there too.'

'We shall be there sometimes. When shall it be?'

'The year after next.'

'Nonsense, Marie.'

'To-morrow.'

'You wouldn't be ready.'

'You may manage it all just as you like with papa. Oh, yes,—kiss me; of course you may. If I'm to belong to you what does it matter? No;—I won't say that I love you. But if ever I do say it, you may be sure it will be true. That's more than you can say of yourself,—John.'

So the interview was over and Nidderdale walked back to the house thinking of his lady love, as far as he was able to bring his mind to any operation of thinking. He was fully determined to go on with it. As far as the girl herself was concerned, she had, in these latter days, become much more attractive to him than when he had first known her. She certainly was not a fool. And, though he could not tell himself that she was altogether like a lady, still she had a manner of her own which made him think that she would be able to live with ladies. And he did think that, in spite of all she said to the contrary, she was becoming fond of him,—as he certainly had become fond of her. 'Have you been up with the ladies?' Melmotte asked him.

'Oh yes.'

'And what does Marie say?'

'That you must fix the day.'

'We'll have it very soon then;—some time next month. You'll want to get away in August. And to tell the truth so shall I. I never was worked so hard in my life as I've been this summer. The election and that horrid dinner had something to do with it. And I don't mind telling you that I've had a fearful weight on my mind in reference to money. I never had to find so many large sums in so short a time! And I'm not quite through it yet.'

'I wonder why you gave the dinner then.'

'My dear boy,'—it was very pleasant to him to call the son of a marquis his dear boy,—'as regards expenditure that was a flea-bite. Nothing that I could spend myself would have the slightest effect upon my condition,—one way or the other.'

'I wish it could be the same way with me,' said Nidderdale.

'If you chose to go into business with me instead of taking Marie's money out, it very soon would be so with you. But the burden is very great. I never know whence these panics arise, or why they come, or whither they go. But when they do come, they are like a storm at sea. It is only the strong ships that can stand the fury of the winds and waves. And then the buffeting which a man gets leaves him only half the man he was. I've had it very hard this time.'

'I suppose you are getting right now.'

'Yes;—I am getting right. I am not in any fear, if you mean that. I don't mind telling you everything as it is settled now that you are to be Marie's husband. I know that you are honest, and that if you could hurt me by repeating what I say you wouldn't do it.'

'Certainly I would not.'

'You see I've no partner,—nobody that is bound to know my affairs. My wife is the best woman in the world, but is utterly unable to understand anything about it. Of course I can't talk freely to Marie. Cohenlupe whom you see so much with me is all very well,—in his way, but I never talk over my affairs with him. He is concerned with me in one or two things,—our American railway for instance, but he has no interest generally in my house. It is all on my own shoulders, and I can tell you the weight is a little heavy. It will be the greatest comfort to me in the world if I can get you to have an interest in the matter.'

'I don't suppose I could ever really be any good at business,' said the modest young lord.

'You wouldn't come and work, I suppose. I shouldn't

expect that. But I should be glad to think that I could tell you how things are going on. Of course you heard all that was said just before the election. For forty-eight hours I had a very bad time of it then. The fact was that Alf and they who were supporting him thought that they could carry the election by running me down. They were at it for a fortnight,—perfectly unscrupulous as to what they said or what harm they might do me and others. I thought that very cruel. They couldn't get their man in, but they could and did have the effect of depreciating my property suddenly by nearly half a million of money. Think what that is!'

'I don't understand how it could be done.'

'Because you don't understand how delicate a thing is credit. They persuaded a lot of men to stay away from that infernal dinner, and consequently it was spread about the town that I was ruined. The effect upon shares which I held was instantaneous and tremendous. The Mexican railway were at 117, and they fell from that in two days to something quite nominal,—so that selling was out of the question. Cohenlupe and I between us had about 8,000 of these shares. Think what that comes to!' Nidderdale tried to calculate what it did come to, but failed altogether. 'That's what I call a blow;—a terrible blow. When a man is concerned as I am with money interests, and concerned largely with them all, he is of course exchanging one property for another every day of his life,—according as the markets go. I don't keep such a sum as that in one concern as an investment. Nobody does. Then when a panic comes, don't you see how it hits?'

'Will they never go up again?'

'Oh yes;—perhaps higher than ever. But it will take time. And in the meantime I am driven to fall back upon property intended for other purposes. That's the meaning of what you hear about that place down in Sussex which I bought for Marie. I was so driven that I was obliged to raise forty or fifty thousand wherever I could. But that will be all right in a week or two. And as for Marie's money,—that, you know, is settled.'

He quite succeeded in making Nidderdale believe every word that he spoke, and he produced also a friendly feeling in the young man's bosom, with something approaching to a desire that he might be of service to his future father-in-law. Hazily, as through a thick fog, Lord Nidderdale thought that he did see something of the troubles, as he had long seen something of the glories, of commerce on an extended scale, and an idea occurred to him that it might be almost more exciting than whist or unlimited loo. He resolved too that whatever the man might tell him should never be divulged. He was on this occasion somewhat captivated by Melmotte, and went away from the interview with a conviction that the financier was a big man;—one with whom he could sympathise, and to whom in a certain way he could become attached.

And Melmotte himself had derived positive pleasure even from a simulated confidence in his son-in-law. It had been pleasant to him to talk as though he were talking to a young friend whom he trusted. It was impossible that he could really admit any one to a participation in his secrets. It was out of the question that he should ever allow himself to be betrayed into speaking the truth of his own affairs. Of course every word he had said to Nidderdale had been a lie, or intended to corroborate lies. But it had not been only on behalf of the lies that he had talked after this fashion. Even though his friendship with the young man were but a mock friendship,—though it would too probably be turned into bitter enmity before three months had passed by,—still there was a pleasure in it. The Grendalls had left him since the day of the dinner,—Miles having sent him a letter up from the country complaining of severe illness. It was a comfort to him to have someone to whom he could speak, and he much preferred Nidderdale to Miles Grendall.

This conversation took place in the smoking-room. When it was over Melmotte went into the House, and Nidderdale strolled away to the Beargarden. The Beargarden had been opened again though with difficulty, and with diminished luxury. Nor could even this be done without rigid laws as to the payment of ready money. Herr Vossner had never more been heard of, but the bills which Vossner had left unpaid were held to be good against the club, whereas every note of hand which he had taken from the members was left in the possession of Mr. Flatfleece. Of course there was sorrow and trouble at the Beargarden; but still the institution had become so absolutely necessary to its members that it had been reopened under a new management. No one had felt this need more strongly during every hour of the day,—of the day as he counted his days, rising as he did about an hour after noon and going to bed three or four hours after midnight,—than did Dolly Longestaffe. The Beargarden had become so much to him that he had begun to doubt whether life would be even possible without such a resort for his hours. But now the club was again open, and Dolly could have his dinner and his bottle of wine with the luxury to which he was accustomed.

But at this time he was almost mad with the sense of injury. Circumstances had held out to him a prospect of almost unlimited ease and indulgence. The arrangement made as to the Pickering estate would pay all his debts, would disembarrass his own property, and would still leave him a comfortable sum in hand. Squercum had told him that if he would stick to his terms he would surely get them. He had stuck to his terms and he had got them. And now the property was sold, and the title-deeds gone,—and he had not received a penny! He did not know whom to be loudest in abusing,—his father, the Bideawhiles, or Mr. Melmotte. And then it was said that he had signed that letter! He was very open in his manner of talking about his misfortune at the club. His father was the most obstinate old fool that ever lived. As for the Bideawhiles,—he would bring an action against them. Squercum had explained all that to him. But Melmotte was the biggest rogue the world had ever produced. 'By George! the world,' he said, 'must be coming to an end. There's that infernal scoundrel sitting in Parliament just as if he had not robbed me of my

property, and forged my name, and—and—by George!
he ought to be hung. If any man ever deserved to be hung,
that man deserves to be hung.' This he spoke openly in the
coffee-room of the club, and was still speaking as Nidderdale was taking his seat at one of the tables. Dolly had
been dining, and had turned round upon his chair so as
to face some half-dozen men whom he was addressing.

Nidderdale leaving his chair walked up to him very
gently. 'Dolly,' said he, 'do not go on in that way about
Melmotte when I am in the room. I have no doubt you
are mistaken, and so you'll find out in a day or two. You
don't know Melmotte.'

'Mistaken!' Dolly still continued to exclaim with a
loud voice. 'Am I mistaken in supposing that I haven't
been paid my money?'

'I don't believe it has been owing very long.'

'Am I mistaken in supposing that my name has been
forged to a letter?'

'I am sure you are mistaken if you think that Melmotte
had anything to do with it.'

'Squercum says——'

'Never mind Squercum. We all know what are the
suspicions of a fellow of that kind.'

'I'd believe Squercum a deuced sight sooner than
Melmotte.'

'Look here, Dolly. I know more probably of Melmotte's affairs than you do or perhaps than anybody
else. If it will induce you to remain quiet for a few days
and to hold your tongue here,—I'll make myself responsible for the entire sum he owes you.'

'The devil you will.'

'I will indeed.'

Nidderdale was endeavouring to speak so that only
Dolly should hear him, and probably nobody else did
hear him; but Dolly would not lower his voice. 'That's
out of the question, you know,' he said. 'How could I
take your money? The truth is, Nidderdale, the man is
a thief, and so you'll find out, sooner or later. He has
broken open a drawer in my father's room and forged
my name to a letter. Everybody knows it. Even my

governor knows it now,—and Bideawhile. Before many
days are over you'll find that he will be in gaol for
forgery.'

This was very unpleasant, as every one knew that
Nidderdale was either engaged or becoming engaged
to Melmotte's daughter. 'Since you will speak about it
in this public way——' began Nidderdale.

'I think it ought to be spoken about in a public way,'
said Dolly.

'I deny it as publicly. I can't say anything about the
letter except that I am sure Mr. Melmotte did not put
your name to it. From what I understand there seems
to have been some blunder between your father and his
lawyer.'

'That's true enough,' said Dolly; 'but it doesn't excuse
Melmotte.'

'As to the money, there can be no more doubt that it
will be paid than that I stand here. What is it?—twenty-
five thousand, isn't it?'

'Eighty thousand, the whole.'

'Well,—eighty thousand. It's impossible to suppose
that such a man as Melmotte shouldn't be able to raise
eighty thousand pounds.'

'Why don't he do it then?' asked Dolly.

All this was very unpleasant and made the club less
social than it used to be in old days. There was an
attempt that night to get up a game of cards; but Nidderdale would not play because he was offended with Dolly
Longestaffe; and Miles Grendall was away in the country,
—a fugitive from the face of Melmotte, and Carbury was
in hiding at home with his countenance from top to bottom supported by plasters, and Montague in these days
never went to the club. At the present moment he was
again in Liverpool, having been summoned thither by
Mr. Ramsbottom. 'By George,' said Dolly, as he filled
another pipe and ordered more brandy and water, 'I
think everything is going to come to an end. I do indeed.
I never heard of such a thing before as a man being done
in this way. And then Vossner has gone off, and it seems
everybody is to pay just what he says they owed him.

And now one can't even get up a game of cards. I feel as though there were no good in hoping that things would ever come right again.'

The opinion of the club was a good deal divided as to the matter in dispute between Lord Nidderdale and Dolly Longestaffe. It was admitted by some to be 'very fishy.' If Melmotte were so great a man why didn't he pay the money, and why should he have mortgaged the property before it was really his own? But the majority of the men thought that Dolly was wrong. As to the signature of the letter, Dolly was a man who would naturally be quite unable to say what he had and what he had not signed. And then, even into the Beargarden there had filtered, through the outer world, a feeling that people were not now bound to be so punctilious in the paying of money as they were a few years since. No doubt it suited Melmotte to make use of the money, and therefore,—as he had succeeded in getting the property into his hands,— he did make use of it. But it would be forthcoming sooner or later! In this way of looking at the matter the Beargarden followed the world at large. The world at large, in spite of the terrible falling-off at the Emperor of China's dinner, in spite of all the rumours, in spite of the ruinous depreciation of the Mexican Railway stock, and of the undoubted fact that Dolly Longestaffe had not received his money, was inclined to think that Melmotte would 'pull through.'

## Chapter LXXV

### IN BRUTON STREET

MR. SQUERCUM all this time was in a perfect fever of hard work and anxiety. It may be said of him that he had been quite sharp enough to perceive the whole truth. He did really know it all,—if he could prove that which he knew. He had extended his inquiries in the city till he had convinced himself that,

whatever wealth Melmotte might have had twelve
months ago, there was not enough of it left at present
to cover the liabilities. Squercum was quite sure that
Melmotte was not a falling, but a fallen star,—perhaps
not giving sufficient credence to the recuperative powers
of modern commerce. Squercum told a certain stock-
broker in the City, who was his specially confidential
friend, that Melmotte was a 'gone coon.' The stock-
broker made also some few inquiries, and on that evening agreed with Squercum that Melmotte was a 'gone
coon.' If such were the case it would positively be the
making of Squercum if it could be so managed that he
should appear as the destroying angel of this offensive
dragon. So Squercum raged among the Bideawhiles,
who were unable altogether to shut their doors against
him. They could not dare to bid defiance to Squercum,
—feeling that they had themselves blundered, and feeling also that they must be careful not to seem to screen a
fault by a falsehood. 'I suppose you give it up about the
letter having been signed by my client,' said Squercum
to the elder of the two younger Bideawhiles.

'I give up nothing and I assert nothing,' said the
superior attorney. 'Whether the letter be genuine or
not we had no reason to believe it to be otherwise. The
young gentleman's signature is never very plain, and
this one is about as like any other as that other would be
like the last.'

'Would you let me look at it again, Mr. Bideawhile?'
Then the letter which had been very often inspected
during the last ten days was handed to Mr. Squercum.
'It's a stiff resemblance;—such as he never could have
written had he tried it ever so.'

'Perhaps not, Mr. Squercum. We are not generally
on the look out for forgeries in letters from our clients or
our clients' sons.'

'Just so, Mr. Bideawhile. But then Mr. Longestaffe
had already told you that his son would not sign the
letter.'

'How is one to know when and how and why a young
man like that will change his purpose?'

'Just so, Mr. Bideawhile. But you see, after such a declaration as that on the part of my client's father, the letter,—which is in itself a little irregular perhaps——'

'I don't know that it's irregular at all.'

'Well;—it didn't reach you in a very confirmatory manner. We'll just say that. What Mr. Longestaffe can have been at to wish to give up his title-deeds without getting anything for them——'

'Excuse me, Mr. Squercum, but that's between Mr. Longestaffe and us.'

'Just so;—but as Mr. Longestaffe and you have jeopardised my client's property it is natural that I should make a few remarks. I think you'd have made a few remarks yourself, Mr. Bideawhile, if the case had been reversed. I shall bring the matter before the Lord Mayor, you know.' To this Mr. Bideawhile said not a word. 'And I think I understand you now that you do not intend to insist on the signature as being genuine.'

'I say nothing about it, Mr. Squercum. I think you'll find it very hard to prove that it's not genuine.'

'My client's oath, Mr. Bideawhile.'

'I'm afraid your client is not always very clear as to what he does.'

'I don't know what you mean by that, Mr. Bideawhile. I fancy that if I were to speak in that way of your client you would be very angry with me. Besides, what does it all amount to? Will the old gentleman say that he gave the letter into his son's hands, so that, even if such a freak should have come into my client's head, he could have signed it and sent it off? If I understand, Mr. Longestaffe says that he locked the letter up in a drawer in the very room which Melmotte occupied, and that he afterwards found the drawer open. It won't, I suppose, be alleged that my client knew so little what he was about that he broke open the drawer in order that he might get at the letter. Look at it whichever way you will, he did not sign it, Mr. Bideawhile.'

'I have never said he did. All I say is that we had fair ground for supposing that it was his letter. I really don't know that I can say anything more.'

'Only that we are to a certain degree in the same boat together in this matter.'

'I won't admit even that, Mr. Squercum.'

'The difference being that your client by his fault has jeopardised his own interests and those of my client, while my client has not been in fault at all. I shall bring the matter forward before the Lord Mayor to-morrow, and as at present advised shall ask for an investigation with reference to a charge of fraud. I presume you will be served with a subpœna to bring the letter into court.'

'If so you may be sure that we shall produce it.' Then Mr. Squercum took his leave and went straight away to Mr. Bumby, a barrister well known in the City. The game was too powerful to be hunted down by Mr. Squercum's unassisted hands. He had already seen Mr. Bumby on the matter more than once. Mr. Bumby was inclined to doubt whether it might not be better to get the money, or some guarantee for the money. Mr. Bumby thought that if a bill at three months could be had for Dolly's share of the property it might be expedient to take it. Mr. Squercum suggested that the property itself might be recovered, no genuine sale having been made. Mr. Bumby shook his head. 'Title-deeds give possession, Mr. Squercum. You don't suppose that the company which has lent money to Melmotte on the title-deeds would have to lose it. Take the bill; and if it is dishonoured run your chance of what you'll get out of the property. There must be assets.'

'Every rap will have been made over,' said Mr. Squercum.

This took place on the Monday, the day on which Melmotte had offered his full confidence to his proposed son-in-law. On the following Wednesday three gentlemen met together in the study in the house in Bruton Street from which it was supposed that the letter had been abstracted. There were Mr. Longestaffe, the father, Dolly Longestaffe, and Mr. Bideawhile. The house was still in Melmotte's possession, and Melmotte and Mr. Longestaffe were no longer on friendly terms. Direct application for permission to have this meeting in this place had been formally made to Mr. Melmotte, and he had complied. The meeting took place at eleven o'clock—a terribly early hour. Dolly had at first hesitated as to placing himself as he thought between the fire of two enemies, and Mr. Squercum had told him that as the matter would probably soon be made public, he could not judiciously refuse to meet his father and the old family lawyer. Therefore Dolly had attended, at great personal inconvenience to himself. 'By George, it's hardly worth having if one is to take all this trouble about it,' Dolly had said to Lord Grasslough, with whom he had fraternised since the quarrel with Nidderdale. Dolly entered the room last, and at that time neither Mr. Longestaffe nor Mr. Bidewhile had touched the drawer, or even the table, in which the letter had been deposited.

'Now, Mr. Longestaffe,' said Mr. Bidewhile, 'perhaps you will show us where you think you put the letter.'

'I don't think at all,' said he. 'Since the matter has been discussed the whole thing has come back upon my memory.'

'I never signed it,' said Dolly, standing with his hands in his pockets and interrupting his father.

'Nobody says you did, sir,' rejoined the father with an angry voice. 'If you will condescend to listen we may perhaps arrive at the truth.'

'But somebody has said that I did. I've been told that Mr. Bidewhile says so.'

'No, Mr. Longestaffe; no. We have never said so. We have only said that we had no reason for supposing the letter to be other than genuine. We have never gone beyond that.'

'Nothing on earth would have made me sign it,' said Dolly. 'Why should I have given my property up before I got my money? I never heard such a thing in my life.'

The father looked up at the lawyer and shook his head, testifying as to the hopelessness of his son's obstinacy. 'Now, Mr. Longestaffe,' continued the lawyer, 'let us see where you put the letter.'

Then the father very slowly, and with much dignity of deportment, opened the drawer,—the second drawer from the top, and took from it a bundle of papers very carefully folded and docketed, 'There,' said he, 'the letter was not placed in the envelope but on the top of it, and the two were the two first documents in the bundle.' He went on to say that as far as he knew no other paper had been taken away. He was quite certain that he had left the drawer locked. He was very particular in regard to that particular drawer, and he remembered that about this time Mr. Melmotte had been in the room with him when he had opened it, and,—as he was certain, —had locked it again. At that special time there had been, he said, considerable intimacy between him and Melmotte. It was then that Mr. Melmotte had offered him a seat at the Board of the Mexican railway.

'Of course he picked the lock, and stole the letter,' said Dolly. 'It's as plain as a pikestaff. It's clear enough to hang any man.'

'I am afraid that it falls short of evidence, however strong and just may be the suspicion induced,' said the lawyer. 'Your father for a time was not quite certain about the letter.'

'He thought that I had signed it,' said Dolly.

'I am quite certain now,' rejoined the father angrily. 'A man has to collect his memory before he can be sure of anything.'

'I am thinking you know how it would go to a jury.'

'What I want to know is how are we to get the money,' said Dolly. 'I should like to see him hung,—of course; but I'd sooner have the money. Squercum says——'

'Adolphus, we don't want to know here what Mr. Squercum says.'

'I don't know why what Mr. Squercum says shouldn't be as good as what Mr. Bideawhile says. Of course Squercum doesn't sound very aristocratic.'

'Quite as much so as Bideawhile, no doubt,' said the lawyer laughing.

'No; Squercum isn't aristocratic, and Fetter Lane is a good deal lower than Lincoln's Inn. Nevertheless Squercum may know what he's about. It was Squercum who was first down upon Melmotte in this matter, and if it wasn't for Squercum we shouldn't know as much about it as we do at present.' Squercum's name was odious to the elder Longestaffe. He believed, probably without much reason, that all his family troubles came to him from Squercum, thinking that if his son would have left his affairs in the hands of the old Slows and the old Bideawhiles, money would never have been scarce with him, and that he would not have made this terrible blunder about the Pickering property. And the sound of Squercum, as his son knew, was horrid to his ears. He hummed and hawed, and fumed and fretted about the room, shaking his head and frowning. His son looked at him as though quite astonished at his displeasure. 'There's nothing more to be done here, sir, I suppose,' said Dolly putting on his hat.

'Nothing more,' said Mr. Bideawhile. 'It may be that I shall have to instruct counsel, and I thought it well that I should see in the presence of both of you exactly how the thing stood. You speak so positively, Mr. Longestaffe, that there can be no doubt?'

'There is no doubt.'

'And now perhaps you had better lock the drawer in our presence. Stop a moment—I might as well see whether there is any sign of violence having been used.' So saying Mr. Bideawhile knelt down in front of the table and began to examine the lock. This he did very carefully and satisfied himself that there was 'no sign of violence.' 'Whoever has done it, did it very well,' said Bideawhile.

'Of course Melmotte did it,' said Dolly Longestaffe standing immediately over Bideawhile's shoulder.

At that moment there was a knock at the door,—a very distinct, and, we may say, a formal knock. There are those who knock and immediately enter without waiting for the sanction asked. Had he who knocked done so on this occasion Mr. Bideawhile would have been found still on his knees, with his nose down to the level of the keyhole. But the intruder did not intrude rapidly, and the lawyer jumped on to his feet, almost upsetting Dolly with the effort. There was a pause, during which Mr.

Bideawhile moved away from the table,—as he might have done had he been picking a lock;—and then Mr. Longestaffe bade the stranger come in with a sepulchral voice. The door was opened, and Mr. Melmotte appeared.

Now Mr. Melmotte's presence certainly had not been expected. It was known that it was his habit to be in the City at this hour. It was known also that he was well aware that this meeting was to be held in this room at this special hour,—and he might well have surmised with what view. There was now declared hostility between both the Longestaffes and Mr. Melmotte, and it certainly was supposed by all the gentlemen concerned that he would not have put himself out of the way to meet them on this occasion. 'Gentlemen,' he said, 'perhaps you think that I am intruding at the present moment.' No one said that he did not think so. The elder Longestaffe simply bowed very coldly. Mr. Bideawhile stood upright and thrust his thumbs into his waistcoat pockets. Dolly, who at first forgot to take his hat off, whistled a bar, and then turned a pirouette on his heel. That was his mode of expressing his thorough surprise at the appearance of his debtor. 'I fear that you do think I am intruding,' said Melmotte, 'but I trust that what I have to say will be held to excuse me. I see, sir,' he said, turning to Mr. Longestaffe, and glancing at the still open drawer, 'that you have been examining your desk. I hope that you will be more careful in locking it than you were when you left it before.'

'The drawer was locked when I left it,' said Mr. Longestaffe. 'I make no deductions and draw no conclusions, but the drawer was locked.'

'Then I should say it must have been locked when you returned to it.'

'No, sir, I found it open. I make no deductions and draw no conclusions,—but I left it locked and I found it open.'

'I should make a deduction and draw a conclusion,' said Dolly; 'and that would be that somebody else had opened it.'

'This can answer no purpose at all,' said Bideawhile.

'It was but a chance remark,' said Melmotte. 'I did not come here out of the City at very great personal inconvenience to myself to squabble about the lock of the drawer. As I was informed that you three gentlemen would be here together, I thought the opportunity a suitable one for meeting you and making you an offer about this unfortunate business.' He paused a moment; but neither of the three spoke. It did occur to Dolly to ask them to wait while he should fetch Squercum; but on second thoughts he reflected that a great deal of trouble would have to be taken, and probably for no good. 'Mr. Bideawhile, I believe,' suggested Melmotte; and the lawyer bowed his head. 'If I remember rightly I wrote to you offering to pay the money due to your clients——'

'Squercum is my lawyer,' said Dolly.

'That will make no difference.'

'It makes a deal of difference,' said Dolly.

'I wrote,' continued Melmotte, 'offering my bills at three and six months' date.'

'They couldn't be accepted, Mr. Melmotte.'

'I would have allowed interest. I never have had my bills refused before.'

'You must be aware, Mr. Melmotte,' said the lawyer, 'that the sale of a property is not like an ordinary mercantile transaction in which bills are customarily given and taken. The understanding was that money should be paid in the usual way. And when we learned, as we did learn, that the property had been at once mortgaged by you, of course we became,—well, I think I may be justified in saying more than suspicious. It was a most,—most—unusual proceeding. You say you have another offer to make, Mr. Melmotte.'

'Of course I have been short of money. I have had enemies whose business it has been for some time past to run down my credit, and, with my credit, has fallen the value of stocks in which it has been known that I have been largely interested. I tell you the truth openly. When I purchased Pickering I had no idea that the payment of such a sum of money could inconvenience me in the least. When the time came at which I should pay it, stocks were so depreciated that it was impossible to sell. Very hostile proceedings are threatened against me now. Accusations are made, false as hell,'—Mr. Melmotte as he spoke raised his voice and looked round the room,—'but which at the present crisis may do me most cruel damage. I have come to say that, if you will undertake to stop proceedings which have been commenced in the City, I will have fifty thousand pounds,—which is the amount due to these two gentlemen,—ready for payment on Friday at noon.'

'I have taken no proceedings as yet,' said Bideawhile.

'It's Squercum,' says Dolly.

'Well, sir,' continued Melmotte addressing Dolly, 'let me assure you that if these proceedings are stayed the money will be forthcoming;—but if not, I cannot produce the money. I little thought two months ago that I should ever have to make such a statement in reference to such a sum as fifty thousand pounds. But so it is. To raise that money by Friday, I shall have to cripple my resources frightfully. It will be done at a terrible cost. But what Mr. Bideawhile says is true. I have no right to suppose that the purchase of this property should be looked upon as an ordinary commercial transaction. The money should have been paid,—and, if you will now take my word, the money shall be paid. But this cannot be done if I am made to appear before the Lord Mayor to-morrow. The accusations brought against me are damnably false. I do not know with whom they have originated. Whoever did originate them, they are damnably false. But unfortunately, false as they are, in the present crisis, they may be ruinous to me. Now gentlemen, perhaps you will give me an answer.'

Both the father and the lawyer looked at Dolly. Dolly was in truth the accuser through the mouthpiece of his attorney Squercum. It was at Dolly's instance that these proceedings were being taken. 'I, on behalf of my client,' said Mr. Bideawhile, 'will consent to wait till Friday at noon.'

'I presume, Adolphus, that you will say as much,' said the elder Longestaffe.

Dolly Longestaffe was certainly not an impressionable person, but Melmotte's eloquence had moved even him. It was not that he was sorry for the man, but that at the present moment he believed him. Though he had been absolutely sure that Melmotte had forged his name or caused it to be forged,—and did not now go so far into the matter as to abandon that conviction,—he had been talked into crediting the reasons given for Melmotte's temporary distress, and also into a belief that the money would be paid on Friday. Something of the effect which Melmotte's false confessions had had upon Lord Nidderdale, they now also had on Dolly Longestaffe. 'I'll ask Squercum, you know,' he said.

'Of course Mr. Squercum will act as you instruct him,' said Bideawhile.

'I'll ask Squercum. I'll go to him at once. I can't do any more than that. And upon my word, Mr. Melmotte, you've given me a great deal of trouble.'

Melmotte with a smile apologized. Then it was settled that they three should meet in that very room on Friday at noon, and that the payment should then be made,— Dolly stipulating that as his father would be attended by Bideawhile, so would he be attended by Squercum. To this Mr. Longestaffe senior yielded with a very bad grace.

## Chapter LXXVI

### HETTA AND HER LOVER

LADY CARBURY was at this time so miserable in regard to her son that she found herself unable to be active as she would otherwise have been in her endeavours to separate Paul Montague and her daughter. Roger had come up to town and given his opinion, very freely at any rate with regard to Sir Felix. But Roger had immediately returned to Suffolk, and the poor mother in want of assistance and consolation turned naturally to Mr. Broune, who came to see her for a few minutes almost every evening. It had now become almost a part of Mr. Broune's life to see Lady Carbury once in the day. She told him of the two propositions which Roger had made: first, that she should fix her residence in some second-rate French or German town, and that Sir Felix should be made to go with her; and, secondly, that she should take possession of Carbury manor for six months. 'And where would Mr. Carbury go?' asked Mr. Broune.

'He's so good that he doesn't care what he does with himself. There's a cottage on the place, he says, that he would move to.' Mr. Broune shook his head. Mr. Broune did not think that an offer so quixotically generous as this should be accepted. As to the German or French town, Mr. Broune said that the plan was no doubt feasible, but he doubted whether the thing to be achieved was worth the terrible sacrifice demanded. He was inclined to think that Sir Felix should go to the colonies. 'That he might drink himself to death,' said Lady Carbury, who now had no secrets from Mr. Broune. Sir Felix in the meantime was still in the doctor's hands upstairs. He had no doubt been very severely thrashed, but there was not in truth very much ailing him beyond the cuts on his face. He was, however, at the present moment better satisfied to be an invalid than to have to come out of his room and to meet the world. 'As to Melmotte,' said Mr. Broune, 'they say now that he is in some terrible mess which will ruin him and all who have trusted him.'

'And the girl?'

'It is impossible to understand it at all. Melmotte was to have been summoned before the Lord Mayor to-day on some charge of fraud;—but it was postponed. And I was told this morning that Nidderdale still means to marry the girl. I don't think anybody knows the truth about it. We shall hold our tongue about him till we really do know something.' The 'we' of whom Mr. Broune spoke was, of course, the 'Morning Breakfast Table.'

But in all this there was nothing about Hetta. Hetta, however, thought very much of her own condition, and found herself driven to take some special step by the receipt of two letters from her lover, written to her from Liverpool. They had never met since she had confessed her love to him. The first letter she did not at once answer, as she was at that moment waiting to hear what Roger Carbury would say about Mrs. Hurtle. Roger Carbury had spoken, leaving a conviction on her mind that Mrs. Hurtle was by no means a fiction,—but indeed a fact very injurious to her happiness. Then Paul's second love-letter had come, full of joy, and love, and contentment,—with not a word in it which seemed to have been in the slightest degree influenced by the existence of a Mrs. Hurtle. Had there been no Mrs. Hurtle, the letter would have been all that Hetta could have desired; and she could have answered it, unless forbidden by her mother, with all a girl's usual enthusiastic affection for her chosen lord. But it was impossible that she should now answer it in that strain;—and it was equally impossible that she should leave such letters unanswered. Roger had told her to 'ask himself;' and she now found herself constrained to bid him either come to her and answer the question, or, if he thought it better, to give her some written account of Mrs. Hurtle,—so that she might know who the lady was, and whether the lady's condition did in any way interfere with her own happiness. So she wrote to Paul, as follows:—

'Welbeck Street, 16th July, 18—.

'MY DEAR PAUL.' She found that after that which had passed between them she could not call him 'My dear Sir,' or 'My dear Mr. Montague,' and that it must either be 'Sir' or 'My dear Paul.' He was dear to her,—very dear; and she thought that he had not been as yet convicted of any conduct bad enough to force her to treat him as an outcast. Had there been no Mrs. Hurtle he would have been her 'Dearest Paul,'—but she made her choice, and so commenced.

'MY DEAR PAUL,

'A strange report has come round to me about a lady called Mrs. Hurtle. I have been told that she is an American lady living in London, and that she is engaged to be your wife. I cannot believe this. It is too horrid to be true. But I fear,—I fear there is something true that will be very very sad for me to hear. It was from my brother I first heard it,—who was of course bound to tell me anything he knew. I have talked to mamma about it, and to my cousin Roger. I am sure Roger knows it all;—but he will not tell me. He said,— "Ask himself." And so I ask you. Of course I can write about nothing else till I have heard about this. I am sure I need not tell you that it has made me very unhappy. If you cannot come and see me at once, you had better write. I have told mamma about this letter.' Then came the difficulty of the signature, with the declaration which must naturally be attached to it. After some hesitation she subscribed herself,

'Your affectionate friend,
'HENRIETTA CARBURY.'

'Most affectionately your own Hetta' would have been the form in which she would have wished to finish the first letter she had ever written to him.

Paul received it at Liverpool on the Wednesday morning, and on the Wednesday evening he was in Welbeck Street. He had been quite aware that it had been incumbent on him to tell her the whole history of Mrs. Hurtle. He had meant to keep back—almost nothing. But it had been impossible for him to do so on that one occasion on which he had pleaded his love to her successfully. Let any reader who is intelligent in such matters say whether it would have been possible for him then to have commenced the story of Mrs. Hurtle and to have told it to the bitter end. Such a story must be postponed for a second or third interview. Or it may, indeed, be communicated by letter. When Paul was called away to Liverpool he did consider whether he should write the story. But there are many reasons strong against such written communications. A man may desire that the woman he loves should hear the record of his folly,—so that, in after days, there may be nothing to detect: so that, should the Mrs. Hurtle of his life at any time intrude upon his happiness, he may with a clear brow and un-daunted heart say to his beloved one,—'Ah, this is the trouble of which I spoke to you.' And then he and his beloved one will be in one cause together. But he hardly wishes to supply his beloved one with a written record of his folly. And then who does not know how much tenderness a man may show to his own faults by the tone of his voice, by half-spoken sentences, and by an admixture of words of love for the lady who has filled up the vacant space once occupied by the Mrs. Hurtle of his romance? But the written record must go through from beginning to end, self-accusing, thoroughly perspicuous, with no sweet, soft falsehoods hidden under the half-expressed truth. The soft falsehoods which would be sweet as the scent of violets in a personal interview, would stand in danger of being denounced as deceit added to deceit, if sent in a letter. I think therefore that Paul Montague did quite right in hurrying up to London.

He asked for Miss Carbury, and when told that Miss Henrietta was with her mother, he sent his name up and said that he would wait in the dining-room. He had thoroughly made up his mind to this course. They should know that he had come at once; but he would not, if it could be helped, make his statement in the presence of Lady Carbury. Then, upstairs, there was a little dis-cussion. Hetta pleaded her right to see him alone. She had done what Roger had advised, and had done it with her mother's consent. Her mother might be sure that she would not again accept her lover till this story of Mrs. Hurtle had been sifted to the very bottom. But she must herself hear what her lover had to say for himself. Felix was at the time in the drawing-room and suggested that he should go down and see Paul Montague on his sister's behalf;—but his mother looked at him with scorn, and his sister quietly said that she would rather see Mr. Montague herself. Felix had been so cowed by circumstances that he did not say another word, and Hetta left the room alone.

When she entered the parlour Paul stept forward to take her in his arms. That was a matter of course. She knew it would be so, and she had prepared herself for it. 'Paul,' she said, 'let me hear about all this—first.' She sat down at some distance from him,—and he found himself compelled to seat himself at some distance from her.

'And so you have heard of Mrs. Hurtle,' he said, with a faint attempt at a smile.

'Yes;—Felix told me, and Roger evidently had heard about her.'

'Oh yes; Roger Carbury has heard about her from the beginning;—knows the whole history almost as well as I know it myself. I don't think your brother is as well informed.'

'Perhaps not. But—isn't it a story that—concerns me?'

'Certainly it so far concerns you, Hetta, that you ought to know it. And I trust you will believe that it was my intention to tell it you.'

'I will believe anything that you will tell me.'

'If so, I don't think that you will quarrel with me when you know all. I was engaged to marry Mrs. Hurtle.'

'Is she a widow?'—He did not answer this at once. 'I suppose she must be a widow if you were going to marry her.'

'Yes;—she is a widow. She was divorced.'

'Oh, Paul! And she is an American?'

'Yes.'

'And you loved her?'

Montague was desirous of telling his own story, and did not wish to be interrogated. 'If you will allow me I will tell it you all from beginning to end.'

'Oh, certainly. But I suppose you loved her. If you meant to marry her you must have loved her.' There was a frown upon Hetta's brow and a tone of anger in her voice which made Paul uneasy.

'Yes;—I loved her once; but I will tell you all.' Then he did tell his story, with a repetition of which the reader need not be detained. Hetta listened with fair attention,

—not interrupting very often, though when she did interrupt, the little words which she spoke were bitter enough. But she heard the story of the long journey across the American continent, of the ocean journey before the end of which Paul had promised to make this woman his wife. 'Had she been divorced then?' asked Hetta,—'because I believe they get themselves divorced just when they like.' Simple as the question was he could not answer it. 'I could only know what she told me,' he said, as he went on with his story. Then Mrs. Hurtle had gone on to Paris, and he, as soon as he reached Carbury, had revealed everything to Roger. 'Did you give her up then?' demanded Hetta with stern severity. No,—not then. He had gone back to San Francisco, and,—he had not intended to say that the engagement had been renewed, but he was forced to acknowledge that it had not been broken off. Then he had written to her on his second return to England,—and then she had appeared in London at Mrs. Pipkin's lodgings in Islington. 'I can hardly tell you how terrible that was to me,' he said, 'for I had by that time become quite aware that my happiness must depend upon you.' He tried the gentle, soft falsehoods that should have been as sweet as violets. Perhaps they were sweet. It is odd how stern a girl can be, while her heart is almost breaking with love. Hetta was very stern.

'But Felix says you took her to Lowestoft,—quite the other day.'

Montague had intended to tell all,—almost all. There was a something about the journey to Lowestoft which it would be impossible to make Hetta understand, and he thought that that might be omitted. 'It was on account of her health.'

'Oh;—on account of her health. And did you go to the play with her?'

'I did.'

'Was that for her—health?'

'Oh, Hetta, do not speak to me like that! Cannot you understand that when she came here, following me, I could not desert her?'

'I cannot understand why you deserted her at all,' said Hetta. 'You say you loved her, and you promised to marry her. It seems horrid to me to marry a divorced woman,—a woman who just says that she was divorced. But that is because I don't understand American ways. And I am sure you must have loved her when you took her to the theatre, and down to Lowestoft,—for her health. That was only a week ago.'

'It was nearly three weeks,' said Paul in despair.

'Oh;—nearly three weeks! That is not such a very long time for a gentleman to change his mind on such a matter. You were engaged to her, not three weeks ago.'

'No, Hetta, I was not engaged to her then.'

'I suppose she thought you were when she went to Lowestoft with you.'

'She wanted then to force me to—to—to—. Oh, Hetta, it is so hard to explain, but I am sure that you understand. I do know that you do not, cannot think that I have, even for one moment, been false to you.'

'But why should you be false to her? Why should I step in and crush all her hopes? I can understand that Roger should think badly of her because she was— divorced. Of course he would. But an engagement is an engagement. You had better go back to Mrs. Hurtle and tell her that you are quite ready to keep your promise.'

'She knows now that it is all over.'

'I dare say you will be able to persuade her to reconsider it. When she came all the way here from San Francisco after you, and when she asked you to take her to the theatre, and to Lowestoft—because of her health, she must be very much attached to you. And she is waiting here,—no doubt on purpose for you. She is a very old friend,—very old,—and you ought not to treat her unkindly. Good bye, Mr. Montague. I think you had better lose no time in going—back to Mrs. Hurtle.' All this she said with sundry little impedimentary gurgles in her throat, but without a tear and without any sign of tenderness.

'You don't mean to tell me, Hetta, that you are going to quarrel with me!'

'I don't know about quarrelling. I don't wish to quarrel with any one. But of course we can't be friends when you have married—Mrs. Hurtle.'

'Nothing on earth would induce me to marry her.'

'Of course I cannot say anything about that. When they told me this story I did not believe them. No; I hardly believed Roger when,—he would not tell it for he was too kind,—but when he would not contradict it. It seemed to be almost impossible that you should have come to me just at the very same moment. For, after all, Mr. Montague, nearly three weeks is a very short time. That trip to Lowestoft couldn't have been much above a week before you came to me.'

'What does it matter?'

'Oh no; of course not;—nothing to you. I think I will go away now, Mr. Montague. It was very good of you to come and tell me all. It makes it so much easier.'

'Do you mean to say that—you are going to—throw me over?'

'I don't want you to throw Mrs. Hurtle over. Good bye.'

'Hetta!'

'No; I will not have you lay your hand upon me. Good night, Mr. Montague.' And so she left him.

Paul Montague was beside himself with dismay as he left the house. He had never allowed himself for a moment to believe that this affair of Mrs. Hurtle would really separate him from Hetta Carbury. If she could only really know it all, there could be no such result. He had been true to her from the first moment in which he had seen her, never swerving from his love. It was to be supposed that he had loved some woman before; but, as the world goes, that would not, could not, affect her. But her anger was founded on the presence of Mrs. Hurtle in London,—which he would have given half his possessions to have prevented. But when she did come, was he to have refused to see her? Would Hetta have wished him to be cold and cruel like that? No doubt he had behaved badly to Mrs. Hurtle;—but that trouble he had overcome. And now Hetta was quarrelling with him, though he certainly had never behaved badly to her.

He was almost angry with Hetta as he walked home. Everything that he could do he had done for her. For her sake he had quarrelled with Roger Carbury. For her sake,—in order that he might be effectually free from Mrs. Hurtle,—he had determined to endure the spring of the wild cat. For her sake,—so he told himself,—he had been content to abide by that odious railway company, in order that he might if possible preserve an income on which to support her. And now she told him that they must part,—and that only because he had not been cruelly indifferent to the unfortunate woman who had followed him from America. There was no logic in it, no reason,—and, as he thought, very little heart. 'I don't want you to throw Mrs. Hurtle over,' she had said. Why should Mrs. Hurtle be anything to her? Surely she might have left Mrs. Hurtle to fight her own battles. But they were all against him. Roger Carbury, Lady Carbury, and Sir Felix; and the end of it would be that she would be forced into marriage with a man almost old enough to be her father! She could not ever really have loved him. That was the truth. She must be incapable of such love as was his own for her. True love always forgives. And here there was really so very little to forgive! Such were his thoughts as he went to bed that night. But he probably omitted to ask himself whether he would have forgiven her very readily had he found that she had been living 'nearly three weeks ago' in close intercourse with another lover of whom he had hitherto never even heard the name. But then,—as all the world knows,—there is a wide difference between young men and young women!

Hetta, as soon as she had dismissed her lover, went up at once to her own room. Thither she was soon followed by her mother, whose anxious ear had heard the closing of the front door. 'Well; what has he said?' asked Lady Carbury. Hetta was in tears,—or very nigh to tears,—struggling to repress them, and struggling almost successfully. 'You have found that what we told you about that woman was all true.'

'Enough of it was true,' said Hetta, who, angry as she

was with her lover, was not on that account less angry with her mother for disturbing her bliss.

'What do you mean by that, Hetta? Had you not better speak to me openly?'

'I say, mamma, that enough was true. I do not know how to speak more openly. I need not go into all the miserable story of the woman. He is like other men, I suppose. He has entangled himself with some abominable creature and then when he is tired of her thinks that he has nothing to do but to say so,—and to begin with somebody else.'

'Roger Carbury is very different.'

'Oh, mamma, you will make me ill if you go on like that. It seems to me that you do not understand in the least.'

'I say he is not like that.'

'Not in the least. Of course I know that he is not in the least like that.'

'I say that he can be trusted.'

'Of course he can be trusted. Who doubts it?'

'And that if you would give yourself to him, there would be no cause for any alarm.'

'Mamma,' said Hetta jumping up, 'how can you talk to me in that way? As soon as one man doesn't suit, I am to give myself to another! Oh, mamma, how can you propose it? Nothing on earth will ever induce me to be more to Roger Carbury than I am now.'

'You have told Mr. Montague that he is not to come here again?'

'I don't know what I told him, but he knows very well what I mean.'

'That it is all over?' Hetta made no reply. 'Hetta, I have a right to ask that, and I have a right to expect a reply. I do not say that you have hitherto behaved badly about Mr. Montague.'

'I have not behaved badly. I have told you everything. I have done nothing that I am ashamed of.'

'But we have now found out that he has behaved very badly. He has come here to you,—with unexampled treachery to your cousin Roger——'

'I deny that,' exclaimed Hetta.

'And at the very time was almost living with this woman who says that she is divorced from her husband in America! Have you told him that you will see him no more?'

'He understood that.'

'If you have not to'ld him so plainly, I must tell him.'

'Mamma, you need not trouble yourself. I have told him very plainly.' Then Lady Carbury expressed herself satisfied for the moment, and left her daughter to her solitude.

## Chapter LXXVII

### ANOTHER SCENE IN BRUTON STREET

WHEN Mr. Melmotte made his promise to Mr. Longestaffe and to Dolly, in the presence of Mr. Bideawhile, that he would, on the next day but one, pay to them a sum of fifty thousand pounds, thereby completing, satisfactorily as far as they were concerned, the purchase of the Pickering property, he intended to be as good as his word. The reader knows that he had resolved to face the Longestaffe difficulty,—that he had resolved that at any rate he would not get out of it by sacrificing the property to which he had looked forward as a safe haven when storms should come. But, day by day, every resolution that he made was forced to undergo some change. Latterly he had been intent on purchasing a noble son-in-law with this money,—still trusting to the chapter of chances for his future escape from the Longestaffe and other difficulties. But Squercum had been very hard upon him; and in connexion with this accusation as to the Pickering property, there was another, which he would be forced to face also, respecting certain property in the East of London, with which the reader need not much trouble himself specially, but in reference to which it was stated that he had induced a foolish old gentleman to consent to accept railway shares in lieu of money. The old gentleman had died during the transaction, and it was asserted that the old gentleman's letter was hardly genuine. Melmotte had certainly raised between twenty and thirty thousand pounds on the property, and had made payment for it in stock which was now worth—almost nothing at all. Melmotte thought that he might face this matter successfully if the matter came upon him single-handed;—but in regard to the Longestaffes he considered that now, at this last moment, he had better pay for Pickering.

The property from which he intended to raise the necessary funds was really his own. There could be no doubt about that. It had never been his intention to make it over to his daughter. When he had placed it in her name, he had done so simply for security,—feeling that his control over his only daughter would be perfect and free from danger. No girl apparently less likely to take it into her head to defraud her father could have crept quietly about a father's house. Nor did he now think that she would disobey him when the matter was explained to her. Heavens and earth! That he should be robbed by his own child,—robbed openly, shamefully, with brazen audacity! It was impossible. But still he had felt the necessity of going about this business with some little care. It might be that she would disobey him if he simply sent for her and bade her to affix her signature here and there. He thought much about it and considered that it would be wise that his wife should be present on the occasion, and that a full explanation should be given to Marie, by which she might be made to understand that the money had in no sense become her own. So he gave instructions to his wife when he started into the city that morning; and when he returned, for the sake of making his offer to the Longestaffes, he brought with him the deeds which it would be necessary that Marie should sign, and he brought also Mr. Croll, his clerk, that Mr. Croll might witness the signature.

When he left the Longestaffes and Mr. Bideawhile he went at once to his wife's room. 'Is she here?' he asked.

'I will send for her. I have told her.'

'You haven't frightened her?'

'Why should I frighten her? It is not very easy to frighten her, Melmotte. She is changed since these young men have been so much about her.'

'I shall frighten her if she does not do as I bid her. Bid her come now.' This was said in French. Then Madame Melmotte left the room, and Melmotte arranged a lot of papers in order upon a table. Having done so, he called to Croll, who was standing on the landing-place, and told him to seat himself in the back drawing-room till he should be called. Melmotte then stood with his back to the fireplace in his wife's sitting-room, with his hands in his pockets, contemplating what might be the incidents of the coming interview. He would be very gracious,—affectionate if it were possible,—and, above all things, explanatory. But, by heavens, if there were continued opposition to his demand,—to his just demand,—if this girl should dare to insist upon exercising her power to rob him, he would not then be affectionate, —nor gracious! There was some little delay in the coming of the two women, and he was already beginning to lose his temper when Marie followed Madame Melmotte into the room. He at once swallowed his rising anger—with an effort. He would put a constraint upon himself. The affection and the graciousness should be all there,—as long as they might secure the purpose in hand.

'Marie,' he began, 'I spoke to you the other day about some property which for certain purposes was placed in your name just as we were leaving Paris.'

'Yes, papa.'

'You were such a child then,—I mean when we left Paris,—that I could hardly explain to you the purpose of what I did.'

'I understood it, papa.'

'You had better listen to me, my dear. I don't think you did quite understand it. It would have been very odd if you had, as I never explained it to you.'

'You wanted to keep it from going away if you got into trouble.'

This was so true that Melmotte did not know how at the moment to contradict the assertion. And yet he had not intended to talk of the possibility of trouble. 'I wanted to lay aside a large sum of money which should not be liable to the ordinary fluctuations of commercial enterprise.'

'So that nobody could get at it.'

'You are a little too quick, my dear.'

'Marie, why can't you let your papa speak?' said Madame Melmotte.

'But of course, my dear,' continued Melmotte, 'I had no idea of putting the money beyond my own reach. Such a transaction is very common; and in such cases a man naturally uses the name of some one who is very near and dear to him, and in whom he is sure that he can put full confidence. And it is customary to choose a young person, as there will then be less danger of the accident of death. It was for these reasons, which I am sure that you will understand, that I chose you. Of course the property remained exclusively my own.'

'But it is really mine,' said Marie.

'No, miss; it was never yours,' said Melmotte, almost bursting out into anger, but restraining himself. 'How could it become yours, Marie? Did I ever make you a gift of it?'

'But I know that it did become mine,—legally.'

'By a quibble of law,—yes; but not so as to give you any right to it. I always draw the income.'

'But I could stop that, papa,—and if I were married, of course it would be stopped.'

Then, quick as a flash of lightning, another idea occurred to Melmotte, who feared that he already began to see that this child of his might be stiff-necked. 'As we are thinking of your marriage,' he said, 'it is necessary that a change should be made. Settlements must be drawn for the satisfaction of Lord Nidderdale and his father. The old Marquis is rather hard upon me, but the marriage is so splendid that I have consented. You must now sign these papers in four or five places. Mr. Croll is here, in the next room, to witness your signature, and I will call him.'

'Wait a moment, papa.'

'Why should we wait?'

'I don't think I will sign them.'

'Why not sign them? You can't really suppose that the property is your own. You could not even get it if you did think so.'

'I don't know how that may be; but I had rather not sign them. If I am to be married, I ought not to sign anything except what he tells me.'

'He has no authority over you yet. I have authority over you. Marie, do not give more trouble. I am very much pressed for time. Let me call in Mr. Croll.'

'No, papa,' she said.

Then came across his brow that look which had probably first induced Marie to declare that she would endure to be 'cut to pieces,' rather than to yield in this or that direction. The lower jaw squared itself, and the teeth became set, and the nostrils of his nose became extended, —and Marie began to prepare herself to be 'cut to pieces.' But he reminded himself that there was another game which he had proposed to play before he resorted to anger and violence. He would tell her how much depended on her compliance. Therefore he relaxed the frown,—as well as he knew how, and softened his face towards her, and turned again to his work. 'I am sure, Marie, that you will not refuse to do this when I explain to you its importance to me. I must have that property for use in the city to-morrow, or——I shall be ruined.' The statement was very short, but the manner in which he made it was not without effect.

'Oh!' shrieked his wife.

'It is true. These harpies have so beset me about the election that they have lowered the price of every stock in which I am concerned, and have brought the Mexican Railway so low that they cannot be sold at all. I don't like bringing my troubles home from the city; but on this occasion I cannot help it. The sum locked up here is very large, and I am compelled to use it. In point of fact it is necessary to save us from destruction.' This he said, very slowly, and with the utmost solemnity.

'But you told me just now you wanted it because I was going to be married,' rejoined Marie.

A liar has many points to his favour,—but he has this

against him, that unless he devote more time to the management of his lies than life will generally allow, he cannot make them tally. Melmotte was thrown back for a moment, and almost felt that the time for violence had come. He longed to be at her that he might shake the wickedness, and the folly, and the ingratitude out of her. But he once more condescended to argue and to explain. 'I think you misunderstood me, Marie. I meant you to understand that settlements must be made, and that of course I must get my own property back into my own hands before anything of that kind can be done. I tell you once more, my dear, that if you do not do as I bid you, so that I may use that property the first thing to-morrow, we are all ruined. Everything will be gone.'

'This can't be gone,' said Marie, nodding her head at the papers.

'Marie,—do you wish to see me disgraced and ruined? I have done a great deal for you.'

'You turned away the only person I ever cared for,' said Marie.

'Marie, how can you be so wicked? Do as your papa bids you,' said Madame Melmotte.

'No!' said Melmotte. 'She does not care who is ruined, because we saved her from that reprobate.'

'She will sign them now,' said Madame Melmotte.

'No;—I will not sign them,' said Marie. 'If I am to be married to Lord Nidderdale as you all say, I am sure I ought to sign nothing without telling him. And if the property was once made to be mine, I don't think I ought to give it up again because papa says that he is going to be ruined. I think that's a reason for not giving it up again.'

'It isn't yours to give. It's mine,' said Melmotte gnashing his teeth.

'Then you can do what you like with it without my signing,' said Marie.

He paused a moment, and then laying his hand gently upon her shoulder, he asked her yet once again. His voice was changed, and was very hoarse. But he still tried to be gentle with her. 'Marie,' he said, 'will you do this to save your father from destruction?'

But she did not believe a word that he said to her. How could she believe him? He had taught her to regard him as her natural enemy, making her aware that it was his purpose to use her as a chattel for his own advantage, and never allowing her for a moment to suppose that aught that he did was to be done for her happiness. And now, almost in a breath, he had told her that this money was wanted that it might be settled on her and the man to whom she was to be married, and then that it might be used to save him from instant ruin. She believed neither one story nor the other. That she should have done as she was desired in this matter can hardly be disputed. The father had used her name because he thought that he could trust her. She was his daughter and should not have betrayed his trust. But she had steeled herself to obstinacy against him in all things. Even yet, after all that had passed, although she had consented to marry Lord Nidderdale, though she had been forced by what she had learned to despise Sir Felix Carbury, there was present to her an idea that she might escape with the man she really loved. But any such hope could depend only on the possession of the money which she now claimed as her own. Melmotte had endeavoured to throw a certain supplicatory pathos into the question he had asked her; but, though he was in some degree successful with his voice, his eyes and his mouth and his forehead still threatened her. He was always threatening her. All her thoughts respecting him reverted to that inward assertion that he might 'cut her to pieces' if he liked. He repeated his question in the pathetic strain. 'Will you do this now,—to save us all from ruin?' But his eyes still threatened her.

'No;' she said, looking up into his face as though watching for the personal attack which would be made upon her; 'no, I won't.'

'Marie!' exclaimed Madame Melmotte.

She glanced round for a moment at her pseudo-mother with contempt. 'No;' she said. 'I don't think I ought,—and I won't.'

'You won't!' shouted Melmotte. She merely shook her head. 'Do you mean that you, my own child, will attempt to rob your father just at the moment you can destroy him by your wickedness?' She shook her head but said no other word.

'Nec pueros coram populo Medea trucidet.'

'Let not Medea with unnatural rage
Slaughter her mangled infants on the stage.'*

Nor will I attempt to harrow my readers by a close description of the scene which followed. Poor Marie! That cutting her up into pieces was commenced after a most savage fashion. Marie crouching down hardly uttered a sound. But Madame Melmotte frightened beyond endurance screamed at the top of her voice,—'Ah, Melmotte, tu la tueras!' And then she tried to drag him from his prey. 'Will you sign them now?' said Melmotte, panting. At that moment Croll, frightened by the screams, burst into the room. It was perhaps not the first time that he had interfered to save Melmotte from the effects of his own wrath.

'Oh, Mr. Melmotte, vat is de matter?' asked the clerk.

Melmotte was out of breath and could hardly tell his story. Marie gradually recovered herself, and crouched, cowering, in the corner of a sofa, by no means vanquished in spirit, but with a feeling that the very life had been crushed out of her body. Madame Melmotte was standing weeping copiously, with her handkerchief up to her eyes. 'Will you sign the papers?' Melmotte demanded. Marie, lying as she was, all in a heap, merely shook her head. 'Pig!' said Melmotte,—'wicked, ungrateful pig.'

'Ah, Ma'am-moiselle,' said Croll, 'you should oblige your fader.'

'Wretched, wicked girl!' said Melmotte, collecting the papers together. Then he left the room, and followed by Croll descended to the study, whence the Longestaffes and Mr. Bideawhile had long since taken their departure.

Madame Melmotte came and stood over the girl, but for some minutes spoke never a word. Marie lay on the sofa, all in a heap, with her hair dishevelled and her dress disordered, breathing hard, but uttering no sobs and shedding no tears. The stepmother,—if she might so be called,—did not think of attempting to persuade where her husband had failed. She feared Melmotte so thoroughly, and was so timid in regard to her own person, that she could not understand the girl's courage. Melmotte was to her an awful being, powerful as Satan, —whom she never openly disobeyed, though she daily deceived him, and was constantly detected in her deceptions. Marie seemed to her to have all her father's stubborn, wicked courage, and very much of his power. At the present moment she did not dare to tell the girl that she had been wrong. But she had believed her husband when he had said that destruction was coming, and had partly believed him when he declared that the destruction might be averted by Marie's obedience. Her life had been passed in almost daily fear of destruction. To Marie the last two years of splendour had been so long that they had produced a feeling of security. But to the elder woman the two years had not sufficed to eradicate the remembrance of former reverses, and never for a moment had she felt herself to be secure. At last she asked the girl what she would like to have done for her. 'I wish he had killed me,' Marie said, slowly dragging herself up from the sofa, and retreating without another word to her own room.

In the meantime another scene was being acted in the room below. Melmotte after he reached the room hardly made a reference to his daughter,—merely saying that nothing would overcome her wicked obstinacy. He made no allusion to his own violence, nor had Croll the courage to expostulate with him now that the immediate danger was over. The Great Financier again arranged the papers, just as they had been laid out before,—as though he thought that the girl might be brought down to sign them there. And then he went on to explain to Croll what he had wanted to have done,—how necessary it was that the thing should be done, and how terribly cruel it was to him that in such a crisis of his life he should be hampered, impeded,—he did not venture to his clerk to say ruined,—by the ill-conditioned obstinacy of a girl!

He explained very fully how absolutely the property was his own, how totally the girl was without any right to withhold it from him! How monstrous in its injustice was the present position of things! In all this Croll fully agreed. Then Melmotte went on to declare that he would not feel the slightest scruple in writing Marie's signature to the papers himself. He was the girl's father and was justified in acting for her. The property was his own property, and he was justified in doing with it as he pleased. Of course he would have no scruple in writing his daughter's name. Then he looked up at the clerk. The clerk again assented,—after a fashion, not by any means with the comfortable certainty with which he had signified his accordance with his employer's first propositions. But he did not, at any rate, hint any disapprobation of the step which Melmotte proposed to take. Then Melmotte went a step farther, and explained that the only difficulty in reference to such a transaction would be that the signature of his daughter would be required to be corroborated by that of a witness before he could use it. Then he again looked up at Croll;—but on this occasion Croll did not move a muscle of his face. There certainly was no assent. Melmotte continued to look at him; but then came upon the old clerk's countenance a stern look which amounted to very strong dissent. And yet Croll had been conversant with some irregular doings in his time, and Melmotte knew well the extent of Croll's experience. Then Melmotte made a little remark to himself. 'He knows that the game is pretty well over.' 'You had better return to the city now,' he said aloud. 'I shall follow you in half an hour. It is quite possible that I may bring my daughter with me. If I can make her understand this thing I shall do so. In that case I shall want you to be ready.' Croll again smiled, and again assented, and went his way.

But Melmotte made no further attempt upon his daughter. As soon as Croll was gone he searched among various papers in his desk and drawers, and having found two signatures, those of his daughter and of this German clerk, set to work tracing them with some thin tissue paper. He commenced his present operation by bolting his door and pulling down the blinds. He practised the two signatures for the best part of an hour. Then he forged them on the various documents;—and, having completed the operation, refolded them, placed them in a locked bag of which he had always kept the key in his purse, and then, with the bag in his hand, was taken in his brougham into the city.

## Chapter LXXVIII

### MISS LONGESTAFFE AGAIN AT CAVERSHAM

ALL this time Mr. Longestaffe was necessarily detained in London while the three ladies of his family were living forlornly at Caversham. He had taken his younger daughter home on the day after his visit to Lady Monogram, and in all his intercourse with her had spoken of her suggested marriage with Mr. Brehgert as a thing utterly out of the question. Georgiana had made one little fight for her independence at the Jermyn Street Hotel. 'Indeed, papa, I think it's very hard,' she said.

'What's hard? I think a great many things are hard; but I have to bear them.'

'You can do nothing for me.'

'Do nothing for you! Haven't you got a home to live in, and clothes to wear, and a carriage to go about in,—and books to read if you choose to read them? What do you expect?'

'You know, papa, that's nonsense.'

'How do you dare to tell me that what I say is nonsense?'

'Of course there's a house to live in and clothes to wear; but what's to be the end of it? Sophia, I suppose, is going to be married.'

'I am happy to say she is,—to a most respectable young man and a thorough gentleman.'

'And Dolly has his own way of going on.'

'You have nothing to do with Adolphus.'

'Nor will he have anything to do with me. If I don't marry what's to become of me? It isn't that Mr. Brehgert is the sort of man I should choose.'

'Do not mention his name to me.'

'But what am I to do? You give up the house in town, and how am I to see people? It was you sent me to Mr. Melmotte.'

'I didn't send you to Mr. Melmotte.'

'It was at your suggestion I went there, papa. And of course I could only see the people he had there. I like nice people as well as anybody.'

'There's no use talking any more about it.'

'I don't see that. I must talk about it, and think about it too. If I can put up with Mr. Brehgert I don't see why you and mamma should complain.'

'A Jew!'

'People don't think about that as they used to, papa. He has a very fine income, and I should always have a house in——'

Then Mr. Longestaffe became so furious and loud, that he stopped her for that time. 'Look here,' he said, 'if you mean to tell me that you will marry that man without my consent, I can't prevent it. But you shall not marry him as my daughter. You shall be turned out of my house, and I will never have your name pronounced in my presence again. It is disgusting,—degrading,—disgraceful!' And then he left her.

On the next morning before he started for Caversham he did see Mr. Brehgert; but he told Georgiana nothing of the interview, nor had she the courage to ask him. The objectionable name was not mentioned again in her father's hearing, but there was a sad scene between herself, Lady Pomona, and her sister. When Mr. Longestaffe and his younger daughter arrived, the poor mother did not go down into the hall to meet her child,—from whom she had that morning received the dreadful tidings about the Jew. As to these tidings she had as yet heard no direct condemnation from her husband. The effect upon Lady Pomona had been more grievous even than that made upon the father. Mr. Longestaffe had been able to declare immediately that the proposed marriage was out of the question, that nothing of the kind should be allowed, and could take upon himself to see the Jew with the object of breaking off the engagement. But poor Lady Pomona was helpless in her sorrow. If Georgiana chose to marry a Jew tradesman she could not help it. But such an occurrence in the family would, she felt, be to her as though the end of all things had come. She could never again hold up her head, never go into society, never take pleasure in her powdered footmen. When her daughter should have married a Jew, she didn't think that she could pluck up the courage to look even her neighbours Mrs. Yeld and Mrs. Hepworth in the face. Georgiana found no one in the hall to meet her, and dreaded to go to her mother. She first went with her maid to her own room, and waited there till Sophia came to her. As she sat pretending to watch the process of unpacking, she strove to regain her courage. Why need she be afraid of anybody? Why, at any rate, should she be afraid of other females? Had she not always been dominant over her mother and sister? 'Oh, Georgey,' said Sophia, 'this is wonderful news!'

'I suppose it seems wonderful that anybody should be going to be married except yourself.'

'No;—but such a very odd match!'

'Look here, Sophia. If you don't like it, you need not talk about it. We shall always have a house in town, and you will not. If you don't like to come to us, you needn't. That's about all.'

'George wouldn't let me go there at all,' said Sophia.

'Then—George—had better keep you at home at Toodlam. Where's mamma? I should have thought somebody might have come and met me to say a word to me, instead of allowing me to creep into the house like this.'

'Mamma isn't at all well; but she's up in her own room. You mustn't be surprised, Georgey, if you find mamma very—very much cut up about this.' Then Georgiana understood that she must be content to stand all alone in the world, unless she made up her mind to give up Mr. Brehgert.

'So I've come back,' said Georgiana, stooping down and kissing her mother.

'Oh, Georgiana; oh, Georgiana!' said Lady Pomona, slowly raising herself and covering her face with one of her hands. 'This is dreadful. It will kill me. It will indeed. I didn't expect it from you.'

'What is the good of all that, mamma?'

'It seems to me that it can't be possible. It's unnatural. It's worse than your wife's sister.* I'm sure there's something in the Bible against it. You never would read your Bible, or you wouldn't be going to do this.'

'Lady Julia Start has done just the same thing,—and she goes everywhere.'

'What does your papa say? I'm sure your papa won't allow it. If he's fixed about anything, it's about the Jews. An accursed race;—think of that, Georgiana;—expelled from Paradise.'

'Mamma, that's nonsense.'

'Scattered about all over the world, so that nobody knows who anybody is. And it's only since those nasty Radicals came up that they have been able to sit in Parliament.'

'One of the greatest judges in the land is a Jew,'*said Georgiana, who had already learned to fortify her own case.

'Nothing that the Radicals can do can make them anything else but what they are. I'm sure that Mr. Whitstable, who is to be your brother-in-law, will never condescend to speak to him.'

Now if there was anybody whom Georgiana Longe-staffe had despised from her youth upwards it was George Whitstable. He had been a laughing-stock to her when they were children, had been regarded as a lout when he left school, and had been her common example of rural dullness since he had become a man. He certainly was neither beautiful nor bright;—but he was a Conservative squire born of Tory parents. Nor was he rich;—having but a moderate income, sufficient to maintain a moderate country house and no more. When first there came indications that Sophia intended to put

up with George Whitstable, the more ambitious sister did
not spare the shafts of her scorn. And now she was told
that George Whitstable would not speak to her future
husband! She was not to marry Mr. Brehgert lest she
should bring disgrace, among others, upon George Whitstable! This was not to be endured.

'Then Mr. Whitstable may keep himself at home at
Toodlam and not trouble his head at all about me or my
husband. I'm sure I shan't trouble myself as to what a
poor creature like that may think about me. George
Whitstable knows as much about London as I do about
the moon.'

'He has always been in county society,' said Sophia,
'and was staying only the other day at Lord Cantab's.'

'Then there were two fools together,' said Georgiana,
who at this moment was very unhappy.

'Mr. Whitstable is an excellent young man, and I am
sure he will make your sister happy; but as for Mr.
Brehgert,—I can't bear to have his name mentioned in
my hearing.'

'Then, mamma, it had better not be mentioned. At
any rate it shan't be mentioned again by me.' Having so
spoken, Georgiana bounced out of the room and did not
meet her mother and sister again till she came down into
the drawing-room before dinner.

Her position was one very trying both to her nerves
and to her feelings. She presumed that her father had
seen Mr. Brehgert, but did not in the least know what
had passed between them. It might be that her father
had been so decided in his objection as to induce Mr.
Brehgert to abandon his intention,—and if this were so,
there could be no reason why she should endure the
misery of having the Jew thrown in her face. Among
them all they had made her think that she would never
become Mrs. Brehgert. She certainly was not prepared
to nail her colours upon the mast and to live and die for
Brehgert. She was almost sick of the thing herself. But
she could not back out of it so as to obliterate all traces
of the disgrace. Even if she should not ultimately marry
the Jew, it would be known that she had been engaged to

a Jew,—and then it would certainly be said afterwards that the Jew had jilted her. She was thus vacillating in her mind, not knowing whether to go on with Brehgert or to abandon him. That evening Lady Pomona retired immediately after dinner, being 'far from well.' It was of course known to them all that Mr. Brehgert was her ailment. She was accompanied by her elder daughter, and Georgiana was left with her father. Not a word was spoken between them. He sat behind his newspaper till he went to sleep, and she found herself alone and deserted in that big room. It seemed to her that even the servants treated her with disdain. Her own maid had already given her notice. It was manifestly the intention of her family to ostracise her altogether. Of what service would it be to her that Lady Julia Goldsheiner should be received everywhere, if she herself were to be left without a single Christian friend? Would a life passed exclusively among the Jews content even her lessened ambition? At ten o'clock she kissed her father's head and went to bed. Her father grunted less audibly than usual under the operation. She had always given herself credit for high spirits, but she began to fear that her courage would not suffice to carry her through sufferings such as these.

On the next day her father returned to town, and the three ladies were left alone. Great preparations were going on for the Whitstable wedding. Dresses were being made and linen marked, and consultations held,—from all which things Georgiana was kept quite apart. The accepted lover came over to lunch, and was made as much of as though the Whitstables had always kept a town house. Sophy loomed so large in her triumph and happiness, that it was not to be borne. All Caversham treated her with a new respect. And yet if Toodlam was a couple of thousand a year, it was all it was;—and there were two unmarried sisters! Lady Pomona went half into hysterics every time she saw her younger daughter, and became in her way a most oppressive parent. Oh, heavens;—was Mr. Brehgert with his two houses worth all this? A feeling of intense regret for the things she was losing came over her. Even Caversham, the Caversham of old days which she had hated, but in which she had made herself respected and partly feared by everybody about the place,—had charms for her which seemed to her delightful now that they were lost for ever. Then she had always considered herself to be the first personage in the house,—superior even to her father;—but now she was decidedly the last.

Her second evening was worse even than the first. When Mr. Longestaffe was not at home the family sat in a small dingy room between the library and the dining-room, and on this occasion the family consisted only of Georgiana. In the course of the evening she went up-stairs and calling her sister out into the passage de-manded to be told why she was thus deserted. 'Poor mamma is very ill,' said Sophy.

'I won't stand it if I'm to be treated like this,' said Georgiana. 'I'll go away somewhere.'

'How can I help it, Georgey? It's your own doing. Of course you must have known that you were going to separate yourself from us.'

On the next morning there came a dispatch from Mr. Longestaffe,—of what nature Georgey did not know as it was addressed to Lady Pomona. But one enclosure she was allowed to see. 'Mamma,' said Sophy, 'thinks you ought to know how Dolly feels about it.' And then a letter from Dolly to his father was put into Georgey's hands. The letter was as follows:—

'MY DEAR FATHER,—

'Can it be true that Georgey is thinking of marrying that horrid vulgar Jew, old Brehgert? The fellows say so; but I can't believe it. I'm sure you wouldn't let her. You ought to lock her up.

'Yours affectionately,
'A. LONGESTAFFE.'

Dolly's letters made his father very angry, as, short as they were, they always contained advice or instruction, such as should come from a father to a son, rather than from a son to a father. This letter had not been received with a welcome. Nevertheless the head of the family had thought it worth his while to make use of it, and had sent it to Caversham in order that it might be shown to his rebellious daughter.

And so Dolly had said that she ought to be locked up! She'd like to see somebody do it! As soon as she had read her brother's epistle she tore it into fragments and threw it away in her sister's presence. 'How can mamma be such a hypocrite as to pretend to care what Dolly says? Who doesn't know that he's an idiot? And papa has thought it worth his while to send that down here for me to see! Well, after that I must say that I don't much care what papa does.'

'I don't see why Dolly shouldn't have an opinion as well as anybody else,' said Sophy.

'As well as George Whitstable? As far as stupidness goes they are about the same. But Dolly has a little more knowledge of the world.'

'Of course we all know, Georgiana,' rejoined the elder sister, 'that for cuteness and that kind of thing one must look among the commercial classes, and especially among a certain sort.'

'I've done with you all,' said Georgey, rushing out of the room. 'I'll have nothing more to do with any one of you.'

But it is very difficult for a young lady to have done with her family! A young man may go anywhere, and may be lost at sea; or come and claim his property after twenty years.* A young man may demand an allowance, and has almost a right to live alone. The young male bird is supposed to fly away from the paternal nest. But the daughter of a house is compelled to adhere to her father till she shall get a husband. The only way in which Georgey could 'have done' with them all at Caversham would be by trusting herself to Mr. Brehgert, and at the present moment she did not know whether Mr. Brehgert did or did not consider himself as engaged to her.

That day also passed away with ineffable tedium. At one time she was so beaten down by ennui that she almost offered her assistance to her sister in reference to the wedding garments. In spite of the very bitter words which had been spoken in the morning she would have done so had Sophy afforded her the slightest opportunity. But Sophy was heartlessly cruel in her indifference. In her younger days she had had her bad things, and now,—with George Whitstable by her side,—she meant to have good things, the goodness of which was infinitely enhanced by the badness of her sister's things. She had been so greatly despised that the charm of despising again was irresistible. And she was able to reconcile her cruelty to her conscience by telling herself that duty required her to show implacable resistance to such a marriage as this which her sister contemplated. Therefore Georgiana dragged out another day, not in the least knowing what was to be her fate.

## Chapter LXXIX

### THE BREHGERT CORRESPONDENCE

MR. LONGESTAFFE had brought his daughter down to Caversham on a Wednesday. During the Thursday and Friday she had passed a very sad time, not knowing whether she was or was not engaged to marry Mr. Brehgert. Her father had declared to her that he would break off the match, and she believed that he had seen Mr. Brehgert with that purpose. She had certainly given no consent, and had never hinted to any one of the family an idea that she was disposed to yield. But she felt that, at any rate with her father, she had not adhered to her purpose with tenacity, and that she had allowed him to return to London with a feeling that she might still be controlled. She was beginning to be angry with Mr. Brehgert, thinking that he had taken his dismissal from her father without consulting her. It was necessary that something should be settled, something known. Life such as she was leading now would drive her mad. She had all the disadvantages of the Brehgert connection and none of the advantages. She could not comfort herself with thinking of the Brehgert wealth and the Brehgert houses, and yet she was living under the general ban of Caversham on account of her Brehgert associations. She was beginning to think that she herself must write to Mr. Brehgert,—only she did not know what to say to him.

But on the Saturday morning she got a letter from Mr. Brehgert. It was handed to her as she was sitting at breakfast with her sister,—who at that moment was triumphant with a present of gooseberries which had been sent over from Toodlam. The Toodlam gooseberries were noted throughout Suffolk, and when the letters were being brought in Sophia was taking her lover's offering from the basket with her own fair hands. 'Well!' Georgey had exclaimed, 'to send a pottle of gooseberries to his lady love across the country! Who but George Whitstable would do that?'

'I dare say you get nothing but gems and gold,' Sophy retorted. 'I don't suppose that Mr. Brehgert knows what a gooseberry is.' At that moment the letter was brought in, and Georgiana knew the writing. 'I suppose that's from Mr. Brehgert,' said Sophy.

'I don't think it matters much to you who it's from.' She tried to be composed and stately, but the letter was too important to allow of composure, and she retired to read it in privacy.

The letter was as follows:—

'MY DEAR GEORGIANA,

'Your father came to me the day after I was to have met you at Lady Monogram's party. I told him then that I would not write to you till I had taken a day or two to consider what he said to me;—and also that I thought it better that you should have a day or two to consider what he might say to you. He has now repeated what he said at our first interview, almost with more violence; for I must say that I think he has allowed himself to be violent when it was surely unnecessary.

'The long and short of it is this. He altogether disapproves of your promise to marry me. He has given three reasons;—first that I am in trade; secondly that I am much older than you, and have a family; and thirdly that I am a Jew. In regard to the first I can hardly think that he is earnest. I have explained to him that my business is that of a banker; and I can hardly conceive it to be possible that any gentleman in England should object to his daughter marrying a banker, simply because the man is a banker. There would be a blindness of arrogance in such a proposition of which I think your father to be incapable. This has merely been added in to strengthen his other objections.

'As to my age, it is just fifty-one. I do not at all think myself too old to be married again. Whether I am too old for you is for you to judge,—as is also that question of my children who, of course, should you become my wife will be to some extent a care upon your shoulders. As this is all very serious you will not, I hope, think me wanting in gallantry if I say that I should hardly have ventured to address you if you had been quite a young girl. No doubt there are many years between us;—and so I think there should be. A man of my age hardly looks to marry a woman of the same standing as himself. But the question is one for the lady to decide,—and you must decide it now.

'As to my religion, I acknowledge the force of what your father says,—though I think that a gentleman brought up with fewer prejudices would have expressed himself in language less likely to give offence. However I am a man not easily offended; and on this occasion I am ready to take what he has said in good part. I can easily conceive that there should be those who think that the husband and wife should agree in religion. I am indifferent to it myself. I shall not interfere with you if you make me happy by becoming my wife, nor, I suppose, will you with me. Should you have a daughter or daughters I am quite willing that they should be brought up subject to your influence.' There was a plain-speaking in this which made Georgiana look round the room as though to see whether any one was watching her as she read it. 'But no doubt your father objects to me specially because I am a Jew. If I were an atheist he might, perhaps, say nothing on the subject of religion. On this matter as well as on others it seems to me that your father has hardly kept pace with the movements of the age. Fifty years ago, whatever claim a Jew might have to be as well considered as a Christian, he certainly was not so considered. Society was closed against him, except under special circumstances, and so were all the privileges of high position. But that has been altered. Your father does not admit the change; but I think he is blind to it, because he does not wish to see.

'I say all this more as defending myself than as combating his views with you. It must be for you and for you alone to decide how far his views shall govern you. He has told me, after a rather peremptory fashion, that I have behaved badly to him and to his family because I did not go to him in the first instance when I thought of obtaining the honour of an alliance with his daughter. I have been obliged to tell him that in this matter I disagree with him entirely, though in so telling him I endeavoured to restrain myself from any appearance of warmth. I had not the pleasure of meeting you in his house, nor had I any aquaintance with him. And again, at the risk of being thought uncourteous, I must say that you are to a certain degree emancipated by age from that positive subordination to which a few years ago you probably submitted without a question. If a gentleman meets a lady in society, as I met you in the home of our friend Mr. Melmotte, I do not think that the gentleman is to be debarred from expressing his feelings because the lady may possibly have a parent. Your father, no doubt with propriety, had left you to be the guardian of yourself, and I cannot submit to be accused of improper conduct because, finding you in that condition, I availed myself of it.

'And now, having said so much, I must leave the question to be decided entirely by yourself. I beg you to understand that I do not at all wish to hold you to a promise merely because the promise has been given. I readily acknowledge that the opinion of your family should be considered by you, though I will not admit

that I was bound to consult that opinion before I spoke to
you. It may well be that your regard for me or your appreciation of the comforts with which I may be able to
surround you, will not suffice to reconcile you to such a
breach from your own family as your father, with much
repetition, has assured me will be inevitable. Take a day
or two to think of this and turn it well over in your mind.
When I last had the happiness of speaking to you, you
seemed to think that your parents might raise objections,
but that those objections would give way before an expression of your own wishes. I was flattered by your so
thinking; but, if I may form any judgment from your
father's manner, I must suppose that you were mistaken.
You will understand that I do not say this as any reproach to you. Quite the contrary. I think your father is
irrational; and you may well have failed to anticipate
that he should be so.

'As to my own feelings they remain exactly as they
were when I endeavoured to explain them to you.
Though I do not find myself to be too old to marry, I do
think myself too old to write love letters. I have no doubt
you believe me when I say that I entertain a most sincere
affection for you; and I beseech you to believe me in
saying further that should you become my wife it shall be
the study of my life to make you happy.

'It is essentially necessary that I should allude to one
other matter, as to which I have already told your father
what I will now tell you. I think it probable that within this week I shall find myself a loser of a very large sum
of money through the failure of a gentleman whose bad
treatment of me I will the more readily forgive because
he was the means of making me known to you. This you
must understand is private between you and me, though
I have thought it proper to inform your father. Such loss,
if it fall upon me, will not interfere in the least with the
income which I have proposed to settle upon you for your
use after my death; and, as your father declares that in the
event of your marrying me he will neither give to you nor
bequeath to you a shilling, he might have abstained from
telling me to my face that I was a bankrupt merchant

when I myself told him of my loss. I am not a bankrupt merchant nor at all likely to become so. Nor will this loss at all interfere with my present mode of living. But I have thought it right to inform you of it, because, if it occur,—as I think it will,—I shall not deem it right to keep a second establishment probably for the next two or three years. But my house at Fulham and my stables there will be kept up just as they are at present.

'I have now told you everything which I think it is necessary you should know, in order that you may determine either to adhere to or to recede from your engagement. When you have resolved you will let me know,—but a day or two may probably be necessary for your decision. I hope I need not say that a decision in my favour will make me a happy man.

'I am, in the meantime, your affectionate friend,
'EZEKIEL BREHGERT.'

This very long letter puzzled Georgey a good deal, and left her, at the time of reading it, very much in doubt as to what she would do. She could understand that it was a plain-spoken and truth-telling letter. Not that she, to herself, gave it praise for those virtues; but that it imbued her unconsciously with a thorough belief. She was apt to suspect deceit in other people;—but it did not occur to her that Mr. Brehgert had written a single word with an attempt to deceive her. But the single-minded genuine honesty of the letter was altogether thrown away upon her. She never said to herself, as she read it, that she might safely trust herself to this man, though he were a Jew, though greasy and like a butcher, though over fifty and with a family, because he was an honest man. She did not see that the letter was particularly sensible;—but she did allow herself to be pained by the total absence of romance. She was annoyed at the first allusion to her age, and angry at the second; and yet she had never supposed that Brehgert had taken her to be younger than she was. She was well aware that the world in general attributes more years to unmarried women than they have lived, as a sort of equalising counter-weight against the pretences which young women make on the other side, or the lies which are told on their behalf. Nor had she wished to appear peculiarly young in his eyes. But, nevertheless, she regarded the reference to be uncivil,—perhaps almost butcher-like,—and it had its effect upon her. And then the allusion to the 'daughter or daughters' troubled her. She told herself that it was vulgar,—just what a butcher might have said. And although she was quite prepared to call her father the most irrational, the most prejudiced, and most ill-natured of men, yet she was displeased that Mr. Brehgert should take such a liberty with him. But the passage in Mr. Brehgert's letter which was most distasteful to her was that which told her of the loss which he might probably incur through his connection with Melmotte. What right had he to incur a loss which would incapacitate him from keeping his engagements with her? The town-house had been the great persuasion, and now he absolutely had the face to tell her that there was to be no town-house for three years. When she read this she felt that she ought to be indignant, and for a few moments was minded to sit down without further consideration and tell the man with considerable scorn that she would have nothing more to say to him.

But on that side too there would be terrible bitterness. How would she have fallen from her greatness when, barely forgiven by her father and mother for the vile sin which she had contemplated, she should consent to fill a common bridesmaid place at the nuptials of George Whitstable! And what would then be left to her in life? This episode of the Jew would make it quite impossible for her again to contest the question of the London house with her father. Lady Pomona and Mrs. George Whitstable would be united with him against her. There would be no 'season' for her, and she would be nobody at Caversham. As for London, she would hardly wish to go there! Everybody would know the story of the Jew. She thought that she could have plucked up courage to face the world as the Jew's wife, but not as the young woman who had wanted to marry the Jew and had failed. How would her future life go with her, should she now make up her mind to retire from the proposed alliance? If she could get her father to take her abroad at once, she would do it; but she was not now in a condition to make any terms with her father. As all this gradually passed through her mind, she determined that she would so far take Mr. Brehgert's advice as to postpone her answer till she had well considered the matter.

She slept upon it, and the next day she asked her mother a few questions. 'Mamma, have you any idea what papa means to do?'

'In what way, my dear?' Lady Pomona's voice was not gracious, as she was free from that fear of her daughter's ascendency which had formerly affected her.

'Well;—I suppose he must have some plan.'

'You must explain yourself. I don't know why he should have any particular plan.'

'Will he go to London next year?'

'That depends upon money, I suppose. What makes you ask?'

'Of course I have been very cruelly circumstanced. Everybody must see that. I'm sure you do, mamma. The long and short of it is this;—if I give up my engagement, will he take us abroad for a year?'

'Why should he?'

'You can't suppose that I should be very comfortable in England. If we are to remain here at Caversham, how am I to hope ever to get settled?'

'Sophy is doing very well.'

'Oh, mamma, there are not two George Whitstables;—thank God.' She had meant to be humble and supplicating, but she could not restrain herself from the use of that one shaft. 'I don't mean but what Sophy may be very happy, and I am sure that I hope she will. But that won't do me any good. I should be very unhappy here.'

'I don't see how you are to find any one to marry you by going abroad,' said Lady Pomona, 'and I don't see why your papa is to be taken away from his own home. He likes Caversham.'

'Then I am to be sacrificed on every side,' said Georgey

stalking out of the room. But still she could not make up her mind what letter she would write to Mr. Brehgert, and she slept upon it another night.

On the next day after breakfast she did write her letter, though when she sat down to her task she had not clearly made up her mind what she would say. But she did get it written, and here it is.

'Caversham, Monday.

'My dear Mr. Brehgert,

'As you told me not to hurry, I have taken a little time to think about your letter. Of course it would be very disagreeable to quarrel with papa and mamma and everybody. And if I do do so, I'm sure somebody ought to be very grateful. But papa has been very unfair in what he has said. As to not asking him, it could have been of no good, for of course he would be against it. He thinks a great deal of the Longestaffe family, and so, I suppose, ought I. But the world does change so quick that one doesn't think of anything now as one used to do. Anyway, I don't feel that I'm bound to do what papa tells me just because he says it. Though I'm not quite so old as you seem to think, I'm old enough to judge for myself,—and I mean to do so. You say very little about affection, but I suppose I am to take all that for granted.

'I don't wonder at papa being annoyed about the loss of the money. It must be a very great sum when it will prevent your having a house in London,—as you agreed. It does make a great difference, because, of course, as you have no regular place in the country, one could only see one's friends in London. Fulham is all very well now and then, but I don't think I should like to live at Fulham all the year through. You talk of three years, which would be dreadful. If as you say it will not have any lasting effect, could you not manage to have a house in town? If you can do it in three years, I should think you could do it now. I should like to have an answer to this question. I do think so much about being the season in town!

'As for the other parts of your letter, I knew very well

beforehand that papa would be unhappy about it. But
I don't know why I'm to let that stand in my way when
so very little is done to make me happy. Of course you
will write to me again, and I hope you will say something
satisfactory about the house in London.

'Yours always sincerely,

'GEORGIANA LONGESTAFFE.'

It probably never occurred to Georgey that Mr. Brehgert would under any circumstances be anxious to go
back from his engagement. She so fully recognised her
own value as a Christian lady of high birth and position
giving herself to a commercial Jew, that she thought that
under any circumstances Mr. Brehgert would be only too
anxious to stick to his bargain. Nor had she any idea
that there was anything in her letter which could probably offend him. She thought that she might at any
rate make good her claim to the house in London; and
that as there were other difficulties on his side, he would
yield to her on this point. But as yet she hardly knew Mr.
Brehgert. He did not lose a day in sending to her a
second letter. He took her letter with him to his office in
the city, and there he answered it without a moment's
delay.

'No. 7, St. Cuthbert's Court, London,
'Tuesday, July 16, 18—.

'MY DEAR MISS LONGESTAFFE,

'You say it would be very disagreeable to you to
quarrel with your papa and mamma; and as I agree with
you, I will take your letter as concluding our intimacy.
I should not, however, be dealing quite fairly with you or
with myself if I gave you to understand that I felt myself
to be coerced to this conclusion simply by your qualified
assent to your parents' views. It is evident to me from
your letter that you would not wish to be my wife unless
I can supply you with a house in town as well as with one
in the country. But this for the present is out of my
power. I would not have allowed my losses to interfere
with your settlement because I had stated a certain

income; and must therefore to a certain extent have compromised my children. But I should not have been altogether happy till I had replaced them in their former position, and must therefore have abstained from increased expenditure till I had done so. But of course I have no right to ask you to share with me the discomfort of a single home. I may perhaps add that I had hoped that you would have looked to your happiness to another source, and that I will bear my disappointment as best I may.

'As you may perhaps under these circumstances be unwilling that I should wear the ring you gave me, I return it by post. I trust you will be good enough to keep the trifle you were pleased to accept from me, in remembrance of one who will always wish you well.

'Yours sincerely,
'EZEKIEL BREHGERT.'

And so it was all over! Georgey, when she read this letter, was very indignant at her lover's conduct. She did not believe that her own letter had at all been of a nature to warrant it. She had regarded herself as being quite sure of him, and only so far doubting herself, as to be able to make her own terms because of such doubts. And now the Jew had rejected her! She read this last letter over and over again, and the more she read it the more she felt that in her heart of hearts she had intended to marry him. There would have been inconveniences no doubt, but they would have been less than the sorrow on the other side. Now she saw nothing before her but a long vista of Caversham dullness, in which she would be trampled upon by her father and mother, and scorned by Mr. and Mrs. George Whitstable.

She got up and walked about the room thinking of vengeance. But what vengeance was possible to her? Everybody belonging to her would take the part of the Jew in that which he had now done. She could not ask Dolly to beat him; nor could she ask her father to visit him with a stern frown of paternal indignation. There could be no revenge. For a time,—only a few seconds,—she

thought that she would write to Mr. Brehgert and tell
him that she had not intended to bring about this termination of their engagement. This, no doubt, would
have been an appeal to the Jew for mercy;—and she
could not quite descend to that. But she would keep the
watch and chain he had given her, and which somebody
had told her had not cost less than a hundred and fifty
guineas. She could not wear them, as people would know
whence they had come; but she might exchange them
for jewels which she could wear.

At lunch she said nothing to her sister, but in the
course of the afternoon she thought it best to inform her
mother. 'Mamma,' she said, 'as you and papa take it so
much to heart, I have broken off everything with Mr.
Brehgert.'

'Of course it must be broken off,' said Lady Pomona.
This was very ungracious,—so much so that Georgey
almost flounced out of the room. 'Have you heard from
the man?' asked her ladyship.

'I have written to him, and he has answered me; and
it is all settled. I thought that you would have said
something kind to me.' And the unfortunate young
woman burst out into tears.

'It was so dreadful,' said Lady Pomona;—'so very
dreadful. I never heard of anything so bad. When young
what's-his-name married the tallow-chandler's daughter
I thought it would have killed me if it had been Dolly;
but this was worse than that. Her father was a methodist.'

'They had neither of them a shilling of money,' said
Georgey through her tears.

'And your papa says this man was next door to a
bankrupt. But it's all over?'

'Yes, mamma.'

'And now we must all remain here at Caversham till
people forget it. It has been very hard upon George
Whitstable, because of course everybody has known it
through the county. I once thought he would have been
off, and I really don't know that we could have said
anything.' At that moment Sophy entered the room.
'It's all over between Georgiana and the—man,' said

Lady Pomona, who hardly saved herself from stigma-
tising him by a further reference to his religion.

'I knew it would be,' said Sophia.

'Of course it could never have really taken place,' said
their mother.

'And now I beg that nothing more may be said about
it,' said Georgiana. 'I suppose, mamma, you will write
to papa?'

'You must send him back his watch and chain,
Georgey,' said Sophia.

'What business is that of yours?'

'Of course she must. Her papa would not let her keep
it.'

To such a miserable depth of humility had the younger
Miss Longestaffe been brought by her ill-considered
intimacy with the Melmottes! Georgiana, when she
looked back on this miserable episode in her life, always
attributed her grief to the scandalous breach of compact
of which her father had been guilty.

## Chapter LXXX

### RUBY PREPARES FOR SERVICE

OUR poor old honest friend John Crumb was taken
away to durance vile after his performance in the
street with Sir Felix, and was locked up for the remainder
of the night. This indignity did not sit so heavily on his
spirits as it might have done on those of a quicker nature.
He was aware that he had not killed the baronet, and that
he had therefore enjoyed his revenge without the necessity
of 'swinging for it at Bury.' That in itself was a comfort to
him. Then it was a great satisfaction to think that he had
'served the young man out' in the actual presence of his
Ruby. He was not prone to give himself undue credit for
his capability and willingness to knock his enemies about;
but he did think that Ruby must have observed on this
occasion that he was the better man of the two. And, to

John, a night in the station-house was no great personal
inconvenience. Though he was very proud of his four-
post bed at home, he did not care very much for such
luxuries as far as he himself was concerned. Nor did
he feel any disgrace from being locked up for the night.
He was very good-humoured with the policeman, who
seemed perfectly to understand his nature, and was as
meek as a child when the lock was turned upon him. As
he lay down on the hard bench, he comforted himself
with thinking that Ruby would surely never care any
more for the 'baronite' since she had seen him go down
like a cur without striking a blow. He thought a good
deal about Ruby, but never attributed any blame to her
for her share in the evils that had befallen him.

The next morning he was taken before the magistrates,
but was told at an early hour of the day that he was
again free. Sir Felix was not much the worse for what
had happened to him, and had refused to make any
complaint against the man who had beaten him. John
Crumb shook hands cordially with the policeman who
had had him in charge, and suggested beer. The
constable, with regrets, was forced to decline, and bade
adieu to his late prisoner with the expression of a hope
that they might meet again before long. 'You come
down to Bungay,' said John, 'and I'll show you how we
live there.'

From the police-office he went direct to Mrs. Pipkin's
house, and at once asked for Ruby. He was told that
Ruby was out with the children, and was advised both
by Mrs. Pipkin and Mrs. Hurtle not to present himself
before Ruby quite yet. 'You see,' said Mrs. Pipkin, 'she's
a thinking how heavy you were upon that young gentleman.'

'But I wasn't;—not particular. Lord love you, he ain't
a hair the wuss.'

'You let her alone for a time,' said Mrs. Hurtle. 'A
little neglect will do her good.'

'Maybe,' said John,—'only I wouldn't like her to have
it bad. You'll let her have her wittles regular, Mrs.
Pipkin.'

It was then explained to him that the neglect proposed should not extend to any deprivation of food, and he took his leave, receiving an assurance from Mrs. Hurtle that he should be summoned to town as soon as it was thought that his presence there would serve his purposes; and with loud promises repeated to each of the friendly women that as soon as ever a 'line should be dropped' he would appear again upon the scene, he took Mrs. Pipkin aside, and suggested that if there were 'any hextras,' he was ready to pay for them. Then he took his leave without seeing Ruby, and went back to Bungay.

When Ruby returned with the children she was told that John Crumb had called. 'I thought as he was in prison,' said Ruby.

'What should they keep him in prison for?' said Mrs. Pipkin. 'He hasn't done nothing as he oughtn't to have done. That young man was dragging you about as far as I can make out, and Mr. Crumb just did as anybody ought to have done to prevent it. Of course they weren't going to keep him in prison for that. Prison indeed! It isn't him as ought to be in prison.'

'And where is he now, aunt?'

'Gone down to Bungay to mind his business, and won't be coming here any more of a fool's errand. He must have seen now pretty well what's worth having, and what ain't. Beauty is but skin deep, Ruby.'

'John Crumb 'd be after me again to-morrow, if I'd give him encouragement,' said Ruby. 'If I'd hold up my finger he'd come.'

'Then John Crumb's a fool for his pains, that's all; and now do you go about your work.' Ruby didn't like to be told to go about her work, and tossed her head, and slammed the kitchen door, and scolded the servant girl, and then sat down to cry. What was she to do with herself now? She had an idea that Felix would not come back to her after the treatment he had received;—and a further idea that if he did come he was not, as she phrased it to herself, 'of much account.' She certainly did not like him the better for having been beaten, though, at the time, she had been disposed to take his part. She did not

believe that she would ever dance with him again. That
had been the charm of her life in London, and that was
now all over. And as for marrying her,—she began to
feel certain that he did not intend it. John Crumb was
a big, awkward, dull, uncouth lump of a man, with
whom Ruby thought it impossible that a girl should be
in love. Love and John Crumb were poles asunder.
But——! Ruby did not like wheeling the perambulator
about Islington, and being told by her aunt Pipkin to
go about her work. What Ruby did like was being in
love and dancing; but if all that must come to an end,
then there would be a question whether she could not do
better for herself, than by staying with her aunt and
wheeling the perambulator about Islington.

Mrs. Hurtle was still living in solitude in the lodgings,
and having but little to do on her own behalf, had devoted herself to the interest of John Crumb. A man more
unlike one of her own countrymen she had never seen.
'I wonder whether he has any ideas at all in his head,'
she had said to Mrs. Pipkin. Mrs. Pipkin had replied
that Mr. Crumb had certainly a very strong idea of
marrying Ruby Ruggles. Mrs. Hurtle had smiled,
thinking that Mrs. Pipkin was also very unlike her own
countrywomen. But she was very kind to Mrs. Pipkin,
ordering rice-puddings on purpose that the children
might eat them, and she was quite determined to give
John Crumb all the aid in her power.

In order that she might give effectual aid she took
Mrs. Pipkin into confidence, and prepared a plan of
action in reference to Ruby. Mrs. Pipkin was to appear
as chief actor on the scene, but the plan was altogether
Mrs. Hurtle's plan. On the day following John's return
to Bungay Mrs. Pipkin summoned Ruby into the back
parlour, and thus addressed her. 'Ruby, you know, this
must come to an end now.'

'What must come to an end?'

'You can't stay here always, you know.'

'I'm sure I work hard, Aunt Pipkin, and I don't get no
wages.'

'I can't do with more than one girl,—and there's the

keep if there isn't wages. Besides, there's other reasons. Your grandfather won't have you back there; that's certain.'

'I wouldn't go back to grandfather, if it was ever so.'

'But you must go somewheres. You didn't come to stay here always,—nor I couldn't have you. You must go into service.'

'I don't know anybody as 'd have me,' said Ruby.

'You must put a 'vertisement into the paper. You'd better say as nursemaid, as you seems to take kindly to children. And I must give you a character;—only I shall say just the truth. You mustn't ask much wages just at first.' Ruby looked very sorrowful, and the tears were near her eyes. The change from the glories of the music hall was so startling and so oppressive! 'It has got to be done sooner or later, so you may as well put the 'vertisement in this afternoon.'

'Your going to turn me out, Aunt Pipkin.'

'Well;—if that's turning out, I am. You see you never would be said by me as though I was your mistress. You would go out with that rapscallion when I bid you not. Now when you're in a regular place like, you must mind when you're spoke to, and it will be best for you. You've had your swing, and now you see you've got to pay for it. You must earn your bread, Ruby, as you've quarrelled both with your lover and your grandfather.'

There was no possible answer to this, and therefore the necessary notice was put into the paper,—Mrs. Hurtle paying for its insertion. 'Because, you know,' said Mrs. Hurtle, 'she must stay here really, till Mr. Crumb comes and takes her away.' Mrs. Pipkin expressed her opinion that Ruby was a 'baggage' and John Crumb a 'soft.' Mrs. Pipkin was perhaps a little jealous at the interest which her lodger took in her niece, thinking perhaps that all Mrs. Hurtle's sympathies were due to herself.

Ruby went hither and thither for a day or two, calling upon the mothers of children who wanted nursemaids. The answers which she had received had not come from the highest members of the aristocracy, and the houses which she visited did not appal her by their splendour. Many objections were made to her. A character from an aunt was objectionable. Her ringlets were objectionable. She was a deal too flighty-looking. She spoke up much too free. At last one happy mother of five children offered to take her on approval for a month, at £12 a year, Ruby to find her own tea and wash for herself. This was slavery;—abject slavery. And she too, who had been the beloved of a baronet, and who might even now be the mistress of a better house than that into which she was to go as a servant,—if she would only hold up her finger! But the place was accepted, and with broken-hearted sobbings Ruby prepared herself for her departure from Aunt Pipkin's roof.

'I hope you like your place, Ruby,' Mrs. Hurtle said on the afternoon of her last day.

'Indeed then I don't like it at all. They're the ugliest children you ever see, Mrs. Hurtle.'

'Ugly children must be minded as well as pretty ones.'

'And the mother of 'em is as cross as cross.'

'It's your own fault, Ruby; isn't it?'

'I don't know as I've done anything out of the way.'

'Don't you think it's anything out of the way to be engaged to a young man and then to throw him over? All this has come because you wouldn't keep your word to Mr. Crumb. Only for that your grandfather wouldn't have turned you out of his house.'

'He didn't turn me out. I ran away. And it wasn't along of John Crumb, but because grandfather hauled me about by the hair of my head.'

'But he was angry with you about Mr. Crumb.. When a young woman becomes engaged to a young man, she ought not to go back from her word.' No doubt Mrs. Hurtle, when preaching this doctrine, thought that the same law might be laid down with propriety for the conduct of young men. 'Of course you have brought trouble on yourself. I am sorry you don't like the place. I'm afraid you must go to it now.'

'I am agoing,—I suppose,' said Ruby, probably feeling that if she could but bring herself to condescend so far there might yet be open for her a way of escape.

'I shall write and tell Mr. Crumb where you are placed.'

'Oh, Mrs. Hurtle, don't. What should you write to him for? It ain't nothing to him.'

'I told him I'd let him know if any steps were taken.'

'You can forget that, Mrs. Hurtle. Pray don't write. I don't want him to know as I'm in service.'

'I must keep my promise. Why shouldn't he know? I don't suppose you care much now what he hears about you.'

'Yes I do. I wasn't never in service before, and I don't want him to know.'

'What harm can it do you?'

'Well, I don't want him to know. It is such a come down, Mrs. Hurtle.'

'There is nothing to be ashamed of in that. What you have to be ashamed of is jilting him. It was a bad thing to do;—wasn't it, Ruby?'

'I didn't mean nothing bad, Mrs. Hurtle; only why couldn't he say what he had to say himself, instead of bringing another to say it for him? What would you feel, Mrs. Hurtle, if a man was to come and say it all out of another man's mouth?'

'I don't think I should much care if the thing was well said at last. You know he meant it.'

'Yes;—I did know that.'

'And you know he means it now?'

'I'm not so sure about that. He's gone back to Bungay, and he isn't no good at writing letters no more than at speaking. Oh,—he'll go and get somebody else now.'

'Of course he will if he hears nothing about you. I think I'd better tell him. I know what would happen.'

'What would happen, Mrs. Hurtle?'

'He'd be up in town again in half a jiffey to see what sort of a place you'd got. Now, Ruby, I'll tell you what I'll do, if you'll say the word. I'll have him up here at once and you shan't go to Mrs. Buggins'.' Ruby dropped her hands and stood still, staring at Mrs. Hurtle. 'I will. But if he comes you mustn't behave this time as you did before.'

'But I'm to go to Mrs. Buggins' to-morrow.'

'We'll send to Mrs. Buggins and tell her to get some-body else. You're breaking your heart about going there;—are you not?'

'I don't like it, Mrs. Hurtle.'

'And this man will make you mistress of his house. You say he isn't good at speaking; but I tell you I never came across an honester man in the whole course of my life, or one who I think would treat a woman better. What's the use of a glib tongue if there isn't a heart with it? What's the use of a lot of tinsel and lacker, if the real metal isn't there? Sir Felix Carbury could talk, I dare say, but you don't think now he was a very fine fellow.'

'He was so beautiful, Mrs. Hurtle!'

'But he hadn't the spirit of a mouse in his bosom. Well, Ruby, you have one more choice left you. Shall it be John Crumb or Mrs. Buggins?'

'He wouldn't come, Mrs. Hurtle.'

'Leave that to me, Ruby. May I bring him if I can?' Then Ruby in a very low whisper told Mrs. Hurtle, that if she thought proper she might bring John Crumb back again. 'And there shall be no more nonsense?'

'No,' whispered Ruby.

On that same night a letter was sent to Mrs. Buggins, which Mrs. Hurtle also composed, informing that lady that unforeseen circumstances prevented Ruby Ruggles from keeping the engagement she had made; to which a verbal answer was returned that Ruby Ruggles was an impudent hussey. And then Mrs. Hurtle in her own name wrote a short note to Mr. John Crumb.

'DEAR MR. CRUMB,

'If you will come back to London I think you will find Miss Ruby Ruggles all that you desire.

'Yours faithfully,

'WINIFRED HURTLE.'

'She's had a deal more done for her than I ever knew to be done for young women in my time,' said Mrs. Pipkin, 'and I'm not at all so sure that she has deserved it.'

'John Crumb will think she has.'

'John Crumb's a fool;—and as to Ruby; well, I haven't got no patience with girls like them. Yes; it is for the best; and as for you, Mrs. Hurtle, there's no words to say how good you've been. I hope, Mrs. Hurtle, you ain't thinking of going away because this is all done.'

## Chapter LXXXI

### MR. COHENLUPE LEAVES LONDON

DOLLY LONGESTAFFE had found himself compelled to go to Fetter Lane immediately after that meeting in Bruton Street at which he had consented to wait two days longer for the payment of his money. This was on a Wednesday, the day appointed for the payment being Friday. He had undertaken that, on his part, Squercum should be made to desist from further immediate proceedings, and he could only carry out his word by visiting Squercum. The trouble to him was very great, but he began to feel that he almost liked it. The excitement was nearly as good as that of loo. Of course it was a 'horrid bore,'—this having to go about in cabs under the sweltering sun of a London July day. Of course it was a 'horrid bore,'—this doubt about his money. And it went altogether against the grain with him that he should be engaged in any matter respecting the family property in agreement with his father and Mr. Bideawhile. But there was an importance in it that sustained him amidst his troubles. It is said that if you were to take a man of moderate parts and make him Prime Minister out of hand, he might probably do as well as other Prime Ministers, the greatness of the work elevating the man to its own level. In that way Dolly was elevated to the level of a man of business, and felt and enjoyed his own capacity. 'By George!' It depended chiefly upon him whether such a man as Melmotte should or should not be charged before the Lord Mayor. 'Perhaps I oughtn't to have promised,' he said to Squercum, sitting in the lawyer's office on a high-legged stool with a cigar in his mouth. He preferred Squercum to any other lawyer he had met because Squercum's room was untidy and homely, because there was nothing awful about it, and because he could sit in what position he pleased, and smoke all the time.

'Well; I don't think you ought, if you ask me,' said Squercum.

'You weren't there to be asked, old fellow.'

'Bideawhile shouldn't have asked you to agree to anything in my absence,' said Squercum indignantly. 'It was a very unprofessional thing on his part, and so I shall take an opportunity of telling him.'

'It was you told me to go.'

'Well;—yes. I wanted you to see what they were at in that room; but I told you to look on and say nothing.'

'I didn't speak half-a-dozen words.'

'You shouldn't have spoken those words. Your father then is quite clear that you did not sign the letter?'

'Oh, yes;—the governor is pig-headed, you know, but he's honest.'

'That's a matter of course,' said the lawyer. 'All men are honest; but they are generally specially honest to their own side. Bideawhile's honest; but you've got to fight him deuced close to prevent his getting the better of you. Melmotte has promised to pay the money on Friday, has he?'

'He's to bring it with him to Bruton Street.'

'I don't believe a word of it;—and I'm sure Bideawhile doesn't. In what shape will he bring it? He'll give you a cheque dated on Monday, and that'll give him two days more, and then on Monday there'll be a note to say the money can't be lodged till Wednesday. There should be no compromising with such a man. You only get from one mess into another. I told you neither to do anything or to say anything.'

'I suppose we can't help ourselves now. You're to be there on Friday. I particularly bargained for that. If you're there, there won't be any more compromising.'

Squercum made one or two further remarks to his client, not at all flattering to Dolly's vanity,—which might have caused offence had not there been such perfectly good feeling between the attorney and the young man. As it was, Dolly replied to everything that was said with increased flattery. 'If I was a sharp fellow like you, you know,' said Dolly, 'of course I should get along better; but I ain't, you know.' It was then settled that they should meet each other, and also meet Mr. Longestaffe senior, Bideawhile, and Melmotte, at twelve o'clock on Friday morning in Bruton Street.

Squercum was by no means satisfied. He had busied himself in this matter, and had ferreted things out, till he had pretty nearly got to the bottom of that affair about the houses in the East, and had managed to induce the heirs of the old man who had died to employ him. As to the Pickering property he had not a doubt on the subject. Old Longestaffe had been induced by promises of wonderful aid and by the bribe of a seat at the Board of the South Central Pacific and Mexican Railway to give up the title-deeds of the property,—as far as it was in his power to give them up; and had endeavoured to induce Dolly to do so also. As he had failed, Melmotte had supplemented his work by ingenuity, with which the reader is acquainted. All this was perfectly clear to Squercum, who thought that he saw before him a most attractive course of proceeding against the Great Financier. It was pure ambition rather than any hope of lucre that urged him on. He regarded Melmotte as a grand swindler,—perhaps the grandest that the world had ever known,—and he could conceive no greater honour than the detection, successful prosecution, and ultimate destroying of so great a man. To have hunted down Melmotte would make Squercum as great almost as Melmotte himself. But he felt himself to have been unfairly hampered by his own client. He did not believe that the money would be paid; but delay might rob him of his Melmotte. He had heard a good many things in the City, and believed it to be quite out of the question that Melmotte should raise the money,—but there were various ways in which a man might escape.

It may be remembered that Croll, the German clerk, preceded Melmotte into the City on Wednesday after Marie's refusal to sign the deeds. He, too, had his eyes open, and had perceived that things were not looking as well as they used to look. Croll had for many years been true to his patron, having been, upon the whole, very well paid for such truth. There had been times when things had gone badly with him, but he had believed in Melmotte, and, when Melmotte rose, had been rewarded for his faith. Mr. Croll at the present time had little investments of his own, not made under his employer's auspices, which would leave him not absolutely without bread for his family should the Melmotte affairs at any time take an awkward turn. Melmotte had never required from him service that was actually fraudulent,— had at any rate never required it by spoken words. Mr. Croll had not been over-scrupulous, and had occasionally been very useful to Mr. Melmotte. But there must be a limit to all things; and why should any man sacrifice himself beneath the ruins of a falling house,— when convinced that nothing he can do can prevent the fall? Mr. Croll would have been of course happy to witness Miss Melmotte's signature; but as for that other kind of witnessing,—this clearly to his thinking was not the time for such good-nature on his part.

'You know what's up now;—don't you?' said one of the junior clerks to Mr. Croll when he entered the office in Abchurch Lane.

'A good deal will be up soon,' said the German.

'Cohenlupe has gone!'

'And to vere has Mr. Cohenlupe gone?'

'He hasn't been civil enough to leave his address. I fancy he don't want his friends to have to trouble themselves by writing to him. Nobody seems to know what's become of him.'

'New York,' suggested Mr. Croll.

'They seem to think not. They're too hospitable in New York for Mr. Cohenlupe just at present. He's travelling private. He's on the continent somewhere,—

half across France by this time; but nobody knows what route he has taken. That'll be a poke in the ribs for the old boy;—eh, Croll?' Croll merely shook his head. 'I wonder what has become of Miles Grendall,' continued the clerk.

'Ven de rats is going avay it is bad for de house. I like de rats to stay.'

'There seems to have been a regular manufactory of Mexican Railway scrip.'

'Our governor knew noding about dat,' said Croll.

'He has a hat full of them at any rate. If they could have been kept up another fortnight they say Cohenlupe would have been worth nearly a million of money, and the governor would have been as good as the bank. Is it true they are going to have him before the Lord Mayor about the Pickering title-deeds?' Croll declared that he knew nothing about the matter, and settled himself down to his work.

In little more than two hours he was followed by Melmotte, who thus reached the City late in the afternoon. It was he knew too late to raise the money on that day, but he hoped that he might pave the way for getting it on the next day, which would be Thursday. Of course the first news which he heard was of the defection of Mr. Cohenlupe. It was Croll who told him. He turned back, and his jaw fell, but at first he said nothing.

'It's a bad thing,' said Mr. Croll.

'Yes;—it is bad. He had a vast amount of my property in his hands. Where has he gone?' Croll shook his head. 'It never rains but it pours,' said Melmotte. 'Well; I'll weather it all yet. I've been worse than I am now, Croll, as you know, and have had a hundred thousand pounds at my banker's,—loose cash,—before the month was out.'

'Yes, indeed,' said Croll.

'But the worst of it is that every one around me is so damnably jealous. It isn't what I've lost that will crush me, but what men will say that I've lost. Ever since I began to stand for Westminster there has been a dead set against me in the City. The whole of that affair of the dinner was planned,—planned, by G——, that it might ruin me. It was all laid out just as you would lay the foundation of a building. It is hard for one man to stand against all that when he has dealings so large as mine.'

'Very hard, Mr. Melmotte.'

'But they'll find they're mistaken yet. There's too much of the real stuff, Croll, for them to crush me. Property's a kind of thing that comes out right at last. It's cut and come again, you know, if the stuff is really there. But I mustn't stop talking here. I suppose I shall find Brehgert in Cuthbert's Court.'

'I should say so, Mr. Melmotte. Mr. Brehgert never leaves much before six.'

Then Mr. Melmotte took his hat and gloves, and the stick that he usually carried, and went out with his face carefully dressed in its usually jaunty air. But Croll as he went heard him mutter the name of Cohenlupe between his teeth. The part which he had to act is one very difficult to any actor. The carrying an external look of indifference when the heart is sinking within,—or has sunk almost to the very ground,—is more than difficult; it is an agonizing task. In all mental suffering the sufferer longs for solitude,—for permission to cast himself loose along the ground, so that every limb and every feature of his person may faint in sympathy with his heart. A grandly urbane deportment over a crushed spirit and ruined hopes is beyond the physical strength of most men;—but there have been men so strong. Melmotte very nearly accomplished it. It was only to the eyes of such a one as Herr Croll that the failure was perceptible.

Melmotte did find Mr. Brehgert. At this time Mr. Brehgert had completed his correspondence with Miss Longestaffe, in which he had mentioned the probability of great losses from the anticipated commercial failure in Mr. Melmotte's affairs. He had now heard that Mr. Cohenlupe had gone upon his travels, and was therefore nearly sure that his anticipation would be correct. Nevertheless, he received his old friend with a smile. When large sums of money are concerned there is seldom much of personal indignation between man and man. The loss of fifty pounds or of a few hundreds may create personal wrath;—but fifty thousand require equanimity. 'So Cohenlupe hasn't been seen in the City to-day,' said Brehgert.

'He has gone,' said Melmotte hoarsely.

'I think I once told you that Cohenlupe was not the man for large dealings.'

'Yes, you did,' said Melmotte.

'Well;—it can't be helped; can it? And what is it now?' Then Melmotte explained to Mr. Brehgert what it was that he wanted then, taking the various documents out of the bag which throughout the afternoon he had carried in his hand. Mr. Brehgert understood enough of his friend's affairs, and enough of affairs in general, to understand readily all that was required. He examined the documents, declaring, as he did so, that he did not know how the thing could be arranged by Friday. Melmotte replied that £50,000 was not a very large sum of money, that the security offered was worth twice as much as that. 'You will leave them with me this evening,' said Brehgert. Melmotte paused for a moment, and said that he would of course do so. He would have given much, very much, to have been sufficiently master of himself to have assented without hesitation;—but then the weight within was so very heavy!

Having left the papers and the bag with Mr. Brehgert, he walked westwards to the House of Commons. He was accustomed to remain in the City later than this, often not leaving it till seven,—though during the last week or ten days he had occasionally gone down to the House in the afternoon. It was now Wednesday, and there was no evening sitting;—but his mind was too full of other things to allow him to remember this. As he walked along the Embankment, his thoughts were very heavy. How would things go with him?—What would be the end of it? Ruin;—yes, but there were worse things than ruin. And a short time since he had been so fortunate;— had made himself so safe! As he looked back at it, he could hardly say how it had come to pass that he had been driven out of the track that he had laid down for himself. He had known that ruin would come, and had made himself so comfortably safe, so brilliantly safe, in spite of ruin. But insane ambition had driven him away from his anchorage. He told himself over and over again that the fault had been not in circumstances,—not in that which men call Fortune,—but in his own incapacity to bear his position. He saw it now. He felt it now. If he could only begin again, how different would his conduct be!

But of what avail were such regrets as these? He must take things as they were now, and see that, in dealing with them, he allowed himself to be carried away neither by pride nor cowardice. And if the worst should come to the worst, then let him face it like a man! There was a certain manliness about him which showed itself perhaps as strongly in his own self-condemnation as in any other part of his conduct at this time. Judging of himself, as though he were standing outside himself and looking on to another man's work, he pointed out to himself his own shortcomings. If it were all to be done again he thought that he could avoid this bump against the rocks on one side, and that terribly shattering blow on the other. There was much that he was ashamed of,—many a little act which recurred to him vividly in this solitary hour as a thing to be repented of with inner sackcloth and ashes. But never once, not for a moment, did it occur to him that he should repent of the fraud in which his whole life had been passed. No idea ever crossed his mind of what might have been the result had he lived the life of an honest man. Though he was inquiring into himself as closely as he could, he never even told himself that he had been dishonest. Fraud and dishonesty had been the very principle of his life, and had so become a part of his blood and bones that even in this extremity of his misery he made no question within himself as to his right judgment in regard to them. Not to cheat, not to be a scoundrel, not to live more luxuriously than others by cheating more brilliantly, was a condition of things to which his mind had never turned itself. In that respect

he accused himself of no want of judgment. But why
had he, so unrighteous himself, not made friends to himself of the Mammon of unrighteousness? Why had he
not conciliated Lord Mayors? Why had he trod upon
all the corns of all his neighbours? Why had he been
insolent at the India Office? Why had he trusted any
man as he had trusted Cohenlupe? Why had he not
stuck to Abchurch Lane instead of going into Parliament? Why had he called down unnecessary notice on
his head by entertaining the Emperor of China? It was
too late now, and he must bear it; but these were the
things that had ruined him.

He walked into Palace Yard and across it, to the door
of Westminster Abbey, before he found out that Parliament was not sitting. 'Oh, Wednesday! Of course it is,'
he said, turning round and directing his steps towards
Grosvenor Square. Then he remembered that in the
morning he had declared his purpose of dining at home,
and now he did not know what better use to make of the
present evening. His house could hardly be very comfortable to him. Marie no doubt would keep out of his
way, and he did not habitually receive much pleasure
from his wife's company. But in his own house he could
at least be alone. Then, as he walked slowly across the
park, thinking so intently on matters as hardly to observe
whether he himself were observed or no, he asked himself
whether it still might not be best for him to keep the
money which was settled on his daughter, to tell the
Longestaffes that he could make no payment, and to face
the worst that Mr. Squercum could do to him,—for he
knew already how busy Mr. Squercum was in the matter.
Though they should put him on his trial for forgery, what
of that? He had heard of trials in which the accused
criminals had been heroes to the multitude while their
cases were in progress,—who had been fêted from the
beginning to the end though no one had doubted their
guilt,—and who had come out unscathed at the last.
What evidence had they against him? It might be that
the Longestaffes and Bideawhiles and Squercums should
know that he was a forger, but their knowledge would

not produce a verdict. He, as member for Westminster, as the man who had entertained the Emperor, as the owner of one of the most gorgeous houses in London, as the great Melmotte, could certainly command the best half of the bar. He already felt what popular support might do for him. Surely there need be no despondency while so good a hope remained to him! He did tremble as he remembered Dolly Longestaffe's letter, and the letter of the old man who was dead. And he knew that it was possible that other things might be adduced; but would it not be better to face it all than surrender his money and become a pauper, seeing, as he did very clearly, that even by such surrender he could not cleanse his character?

But he had given those forged documents into the hands of Mr. Brehgert! Again he had acted in a hurry, —without giving sufficient thought to the matter in hand. He was angry with himself for that also. But how is a man to give sufficient thought to his affairs when no step that he takes can be other than ruinous? Yes;—he had certainly put into Brehgert's hands means of proving him to have been absolutely guilty of forgery. He did not think that Marie would disclaim the signatures, even though she had refused to sign the deeds, when she should understand that her father had written her name; nor did he think that his clerk would be urgent against him, as the forgery of Croll's name could not injure Croll. But Brehgert, should he discover what had been done, would certainly not permit him to escape. And now he had put these forgeries without any guard into Brehgert's hands.

He would tell Brehgert in the morning that he had changed his mind. He would see Brehgert before any action could have been taken on the documents, and Brehgert would no doubt restore them to him. Then he would instruct his daughter to hold the money fast, to sign no paper that should be put before her, and to draw the income herself. Having done that, he would let his foes do their worst. They might drag him to gaol. They probably would do so. He had an idea that he could not be admitted to bail if accused of forgery. But he would bear all that. If convicted he would bear the punishment, still hoping that an end might come. But how great was the chance that they might fail to convict him! As to the dead man's letter, and as to Dolly Longe-staffe's letter, he did not think that any sufficient evidence could be found. The evidence as to the deeds by which Marie was to have released the property was indeed conclusive; but he believed that he might still recover those documents. For the present it must be his duty to do nothing,—when he should have recovered and destroyed those documents,—and to live before the eyes of men as though he feared nothing.

He dined at home alone, in the study, and after dinner carefully went through various bundles of papers, pre-paring them for the eyes of those ministers of the law who would probably before long have the privilege of searching them. At dinner, and while he was thus em-ployed, he drank a bottle of champagne,—feeling himself greatly comforted by the process. If he could only hold up his head and look men in the face, he thought that he might still live through it all. How much had he done by his own unassisted powers! He had once been imprisoned for fraud at Hamburg, and had come out of gaol a pauper; friendless, with all his wretched antecedents against him. Now he was a member of the British House of Parliament, the undoubted owner of perhaps the most gorgeously furnished house in London, a man with an established character for high finance,—a commercial giant whose name was a familiar word on all the ex-changes of the two hemispheres. Even though he should be condemned to penal servitude for life, he would not all die. He rang the bell and desired that Madame Melmotte might be sent to him, and bade the servant bring him brandy.

In ten minutes his poor wife came crawling into the room. Every one connected with Melmotte regarded the man with a certain amount of awe,—every one except Marie, to whom alone he had at times been himself almost gentle. The servants all feared him, and his wife obeyed him implicitly when she could not keep away from him. She came in now and stood opposite him, while he spoke to her. She never sat in his presence in that room. He asked her where she and Marie kept their jewelry;—for during the last twelve months rich trinkets had been supplied to both of them. Of course she answered by another question. 'Is anything going to happen, Melmotte?'

'A good deal is going to happen. Are they here in this house, or in Grosvenor Square?'

'They are here.'

'Then have them all packed up,—as small as you can; never mind about wool and cases and all that. Have them close to your hand so that if you have to move you can take them with you. Do you understand?'

'Yes; I understand.'

'Why don't you speak, then?'

'What is going to happen, Melmotte?'

'How can I tell? You ought to know by this time that when a man's work is such as mine, things will happen. You'll be safe enough. Nothing can hurt you.'

'Can they hurt you, Melmotte?'

'Hurt me! I don't know what you call hurting. Whatever there is to be borne, I suppose it is I must bear it. I have not had it very soft all my life hitherto, and I don't think it's going to be very soft now.'

'Shall we have to move?'

'Very likely. Move! What's the harm of moving? You talk of moving as though that were the worst thing that could happen. How would you like to be in some place where they wouldn't let you move?'

'Are they going to send you to prison?'

'Hold your tongue.'

'Tell me, Melmotte;—are they going to?' Then the poor woman did sit down, overcome by her feelings.

'I didn't ask you to come here for a scene,' said Melmotte. 'Do as I bid you about your own jewels, and Marie's. The thing is to have them in small compass, and that you should not have it to do at the last moment, when you will be flurried and incapable. Now you needn't stay any longer, and it's no good asking any questions because I shan't answer them.' So dismissed, the poor woman crept out again, and immediately, after her own slow fashion, went to work with her ornaments.

Melmotte sat up during the greater part of the night sometimes sipping brandy and water, and sometimes smoking. But he did no work, and hardly touched a paper after his wife left him.

## Chapter LXXXII

### MARIE'S PERSEVERANCE

VERY early the next morning, very early that is for London life, Melmotte was told by a servant that Mr. Croll had called and wanted to see him. Then it immediately became a question with him whether he wanted to see Croll. 'Is it anything special?' he asked. The man thought that it was something special, as Croll had declared his purpose of waiting when told that Mr. Melmotte was not as yet dressed. This happened at about nine o'clock in the morning. Melmotte longed to know every detail of Croll's manner,—to know even the servant's opinion of the clerk's manner,—but he did not dare to ask a question. Melmotte thought that it might be well to be gracious. 'Ask him if he has breakfasted, and if not give him something in the study.' But Mr. Croll had breakfasted and declined any further refreshment.

Nevertheless Melmotte had not as yet made up his mind that he would meet his clerk. His clerk was his clerk. It might perhaps be well that he should first go into the City and send word to Croll, bidding him wait for his return. Over and over again, against his will, the question of flying would present itself to him; but, though he discussed it within his own bosom in every form, he knew that he could not fly. And if he stood his ground,—as most assuredly he would do,—then must he not be afraid

to meet any man, let the man come with what thunder-
bolts in his hand he might. Of course sooner or later
some man must come with a thunderbolt,—and why not
Croll as well as another? He stood against a press in his
chamber, with a razor in his hand, and steadied himself.
How easily might he put an end to it all! Then he rang
his bell and desired that Croll might be shown up into
his room.

The three or four minutes which intervened seemed to
him to be very long. He had absolutely forgotten in his
anxiety that the lather was still upon his face. But he
could not smother his anxiety. He was fighting with it
at every turn, but he could not conquer it. When the
knock came at his door, he grasped at his own breast as
though to support himself. With a hoarse voice he told
the man to come in, and Croll himself appeared, opening
the door gently and very slowly. Melmotte had left the
bag which contained the papers in possession of Mr.
Brehgert, and he now saw, at a glance, that Croll had
got the bag in his hand,—and could see also by the shape
of the bag that the bag contained the papers. The man
therefore had in his own hands, in his own keeping, the
very documents to which his own name had been forged!
There was no longer a hope, no longer a chance that
Croll should be ignorant of what had been done. 'Well,
Croll,' he said with an attempt at a smile, 'what brings
you here so early?' He was pale as death, and let him
struggle as he would, could not restrain himself from
trembling.

'Herr Brehgert vas vid me last night,' said Croll.

'Eh!'

'And he thought I had better bring these back to you.
That's all.' Croll spoke in a very low voice, with his eyes
fixed on his master's face, but with nothing of a threat in
his attitude or manner.

'Eh!' repeated Melmotte. Even though he might have
saved himself from all coming evils by a bold demeanour
at that moment, he could not assume it. But it all flashed
upon him at a moment. Brehgert had seen Croll after
he, Melmotte, had left the City, had then discovered the

forgery, and had taken this way of sending back all the
forged documents. He had known Brehgert to be of all
men who ever lived the most good-natured, but he could
hardly believe in pure good-nature such as this. It
seemed that the thunderbolt was not yet to fall.

'Mr. Brehgert came to me,' continued Croll, 'because
one signature was wanting. It was very late, so I took
them home with me. I said I'd bring them to you in the
morning.'

They both knew that he had forged the documents,
Brehgert and Croll; but how would that concern him,
Melmotte, if these two friends had resolved together
that they would not expose him? He had desired to get
the documents back into his own hands, and here they
were! Melmotte's immediate trouble arose from the
difficulty of speaking in a proper manner to his own
servant who had just detected him in forgery. He
couldn't speak. There were no words appropriate to
such an occasion. 'It vas a strong order, Mr. Melmotte,'
said Croll. Melmotte tried to smile but only grinned.
'I vill not be back in the Lane, Mr. Melmotte.'

'Not back at the office, Croll?'

'I tink not;—no. De leetle money coming to me, you
will send it. Adieu.' And so Mr. Croll took his final
leave of his old master after an intercourse which had
lasted twenty years. We may imagine that Herr Croll
found his spirits to be oppressed and his capacity for
business to be obliterated by his patron's misfortunes
rather than by his patron's guilt. But he had not behaved
unkindly. He had merely remarked that the forgery of
his own name half-a-dozen times over was a 'strong
order.'

Melmotte opened the bag, and examined the documents one by one. It had been necessary that Marie
should sign her name some half-dozen times, and Marie's
father had made all the necessary forgeries. It had been
of course necessary that each name should be witnessed;
—but here the forger had scamped his work. Croll's
name he had written five times; but one forged signature
he had left unattested! Again he had himself been at

fault. Again he had aided his own ruin by his own care-
lessness. One seems inclined to think sometimes that any
fool might do an honest business. But fraud requires a
man to be alive and wide awake at every turn!

Melmotte had desired to have the documents back in
his own hands, and now he had them. Did it matter
much that Brehgert and Croll both knew the crime which
he had committed? Had they meant to take legal steps
against him they would not have returned the forgeries
to his own hands. Brehgert, he thought, would never tell
the tale;—unless there should arise some most improbable emergency in which he might make money by telling it; but he was by no means so sure of Croll. Croll had
signified his intention of leaving Melmotte's service, and
would therefore probably enter some rival service, and
thus become an enemy to his late master. There could
be no reason why Croll should keep the secret. Even if he
got no direct profit by telling it, he would curry favour
by making it known. Of course Croll would tell it.

But what harm could the telling of such a secret do
him? The girl was his own daughter! The money had
been his own money! The man had been his own servant!
There had been no fraud; no robbery; no purpose of
peculation. Melmotte, as he thought of this, became
almost proud of what he had done, thinking that if the
evidence were suppressed the knowledge of the facts
could do him no harm. But the evidence must be suppressed, and with the view of suppressing it he took the
little bag and all the papers down with him to the study.
Then he ate his breakfast,—and suppressed the evidence
by the aid of his gas lamp.

When this was accomplished he hesitated as to the
manner in which he would pass his day. He had now
given up all idea of raising the money for Longestaffe.
He had even considered the language in which he would
explain to the assembled gentlemen on the morrow the
fact that a little difficulty still presented itself, and that
as he could not exactly name a day, he must leave the
matter in their hands. For he had resolved that he would
not evade the meeting. Cohenlupe had gone since he had

made his promise, and he would throw all the blame on Cohenlupe. Everybody knows that when panics arise the breaking of one merchant causes the downfall of another. Cohenlupe should bear the burden. But as that must be so, he could do no good by going into the City. His pecuniary downfall had now become too much a matter of certainty to be staved off by his presence; and his personal security could hardly be assisted by it. There would be nothing for him to do. Cohenlupe had gone. Miles Grendall had gone. Croll had gone. He could hardly go to Cuthbert's Court and face Mr. Brehgert! He would stay at home till it was time for him to go down to the House, and then he would face the world there. He would dine down at the House, and stand about in the smoking-room with his hat on, and be visible in the lobbies, and take his seat among his brother legislators,—and, if it were possible, rise on his legs and make a speech to them. He was about to have a crushing fall,—but the world should say that he had fallen like a man.

About eleven his daughter came to him as he sat in the study. It can hardly be said that he had ever been kind to Marie, but perhaps she was the only person who in the whole course of his career had received indulgence at his hands. He had often beaten her; but he had also often made her presents and smiled on her, and in the periods of his opulence, had allowed her pocket-money almost without limit. Now she had not only disobeyed him, but by most perverse obstinacy on her part had driven him to acts of forgery which had already been detected. He had cause to be angry now with Marie if he had ever had cause for anger. But he had almost forgotten the transaction. He had at any rate forgotten the violence of his own feelings at the time of its occurrence. He was no longer anxious that the release should be made, and therefore no longer angry with her for her refusal.

'Papa,' she said, coming very gently into the room, 'I think that perhaps I was wrong yesterday.'

'Of course you were wrong;—but it doesn't matter now.'

'If you wish it I'll sign those papers. I don't suppose Lord Nidderdale means to come any more;—and I'm sure I don't care whether he does or not.'

'What makes you think that, Marie?'

'I was out last night at Lady Julia Goldsheiner's, and he was there. I'm sure he doesn't mean to come here any more.'

'Was he uncivil to you?'

'Oh dear no. He's never uncivil. But I'm sure of it. Never mind how. I never told him that I cared for him and I never did care for him. Papa, is there something going to happen?'

'What do you mean?'

'Some misfortune! Oh, papa, why didn't you let me marry that other man?'

'He is a penniless adventurer.'

'But he would have had this money that I call my money, and then there would have been enough for us all. Papa, he would marry me still if you would let him.'

'Have you seen him since you went to Liverpool?'

'Never, papa.'

'Or heard from him?'

'Not a line.'

'Then what makes you think he would marry you?'

'He would if I got hold of him and told him. And he is a baronet. And there would be plenty of money for us all. And we could go and live in Germany.'

'We could do that just as well without your marrying.'

'But I suppose, papa, I am to be considered as somebody. I don't want after all to run away from London, just as if everybody had turned up their noses at me. I like him, and I don't like anybody else.'

'He wouldn't take the trouble to go to Liverpool with you.'

'He got tipsy. I know all about that. I don't mean to say that he's anything particularly grand. I don't know that anybody is very grand. He's as good as anybody else.'

'It can't be done, Marie.'

'Why can't it be done?'

'There are a dozen reasons. Why should my money be given up to him? And it is too late. There are other things to be thought of now than marriage.'

'You don't want me to sign the papers?'

'No;—I haven't got the papers. But I want you to remember that the money is mine and not yours. It may be that much may depend on you, and that I shall have to trust to you for nearly everything. Do not let me find myself deceived by my daughter.'

'I won't,—if you'll let me see Sir Felix Carbury once more.'

Then the father's pride again reasserted itself and he became angry. 'I tell you, you little fool, that it is out of the question. Why cannot you believe me? Has your mother spoken to you about your jewels? Get them packed up, so that you can carry them away in your hand if we have to leave this suddenly. You are an idiot to think of that young man. As you say, I don't know that any of them are very good, but among them all he is about the worst. Go away and do as I bid you.'

That afternoon the page in Welbeck Street came up to Lady Carbury and told her that there was a young lady downstairs who wanted to see Sir Felix. At this time the dominion of Sir Felix in his mother's house had been much curtailed. His latch-key had been surreptitiously taken away from him, and all messages brought for him reached his hands through those of his mother. The plasters were not removed from his face, so that he was still subject to that loss of self-assertion with which we are told that hitherto dominant cocks become afflicted when they have been daubed with mud. Lady Carbury asked sundry questions about the lady, suspecting that Ruby Ruggles, of whom she had heard, had come to seek her lover. The page could give no special description, merely saying that the young lady wore a black veil. Lady Carbury directed that the young lady should be shown into her own presence,—and Marie Melmotte was ushered into the room. 'I dare say you don't remember me, Lady Carbury,' Marie said. 'I am Marie Melmotte.'

At first Lady Carbury had not recognized her visitor;

—but she did so before she replied. 'Yes, Miss Melmotte, I remember you.'

'Yes;—I am Mr. Melmotte's daughter. How is your son? I hope he is better. They told me he had been horribly used by a dreadful man in the street.'

'Sit down, Miss Melmotte. He is getting better.' Now Lady Carbury had heard within the last two days from Mr. Broune that 'it was all over' with Melmotte. Broune had declared his very strong belief, his thorough conviction, that Melmotte had committed various forgeries, that his speculations had gone so much against him as to leave him a ruined man, and, in short, that the great Melmotte bubble was on the very point of bursting. 'Everybody says that he'll be in gaol before a week is over.'. That was the information which had reached Lady Carbury about the Melmottes only on the previous evening.

'I want to see him,' said Marie. Lady Carbury, hardly knowing what answer to make, was silent for a while. 'I suppose he told you everything;—didn't he? You know that we were to have been married? I loved him very much, and so I do still. I am not ashamed of coming and telling you.'

'I thought it was all off,' said Lady Carbury.

'I never said so. Does he say so? Your daughter came to me and was very good to me. I do so love her. She said that it was all over; but perhaps she was wrong. It shan't be all over if he will be true.'

Lady Carbury was taken greatly by surprise. It seemed to her at the moment that this young lady, knowing that her own father was ruined, was looking out for another home, and was doing so with a considerable amount of audacity. She gave Marie little credit either for affection or for generosity; but yet she was unwilling to answer her roughly. 'I am afraid,' she said, 'that it would not be suitable.'

'Why should it not be suitable? They can't take my money away. There is enough for all of us even if papa wanted to live with us;—but it is mine. It is ever so much;—I don't know how much, but a great deal. We should be quite rich enough. I ain't a bit ashamed to come and tell you, because we were engaged. I know he isn't rich, and I should have thought it would be suitable.'

It then occurred to Lady Carbury that if this were true the marriage after all might be suitable. But how was she to find out whether it was true? 'I understand that your papa is opposed to it,' she said.

'Yes, he is;—but papa can't prevent me, and papa can't make me give up the money. It's ever so many thousands a year, I know. If I can dare to do it, why can't he?'

Lady Carbury was so beside herself with doubts, that she found it impossible to form any decision. It would be necessary that she should see Mr. Broune. What to do with her son, how to bestow him, in what way to get rid of him so that in ridding herself of him she might not aid in destroying him,—this was the great trouble of her life, the burden that was breaking her back. Now this girl was not only willing but persistently anxious to take her black sheep and to endow him,—as she declared,—with ever so many thousands a year. If the thousands were there,—or even an income of a single thousand a year,—then what a blessing would such a marriage be! Sir Felix had already fallen so low that his mother on his behalf would not be justified in declining a connection with the Melmottes because the Melmottes had fallen. To get any niche in the world for him in which he might live with comparative safety would now be to her a heaven-sent comfort. 'My son is upstairs,' she said. 'I will go up and speak to him.'

'Tell him I am here and that I have said that I will forgive him everything, and that I love him still, and that if he will be true to me, I will be true to him.'

'I couldn't go down to her,' said Sir Felix, 'with my face all in this way.'

'I don't think she would mind that.'

'I couldn't do it. Besides, I don't believe about her money. I never did believe it. That was the real reason why I didn't go to Liverpool.'

'I think I would see her if I were you, Felix. We could find out to a certainty about her fortune. It is evident at any rate that she is very fond of you.'

'What's the use of that, if he is ruined?' He would not go down to see the girl,—because he could not endure to expose his face, and was ashamed of the wounds which he had received in the street. As regarded the money he half-believed and half-disbelieved Marie's story. But the fruition of the money, if it were within his reach, would be far off and to be attained with much trouble; whereas the nuisance of a scene with Marie would be immediate. How could he kiss his future bride, with his nose bound up with a bandage?

'What shall I say to her?' asked his mother.

'She oughtn't to have come. I should tell her just that. You might send the maid to her to tell her that you couldn't see her again.'

But Lady Carbury could not treat the girl after that fashion. She returned to the drawing-room, descending the stairs very slowly, and thinking what answer she would make. 'Miss Melmotte,' she said, 'my son feels that everything has been so changed since he and you last met, that nothing can be gained by a renewal of your acquaintance.'

'That is his message;—is it?' Lady Carbury remained silent. 'Then he is indeed all that they have told me; and I am ashamed that I should have loved him. I am ashamed;—not of coming here, although you will think that I have run after him. I don't see why a girl should not run after a man if they have been engaged together. But I'm ashamed of thinking so much of so mean a person. Goodbye, Lady Carbury.'

'Good-bye, Miss Melmotte. I don't think you should be angry with me.'

'No;—no. I am not angry with you. You can forget me now as soon as you please, and I will try to forget him.'

Then with a rapid step she walked back to Bruton Street, going round by Grosvenor Square and in front of her old house on the way. What should she now do with herself? What sort of life should she endeavour to prepare for herself? The life that she had led for the last year had been thoroughly wretched. The poverty and hardship which she remembered in her early days had been more endurable. The servitude to which she had been subjected before she had learned by intercourse with the world to assert herself, had been preferable. In these days of her grandeur, in which she had danced with princes, and seen an emperor in her father's house, and been affianced to lords, she had encountered degradation which had been abominable to her. She had really loved; —but had found out that her golden idol was made of the basest clay. She had then declared to herself that bad as the clay was she would still love it;—but even the clay had turned away from her and had refused her love!

She was well aware that some catastrophe was about to happen to her father. Catastrophes had happened before, and she had been conscious of their coming. But now the blow would be a very heavy blow. They would again be driven to pack up and move and seek some other city,—probably in some very distant part. But go where she might, she would now be her own mistress. That was the one resolution she succeeded in forming before she re-entered the house in Bruton Street.

## Chapter LXXXIII

### MELMOTTE AGAIN AT THE HOUSE

ON that Thursday afternoon it was known everywhere that there was to be a general ruin of all the Melmotte affairs. As soon as Cohenlupe had gone, no man doubted. The City men who had not gone to the dinner prided themselves on their foresight, as did also the politicians who had declined to meet the Emperor of China at the table of the suspected Financier. They who had got up the dinner and had been instrumental in taking the Emperor to the house in Grosvenor Square, and they also who had brought him forward at Westminster and had fought his battle for him, were aware that they would have to defend themselves against heavy attacks. No one now had a word to say in his favour, or a doubt as to his guilt. The Grendalls had retired altogether out of town, and were no longer even heard of. Lord Alfred had not been seen since the day of the dinner. The Duchess of Albury, too, went into the country some weeks earlier than usual, quelled, as the world said, by the general Melmotte failure. But this departure had not as yet taken place at the time at which we have now arrived.

When the Speaker took his seat in the House, soon after four o'clock, there were a great many members present, and a general feeling prevailed that the world was more than ordinarily alive because of Melmotte and his failures. It had been confidently asserted throughout the morning that he would be put upon his trial for forgery in reference to the purchase of the Pickering property from Mr. Longestaffe, and it was known that he had not as yet shown himself anywhere on this day. People had gone to look at the house in Grosvenor Square,—not knowing that he was still living in Mr. Longestaffe's house in Bruton Street, and had come away with the impression that the desolation of ruin and crime was already plainly to be seen upon it. 'I wonder where he is,' said Mr. Lupton to Mr. Beauchamp Beauclerk in one of the lobbies of the house.

'They say he hasn't been in the City all day. I suppose he's in Longestaffe's house. That poor fellow has got it heavy all round. The man has got his place in the country and his house in town. There's Nidderdale. I wonder what he thinks about it all.'

'This is awful;—ain't it?' said Nidderdale.

'It might have been worse, I should say, as far as you are concerned,' replied Mr. Lupton.

'Well, yes. But I'll tell you what, Lupton. I don't quite understand it all yet. Our lawyer said three days ago that the money was certainly there.'

'And Cohenlupe was certainly here three days ago,' said Lupton,—'but he isn't here now. It seems to me

that it has just happened in time for you.' Lord Nidderdale shook his head and tried to look very grave.

'There's Brown,' said Sir Orlando Drought, hurrying
up to the commercial gentleman whose mistakes about
finance Mr. Melmotte on a previous occasion had been
anxious to correct. 'He'll be able to tell us where he is.
It was rumoured, you know, an hour ago, that he was off
to the continent after Cohenlupe.' But Mr. Brown shook
his head. Mr. Brown didn't know anything. But Mr.
Brown was very strongly of opinion that the police would
know all that there was to be known about Mr. Melmotte
before this time on the following day. Mr. Brown had
been very bitter against Melmotte since that memorable
attack made upon him in the House.

Even ministers as they sat to be badgered by the
ordinary question-mongers of the day were more intent
upon Melmotte than upon their own defence. 'Do you
know anything about it?' asked the Chancellor of the
Exchequer of the Secretary of State for the Home Department.

'I understand that no order has been given for his
arrest. There is a general opinion that he has committed
forgery; but I doubt whether they've got their evidence
together.'

'He's a ruined man, I suppose,' said the Chancellor.

'I doubt whether he ever was a rich man. But I'll tell
you what;—he has been about the grandest rogue we've
seen yet. He must have spent over a hundred thousand
pounds during the last twelve months on his personal
expenses. I wonder how the Emperor will like it when
he learns the truth.' Another minister sitting close to
the Secretary of State was of opinion that the Emperor
of China would not care half so much about it as our own
First Lord of the Treasury.

At this moment there came a silence over the House
which was almost audible. They who know the sensation
which arises from the continued hum of many suppressed
voices will know also how plain to the ear is the feeling
caused by the discontinuance of the sound. Everybody
looked up, but everybody looked up in perfect silence.

An Under-Secretary of State had just got upon his legs to answer a most indignant question as to an alteration of the colour of the facings of a certain regiment, his prepared answer to which, however, was so happy as to allow him to anticipate quite a little triumph. It is not often that such a Godsend comes in the way of an undersecretary; and he was intent upon his performance. But even he was startled into momentary oblivion of his well-arranged point. Augustus Melmotte, the member for Westminster, was walking up the centre of the House.

He had succeeded by this time in learning so much of the forms of the House as to know what to do with his hat,—when to wear it, and when to take it off,—and how to sit down. As he entered by the door facing the Speaker, he wore his hat on the side of his head, as was his custom. Much of the arrogance of his appearance had come from this habit, which had been adopted probably from a conviction that it added something to his powers of self-assertion. At this moment he was more determined than ever that no one should trace in his outer gait or in any feature of his face any sign of that ruin which, as he well knew, all men were anticipating. Therefore, perhaps, his hat was a little more cocked than usual, and the lappels of his coat were thrown back a little wider, displaying the large jewelled studs which he wore in his shirt; and the arrogance conveyed by his mouth and chin was specially conspicuous. He had come down in his brougham, and as he had walked up Westminster Hall and entered the House by the private door of the members, and then made his way in across the great lobby and between the doorkeepers,—no one had spoken a word to him. He had of course seen many whom he had known. He had indeed known nearly all whom he had seen;—but he had been aware, from the beginning of this enterprise of the day, that men would shun him, and that he must bear their cold looks and colder silence without seeming to notice them. He had schooled himself to the task, and he was now performing it. It was not only that he would have to move among men without being noticed, but that he must endure to pass the whole evening in the same plight. But he was resolved, and he was now doing it. He bowed to the Speaker with more than usual courtesy, raising his hat with more than usual care, and seated himself, as usual, on the third opposition-bench, but with more than his usual fling. He was a big man, who always endeavoured to make an effect by deportment, and was therefore customarily conspicuous in his movements. He was desirous now of being as he was always, neither more nor less demonstrative;—but, as a matter of course, he exceeded; and it seemed to those who looked at him that there was a special impudence in the manner in which he walked up the House and took his seat. The Under-Secretary of State, who was on his legs, was struck almost dumb, and his morsel of wit about the facings was lost to Parliament for ever.

That unfortunate young man, Lord Nidderdale, occupied the seat next to that on which Melmotte had placed himself. It had so happened three or four times since Melmotte had been in the House, as the young lord, fully intending to marry the Financier's daughter, had resolved that he would not be ashamed of his father-in-law. He understood that countenance of the sort which he as a young aristocrat could give to the man of millions who had risen no one knew whence, was part of the bargain in reference to the marriage, and he was gifted with a mingled honesty and courage which together made him willing and able to carry out his idea. He had given Melmotte little lessons as to ordinary forms of the House, and had done what in him lay to earn the money which was to be forthcoming. But it had become manifest both to him and to his father during the last two days,—very painfully manifest to his father,—that the thing must be abandoned. And if so,—then why should he be any longer gracious to Melmotte? And, moreover, though he had been ready to be courteous to a very vulgar and a very disagreeable man, he was not anxious to extend his civilities to one who, as he was now assured, had been certainly guilty of forgery. But to get up at once and leave his seat because Melmotte had placed himself by his side, did not suit the turn of his mind. He looked round to his neighbour on the right with a half-comic look of misery, and then prepared himself to bear his punishment, whatever it might be.

'Have you been up with Marie to-day?' said Melmotte.

'No;—I've not,' replied the lord.

'Why don't you go? She's always asking about you now. I hope we shall be in our own house again next week, and then we shall be able to make you comfortable.'

Could it be possible that the man did not know that all the world was united in accusing him of forgery? 'I'll tell you what it is,' said Nidderdale. 'I think you had better see my governor again, Mr. Melmotte.'

'There's nothing wrong, I hope.'

'Well;—I don't know. You'd better see him. I'm going now. I only just came down to enter an appearance.' He had to cross Melmotte on his way out, and as he did so Melmotte grasped him by the hand. 'Good night, my boy,' said Melmotte quite aloud,—in a voice much louder than that which members generally allow themselves for conversation. Nidderdale was confused and unhappy; but there was probably not a man in the House who did not understand the whole thing. He rushed down through the gangway and out through the doors with a hurried step, and as he escaped into the lobby he met Lionel Lupton, who, since his little conversation with Mr. Beauclerk, had heard further news.

'You know what has happened, Nidderdale?'

'About Melmotte, you mean?'

'Yes, about Melmotte,' continued Lupton. 'He has been arrested in his own house within the last half-hour on a charge of forgery.'

'I wish he had,' said Nidderdale, 'with all my heart. If you go in you'll find him sitting there as large as life. He has been talking to me as though everything were all right.'

'Compton was here not a moment ago, and said that he had been taken under a warrant from the Lord Mayor.'

'The Lord Mayor is a member and had better come and fetch his prisoner himself. At any rate he's there. I shouldn't wonder if he wasn't on his legs before long.'

Melmotte kept his seat steadily till seven, at which hour the House adjourned till nine. He was one of the last to leave, and then with a slow step,—with almost majestic steps,—he descended to the dining-room and ordered his dinner. There were many men there, and some little difficulty about a seat. No one was very willing to make room for him. But at last he secured a place, almost jostling some unfortunate who was there before him. It was impossible to expel him,—almost as impossible to sit next him. Even the waiters were unwilling to serve him;—but with patience and endurance he did at last get his dinner. He was there in his right, as a member of the House of Commons, and there was no ground on which such service as he required could be refused to him. It was not long before he had the table all to himself. But of this he took no apparent notice. He spoke loudly to the waiters and drank his bottle of champagne with much apparent enjoyment. Since his friendly intercourse with Nidderdale no one had spoken to him, nor had he spoken to any man. They who watched him declared among themselves that he was happy in his own audacity;—but in truth he was probably at that moment the most utterly wretched man in London. He would have better studied his personal comfort had he gone to his bed, and spent his evening in groans and wailings. But even he, with all the world now gone from him, with nothing before him but the extremest misery which the indignation of offended laws could inflict, was able to spend the last moments of his freedom in making a reputation at any rate for audacity. It was thus that Augustus Melmotte wrapped his toga around him before his death!

He went from the dining-room to the smoking-room, and there, taking from his pocket a huge case which he always carried, proceeded to light a cigar about eight inches long. Mr. Brown, from the City, was in the room, and Melmotte, with a smile and a bow, offered Mr.

Brown one of the same. Mr. Brown was a short, fat, round little man, over sixty, who was always endeavouring to give to a somewhat commonplace set of features an air of importance by the contraction of his lips and the knitting of his brows. It was as good as a play to see Mr. Brown jumping back from any contact with the wicked one, and putting on a double frown as he looked at the impudent sinner. 'You needn't think so much, you know, of what I said the other night. I didn't mean any offence.' So spoke Melmotte, and then laughed with a loud, hoarse laugh, looking round upon the assembled crowd as though he were enjoying his triumph.

He sat after that and smoked in silence. Once again he burst out into a laugh, as though peculiarly amused with his own thoughts;—as though he were declaring to himself with much inward humour that all these men around him were fools for believing the stories which they had heard; but he made no further attempt to speak to any one. Soon after nine he went back again into the House, and again took his old place. At this time he had swallowed three glasses of brandy and water, as well as the champagne, and was brave enough almost for anything. There was some debate going on in reference to the game laws,—a subject on which Melmotte was as ignorant as one of his housemaids,—but, as some speaker sat down, he jumped up to his legs. Another gentleman had also risen, and when the House called to that other gentleman Melmotte gave way. The other gentleman had not much to say, and in a few minutes Melmotte was again on his legs. Who shall dare to describe the thoughts which would cross the august mind of a Speaker of the House of Commons at such a moment? Of Melmotte's villainy he had no official knowledge. And even could he have had such knowledge it was not for him to act upon it. The man was a member of the House, and as much entitled to speak as another. But it seemed on that occasion that the Speaker was anxious to save the House from disgrace;—for twice and thrice he refused to have his 'eye caught' by the member for Westminster. As long as any other member would rise he would not have

his eye caught. But Melmotte was persistent, and determined not to be put down. At last no one else would
speak, and the House was about to negative the motion
without a division,—when Melmotte was again on his
legs, still persisting. The Speaker scowled at him and
leaned back in his chair. Melmotte standing erect, turning his head round from one side of the House to another,
as though determined that all should see his audacity,
propping himself with his knees against the seat before
him, remained for half a minute perfectly silent. He was
drunk,—but better able than most drunken men to steady
himself, and showing in his face none of those outward
signs of intoxication by which drunkenness is generally
made apparent. But he had forgotten in his audacity
that words are needed for the making of a speech, and
now he had not a word at his command. He stumbled
forward, recovered himself, then looked once more round
the House with a glance of anger, and after that toppled
headlong over the shoulders of Mr. Beauchamp Beauclerk,
who was sitting in front of him.

He might have wrapped his toga around him better
perhaps had he remained at home, but if to have himself
talked about was his only object, he could hardly have
taken a surer course. The scene, as it occurred, was one
very likely to be remembered when the performer should
have been carried away into enforced obscurity. There
was much commotion in the House. Mr. Beauclerk, a
man of natural good nature, though at the moment put
to considerable personal inconvenience, hastened, when
he recovered his own equilibrium, to assist the drunken
man. But Melmotte had by no means lost the power of
helping himself. He quickly recovered his legs, and then
reseating himself, put his hat on, and endeavoured to
look as though nothing special had occurred. The House
resumed its business, taking no further notice of Melmotte,
and having no special rule of its own as to the treatment
to be adopted with drunken members. But the member
for Westminster caused no further inconvenience. He
remained in his seat for perhaps ten minutes, and then,
not with a very steady step, but still with capacity suffi-

cient for his own guidance, he made his way down to the doors. His exit was watched in silence, and the moment was an anxious one for the Speaker, the clerks, and all who were near him. Had he fallen some one,—or rather some two or three,—must have picked him up and carried him out. But he did not fall either there or in the lobbies, or on his way down to Palace Yard. Many were looking at him, but none touched him. When he had got through the gates, leaning against the wall he hallooed for his brougham, and the servant who was waiting for him soon took him home to Bruton Street. That was the last which the British Parliament saw of its new member for Westminster.

Melmotte as soon as he reached home got into his own sitting-room without difficulty, and called for more brandy and water. Between eleven and twelve he was left there by his servant with a bottle of brandy, three or four bottles of sodawater, and his cigar-case. Neither of the ladies of the family came to him, nor did he speak of them. Nor was he so drunk then as to give rise to any suspicion in the mind of the servant. He was habitually left there at night, and the servant as usual went to his bed. But at nine o'clock on the following morning the maid-servant found him dead upon the floor. Drunk as he had been,—more drunk as he probably became during the night,—still he was able to deliver himself from the indignities and penalties to which the law might have subjected him by a dose of prussic acid.

## Chapter LXXXIV

### PAUL MONTAGUE'S VINDICATION

IT is hoped that the reader need hardly be informed that Hetta Carbury was a very miserable young woman as soon as she decided that duty compelled her to divide herself altogether from Paul Montague. I think that she was irrational; but to her it seemed that the offence

against herself,—the offence against her own dignity as
a woman,—was too great to be forgiven. There can be
no doubt that it would all have been forgiven with the
greatest ease had Paul told the story before it had reached
her ears from any other source. Had he said to her,—
when her heart was softest towards him,—I once loved
another woman, and that woman is here now in London,
a trouble to me, persecuting me, and her history is so
and so, and the history of my love for her was after this
fashion, and the history of my declining love is after that
fashion, and of this at any rate you may be sure, that this
woman has never been near my heart from the first
moment in which I saw you;—had he told it to her thus,
there would not have been an opening for anger. And he
doubtless would have so told it, had not Hetta's brother
interfered too quickly. He was then forced to exculpate
himself, to confess rather than to tell his own story,—and
to admit facts which wore the air of having been concealed, and which had already been conceived to be altogether damning if true. It was that journey to Lowestoft,
not yet a month old, which did the mischief,—a journey
as to which Hetta was not slow in understanding all that
Roger Carbury had thought about it, though Roger
would say nothing of it to herself. Paul had been staying
at the seaside with this woman in amicable intimacy,—
this horrid woman,—in intimacy worse than amicable,
and had been visiting her daily at Islington! Hetta felt
quite sure that he had never passed a day without going
there since the arrival of the woman; and everybody
would know what that meant. And during this very hour
he had been,—well, perhaps not exactly making love to
herself, but looking at her and talking to her, and behaving to her in a manner such as could not but make her
understand that he intended to make love to her. Of
course they had really understood it, since they had met
at Madame Melmotte's first ball, when she had made a
plea that she could not allow herself to dance with him
more than,—say half-a-dozen times. Of course she had
not intended him then to know that she would receive his
love with favour; but equally of course she had known that

he must so feel it. She had not only told herself, but had told her mother, that her heart was given away to this man; and yet the man during this very time was spending his hours with a—woman, with a strange American woman, to whom he acknowledged that he had been once engaged. How could she not quarrel with him? How could she refrain from telling him that everything must be over between them? Everybody was against him,—her mother, her brother, and her cousin: and she felt that she had not a word to say in his defence. A horrid woman! A wretched, bad, bold American intriguing woman! It was terrible to her that a friend of hers should ever have attached himself to such a creature;— but that he should have come to her with a second tale of love long, long before he had cleared himself from the first;—perhaps with no intention of clearing himself from the first! Of course she could not forgive him! No;—she would never forgive him. She would break her heart for him. That was a matter of course; but she would never forgive him. She knew well what it was that her mother wanted. Her mother thought that by forcing her into a quarrel with Montague she would force her also into a marriage with Roger Carbury. But her mother would find out that in that she was mistaken. She would never marry her cousin, though she would be always ready to acknowledge his worth. She was sure now that she would never marry any man. As she made this resolve she had a wicked satisfaction in feeling that it would be a trouble to her mother;—for though she was altogether in accord with Lady Carbury as to the iniquities of Paul Montague she was not the less angry with her mother for being so ready to expose those iniquities.

Oh, with what slow, cautious fingers, with what heart-broken tenderness did she take out from its guardian case the brooch which Paul had given her! It had as yet been an only present, and in thanking him for it, which she had done with full, free-spoken words of love, she had begged him to send her no other, so that that might ever be to her,—to her dying day,—the one precious thing that had been given to her by her lover while she was yet a girl. Now it must be sent back;—and, no doubt, it would go to that abominable woman! But her fingers lingered over it as she touched it, and she would fain have kissed it, had she not told herself that she would have been disgraced, even in her solitude, by such a demonstration of affection. She had given her answer to Paul Montague; and, as she would have no further personal correspondence with him, she took the brooch to her mother with a request that it might be returned.

'Of course, my dear, I will send it back to him. Is there nothing else?'

'No, mamma;—nothing else. I have no letters, and no other present. You always knew everything that took place. If you will just send that back to him,—without a word. You won't say anything, will you, mamma?'

'There is nothing for me to say if you have really made him understand you.'

'I think he understood me, mamma. You need not doubt about that.'

'He has behaved very, very badly,—from the beginning,' said Lady Carbury.

But Hetta did not really think that the young man had behaved very badly from the beginning, and certainly did not wish to be told of his misbehaviour. No doubt she thought that the young man had behaved very well in falling in love with her directly he saw her; —only that he had behaved so badly in taking Mrs. Hurtle to Lowestoft afterwards! 'It's no good talking about that, mamma. I hope you will never talk of him any more.'

'He is quite unworthy,' said Lady Carbury.

'I can't bear to—have him—abused,' said Hetta sobbing.

'My dear Hetta, I have no doubt this has made you for the time unhappy. Such little accidents do make people unhappy—for the time. But it will be much for the best that you should endeavour not to be so sensitive about it. The world is too rough and too hard for people to allow their feelings full play. You have to look out for the future, and you can best do so by resolving that Paul Montague shall be forgotten at once.'

'Oh, mamma, don't. How is a person to resolve? Oh, mamma, don't say any more.'

'But, my dear, there is more that I must say. Your future life is before you, and I must think of it, and you must think of it. Of course you must be married.'

'There is no of course at all.'

'Of course you must be married,' continued Lady Carbury, 'and of course it is your duty to think of the way in which this may be best done. My income is becoming less and less every day. I already owe money to your cousin, and I owe money to Mr. Broune.'

'Money to Mr. Broune!'

'Yes,—to Mr. Broune. I had to pay a sum for Felix which Mr. Broune told me ought to be paid. And I owe money to tradesmen. I fear that I shall not be able to keep on this house. And they tell me,—your cousin and Mr. Broune,—that it is my duty to take Felix out of London,—probably abroad.'

'Of course I shall go with you.'

'It may be so at first; but, perhaps, even that may not be necessary. Why should you? What pleasure could you have in it? Think what my life must be with Felix in some French or German town!'

'Mamma, why don't you let me be a comfort to you? Why do you speak of me always as though I were a burden?'

'Everybody is a burden to other people. It is the way of life. But you,—if you will only yield in ever so little,—you may go where you will be no burden, where you will be accepted simply as a blessing. You have the opportunity of securing comfort for your whole life, and of making a friend, not only for yourself, but for me and your brother, of one whose friendship we cannot fail to want.'

'Mamma, you cannot really mean to talk about that now?'

'Why should I not mean it? What is the use of

indulging in high-flown nonsense? Make up your mind
to be the wife of your cousin Roger.'

'This is horrid,' said Hetta, bursting out in her agony.
'Cannot you understand that I am broken-hearted about
Paul, that I love him from my very soul, that parting
from him is like tearing my heart in pieces? I know that
I must, because he has behaved so very badly,—and
because of that wicked woman! And so I have. But I
did not think that in the very next hour you would bid
me give myself to somebody else! I will never marry
Roger Carbury. You may be quite—quite sure that I
shall never marry any one. If you won't take me with
you when you go away with Felix, I must stay behind and
try and earn my bread. I suppose I could go out as a
nurse.' Then, without waiting for a reply, she left the
room and betook herself to her own apartment.

Lady Carbury did not even understand her daughter.
She could not conceive that she had in any way acted
unkindly in taking the opportunity of Montague's rejec-
tion for pressing the suit of the other lover. She was
simply anxious to get a husband for her daughter,—as
she had been anxious to get a wife for her son,—in order
that her child might live comfortably. But she felt that
whenever she spoke common sense to Hetta, her daughter
took it as an offence, and flew into tantrums, being altogether unable to accommodate herself to the hard truths
of the world. Deep as was the sorrow which her son
brought upon her, and great as was the disgrace, she
could feel more sympathy for him than for the girl. If
there was anything that she could not forgive in life it was
romance. And yet she, at any rate, believed that she
delighted in romantic poetry! At the present moment she
was very wretched; and was certainly unselfish in her
wish to see her daughter comfortably settled before she
commenced those miserable roamings with her son which
seemed to be her coming destiny.

In these days she thought a good deal of Mr. Broune's
offer, and of her own refusal. It was odd that since that
refusal she had seen more of him, and had certainly known
much more of him than she had ever seen or known before.

Previous to that little episode their intimacy had been very fictitious, as are many intimacies. They had played at being friends, knowing but very little of each other. But now, during the last five or six weeks,—since she had refused his offer,—they had reàlly learned to know each other. In the exquisite misery of her troubles, she had told him the truth about herself and her son, and he had responded, not by compliments, but by real aid and true counsel. His whole tone was altered to her, as was hers to him. There was no longer any egregious flattery between them,—and he, in speaking to her, would be almost rough to her. Once he had told her that she would be a fool if she did not do so and so. The consequence was that she almost regretted that she had allowed him to escape. But she certainly made no effort to recover the lost prize, for she told him all her troubles. It was on that afternoon, after her disagreement with her daughter, that Marie Melmotte came to her. And, on the same evening, closeted with Mr. Broune in her back room, she told him of both occurrences. 'If the girl has got the money——,' she began, regretting her son's obstinacy.

'I don't believe a bit of it,' said Broune. 'From all that I can hear, I don't think that there is any money. And if there is, you may be sure that Melmotte would not let it slip through his fingers in that way. I would not have anything to do with it.'

'You think it is all over with the Melmottes?'

'A rumour reached me just now that he had been already arrested.' It was now between nine and ten in the evening. 'But as I came away from my room, I heard that he was down at the House. That he will have to stand a trial for forgery, I think there cannot be a doubt, and I imagine that it will be found that not a shilling will be saved out of the property.'

'What a wonderful career it has been!'

'Yes,—the strangest thing that has come up in our days. I am inclined to think that the utter ruin at this moment has been brought about by his reckless personal expenditure.'

'Why did he spend such a lot of money?'

'Because he thought he could conquer the world by it, and obtain universal credit. He very nearly succeeded too. Only he had forgotten to calculate the force of the envy of his competitors.'

'You think he has committed forgery?'

'Certainly, I think so. Of course we know nothing as yet.'

'Then I suppose it is better that Felix should not have married her.'

'Certainly better. No redemption was to have been had on that side, and I don't think you should regret the loss of such money as his.' Lady Carbury shook her head, meaning probably to imply that even Melmotte's money would have had no bad odour to one so dreadfully in want of assistance as her son. 'At any rate do not think of it any more.' Then she told him her grief about Hetta. 'Ah, there,' said he, 'I feel myself less able to express an authoritative opinion.'

'He doesn't owe a shilling,' said Lady Carbury, 'and he is really a fine gentleman.'

'But if she doesn't like him?'

'Oh, but she does. She thinks him to be the finest person in the world. She would obey him a great deal sooner than she would me. But she has her mind stuffed with nonsense about love.'

'A great many people, Lady Carbury, have their minds stuffed with that nonsense.'

'Yes;—and ruin themselves with it, as she will do. Love is like any other luxury. You have no right to it unless you can afford it. And those who will have it when they can't afford it, will come to the ground like this Mr. Melmotte. How odd it seems! It isn't a fortnight since we all thought him the greatest man in London.' Mr. Broune only smiled, not thinking it worth his while to declare that he had never held that opinion about the late idol of Abchurch Lane.

On the following morning, very early, while Melmotte was still lying, as yet undiscovered, on the floor of Mr. Longestaffe's room, a letter was brought up to Hetta by the maid-servant, who told her that Mr. Montague had delivered it with his own hands. She took it greedily, and then repressing herself, put it with an assumed gesture of indifference beneath her pillow. But as soon as the girl had left the room she at once seized her treasure. It never occurred to her as yet to think whether she would or would not receive a letter from her dismissed lover. She had told him that he must go, and go for ever, and had taken it for granted that he would do so,—probably willingly. No doubt he would be delighted to return to the American woman. But now that she had the letter, she allowed no doubt to come between her and the reading of it. As soon as she was alone she opened it, and she ran through its contents without allowing herself a moment for thinking, as she went on, whether the excuses made by her lover were or were not such as she ought to accept.

'DEAREST HETTA,

'I think you have been most unjust to me, and if you have ever loved me I cannot understand your injustice. I have never deceived you in anything, not by a word, or for a moment. Unless you mean to throw me over because I did once love another woman, I do not know what cause of anger you have. I could not tell you about Mrs. Hurtle till you had accepted me, and, as you yourself must know, I had had no opportunity to tell you anything afterwards till the story had reached your ears. I hardly know what I said the other day, I was so miserable at your accusation. But I suppose I said then, and I again declare now, that I had made up my mind that circumstances would not admit of her becoming my wife before I had ever seen you, and that I have certainly never wavered in my determination since I saw you. I can with safety refer to Roger as to this, because I was with him when I so determined, and made up my mind very much at his instance. This was before I had ever even met you.

'If I understand it all right you are angry because I have associated with Mrs. Hurtle since I so determined. I am not going back to my first acquaintance with her now. You may blame me for that if you please,—though it cannot have been a fault against you. But, after what had occurred, was I to refuse to see her when she came to England to see me? I think that would have been cowardly. Of course I went to her. And when she was all alone here, without a single other friend and telling me that she was unwell, and asking me to take her down to the seaside, was I to refuse? I think that that would have been unkind. It was a dreadful trouble to me. But of course I did it.

'She asked me to renew my engagement. I am bound to tell you that, but I know in telling you that it will go no farther. I declined, telling her that it was my purpose to ask another woman to be my wife. Of course there has been anger and sorrow,—anger on her part and sorrow on mine. But there has been no doubt. And at last she yielded. As far as she was concerned my trouble was over, —except in so far that her unhappiness has been a great trouble to me,—when, on a sudden, I found that the story had reached you in such a form as to make you determined to quarrel with me!

'Of course you do not know it all, for I cannot tell you all without telling her history. But you know everything that in the least concerns yourself, and I do say that you have no cause whatever for anger. I am writing at night. This evening your brooch was brought to me with three or four cutting words from your mother. But I cannot understand that if you really love me, you should wish to separate yourself from me,—or that, if you ever loved me, you should cease to love me now because of Mrs. Hurtle.

'I am so absolutely confused by the blow that I hardly know what I am writing, and take first one outrageous idea into my head and then another. My love for you is so thorough and so intense that I cannot bring myself to look forward to living without you, now that you have once owned that you have loved me. I cannot think it possible that love, such as I suppose yours must have been, could be made to cease all at a moment. Mine can't. I don't think it is natural that we should be parted.

'If you want corroboration of my story go yourself to Mrs. Hurtle. Anything is better than that we both should be broken-hearted.

'Yours most affectionately,
'PAUL MONTAGUE.'

## Chapter LXXXV

### BREAKFAST IN BERKELEY SQUARE

LORD NIDDERDALE was greatly disgusted with his own part of the performance when he left the House of Commons, and was, we may say, disgusted with his own position generally, when he considered all its circumstances. That had been at the commencement of the evening, and Melmotte had not then been tipsy; but he had behaved with unsurpassable arrogance and vulgarity, and had made the young lord drink the cup of his own disgrace to the very dregs. Everybody now knew it as a positive fact that the charges made against the man were to become matter of investigation before the chief magistrate for the City, everybody knew that he had committed forgery upon forgery, everybody knew that he could not pay for the property which he had pretended to buy, and that actually he was a ruined man;—and yet he had seized Nidderdale by the hand, and called the young lord 'his dear boy' before the whole House.

And then he had made himself conspicuous as this man's advocate. If he had not himself spoken openly of his coming marriage with the girl, he had allowed other men to speak to him about it. He had quarrelled with one man for saying that Melmotte was a rogue, and had confidentially told his most intimate friends that in spite of a little vulgarity of manner, Melmotte at bottom was a very good fellow. How was he now to back out of his intimacy with the Melmottes generally? He was engaged to marry the girl, and there was nothing of which he

could accuse her. He acknowledged to himself that she
deserved well at his hands. Though at this moment he
hated the father most bitterly, as those odious words, and
the tone in which they had been pronounced, rang in his
ears, nevertheless he had some kindly feeling for the girl.
Of course he could not marry her now. That was manifestly out of the question. She herself, as well as all others,
had known that she was to be married for her money,
and now that bubble had been burst. But he felt that he
owed it to her, as to a comrade who had on the whole
been loyal to him, to have some personal explanation
with herself. He arranged in his own mind the sort of
speech that he would make to her. 'Of course you know
it can't be. It was all arranged because you were to have
a lot of money, and now it turns out that you haven't
got any. And I haven't got any, and we should have
nothing to live upon. It's out of the question. But, upon
my word, I'm very sorry, for I like you very much, and
I really think we should have got on uncommon well
together.' That was the kind of speech that he suggested
to himself, but he did not know how to find for himself
the opportunity of making it. He thought that he must
put it all into a letter. But then that would be tantamount to a written confession that he had made her an
offer of marriage, and he feared that Melmotte,—or
Madame Melmotte on his behalf, if the great man himself were absent, in prison,—might make an ungenerous
use of such an admission.

Between seven and eight he went into the Beargarden,
and there he saw Dolly Longestaffe and others. Everybody was talking about Melmotte, the prevailing belief
being that he was at this moment in custody. Dolly was
full of his own griefs; but consoled amidst them by a
sense of his own importance. 'I wonder whether it's true,'
he was saying to Lord Grasslough. 'He has an appointment to meet me and my governor at twelve o'clock
to-morrow, and to pay us what he owes us. He swore
yesterday that he would have the money to-morrow. But
he can't keep his appointment, you know, if he's in
prison.'

'You won't see the money, Dolly, you may swear to that,' said Grasslough.

'I don't suppose I shall. By George, what an ass my governor has been. He had no more right than you have to give up the property. Here's Nidderdale. He could tell us where he is; but I'm afraid to speak to him since he cut up so rough the other night.'

In a moment the conversation was stopped; but when Lord Grasslough asked Nidderdale in a whisper whether he knew anything about Melmotte, the latter answered out loud, 'Yes;—I left him in the House half an hour ago.'

'People are saying that he has been arrested.'

'I heard that also; but he certainly had not been arrested when I left the House.' Then he went up and put his hand on Dolly Longestaffe's shoulder, and spoke to him. 'I suppose you were about right the other night and I was about wrong; but you could understand what it was that I meant. I'm afraid this is a bad look out for both of us.'

'Yes;—I understand. It's deuced bad for me,' said Dolly. 'I think you're very well out of it. But I'm glad there's not to be a quarrel. Suppose we have a rubber of whist.'

Later on in the night news was brought to the club that Melmotte had tried to make a speech in the House, that he had been very drunk, and that he had tumbled over, upsetting Beauchamp Beauclerk in his fall. 'By George, I should like to have seen that!' said Dolly.

'I am very glad I was not there,' said Nidderdale. It was three o'clock before they left the card table, at which time Melmotte was lying dead upon the floor in Mr. Longestaffe's house.

On the following morning, at ten o'clock, Lord Nidderdale sat at breakfast with his father in the old lord's house in Berkeley Square. From thence the house which Melmotte had hired was not above a few hundred yards distant. At this time the young lord was living with his father, and the two had now met by appointment in order that something might be settled between them as to the proposed marriage. The Marquis was not a very pleasant

companion when the affairs in which he was interested
did not go exactly as he would have them. He could be
very cross and say most disagreeable words,—so that the
ladies of the family, and others connected with him, for
the most part, found it impossible to live with him. But
his eldest son had endured him;—partly perhaps because,
being the eldest, he had been treated with a nearer
approach to courtesy, but chiefly by means of his own
extreme good humour. What did a few hard words
matter? If his father was ungracious to him, of course he
knew what all that meant. As long as his father would
make fair allowance for his own peccadilloes,—he also
would make allowances for his father's roughness. All
this was based on his grand theory of live and let live.
He expected his father to be a little cross on this occasion,
and he acknowledged to himself that there was cause for it.

He was a little late himself, and he found his father
already buttering his toast. 'I don't believe you'd get
out of bed a moment sooner than you liked if you could
save the whole property by it.'

'You show me how I can make a guinea by it, sir, and
see if I don't earn the money.' Then he sat down and
poured himself out a cup of tea, and looked at the kidneys and looked at the fish.

'I suppose you were drinking last night,' said the old
lord.

'Not particular.' The old man turned round and
gnashed his teeth at him. 'The fact is, sir, I don't drink.
Everybody knows that.'

'I know when you're in the country you can't live
without champagne. Well;—what have you got to say
about all this?'

'What have you got to say?'

'You've made a pretty kettle of fish of it.'

'I've been guided by you in everything. Come, now;
you ought to own that. I suppose the whole thing is
over?'

'I don't see why it should be over. I'm told she has got
her own money.' Then Nidderdale described to his father
Melmotte's behaviour in the House on the preceding even-

ing. 'What the devil does that matter?' said the old man.
'You're not going to marry the man himself.'

'I shouldn't wonder if he's in gaol now.'

'And what does that matter? She's not in gaol. And
if the money is hers, she can't lose it because he goes to
prison. Beggars mustn't be choosers. How do you mean
to live if you don't marry this girl?'

'I shall scrape on, I suppose. I must look for somebody
else.' The Marquis showed very plainly by his demeanour
that he did not give his son much credit either for diligence or for ingenuity in making such a search. 'At any
rate, sir, I can't marry the daughter of a man who is to be
put upon his trial for forgery.'

'I can't see what that has to do with you.'

'I couldn't do it, sir. I'd do anything else to oblige you,
but I couldn't do that. And, moreover, I don't believe
in the money.'

'Then you may just go to the devil,' said the old Marquis turning himself round in his chair, and lighting a
cigar as he took up the newspaper. Nidderdale went on
with his breakfast with perfect equanimity, and when he
had finished lighted his cigar. 'They tell me,' said the old
man, 'that one of those Goldsheiner girls will have a lot
of money.'

'A Jewess,' suggested Nidderdale.

'What difference does that make?'

'Oh no;—not in the least;—if the money's really there.
Have you heard any sum named, sir?' The old man only
grunted. 'There are two sisters and two brothers. I don't
suppose the girls would have a hundred thousand each.'

'They say the widow of that brewer who died the other
day has about twenty thousand a year.'

'It's only for her life, sir.'

'She could insure her life. D—— me, sir, we must do
something. If you turn up your nose at one woman after
another how do you mean to live?'

'I don't think that a woman of forty with only a life
interest would be a good speculation. Of course I'll think
of it if you press it.' The old man growled again. 'You see,
sir, I've been so much in earnest about this girl that I

haven't thought of inquiring about any one else. There always is some one up with a lot of money. It's a pity there shouldn't be a regular statement published with the amount of money, and what is expected in return. It'd save a deal of trouble.'

'If you can't talk more seriously than that you'd better go away,' said the old Marquis.

At that moment a footman came into the room and told Lord Nidderdale that a man particularly wished to see him in the hall. He was not always anxious to see those who called on him, and he asked the servant whether he knew who the man was. 'I believe, my lord, he's one of the domestics from Mr. Melmotte's in Bruton Street,' said the footman, who was no doubt fully acquainted with all the circumstances of Lord Nidderdale's engagement. The son, who was still smoking, looked at his father as though in doubt. 'You'd better go and see,' said the Marquis. But Nidderdale before he went asked a question as to what he had better do if Melmotte had sent for him. 'Go and see Melmotte. Why should you be afraid to see him? Tell him you are ready to marry the girl if you can see the money down, but that you won't stir a step till it has been actually paid over.'

'He knows that already,' said Nidderdale as he left the room.

In the hall he found a man whom he recognized as Melmotte's butler, a ponderous, elderly, heavy man who now had a letter in his hand. But the lord could tell by the man's face and manner that he himself had some story to tell. 'Is there anything the matter?'

'Yes, my lord,—yes. Oh, dear,—oh, dear! I think you'll be sorry to hear it. There was none who came there he seemed to take to so much as your lordship.'

'They've taken him to prison!' exclaimed Nidderdale. But the man shook his head. 'What is it then? He can't be dead.' Then the man nodded his head, and, putting his hand up to his face, burst into tears. 'Mr. Melmotte dead! He was in the House of Commons last night. I saw him myself. How did he die?' But the fat, ponderous man was so affected by the tragedy he had witnessed, that he could not as yet give any account of the scene of his master's death, but simply handed the note which he had in his hand to Lord Nidderdale. It was from Marie, and had been written within half an hour of the time at which news had been brought to her of what had occurred. The note was as follows:—

'DEAR LORD NIDDERDALE,

'The man will tell you what has happened. I feel as though I was mad. I do not know who to send to. Will you come to me, only for a few minutes?

'MARIE.'

He read it standing up in the hall, and then again asked the man as to the manner of his master's death. And now the Marquis, gathering from a word or two that he heard and from his son's delay that something special had occurred, hobbled out into the hall. 'Mr. Melmotte is—dead,' said his son. The old man dropped his stick, and fell back against the wall. 'This man says that he is dead, and here is a letter from Marie asking me to go there. How was it that he—died?'

'It was—poison,' said the butler solemnly. 'There has been a doctor already, and there isn't no doubt of that. He took it all by himself last night. He came home, perhaps a little fresh, and he had in brandy and soda and cigars;—and sat himself down all to himself. Then in the morning, when the young woman went in,—there he was, —poisoned! I see him lay on the ground, and I helped to lift him up, and there was that smell of prussic acid that I knew what he had been and done just the same as when the doctor came and told us.'

Before the man could be allowed to go back, there was a consultation between the father and son as to a compliance with the request which Marie had made in her first misery. The Marquis thought that his son had better not go to Bruton Street. 'What's the use? What good can you do? She'll only be falling into your arms, and that's what you've got to avoid,—at any rate, till you know how things are.'

But Nidderdale's better feelings would not allow him to submit to this advice. He had been engaged to marry the girl, and she in her abject misery had turned to him as the friend she knew best. At any rate for the time the heartlessness of his usual life deserted him, and he felt willing to devote himself to the girl not for what he could get,—but because she had so nearly been so near to him. 'I couldn't refuse her,' he said over and over again. 'I couldn't bring myself to do it. Oh, no;—I shall certainly go.'

'You'll get into a mess if you do.'

'Then I must get into a mess. I shall certainly go. I will go at once. It is very disagreeable, but I cannot possibly refuse. It would be abominable.' Then going back to the hall, he sent a message by the butler to Marie, saying that he would be with her in less than half an hour.

'Don't you go and make a fool of yourself,' his father said to him when he was alone. 'This is just one of those times when a man may ruin himself by being soft-hearted.' Nidderdale simply shook his head as he took his hat and gloves to go across to Bruton Street.

## *Chapter LXXXVI*

### THE MEETING IN BRUTON STREET

WHEN the news of her husband's death was in some very rough way conveyed to Madame Melmotte, it crushed her for the time altogether. Marie first heard that she no longer had a living parent as she stood by the poor woman's bedside, and she was enabled, as much perhaps by the necessity incumbent upon her of attending to the wretched woman as by her own superior strength of character, to save herself from that prostration and collapse of power which a great and sudden blow is apt to produce. She stared at the woman who first conveyed to her tidings of the tragedy, and then for a moment seated herself at the bedside. But the violent sobbings and hysterical screams of Madame Melmotte soon brought her again to her feet, and from that moment she was not only active but efficacious. No;—she would not go down to the room; she could do no good by going thither. But they must send for a doctor. They should send for a doctor immediately. She was then told that a doctor and an inspector of police were already in the rooms below. The necessity of throwing whatever responsibility there might be on to other shoulders had been at once apparent to the servants, and they had sent out right and left, so that the house might be filled with persons fit to give directions in such an emergency. The officers from the police station were already there when the woman who now filled Didon's place in the house communicated to Madame Melmotte the fact that she was a widow.

It was afterwards said by some of those who had seen her at the time, that Marie Melmotte had shown a hard heart on the occasion. But the condemnation was wrong. Her feeling for her father was certainly not that which we are accustomed to see among our daughters and sisters. He had never been to her the petted divinity of the household, whose slightest wish had been law, whose little comforts had become matters of serious care, whose frowns were horrid clouds, whose smiles were glorious sunshine, whose kisses were daily looked for, and if missed would be missed with mourning. How should it have been so with her? In all the intercourses of her family, since the first rough usage which she remembered, there had never been anything sweet or gracious. Though she had recognized a certain duty, as due from herself to her father, she had found herself bound to measure it, so that more should not be exacted from her than duty required. She had long known that her father would fain make her a slave for his own purposes, and that if she put no limits to her own obedience he certainly would put none. She had drawn no comparison between him and other fathers, or between herself and other daughters, because she had never become conversant with the ways of other families. After a fashion she had loved him, because nature creates

love in a daughter's heart; but she had never respected
him, and had spent the best energies of her character on
a resolve that she would never fear him. 'He may cut me
into pieces, but he shall not make me do for his advantage that which I do not think he has a right to exact
from me.' That had been the state of her mind towards
her father; and now that he had taken himself away with
terrible suddenness, leaving her to face the difficulties of
the world with no protector and no assistance, the feeling
which dominated her was no doubt one of awe rather
than of broken-hearted sorrow. Those who depart must
have earned such sorrow before it can be really felt. They
who are left may be overwhelmed by the death—even
of their most cruel tormentors. Madame Melmotte was
altogether overwhelmed; but it could not probably be
said of her with truth that she was crushed by pure grief.
There was fear of all things, fear of solitude, fear of sudden
change, fear of terrible revelations, fear of some necessary
movement she knew not whither, fear that she might be
discovered to be a poor wretched impostor who never
could have been justified in standing in the same presence
with emperors and princes, with duchesses and cabinet
ministers. This and the fact that the dead body of the
man who had so lately been her tyrant was lying near
her, so that she might hardly dare to leave her room lest
she should encounter him dead, and thus more dreadful
even than when alive, utterly conquered her. Feelings of
the same kind, the same fears, and the same awe were
powerful also with Marie;—but they did not conquer her.
She was strong and conquered them; and she did not care
to affect a weakness to which she was in truth superior.
In such a household the death of such a father after such
a fashion will hardly produce that tender sorrow which
comes from real love.

She soon knew it all. Her father had destroyed himself, and had doubtless done so because his troubles in
regard to money had been greater than he could bear.
When he had told her that she was to sign those deeds
because ruin was impending, he must indeed have told
her the truth. He had so often lied to her that she had

had no means of knowing whether he was lying then or telling her a true story. But she had offered to sign the deeds since that, and he had told her that it would be of no avail,—and at that time had not been angry with her as he would have been had her refusal been the cause of his ruin. She took some comfort in thinking of that.

But what was she to do? What was to be done generally by that over-cumbered household? She and her pseudo-mother had been instructed to pack up their jewellery, and they had both obeyed the order. But she herself at this moment cared but little for any property. How ought she to behave herself? Where should she go? On whose arm could she lean for some support at this terrible time? As for love, and engagements, and marriage,—that was all over. In her difficulty she never for a moment thought of Sir Felix Carbury. Though she had been silly enough to love the man because he was pleasant to look at, she had never been so far gone in silliness as to suppose that he was a staff upon which any one might lean. Had that marriage taken place, she would have been the staff. But it might be possible that Lord Nidderdale would help her. He was good-natured and manly, and would be efficacious,—if only he would come to her. He was near, and she thought that at any rate she would try. So she had written her note and sent it by the butler,—thinking as she did so of the words she would use to make the young man understand that all the nonsense they had talked as to marrying each other was, of course, to mean nothing now.

It was past eleven when he reached the house, and he was shown upstairs into one of the sitting-rooms on the first-floor. As he passed the door of the study, which was at the moment partly open, he saw the dress of a police-man within, and knew that the body of the dead man was still lying there. But he went by rapidly without a glance within, remembering the look of the man as he had last seen his burly figure, and that grasp of his hand, and those odious words. And now the man was dead,—having destroyed his own life. Surely the man must have known when he uttered those words what it was that he

intended to do! When he had made that last appeal
about Marie, conscious as he was that every one was de-
serting him, he must even then have looked his fate in
the face and have told himself that it was better that he
should die! His misfortunes, whatever might be their
nature, must have been heavy on him then with all their
weight; and he himself and all the world had known that
he was ruined. And yet he had pretended to be anxious
about the girl's marriage, and had spoken of it as though
he still believed that it would be accomplished!

Nidderdale had hardly put his hat down on the table
before Marie was with him. He walked up to her, took
her by both hands, and looked into her face. There was
no trace of a tear, but her whole countenance seemed
to him to be altered. She was the first to speak.

'I thought you would come when I sent for you.'

'Of course I came.'

'I knew you would be a friend, and I knew no one else
who would. You won't be afraid, Lord Nidderdale, that
I shall ever think any more of all those things which he
was planning?' She paused a moment, but he was not
ready enough to have a word to say in answer to this.
'You know what has happened?'

'Your servant told us.'

'What are we to do? Oh, Lord Nidderdale, it is so
dreadful! Poor papa! Poor papa! When I think of all
that he must have suffered I wish that I could be dead too.'

'Has your mother been told?'

'Oh yes. She knows. No one tried to conceal anything
for a moment. It was better that it should be so;—better
at last. But we have no friends who would be considerate
enough to try to save us from sorrow. But I think it was
better. Mamma is very bad. She is always nervous and
timid. Of course this has nearly killed her. What ought
we to do? It is Mr. Longestaffe's house, and we were to
have left it to-morrow.'

'He will not mind that now.'

'Where must we go? We can't go back to that big
place in Grosvenor Square. Who will manage for us?
Who will see the doctor and the policemen?'

'I will do that.'

'But there will be things that I cannot ask you to do. Why should I ask you to do anything?'

'Because we are friends.'

'No,' she said, 'no. You cannot really regard me as a friend. I have been an impostor. I know that. I had no business to know a person like you at all. Oh, if the next six months could be over! Poor papa;—poor papa!' And then for the first time she burst into tears.

'I wish I knew what might comfort you,' he said.

'How can there be any comfort? There never can be comfort again! As for comfort, when were we ever comfortable? It has been one trouble after another,—one fear after another! And now we are friendless and homeless. I suppose they will take everything that we have.'

'Your papa had a lawyer, I suppose?'

'I think he had ever so many,—but I do not know who they were. His own clerk, who had lived with him for over twenty years, left him yesterday. I suppose they will know something in Abchurch Lane; but now that Herr Croll has gone I am not acquainted even with the name of one of them. Mr. Miles Grendall used to be with him.'

'I do not think that he could be of much service.'

'Nor Lord Alfred? Lord Alfred was always with him till very lately.' Nidderdale shook his head. 'I suppose not. They only came because papa had a big house.' The young lord could not but feel that he was included in the same rebuke. 'Oh, what a life it has been! And now,—now it's over.' As she said this it seemed that for the moment her strength failed her, for she fell backwards on the corner of the sofa. He tried to raise her, but she shook him away, burying her face in her hands. He was standing close to her, still holding her arm, when he heard a knock at the front door, which was immediately opened, as the servants were hanging about in the hall. 'Who are they?' said Marie, whose sharp ears caught the sound of various steps. Lord Nidderdale went out on to the head of the stairs, and immediately heard the voice of Dolly Longestaffe.

Dolly Longestaffe had on that morning put himself

early into the care of Mr. Squercum, and it had happened
that he with his lawyer had met his father with Mr. Bideawhile at the corner of the square. They were all coming
according to appointment to receive the money which
Mr. Melmotte had promised to pay them at this very
hour. Of course they had none of them as yet heard of
the way in which the Financier had made his last grand
payment, and as they walked together to the door had
been intent only in reference to their own money. Squercum, who had heard a good deal on the previous day,
was very certain that the money would not be forthcoming, whereas Bideawhile was sanguine of success.
'Don't we wish we may get it?' Dolly had said, and by
saying so had very much offended his father, who had
resented the want of reverence implied in the use of that
word 'we'. They had all been admitted together, and
Dolly had at once loudly claimed an old acquaintance
with some of the articles around him. 'I knew I'd got a
coat just like that,' said Dolly, 'and I never could make
out what my fellow had done with it.' This was the
speech which Nidderdale had heard, standing on the top
of the stairs.

The two lawyers had at once seen, from the face of the
man who had opened the door and from the presence of
three or four servants in the hall, that things were not
going on in their usual course. Before Dolly had completed
his buffoonery the butler had whispered to Mr. Bideawhile that Mr. Melmotte—'was no more.'

'Dead!' exclaimed Mr. Bideawhile. Squercum put his
hands into his trousers pockets and opened his mouth
wide. 'Dead!' muttered Mr. Longestaffe senior. 'Dead!'
said Dolly. 'Who's dead?' The butler shook his head.
Then Squercum whispered a word into the butler's ear,
and the butler thereupon nodded his head. 'It's about
what I expected,' said Squercum. Then the butler
whispered the word to Mr. Longestaffe, and whispered
it also to Mr. Bideawhile, and they all knew that the
millionaire had swallowed poison during the night.

It was known to the servants that Mr. Longestaffe was
the owner of the house, and he was therefore, as having

authority there, shown into the room where the body of Melmotte was lying on a sofa. The two lawyers and Dolly of course followed, as did also Lord Nidderdale, who had now joined them from the lobby above. There was a policeman in the room who seemed to be simply watching the body, and who rose from his seat when the gentlemen entered. Two or three of the servants followed them, so that there was almost a crowd round the dead man's bier. There was no further tale to be told. That Melmotte had been in the House on the previous night, and had there disgraced himself by intoxication, they had known already. That he had been found dead that morning had been already announced. They could only stand round and gaze on the square, sullen, livid features of the big-framed man, and each lament that he had ever heard the name of Melmotte.

'Are you in the house here?' said Dolly to Lord Nidderdale in a whisper.

'She sent for me. We live quite close, you know. She wanted somebody to tell her something. I must go up to her again now.'

'Had you seen him before?'

'No indeed. I only came down when I heard your voices. I fear it will be rather bad for you;—won't it?'

'He was regularly smashed, I suppose?' asked Dolly.

'I know nothing myself. He talked to me about his affairs once, but he was such a liar that not a word that he said was worth anything. I believed him then. How it will go, I can't say.'

'That other thing is all over of course,' suggested Dolly.

Nidderdale intimated by a gesture of his head that the other thing was all over, and then returned to Marie. There was nothing further that the four gentlemen could do, and they soon departed from the house;—not, however, till Mr. Bideawhile had given certain short injunctions to the butler concerning the property contained in Mr. Longestaffe's town residence.

'They had come to see him,' said Lord Nidderdale in a whisper. 'There was some appointment. He had told them to be all here at this hour.'

'They didn't know, then?' asked Marie.

'Nothing,—till the man told them.'

'And did you go in?'

'Yes; we all went into the room.' Marie shuddered, and again hid her face. 'I think the best thing I can do,' said Nidderdale, 'is to go to Abchurch Lane, and find out from Smith who is the lawyer whom he chiefly trusted. I know Smith had to do with his own affairs, because he has told me so at the Board; and if necessary I will find out Croll. No doubt I can trace him. Then we had better employ the lawyer to arrange everything for you.'

'And where had we better go to?'

'Where would Madame Melmotte wish to go?'

'Anywhere, so that we could hide ourselves. Perhaps Frankfort would be the best. But shouldn't we stay till something has been done here? And couldn't we have lodgings, so as to get away from Mr. Longestaffe's house?' Nidderdale promised that he himself would look for lodgings, as soon as he had seen the lawyer. 'And now, my lord, I suppose that I never shall see you again,' said Marie.

'I don't know why you should say that.'

'Because it will be best. Why should you? All this will be trouble enough to you when people begin to say what we are. But I don't think it has been my fault.'

'Nothing has ever been your fault.'

'Good-bye, my lord. I shall always think of you as one of the kindest people I ever knew. I thought it best to send to you for different reasons, but I do not want you to come back.'

'Good-bye, Marie. I shall always remember you.' And so they parted.

After that he did go into the City, and succeeded in finding both Mr. Smith and Herr Croll. When he reached Abchurch Lane, the news of Melmotte's death had already been spread abroad; and more was known, or said to be known, of his circumstances than Nidderdale had as yet heard. The crushing blow to him, so said Herr Croll, had been the desertion of Cohenlupe,—that and the sudden fall in the value of the South Central Pacific and Mexican Railway shares, consequent on the rumours spread about the City respecting the Pickering property. It was asserted in Abchurch Lane that had he not at that moment touched the Pickering property, or entertained the Emperor, or stood for Westminster, he must, by the end of the autumn, have been able to do any or all of those things without danger, simply as the result of the money which would then have been realized by the railway. But he had allowed himself to become hampered by the want of comparatively small sums of ready money, and in seeking relief had rushed from one danger to another, till at last the waters around him had become too deep even for him, and had overwhelmed him. As to his immediate death, Herr Croll expressed not the slightest astonishment. It was just the thing, Herr Croll said, that he had been sure that Melmotte would do, should his difficulties ever become too great for him. 'And dere vas a leetle ting he lay himself open by de oder day,' said Croll, 'dat vas nasty,—very nasty.' Nidderdale shook his head, but asked no questions. Croll had alluded to the use of his own name, but did not on this occasion make any further revelation. Then Croll made a further statement to Lord Nidderdale, which I think he must have done in pure good-nature. 'My lor,' he said, whispering very gravely, 'de money of de yong lady is all her own.' Then he nodded his head three times. 'Nobody can toch it, not if he vas in debt millions.' Again he nodded his head.

'I am very glad to hear it for her sake,' said Lord Nidderdale as he took his leave.

## Chapter LXXXVII

### DOWN AT CARBURY

WHEN Roger Carbury returned to Suffolk, after seeing his cousins in Welbeck Street, he was by no means contented with himself. That he should be discontented generally with the circumstances of his life was a matter of course. He knew that he was farther removed than ever from the object on which his whole mind was set. Had Hetta Carbury learned all the circumstances of Paul's engagement with Mrs. Hurtle before she had confessed her love to Paul,—so that her heart might have been turned against the man before she had made her confession,—then, he thought, she might at last have listened to him. Even though she had loved the other man, she might have at last done so, as her love would have been buried in her own bosom. But the tale had been told after the fashion which was most antagonistic to his own interests. Hetta had never heard Mrs. Hurtle's name till she had given herself away, and had declared to all her friends that she had given herself away to this man, who was so unworthy of her. The more Roger thought of this, the more angry he was with Paul Montague, and the more convinced that that man had done him an injury which he could never forgive.

But his grief extended even beyond that. Though he was never tired of swearing to himself that he would not forgive Paul Montague, yet there was present to him a feeling that an injury was being done to the man, and that he was in some sort responsible for that injury. He had declined to tell Hetta any part of the story about Mrs. Hurtle,—actuated by a feeling that he ought not to betray the trust put in him by a man who was at the time his friend; and he had told nothing. But no one knew so well as he did the fact that all the attention latterly given by Paul to the American woman had by no means been the effect of love, but had come from a feeling on Paul's part that he could not desert the woman he had once loved, when she asked him for his kindness. If Hetta could know everything exactly,—if she could look back and read the state of Paul's mind as he, Roger, could read it,—then she would probably forgive the man, or perhaps tell herself that there was nothing for her to forgive. Roger was anxious that Hetta's anger should burn hot,—because of the injury done to himself. He thought that there were ample reasons why Paul Montague should be punished,—why Paul should be utterly expelled from among them, and allowed to go his own course. But it was not right that the man should be punished on false grounds. It seemed to Roger now that he was doing an injustice to his enemy by refraining from telling all that he knew.

As to the girl's misery in losing her lover, much as he loved her, true as it was that he was willing to devote himself and all that he had to her happiness, I do not think that at the present moment he was disturbed in that direction. It is hardly natural, perhaps, that a man should love a woman with such devotion as to wish to make her happy by giving her to another man. Roger told himself that Paul would be an unsafe husband, a fickle husband,—one who might be carried hither and thither both in his circumstances and his feelings,—and that it would be better for Hetta that she should not marry him; but at the same time he was unhappy as he reflected that he himself was a party to a certain amount of deceit.

And yet he had said not a word. He had referred Hetta to the man himself. He thought that he knew, and he did indeed accurately know, the state of Hetta's mind. She was wretched because she thought that while her lover was winning her love, while she herself was willingly allowing him to win her love, he was dallying with another woman, and making to that other woman promises the same as those he made to her. This was not true. Roger knew that it was not true. But when he tried to quiet his conscience by saying that they must fight it out among themselves, he felt himself to be uneasy under that assurance.

His life at Carbury, at this time, was very desolate. He had become tired of the priest, who, in spite of various repulses, had never for a moment relaxed his efforts to convert his friend. Roger had told him once that he must beg that religion might not be made the subject of further conversation between them. In answer to this, Father Barham had declared that he would never consent to remain as an intimate associate with any man on those terms. Roger had persisted in his stipulation, and the priest had then suggested that it was his host's intention

to banish him from Carbury Hall. Roger had made
no reply, and the priest had of course been banished.
But even this added to his misery. Father Barham was
a gentleman, was a good man, and in great penury. To
ill-treat such a one, to expel such a one from his house,
seemed to Roger to be an abominable cruelty. He was
unhappy with himself about the priest, and yet he could
not bid the man come back to him. It was already being
said of him among his neighbours, at Eardly, at Caversham, and at the Bishop's palace, that he either had
become or was becoming a Roman Catholic, under the
priest's influence. Mrs. Yeld had even taken upon herself to write to him a most affectionate letter, in which
she said very little as to any evidence that had reached
her as to Roger's defection, but dilated at very great
length on the abominations of a certain lady who is supposed to indulge in gorgeous colours.

He was troubled, too, about old Daniel Ruggles, the
farmer at Sheep's Acre, who had been so angry because
his niece would not marry John Crumb. Old Ruggles,
when abandoned by Ruby and accused by his neighbours of personal cruelty to the girl, had taken freely to
that source of consolation which he found to be most
easily within his reach. Since Ruby had gone he had
been drunk every day, and was making himself generally
a scandal and a nuisance. His landlord had interfered
with his usual kindness, and the old man had always
declared that his niece and John Crumb were the cause
of it all; for now, in his maudlin misery, he attributed as
much blame to the lover as he did to the girl. John Crumb
wasn't in earnest. If he had been in earnest he would
have gone after her to London at once. No;—he wouldn't
invite Ruby to come back. If Ruby would come back,
repentant, full of sorrow,—and hadn't been and made a
fool of herself in the meantime,—then he'd think of taking
her back. In the meantime, with circumstances in their
present condition, he evidently thought that he could
best face the difficulties of the world by an unfaltering
adhesion to gin, early in the day and all day long. This,
too, was a grievance to Roger Carbury.

But he did not neglect his work, the chief of which at the present moment was the care of the farm which he kept in his own hands. He was making hay at this time in certain meadows down by the river side; and was standing by while the men were loading a cart, when he saw John Crumb approaching across the field. He had not seen John since the eventful journey to London; nor had he seen him in London; but he knew well all that had occurred,—how the dealer in pollard had thrashed his cousin, Sir Felix, how he had been locked up by the police and then liberated,—and how he was now re-garded in Bungay as a hero, as far as arms were con-cerned, but as being very 'soft' in the matter of love. The reader need hardly be told that Roger was not at all disposed to quarrel with Mr. Crumb, because the victim of Crumb's heroism had been his own cousin. Crumb had acted well, and had never said a word about Sir Felix since his return to the country. No doubt he had now come to talk about his love,—and in order that his confessions might not be made before all the assembled haymakers, Roger Carbury hurried to meet him. There was soon evident on Crumb's broad face a whole sun-shine of delight. As Roger approached him he began to laugh aloud, and to wave a bit of paper that he had in his hands. 'She's a coomin; she's a coomin,' were the first words he uttered. Roger knew very well that in his friend's mind there was but one 'she' in the world, and that the name of that she was Ruby Ruggles.

'I am delighted to hear it,' said Roger. 'She has made it up with her grandfather?'

'Don't know now't about grandfeyther. She have made it up wi' me. Know'd she would when I'd polish'd t'other un off a bit;—know'd she would.'

'Has she written to you, then?'

'Well, squoire,—she ain't; not just herself. I do sup-pose that isn't the way they does it. But it's all as one.' And then Mr. Crumb thrust Mrs. Hurtle's note into Roger Carbury's hand.

Roger certainly was not predisposed to think well or

kindly of Mrs. Hurtle. Since he had first known Mrs.
Hurtle's name, when Paul Montague had told the story
of his engagement on his return from America, Roger
had regarded her as a wicked, intriguing, bad woman.
It may, perhaps, be confessed that he was prejudiced
against all Americans, looking upon Washington much
as he did upon Jack Cade or Wat Tyler; and he pictured
to himself all American women as being loud, masculine,
and atheistical. But it certainly did seem that in this
instance Mrs. Hurtle was endeavouring to do a good
turn from pure charity. 'She is a lady,' Crumb began
to explain, 'who do be living with Mrs. Pipkin; and she
is a lady as is a lady.'

Roger could not fully admit the truth of this assertion;
but he explained that he, too, knew something of Mrs.
Hurtle, and that he thought it probable that what she
said of Ruby might be true. 'True, squoire!' said Crumb,
laughing with his whole face. 'I ha' nae a doubt it's true.
What's again its being true? When I had dropped into
t'other fellow, of course she made her choice. It was me
as was to blame, because I didn't do it before. I ought
to ha' dropped into him when I first heard as he was arter
her. It's that as girls like. So, squoire, I'm just going
again to Lon'on right away.'

Roger suggested that old Ruggles would, of course,
receive his niece; but as to this John expressed his supreme
indifference. The old man was nothing to him. Of course
he would like to have the old man's money; but the old
man couldn't live for ever, and he supposed that things
would come right in time. But this he knew,—that he
wasn't going to cringe to the old man about his money.
When Roger observed that it would be better that Ruby
should have some home to which she might at once
return, John adverted with a renewed grin to all the
substantial comforts of his own house. It seemed to be
his idea, that on arriving in London he would at once
take Ruby away to church and be married to her out of
hand. He had thrashed his rival, and what cause could
there now be for delay?

But before he left the field he made one other speech

to the squire. 'You ain't a'taken it amiss, squoire, 'cause
he was coosin to yourself?'

'Not in the least, Mr. Crumb.'

'That's koind now. I ain't a done the yong man a
ha'porth o' harm, and I don't feel no grudge again him,
and when me and Ruby's once spliced, I'm darned if I
don't give 'un a bottle of wine the first day as he'll come
to Bungay.'

Roger did not feel himself justified in accepting this
invitation on the part of Sir Felix; but he renewed his
assurance that he, on his own part, thought that Crumb
had behaved well in that matter of the street encounter,
and he expressed a strong wish for the immediate and
continued happiness of Mr. and Mrs. John Crumb.

'Oh, ay, we'll be 'appy, squoire,' said Crumb as he
went exulting out of the field.

On the day after this Roger Carbury received a letter
which disturbed him very much, and to which he hardly
knew whether to return any answer, or what answer.
It was from Paul Montague, and was written by him
but a few hours after he had left his letter for Hetta with
his own hands, at the door of her mother's house. Paul's
letter to Roger was as follows:—

'My dear Roger,—

'Though I know that you have cast me off from you
I cannot write to you in any other way, as any other way
would be untrue. You can answer me, of course, as you
please, but I do think that you will owe me an answer,
as I appeal to you in the name of justice.

'You know what has taken place between Hetta and
myself. She had accepted me, and therefore I am justified in feeling sure that she must have loved me. But she
has now quarrelled with me altogether, and has told me
that I am never to see her again. Of course I don't mean
to put up with this. Who would? You will say that it is
no business of yours. But I think that you would not wish
that she should be left under a false impression, if you
could put her right.

'Somebody has told her the story of Mrs. Hurtle. I

suppose it was Felix, and that he had learned it from those people at Islington. But she has been told that which is untrue. Nobody knows and nobody can know the truth as you do. She supposes that I have willingly been passing my time with Mrs. Hurtle during the last two months, although during that very time I have asked for and received the assurance of her love. Now, whether or no I have been to blame about Mrs. Hurtle,—as to which nothing at present need be said,—it is certainly the truth that her coming to England was not only not desired by me, but was felt by me to be the greatest possible misfortune. But after all that had passed I certainly owed it to her not to neglect her;—and this duty was the more incumbent on me as she was a foreigner and unknown to any one. I went down to Lowestoft with her at her request, having named the place to her as one known to myself, and because I could not refuse her so small a favour. You know that it was so, and you know also, as no one else does, that whatever courtesy I have shown to Mrs. Hurtle in England, I have been constrained to show her.

'I appeal to you to let Hetta know that this is true. She had made me understand that not only her mother and brother, but you also, are well acquainted with the story of my acquaintance with Mrs. Hurtle. Neither Lady Carbury nor Sir Felix has ever known anything about it. You, and you only, have known the truth. And now, though at the present you are angry with me, I call upon you to tell Hetta the truth as you know it. You will understand me when I say that I feel that I am being destroyed by a false representation. I think that you, who abhor a falsehood, will see the justice of setting me right, at any rate as far as the truth can do so. I do not want you to say a word for me beyond that.

'Yours always,
'Paul Montague.'

'What business is all that of mine?' This, of course, was the first feeling produced in Roger's mind by Montague's letter. If Hetta had received any false impression, it had

not come from him. He had told no stories against his
rival, whether true or false. He had been so scrupulous
that he had refused to say a word at all. And if any false
impression had been made on Hetta's mind, either by
circumstances or by untrue words, had not Montague
deserved any evil that might fall upon him? Though
every word in Montague's letter might be true, nevertheless, in the end, no more than justice would be done
him, even should he be robbed at last of his mistress
under erroneous impressions. The fact that he had once
disgraced himself by offering to make Mrs. Hurtle his
wife, rendered him unworthy of Hetta Carbury. Such,
at least, was Roger Carbury's verdict as he thought over
all the circumstances. At any rate, it was no business
of his to correct these wrong impressions.

And yet he was ill at ease as he thought of it all. He
did believe that every word in Montague's letter was
true. Though he had been very indignant when he met
Roger and Mrs. Hurtle together on the sands at Lowestoft, he was perfectly convinced that the cause of their
coming there had been precisely that which Montague
had stated. It took him two days to think over all this,
two days of great discomfort and unhappiness. After all,
why should he be a dog in the manger? The girl did not
care for him,—looked upon him as an old man to be
regarded in a fashion altogether different from that in
which she regarded Paul Montague. He had let his time
for love-making go by, and now it behoved him, as a man,
to take the world as he found it, and not to lose himself
in regrets for a kind of happiness which he could never
attain. In such an emergency as this he should do what
was fair and honest, without reference to his own feelings.
And yet the passion which dominated John Crumb altogether, which made the mealman so intent on the attain-
ment of his object as to render all other things indifferent
to him for the time, was equally strong with Roger Carbury. Unfortunately for Roger, strong as his passion was,
it was embarrassed by other feelings. It never occurred
to Crumb to think whether he was a fit husband for
Ruby, or whether Ruby, having a decided preference

for another man, could be a fit wife for him. But with Roger there were a thousand surrounding difficulties to hamper him. John Crumb never doubted for a moment what he should do. He had to get the girl, if possible, and he meant to get her whatever she might cost him. He was always confident though sometimes perplexed. But Roger had no confidence. He knew that he should never win the game. In his sadder moments he felt that he ought not to win it. The people around him, from old fashion, still called him the young squire! Why;—he felt himself at times to be eighty years old,—so old that he was unfitted for intercourse with such juvenile spirits as those of his neighbour the bishop, and of his friend Hepworth. Could he, by any training, bring himself to take her happiness in hand, altogether sacrificing his own?

In such a mood as this he did at last answer his enemy's letter,—and he answered it as follows:—

'I do not know that I am concerned to meddle in your affairs at all. I have told no tale against you, and I do not know that I have any that I wish to tell in your favour, or that I could so tell if I did wish. I think that you have behaved badly to me, cruelly to Mrs. Hurtle, and disrespectfully to my cousin. Nevertheless, as you appeal to me on a certain point for evidence which I can give, and which you say no one else can give, I do acknowledge that, in my opinion, Mrs. Hurtle's presence in England has not been in accordance with your wishes, and that you accompanied her to Lowestoft, not as her lover but as an old friend whom you could not neglect.

'ROGER CARBURY.

'Paul Montague, Esq.

'You are at liberty to show this letter to Miss Carbury, if you please; but if she reads part she should read the whole!'

There was more perhaps of hostility in this letter than of that spirit of self-sacrifice to which Roger intended to train himself; and so he himself felt after the letter had been dispatched.

## Chapter LXXXVIII

### THE INQUEST

MELMOTTE had been found dead on Friday morning, and late on the evening of the same day Madame Melmotte and Marie were removed to lodgings far away from the scene of the tragedy, up at Hampstead. Herr Croll had known of the place, and at Lord Nidderdale's instance had busied himself in the matter, and had seen that the rooms were made instantly ready for the widow of his late employer. Nidderdale himself had assisted them in their departure; and the German, with the poor woman's maid, with the jewels also, which had been packed according to Melmotte's last orders to his wife, followed the carriage which took the mother and the daughter. They did not start till nine o'clock in the evening, and Madame Melmotte at the moment would fain have been allowed to rest one other night in Bruton Street. But Lord Nidderdale, with one hardly uttered word, made Marie understand that the inquest would be held early on the following morning, and Marie was imperious with her mother and carried her point. So the poor woman was taken away from Mr. Longestaffe's residence, and never again saw the grandeur of her own house in Grosvenor Square, which she had not visited since the night on which she had helped to entertain the Emperor of China.

On Saturday morning the inquest was held. There was not the slightest doubt as to any one of the incidents of the catastrophe. The servants, the doctor, and the inspector of police between them, learned that he had come home alone, that nobody had been near him during the night, that he had been found dead, and that he had undoubtedly been poisoned by prussic acid. It was also proved that he had been drunk in the House of Commons, a fact to which one of the clerks of the House, very much against his will, was called upon to testify. That he had destroyed himself there was no doubt,—nor was there any doubt as to the cause.

In such cases as this it is for the jury to say whether the unfortunate one who has found his life too hard for endurance, and has rushed away to see whether he could not find an improved condition of things elsewhere, has or has not been mad at the moment. Surviving friends are of course anxious for a verdict of insanity, as in that case no further punishment is exacted. The body can be buried like any other body, and it can always be said afterwards that the poor man was mad. Perhaps it would be well that all suicides should be said to have been mad, for certainly the jurymen are not generally guided in their verdicts by any accurately ascertained facts. If the poor wretch has, up to his last days, been apparently living a decent life; if he be not hated, or has not in his last moments made himself specially obnoxious to the world at large, then he is declared to have been mad. Who would be heavy on a poor clergyman who has been at last driven by horrid doubts to rid himself of a difficulty from which he saw no escape in any other way? Who would not give the benefit of the doubt to the poor woman whose lover and lord had deserted her? Who would remit to unhallowed earth the body of the once beneficent philosopher who has simply thought that he might as well go now, finding himself powerless to do further good upon earth? Such, and such like, have of course been temporarily insane, though no touch even of strangeness may have marked their conduct up to their last known dealings with their fellow-mortals. But let a Melmotte be found dead, with a bottle of prussic acid by his side —a man who has become horrid to the world because of his late iniquities, a man who has so well pretended to be rich that he has been able to buy and to sell properties without paying for them, a wretch who has made himself odious by his ruin to friends who had taken him up as a pillar of strength in regard to wealth, a brute who had got into the House of Commons by false pretences, and had disgraced the House by being drunk there,— and, of course, he will not be saved by a verdict of insanity from the cross roads, or whatever scornful grave may be allowed to those who have killed themselves with

their wits about them. Just at this moment there was a
very strong feeling against Melmotte, owing perhaps as
much to his having tumbled over poor Mr. Beauchamp
in the House of Commons as to the stories of the forgeries
he had committed, and the virtue of the day vindicated
itself by declaring him to have been responsible for his
actions when he took the poison. He was *felo de se*, and
therefore carried away to the cross roads—or elsewhere.
But it may be imagined, I think, that during that night he
may have become as mad as any other wretch, have been
driven as far beyond his powers of endurance as any other
poor creature who ever at any time felt himself constrained to go. He had not been so drunk but that he
knew all that happened, and could foresee pretty well
what would happen. The summons to attend upon the
Lord Mayor had been served upon him. There were
some, among them Croll and Mr. Brehgert, who absolutely knew that he had committed forgery. He had no
money for the Longestaffes, and he was well aware what
Squercum would do at once. He had assured himself
long ago,—he had assured himself indeed not very long
ago,—that he would brave it all like a man. But we
none of us know what load we can bear, and what would
break our backs. Melmotte's back had been so utterly
crushed that I almost think that he was mad enough to
have justified a verdict of temporary insanity.

But he was carried away, no one knew whither, and
for a week his name was hateful. But after that, a certain
amount of whitewashing took place, and, in some degree,
a restitution of fame was made to the manes* of the
departed. In Westminster he was always odious. Westminster, which had adopted him, never forgave him.
But in other districts it came to be said of him that he had
been more sinned against than sinning; and that, but for
the jealousy of the old stagers in the mercantile world,
he would have done very wonderful things. Marylebone,
which is always merciful, took him up quite with affection, and would have returned his ghost to Parliament
could his ghost have paid for committee rooms. Finsbury
delighted for a while to talk of the great Financier, and

even Chelsea thought that he had been done to death by ungenerous tongues. It was, however, Marylebone alone that spoke of a monument.

Mr. Longestaffe came back to his house, taking formal possession of it a few days after the verdict. Of course he was alone. There had been no further question of bringing the ladies of the family up to town; and Dolly altogether declined to share with his father the honour of encountering the dead man's spirit. But there was very much for Mr. Longestaffe to do, and very much also for his son. It was becoming a question with both of them how far they had been ruined by their connection with the horrible man. It was clear that they could not get back the title-deeds of the Pickering property without paying the amount which had been advanced upon them, and it was equally clear that they could not pay that sum unless they were enabled to do so by funds coming out of the Melmotte estate. Dolly, as he sat smoking upon the stool in Mr. Squercum's office, where he now passed a considerable portion of his time, looked upon himself as a miracle of ill-usage.

'By George, you know, I shall have to go to law with the governor. There's nothing else for it; is there, Squercum?'

Squercum suggested that they had better wait till they found what pickings there might be out of the Melmotte estate. He had made inquiries too about that, and had been assured that there must be property, but property so involved and tied up as to make it impossible to lay hands upon it suddenly. 'They say that the things in the square, and the plate, and the carriages and horses, and all that, ought to fetch between twenty and thirty thousand. There were a lot of jewels, but the women have taken them,' said Squercum.

'By George, they ought to be made to give up everything. Did you ever hear of such a thing;—the very house pulled down;—my house; and all done without a word from me in the matter? I don't suppose such a thing was ever known before, since properties were properties.' Then he uttered sundry threats against the Bideawhiles, in reference to whom he declared his intention of 'making it very hot for them.'

It was an annoyance added to the elder Mr. Longe-staffe that the management of Melmotte's affairs fell at last almost exclusively into the hands of Mr. Brehgert. Now Brehgert, in spite of his many dealings with Mel-motte, was an honest man, and, which was perhaps of as much immediate consequence, both an energetic and a patient man. But then he was the man who had wanted to marry Georgiana Longestaffe, and he was the man to whom Mr. Longestaffe had been particularly uncivil. Then there arose necessities for the presence of Mr. Brehgert in the house in which Melmotte had lately lived and had died. The dead man's papers were still there,—deeds, documents, and such letters as he had not chosen to destroy;—and these could not be moved quite at once. 'Mr. Brehgert must of course have access to my private room, as long as it is necessary,—absolutely neces-sary,' said Mr. Longestaffe in answer to a message which was brought to him; 'but he will of course see the ex-pediency of relieving me from such intrusion as soon as possible.' But he soon found it preferable to come to terms with the rejected suitor, especially as the man was singularly good-natured and forbearing after the injuries he had received.

All minor debts were to be paid at once; an arrange-ment to which Mr. Longestaffe cordially agreed, as it included a sum of £300 due to him for the rent of his house in Bruton Street. Then by degrees it became known that there would certainly be a dividend of not less than fifty per cent. payable on debts which could be proved to have been owing by Melmotte, and perhaps of more;—an arrangement which was very comfortable to Dolly, as it had been already agreed between all the parties interested that the debt due to him should be satisfied before the father took anything. Mr. Longestaffe resolved during these weeks that he remained in town that, as regarded himself and his own family, the house in London should not only not be kept up, but that it should be absolutely sold, with all its belongings, and that

the servants at Caversham should be reduced in number
and should cease to wear powder. All this was communicated to Lady Pomona in a very long letter, which she
was instructed to read to her daughters. 'I have suffered
great wrongs,' said Mr. Longestaffe, 'but I must submit
to them, and as I submit so must my wife and children.
If our son were different from what he is the sacrifice
might probably be made lighter. His nature I cannot
alter, but from my daughters I expect cheerful obedience.'
From what incidents of his past life he was led to expect
cheerfulness at Caversham it might be difficult to say;
but the obedience was there. Georgey was for the time
broken down; Sophia was satisfied with her nuptial prospects, and Lady Pomona had certainly no spirits left for
a combat. I think the loss of the hair-powder afflicted
her most; but she said not a word even about that.

But in all this the details necessary for the telling of our
story are anticipated. Mr. Longestaffe had remained in
London actually over the 1st of September, which in
Suffolk is the one great festival of the year,* before the
letter was written to which allusion has been made. In
the meantime he saw much of Mr. Brehgert, and absolutely formed a kind of friendship for that gentleman, in
spite of the abomination of his religion,—so that on one
occasion he even condescended to ask Mr. Brehgert to
dine alone with him in Bruton Street. This, too, was in
the early days of the arrangement of the Melmotte affairs,
when Mr. Longestaffe's heart had been softened by that
arrangement with reference to the rent. Mr. Brehgert
came, and there arose a somewhat singular conversation
between the two gentlemen as they sat together over a
bottle of Mr. Longestaffe's old port wine. Hitherto not
a word had passed between them respecting the connection which had once been proposed, since the day on
which the young lady's father had said so many bitter
things to the expectant bridegroom. But in this evening
Mr. Brehgert, who was by no means a coward in such
matters and whose feelings were not perhaps painfully
fine, spoke his mind in a way that at first startled Mr.
Longestaffe. The subject was introduced by a reference

which Brehgert had made to his own affairs. His loss would be, at any rate, double that which Mr. Longe-staffe would have to bear;—but he spoke of it in an easy way, as though it did not sit very near his heart. 'Of course there's a difference between me and you,' he said. Mr. Longestaffe bowed his head graciously, as much as to say that there was of course a very wide difference. 'In our affairs,' continued Brehgert, 'we expect gains, and of course look for occasional losses. When a gentle-man in your position sells a property he expects to get the purchase-money.'

'Of course he does, Mr. Brehgert. That's what made it so hard.'

'I can't even yet quite understand how it was with him, or why he took upon himself to spend such an enormous deal of money here in London. His business was quite irregular, but there was very much of it, and some of it immensely profitable. He took us in completely.'

'I suppose so.'

'It was old Mr. Todd that first took to him;—but I was deceived as much as Todd, and then I ventured on a speculation with him outside of our house. The long and short of it is that I shall lose something about sixty thou-sand pounds.'

'That's a large sum of money.'

'Very large;—so large as to affect my daily mode of life. In my correspondence with your daughter, I con-sidered it to be my duty to point out to her that it would be so. I do not know whether she told you.'

This reference to his daughter for the moment alto-gether upset Mr. Longestaffe. The reference was cer-tainly most indelicate, most deserving of censure; but Mr. Longestaffe did not know how to pronounce his censure on the spur of the moment, and was moreover at the present time so very anxious for Brehgert's assistance in the arrangement of his affairs that, so to say, he could not afford to quarrel with the man. But he assumed something more than his normal dignity as he asserted that his daughter had never mentioned the fact.

'It was so,' said Brehgert.

'No doubt;'—and Mr. Longestaffe assumed a great deal of dignity.

'Yes; it was so. I had promised your daughter when she was good enough to listen to the proposition which I made to her, that I would maintain a second house when we should be married.'

'It was impossible,' said Mr. Longestaffe,—meaning to assert that such hymeneals were altogether unnatural and out of the question.

'It would have been quite possible as things were when that proposition was made. But looking forward to the loss which I afterwards anticipated from the affairs of our deceased friend, I found it to be prudent to relinquish my intention for the present, and I thought myself bound to inform Miss Longestaffe.'

'There were other reasons,' muttered Mr. Longestaffe, in a suppressed voice, almost in a whisper,—in a whisper which was intended to convey a sense of present horror and a desire for future reticence.

'There may have been; but in the last letter which Miss Longestaffe did me the honour to write to me,—a letter with which I have not the slightest right to find any fault,—she seemed to me to confine herself almost exclusively to that reason.'

'Why mention this now, Mr. Brehgert; why mention this now? The subject is painful.'

'Just because it is not painful to me, Mr. Longestaffe; and because I wish that all they who have heard of the matter should know that it is not painful. I think that throughout I behaved like a gentleman.' Mr. Longestaffe, in an agony, first shook his head twice, and then bowed it three times, leaving the Jew to take what answer he could from so dubious an oracle. 'I am sure,' continued Brehgert, 'that I behaved like an honest man; and I didn't quite like that the matter should be passed over as if I was in any way ashamed of myself.'

'Perhaps on so delicate a subject the less said the soonest mended.'

'I've nothing more to say, and I've nothing at all to mend.' Finishing the conversation with this little speech

Brehgert arose to take his leave, making some promise at
the time that he would use all the expedition in his power
to complete the arrangement of the Melmotte affairs.

As soon as he was gone Mr. Longestaffe opened the
door and walked about the room and blew out long puffs
of breath, as though to cleanse himself from the impuri-
ties of his late contact. He told himself that he could not
touch pitch and not be defiled! How vulgar had the man
been, how indelicate, how regardless of all feeling, how
little grateful for the honour which Mr. Longestaffe had
conferred upon him by asking him to dinner! Yes;—
yes! A horrid Jew! Were not all Jews necessarily an
abomination? Yet Mr. Longestaffe was aware that in
the present crisis of his fortunes he could not afford to
quarrel with Mr. Brehgert.


## Chapter LXXXIX

### 'THE WHEEL OF FORTUNE'

IT was a long time now since Lady Carbury's great
historical work on the Criminal Queens of the World
had been completed and given to the world. Any reader
careful as to dates will remember that it was as far back
as in February that she had solicited the assistance of
certain of her literary friends who were connected with the
daily and weekly press. These gentlemen had responded
to her call with more or less zealous aid, so that the
'Criminal Queens' had been regarded in the trade as one
of the successful books of the season. Messrs. Leadham
and Loiter had published a second, and then, very
quickly, a fourth and fifth edition; and had been able
in their advertisements to give testimony from various
criticisms showing that Lady Carbury's book was about
the greatest historical work which had emanated from
the press in the present century. With this object a
passage was extracted even from the columns of the
'Evening Pulpit,'—which showed very great ingenuity on

the part of some young man connected with the establishment of Messrs. Leadham and Loiter. Lady Carbury had suffered something in the struggle. What efforts can mortals make as to which there will not be some disappointment? Paper and print cannot be had for nothing, and advertisements are very costly. An edition may be sold with startling rapidity, but it may have been but a scanty edition. When Lady Carbury received from Messrs. Leadham and Loiter their second very moderate cheque, with the expression of a fear on their part that there would not probably be a third,—unless some unforeseen demand should arise,—she repeated to herself those well-known lines from the satirist,—

> 'Oh, Amos Cottle, for a moment think
> What meagre profits spread from pen and ink.'*

But not on that account did she for a moment hesitate as to further attempts. Indeed she had hardly completed the last chapter of her 'Criminal Queens' before she was busy on another work; and although the last six months had been to her a period of incessant trouble, and sometimes of torture, though the conduct of her son had more than once forced her to declare to herself that her mind would fail her, still she had persevered. From day to day, with all her cares heavy upon her, she had sat at her work, with a firm resolve that so many lines should be always forthcoming, let the difficulty of making them be what it might. Messrs. Leadham and Loiter had thought that they might be justified in offering her certain terms for a novel,—terms not very high indeed, and those contingent on the approval of the manuscript by their reader. The smallness of the sum offered, and the want of certainty, and the pain of the work in her present circumstances, had all been felt by her to be very hard. But she had persevered, and the novel was now complete.

It cannot with truth be said of her that she had had any special tale to tell. She had taken to the writing of a novel because Mr. Loiter had told her that upon the whole novels did better than anything else. She would have written a volume of sermons on the same encouragement,

and have gone about the work exactly after the same
fashion. The length of her novel had been her first question. It must be in three volumes,* and each volume
must have three hundred pages. But what fewest number of words might be supposed sufficient to fill a page?
The money offered was too trifling to allow of very
liberal measure on her part. She had to live, and if
possible to write another novel,—and, as she hoped, upon
better terms,—when this should be finished. Then what
should be the name of her novel; what the name of her
hero; and above all what the name of her heroine? It
must be a love story of course; but she thought that she
would leave the complications of the plot to come by
chance,—and they did come. 'Don't let it end unhap-
pily, Lady Carbury,' Mr. Loiter had said, 'because
though people like it in a play, they hate it in a book.
And whatever you do, Lady Carbury, don't be historical.
Your historical novel, Lady Carbury, isn't worth a——*'
Mr. Loiter stopping himself suddenly, and remembering
that he was addressing himself to a lady, satisfied his
energy at last by the use of the word 'straw.' Lady Carbury had followed these instructions with accuracy.

The name for the story had been the great thing. It did
not occur to the authoress that, as the plot was to be
allowed to develop itself and was, at this moment when
she was perplexed as to the title, altogether uncreated,
she might as well wait to see what appellation might best
suit her work when its purpose should have declared
itself. A novel, she knew well, was most unlike a rose,
which by any other name will smell as sweet. 'The
Faultless Father,' 'The Mysterious Mother,' 'The Lame
Lover,'—such names as that she was aware would be
useless now. 'Mary Jane Walker,' if she could be very
simple, would do, or 'Blanche De Veau,' if she were able
to maintain throughout a somewhat high-stilted style of
feminine rapture. But as she considered that she could
best deal with rapid action and strange coincidences, she
thought that something more startling and descriptive
would better suit her purpose. After an hour's thought
a name did occur to her, and she wrote it down, and with

considerable energy of purpose framed her work in
accordance with her chosen title, 'The Wheel of Fortune!'
She had no particular fortune in her mind when she
chose it, and no particular wheel;—but the very idea
conveyed by the words gave her the plot which she
wanted. A young lady was blessed with great wealth, and
lost it all by an uncle, and got it all back by an honest
lawyer, and gave it all up to a distressed lover, and found
it all again in a third volume. And the lady's name was
Cordinga, selected by Lady Carbury as never having
been heard before either in the world of fact or in that of
fiction.

And now with all her troubles thick about her,—while
her son was still hanging about the house in a condition
that would break any mother's heart, while her daughter
was so wretched and sore that she regarded all those
around her as her enemies, Lady Carbury finished her
work, and having just written the last words in which
the final glow of enduring happiness was given to the
young married heroine whose wheel had now come full
round, sat with the sheets piled at her right hand. She
had allowed herself a certain number of weeks for the task,
and had completed it exactly in the time fixed. As she
sat with her hand near the pile, she did give herself credit
for her diligence. Whether the work might have been
better done she never asked herself. I do not think that
she prided herself much on the literary merit of the tale.
But if she could bring the papers to praise it, if she could
induce Mudie to circulate it,* if she could manage that the
air for a month should be so loaded with 'The Wheel of
Fortune,' as to make it necessary for the reading world to
have read or to have said that it had read the book,—
then she would pride herself very much upon her work.

As she was so sitting on a Sunday afternoon, in her
own room, Mr. Alf was announced. According to her
habit, she expressed warm delight at seeing him. Nothing could be kinder than such a visit just at such a
time,—when there was so very much to occupy such a
one as Mr. Alf! Mr. Alf, in his usual mildly satirical way,
declared that he was not peculiarly occupied just at

present. 'The Emperor has left Europe at last,' he said. 'Poor Melmotte poisoned himself on Friday, and the inquest sat yesterday. I don't know that there is anything of interest to-day.' Of course Lady Carbury was intent upon her book, rather even than on the exciting death of a man whom she had herself known. Oh, if she could only get Mr. Alf! She had tried it before, and had failed lamentably. She was well aware of that; and she had a deep-seated conviction that it would be almost impossible to get Mr. Alf. But then she had another deep-seated conviction, that that which is almost impossible may possibly be done. How great would be the glory, how infinite the service! And did it not seem as though Providence had blessed her with this special opportunity, sending Mr. Alf to her just at the one moment at which she might introduce the subject of her novel without seeming premeditation?

'I am so tired,' she said, affecting to throw herself back as though stretching her arms out for ease.

'I hope I am not adding to your fatigue,' said Mr. Alf.

'Oh dear no. It is not the fatigue of the moment, but of the last six months. Just as you knocked at the door, I had finished the novel at which I have been working, oh, with such diligence!'

'Oh,—a novel! When is it to appear, Lády Carbury?'

'You must ask Leadham and Loiter that question. I have done my part of the work. I suppose you never wrote a novel, Mr. Alf?'

'I? Oh dear no; I never write anything.'

'I have sometimes wondered whether I have hated or loved it the most. One becomes so absorbed in one's plot and one's characters! One loves the loveable so intensely, and hates with such fixed aversion those who are intended to be hated. When the mind is attuned to it, one is tempted to think that it is all so good. One cries at one's own pathos, laughs at one's own humour, and is lost in admiration at one's own sagacity and knowledge.'

'How very nice!'

'But then there comes the reversed picture, the other side of the coin. On a sudden everything becomes flat, tedious, and unnatural. The heroine who was yesterday alive with the celestial spark is found to-day to be a lump of motionless clay. The dialogue that was so cheery on the first perusal is utterly uninteresting at a second reading. Yesterday I was sure that there was my monument,' and she put her hand upon the manuscript; 'to-day I feel it to be only too heavy for a gravestone!'

'One's judgement about one's self always does vacillate,' said Mr. Alf in a tone as phlegmatic as were the words.

'And yet it is so important that one should be able to judge correctly of one's own work! I can at any rate trust myself to be honest, which is more perhaps than can be said of all the critics.'

'Dishonesty is not the general fault of the critics, Lady Carbury,—at least not as far as I have observed the business. It is incapacity. In what little I have done in the matter, that is the sin which I have striven to conquer. When we want shoes we go to a professed shoemaker; but for criticism we have certainly not gone to professed critics. I think that when I gave up the "Evening Pulpit," I left upon it a staff of writers who are entitled to be regarded as knowing their business.'

'You given up the "Pulpit"?' asked Lady Carbury with astonishment, readjusting her mind at once, so that she might perceive whether any and if so what advantage might be taken of Mr. Alf's new position. He was no longer editor, and therefore his heavy sense of responsibility would no longer exist;—but he must still have influence. Might he not be persuaded to do one act of real friendship? Might she not succeed if she would come down from her high seat, sink on the ground before him, tell him the plain truth, and beg for a favour as a poor struggling woman?

'Yes, Lady Carbury, I have given it up. It was a matter of course that I should do so when I stood for Parliament. Now that the new member has so suddenly vacated his seat, I shall probably stand again.'

'And you are no longer an editor?'

'I have given it up, and I suppose I have now satisfied

the scruples of those gentlemen who seemed to think that
I was committing a crime against the Constitution in
attempting to get into Parliament while I was managing
a newspaper. I never heard such nonsense. Of course I
know where it came from.'

'Where did it come from?'

'Where should it come from but the "Breakfast Table"?
Broune and I have been very good friends, but I do think
that of all the men I know he is the most jealous.'

'That is so little,' said Lady Carbury. She was really
very fond of Mr. Broune, but at the present moment she
was obliged to humour Mr. Alf.

'It seems to me that no man can be better qualified
to sit in Parliament than an editor of a newspaper,—that
is if he is capable as an editor.'

'No one, I think, has ever doubted that of you.'

'The only question is whether he be strong enough for
the double work. I have doubted about myself, and have
therefore given up the paper. I almost regret it.'

'I dare say you do,' said Lady Carbury, feeling intensely anxious to talk about her own affairs instead of
his. 'I suppose you still retain an interest in the paper?'

'Some pecuniary interest;—nothing more.'

'Oh, Mr. Alf,—you could do me such a favour!'

'Can I? If I can, you may be sure I will.' False-hearted,
false-tongued man! Of course he knew at the moment
what was the favour Lady Carbury intended to ask, and
of course he had made up his mind that he would not do
as he was asked.

'Will you?' And Lady Carbury clasped her hands
together as she poured forth the words of her prayer. 'I
never asked you to do anything for me as long as you
were editing the paper. Did I? I did not think it right,
and I would not do it. I took my chance like others, and
I am sure you must own that I bore what was said of me
with a good grace. I never complained. Did I?'

'Certainly not.'

'But now that you have left it yourself,—if you would
have the "Wheel of Fortune" done for me,—really well
done!'

'The "Wheel of Fortune"!'

'That is the name of my novel,' said Lady Carbur
putting her hand softly upon the manuscript. 'Just a
this moment it would be the making of a fortune for me!
And oh, Mr. Alf, if you could but know how I want such
assistance!'

'I have nothing further to do with the editorial
management, Lady Carbury.'

'Of course you could get it done. A word from you
would make it certain. A novel is different from an
historical work, you know. I have taken so much pains
with it.'

'Then no doubt it will be praised on its own merits.'

'Don't say that, Mr. Alf. The "Evening Pulpit" is like,
—oh, it is like,—like,—like the throne of heaven! Who
can be justified before it? Don't talk about its own
merits, but say that you will have it done. It couldn't do
any man any harm, and it would sell five hundred copies
at once,—that is if it were done really con amore.' Mr.
Alf looked at her almost piteously, and shook his head.
'The paper stands so high, it can't hurt it to do that kind
of thing once. A woman is asking you, Mr. Alf. It is for
my children that I am struggling. The thing is done
every day of the week, with much less noble motives.'

'I do not think that it has ever been done by the
"Evening Pulpit."'

'I have seen books praised.'

'Of course you have.'

'I think I saw a novel spoken highly of.'

Mr. Alf laughed. 'Why not? You do not suppose that
it is the object of the "Pulpit" to cry down novels?'

'I thought it was; but I thought you might make an
exception here. I would be so thankful;—so grateful.'

'My dear Lady Carbury, pray believe me when I say
that I have nothing to do with it. I need not preach to
you sermons about literary virtue.'

'Oh, no,' she said, not quite understanding what he
meant.

'The sceptre has passed from my hands, and I need not
vindicate the justice of my successor.'

'I shall never know your successor.'

'But I must assure you that on no account should I think of meddling with the literary arrangement of the paper. I would not do it for my sister.' Lady Carbury looked greatly pained. 'Send the book out, and let it take its chance. How much prouder you will be to have it praised because it deserves praise, than to know that it has been eulogized as a mark of friendship.'

'No, I shan't,' said Lady Carbury. 'I don't believe that anything like real selling praise is ever given to anybody, except to friends. I don't know how they manage it, but they do.' Mr. Alf shook his head. 'Oh yes; that is all very well from you. Of course you have been a dragon of virtue; but they tell me that the authoress of the "New Cleopatra" is a very handsome woman.' Lady Carbury must have been worried much beyond her wont, when she allowed herself so far to lose her temper as to bring against Mr. Alf the double charge of being too fond of the authoress in question, and of having sacrificed the justice of his columns to that improper affection.

'At this moment I do not remember the name of the lady to whom you allude,' said Mr. Alf, getting up to take his leave; 'and I am quite sure that the gentleman who reviewed the book,—if there be any such lady and any such book,—had never seen her!' And so Mr. Alf departed.

Lady Carbury was very angry with herself, and very angry also with Mr. Alf. She had not only meant to be piteous, but had made the attempt and then had allowed herself to be carried away into anger. She had degraded herself to humility, and had then wasted any possible good result by a foolish fit of chagrin. The world in which she had to live was almost too hard for her. When left alone she sat weeping over her sorrows; but when from time to time she thought of Mr. Alf and his conduct, she could hardly repress her scorn. What lies he had told her! Of course he could have done it had he chosen. But the assumed honesty of the man was infinitely worse to her than his lies. No doubt the 'Pulpit' had two objects

in its criticisms. Other papers probably had but one.
The object common to all papers, that of helping friends
and destroying enemies, of course prevailed with the
'Pulpit.' There was the second purpose of enticing
readers by crushing authors,—as crowds used to be
enticed to see men hanged when executions were done
in public. But neither the one object nor the other
was compatible with that Aristidean justice which
Mr. Alf arrogated to himself and to his paper. She
hoped with all her heart that Mr. Alf would spend a
great deal of money at Westminster, and then lose his
seat.

On the following morning she herself took the manuscript to Messrs. Leadham and Loiter, and was hurt again
by the small amount of respect which seemed to be paid
to the collected sheets. There was the work of six months;
her very blood and brains,—the concentrated essence of
her mind,—as she would say herself when talking with
energy of her own performances; and Mr. Leadham
pitched it across to a clerk, apparently perhaps sixteen
years of age, and the lad chucked the parcel uncere-
moniously under the counter. An author feels that his
work should be taken from him with fast-clutching but
reverential hands, and held thoughtfully, out of harm's
way, till it be deposited within the very sanctum of an
absolutely fireproof safe. Oh, heavens, if it should be
lost!—or burned!—or stolen! Those scraps of paper, so
easily destroyed, apparently so little respected, may
hereafter be acknowledged to have had a value greater,
so far greater, than their weight in gold! If 'Robinson
Crusoe' had been lost! If 'Tom Jones' had been consumed by flames! And who knows but that this may
be another 'Robinson Crusoe,'—a better than 'Tom
Jones'? 'Will it be safe there?' asked Lady Carbury.

'Quite safe,—quite safe,' said Mr. Leadham, who was
rather busy, and perhaps saw Lady Carbury more frequently than the nature and amount of her authorship
seemed to him to require.

'It seemed to be, — put down there, — under the
counter!'

'That's quite right, Lady Carbury. They're left there till they're packed.'

'Packed!'

'There are two or three dozen going to our reader this week. He's down in Skye, and we keep them till there's enough to fill the sack.'

'Do they go by post, Mr. Leadham?'

'Not by post, Lady Carbury. There are not many of them would pay the expense. We send them by long sea to Glasgow, because just at this time of the year there is not much hurry. We can't publish before the winter.' Oh, heavens! If that ship should be lost on its journey by long sea to Glasgow!

That evening, as was now almost his daily habit, Mr. Broune came to her. There was something in the absolute friendship which now existed between Lady Carbury and the editor of the 'Morning Breakfast Table,' which almost made her scrupulous as to asking from him any further literary favour. She fully recognized,—no woman perhaps more fully,—the necessity of making use of all aid and furtherance which might come within reach. With such a son, with such need for struggling before her, would she not be wicked not to catch even at every straw? But this man had now become so true to her, that she hardly knew how to beg him to do that which she, with all her mistaken feelings, did in truth know that he ought not to do. He had asked her to marry him, for which,— though she had refused him,—she felt infinitely grateful. And though she had refused him, he had lent her money, and had supported her in her misery by his continued counsel. If he would offer to do this thing for her she would accept his kindness on her knees,—but even she could not bring herself to ask to have this added to his other favours. Her first word to him was about Mr. Alf. 'So he has given up the paper?'

'Well, yes;—nominally.'

'Is that all?'

'I don't suppose he'll really let it go out of his own hands. Nobody likes to lose power. He'll share the work, and keep the authority. As for Westminster, I don't believe he has a chance. If that poor wretch Melmotte could beat him when everybody was already talking about the forgeries, how is it likely that he should stand against such a candidate as they'll get now?'

'He was here yesterday.'

'And full of triumph, I suppose?'

'He never talks to me much of himself. We were speaking of my new book,—my novel. He assured me most positively that he had nothing further to do with the paper.'

'He did not care to make you a promise, I dare say.'

'That was just it. Of course I did not believe him.'

'Neither will I make a promise, but we'll see what we can do. If we can't be good-natured, at any rate we will say nothing ill-natured. Let me see,—what is the name?'

' "The Wheel of Fortune." ' Lady Carbury as she told the title of her new book to her old friend seemed to be almost ashamed of it.

'Let them send it early,—a day or two before it's out, if they can. I can't answer, of course, for the opinion of the gentleman it will go to, but nothing shall go in that you would dislike. Good-bye. God bless you.' And as he took her hand, he looked at her almost as though the old susceptibility were returning to him.

As she sat alone after he had gone, thinking over it all, —thinking of her own circumstances and of his kindness, —it did not occur to her to call him an old goose again. She felt now that she had mistaken her man when she had so regarded him. That first and only kiss which he had given her, which she had treated with so much derision, for which she had rebuked him so mildly and yet so haughtily, had now a somewhat sacred spot in her memory. Through it all the man must have really loved her! Was it not marvellous that such a thing should be? And how had it come to pass that she in all her tenderness had rejected him when he had given her the chance of becoming his wife?

## Chapter XC

### HETTA'S SORROW

WHEN Hetta Carbury received that letter from her lover which was given to the reader some chapters back, it certainly did not tend in any way to alleviate her misery. Even when she had read it over half-a-dozen times, she could not bring herself to think it possible that she could be reconciled to the man. It was not only that he had sinned against her by giving his society to another woman to whom he had at any rate been engaged not long since, at the very time at which he was becoming engaged to her,—but also that he had done this in such a manner as to make his offence known to all her friends. Perhaps she had been too quick;—but there was the fact that with her own consent she had acceded to her mother's demand that the man should be rejected. The man had been rejected, and even Roger Carbury knew that it was so. After this it was, she thought, impossible that she should recall him. But they should all know that her heart was unchanged. Roger Carbury should certainly know that, if he ever asked her further question on the matter. She would never deny it; and though she knew that the man had behaved badly,—having entangled himself with a nasty American woman,—yet she would be true to him as far as her own heart was concerned.

And now he told her that she had been most unjust to him. He said that he could not understand her injustice. He did not fill his letter with entreaties, but with reproaches. And certainly his reproaches moved her more than any prayer would have done. It was too late now to remedy the evil; but she was not quite sure within her own bosom that she had not been unjust to him. The more she thought of it the more puzzled her mind became. Had she quarrelled with him because he had once been in love with Mrs. Hurtle, or because she had grounds for regarding Mrs. Hurtle as her present rival? She hated Mrs. Hurtle,

and she was very angry with him in that he had ever been
on affectionate terms with a woman she hated;—but
that had not been the reason put forward by her for
quarrelling with him. Perhaps it was true that he, too,
had of late loved Mrs. Hurtle hardly better than she did
herself. It might be that he had been indeed constrained
by hard circumstances to go with the woman to Lowestoft.
Having so gone with her, it was no doubt right that he
should be rejected:—for how can it be that a man who
is engaged shall be allowed to travel about the country
with another woman to whom also he was engaged a few
months back? But still there might be hardship in it.
To her, to Hetta herself, the circumstances were very
hard. She loved the man with all her heart. She could
look forward to no happiness in life without him. But
yet it must be so.

At the end of his letter he had told her to go to Mrs.
Hurtle herself if she wanted corroboration of the story as
told by him. Of course he had known when he wrote it
that she could not and would not go to Mrs. Hurtle. But
when the letter had been in her possession three or four
days,—unanswered, for, as a matter of course, no answer
to it from herself was possible,—and had been read and
re-read till she knew every word of it by heart, she began
to think that if she could hear the story as it might be
told by Mrs. Hurtle, a good deal that was now dark might
become light to her. As she continued to read the letter,
and to brood over it all, by degrees her anger was turned
from her lover to her mother, her brother, and to her
cousin Roger. Paul had of course behaved badly, very
badly,—but had it not been for them she might have had
an opportunity of forgiving him. They had driven her
on to the declaration of a purpose from which she could
now see no escape. There had been a plot against her,
and she was a victim. In the first dismay and agony
occasioned by that awful story of the American woman,
—which had, at the moment, struck her with a horror
which was now becoming less and less every hour,—she
had fallen head foremost into the trap laid for her. She
acknowledged to herself that it was too late to recover

her ground. She was, at any rate, almost sure that it must be too late. But yet she was disposed to do battle with her mother and her cousin in the matter—if only with the object of showing that she would not submit her own feelings to their control. She was savage to the point of rebellion against all authority. Roger Carbury would of course think that any communication between herself and Mrs. Hurtle must be improper,—altogether indelicate. Two or three days ago she thought so herself. But the world was going so hard with her, that she was beginning to feel herself capable of throwing propriety and delicacy to the winds. This man whom she had once accepted, whom she altogether loved, and who, in spite of all his faults, certainly still loved her,—of that she was beginning to have no further doubt,—accused her of dishonesty, and referred her to her rival for a corroboration of his story. She would appeal to Mrs. Hurtle. The woman was odious, abominable, a nasty intriguing American female. But her lover desired that she should hear the woman's story; and she would hear the story,—if the woman would tell it.

So resolving, she wrote as follows to Mrs. Hurtle, finding great difficulty in the composition of a letter which should tell neither too little nor too much, and determined that she would be restrained by no mock modesty, by no girlish fear of declaring the truth about herself. The letter at last was stiff and hard, but it sufficed for its purpose.

'Madam,—

'Mr. Paul Montague has referred me to you as to certain circumstances which have taken place between him and you. It is right that I should tell you that I was a short time since engaged to marry him, but that I have found myself obliged to break off that engagement in consequence of what I have been told as to his acquaintance with you. I make this proposition to you, not thinking that anything you will say to me can change my mind, but because he has asked me to do so, and has, at the same time, accused me of injustice towards him. I do

not wish to rest under an accusation of injustice from one
to whom I was once warmly attached. If you will receive
me, I will make it my business to call any afternoon you
may name.

'Yours truly,
'HENRIETTA CARBURY.'

When the letter was written she was not only ashamed
of it, but very much afraid of it also. What if the American woman should put it in a newspaper! She had heard
that everything was put into newspapers in America.
What if this Mrs. Hurtle should send back to her some
horribly insolent answer;—or should send such answer to
her mother, instead of herself! And then, again, if the
American woman consented to receive her, would not the
American woman, as a matter of course, trample upon
her with rough words? Once or twice she put the letter
aside, and almost determined that it should not be sent;
—but at last, with desperate fortitude, she took it out
with her and posted it herself. She told no word of it to
any one. Her mother, she thought, had been cruel to her,
had disregarded her feelings, and made her wretched for
ever. She could not ask her mother for sympathy in her
present distress. There was no friend who would sympathize with her. She must do everything alone.

Mrs. Hurtle, it will be remembered, had at last determined that she would retire from the contest and own
herself to have been worsted. It is, I fear, impossible to
describe adequately the various half resolutions which
she formed, and the changing phases of her mind before
she brought herself to this conclusion. And soon after she
had assured herself that this should be the conclusion,—
after she had told Paul Montague that it should be so,—
there came back upon her at times other half resolutions
to a contrary effect. She had written a letter to the man
threatening desperate revenge, and had then abstained
from sending it, and had then shown it to the man,—not
intending to give it to him as a letter upon which he would
have to act, but only that she might ask him whether,
had he received it, he would have said that he had not

deserved it. Then she had parted with him, refusing
either to hear or to say a word of farewell, and had told
Mrs. Pipkin that she was no longer engaged to be married. At that moment everything was done that could
be done. The game had been played and the stakes lost,
—and she had schooled herself into such restraint as to
have abandoned all idea of vengeance. But from time to
time there arose in her heart a feeling that such softness
was unworthy of her. Who had ever been soft to her? Who
had spared her? Had she not long since found out that
she must fight with her very nails and teeth for every inch
of ground, if she did not mean to be trodden into the dust?
Had she not held her own among rough people after a
very rough fashion, and should she now simply retire
that she might weep in a corner like a love-sick school-
girl? And she had been so stoutly determined that she
would at any rate avenge her own wrongs, if she could
not turn those wrongs into triumph! There were moments
in which she thought that she could still seize the man by
the throat, where all the world might see her, and dare
him to deny that he was false, perjured, and mean.

Then she received a long passionate letter from Paul
Montague, written at the same time as those other letters
to Roger Carbury and Hetta, in which he told her all the
circumstances of his engagement to Hetta Carbury, and
implored her to substantiate the truth of his own story.
It was certainly marvellous to her that the man who had
so long been her own lover and who had parted with her
after such a fashion should write such a letter to her. But
it had no tendency to increase either her anger or her
sorrow. Of course she had known that it was so, and
at certain times she had told herself that it was only
natural,—had almost told herself that it was right. She
and this young Englishman were not fit to be mated. He
was to her thinking a tame, sleek household animal,
whereas she knew herself to be wild,—fitter for the woods
than for polished cities. It had been one of the faults of
her life that she had allowed herself to be bound by
tenderness of feeling to this soft over-civilised man. The
result had been disastrous, as might have been expected.

She was angry with him,—almost to the extent of tearing him to pieces,—but she did not become more angry because he wrote to her of her rival.

Her only present friend was Mrs. Pipkin, who treated her with the greatest deference, but who was never tired of asking questions about the lost lover. 'That letter was from Mr. Montague?' said Mrs. Pipkin on the morning after it had been received.

'How can you know that?'

'I'm sure it was. One does get to know handwritings when letters come frequent.'

'It was from him. And why not?'

'Oh dear no;—why not certainly? I wish he'd write every day of his life, so that things would come round again. Nothing ever troubles me so much as broken love. Why don't he come again himself, Mrs. Hurtle?'

'It is not at all likely that he should come again. It is all over, and there is no good in talking of it. I shall return to New York on Saturday week.'

'Oh, Mrs. Hurtle!'

'I can't remain here, you know, all my life doing nothing. I came over here for a certain purpose, and that has——gone by. Now I may just go back again.'

'I know he has ill-treated you. I know he has.'

'I am not disposed to talk about it, Mrs. Pipkin.'

'I should have thought it would have done you good to speak your mind out free. I know it would me if I'd been served in that way.'

'If I had anything to say at all after that fashion it would be to the gentleman, and not to any other else. As it is I shall never speak of it again to any one. You have been very kind to me, Mrs. Pipkin, and I shall be sorry to leave you.'

'Oh, Mrs. Hurtle, you can't understand what it is to me. It isn't only my feelings. The likes of me can't stand by their feelings only, as their betters do. I've never been above telling you what a godsend you've been to me this summer;—have I? I've paid everything, butcher, baker, rates and all, just like clockwork. And now you're going away!' Then Mrs. Pipkin began to sob.

'I suppose I shall see Mr. Crumb before I go,' said Mrs. Hurtle.

'She don't deserve it; do she? And even now she never says a word about him that I call respectful. She looks on him as just being better than Mrs. Buggins's children. That's all.'

'She'll be all right when he has once got her home.'

'And I shall be all alone by myself,' said Mrs. Pipkin, with her apron up to her eyes.

It was after this that Mrs. Hurtle received Hetta's letter. She had as yet returned no answer to Paul Montague,—nor had she intended to send any written answer. Were she to comply with his request she could do so best by writing to the girl who was concerned rather than to him. And though she wrote no such letter she thought of it,—of the words she would use were she to write it, and of the tale which she would have to tell. She sat for hours thinking of it, trying to resolve whether she would tell the tale,—if she told it at all,—in a manner to suit Paul's purpose, or so as to bring that purpose utterly to ship-wreck. She did not doubt that she could cause the shipwreck were she so minded. She could certainly have her revenge after that fashion. But it was a woman's fashion, and, as such, did not recommend itself to Mrs. Hurtle's feelings. A pistol or a horsewhip, a violent seizing by the neck, with sharp taunts and bitter-ringing words, would have made the fitting revenge. If she abandoned that she could do herself no good by telling a story of her wrongs to another woman.

Then came Hetta's note, so stiff, so cold, so true,—so like the letter of an Englishwoman, as Mrs. Hurtle said to herself. Mrs. Hurtle smiled as she read the letter. 'I make this proposition not thinking that anything you can say to me can change my mind.' Of course the girl's mind would be changed. The girl's mind, indeed, re-quired no change. Mrs. Hurtle could see well enough that the girl's heart was set upon the man. Nevertheless she did not doubt but that she could tell the story after such a fashion as to make it impossible that the girl should marry him,—if she chose to do so.

At first she thought that she would not answer the
letter at all. What was it to her? Let them fight their
own lovers' battles out after their own childish fashion.
If the man meant at last to be honest, there could be no
doubt, Mrs. Hurtle thought, that the girl would go to
him. It would require no interference of hers. But after
a while she thought that she might as well see this
English chit who had superseded herself in the affections
of the Englishman she had condescended to love. And
if it were the case that all revenge was to be abandoned,
that no punishment was to be exacted in return for all
the injury that had been done, why should she not say a
kind word so as to smooth away the existing difficulties?
Wild cat as she was, kindness was more congenial to her
nature than cruelty. So she wrote to Hetta making an
appointment.

'DEAR MISS CARBURY,—

'If you could make it convenient to yourself to call
here either Thursday or Friday at any hour between two
and four, I shall be very happy to see you.
                              'Yours sincerely,
                                    'WINIFRED HURTLE.'

## Chapter XCI

### THE RIVALS

DURING these days the intercourse between Lady
Carbury and her daughter was constrained and far
from pleasant. Hetta, thinking that she was ill-used,
kept herself aloof, and would not speak to her mother of
herself or of her troubles. Lady Carbury watching her,
but not daring to say much, was at last almost frightened
at her girl's silence. She had assured herself, when she
found that Hetta was disposed to quarrel with her lover
and to send him back his brooch, that 'things would
come round,' that Paul would be forgotten quickly,—or

laid aside as though he were forgotten,—and that Hetta would soon perceive it to be her interest to marry her cousin. With such a prospect before her, Lady Carbury thought it to be her duty as a mother to show no tendency to sympathize with her girl's sorrow. Such heart-breakings were occurring daily in the world around them. Who were the happy people that were driven neither by ambition, nor poverty, nor greed, nor the cross purposes of unhappy love, to stifle and trample upon their feelings? She had known no one so blessed. She had never been happy after that fashion. She herself had within the last few weeks refused to join her lot with that of a man she really liked, because her wicked son was so grievous a burden on her shoulders. A woman, she thought, if she were unfortunate enough to be a lady without wealth of her own, must give up everything, her body, her heart,—her very soul if she were that way troubled,—to the procuring of a fitting maintenance for herself. Why should Hetta hope to be more fortunate than others? And then the position which chance now offered to her was fortunate. This cousin of hers, who was so devoted to her, was in all respects good. He would not torture her by harsh restraint and cruel temper. He would not drink. He would not spend his money foolishly. He would allow her all the belongings of a fair, free life. Lady Carbury reiterated to herself the assertion that she was manifestly doing a mother's duty by her endeavours to constrain her girl to marry such a man. With a settled purpose she was severe and hard. But when she found how harsh her daughter could be in response to this,—how gloomy, how silent, and how severe in retaliation,—she was almost frightened at what she herself was doing. She had not known how stern and how enduring her daughter could be. 'Hetta,' she said, 'why don't you speak to me?' On this very day it was Hetta's purpose to visit Mrs. Hurtle at Islington. She had said no word of her intention to any one. She had chosen the Friday because on that day she knew her mother would go in the afternoon to her publisher. There should be no deceit. Immediately on her return she would tell her

mother what she had done. But she considered herself
to be emancipated from control. Among them they
had robbed her of her lover. She had submitted to the
robbery, but she would submit to nothing else. 'Hetta,
why don't you speak to me?' said Lady Carbury.

'Because, mamma, there is nothing we can talk about
without making each other unhappy.'

'What a dreadful thing to say! Is there no subject in
the world to interest you except that wretched young
man?'

'None other at all,' said Hetta obstinately.

'What folly it is,—I will not say only to speak like that,
but to allow yourself to entertain such thoughts!'

'How am I to control my thoughts? Do you think,
mamma, that after I had owned to you that I loved a man,
—after I had owned it to him and, worst of all, to myself,
—I could have myself separated from him, and then not
think about it? It is a cloud upon everything. It is as
though I had lost my eyesight and my speech. It is as it
would be to you if Felix were to die. It crushes me.'

There was an accusation in this allusion to her brother
which the mother felt,—as she was intended to feel it,—
but to which she could make no reply. It accused her of
being too much concerned for her son to feel any real
affection for her daughter. 'You are ignorant of the
world, Hetta,' she said.

'I am having a lesson in it now, at any rate.'

'Do you think it is worse than others have suffered
before you? In what little you see around you do you
think that girls are generally able to marry the men
upon whom they set their hearts?' She paused, but
Hetta made no answer to this. 'Marie Melmotte was as
warmly attached to your brother as you can be to Mr.
Montague.'

'Marie Melmotte!'

'She thinks as much of her feelings as you do of yours.
The truth is you are indulging a dream. You must wake
from it, and shake yourself, and find out that you, like
others, have got to do the best you can for yourself in
order that you may live. The world at large has to eat

dry bread, and cannot get cakes and sweetmeats. A girl, when she thinks of giving herself to a husband, has to remember this. If she has a fortune of her own she can pick and choose, but if she have none she must allow herself to be chosen.'

'Then a girl is to marry without stopping even to think whether she likes the man or not?'

'She should teach herself to like the man, if the marriage be suitable. I would not have you take a vicious man because he was rich, or one known to be cruel and imperious. Your cousin Roger, you know——'

'Mamma,' said Hetta, getting up from her seat, 'you may as well believe me. No earthly inducement shall ever make me marry my cousin Roger. It is to me horrible that you should propose it to me when you know that I love that other man with my whole heart.'

'How can you speak so of one who has treated you with the utmost contumely?'

'I know nothing of any contumely. What reasons have I to be offended because he has liked a woman whom he knew before he ever saw me? It has been unfortunate, wretched, miserable; but I do not know that I have any right whatever to be angry with Mr. Paul Montague.' Having so spoken she walked out of the room without waiting for a further reply.

It was all very sad to Lady Carbury. She perceived now that she had driven her daughter to pronounce an absolution of Paul Montague's sins, and that in this way she had lessened and loosened the barrier which she had striven to construct between them. But that which pained her most was the unrealistic, romantic view of life which pervaded all Hetta's thoughts. How was any girl to live in this world who could not be taught the folly of such idle dreams?

That afternoon Hetta trusted herself all alone to the mysteries of the Marylebone underground railway,* and emerged with accuracy at King's Cross. She had studied her geography, and she walked from thence to Islington. She knew well the name of the street and the number at which Mrs. Hurtle lived.* But when she reached the door she did not at first dare to stand and raise the knocker. She passed on to the end of the silent, vacant street, endeavouring to collect her thoughts, striving to find and to arrange the words with which she would commence her strange petition. And she endeavoured to dictate to herself some defined conduct should the woman be insolent to her. Personally she was not a coward, but she doubted her power of replying to a rough speech. She could at any rate escape. Should the worst come to the worst, the woman would hardly venture to impede her departure. Having gone to the end of the street, she returned with a very quick step and knocked at the door. It was opened almost immediately by Ruby Ruggles, to whom she gave her name.

'Oh laws,—Miss Carbury!' said Ruby, looking up into the stranger's face. Yes;—sure enough she must be Felix's sister. But Ruby did not dare to ask any question. She had admitted to all around her that Sir Felix should not be her lover any more, and that John Crumb should be allowed to return. But, nevertheless, her heart twittered as she showed Miss Carbury up to the lodger's sitting-room.

Though it was midsummer Hetta entered the room with her veil down. She adjusted it as she followed Ruby up the stairs, moved by a sudden fear of her rival's scrutiny. Mrs. Hurtle rose from her chair and came forward to greet her visitor, putting out both her hands to do so. She was dressed with the most scrupulous care, —simply, and in black, without an ornament of any kind, without a ribbon or a chain or a flower. But with some woman's purpose at her heart she had so attired herself as to look her very best. Was it that she thought that she would vindicate to her rival their joint lover's first choice, or that she was minded to teach the English girl that an American woman might have graces of her own? As she came forward she was gentle and soft in her movements, and a pleasant smile played round her mouth. Hetta, at the first moment, was almost dumbfounded by her beauty,—by that and by her ease and exquisite self-possession. 'Miss Carbury,' she said with that low, rich voice

which in old days had charmed Paul almost as much as
her loveliness, 'I need not tell you how interested I am in
seeing you. May I not ask you to lay aside your veil, so
that we may look at each other fairly?' Hetta, dumbfounded, not knowing how to speak a word, stood gazing at the woman when she had removed her veil. She
had had no personal description of Mrs. Hurtle, but had
expected something very different from this! She had
thought that the woman would be coarse and big, with
fine eyes and a bright colour. As it was they were both of
the same complexion, both dark, with hair nearly black,
with eyes of the same colour. Hetta thought of all that at
the moment,—but acknowledged to herself that she had
no pretension to beauty such as that which this woman
owned. 'And so you have come to see me,' said Mrs.
Hurtle. 'Sit down so that I may look at you. I am glad
that you have come to see me, Miss Carbury.'

'I am glad at any rate that you are not angry.'

'Why should I be angry? Had the idea been distasteful
to me I should have declined. I know not why, but it is a
sort of pleasure to me to see you. It is a poor time we
women have,—is it not,—in becoming playthings to
men? So this Lothario that was once mine, is behaving
badly to you also. Is it so? He is no longer mine, and you
may ask me freely for aid, if there be any that I can give
you. If he were an American I should say that he had
behaved badly to me;—but as he is an Englishman
perhaps it is different. Now tell me;—what can I do, or
what can I say?'

'He told me that you could tell me the truth.'

'What truth? I will certainly tell you nothing that is
not true. You have quarrelled with him too. It is not so?'

'Certainly I have quarrelled with him.'

'I am not curious;—but perhaps you had better tell me
of that. I know him so well that I can guess that he
should give offence. He can be full of youthful ardour
one day, and cautious as old age itself the next. But I do
not suppose that there has been need for such caution
with you. What is it, Miss Carbury?'

Hetta found the telling of her story to be very difficult.

'Mrs. Hurtle,' she said, 'I had never heard your name when he first asked me to be his wife.'

'I dare say not. Why should he have told you anything of me?'

'Because,—oh, because—. Surely he ought, if it is true that he had once promised to marry you.'

'That is certainly true.'

'And you were here, and I knew nothing of it. Of course I should have been very different to him had I known that,—that,—that—'

'That there was such a woman as Winifred Hurtle interfering with him. Then you heard it by chance, and you were offended. Was it not so?'

'And now he tells me that I have been unjust to him and he bids me ask you. I have not been unjust.'

'I am not so sure of that. Shall I tell you what I think? I think that he has been unjust to me, and that therefore your injustice to him is no more than his due. I cannot plead for him, Miss Carbury. To me he has been the last and worst of a long series of, I think, undeserved misfortune. But whether you will avenge my wrongs must be for you to decide.'

'Why did he go with you to Lowestoft?'

'Because I asked him,—and because, like many men, he cannot be ill-natured although he can be cruel. He would have given a hand not to have gone, but he could not say me nay. As you have come here, Miss Carbury, you may as well know the truth. He did love me, but he had been talked out of his love by my enemies and his own friends long before he had ever seen you. I am almost ashamed to tell you my own part of the story, and yet I know not why I should be ashamed. I followed him here to England—because I loved him. I came after him, as perhaps a woman should not do, because I was true of heart. He had told me that he did not want me;—but I wanted to be wanted, and I hoped that I might lure him back to his troth. I have utterly failed, and I must return to my own country,—I will not say a broken-hearted woman, for I will not admit of such a condition,—but a creature with a broken spirit. He has misused me foully,

and I have simply forgiven him; not because I am a
Christian, but because I am not strong enough to punish
one that I still love. I could not put a dagger into him,—
or I would; or a bullet,—or I would. He has reduced me
to a nothing by his falseness, and yet I cannot injure him!
I, who have sworn to myself that no man should ever lay
a finger on me in scorn without feeling my wrath in
return, I cannot punish him. But if you choose to do so it
is not for me to set you against such an act of justice.'
Then she paused and looked up to Hetta as though
expecting a reply.

But Hetta had no reply to make. All had been said that
she had come to hear. Every word that the woman had
spoken had in truth been a comfort to her. She had told
herself that her visit was to be made in order that she
might be justified in her condemnation of her lover. She
had believed that it was her intention to arm herself with
proof that she had done right in rejecting him. Now she
was told that however false her lover might have been
to this other woman he had been absolutely true to her.
The woman had not spoken kindly of Paul,—had seemed
to intend to speak of him with the utmost severity; but
she had so spoken as to acquit him of all sin against
Hetta. What was it to Hetta that her lover had been
false to this American stranger? It did not seem to her to
be at all necessary that she should be angry with her
lover on that head. Mrs. Hurtle had told her that she
herself must decide whether she would take upon herself
to avenge her rival's wrongs. In saying that, Mrs. Hurtle
had taught her to feel that there were no other wrongs
which she need avenge. It was all done now. If she
could only thank the woman for the pleasantness of her
demeanour, and then go, she could, when alone, make
up her mind as to what she would do next. She had not
yet told herself she would submit herself again to Paul
Montague. She had only told herself that, within her own
breast, she was bound to forgive him. 'You have been
very kind,' she said at last,—speaking only because it was
necessary that she should say something.

'It is well that there should be some kindness where

there has been so much that is unkind. Forgive me, Miss Carbury, if I speak plainly to you. Of course you will go back to him. Of course you will be his wife. You have told me that you love him dearly, as plainly as I have told you the same story of myself. Your coming here would of itself have declared it, even if I did not see your satisfaction at my account of his treachery to me.'

'Oh, Mrs. Hurtle, do not say that of me!'

'But it is true, and I do not in the least quarrel with you on that account. He has preferred you to me, and as far as I am concerned there is an end of it. You are a girl, whereas I am a woman,—and he likes your youth. I have undergone the cruel roughness of the world, which has not as yet touched you; and therefore you are softer to the touch. I do not know that you are very superior in other attractions; but that has sufficed, and you are the victor. I am strong enough to acknowledge that I have nothing to forgive in you;—and am weak enough to forgive all his treachery.' Hetta was now holding the woman by the hand, and was weeping, she knew not why. 'I am so glad to have seen you,' continued Mrs. Hurtle, 'so that I may know what his wife was like. In a few days I shall return to the States, and then neither of you will ever be troubled further by Winifred Hurtle. Tell him that if he will come and see me once before I go, I will not be more unkind to him than I can help.'

When Hetta did not decline to be the bearer of this message she must have at any rate resolved that she would see Paul Montague again,—and to see him would be to tell him that she was again his own. She now got herself quickly out of the room, absolutely kissing the woman whom she had both dreaded and despised. As soon as she was alone in the street she tried to think of it all. How full of beauty was the face of that American female,—how rich and glorious her voice in spite of a slight taint of the well-known nasal twang;—and above all how powerful and at the same time how easy and how gracious was her manner! That she would be an unfit wife for Paul Montague was certain to Hetta, but that he or any man should have loved her and have been loved

by her, and then have been willing to part from her, was
wonderful. And yet Paul Montague had preferred herself, Hetta Carbury, to this woman! Paul had certainly done well for his own cause when he had referred
the younger lady to the elder.

Of her own quarrel of course there must be an end.
She had been unjust to the man, and injustice must of
course be remedied by repentance and confession. As she
walked quickly back to the railway station she brought
herself to love her lover more fondly than she had ever
done. He had been true to her from the first hour of their
acquaintance. What truth higher than that has any
woman a right to desire? No doubt she gave to him a
virgin heart. No other man had ever touched her lips, or
been allowed to press her hand, or to look into her eyes
with unrebuked admiration. It was her pride to give
herself to the man she loved after this fashion, pure and
white as snow on which no foot has trodden. But, in
taking him, all that she wanted was that he should be true
to her now and henceforward. The future must be her
own work. As to the 'now,' she felt that Mrs. Hurtle had
given her sufficient assurance.

She must at once let her mother know this change in
her mind. When she re-entered the house she was no
longer sullen, no longer anxious to be silent, very willing
to be gracious if she might be received with favour,—but
quite determined that nothing should shake her purpose.
She went at once into her mother's room, having heard
from the boy at the door that Lady Carbury had
returned.

'Hetta, wherever have you been?' asked Lady Carbury.

'Mamma,' she said, 'I mean to write to Mr. Montague
and tell him that I have been unjust to him.'

'Hetta, you must do nothing of the kind,' said Lady
Carbury, rising from her seat.

'Yes, mamma. I have been unjust, and I must do so.'

'It will be asking him to come back to you.'

'Yes, mamma:—that is what I mean. I shall tell him
that if he will come, I will receive him. I know he will

come. Oh, mamma, let us be friends, and I will tell you everything. Why should you grudge me my love?'

'You have sent him back his brooch,' said Lady Carbury hoarsely.

'He shall give it me again. Hear what I have done. I have seen that American lady.'

'Mrs. Hurtle!'

'Yes;—I have been to her. She is a wonderful woman.'

'And she has told you wonderful lies.'

'Why should she lie to me? She has told me no lies. She said nothing in his favour.'

'I can well believe that. What can any one say in his favour?'

'But she told me that which has assured me that Mr. Montague has never behaved badly to me. I shall write to him at once. If you like I will show you the letter.'

'Any letter to him, I will tear,' said Lady Carbury, full of anger.

'Mamma, I have told you everything, but in this I must judge for myself.' Then Hetta, seeing that her mother would not relent, left the room without further speech, and immediately opened her desk that the letter might be written.

## Chapter XCII

### HAMILTON K. FISKER AGAIN

TEN days had passed since the meeting narrated in the last chapter,—ten days, during which Hetta's letter had been sent to her lover, but in which she had received no reply,—when two gentlemen met each other in a certain room in Liverpool, who were seen together in the same room in the early part of this chronicle. These were our young friend Paul Montague, and our not much older friend Hamilton K. Fisker. Melmotte had died on the 18th of July, and tidings of the event had been at once sent by telegraph to San Francisco. Some weeks before this Montague had written to his partner, giving his account of the South Central Pacific and Mexican Railway Company,—describing its condition in England as he then believed it to be,—and urging Fisker to come over to London. On receipt of a message from his American correspondent he had gone down to Liverpool, and had there awaited Fisker's arrival, taking counsel with his friend Mr. Ramsbottom. In the meantime Hetta's letter was lying at the Beargarden, Paul having written from his club and having omitted to desire that the answer should be sent to his lodgings. Just at this moment things at the Beargarden were not well managed. They were indeed so ill managed that Paul never received that letter,—which would have had for him charms greater than those of any letter ever before written.

'This is a terrible business,' said Fisker, immediately on entering the room in which Montague was waiting him. 'He was the last man I'd have thought would be cut up in that way.'

'He was utterly ruined.'

'He wouldn't have been ruined,—and couldn't have thought so if he'd known all he ought to have known. The South Central would have pulled him through a'most anything if he'd have understood how to play it.'

'We don't think much of the South Central here now,' said Paul.

'Ah;—that's because you've never above half spirit enough for a big thing. You nibble at it instead of swallowing it whole,—and then, of course, folks see that you're only nibbling. I thought that Melmotte would have had spirit.'

'There is, I fear, no doubt that he had committed forgery. It was the dread of detection as to that which drove him to destroy himself.'

'I call it dam clumsy from beginning to end;—dam clumsy. I took him to be a different man, and I feel more than half ashamed of myself because I trusted such a fellow. That chap Cohenlupe has got off with a lot of swag. Only think of Melmotte allowing Cohenlupe to get the better of him!'

'I suppose the thing will be broken up now at San Francisco,' suggested Paul.

'Bu'st up at Frisco! Not if I know it. Why should it be bu'st up? D'you think we're all going to smash there because a fool like Melmotte blows his brains out in London?'

'He took poison.'

'Or p'ison either. That's not just our way. I'll tell you what I'm going to do; and why I'm over here so uncommon sharp. These shares are at a'most nothing now in London. I'll buy every share in the market. I wired for as many as I dar'd, so as not to spoil our own game, and I'll make a clean sweep of every one of them. Bu'st up! I'm sorry for him because I thought him a biggish man; —but what he's done 'll just be the making of us over there. Will you get out of it, or will you come back to Frisco with me?'

In answer to this Paul asserted most strenuously that he would not return to San Francisco, and, perhaps too ingenuously, gave his partner to understand that he was altogether sick of the great railway, and would under no circumstances have anything more to do with it. Fisker shrugged his shoulders, and was not displeased at the proposed rupture. He was prepared to deal fairly,—nay, generously,—by his partner, having recognized the wisdom of that great commercial rule which teaches us that honour should prevail among associates of a certain class; but he had fully convinced himself that Paul Montague was not a fit partner for Hamilton K. Fisker. Fisker was not only unscrupulous himself, but he had a thorough contempt for scruples in others. According to his theory of life, nine hundred and ninety-nine men were obscure because of their scruples, whilst the thousandth man predominated and cropped up into the splendour of commercial wealth because he was free from such bondage. He had his own theories, too, as to commercial honesty. That which he had promised to do he would do, if it was within his power. He was anxious that his bond should be good, and his word equally so. But the work of robbing mankind in gross by magnificently false representations,

was not only the duty, but also the delight and the
ambition of his life. How could a man so great endure a
partnership with one so small as Paul Montague? 'And
now what about Winifred Hurtle?' asked Fisker.

'What makes you ask? She's in London.'

'Oh yes, I know she's in London, and Hurtle's at
Frisco, swearing that he'll come after her. He would,
only he hasn't got the dollars.'

'He's not dead then?' muttered Paul.

'Dead!—no, nor likely to die. She'll have a bad time
of it with him yet.'

'But she divorced him.'

'She got a Kansas lawyer to say so, and he's got a
Frisco lawyer to say that there's nothing of the kind. She
hasn't played her game badly neither, for she's had the
handling of her own money, and has put it so that he
can't get hold of a dollar. Even if it suited other ways,
you know, I wouldn't marry her myself till I saw my way
clearer out of the wood.'

'I'm not thinking of marrying her,—if you mean that.'

'There was a talk about it in Frisco;—that's all. And I
have heard Hurtle say when he was a little farther gone
than usual that she was here with you, and that he meant
to drop in on you some of these days.' To this Paul made
no answer, thinking that he had now both heard enough
and said enough about Mrs. Hurtle.

On the following day the two men, who were still
partners, went together to London, and Fisker immediately became immersed in the arrangement of
Melmotte's affairs. He put himself into communication
with Mr. Brehgert, went in and out of the offices in Abchurch Lane and the rooms which had belonged to the
Railway Company, cross-examined Croll, mastered the
books of the Company as far as they were to be mastered,
and actually summoned both the Grendalls, father and
son, up to London. Lord Alfred, and Miles with him, had
left London a day or two before Melmotte's death,—
having probably perceived that there was no further
occasion for their services. To Fisker's appeal Lord
Alfred was proudly indifferent. Who was this American

that he should call upon a director of the London Company to appear? Does not every one know that a director of a company need not direct unless he pleases? Lord Alfred, therefore, did not even condescend to answer Fisker's letter;—but he advised his son to run up to town. 'I should just go, because I'd taken a salary from the d—— Company,' said the careful father, 'but when there I wouldn't say a word.' So Miles Grendall, obeying his parent, reappeared upon the scene.

But Fisker's attention was perhaps most usefully and most sedulously paid to Madame Melmotte and her daughter. Till Fisker arrived no one had visited them in their solitude at Hampstead, except Croll, the clerk. Mr. Brehgert had abstained, thinking that a widow, who had become a widow under such terrible circumstances, would prefer to be alone. Lord Nidderdale had made his adieux, and felt that he could do no more. It need hardly be said that Lord Alfred had too much good taste to interfere at such a time, although for some months he had been domestically intimate with the poor woman, or that Sir Felix would not be prompted by the father's death to renew his suit to the daughter. But Fisker had not been two days in London before he went out to Hampstead, and was admitted to Madame Melmotte's presence;—and he had not been there four days before he was aware that in spite of all misfortunes, Marie Melmotte was still the undoubted possessor of a large fortune.

In regard to Melmotte's effects generally the Crown had been induced to abstain from interfering,—giving up the right to all the man's plate and chairs and tables which it had acquired by the finding of the coroner's verdict,—not from tenderness to Madame Melmotte, for whom no great commiseration was felt, but on behalf of such creditors as poor Mr. Longestaffe and his son. But Marie's money was quite distinct from this. She had been right in her own belief as to this property, and had been right, too, in refusing to sign those papers,—unless it may be that that refusal led to her father's act. She herself was sure that it was not so, because she had withdrawn her refusal, and had offered to sign the papers before her father's death. What might have been the ultimate result had she done so when he first made the request, no one could now say. That the money would have gone there could be no doubt. The money was now hers,—a fact which Fisker soon learned with that peculiar cleverness which belonged to him.

Poor Madame Melmotte felt the visits of the American to be a relief to her in her misery. The world makes great mistakes as to that which is and is not beneficial to those whom Death has bereaved of a companion. It may be, no doubt sometimes it is the case, that grief shall be so heavy, so absolutely crushing, as to make any interference with it an additional trouble, and this is felt also in acute bodily pain, and in periods of terrible mental suffering. It may also be, and, no doubt, often is the case, that the bereaved one chooses to affect such overbearing sorrow, and that friends abstain, because even such affectation has its own rights and privileges. But Madame Melmotte was neither crushed by grief nor did she affect to be so crushed. She had been numbed by the suddenness and by the awe of the catastrophe. The man who had been her merciless tyrant for years, who had seemed to her to be a very incarnation of cruel power, had succumbed, and shown himself to be powerless against his own misfortunes. She was a woman of very few words, and had spoken almost none on this occasion even to her own daughter; but when Fisker came to her, and told her more than she had ever known before of her husband's affairs, and spoke to her of her future life, and mixed for her a small glass of brandy-and-water warm, and told her that Frisco would be the fittest place for her future residence, she certainly did not find him to be intrusive.

And even Marie liked Fisker, though she had been wooed and almost won both by a lord and a baronet, and had understood, if not much, at least more than her mother, of the life to which she had been introduced. There was something of real sorrow in her heart for her father. She was prone to love,—though, perhaps, not prone to deep affection. Melmotte had certainly been often cruel to her, but he had also been very indulgent.

And as she had never been specially grateful for the one,
so neither had she ever specially resented the other.
Tenderness, care, real solicitude for her well-being, she
had never known, and had come to regard the unevenness
of her life, vacillating between knocks and knick-knacks,
with a blow one day and a jewel the next, as the condition
of things which was natural to her. When her father was
dead she remembered for a while the jewels and the knick-
knacks, and forgot the knocks and blows. But she was not
beyond consolation, and she also found consolation in
Mr. Fisker's visits.

'I used to sign a paper every quarter,' she said to Fisker,
as they were walking together one evening in the lanes
round Hampstead.

'You'll have to do the same now, only instead of giving
the paper to any one you'll have to leave it in a banker's
hands to draw the money for yourself.'

'And can that be done over in California?'

'Just the same as here. Your bankers will manage it
all for you without the slightest trouble. For the matter
of that I'll do it, if you'll trust me. There's only one thing
against it all, Miss Melmotte.'

'And what's that?'

'After the sort of society you've been used to here, I
don't know how you'll get on among us Americans.
We're a pretty rough lot, I guess. Though, perhaps,
what you lose in the look of the fruit, you'll make up in
the flavour.' This Fisker said in a somewhat plaintive
tone, as though fearing that the manifest substantial
advantages of Frisco would not suffice to atone for the
loss of that fashion to which Miss Melmotte had been used.

'I hate swells,' said Marie, flashing round upon him.

'Do you now?'

'Like poison. What's the use of 'em? They never mean
a word that they say,—and they don't say so many words
either. They're never more than half awake, and don't
care the least about anybody. I hate London.'

'Do you now?'

'Oh, don't I?'

'I wonder whether you'd hate Frisco?'

'I rather think it would be a jolly sort of place.'

'Very jolly I find it. And I wonder whether you'd hate —me?'

'Mr. Fisker, that's nonsense. Why should I hate anybody?'

'But you do. I've found out one or two that you don't love. If you do come to Frisco, I hope you won't just hate me, you know.' Then he took her gently by the arm;— but she, whisking herself away rapidly, bade him behave himself. Then they returned to their lodgings, and Mr. Fisker, before he went back to London, mixed a little warm brandy-and-water for Madame Melmotte. I think that upon the whole Madame Melmotte was more comfortable at Hampstead than she had been either in Grosvenor Square or Bruton Street, although she was certainly not a thing beautiful to look at in her widow's weeds.

'I don't think much of you as a book-keeper, you know,' Fisker said to Miles Grendall in the now almost deserted Board-room of the South Central Pacific and Mexican Railway. Miles, remembering his father's advice, answered not a word, but merely looked with assumed amazement at the impertinent stranger who dared thus to censure his performances. Fisker had made three or four remarks previous to this, and had appealed both to Paul Montague and to Croll, who were present. He had invited also the attendance of Sir Felix Carbury, Lord Nidderdale, and Mr. Longestaffe, who were all Directors; —but none of them had come. Sir Felix had paid no attention to Fisker's letter. Lord Nidderdale had written a short but characteristic reply. 'Dear Mr. Fisker,—I really don't know anything about it. Yours, Nidderdale.' Mr. Longestaffe, with laborious zeal, had closely covered four pages with his reasons for non-attendance, with which the reader shall not be troubled, and which it may be doubted whether even Fisker perused to the end. 'Upon my word,' continued Fisker, 'it's astonishing to me that Melmotte should have put up with this kind of thing. I suppose you understand something of business, Mr. Croll?'

'It vas not my department, Mr. Fisker,' said the German.

'Nor anybody else's either,' said the domineering American. 'Of course it's on the cards, Mr. Grendall, that we shall have to put you into a witness-box, because there are certain things we must get at.' Miles was silent as the grave, but at once made up his mind that he would pass his autumn at some pleasant but economical German retreat, and that his autumnal retirement should be commenced within a very few days;—or perhaps hours might suffice.

But Fisker was not in earnest in his threat. In truth the greater the confusion in the London office, the better, he thought, were the prospects of the Company at San Francisco. Miles underwent purgatory on this occasion for three or four hours, and when dismissed had certainly revealed none of Melmotte's secrets. He did, however, go to Germany, finding that a temporary absence from England would be comfortable to him in more respects than one,—and need not be heard of again in these pages.

When Melmotte's affairs were ultimately wound up there was found to be nearly enough of property to satisfy all his proved liabilities. Very many men started up with huge claims, asserting that they had been robbed, and in the confusion it was hard to ascertain who had been robbed, or who had simply been unsuccessful in their attempts to rob others. Some, no doubt, as was the case with poor Mr. Brehgert, had speculated in dependence on Melmotte's sagacity, and had lost heavily without dishonesty. But of those who, like the Longestaffes, were able to prove direct debts, the condition at last was not very sad. Our excellent friend Dolly got his money early in the day, and was able, under Mr. Squercum's guidance, to start himself on a new career. Having paid his debts, and with still a large balance at his bankers', he assured his friend Nidderdale that he meant to turn over an entirely new leaf. 'I shall just make Squercum allow me so much a month, and I shall have all the bills and that kind of thing sent to him, and he will do everything, and pull me up if I'm getting wrong. I like Squercum.'

'Won't he rob you, old fellow?' suggested Nidderdale.

'Of course he will;—but he won't let any one else do it. One has to be plucked, but it's everything to have it done on a system. If he'll only let me have ten shillings out of every sovereign I think I can get along.' Let us hope that Mr. Squercum was merciful, and that Dolly was enabled to live in accordance with his virtuous resolutions.

But these things did not arrange themselves till late in the winter,—long after Mr. Fisker's departure for California. That, however, was protracted till a day much later than he anticipated before he had become intimate with Madame Melmotte and Marie. Madame Melmotte's affairs occupied him for a while almost exclusively. The furniture and plate were of course sold for the creditors, but Madame Melmotte was allowed to take whatever she declared to be specially her own property: —and, though much was said about the jewels, no attempt was made to recover them. Marie advised Madame Melmotte to give them up, assuring the old woman that she should have whatever she wanted for her maintenance. But it was not likely that Melmotte's widow would willingly abandon any property, and she did not abandon her jewels. It was agreed between her and Fisker that they were to be taken to New York. 'You'll get as much there as in London, if you like to part with them; and nobody 'll say anything about it there. You couldn't sell a locket or chain here without all the world talking about it.'

In all these things Madame Melmotte put herself into Fisker's hands with the most absolute confidence,—and, indeed, with a confidence that was justified by its results. It was not by robbing an old woman that Fisker intended to make himself great. To Madame Melmotte's thinking, Fisker was the finest gentleman she had ever met,—so infinitely pleasanter in his manner than Lord Alfred even when Lord Alfred had been most gracious, with so much more to say for himself than Miles Grendall, understanding her so much better than any man had ever done,—

especially when he supplied her with those small warm beakers of sweet brandy-and-water. 'I shall do whatever he tells me,' she said to Marie. 'I'm sure I've nothing to keep me here in this country.'

'I'm willing to go,' said Marie. 'I don't want to stay in London.'

'I suppose you'll take him if he asks you?'

'I don't know anything about that,' said Marie. 'A man may be very well without one's wanting to marry him. I don't think I'll marry anybody. What's the use? It's only money. Nobody cares for anything else. Fisker's all very well; but he only wants the money. Do you think Fisker'd ask me to marry him if I hadn't got anything? Not he! He ain't slow enough for that.'

'I think he's a very nice young man,' said Madame Melmotte.

## Chapter XCIII

### A TRUE LOVER

HETTA CARBURY, out of the fulness of her heart, having made up her mind that she had been unjust to her lover, wrote to him a letter full of penitence, full of love, telling him at great length all the details of her meeting with Mrs. Hurtle, and bidding him come back to her, and bring the brooch with him. But this letter she had unfortunately addressed to the Beargarden, as he had written to her from that club; and partly through his own fault, and partly through the demoralization of that once perfect establishment, the letter never reached his hands. When, therefore, he returned to London he was justified in supposing that she had refused even to notice his appeal. He was, however, determined that he would still make further struggles. He had, he felt, to contend with many difficulties. Mrs. Hurtle, Roger Carbury, and Hetta's mother were, he thought, all inimical to him. Mrs. Hurtle, though she had declared that she would not rage as a lioness, could hardly be his friend in the matter. Roger had repeatedly declared his determination to regard him as a traitor. And Lady Carbury, as he well knew, had always been and always would be opposed to the match. But Hetta had owned that she loved him, had submitted to his caresses, and had been proud of his admiration. And Paul, though he did not probably analyse very carefully the character of his beloved, still felt instinctively that, having so far prevailed with such a girl, his prospects could not be altogether hopeless. And yet how should he continue the struggle? With what weapons should he carry on the fight? The writing of letters is but a one-sided, troublesome proceeding, when the person to whom they are written will not answer them; and the calling at a door at which the servant has been instructed to refuse a visitor admission, becomes disagreeable,—if not degrading, —after a time.

But Hetta had written a second epistle,—not to her lover, but to one who received his letters with more regularity. When she rashly and with precipitate wrath quarrelled with Paul Montague, she at once communicated the fact to her mother, and through her mother to her cousin Roger. Though she would not recognize Roger as a lover, she did acknowledge him to be the head of her family, and her own special friend, and entitled in some special way to know all that she herself did, and all that was done in regard to her. She therefore wrote to her cousin, telling him that she had made a mistake about Paul, that she was convinced that Paul had always behaved to her with absolute sincerity, and, in short, that Paul was the best, and dearest, and most ill-used of human beings. In her enthusiasm she went on to declare that there could be no other chance of happiness for her in this world than that of becoming Paul's wife, and to beseech her dearest friend and cousin Roger not to turn against her, but to lend her an aiding hand. There are those whom strong words in letters never affect at all,— who, perhaps, hardly read them, and take what they do read as meaning no more than half what is said. But Roger Carbury was certainly not one of these. As he sat

on the garden wall at Carbury, with his cousin's letter
in his hand, her words had their full weight with him.
He did not try to convince himself that all this was the
verbiage of an enthusiastic girl, who might soon be turned
and trained to another mode of thinking by fitting ad-
monitions. To him now, as he read and re-read Hetta's
letter sitting on the wall, there was not at any rate further
hope for himself. Though he was altogether unchanged
himself, though he was altogether incapable of change,
—though he could not rally himself sufficiently to look
forward to even a passive enjoyment of life without the
girl whom he had loved,—yet he told himself what he
believed to be the truth. At last he owned directly and
plainly that, whether happy or unhappy, he must do
without her. He had let time slip by with him too fast
and too far before he had ventured to love. He must now
stomach his disappointment, and make the best he could
of such a broken, ill-conditioned life as was left to him.
But, if he acknowledged this,—and he did acknowledge
it,—in what fashion should he in future treat the man
and woman who had reduced him so low?

At this moment his mind was tuned to high thoughts.
If it were possible he would be unselfish. He could not,
indeed, bring himself to think with kindness of Paul
Montague. He could not say to himself that the man
had not been treacherous to him, nor could he forgive
the man's supposed treason. But he did tell himself
very plainly that in comparison with Hetta the man was
nothing to him. It could hardly be worth his while to
maintain a quarrel with the man if he were once able to
assure Hetta that she, as the wife of another man, should
still be dear to him as a friend might be dear. He was
well aware that such assurance, such forgiveness, must
contain very much. If it were to be so, Hetta's child
must take the name of Carbury, and must be to him as
his heir,—as near as possible his own child. In her favour
he must throw aside that law of primogeniture which to
him was so sacred that he had been hitherto minded to
make Sir Felix his heir in spite of the absolute unfitness
of the wretched young man. All this must be changed,

should he be able to persuade himself to give his consent
to the marriage. In such case Carbury must be the home
of the married couple, as far as he could induce them to
make it so. There must be born the future infant to whose
existence he was already looking forward with some idea
that in his old age he might there find comfort. In such
case, though he should never again be able to love Paul
Montague in his heart of hearts, he must live with him
for her sake on affectionate terms. He must forgive Hetta
altogether,—as though there had been no fault; and he
must strive to forgive the man's fault as best he might.
Struggling as he was to be generous, passionately fond
as he was of justice, yet he did not know how to be just
himself. He could not see that he in truth had been to
no extent ill-used. And ever and again, as he thought of
the great prayer as to the forgiveness of trespasses, he
could not refrain from asking himself whether it could
really be intended that he should forgive such trespass as
that committed against him by Paul Montague! Nevertheless, when he rose from the wall he had resolved that
Hetta should be pardoned entirely, and that Paul
Montague should be treated as though he were pardoned. As for himself,—the chances of the world had
been unkind to him, and he would submit to them!

Nevertheless he wrote no answer to Hetta's letter. Perhaps he felt, with some undefined but still existing hope,
that the writing of such a letter would deprive him of
his last chance. Hetta's letter to himself hardly required
an immediate answer,—did not, indeed, demand any
answer. She had simply told him that, whereas she had
for certain reasons quarrelled with the man she had
loved, she had now come to the conclusion that she
would quarrel with him no longer. She had asked for
her cousin's assent to her own views, but that, as Roger
felt, was to be given rather by the discontinuance of opposition than by any positive action. Roger's influence
with her mother was the assistance which Hetta really
wanted from him, and that influence could hardly be
given by the writing of any letter. Thinking of all this,
Roger determined that he would again go up to London.

He would have the vacant hours of the journey in which
to think of it all again, and tell himself whether it was possible for him to bring his heart to agree to the marriage;
—and then he would see the people, and perhaps learn
something further from their manner and their words,
before he finally committed himself to the abandonment
of his own hopes and the completion of theirs.

He went up to town, and I do not know that those
vacant hours served him much. To a man not accustomed to thinking there is nothing in the world so difficult as to think. After some loose fashion we turn over
things in our mind and ultimately reach some decision,
guided probably by our feelings at the last moment rather
than by any process of ratiocination;—and then we think
that we have thought. But to follow out one argument
to an end, and then to found on the base so reached the
commencement of another, is not common to us. Such
a process was hardly within the compass of Roger's mind,
—who when he was made wretched by the dust, and by
a female who had a basket of objectionable provisions
opposite to him, almost forswore his charitable resolutions of the day before; but who again, as he walked
lonely at night round the square which was near to his
hotel, looking up at the bright moon with a full appreciation of the beauty of the heavens, asked himself what
was he that he should wish to interfere with the happiness of two human beings much younger than himself
and much fitter to enjoy the world. But he had had a
bath, and had got rid of the dust, and had eaten his dinner.

The next morning he was in Welbeck Street at an early
hour. When he knocked he had not made up his mind
whether he would ask for Lady Carbury or her daughter,
and did at last inquire whether 'the ladies' were at home.
The ladies were reported as being at home, and he was
at once shown into the drawing-room, where Hetta was
sitting. She hurried up to him, and he at once took her
in his arms and kissed her. He had never done such a
thing before. He had never even kissed her hand. Though
they were cousins and dear friends, he had never treated
her after that fashion. Her instinct told her immediately

that such a greeting from him was a sign of affectionate compliance with her wishes. That this man should kiss her as her best and dearest relation, as her most trusted friend, as almost her brother, was certainly to her no offence. She could cling to him in fondest love,—if he would only consent not to be her lover. 'Oh, Roger, I am so glad to see you,' she said, escaping gently from his arms.

'I could not write an answer, and so I came.'

'You always do the kindest thing that can be done.'

'I don't know. I don't know that I can do anything now,—kind or unkind. It is all done without any aid from me. Hetta, you have been all the world to me.'

'Do not reproach me,' she said.

'No;—no. Why should I reproach you? You have committed no fault. I should not have come had I intended to reproach any one.'

'I love you so much for saying that.'

'Let it be as you wish it,—if it must. I have made up my mind to bear it, and there shall be an end of it.' As he said this he took her by the hand, and she put her head upon his shoulder and began to weep. 'And still you will be all the world to me,' he continued, with his arm round her waist. 'As you will not be my wife, you shall be my daughter.'

'I will be your sister, Roger.'

'My daughter rather. You shall be all that I have in the world. I will hurry to grow old that I may feel for you as the old feel for the young. And if you have a child, Hetta, he must be my child.' As he thus spoke her tears were renewed. 'I have planned it all out in my mind, dear. There! If there be anything that I can do to add to your happiness, I will do it. You must believe this of me,—that to make you happy shall be the only enjoyment of my life.'

It had been hardly possible for her to tell him as yet that the man to whom he was thus consenting to surrender her had not even condescended to answer the letter in which she had told him to come back to her. And now, sobbing as she was, overcome by the tenderness

of her cousin's affection, anxious to express her intense
gratitude, she did not know how first to mention the
name of Paul Montague. 'Have you seen him?' she said
in a whisper.

'Seen whom?'

'Mr. Montague.'

'No;—why should I have seen him? It is not for his
sake that I am here.'

'But you will be his friend?'

'Your husband shall certainly be my friend;—or, if
not, the fault shall not be mine. It shall all be forgotten,
Hetta,—as nearly as such things may be forgotten.
But I had nothing to say to him till I had seen you.' At
that moment the door was opened and Lady Carbury
entered the room, and, after her greeting with her cousin,
looked first at her daughter and then at Roger. 'I have
come up,' said he, 'to signify my adhesion to this
marriage.' Lady Carbury's face fell very low. 'I need
not speak again of what were my own wishes. I have
learned at last that it could not have been so.'

'Why should you say so?' exclaimed Lady Carbury.

'Pray, pray, mamma——,' Hetta began, but was
unable to find words with which to go on with her prayer.

'I do not know that it need be so at all,' continued
Lady Carbury. 'I think it is very much in your own
hands. Of course it is not for me to press such an arrangement, if it be not in accord with your own wishes.'

'I look upon her as engaged to marry Paul Montague,'
said Roger.

'Not at all,' said Lady Carbury.

'Yes; mamma,—yes,' cried Hetta boldly. 'It is so. I
am engaged to him.'

'I beg to let your cousin know that it is not so with my
consent,—nor, as far as I can understand at present, with
the consent of Mr. Montague himself.'

'Mamma!'

'Paul Montague!' ejaculated Roger Carbury. 'The
consent of Paul Montague! I think I may take upon
myself to say that there can be no doubt as to that.'

'There has been a quarrel,' said Lady Carbury.

'Surely he has not quarrelled with you, Hetta?'

'I wrote to him,—and he has not answered me,' said Hetta piteously.

Then Lady Carbury gave a full and somewhat coloured account of what had taken place, while Roger listened with admirable patience. 'The marriage is on every account objectionable,' she said at last. 'His means are precarious. His conduct with regard to that woman has been very bad. He has been sadly mixed up with that wretched man who destroyed himself. And now, when Henrietta has written to him without my sanction,—in opposition to my express commands,—he takes no notice of her. She, very properly, sent him back a present that he made her, and no doubt he has resented her doing so. I trust that his resentment may be continued.'

Hetta was now seated on a sofa hiding her face and weeping. Roger stood perfectly still, listening with respectful silence till Lady Carbury had spoken her last word. And even then he was slow to answer, considering what he might best say. 'I think I had better see him,' he replied. 'If, as I imagine, he has not received my cousin's letter, that matter will be set at rest. We must not take advantage of such an accident as that. As to his income,—that I think may be managed. His connection with Mr. Melmotte was unfortunate, but was due to no fault of his.' At this moment he could not but remember Lady Carbury's great anxiety to be closely connected with Melmotte, but he was too generous to say a word on that head. 'I will see him, Lady Carbury, and then I will come to you again.'

Lady Carbury did not dare to tell him that she did not wish him so see Paul Montague. She knew that if he really threw himself into the scale against her, her opposition would weigh nothing. He was too powerful in his honesty and greatness of character,—and had been too often admitted by herself to be the guardian angel of the family,—for her to stand against him. But she still thought that had he persevered, Hetta would have become his wife.

It was late that evening before Roger found Paul

Montague, who had only then returned from Liverpool with Fisker,—whose subsequent doings have been recorded somewhat out of their turn.

'I don't know what letter you mean,' said Paul.

'You wrote to her?'

'Certainly I wrote to her. I wrote to her twice. My last letter was one which I think she ought to have answered. She had accepted me, and had given me a right to tell my own story when she unfortunately heard from other sources the story of my journey to Lowestoft with Mrs. Hurtle.' Paul pleaded his own case with indignant heat, not understanding at first that Roger had come to him on a friendly mission.

'She did answer your letter.'

'I have not had a line from her;—not a word!'

'She did answer your letter.'

'What did she say to me?'

'Nay,—you must ask her that.'

'But if she will not see me?'

'She will see you. I can tell you that. And I will tell you this also;—that she wrote to you as a girl writes to the lover whom she does wish to see.'

'Is that true?' exclaimed Paul, jumping up.

'I am here especially to tell you that it is true. I should hardly come on such a message if there were a doubt. You may go to her, and need have nothing to fear,—unless, indeed, it be the opposition of her mother.'

'She is stronger than her mother,' said Paul.

'I think she is. And now I wish you to hear what I have to say.'

'Of course,' said Paul, sitting down suddenly. Up to this moment Roger Carbury, though he had certainly brought glad tidings, had not communicated them as a joyous, sympathetic messenger. His face had been severe, and the tone of his voice almost harsh; and Paul, remembering well the words of the last letter which his old friend had written him, did not expect personal kindness. Roger would probably say very disagreeable things to him, which he must bear with all the patience which he could summon to his assistance.

'You know my what feelings have been,' Roger began, 'and how deeply I have resented what I thought to be an interference with my affections. But no quarrel between you and me, whatever the rights of it may be——'

'I have never quarrelled with you,' Paul began.

'If you will listen to me for a moment it will be better. No anger between you and me, let it arise as it might, should be allowed to interfere with the happiness of her whom I suppose we both love better than all the rest of the world put together.'

'I do,' said Paul.

'And so do I;—and so I always shall. But she is to be your wife. She shall be my daughter. She shall have my property,—or her child shall be my heir. My house shall be her house,—if you and she will consent to make it so. You will not be afraid of me. You know me, I think, too well for that. You may now count on any assistance you could have from me were I a father giving you a daughter in marriage. I do this because I will make the happiness of her life the chief object of mine. Now good night. Don't say anything about it at present. By-and-by we shall be able to talk about these things with more equable temper.' Having so spoken he hurried out of the room, leaving Paul Montague bewildered by the tidings which had been announced to him.

## Chapter XCIV

### JOHN CRUMB'S VICTORY

IN the meantime great preparations were going on down in Suffolk for the marriage of that happiest of lovers, John Crumb. John Crumb had been up to London, had been formally reconciled to Ruby,—who had submitted to his floury embraces, not with the best grace in the world, but still with a submission that had satisfied her future husband,—had been intensely grateful to Mrs. Hurtle, and almost munificent in liberality to Mrs. Pipkin, to whom he presented a purple silk dress, in addition to the cloak which he had given on a former occasion. During this visit he had expressed no anger against Ruby, and no indignation in reference to the baronite. When informed by Mrs. Pipkin, who hoped thereby to please him, that Sir Felix was supposed to be still 'all one mash of gore,' he blandly smiled, remarking that no man could be much worse for a 'few sich taps as them.' He only stayed a few hours in London, but during these few hours he settled everything. When Mrs. Pipkin suggested that Ruby should be married from her house, he winked his eye as he declined the suggestion with thanks. Daniel Ruggles was old, and, under the influence of continued gin and water, was becoming feeble. John Crumb was of opinion that the old man should not be neglected, and hinted that with a little care the five hundred pounds which had originally been promised as Ruby's fortune, might at any rate be secured. He was of opinion that the marriage should be celebrated in Suffolk,—the feast being spread at Sheep's Acre farm, if Dan Ruggles could be talked into giving it,—and if not, at his own house. When both the ladies explained to him that this last proposition was not in strict accordance with the habits of the fashionable world, John expressed an opinion that, under the peculiar circumstances of his marriage, the ordinary laws of the world might be suspended. 'It ain't jist like other folks, after all as we've been through,' said he,—meaning probably to imply that having had to fight for his wife, he was entitled to give a breakfast on the occasion if he pleased. But whether the banquet was to be given by the bride's grandfather or by himself,—he was determined that there should be a banquet, and that he would bid the guests. He invited both Mrs. Pipkin and Mrs. Hurtle, and at last succeeded in inducing Mrs. Hurtle to promise that she would bring Mrs. Pipkin down to Bungay, for the occasion.

Then it was necessary to fix the day, and for this purpose it was of course essential that Ruby should be consulted. During the discussion as to the feast and the bridegroom's entreaties that the two ladies would be present, she had taken no part in the matter in hand.

She was brought up to be kissed, and having been duly
kissed she retired again among the children, having only
expressed one wish of her own,—namely, that Joe Mixet
might not have anything to do with the affair. But the
day could not be fixed without her, and she was summoned. Crumb had been absurdly impatient, proposing next Tuesday,—making his proposition on a Friday.
They could cook enough meat for all Bungay to eat by
Tuesday, and he was aware of no other cause for delay.
'That's out of the question,' Ruby had said decisively,
and as the two elder ladies had supported her Mr. Crumb
yielded with a good grace. He did not himself appreciate the reasons given because, as he remarked, gowns
can be bought ready made at any shop. But Mrs. Pipkin
told him with a laugh that he didn't know anything
about it, and when the 14th of August was named he
only scratched his head and, muttering something about
Thetford fair, agreed that he would, yet once again, allow
love to take precedence of business. If Tuesday would
have suited the ladies as well he thought that he might
have managed to combine the marriage and the fair, but
when Mrs. Pipkin told him that he must not interfere
any further, he yielded with a good grace. He merely
remained in London long enough to pay a friendly visit
to the policeman who had locked him up, and then returned to Suffolk, revolving in his mind how glorious
should be the matrimonial triumph which he had at last
achieved.

Before the day arrived, old Ruggles had been constrained to forgive his granddaughter, and to give a
general assent to the marriage. When John Crumb, with
a sound of many trumpets, informed all Bungay that he
had returned victorious from London, and that after all
the ups and downs of his courtship Ruby was to become
his wife on a fixed day, all Bungay took his part, and
joined in a general attack upon Mr. Daniel Ruggles.
The cross-grained old man held out for a long time,
alleging that the girl was no better than she should be,
and that she had run away with the baronite. But this
assertion was met by so strong a torrent of contradiction,

that the farmer was absolutely driven out of his own convictions. It is to be feared that many lies were told on Ruby's behalf by lips which had been quite ready a fortnight since to take away her character. But it had become an acknowledged fact in Bungay that John Crumb was ready at any hour to punch the head of any man who should hint that Ruby Ruggles had, at any period of her life, done any act or spoken any word unbecoming a young lady; and so strong was the general belief in John Crumb, that Ruby became the subject of general eulogy from all male lips in the town. And though perhaps some slight suspicion of irregular behaviour up in London might be whispered by the Bungay ladies among themselves, still the feeling in favour of Mr. Crumb was so general, and his constancy was so popular, that the grandfather could not stand against it. 'I don't see why I ain't to do as I likes with my own,' he said to Joe Mixet, the baker, who went out to Sheep's Acre Farm as one of many deputations sent by the municipality of Bungay.

'She's your own flesh and blood, Mr. Ruggles,' said the baker.

'No; she ain't;—no more than she's a Pipkin. She's taken up with Mrs. Pipkin jist because I hate the Pipkinses. Let Mrs. Pipkin give 'em a breakfast.'

'She is your own flesh and blood,—and your name, too, Mr. Ruggles. And she's going to be the respectable wife of a respectable man, Mr. Ruggles.'.

'I won't give 'em no breakfast;—that's flat,' said the farmer.

But he had yielded in the main when he allowed himself to base his opposition on one immaterial detail. The breakfast was to be given at the King's Head, and, though it was acknowledged on all sides that no authority could be found for such a practice, it was known that the bill was to be paid by the bridegroom. Nor would Mr. Ruggles pay the five hundred pounds down as in early days he had promised to do. He was very clear in his mind that his undertaking on that head was altogether cancelled by Ruby's departure from Sheep's Acre. When he was reminded that he had nearly pulled his granddaughter's

hair out of her head, and had thus justified her act of
rebellion, he did not contradict the assertion, but implied
that if Ruby did not choose to earn her fortune on such
terms as those, that was her fault. It was not to be supposed that he was to give a girl, who was after all as much
a Pipkin as a Ruggles, five hundred pounds for nothing.
But, in return for that night's somewhat harsh treatment
of Ruby, he did at last consent to have the money settled
upon John Crumb at his death,—an arrangement which
both the lawyer and Joe Mixet thought to be almost as
good as a free gift, being both of them aware that the
consumption of gin and water was on the increase. And
he, moreover, was persuaded to receive Mrs. Pipkin and
Ruby at the farm for the night previous to the marriage.
This very necessary arrangement was made by Mr.
Mixet's mother, a most respectable old lady, who went
out in a fly from the inn attired in her best black silk
gown and an overpowering bonnet, an old lady from
whom her son had inherited his eloquence, who absolutely shamed the old man into compliance,—not, however, till she had promised to send out the tea and white
sugar and box of biscuits which were thought to be necessary for Mrs. Pipkin on the evening preceding the
marriage. A private sitting-room at the inn was secured
for the special accommodation of Mrs. Hurtle,—who was
supposed to be a lady of too high standing to be properly
entertained at Sheep's Acre Farm.

On the day preceding the wedding one trouble for a
moment clouded the bridegroom's brow. Ruby had demanded that Joe Mixet should not be among the per-
formers, and John Crumb, with the urbanity of a lover,
had assented to her demand,—as far, at least, as silence
can give consent. And yet he felt himself unable to
answer such interrogatories as the parson might put to
him without the assistance of his friend, although he
devoted much study to the matter. 'You could come in
behind like, Joe, just as if I knew nothin' about it,' suggested Crumb.

'Don't you say a word of me, and she won't say nothing,
you may be sure. You ain't going to give in to all her

cantraps that way, John?' John shook his head and rubbed the meal about on his forehead. 'It was only just something for her to say. What have I done that she should object to me?'

'You didn't ever go for to—kiss her,—did you, Joe?'

'What a one'er you are! That wouldn't 'a set her again me. It is just because I stood up and spoke for you like a man that night at Sheep's Acre, when her mind was turned the other way. Don't you notice nothing about it. When we're all in the church she won't go back because Joe Mixet's there. I'll bet you a gallon, old fellow, she and I are the best friends in Bungay before six months are gone.'

'Nay, nay; she must have a better friend than thee, Joe, or I must know the reason why.' But John Crumb's heart was too big for jealousy, and he agreed at last that Joe Mixet should be his best man, undertaking to 'square it all' with Ruby, after the ceremony.

He met the ladies at the station and,—for him,—was quite eloquent in his welcome to Mrs. Hurtle and Mrs. Pipkin. To Ruby he said but little. But he looked at her in her new hat, and generally bright in subsidiary wedding garments, with great delight. 'Ain't she bootiful now?' he said aloud to Mrs. Hurtle on the platform, to the great delight of half Bungay, who had accompanied him on the occasion. Ruby, hearing her praises thus sung, made a fearful grimace as she turned round to Mrs. Pipkin, and whispered to her aunt, so that those only who were within a yard or two could hear her: 'He is such a fool!' Then he conducted Mrs. Hurtle in an omnibus up to the Inn, and afterwards himself drove Mrs. Pipkin and Ruby out to Sheep's Acre; in the performance of all which duties he was dressed in the green cutaway coat with brass buttons which had been expressly made for his marriage. 'Thou'rt come back then, Ruby,' said the old man.

'I ain't going to trouble you long, grandfather,' said the girl.

'So best;—so best. And this is Mrs. Pipkin?'

'Yes, Mr. Ruggles; that's my name.'

'I've heard your name. I've heard your name, and I don't know as I ever want to hear it again. But they say as you've been kind to that girl as 'd 'a been on the town only for that.'

'Grandfather, that ain't true,' said Ruby with energy. The old man made no rejoinder, and Ruby was allowed to take her aunt up into the bedroom which they were both to occupy. 'Now, Mrs. Pipkin, just you say,' pleaded Ruby, 'how was it possible for any girl to live with an old man like that?'

'But, Ruby, you might always have gone to live with the young man instead when you pleased.'

'You mean John Crumb.'

'Of course I mean John Crumb, Ruby.'

'There ain't much to choose between 'em. What one says is all spite; and the other man says nothing at all.'

'Oh Ruby, Ruby,' said Mrs. Pipkin, with solemnly persuasive voice, 'I hope you'll come to learn some day, that a loving heart is better nor a fickle tongue,—specially with vittels certain.'

On the following morning the Bungay church bells rang merrily, and half its population was present to see John Crumb made a happy man. He himself went out to the farm and drove the bride and Mrs. Pipkin into the town, expressing an opinion that no hired charioteer would bring them so safely as he would do himself; nor did he think it any disgrace to be seen performing this task before his marriage. He smiled and nodded at every one, now and then pointing back with his whip to Ruby when he met any of his specially intimate friends, as though he would have said, 'See, I've got her at last in spite of all difficulties.' Poor Ruby, in her misery under this treatment, would have escaped out of the cart had it been possible. But now she was altogether in the man's hands and no escape was within her reach. 'What's the odds?' said Mrs. Pipkin as they settled their bonnets in a room at the Inn just before they entered the church. 'Drat it,—you make me that angry I'm half minded to cuff you. Ain't he fond o' you? Ain't he got a house of

his own? Ain't he well to do all round? Manners!
What's manners? I don't see nothing amiss in his
manners. He means what he says, and I call that the
best of good manners.'

Ruby, when she reached the church, had been too
completely quelled by outward circumstances to take any
notice of Joe Mixet, who was standing there, quite unabashed, with a splendid nosegay in his button-hole. She
certainly had no right on this occasion to complain of her
husband's silence. Whereas she could hardly bring herself to utter the responses in a voice loud enough for the
clergyman to catch the familiar words, he made his assertions so vehemently that they were heard throughout the
whole building. 'I, John,—take thee Ruby,—to my wedded wife,—to 'ave and to 'old,—from this day forrard,—
for better nor worser,—for richer nor poorer—'; and so
on to the end. And when he came to the 'worldly goods'
with which he endowed his Ruby, he was very emphatic
indeed. Since the day had been fixed he had employed
all his leisure-hours in learning the words by heart, and
would now hardly allow the clergyman to say them
before him. He thoroughly enjoyed the ceremony, and
would have liked to be married over and over again,
every day for a week, had it been possible.

And then there came the breakfast, to which he marshalled the way up the broad stairs of the inn at Bungay,
with Mrs. Hurtle on one arm and Mrs. Pipkin on the
other. He had been told that he ought to take his wife's
arm on this occasion, but he remarked that he meant to
see a good deal of her in future, and that his opportunities of being civil to Mrs. Hurtle and Mrs. Pipkin
would be rare. Thus it came to pass that, in spite of all
that poor Ruby had said, she was conducted to the
marriage-feast by Joe Mixet himself. Ruby, I think, had
forgotten the order which she had given in reference to
the baker. When desiring that she might see nothing
more of Joe Mixet, she had been in her pride;—but now
she was so tamed and quelled by the outward circumstances of her position, that she was glad to have some
one near her who knew how to behave himself. 'Mrs.

Crumb, you have my best wishes for your continued 'ealth and 'appiness,' said Joe Mixet in a whisper.

'It's very good of you to say so, Mr. Mixet.'

'He's a good 'un; is he.'

'Oh, I dare say.'

'You just be fond of him and stroke him down, and make much of him, and I'm blessed if you mayn't do a'most anything with him,—all's one as a babby.'

'A man shouldn't be all's one as a babby, Mr. Mixet.'

'And he don't drink hard, but he works hard, and go where he will he can hold his own.' Ruby said no more, and soon found herself seated by her husband's side. It certainly was wonderful to her that so many people should pay John Crumb so much respect, and should seem to think so little of the meal and flour which pervaded his countenance.

After the breakfast, or 'bit of dinner,' as John Crumb would call it, Mr. Mixet of course made a speech. 'He had had the pleasure of knowing John Crumb for a great many years, and the honour of being acquainted with Miss Ruby Ruggles,—he begged all their pardons, and should have said Mrs. John Crumb,—ever since she was a child.' 'That's a downright story,' said Ruby in a whisper to Mrs. Hurtle. 'And he'd never known two young people more fitted by the gifts of nature to contribute to one another's 'appinesses. He had understood that Mars and Wenus always lived on the best of terms, and perhaps the present company would excuse him if he likened this 'appy young couple to them two 'eathen gods and goddesses. For Miss Ruby,—Mrs. Crumb he should say,—was certainly lovely as ere a Wenus as ever was; and as for John Crumb, he didn't believe that ever a Mars among 'em could stand again him. He didn't remember just at present whether Mars and Wenus had any young family, but he hoped that before long there would be any number of young Crumbs for the Bungay birds to pick up. 'Appy is the man as 'as his quiver full of 'em,—and the woman too, if you'll allow me to say so, Mrs. Crumb.' The speech, of which only a small sample can be given here, was very much admired by the ladies

and gentlemen present,—with the single exception of
poor Ruby, who would have run away and locked herself
in an inner chamber had she not been certain that she
would be brought back again.

In the afternoon John took his bride to Lowestoft, and
brought her back to all the glories of his own house on the
following day. His honeymoon was short, but its influence on Ruby was beneficent. When she was alone
with the man, knowing that he was her husband, and
thinking something of all that he had done to win her to
be his wife, she did learn to respect him. 'Now, Ruby,
give a fellow a buss,—as though you meant it,' he said,
when the first fitting occasion presented itself.

'Oh, John,—what nonsense!'

'It ain't nonsense to me, I can tell you. I'd sooner have
a kiss from you than all the wine as ever was swallowed.'
Then she did kiss him, 'as though she meant it;' and when
she returned with him to Bungay the next day, she had
made up her mind that she would endeavour to do her
duty by him as his wife.

## Chapter XCV

### THE LONGESTAFFE MARRIAGES

IN another part of Suffolk, not very far from Bungay,
there was a lady whose friends had not managed her
affairs as well as Ruby's friends had done for Ruby. Miss
Georgiana Longestaffe in the early days of August was in
a very miserable plight. Her sister's marriage with Mr.
George Whitstable was fixed for the first of September, a
day which in Suffolk is of all days the most sacred; and
the combined energies of the houses of Caversham and
Toodlam were being devoted to that happy event. Poor
Georgey's position was in every respect wretched, but its
misery was infinitely increased by the triumph of those
hymeneals. It was but the other day that she had looked
down from a very great height on her elder sister, and

had utterly despised the squire of Toodlam. And at that time, still so recent, this contempt from her had been accepted as being almost reasonable. Sophia had hardly ventured to rebel against it, and Mr. Whitstable himself had been always afraid to encounter the shafts of irony with which his fashionable future sister-in-law attacked him. But all that was now changed. Sophia in her pride of place had become a tyrant, and George Whitstable, petted in the house with those sweetmeats which are always showered on embryo bridegrooms, absolutely gave himself airs. At this time Mr. Longestaffe was never at home. Having assured himself that there was no longer any danger of the Brehgert alliance he had remained in London, thinking his presence to be necessary for the winding up of Melmotte's affairs, and leaving poor Lady Pomona to bear her daughter's ill humour. The family at Caversham consisted therefore of the three ladies, and was enlivened by daily visits from Toodlam. It will be owned that in this state of things there was very little consolation for Georgiana.

It was not long before she quarrelled altogether with her sister,—to the point of absolutely refusing to act as bridesmaid. The reader may remember that there had been a watch and chain, and that two of the ladies of the family had expressed an opinion that these trinkets should be returned to Mr. Brehgert who had bestowed them. But Georgiana had not sent them back when a week had elapsed since the receipt of Mr. Brehgert's last letter. The matter had perhaps escaped Lady Pomona's memory, but Sophia was happily alive to the honour of her family. 'Georgey,' she said one morning in their mother's presence, 'don't you think Mr. Brehgert's watch ought to go back to him without any more delay?'

'What have you got to do with anybody's watch? The watch wasn't given to you.'

'I think it ought to go back. When papa finds that it has been kept I'm sure he'll be very angry.'

'It's no business of yours whether he's angry or not.'

'If it isn't sent, George will tell Dolly. You know what would happen then.'

This was unbearable! That George Whitstable should interfere in her affairs,—that he should talk about her watch and chain. 'I never will speak to George Whitstable again the longest day that ever I live,' she said, getting up from her chair.

'My dear, don't say anything so horrible as that,' exclaimed the unhappy mother.

'I do say it. What has George Whitstable to do with me? A miserably stupid fellow! Because you've landed him, you think he's to ride over the whole family.'

'I think Mr. Brehgert ought to have his watch and chain back,' said Sophia.

'Certainly he ought,' said Lady Pomona. 'Georgiana, it must be sent back. It really must,—or I shall tell your papa.'

Subsequently, on the same day, Georgiana brought the watch and chain to her mother, protesting that she had never thought of keeping them, and explaining that she had intended to hand them over to her papa as soon as he should have returned to Caversham. Lady Pomona was now empowered to return them, and they were absolutely confided to the hands of the odious George Whitstable, who about this time made a journey to London in reference to certain garments which he required. But Georgiana, though she was so far beaten, kept up her quarrel with her sister. She would not be bridesmaid. She would never speak to George Whitstable. And she would shut herself up on the day of the marriage.

She did think herself to be very hardly used. What was there left in the world that she could do in furtherance of her future cause? And what did her father and mother expect would become of her? Marriage had ever been so clearly placed before her eyes as a condition of things to be achieved by her own efforts, that she could not endure the idea of remaining tranquil in her father's house and waiting till some fitting suitor might find her out. She had struggled and struggled,—struggling still in vain, —till every effort of her mind, every thought of her daily life, was pervaded by a conviction that as she grew older from year to year, the struggle should be more intense.

The swimmer when first he finds himself in the water, conscious of his skill and confident in his strength, can make his way through the water with the full command of all his powers. But when he begins to feel that the shore is receding from him, that his strength is going, that the footing for which he pants is still far beneath his feet, —that there is peril where before he had contemplated no danger,—then he begins to beat the water with strokes rapid but impotent, and to waste in anxious gaspings the breath on which his very life must depend. So it was with poor Georgey Longestaffe. Something must be done at once, or it would be of no avail. Twelve years had been passed by her since first she plunged into the stream,— the twelve years of her youth,—and she was as far as ever from the bank; nay, farther, if she believed her eyes. She too must strike out with rapid efforts, unless, indeed, she would abandon herself and let the waters close over her head. But immersed as she was here at Caversham, how could she strike at all? Even now the waters were closing upon her. The sound of them was in her ears. The ripple of the wave was already round her lips; robbing her of breath. Ah!—might not there be some last great convulsive effort which might dash her on shore, even if it were upon a rock!

That ultimate failure in her matrimonial projects would be the same as drowning she never for a moment doubted. It had never occurred to her to consider with equanimity the prospect of living as an old maid. It was beyond the scope of her mind to contemplate the chances of a life in which marriage might be well if it came, but in which unmarried tranquillity might also be well should that be her lot. Nor could she understand that others should contemplate it for her. No doubt the battle had been carried on for many years so much under the auspices of her father and mother as to justify her in thinking that their theory of life was the same as her own. Lady Pomona had been very open in her teaching, and Mr. Longestaffe had always given a silent adherence to the idea that the house in London was to be kept open in order that husbands might be caught. And now when they deserted her in her real difficulty,—when they first told her to live at Caversham all the summer, and then sent her up to the Melmottes, and after that forbade her marriage with Mr. Brehgert,—it seemed to her that they were unnatural parents who gave her a stone when she wanted bread, a serpent when she asked for a fish. She had no friend left. There was no one living who seemed to care whether she had a husband or not. She took to walking in solitude about the park, and thought of many things with a grim earnestness which had not hitherto belonged to her character.

'Mamma,' she said one morning when all the care of the household was being devoted to the future comforts, —chiefly in regard to linen,—of Mrs. George Whitstable, 'I wonder whether papa has any intention at all about me.'

'In what sort of way, my dear?'

'In any way. Does he mean me to live here for ever and ever?'

'I don't think he intends to have a house in town again.'

'And what am I to do?'

'I suppose we shall stay here at Caversham.'

'And I'm to be buried just like a nun in a convent,— only that the nun does it by her own consent and I don't! Mamma, I won't stand it. I won't indeed.'

'I think, my dear, that that is nonsense. You see company here, just as other people do in the country;—and as for not standing it, I don't know what you mean. As long as you are one of your papa's family of course you must live where he lives.'

'Oh, mamma, to hear you talk like that!—It is horrible —horrible! As if you didn't know! As if you couldn't understand! Sometimes I almost doubt whether papa does know, and then I think that if he did he would not be so cruel. But you understand it all as well as I do myself. What is to become of me? Is it not enough to drive me mad to be going about here by myself, without any prospect of anything? Should you have liked at my age to have felt that you had no chance of having a house of your own to live in? Why didn't you, among you, let me marry Mr. Breghert?' As she said this she was almost eloquent with passion.

'You know, my dear,' said Lady Pomona, 'that your papa wouldn't hear of it.'

'I know that if you would have helped me I would have done it in spite of papa. What right has he to domineer over me in that way? Why shouldn't I have married the man if I chose? I am old enough to know surely. You talk now of shutting up girls in convents as being a thing quite impossible. This is much worse. Papa won't do anything to help me. Why shouldn't he let me do something for myself?'

'You can't regret Mr. Brehgert!'

'Why can't I regret him? I do regret him. I'd have him to-morrow if he came. Bad as it might be, it couldn't be so bad as Caversham.'

'You couldn't have loved him, Georgiana.'

'Loved him! Who thinks about love nowadays? I don't know any one who loves any one else. You won't tell me that Sophy is going to marry that idiot because she loves him! Did Julia Triplex love that man with the large fortune? When you wanted Dolly to marry Marie Melmotte you never thought of his loving her. I had got the better of all that kind of thing before I was twenty.'

'I think a young woman should love her husband.'

'It makes me sick, mamma, to hear you talk in that way. It does indeed. When one has been going on for a dozen years trying to do something,—and I have never had any secrets from you,—then that you should turn round upon me and talk about love! Mamma, if you would help me I think I could still manage with Mr. Brehgert.' Lady Pomona shuddered. 'You have not got to marry him.'

'It is too horrid.'

'Who would have to put up with it? Not you, or papa, or Dolly. I should have a house of my own at least, and I should know what I had to expect for the rest of my life. If I stay here I shall go mad,—or die.'

'It is impossible.'

'If you will stand to me, mamma, I am sure it may be

done. I would write to him, and say that you would see him.'

'Georgiana, I will never see him.'

'Why not?'

'He is a Jew!'

'What abominable prejudice;—what wicked prejudice! As if you didn't know that all that is changed now! What possible difference can it make about a man's religion? Of course I know that he is vulgar, and old, and has a lot of children. But if I can put up with that, I don't think that you and papa have a right to interfere. As to his religion it cannot signify.'

'Georgiana, you make me very unhappy. I am wretched to see you so discontented. If I could do anything for you, I would. But I will not meddle about Mr. Brehgert. I shouldn't dare to do so. I don't think you know how angry your papa can be.'

'I'm not going to let papa be a bugbear to frighten me. What can he do? I don't suppose he'll beat me. And I'd rather he would than shut me up here. As for you, mamma, I don't think you care for me a bit. Because Sophy is going to be married to that oaf, you are become so proud of her that you haven't half a thought for anybody else.'

'That's very unjust, Georgiana.'

'I know what's unjust,—and I know who's ill-treated. I tell you fairly, mamma, that I shall write to Mr. Brehgert and tell him that I am quite ready to marry him. I don't know why he should be afraid of papa. I don't mean to be afraid of him any more, and you may tell him just what I say.'

All this made Lady Pomona very miserable. She did not communicate her daughter's threat to Mr. Longestaffe, but she did discuss it with Sophia. Sophia was of opinion that Georgiana did not mean it, and gave two or three reasons for thinking so. In the first place had she intended it she would have written her letter without saying a word about it to Lady Pomona. And she certainly would not have declared her purpose of writing such letter after Lady Pomona had refused her assistance. And moreover,—Lady Pomona had received no former hint of the information which was now conveyed to her,—Georgiana was in the habit of meeting the curate of the next parish almost every day in the park.

'Mr. Batherbolt!' exclaimed Lady Pomona.

'She is walking with Mr. Batherbolt almost every day.'

'But he is so very strict.'

'It is true, mamma.'

'And he's five years younger than she! And he's got nothing but his curacy! And he's a celibate!* I heard the bishop laughing at him because he called himself a celibate.'

'It doesn't signify, mamma. I know she is with him constantly. Wilson has seen them,—and I know it. Perhaps papa could get him a living. Dolly has a living of his own that came to him with his property.'

'Dolly would be sure to sell the presentation,' said Lady Pomona.

'Perhaps the bishop would do something,' said the anxious sister, 'when he found that the man wasn't a celibate. Anything, mamma, would be better than the Jew.' To this latter proposition Lady Pomona gave a cordial assent. 'Of course it is a come-down to marry a curate,—but a clergyman is always considered to be decent.'

The preparations for the Whitstable marriage went on without any apparent attention to the intimacy which was growing up between Mr. Batherbolt and Georgiana. There was no room to apprehend anything wrong on that side. Mr. Batherbolt was so excellent a young man, and so exclusively given to religion, that, even should Sophy's suspicion be correct, he might be trusted to walk about the park with Georgiana. Should he at any time come forward and ask to be allowed to make the lady his wife, there would be no disgrace in the matter. He was a clergyman and a gentleman,—and the poverty would be Georgiana's own affair.

Mr. Longestaffe returned home only on the eve of his eldest daughter's marriage, and with him came Dolly. Great trouble had been taken to teach him that duty absolutely required his presence at his sister's marriage, and he had at last consented to be there. It is not generally considered a hardship by a young man that he should have to go into a good partridge country on the 1st of September, and Dolly was an acknowledged sportsman. Nevertheless, he considered that he had made a great sacrifice to his family, and he was received by Lady Pomona as though he were a bright example to other sons. He found the house not in a very comfortable position, for Georgiana still persisted in her refusal either to be a bridesmaid or to speak to Mr. Whitstable; but still his presence, which was very rare at Caversham, gave some assistance: and, as at this moment his money affairs had been comfortably arranged, he was not called upon to squabble with his father. It was a great thing that one of the girls should be married, and Dolly had brought down an enormous china dog, about five feet high, as a wedding present, which added materially to the happiness of the meeting. Lady Pomona had determined that she would tell her husband of those walks in the park, and of other signs of growing intimacy which had reached her ears;—but this she would postpone until after the Whitstable marriage.

But at nine o'clock on the morning set apart for that marriage, they were all astounded by the news that Georgiana had run away with Mr. Batherbolt. She had been up before six. He had met her at the park gate, and had driven her over to catch the early train at Stow-market. Then it appeared, too, that by degrees various articles of her property had been conveyed to Mr. Batherbolt's lodgings in the adjacent village, so that Lady Pomona's fear that Georgiana would not have a thing to wear was needless. When the fact was first known it was almost felt, in the consternation of the moment, that the Whitstable marriage must be postponed. But Sophia had a word to say to her mother on that head, and she said it. The marriage was not postponed. At first Dolly talked of going after his younger sister, and the father did dispatch various telegrams. But the fugitives could not be brought back, and with some little delay,—which

made the marriage perhaps uncanonical*but not illegal,
—Mr. George Whitstable was made a happy man.

It need only be added that in about a month's time
Georgiana returned to Caversham as Mrs. Batherbolt,
and that she resided there with her husband in much
connubial bliss for the next six months. At the end of that
time they removed to a small living, for the purchase of
which Mr. Longestaffe had managed to raise the necessary money.

## Chapter XCVI

### WHERE 'THE WILD ASSES QUENCH THEIR THIRST'*

WE must now go back a little in our story,—about
three weeks,—in order that the reader may be told
how affairs were progressing at the Beargarden. That
establishment had received a terrible blow in the defection
of Herr Vossner. It was not only that he had robbed the
club, and robbed every member of the club who had
ventured to have personal dealings with him. Although
a bad feeling in regard to him was no doubt engendered
in the minds of those who had suffered deeply, it was not
that alone which cast an almost funereal gloom over the
club. The sorrow was in this,—that with Herr Vossner
all their comforts had gone. Of course Herr Vossner had
been a thief. That no doubt had been known to them from
the beginning. A man does not consent to be called out
of bed at all hours in the morning to arrange the gambling
accounts of young gentlemen without being a thief. No
one concerned with Herr Vossner had supposed him to
be an honest man. But then as a thief he had been so
comfortable that his absence was regretted with a tenderness almost amounting to love even by those who had
suffered most severely from his rapacity. Dolly Longestaffe had been robbed more outrageously than any other
member of the club, and yet Dolly Longestaffe had said
since the departure of the purveyor that London was not

worth living in now that Herr Vossner was gone. In a week the Beargarden collapsed,—as Germany would collapse for a period if Herr Vossner's great compatriot were suddenly to remove himself from the scene; but as Germany would strive to live even without Bismarck,* so did the club make its new efforts. But here the parallel must cease. Germany no doubt would at last succeed, but the Beargarden had received a blow from which it seemed that there was no recovery. At first it was proposed that three men should be appointed as trustees,—trustees for paying Vossner's debts, trustees for borrowing more money, trustees for the satisfaction of the landlord who was beginning to be anxious as to his future rent. At a certain very triumphant general meeting of the club it was determined that such a plan should be arranged, and the members assembled were unanimous. It was at first thought that there might be a little jealousy as to the trusteeship. The club was so popular and the authority conveyed by the position would be so great, that A, B, and C might feel aggrieved at seeing so much power conferred on D, E, and F. When at the meeting above mentioned one or two names were suggested, the final choice was postponed, as a matter of detail to be arranged privately, rather from this consideration than with any idea that there might be a difficulty in finding adequate persons. But even the leading members of the Beargarden hesitated when the proposition was submitted to them with all its honours and all its responsibilities. Lord Nidderdale declared from the beginning that he would have nothing to do with it,—pleading his poverty openly. Beauchamp Beauclerk was of opinion that he himself did not frequent the club often enough. Mr. Lupton professed his inability as a man of business. Lord Grasslough pleaded his father. The club from the first had been sure of Dolly Longestaffe's services;—for were not Dolly's pecuniary affairs now in process of satisfactory arrangement, and was it not known by all men that his courage never failed him in regard to money? But even he declined. 'I have spoken to Squercum,' he said to the Committee, 'and Squercum won't hear of it. Squercum has made inquiries and he thinks the club very shaky.' When one of the Committee made a remark as to Mr. Squercum which was not complimentary,—insinuated indeed that Squercum without injustice might be consigned to the infernal deities,—Dolly took the matter up warmly. 'That's all very well for you, Grasslough; but if you knew the comfort of having a fellow who could keep you straight without preaching sermons at you you wouldn't despise Squercum. I've tried to go alone and I find that does not answer. Squercum's my coach, and I mean to stick pretty close to him.' Then it came to pass that the triumphant project as to the trustees fell to the ground, although Squercum himself advised that the difficulty might be lessened if three gentlemen could be selected who lived well before the world and yet had nothing to lose. Whereupon Dolly suggested Miles Grendall. But the committee shook its heads, not thinking it possible that the club could be re-established on a basis of three Miles Grendalls.

Then dreadful rumours were heard. The Beargarden must surely be abandoned. 'It is such a pity,' said Nidderdale, 'because there never has been anything like it.'

'Smoke all over the house!' said Dolly.

'No horrid nonsense about closing,' said Grasslough, 'and no infernal old fogies wearing out the carpets and paying for nothing.'

'Not a vestige of propriety, or any beastly rules to be kept! That's what I liked,' said Nidderdale.

'It's an old story,' said Mr. Lupton, 'that if you put a man into Paradise he'll make it too hot to hold him. That's what you've done here.'

'What we ought to do,' said Dolly, who was pervaded by a sense of his own good fortune in regard to Squercum, 'is to get some fellow like Vossner, and make him tell us how much he wants to steal above his regular pay. Then we could subscribe that among us. I really think that might be done. Squercum would find a fellow, no doubt.' But Mr. Lupton was of opinion that the new Vossner might perhaps not know, when thus consulted, the extent of his own cupidity.

One day, before the Whitstable marriage, when it was understood that the club would actually be closed on the 12th August*unless some new heaven-inspired idea might be forthcoming for its salvation, Nidderdale, Grasslough, and Dolly were hanging about the hall and the steps, and drinking sherry and bitters preparatory to dinner, when Sir Felix Carbury came round the neighbouring corner and, in a creeping, hesitating fashion, entered the hall door. He had nearly recovered from his wounds, though he still wore a bit of court plaster*on his upper lip, and had not yet learned to look or to speak as though he had not had two of his front teeth knocked out. He had heard little or nothing of what had been done at the Beargarden since Vossner's defection. It was now a month since he had been seen at the club. His thrashing had been the wonder of perhaps half nine days, but latterly his existence had been almost forgotten. Now, with difficulty, he had summoned courage to go down to his old haunt, so completely had he been cowed by the latter circumstances of his life; but he had determined that he would pluck up his courage, and talk to his old associates as though no evil thing had befallen him. He had still money enough to pay for his dinner and to begin a small rubber of whist. If fortune should go against him he might glide into I O U's;—as others had done before, so much to his cost. 'By George, here's Carbury!' said Dolly. Lord Grasslough whistled, turned his back, and walked upstairs; but Nidderdale and Dolly consented to have their hands shaken by the stranger.

'Thought you were out of town,' said Nidderdale. 'Haven't seen you for the last ever so long.'

'I have been out of town,' said Felix,—lying; 'down in Suffolk. But I'm back now. How are things going on here?'

'They're not going at all;—they're gone,' said Dolly.

'Everything is smashed,' said Nidderdale. 'We shall all have to pay, I don't know how much.'

'Wasn't Vossner ever caught?' asked the baronet.

'Caught!' ejaculated Dolly. 'No;—but he has caught us. I don't know that there has ever been much idea of catching Vossner. We close altogether next Monday, and the furniture is to be gone to law for. Flatfleece says it belongs to him under what he calls a deed of sale. Indeed, everything that everybody has seems to belong to Flatfleece. He's always in and out of the club, and has got the key of the cellar.'

'That don't matter,' said Nidderdale, 'as Vossner took care that there shouldn't be any wine.'

'He's got most of the forks and spoons, and only lets us use what we have as a favour.'

'I suppose one can get a dinner here?'

'Yes; to-day you can, and perhaps to-morrow.'

'Isn't there any playing?' asked Felix with dismay.

'I haven't seen a card this fortnight,' said Dolly. 'There hasn't been anybody to play. Everything has gone to the dogs. There has been the affair of Melmotte, you know; —though, I suppose, you do know all about that.'

'Of course I know he poisoned himself.'

'Of course that had effect,' said Dolly, continuing his history. 'Though why fellows shouldn't play cards because another fellow like that takes poison, I can't understand. Last year the only day I managed to get down in February, the hounds didn't come because some old cove had died. What harm could our hunting have done him? I call it rot.'

'Melmotte's death was rather awful,' said Nidderdale.

'Not half so awful as having nothing to amuse one. And now they say the girl is going to be married to Fisker. I don't know how you and Nidderdale like that. I never went in for her myself. Squercum never seemed to see it.'

'Poor dear!' said Nidderdale. 'She's welcome for me, and I dare say she couldn't do better with herself. I was very fond of her;—I'll be shot if I wasn't.'

'And Carbury too, I suppose,' said Dolly.

'No; I wasn't. If I'd really been fond of her I suppose it would have come off. I should have had her safe enough to America, if I'd cared about it.' This was Sir Felix's view of the matter.

'Come into the smoking-room, Dolly,' said Nidderdale. 'I can stand most things, and I try to stand everything;

but, by George, that fellow is such a cad that I cannot stand him. You and I are bad enough,—but I don't think we're so heartless as Carbury.'

'I don't think I'm heartless at all,' said Dolly. 'I'm good-natured to everybody that is good-natured to me,—and to a great many people who ain't. I'm going all the way down to Caversham next week to see my sister married, though I hate the place and hate marriages, and if I was to be hung for it I couldn't say a word to the fellow who is going to be my brother-in-law. But I do agree about Carbury. It's very hard to be good-natured to him.'

But, in the teeth of these adverse opinions Sir Felix managed to get his dinner-table close to theirs and to tell them at dinner something of his future prospects. He was going to travel and see the world. He had, according to his own account, completely run through London life and found that it was all barren.

> 'In life I've rung all changes through,
>     Run every pleasure down,
> 'Midst each excess of folly too,
>     And lived with half the town.'*

Sir Felix did not exactly quote the old song, probably having never heard the words. But that was the burden of his present story. It was his determination to seek new scenes, and in search of them to travel over the greater part of the known world.

'How jolly for you!' said Dolly.

'It will be a change, you know.'

'No end of a change. Is any one going with you?'

'Well;—yes. I've got a travelling companion;—a very pleasant fellow, who knows a lot, and will be able to coach me up in things. There's a deal to be learned by going abroad, you know.'

'A sort of a tutor,' said Nidderdale.

'A parson, I suppose,' said Dolly.

'Well;—he is a clergyman. Who told you?'

'It's only my inventive genius. Well;—yes; I should say that would be nice,—travelling about Europe with a clergyman. I shouldn't get enough advantage out of it to make it pay, but I fancy it will just suit you.'

'It's an expensive sort of thing;—isn't it?' asked Nidderdale.

'Well;—it does cost something. But I've got so sick of this kind of life;—and then that railway Board coming to an end, and the club smashing up, and——'

'Marie Melmotte marrying Fisker,' suggested Dolly.

'That too, if you will. But I want a change, and a change I mean to have. I've seen this side of things, and now I'll have a look at the other.'

'Didn't you have a row in the street with some one the other day?' This question was asked very abruptly by Lord Grasslough, who, though he was sitting near them, had not yet joined in the conversation, and who had not before addressed a word to Sir Felix. 'We heard something about it, but we never got the right story.' Nidderdale glanced across the table at Dolly, and Dolly whistled. Grasslough looked at the man he addressed as one does look when one expects an answer. Mr. Lupton, with whom Grasslough was dining, also sat expectant. Dolly and Nidderdale were both silent.

It was the fear of this that had kept Sir Felix away from the club. Grasslough, as he had told himself, was just the fellow to ask such a question,—ill-natured, insolent, and obtrusive. But the question demanded an answer of some kind. 'Yes,' said he; 'a fellow attacked me in the street, coming behind me when I had a girl with me. He didn't get much the best of it though.'

'Oh;—didn't he?' said Grasslough. 'I think, upon the whole, you know, you're right about going abroad.'

'What business is it of yours?' asked the baronet.

'Well;—as the club is being broken up, I don't know that it is very much the business of any of us.'

'I was speaking to my friends, Lord Nidderdale and Mr. Longestaffe, and not to you.'

'I quite appreciate the advantage of the distinction,' said Lord Grasslough, 'and am sorry for Lord Nidderdale and Mr. Longestaffe.'

'What do you mean by that?' said Sir Felix, rising

from his chair. His present opponent was not horrible to
him as had been John Crumb, as men in clubs do not
now often knock each others' heads or draw swords one
upon another.

'Don't let's have a quarrel here,' said Mr. Lupton. 'I
shall leave the room if you do.'

'If we must break up, let us break up in peace and
quietness,' said Nidderdale.

'Of course, if there is to be a fight, I'm good to go out
with anybody,' said Dolly. 'When there's any beastly
thing to be done, I've always got to do it. But don't you
think that kind of thing is a little slow?'

'Who began it?' said Sir Felix, sitting down again.
Whereupon Lord Grasslough, who had finished his
dinner, walked out of the room. 'That fellow is always
wanting to quarrel.'

'There's one comfort, you know,' said Dolly. 'It wants
two men to make a quarrel.'

'Yes; it does,' said Sir Felix, taking this as a friendly
observation; 'and I'm not going to be fool enough to be
one of them.'

'Oh, yes, I meant it fast enough,' said Grasslough
afterwards up in the card-room. The other men who had
been together had quickly followed him, leaving Sir Felix
alone, and they had collected themselves there not with
the hope of play, but thinking that they would be less
interrupted than in the smoking-room. 'I don't suppose
we shall ever any of us be here again, and as he did come
in I thought I would tell him my mind.'

'What's the use of taking such a lot of trouble?' said
Dolly. 'Of course he's a bad fellow. Most fellows are bad
fellows in one way or another.'

'But he's bad all round,' said the bitter enemy.

'And so this is to be the end of the Beargarden,' said
Lord Nidderdale with a peculiar melancholy. 'Dear old
place! I always felt it was too good to last. I fancy it
doesn't do to make things too easy;—one has to pay so
uncommon dear for them! And then, you know, when
you've got things easy, then they get rowdy;—and, by
George, before you know where you are, you find your-

self among a lot of blackguards. If one wants to keep one's self straight, one has to work hard at it, one way or the other. I suppose it all comes from the fall of Adam.'

'If Solomon, Solon, and the Archbishop of Canterbury were rolled into one, they couldn't have spoken with more wisdom,' said Mr. Lupton.

'Live and learn,' continued the young lord. 'I don't think anybody has liked the Beargarden so much as I have, but I shall never try this kind of thing again. I shall begin reading blue books*to-morrow, and shall dine at the Carlton. Next session I shan't miss a day in the House, and I'll bet anybody a fiver that I make a speech before Easter. I shall take to claret at 20s. a dozen, and shall go about London on the top of an omnibus.'

'How about getting married?' asked Dolly.

'Oh;—that must be as it comes. That's the governor's affair. None of you fellows will believe me, but, upon my word, I liked that girl; and I'd 've stuck to her at last,— only there are some things a fellow can't do. He was such a thundering scoundrel!'

After a while Sir Felix followed them upstairs, and entered the room as though nothing unpleasant had happened below. 'We can make up a rubber;—can't we?' said he.

'I should say not,' said Nidderdale.

'I shall not play,' said Mr. Lupton.

'There isn't a pack of cards in the house,' said Dolly. Lord Grasslough didn't condescend to say a word. Sir Felix sat down with his cigar in his mouth, and the others continued to smoke in silence.

'I wonder what has become of Miles Grendall,' asked Sir Felix. But no one made any answer, and they smoked on in silence. 'He hasn't paid me a shilling yet of the money he owes me.' Still there was not a word. 'And I don't suppose he ever will.' There was another pause. 'He is the biggest scoundrel I ever met,' said Sir Felix.

'I know one as big,' said Lord Grasslough,—'or, at any rate, as little.'

There was another pause of a minute, and then Sir Felix left the room muttering something as to the stupidity of having no cards;—and so brought to an end his connection with his associates of the Beargarden. From that time forth he was never more seen by them,—or, if seen, was never known.

The other men remained there till well on into the night, although there was not the excitement of any special amusement to attract them. It was felt by them all that this was the end of the Beargarden, and, with a melancholy seriousness befitting the occasion, they whispered sad things in low voices, consoling themselves simply with tobacco. 'I never felt so much like crying in my life,' said Dolly, as he asked for a glass of brandy-and-water at about midnight. 'Good-night, old fellows; good-bye. I'm going down to Caversham, and I shouldn't wonder if I didn't drown myself.'

How Mr. Flatfleece went to law, and tried to sell the furniture, and threatened everybody, and at last singled out poor Dolly Longestaffe as his special victim; and how Dolly Longestaffe, by the aid of Mr. Squercum, utterly confounded Mr. Flatfleece, and brought that ingenious but unfortunate man, with his wife and small family, to absolute ruin, the reader will hardly expect to have told to him in detail in this chronicle.

## Chapter XCVII

### MRS. HURTLE'S FATE

MRS. HURTLE had consented at the joint request of Mrs. Pipkin and John Crumb to postpone her journey to New York and to go down to Bungay and grace the marriage of Ruby Ruggles, not so much from any love for the persons concerned, not so much even from any desire to witness a phase of English life, as from an irresistible tenderness towards Paul Montague. She not only longed to see him once again, but she could with difficulty bring herself to leave the land in which he was living. There was no hope for her. She was sure of that.

She had consented to relinquish him. She had condoned his treachery to her,—and for his sake had even been kind to the rival who had taken her place. But still she lingered near him. And then, though, in all her very restricted intercourse with such English people as she met, she never ceased to ridicule things English, yet she dreaded a return to her own country. In her heart of hearts she liked the somewhat stupid tranquillity of the life she saw, comparing it with the rough tempests of her past days. Mrs. Pipkin, she thought, was less intellectual than any American woman she had ever known; and she was quite sure that no human being so heavy, so slow, and so incapable of two concurrent ideas as John Crumb had ever been produced in the United States;—but, nevertheless, she liked Mrs. Pipkin, and almost loved John Crumb. How different would her life have been could she have met a man who would have been as true to her as John Crumb was to his Ruby!

She loved Paul Montague with all her heart, and she despised herself for loving him. How weak he was;—how inefficient; how unable to seize glorious opportunities; how swathed and swaddled by scruples and prejudices;—how unlike her own countrymen in quickness of apprehension and readiness of action! But yet she loved him for his very faults, telling herself that there was something sweeter in his English manners than in all the smart intelligence of her own land. The man had been false to her,—false as hell; had sworn to her and had broken his oath; had ruined her whole life; had made everything blank before her by his treachery! But then she also had not been quite true with him. She had not at first meant to deceive;—nor had he. They had played a game against each other; and he, with all the inferiority of his intellect to weigh him down, had won,—because he was a man. She had much time for thinking, and she thought much about these things. He could change his love as often as he pleased, and be as good a lover at the end as ever;—whereas she was ruined by his defection. He could look about for a fresh flower and boldly seek his honey; whereas she could only sit and mourn for the sweets of which she had been rifled. She was not quite sure that such mourning would not be more bitter to her in California than in Mrs. Pipkin's solitary lodgings at Islington.

'So he was Mr. Montague's partner,—was he now?' asked Mrs. Pipkin a day or two after their return from the Crumb marriage. For Mr. Fisker had called on Mrs. Hurtle, and Mrs. Hurtle had told Mrs. Pipkin so much. 'To my thinking now he's a nicer man than Mr. Montague.' Mrs. Pipkin perhaps thought that as her lodger had lost one partner she might be anxious to secure the other;—perhaps felt, too, that it might be well to praise an American at the expense of an Englishman.

'There's no accounting for tastes, Mrs. Pipkin.'

'And that's true, too, Mrs. Hurtle.'

'Mr. Montague is a gentleman.'

'I always did say that of him, Mrs. Hurtle.'

'And Mr. Fisker is—an American citizen.' Mrs. Hurtle when she said this was very far gone in tenderness.

'Indeed now!' said Mrs. Pipkin, who did not in the least understand the meaning of her friend's last remark.

'Mr. Fisker came to me with tidings from San Francisco which I had not heard before, and has offered to take me back with him.' Mrs. Pipkin's apron was immediately at her eyes. 'I must go some day, you know.'

'I suppose you must. I couldn't hope as you'd stay here always. I wish I could. I never shall forget the comfort it's been. There hasn't been a week without everything settled; and most ladylike,—most ladylike! You seem to me, Mrs. Hurtle, just as though you had the bank in your pocket.' All this the poor woman said, moved by her sorrow to speak the absolute truth.

'Mr. Fisker isn't in any way a special friend of mine. But I hear that he will be taking other ladies with him, and I fancy I might as well join the party. It will be less dull for me, and I shall prefer company just at present for many reasons. We shall start on the first of September.' As this was said about the middle of August there was still some remnant of comfort for poor Mrs. Pipkin. A fortnight gained was something; and as Mr. Fisker had come to England on business, and as business is always uncertain, there might possibly be further delay. Then Mrs. Hurtle made a further communication to Mrs. Pipkin, which, though not spoken till the latter lady had her hand on the door, was, perhaps, the one thing which Mrs. Hurtle had desired to say. 'By-the-bye, Mrs. Pipkin, I expect Mr. Montague to call to-morrow at eleven. Just show him up when he comes.' She had feared that unless some such instructions were given, there might be a little scene at the door when the gentleman came.

'Mr. Montague;—oh! Of course, Mrs. Hurtle,—of course. I'll see to it myself.' Then Mrs. Pipkin went away abashed,—feeling that she had made a great mistake in preferring any other man to Mr. Montague, if, after all, recent difficulties were to be adjusted.

On the following morning Mrs. Hurtle dressed herself with almost more than her usual simplicity, but certainly with not less than her usual care, and immediately after breakfast seated herself at her desk, nursing an idea that she would work as steadily for the next hour as though she expected no special visitor. Of course she did not write a word of the task which she had prescribed to herself. Of course she was disturbed in her mind, though she had dictated to herself absolute quiescence.

She almost knew that she had been wrong even to desire to see him. She had forgiven him, and what more was there to be said? She had seen the girl, and had in some fashion approved of her. Her curiosity had been satisfied, and her love of revenge had been sacrificed. She had no plan arranged as to what she would now say to him, nor did she at this moment attempt to make a plan. She could tell him that she was about to return to San Francisco with Fisker, but she did not know that she had anything else to say. Then came the knock at the door. Her heart leaped within her, and she made a last great effort to be tranquil. She heard the steps on the stairs, and then the door was opened and Mr. Montague was announced by Mrs. Pipkin herself. Mrs. Pipkin, however, quite conquered by a feeling of gratitude to her lodger, did not once look in through the door, nor did she pause a moment to listen at the keyhole. 'I thought you would come and see me once again before I went,' said Mrs. Hurtle, not rising from her sofa, but putting out her hand to greet him. 'Sit there opposite, so that we can look at one another. I hope it has not been a trouble to you.'

'Of course I came when you left word for me to do so.'

'I certainly should not have expected it from any wish of your own.'

'I should not have dared to come, had you not bade me. You know that.'

'I know nothing of the kind;—but as you are here we will not quarrel as to your motives. Has Miss Carbury pardoned you as yet? Has she forgiven your sins?'

'We are friends,—if you mean that.'

'Of course you are friends. She only wanted to have somebody to tell her that somebody had maligned you. It mattered not much who it was. She was ready to believe any one who would say a good word for you. Perhaps I wasn't just the person to do it, but I believe even I was sufficient to serve the turn.'

'Did you say a good word for me?'

'Well; no;' replied Mrs. Hurtle. 'I will not boast that I did. I do not want to tell you fibs at our last meeting. I said nothing good of you. What could I say of good? But I told her what was quite as serviceable to you as though I had sung your virtues by the hour without ceasing. I explained to her how very badly you had behaved to me. I let her know that from the moment you had seen her, you had thrown me to the winds.'

'It was not so, my friend.'

'What did that matter? One does not scruple a lie for a friend, you know! I could not go into all the little details of your perfidies. I could not make her understand during one short and rather agonizing interview how you had allowed yourself to be talked out of your love for me by English propriety even before you had seen her beautiful eyes. There was no reason why I should tell her all my disgrace,—anxious as I was to be of service. Besides, as I put it, she was sure to be better

pleased. But I did tell her how unwillingly you had
spared me an hour of your company;—what a trouble
I had been to you;—how you would have shirked me if
you could!'

'Winifred, that is untrue.'

'That wretched journey to Lowestoft was the great
crime. Mr. Roger Carbury, who I own is poison to
me——'

'You do not know him.'

'Knowing him or not I choose to have my own opinion,
sir. I say that he is poison to me, and I say that he had
so stuffed her mind with the flagrant sin of that journey,
with the peculiar wickedness of our having lived for two
nights under the same roof, with the awful fact that we
had travelled together in the same carriage, till that had
become the one stumbling-block on your path to happiness.'

'He never said a word to her of our being there.'

'Who did then? But what matters? She knew it;—
and, as the only means of whitewashing you in her eyes,
I did tell her how cruel and how heartless you had been
to me. I did explain how the return of friendship which
you had begun to show me, had been frozen, harder than
Wenham ice,* by the appearance of Mr. Carbury on the
sands. Perhaps I went a little farther and hinted that the
meeting had been arranged as affording you the easiest
means of escape from me.'

'You do not believe that.'

'You see I had your welfare to look after; and the baser
your conduct had been to me, the truer you were in her
eyes. Do I not deserve some thanks for what I did?
Surely you would not have had me tell her that your conduct to me had been that of a loyal, loving gentleman.
I confessed to her my utter despair;—I abased myself in
the dust, as a woman is abased who has been treacherously
ill-used, and has failed to avenge herself. I knew that
when she was sure that I was prostrate and hopeless she
would be triumphant and contented. I told her on your
behalf how I had been ground to pieces under your
chariot wheels. And now you have not a word of thanks
to give me!'

'Every word you say is a dagger.'

'You know where to go for salve for such skin-deep scratches as I make. Where am I to find a surgeon who can put together my crushed bones? Daggers, indeed! Do you not suppose that in thinking of you I have often thought of daggers? Why have I not thrust one into your heart, so that I might rescue you from the arms of this puny, spiritless English girl?' All this time she was still seated, looking at him, leaning forward towards him with her hands upon her brow. 'But, Paul, I spit out my words to you, like any common woman, not because they will hurt you, but because I know I may take that comfort, such as it is, without hurting you. You are uneasy for a moment while you are here, and I have a cruel pleasure in thinking that you cannot answer me. But you will go from me to her, and then will you not be happy? When you are sitting with your arm round her waist, and when she is playing with your smiles, will the memory of my words interfere with your joy then? Ask yourself whether the prick will last longer than the moment. But where am I to go for happiness and joy? Can you understand what it is to have to live only on retrospects?'

'I wish I could say a word to comfort you.'

'You cannot say a word to comfort me, unless you will unsay all that you have said since I have been in England. I never expect comfort again. But, Paul, I will not be cruel to the end. I will tell you all that I know of my concerns, even though my doing so should justify your treatment of me. He is not dead.'

'You mean Mr. Hurtle.'

'Whom else should I mean? And he himself says that the divorce which was declared between us was no divorce. Mr. Fisker came here to me with tidings. Though he is not a man whom I specially love,—though I know that he has been my enemy with you,—I shall return with him to San Francisco.'

'I am told that he is taking Madame Melmotte with him, and Melmotte's daughter.'

'So I understand. They are adventurers,—as I am, and I do not see why we should not suit each other.'

'They say also that Fisker will marry Miss Melmotte.'

'Why should I object to that? I shall not be jealous of Mr. Fisker's attentions to the young lady. But it will suit me to have some one to whom I can speak on friendly terms when I am back in California. I may have a job of work to do there which will require the backing of some friends. I shall be hand-and-glove with these people before I have travelled half across the ocean with them.'

'I hope they will be kind to you,' said Paul.

'No;—but I will be kind to them. I have conquered others by being kind, but I have never had much kindness myself. Did I not conquer you, sir, by being gentle and gracious to you? Ah, how kind I was to that poor wretch, till he lost himself in drink! And then, Paul, I used to think of better people, perhaps of softer people, of things that should be clean and sweet and gentle,—of things that should smell of lavender instead of wild garlic. I would dream of fair, feminine women,—of women who would be scared by seeing what I saw, who would die rather than do what I did. And then I met you, Paul, and I said that my dreams should come true. I ought to have known that it could not be so. I did not dare quite to tell you all the truth. I know I was wrong, and now the punishment has come upon me. Well;—I suppose you had better say good-bye to me. What is the good of putting it off?' Then she rose from her chair and stood before him with her arms hanging listlessly by her side.

'God bless you, Winifred!' he said, putting out his hand to her.

'But he won't. Why should he,—if we are right in supposing that they who do good will be blessed for their good, and those who do evil cursed for their evil? I cannot do good. I cannot bring myself now not to wish that you would return to me. If you would come I should care nothing for the misery of that girl,—nothing, at least nothing now, for the misery I should certainly bring upon you. Look here;—will you have this back?' As she asked this she took from out her bosom a small miniature portrait of himself which he had given her in New York, and held it towards him.

'If you wish it I will,—of course,' he said.

'I would not part with it for all the gold in California. Nothing on earth shall ever part me from it. Should I ever marry another man,—as I may do,—he must take me and this together. While I live it shall be next my heart. As you know, I have little respect for the proprieties of life. I do not see why I am to abandon the picture of the man I love because he becomes the husband of another woman. Having once said that I love you I shall not contradict myself because you have deserted me. Paul, I have loved you, and do love you,—oh, with my very heart of hearts.' So speaking she threw herself into his arms and covered his face with kisses. 'For one moment you shall not banish me. For one short minute I will be here. Oh, Paul, my love;—my love!'

All this to him was simply agony,—though as she had truly said it was an agony he would soon forget. But to be told by a woman of her love,—without being able even to promise love in return,—to be so told while you are in the very act of acknowledging your love for another woman,—carries with it but little of the joy of triumph. He did not want to see her raging like a tigress, as he had once thought might be his fate; but he would have preferred the continuance of moderate resentment to this flood of tenderness. Of couse he stood with his arm round her waist, and of course he returned her caresses; but he did it with such stiff constraint that she at once felt how chill they were. 'There,' she said, smiling through her bitter tears,—'there; you are released now, and not even my fingers shall ever be laid upon you again. If I have annoyed you, at this our last meeting, you must forgive me.'

'No;—but you cut me to the heart.'

'That we can hardly help;—can we? When two persons have made fools of themselves as we have, there must I suppose be some punishment. Yours will never be heavy after I am gone. I do not start till the first of next month because that is the day fixed by our friend, Mr. Fisker, and I shall remain here till then because my presence is convenient to Mrs. Pipkin; but I need not trouble you to come to me again. Indeed it will be better that you should not. Good-bye.'

He took her by the hand, and stood for a moment looking at her, while she smiled and gently nodded her head at him. Then he essayed to pull her towards him as though he would again kiss her. But she repulsed him, still smiling the while. 'No, sir; no; not again; never again, never,—never,—never again.' By that time she had recovered her hand and stood apart from him. 'Good-bye, Paul;—and now go.' Then he turned round and left the room without uttering a word.

She stood still, without moving a limb, as she listened to his step down the stairs and to the opening and the closing of the door. Then hiding herself at the window with the scanty drapery of the curtain she watched him as he went along the street. When he had turned the corner she came back to the centre of the room, stood for a moment with her arms stretched out towards the walls, and then fell prone upon the floor. She had spoken the very truth when she said that she had loved him with all her heart.

But that evening she bade Mrs. Pipkin drink tea with her and was more gracious to the poor woman than ever. When the obsequious but still curious landlady asked some question about Mr. Montague, Mrs. Hurtle seemed to speak very freely on the subject of her late lover,—and to speak without any great pain. They had put their heads together, she said, and had found that the marriage would not be suitable. Each of them preferred their own country, and so they had agreed to part. On that evening Mrs. Hurtle made herself more than usually pleasant, having the children up into her room, and giving them jam and bread-and-butter. During the whole of the next fortnight she seemed to take a delight in doing all in her power for Mrs. Pipkin and her family. She gave toys to the children, and absolutely bestowed upon Mrs. Pipkin a new carpet for the drawing-room. Then Mr. Fisker came and took her away with him to America; and Mrs. Pipkin was left,—a desolate but grateful woman.

'They do tell bad things about them Americans,' she

said to a friend in the street, 'and I don't pretend to know. But for a lodger, I only wish Providence would send me another just like the one I have lost. She had that good nature about her she liked to see the bairns eating pudding just as if they was her own.'

I think Mrs. Pipkin was right, and that Mrs. Hurtle, with all her faults, was a good-natured woman.

## Chapter XCVIII

### MARIE MELMOTTE'S FATE

IN the meantime Marie Melmotte was living with Madame Melmotte in their lodgings up at Hampstead, and was taking quite a new look out into the world. Fisker had become her devoted servant,—not with that old-fashioned service which meant making love, but with perhaps a truer devotion to her material interests. He had ascertained on her behalf that she was the undoubted owner of the money which her father had made over to her on his first arrival in England,—and she also had made herself mistress of that fact with equal precision. It would have astonished those who had known her six months since could they now have seen how excellent a woman of business she had become, and how capable she was of making the fullest use of Mr. Fisker's services. In doing him justice it must be owned that he kept nothing back from her of that which he learned, probably feeling that he might best achieve success in his present project by such honesty,—feeling also, no doubt, the girl's own strength in discovering truth and falsehood. 'She's her father's own daughter,' he said one day to Croll in Abchurch Lane;—for Croll, though he had left Melmotte's employment when he found that his name had been forged, had now returned to the service of the daughter in some undefined position, and had been engaged to go with her and Madame Melmotte to New York.

'Ah; yees,' said Croll, 'but bigger. He vas passionate, and did lose his 'ead; and vas blow'd up vid bigness.' Whereupon Croll made an action as though he were a frog swelling himself to the dimensions of an ox. ''E bursted himself, Mr. Fisker. 'E vas a great man; but the greater he grew he vas always less and less vise. 'E ate so much that he became too fat to see to eat his vittels.' It was thus that Herr Croll analysed the character of his late master. 'But Ma'me'selle,—ah, she is different. She vill never eat too moch, but vill see to eat alvays.' Thus too he analysed the character of his young mistress.

At first things did not arrange themselves pleasantly between Madame Melmotte and Marie. The reader will perhaps remember that they were in no way connected by blood. Madame Melmotte was not Marie's mother, nor, in the eye of the law, could Marie claim Melmotte as her father. She was alone in the world, absolutely without a relation, not knowing even what had been her mother's name,—not even knowing what was her father's true name, as in the various biographies of the great man which were, as a matter of course, published within a fortnight of his death, various accounts were given as to his birth, parentage, and early history. The general opinion seemed to be that his father had been a noted coiner in New York,—an Irishman of the name of Melmody,—and, in one memoir, the probability of the descent was argued from Melmotte's skill in forgery. But Marie, though she was thus isolated, and now altogether separated from the lords and duchesses who a few weeks since had been interested in her career, was the undoubted owner of the money,—a fact which was beyond the comprehension of Madame Melmotte. She could understand,—and was delighted to understand,—that a very large sum of money had been saved from the wreck, and that she might therefore look forward to prosperous tranquillity for the rest of her life. Though she never acknowledged so much to herself, she soon learned to regard the removal of her husband as the end of her troubles. But she could not comprehend why Marie should claim all the money as her own. She declared herself to be quite willing to divide the spoil,—and suggested such an arrangement both to Marie and to Croll. Of Fisker she was afraid, thinking that the iniquity of giving all the money to Marie originated with him, in order that he might obtain it by marrying the girl. Croll, who understood it all perfectly, told her the story a dozen times,—but quite in vain. She made a timid suggestion of employing a lawyer on her own behalf, and was only deterred from doing so by Marie's ready assent to such an arrangement. Marie's equally ready surrender of any right she might have to a portion of the jewels which had been saved had perhaps some effect in softening the elder lady's heart. She thus was in possession of a treasure of her own,—though a treasure small in comparison with that of the younger woman; and the younger woman had promised that in the event of her marriage she would be liberal.

It was distinctly understood that they were both to go to New York under Mr. Fisker's guidance as soon as things should be sufficiently settled to allow of their departure; and Madame Melmotte was told, about the middle of August, that their places had been taken for the 3rd of September. But nothing more was told her. She did not as yet know whether Marie was to go out free or as the affianced bride of Hamilton Fisker. And she felt herself injured by being left so much in the dark. She herself was inimical to Fisker, regarding him as a dark, designing man, who would ultimately swallow up all that her husband had left behind him,—and trusted herself entirely to Croll, who was personally attentive to her. Fisker was, of course, going on to San Francisco. Marie also had talked of crossing the American continent. But Madame Melmotte was disposed to think that for her, with her jewels, and such share of the money as Marie might be induced to give her, New York would be the most fitting residence. Why should she drag herself across the continent to California? Herr Croll had declared his purpose of remaining in New York. Then it occurred to the lady that as Melmotte was a name which might be too well known in New York, and which it therefore might be wise to change, Croll would do as well as any other. She and Herr Croll had known each other for a great many years, and were, she thought, of about the same age. Croll had some money saved. She had, at any rate, her jewels,—and Croll would probably be able to get some portion of all that money, which ought to be hers, if his affairs were made to be identical with her own. So she smiled upon Croll, and whispered to him; and when she had given Croll two glasses of Curaçao,—which comforter she kept in her own hands, as safe guarded almost as the jewels,—then Croll understood her.

But it was essential that she should know what Marie intended to do. Marie was anything but communicative, and certainly was not in any way submissive. 'My dear,' she said one day, asking the question in French, without any preface or apology, 'are you going to be married to Mr. Fisker?'

'What makes you ask that?'

'It is so important I should know. Where am I to live? What am I to do? What money shall I have? Who will be a friend to me? A woman ought to know. You will marry Fisker if you like him. Why cannot you tell me?'

'Because I do not know. When I know I will tell you. If you go on asking me till to-morrow morning I can say no more.'

And this was true. She did not know. It certainly was not Fisker's fault that she should still be in the dark as to her own destiny, for he had asked her often enough, and had pressed his suit with all his eloquence. But Marie had now been wooed so often that she felt the importance of the step which was suggested to her. The romance of the thing was with her a good deal worn, and the material view of matrimony had also been damaged in her sight. She had fallen in love with Sir Felix Carbury, and had assured herself over and over again that she worshipped the very ground on which he stood. But she had taught herself this business of falling in love as a lesson, rather than felt it. After her father's first attempts to marry her to this and that suitor because of her wealth,—attempts which she had hardly opposed amidst the consternation and glitter of the world to which she was suddenly introduced,—she had learned from novels that it would be right that she should be in love, and she had chosen Sir Felix as her idol. The reader knows what had been the end of that episode in her life. She certainly was not now in love with Sir Felix Carbury. Then she had as it were relapsed into the hands of Lord Nidderdale,—one of her early suitors,—and had felt that as love was not to prevail, and as it would be well that she should marry some one, he might probably be as good as any other, and certainly better than many others. She had almost learned to like Lord Nidderdale and to believe that he liked her, when the tragedy came. Lord Nidderdale had been very good-natured,—but he had deserted her at last. She had never allowed herself to be angry with him for a moment. It had been a matter of course that he should do so. Her fortune was still large, but not so large as the sum named in the bargain made. And it was moreover weighted with her father's blood. From the moment of her father's death she had never dreamed that he would marry her. Why should he? Her thoughts in reference to Sir Felix were bitter enough;—but as against Nidderdale they were not at all bitter. Should she ever meet him again she would shake hands with him and smile,—if not pleasantly as she thought of the things which were past,—at any rate with good humour. But all this had not made her much in love with matrimony generally. She had over a hundred thousand pounds of her own, and, feeling conscious of her own power in regard to her own money, knowing that she could do as she pleased with her wealth, she began to look out into life seriously.

What could she do with her money, and in what way would she shape her life, should she determine to remain her own mistress? Were she to refuse Fisker how should she begin? He would then be banished, and her only remaining friends, the only persons whose names she would even know in her own country, would be her father's widow and Herr Croll. She already began to see Madame Melmotte's purport in reference to Croll, and could not reconcile herself to the idea of opening an establishment with them on a scale commensurate with her fortune. Nor could she settle in her own mind any pleasant position for herself as a single woman, living alone in perfect independence. She had opinions of women's rights,—especially in regard to money; and she entertained also a vague notion that in America a young woman would not need support so essentially as in England. Nevertheless, the idea of a fine house for herself in Boston, or Philadelphia,—for in that case she would have to avoid New York as the chosen residence of Madame Melmotte,—did not recommend itself to her. As to Fisker himself,—she certainly liked him. He was not beautiful like Felix Carbury, nor had he the easy good-humour of Lord Nidderdale. She had seen enough of English gentlemen to know that Fisker was very unlike them. But she had not seen enough of English gentlemen to make Fisker distasteful to her. He told her that he had a big house at San Francisco, and she certainly desired to live in a big house. He represented himself to be a thriving man, and she calculated that he certainly would not be here, in London, arranging her father's affairs, were he not possessed of commercial importance. She had contrived to learn that, in the United States, a married woman has greater power over her own money than in England, and this information acted strongly in Fisker's favour. On consideration of the whole subject she was inclined to think that she would do better in the world as Mrs. Fisker than as Marie Melmotte,—if she could see her way clearly in the matter of her own money.

'I have got excellent berths,' Fisker said to her one morning at Hampstead. At these interviews, which were devoted first to business and then to love, Madame Melmotte was never allowed to be present.

'I am to be alone?'

'Oh, yes. There is a cabin for Madame Melmotte and the maid, and a cabin for you. Everything will be comfortable. And there is another lady going,—Mrs. Hurtle, —whom I think you will like.'

'Has she a husband?'

'Not going with us,' said Mr. Fisker evasively.

'But she has one?'

'Well, yes;—but you had better not mention him. He is not exactly all that a husband should be.'

'Did she not come over here to marry some one else?'— For Marie in the days of her sweet intimacy with Sir Felix Carbury had heard something of Mrs. Hurtle's story.

'There is a story, and I dare say I shall tell you all about it some day. But you may be sure I should not ask you to associate with any one you ought not to know.'

'Oh,—I can take care of myself.'

'No doubt, Miss Melmotte,—no doubt. I feel that quite strongly. But what I meant to observe was this,— that I certainly should not introduce a lady whom I aspire to make my own lady to any lady whom a lady oughtn't to know. I hope I make myself understood, Miss Melmotte.'

'Oh, quite.'

'And perhaps I may go on to say that if I could go on board that ship as your accepted lover, I could do a deal more to make you comfortable, particularly when you land, than just as a mere friend, Miss Melmotte. You can't doubt my heart.'

'I don't see why I shouldn't. Gentlemen's hearts are things very much to be doubted as far as I've seen 'em. I don't think many of 'em have 'em at all.'

'Miss Melmotte, you do not know the glorious west. Your past experiences have been drawn from this effete and stone-cold country in which passion is no longer allowed to sway. On those golden shores which the Pacific washes man is still true,—and woman is still tender.'

'Perhaps I'd better wait and see, Mr. Fisker.'

But this was not Mr. Fisker's view of the case. There might be other men desirous of being true on those golden shores. 'And then,' said he, pleading his cause not without skill, 'the laws regulating woman's property there are just the reverse of those which the greediness of man has established here. The wife there can claim her share of her husband's property, but hers is exclusively her own. America is certainly the country for women,—and especially California.'*

'Ah;—I shall find out all about it, I suppose, when I've been there a few months.'

'But you would enter San Francisco, Miss Melmotte, under such much better auspices,—if I may be allowed to say so,—as a married lady or as a lady just going to be married.'

'Ain't single ladies much thought of in California?'

'It isn't that. Come, Miss Melmotte, you know what I mean.'

'Yes, I do.'

'Let us go in for life together. We've both done uncommon well. I'm spending 30,000 dollars a year,—at that rate,—in my own house. You'll see it all. If we put them both together,—what's yours and what's mine,—we can put our foot out as far as about any one there, I guess.'

'I don't know that I care about putting my foot out. I've seen something of that already, Mr. Fisker. You shouldn't put your foot out farther than you can draw it in again.'

'You needn't fear me as to that, Miss Melmotte. I shouldn't be able to touch a dollar of your money. It would be such a triumph to go into Francisco as man and wife.'

'I shouldn't think of being married till I had been there a while and looked about me.'

'And seen the house! Well;—there's something in that. The house is all there, I can tell you. I'm not a bit afraid but what you'll like the house. But if we were engaged, I could do everything for you. Where would you be, going into San Francisco all alone? Oh, Miss Melmotte, I do admire you so much!'

I doubt whether this last assurance had much efficacy. But the arguments with which it was introduced did prevail to a certain extent. 'I'll tell you how it must be then,' she said.

'How shall it be?' and as he asked the question he jumped up and put his arm round her waist.

'Not like that, Mr. Fisker,' she said, withdrawing herself. 'It shall be in this way. You may consider yourself engaged to me.'

'I'm the happiest man on this continent,' he said, forgetting in his ecstasy that he was not in the United States.

'But if I find when I get to Francisco anything to induce me to change my mind, I shall change it. I like you very well, but I'm not going to take a leap in the dark, and I'm not going to marry a pig in a poke.'

'There you're quite right,' he said,—'quite right.'

'You may give it out on board the ship that we're engaged, and I'll tell Madame Melmotte the same. She and Croll don't mean going any farther than New York.'

'We needn't break our hearts about that;—need we?'

'It don't much signify. Well;—I'll go on with Mrs. Hurtle, if she'll have me.'

'Too much delighted she'll be.'

'And she shall be told we're engaged.'

'My darling!'

'But if I don't like it when I get to Frisco, as you call it, all the ropes in California shan't make me do it. Well;— yes; you may give me a kiss I suppose now if you care about it.' And so,—or rather so far,—Mr. Fisker and Marie Melmotte became engaged to each other as man and wife.

After that Mr. Fisker's remaining business in England went very smoothly with him. It was understood up at Hampstead that he was engaged to Marie Melmotte,— and it soon came to be understood also that Madame Melmotte was to be married to Herr Croll. No doubt the father of the one lady and the husband of the other had died so recently as to make these arrangements subject to certain censorious objections. But there was a feeling that Melmotte had been so unlike other men, both in his life and in his death, that they who had been concerned with him were not to be weighed by ordinary scales. Nor did it much matter, for the persons concerned took their departure soon after the arrangement was made, and Hampstead knew them no more.

On the 3rd of September Madame Melmotte, Marie, Mrs. Hurtle, Hamilton K. Fisker, and Herr Croll left Liverpool for New York; and the three ladies were deter-

mined that they never would revisit a country of which
their reminiscences certainly were not happy. The writer
of the present chronicle may so far look forward,—
carrying his reader with him,—as to declare that Marie
Melmotte did become Mrs. Fisker very soon after her
arrival at San Francisco.

## Chapter XCIX

### LADY CARBURY AND MR. BROUNE

WHEN Sir Felix Carbury declared to his friends at the
Beargarden that he intended to devote the next few
months of his life to foreign travel, and that it was his
purpose to take with him a Protestant divine,—as was
much the habit with young men of rank and fortune some
years since,—he was not altogether lying. There was
indeed a sounder basis of truth than was usually to be
found attached to his statements. That he should have
intended to produce a false impression was a matter of
course,— and nearly equally so that he should have made
his attempt by asserting things which he must have known
that no one would believe. He was going to Germany,
and he was going in company with a clergyman, and it
had been decided that he should remain there for the
next twelve months. A representation had lately been
made to the Bishop of London that the English Protestants settled in a certain commercial town in the north-
eastern district of Prussia were without pastoral aid, and
the bishop had stirred himself in the matter. A clergyman
was found willing to expatriate himself, but the income
suggested was very small. The Protestant English population of the commercial town in question, though pious,
was not liberal. It had come to pass that the 'Morning
Breakfast Table' had interested itself in the matter,
having appealed for subscriptions after a manner not
unusual with that paper. The bishop and all those concerned in the matter had fully understood that if the

'Morning Breakfast Table' could be got to take the matter up heartily, the thing would be done. The heartiness had been so complete that it had at last devolved upon Mr. Broune to appoint the clergyman; and, as with all the aid that could be found, the income was still small, the Rev. Septimus Blake,—a brand snatched from the burning of Rome,—had been induced to undertake the maintenance and total charge of Sir Felix Carbury for a consideration. Mr. Broune imparted to Mr. Blake all that there was to know about the baronet, giving much counsel as to the management of the young man, and specially enjoining on the clergyman that he should on no account give Sir Felix the means of returning home. It was evidently Mr. Broune's anxious wish that Sir Felix should see as much as possible of German life, at a comparatively moderate expenditure, and under circumstances that should be externally respectable if not absolutely those which a young gentleman might choose for his own comfort or profit;—but especially that those circumstances should not admit of the speedy return to England of the young gentleman himself.

Lady Carbury had at first opposed the scheme. Terribly difficult as was to her the burden of maintaining her son, she could not endure the idea of driving him into exile. But Mr. Broune was very obstinate, very reasonable, and, as she thought, somewhat hard of heart. 'What is to be the end of it then?' he said to her, almost in anger. For in those days the great editor, when in presence of Lady Carbury, differed very much from that Mr. Broune who used to squeeze her hand and look into her eyes. His manner with her had become so different that she regarded him as quite another person. She hardly dared to contradict him, and found herself almost compelled to tell him what she really felt and thought. 'Do you mean to let him eat up everything you have to your last shilling, and then go to the workhouse with him?'

'Oh, my friend, you know how I am struggling! Do not say such horrid things.'

'It is because I know how you are struggling that I find

myself compelled to say anything on the subject. What hardship will there be in his living for twelve months with a clergyman in Prussia? What can he do better? What better chance can he have of being weaned from the life he is leading?'

'If he could only be married!'

'Married! Who is to marry him? Why should any girl with money throw herself away upon him?'

'He is so handsome.'

'What has his beauty brought him to? Lady Carbury, you must let me tell you that all that is not only foolish but wrong. If you keep him here you will help to ruin him, and will certainly ruin yourself. He has agreed to go;—let him go.'

She was forced to yield. Indeed, as Sir Felix had himself assented, it was almost impossible that she should not do so. Perhaps Mr. Broune's greatest triumph was due to the talent and firmness with which he persuaded Sir Felix to start upon his travels. 'Your mother,' said Mr. Broune, 'has made up her mind that she will not absolutely beggar your sister and herself in order that your indulgence may be prolonged for a few months. She cannot make you go to Germany of course. But she can turn you out of her house, and, unless you go, she will do so.'

'I don't think she ever said that, Mr. Broune.'

'No;—she has not said so. But I have said it for her in her presence; and she has acknowledged that it must necessarily be so. You may take my word as a gentleman that it will be so. If you take my advice £175 a year will be paid for your maintenance;—but if you remain in England not a shilling further will be paid.' He had no money. His last sovereign was all but gone. Not a tradesman would give him credit for a coat or a pair of boots. The key of the door had been taken away from him. The very page treated him with contumely. His clothes were becoming rusty. There was no prospect of amusement for him during the coming autumn or winter. He did not anticipate much excitement in Eastern Prussia, but he thought that any change must be a change for the better.

He assented, therefore, to the proposition made by Mr.
Broune, was duly introduced to the Rev. Septimus
Blake, and, as he spent his last sovereign on a last dinner
at the Beargarden, explained his intentions for the immediate future to those friends at his club who would no
doubt mourn his departure.

Mr. Blake and Mr. Broune between them did not allow
the grass to grow under their feet. Before the end of
August Sir Felix, with Mr. and Mrs. Blake and the young
Blakes, had embarked from Hull for Hamburg,—having
extracted at the very hour of parting a last five pound
note from his foolish mother. 'It will be just enough to
bring him home,' said Mr. Broune with angry energy
when he was told of this. But Lady Carbury, who knew
her son well, assured him that Felix would be restrained
in his expenditure by no such prudence as such a purpose
would indicate. 'It will be gone,' she said, 'long before
they reach their destination.'

'Then why the deuce should you give it him?' said
Mr. Broune.

Mr. Broune's anxiety had been so intense that he had
paid half a year's allowance in advance to Mr. Blake out
of his own pocket. Indeed, he had paid various sums for
Lady Carbury,—so that that unfortunate woman would
often tell herself that she was becoming subject to the
great editor, almost like a slave. He came to her, three
or four times a week, at about nine o'clock in the evening,
and gave her instructions as to all that she should do.
'I wouldn't write another novel if I were you,' he said.
This was hard, as the writing of novels was her great
ambition, and she had flattered herself that the one novel
which she had written was good. Mr. Broune's own
critic had declared it to be very good in glowing language. The 'Evening Pulpit' had of course abused it,—
because it is the nature of the 'Evening Pulpit' to abuse. So
she had argued with herself, telling herself that the praise
was all true, whereas the censure had come from malice.
After that article in the 'Breakfast Table,' it did seem
hard that Mr. Broune should tell her to write no more
novels. She looked up at him piteously but said nothing.

'I don't think you'd find it answer. Of course you can do it as well as a great many others. But then that is saying so little!'

'I thought I could make some money.'

'I don't think Mr. Leadham would hold out to you very high hopes;—I don't, indeed. I think I would turn to something else.'

'It is so very hard to get paid for what one does.'

To this Mr. Broune made no immediate answer; but, after sitting for a while, almost in silence, he took his leave. On that very morning Lady Carbury had parted from her son. She was soon about to part from her daughter, and she was very sad. She felt that she could hardly keep up that house in Welbeck Street for herself, even if her means permitted it. What should she do with herself? Whither should she take herself? Perhaps the bitterest drop in her cup had come from those words of Mr. Broune forbidding her to write more novels. After all, then, she was not a clever woman,—not more clever than other women around her! That very morning she had prided herself on her coming success as a novelist, basing all her hopes on that review in the 'Breakfast Table.' Now, with that reaction of spirits which is so common to all of us, she was more than equally despondent. He would not thus have crushed her without a reason. Though he was hard to her now,—he who used to be so soft,—he was very good. It did not occur to her to rebel against him. After what he had said, of course there would be no more praise in the 'Breakfast Table,'—and, equally of course, no novel of hers could succeed without that. The more she thought of him, the more omnipotent he seemed to be. The more she thought of herself, the more absolutely prostrate she seemed to have fallen from those high hopes with which she had begun her literary career not much more than twelve months ago.

On the next day he did not come to her at all, and she sat idle, wretched, and alone. She could not interest herself in Hetta's coming marriage, as that marriage was in direct opposition to one of her broken schemes. She had not ventured to confess so much to Mr. Broune, but she had in truth written the first pages of the first chapter of a second novel. It was impossible now that she should even look at what she had written. All this made her very sad. She spent the evening quite alone; for Hetta was staying down in Suffolk, with her cousin's friend, Mrs. Yeld, the bishop's wife; and as she thought of her life past and her life to come, she did, perhaps, with a broken light, see something of the error of her ways, and did, after a fashion, repent. It was all 'leather or prunello,'* as she said to herself;—it was all vanity,— and vanity,— and vanity! What real enjoyment had she found in anything? She had only taught herself to believe that some day something would come which she would like;—but she had never as yet in truth found anything to like. It had all been in anticipation,—but now even her anticipations were at an end. Mr. Broune had sent her son away, had forbidden her to write any more novels,—and had been refused when he had asked her to marry him!

The next day he came to her as usual, and found her still very wretched. 'I shall give up this house,' she said. 'I can't afford to keep it; and in truth I shall not want it. I don't in the least know where to go, but I don't think that it much signifies. Any place will be the same to me now.'

'I don't see why you should say that.'

'What does it matter?'

'You wouldn't think of going out of London.'

'Why not? I suppose I had better go wherever I can live cheapest.'

'I should be sorry that you should be settled where I could not see you,' said Mr. Broune plaintively.

'So shall I,—very. You have been more kind to me than anybody. But what am I to do? If I stay in London I can live only in some miserable lodgings. I know you will laugh at me, and tell me that I am wrong; but my idea is that I shall follow Felix wherever he goes, so that I may be near him and help him when he needs help. Hetta doesn't want me. There is nobody else that I can do any good to.'

'I want you,' said Mr. Broune, very quietly.

'Ah,—that is so kind of you. There is nothing makes one so good as goodness;—nothing binds your friend to you so firmly as the acceptance from him of friendly actions. You say you want me, because I have so sadly wanted you. When I go you will simply miss an almost daily trouble, but where shall I find a friend?'

'When I said I wanted you, I meant more than that, Lady Carbury. Two or three months ago I asked you to be my wife. You declined, chiefly, if I understood you rightly, because of your son's position. That has been altered, and therefore I ask you again. I have quite convinced myself,—not without some doubts, for you shall know all; but, still, I have quite convinced myself,—that such a marriage will best contribute to my own happiness. I do not think, dearest, that it would mar yours.'

This was said with so quiet a voice and so placid a demeanour, that the words, though they were too plain to be misunderstood, hardly at first brought themselves home to her. Of course he had renewed his offer of marriage, but he had done so in a tone which almost made her feel that the proposition could not be an earnest one. It was not that she believed that he was joking with her or paying her a poor insipid compliment. When she thought about it at all, she knew that it could not be so. But the thing was so improbable! Her opinion of herself was so poor, she had become so sick of her own vanities and littlenesses and pretences, that she could not understand that such a man as this should in truth want to make her his wife. At this moment she thought less of herself and more of Mr. Broune than either perhaps deserved. She sat silent, quite unable to look him in the face, while he kept his place in his arm-chair, lounging back, with his eyes intent on her countenance. 'Well,' he said; 'what do you think of it? I never loved you better than I did for refusing me before, because I thought that you did so because it was not right that I should be embarrassed by your son.'

'That was the reason,' she said, almost in a whisper.

'But I shall love you better still for accepting me now, —if you will accept me.'

The long vista of her past life appeared before her eyes. The ambition of her youth which had been taught to look only to a handsome maintenance, the cruelty of her husband which had driven her to run from him, the further cruelty of his forgiveness when she returned to him; the calumny which had made her miserable, though she had never confessed her misery; then her attempts at life in London, her literary successes and failures, and the wretchedness of her son's career;—there had never been happiness, or even comfort, in any of it. Even when her smiles had been sweetest her heart had been heaviest. Could it be that now at last real peace should be within her reach, and that tranquillity which comes from an anchor holding to a firm bottom? Then she remembered that first kiss,—or attempted kiss,—when, with a sort of pride in her own superiority, she had told herself that the man was a susceptible old goose. She certainly had not thought then that his susceptibility was of this nature. Nor could she quite understand now whether she had been right then, and that the man's feelings, and almost his nature, had since changed,—or whether he had really loved her from first to last. As he remained silent it was necessary that she should answer him. 'You can hardly have thought of it enough,' she said.

'I have thought of it a good deal too. I have been thinking of it for six months at least.'

'There is so much against me.'

'What is there against you?'

'They say bad things of me in India.'

'I know all about that,' replied Mr. Broune.

'And Felix!'

'I think I may say that I know all about that also.'

'And then I have become so poor!'

'I am not proposing to myself to marry you for your money. Luckily for me,—I hope luckily for both of us,—i tis not necessary that I should do so.'

'And then I seem so to have fallen through in everything. I don't know what I've got to give to a man in eturn for all that you offer to give to me.'

'Yourself,' he said, stretching out his right hand to her.

And there he sat with it stretched out,—so that she found herself compelled to put her own into it, or to refuse to do so with very absolute words. Very slowly she put out her own, and gave it to him without looking at him. Then he drew her towards him, and in a moment she was kneeling at his feet, with her face buried on his knees. Considering their ages perhaps we must say that their attitude was awkward. They would certainly have thought so themselves had they imagined that any one could have seen them. But how many absurdities of the kind are not only held to be pleasant, but almost holy,—as long as they remain mysteries inspected by no profane eyes! It is not that Age is ashamed of feeling passion and acknowledging it,—but that the display of it is without the graces of which Youth is proud, and which Age regrets.

On that occasion there was very little more said between them. He had certainly been in earnest, and she had now accepted him. As he went down to his office he told himself now that he had done the best, not only for her but for himself also. And yet I think that she had won him more thoroughly by her former refusal than by any other virtue.

She, as she sat alone, late into the night, became subject to a thorough reaction of spirit. That morning the world had been a perfect blank to her. There was no single object of interest before her. Now everything was rose-coloured. This man who had thus bound her to him, who had given her such assured proofs of his affection and truth, was one of the considerable ones of the world: a man than whom few,—so she told herself,—were greater or more powerful. Was it not a career enough for any woman to be the wife of such a man, to receive his friends, and to shine with his reflected glory?

Whether her hopes were realised, or,—as human hopes never are realised,—how far her content was assured, these pages cannot tell; but they must tell that, before the coming winter was over, Lady Carbury became the wife of Mr. Broune, and, in furtherance of her own resolve, took her husband's name. The house in Welbeck Street was kept, and Mrs. Broune's Tuesday evenings were much more regarded by the literary world than had been those of Lady Carbury.

## Chapter C

### DOWN IN SUFFOLK

IT need hardly be said that Paul Montague was not long in adjusting his affairs with Hetta after the visit which he received from Roger Carbury. Early on the following morning he was once more in Welbeck Street, taking the brooch with him; and though at first Lady Carbury kept up her opposition, she did it after so weak a fashion as to throw in fact very little difficulty in his way. Hetta understood perfectly that she was in this matter stronger than her mother and that she need fear nothing, now that Roger Carbury was on her side. 'I don't know what you mean to live on,' Lady Carbury said, threatening future evils in a plaintive tone. Hetta repeated, though in other language, the assurance which the young lady made who declared that if her future husband would consent to live on potatoes, she would be quite satisfied with the potato-peelings; while Paul made some vague allusion to the satisfactory nature of his final arrangements with the house of Fisker, Montague, and Montague. 'I don't see anything like an income,' said Lady Carbury; 'but I suppose Roger will make it right. He takes everything upon himself now it seems.' But this was before the halcyon day of Mr. Broune's second offer.

It was at any rate decided that they were to be married, and the time fixed for the marriage was to be the following spring. When this was finally arranged Roger Carbury, who had returned to his own home, conceived the idea that it would be well that Hetta should pass the autumn and if possible the winter also down in Suffolk, so that she might get used to him in the capacity which

he now aspired to fill; and with that object he induced
Mrs. Yeld, the Bishop's wife, to invite her down to the
palace. Hetta accepted the invitation and left London
before she could hear the tidings of her mother's engagement with Mr. Broune.

Roger Carbury had not yielded in this matter,—had
not brought himself to determine that he would recognize
Paul and Hetta as acknowledged lovers,—without a
fierce inward contest. Two convictions had been strong
in his mind, both of which were opposed to this recogni-
tion,—the first telling him that he would be a fitter
husband for the girl than Paul Montague, and the second
assuring him that Paul had ill-treated him in such a
fashion that forgiveness would be both foolish and unmanly. For Roger, though he was a religious man, and
one anxious to conform to the spirit of Christianity, would
not allow himself to think that an injury should be forgiven unless the man who did the injury repented of his
own injustice. As to giving his coat to the thief who had
taken his cloak,—he told himself that were he and others
to be guided by that precept honest industry would go
naked in order that vice and idleness might be comfortably clothed. If any one stole his cloak he would certainly
put that man in prison as soon as possible and not commence his lenience till the thief should at any rate affect
to be sorry for his fault. Now, to his thinking, Paul
Montague had stolen his cloak, and were he, Roger, to
give way in this matter of his love, he would be giving
Paul his coat also. No! He was bound after some fashion
to have Paul put into prison; to bring him before a jury,
and to get a verdict against him, so that some sentence
of punishment might be at least pronounced. How then
could he yield?

And Paul Montague had shown himself to be very
weak in regard to women. It might be,—no doubt it was
true,—that Mrs. Hurtle's appearance in England had
been distressing to him. But still he had gone down with
her to Lowestoft as her lover, and, to Roger's thinking, a
man who could do that was quite unfit to be the husband
of Hetta Carbury. He would himself tell no tales against

Montague on that head. Even when pressed to do so he had told no tale. But not the less was his conviction strong that Hetta ought to know the truth, and to be induced by that knowledge to reject her younger lover.

But then over these convictions there came a third,—equally stong,—which told him that the girl loved the younger man and did not love him, and that if he loved the girl it was his duty as a man to prove his love by doing what he could to make her happy. As he walked up and down the walk by the moat, with his hands clasped behind his back, stopping every now and again to sit on the terrace wall,—walking there, mile after mile, with his mind intent on the one idea,—he schooled himself to feel that that, and that only, could be his duty. What did love mean if not that? What could be the devotion which men so often affect to feel if it did not tend to self-sacrifice on behalf of the beloved one? A man would incur any danger for a woman, would subject himself to any toil,—would even die for her! But if this were done simply with the object of winning her, where was that real love of which sacrifice of self on behalf of another is the truest proof? So, by degrees, he resolved that the thing must be done. The man, though he had been bad to his friend, was not all bad. He was one who might become good in good hands. He, Roger, was too firm of purpose and too honest of heart to buoy himself up into new hopes by assurances of the man's unfitness. What right had he to think that he could judge of that better than the girl herself? And so, when many many miles had been walked, he succeeded in conquering his own heart,—though in conquering it he crushed it,—and in bringing himself to the resolve that the energies of his life should be devoted to the task of making Mrs. Paul Montague a happy woman. We have seen how he acted up to this resolve when last in London, withdrawing at any rate all signs of anger from Paul Montague and behaving with the utmost tenderness to Hetta.

When he had accomplished that task of conquering his own heart and of assuring himself thoroughly that Hetta was to become his rival's wife, he was, I think, more at

ease and less troubled in his spirit than he had been
during these months in which there had still been doubt.
The sort of happiness which he had once pictured to himself could certainly never be his. That he would never
marry he was quite sure. Indeed he was prepared to
settle Carbury on Hetta's eldest boy on condition that
such boy should take the old name. He would never have
a child whom he could in truth call his own. But if he
could induce these people to live at Carbury, or to live
there for at least a part of the year, so that there should
be some life in the place, he thought that he could awaken
himself again, and again take an interest in the property.
But as a first step to this he must learn to regard himself
as an old man,—as one who had let life pass by too far
for the purposes of his own home, and who must therefore
devote himself to make happy the homes of others.

So thinking of himself and so resolving, he had told
much of his story to his friend the Bishop, and as a consequence of those revelations Mrs. Yeld had invited
Hetta down to the palace. Roger felt that he had still
much to say to his cousin before her marriage which
could be said in the country much better than in town,
and he wished to teach her to regard Suffolk as the county
to which she should be attached and in which she was to
find her home. The day before she came he was over at
the palace with the pretence of asking permission to come
and see his cousin soon after her arrival, but in truth with
the idea of talking about Hetta to the only friend to whom
he had looked for sympathy in his trouble. 'As to settling
your property on her or her children,' said the Bishop,
'it is quite out of the question. Your lawyer would not
allow you to do it. Where would you be if after all you
were to marry?'

'I shall never marry.'

'Very likely not,—but yet you may. How is a man of
your age to speak with certainty of what he will do or
what he will not do in that respect? You can make your
will, doing as you please with your property;—and the
will, when made, can be revoked.'

'I think you hardly understand just what I feel,' said

Roger, 'and I know very well that I am unable to explain it. But I wish to act exactly as I would do if she were my daughter, and as if her son, if she had a son, would be my natural heir.'

'But, if she were your daughter, her son wouldn't be your natural heir as long as there was a probability or even a chance that you might have a son of your own. A man should never put the power, which properly belongs to him, out of his own hands. If it does properly belong to you it must be better with you than elsewhere. I think very highly of your cousin, and I have no reason to think otherwise than well of the gentleman whom she intends to marry. But it is only human nature to suppose that the fact that your property is still at your own disposal should have some effect in producing the more complete observance of your wishes.'

'I do not believe it in the least, my lord,' said Roger somewhat angrily.

'That is because you are so carried away by enthusiasm at the present moment as to ignore the ordinary rules of life. There are not, perhaps, many fathers who have Regans and Gonerils for their daughters;—but there are very many who may take a lesson from the folly of the old king. "Thou hadst little wit in thy bald crown," the fool said to him, "when thou gav'st thy golden one away."* The world, I take it, thinks that the fool was right.'

The Bishop did so far succeed that Roger abandoned the idea of settling his property on Paul Montague's children. But he was not on that account the less resolute in his determination to make himself and his own interests subordinate to those of his cousin. When he came over, two days afterwards, to see her he found her in the garden, and walked there with her for a couple of hours. 'I hope all our troubles are over now,' he said smiling.

'You mean about Felix,' said Hetta,—'and mamma?'

'No, indeed. As to Felix I think that Lady Carbury has done the best thing in her power. No doubt she has been advised by Mr. Broune, and Mr. Broune seems to be a prudent man. And about your mother herself, I hope that she may now be comfortable. But I was not alluding to Felix and your mother. I was thinking of you —and of myself.'

'I hope that you will never have any troubles.'

'I have had troubles. I mean to speak very freely to you now, dear. I was nearly upset,—what I suppose people call broken-hearted,—when I was assured that you certainly would never become my wife. I ought not to have allowed myself to get into such a frame of mind. I should have known that I was too old to have a chance.'

'Oh, Roger,—it was not that.'

'Well,—that and other things. I should have known it sooner, and have got over my misery quicker. I should have been more manly and stronger. After all, though love is a wonderful incident in a man's life, it is not that only that he is here for. I have duties plainly marked out for me; and as I should never allow myself to be withdrawn from them by pleasure, so neither should I by sorrow. But it is done now. I have conquered my regrets, and I can say with safety that I look forward to your presence and Paul's presence at Carbury as the source of all my future happiness. I will make him welcome as though he were my brother, and you as though you were my daughter. All I ask of you is that you will not be chary of your presence there.' She only answered him by a close pressure on his arm. 'That is what I wanted to say to you. You will teach yourself to regard me as your best and closest friend,—as he on whom you have the strongest right to depend, of all,—except your husband?'

'There is no teaching necessary for that,' she said.

'As a daughter leans on a father I would have you lean on me, Hetta. You will soon come to find that I am very old. I grow old quickly, and already feel myself to be removed from everything that is young and foolish.'

'You never were foolish.'

'Nor young either, I sometimes think. But now you must promise me this. You will do all that you can to induce him to make Carbury his residence.'

'We have no plans as yet at all, Roger.'

'Then it will be certainly so much the easier for you to

fall into my plan. Of course you will be married at Carbury?'

'What will mamma say?'

'She will come here, and I am sure will enjoy it. That I regard as settled. Then, after that, let this be your home,—so that you should learn really to care about and to love the place. It will be your home really, you know, some of these days. You will have to be Squire of Carbury yourself when I am gone, till you have a son old enough to fill that exalted position.' With all his love to her and his good-will to them both, he could not bring himself to say that Paul Montague should be Squire of Carbury.

'Oh, Roger, please do not talk like that.'

'But it is necessary, my dear. I want you to know what my wishes are, and, if it be possible, I would learn what are yours. My mind is quite made up as to my future life. Of course, I do not wish to dictate to you,—and if I did, I could not dictate to Mr. Montague.'

'Pray,—pray do not call him Mr. Montague.'

'Well, I will not;—to Paul then. There goes the last of my anger.' He threw his hands up as though he were scattering his indignation to the air. 'I would not dictate either to you or to him, but it is right that you should know that I hold my property as steward for those who are to come after me, and that the satisfaction of my stewardship will be infinitely increased if I find that those for whom I act share the interest which I shall take in the matter. It is the only payment which you and he can make me for my trouble.'

'But Felix, Roger!'

His brow became a little black as he answered her. 'To a sister,' he said very solemnly, 'I will not say a word against her brother; but on that subject I claim a right to come to a decision on my own judgment. It is a matter in which I have thought much, and, I may say, suffered much. I have ideas, old-fashioned ideas, on the matter, which I need not pause to explain to you now. If we are as much together as I hope we shall be, you will, no doubt, come to understand them. The disposition of a family property, even though it be one so small as mine, is, to my thinking, a matter which a man should not make in accordance with his own caprices,—or even with his own affections. He owes a duty to those who live on his land, and he owes a duty to his country. And, though it may seem fantastic to say so, I think he owes a duty to those who have been before him, and who have manifestly wished that the property should be continued in the hands of their descendants. These things are to me very holy. In what I am doing I am in some respects departing from the theory of my life,—but I do so under a perfect conviction that by the course I am taking I shall best perform the duties to which I have alluded. I do not think, Hetta, that we need say any more about that.' He had spoken so seriously, that, though she did not quite understand all that he had said, she did not venture to dispute his will any further. He did not endeavour to exact from her any promise, but having explained his purposes, kissed her as he would have kissed a daughter, and then left her and rode home without going into the house.

Soon after that, Paul Montague came down to Carbury, and the same thing was said to him, though in a much less solemn manner. Paul was received quite in the old way. Having declared that he would throw all anger behind him, and that Paul should be again Paul, he rigidly kept his promise, whatever might be the cost to his own feelings. As to his love for Hetta, and his old hopes, and the disappointment which had so nearly unmanned him, he said not another word to his fortunate rival. Montague knew it all, but there was now no necessity that any allusion should be made to past misfortunes. Roger indeed made a solemn resolution that to Paul he would never again speak of Hetta as the girl whom he himself had loved, though he looked forward to a time, probably many years hence, when he might perhaps remind her of his fidelity. But he spoke much of the land and of the tenants and the labourers, of his own farm, of the amount of the income, and of the necessity of so living that the income might always be more than sufficient for the wants of the household.

When the spring came round, Hetta and Paul were married by the Bishop at the parish church of Carbury, and Roger Carbury gave away the bride. All those who saw the ceremony declared that the squire had not seemed to be so happy for many a long year. John Crumb, who was there with his wife,—himself now one of Roger's tenants, having occupied the land which had become vacant by the death of old Daniel Ruggles,—declared that the wedding was almost as good fun as his own. 'John, what a fool you are!' Ruby said to her spouse, when this opinion was expressed with rather a loud voice. 'Yes, I be,' said John,—'but not such a fool as to a missed a having o' you.' 'No, John; it was I was the fool then,' said Ruby. 'We'll see about that when the bairn's born,' said John,—equally aloud. Then Ruby held her tongue. Mrs. Broune, and Mr. Broune, were also at Carbury,—thus doing great honour to Mr. and Mrs. Paul Montague, and showing by their presence that all family feuds were at an end. Sir Felix was not there. Happily up to this time Mr. Septimus Blake had continued to keep that gentleman as one of his Protestant population in the German town,—no doubt not without considerable trouble to himself.

**THE END**

## I

There are a number of interesting plans and layouts for
the novel in the Trollope collection at the Bodleian
Library. The most substantial is a *dramatis personae* which
the novelist drew up for his first spell of composition
(numbers 1–3, May 1873). His early conception of the
work as 'the Carbury novel' is here very pronounced.
Since a slightly abbreviated transcription of this plan is
given as an appendix to Sadleir's *Commentary*, I shall
restrict comment to points of outstanding interest.

The first entry is on Lady Carbury, '*the chief character*'.
It encapsulates the main features of her character and
background which we are to discover in Chapters I and
II: her late husband's brutality, her poverty, her am-
bitions in authorship, her want of principle. All her vices
are set against her one virtue: she is 'capable of great
sacrifice for her son'. Crossings out indicate that originally Lady Carbury was to be forty-seven rather than
fory-three (which would have inhibited the flirtatious-
ness Trollope makes note of) and she was going to live in
Marylebone, closer to the novelist's new London house.

The second entry is on Felix. His 'beauty' and his
profligacy are stressed together with the fact that he has
sold out from the Guards. In outline, it is pretty much
as we are introduced to the young baronet in Chapter II.
But it is strongly suggested that Trollope's first conception
of Felix was as another Burgo Fitzgerald: 'reckless from
utter thoughtlessness, debts paid by mother, by sister's
lover, by the lady who loves him' (these last two benefac-
tors do not turn up in the novel, incidentally). Most
intriguingly, the last observation (which Sadleir omits) is
'Dies.' Felix in the novel does not die; did he do so, it

would be another link with *Can You Forgive Her*'s doomed
Byronic hero.    As an afterthought, in the margin,
Trollope added: 'Felix a coward.'    And this is very much
the cad whom we actually encounter in *The Way We Live
Now*.

The next entry is on Hetta Carbury.    There is nothing
very noteworthy except that she 'loves her brother', which
she doesn't particularly in the written novel (was Trollope
thinking of Burgo-Felix?).    And there is some complicated
inheritance business with £6,000 which does not figure
in the event.    At this primary stage, however, Trollope
clearly preconceived the Paul, Roger, Hetta triangle
and meant it to feature centrally.

The next entry is on Roger Carbury and its prefigur-
ation is somewhat different from what emerges in the
narrative.    Roger is 'very good' and the 'Hero of the
book'; he will 'sacrifice himself at last'.    Although he does
come out as virtuous and self-denying in his love, the
novel's Roger can surely not be termed 'hero'.    Life at
Carbury Hall (originally in Norfolk) was evidently to
figure more than it eventually does.    Most interestingly,
'Doubts about his religion' were to be important—hence
the large build-up early in the novel of the characters of
the Bishop and Father Barham.

The fifth, which is the last substantial entry, is on Paul
Montagu (*sic*, after the Square where Trollope was now
living).    'Gets into some scrapes which must be devised',
noted Trollope vaguely.    In the margin, later evidently,
he specified those scrapes: 'Mrs Hurtle Winifred . . .
Caradoc Carson Hurtle . . . Montagu's pledge' (i.e. to
marry the supposed widow).    Nonetheless the happy
ending—'marries at last under the auspices of Roger'—
was manifestly one of the first things Trollope thought of.
But another first thought, that Paul should be politically
radical and disgust Roger, was, like the other's religious
doubts, dropped.

These five entries make up over half the plan, and
define the nucleus of the 'Carbury novel' which Trollope
superseded with the Melmotte novel.    The remaining
notes are on secondary characters (as they were orig-

inally ranked). The Bishop of Elmham Trollope simply described as 'old Longley'; that is to say, the recently deceased Archbishop of Canterbury who had once been the novelist's headmaster. Trollope playfully reverses this, with a little doodle, into 'Yelgnol', which is then changed to the 'Yeld' of the novel. Subsequent notes briefly mention the Hepworths and the Longestaffes. On the Longestaffe entry Squercum is added as an afterthought on one margin, and Pickering Park on the other.

There is some interest, perhaps, in Broune's originally being 'Balfe' and Booker 'Alfred Shand', since these too may also be references to real people. But in what is little more than a name-list the main interest attaches to Augustus Melmotte. He is only mentioned parenthetically 'Marie Melmotte. The heiress. Daughter of Augustus Melmotte, great French swindler.' Originally Melmotte and his daughter (first thought of as 'Maryanne') had a surname I can't read, and the swindler's forename was first 'Emanuel', then 'Samuel' and only at the third try 'Augustus'. And his nationality was first 'American', later crossed out and replaced with 'French'.

From all of which one deduces that although Melmotte was a fairly minor character as first thought of, Trollope none the less saw him as an interesting amalgam. Was he American (like Fisker), Jewish (like Cohenlupe, who eventually gets the 'Samuel' first name) or French? Probably the case of Charles Lefevre persuaded Trollope to the last; though the American link remains in the shadowy New York father, Melmody, whom we are told about after the financier's death.

The memorandum finishes with references to the South Central Pacific and Mexican Railway and Hamilton K. Fisker's visit to England. This too suggests that the commercial melodrama which makes up the main action of the written novel was latently in Trollope's mind, even at this early stage.

## II

Of the other notes the shortest is a collection of fairly random jottings in pencil on a corner of the sheet of paper which later contained Trollope's ink-written dating scheme. They record Trollope's thoughts just after the first number:

> Lady Carbury's elopement—
> Melmotte had arrived within the last 12 months.
> Page 21? can this be altered.
> Melmotte's house south side of square
> Melmotte has been in prison at Hamburgh.

Lady Carbury's possible infidelity when she left her husband obviously worried Trollope somewhat. In Chapter II his description of the event is very delicate, even evasive ('Her life at that period is of little moment to our story'). The Melmotte entries (again, it is interesting that he should have preoccupied Trollope so early) are easily explained. In Chapter IV, 'Madame Melmotte's Ball', we are introduced to the financier; around page 21 of the first number we are told he has come from abroad within the 'last two years'. Trollope perhaps felt that more would be known about a tycoon who had been in the City so long. Since it couldn't be altered, presumably it was already set up in print (possibly as a trial number, to get length right; as we have seen, the contract did not require Trollope to give over any manuscript until the novel was half finished). We are told in the same chapter that Melmotte's house is indeed on the South side of Grosvenor Square; Trollope must have had an actual mansion in mind. And the business about Melmotte's having been imprisoned in Hamburg does not come out, in the printed novel, until much later in the narrative.

A fuller set of plans was drawn up to cover the last number in the first volume (Chapters XLVI–L) and most of the chapters in the second from LI–LXXX. These notes take the form of brief content descriptions which are similar, though rarely the same, as the published chapter titles. They are accompanied by calculations which bear out Trollope's unremittingly precise quantification of the act of writing fiction. Thus the entry for the first chapter of Volume II runs:

51  11–2  Paul and Mrs Hurtle.  1A  (12)

'51' refers to the number of the chapter. It is the eleventh
number, and the second volume. '1A (12)' would seem
to have something to do with manuscript page length.
In the printed novel Chapter LI is entitled 'Which shall
it be?' and is entirely concerned with Paul's involvement
with Winifred.

There is, as I say, a general equivalence between the
notes' descriptions and the eventual chapter titles. But
there are also some interesting anomalies. Thus Chapter
LIV is given in the notes as 'Melmotte's Election.' In
fact, in the novel, it deals with Melmotte's adoption as a
candidate. In the notes, Chapter LVI is 'Roger and
the Priest'; in the novel that chapter deals with Father
John Barham's unlucky brush with Melmotte in
Grosvenor Square.

Although they form a fairly comprehensive list, many
of these chapter notes are out of sequence (thus one section runs 68, 63, 59). This suggests to me that Trollope
did not cut off writing the strands of his multi-plotted
novel exactly as now appears in the printed novel. Precise carpentry of the narrative into the five-chapter
number units would seem to have been a later process,
as was the final naming of the chapters.

As this plan progresses it seems less a reflection of writing in progress than a prediction of writing to come. In
some cases, too, Trollope apparently changed his plan
quite drastically. Thus, for Chapter LXXII, he writes:

> Hetta again refuses Roger ['Paul' crossed out] and
> tells him at 25

Now in Chapter LXXII there is indeed an interview
between Roger and Hetta in which, as usual, he declares
his undying love. But she by no means tells him—as the
note would suggest—that she will give him an answer
when she is twenty-five years old. Instead she insists on
her love for Paul, and requests Roger to tell her whether
his American rival is free to marry her. 'Ask himself' is
Roger's curt reply, and the title of the chapter as published.

Another change of direction is indicated by the note

for Chapter LXXIX: 'Miles and Felix both expelled.'
As it happens, neither of these scapegraces is expelled from
the Beargarden, since it collapses before their misdeeds
can be judged by a committee who probably would be
too indulgent to take such a step anyway.

Even more intriguing is Trollope's note for Chapter 78.
This runs: 'Lady Pomona's despair at the trial [crossed
out] marriage.' In the printed novel, the chapter is entitled 'Miss Longestaffe again at Caversham' and deals
with Lady Pomona's distress at Georgiana's planned
marriage with Brehgert. But the deleted 'trial' seems to
have been a slip of the pen which Trollope committed
thinking of Melmotte's final act. Chapter LXXVII, in
the notes, is written as 'Melmotte at the trial [crossed
out] with Marie.' In the novel, as published, that chapter is 'Another scene in Bruton Street', and centres on the
bitter and violent argument between Melmotte and
Marie over 'Melmotte's' money. This possible trial of
Melmotte is even more evident in the last of the notes, as
the list peters out. (The numbers which follow the entries
may refer to expected second volume chapter numbers.)

> Scene in Grosvenor Square 42
> The Trial [crossed out] Melmotte dead 43
> Delay [crossed out] 45
> Lady Carbury's despair 44
> Melmotte [illegible] imprisoned [?] 47 [all crossed out]
> After [?] [illegible] the trial 48

P. D. Edwards has drawn attention to Trollope's change
of intention about the trial or suicide of Melmotte (see
*Nineteenth-Century Fiction*, pp. 89–93 (1963)). I wonder,
too, if Lady Carbury's 'despair' was expected to be a
consequence of Felix's death—an eventuality held out by
the first plan.

### III

The last set of notes is a date list which was apparently
drawn up after the novel was finished, for correction's
sake. It runs from Chapter X to Chapter XCVI. The

chapter descriptions, where they occur, are very precise and in most cases identical with printed chapter headings. The fact that Trollope should have made up this chronology (with an entry for every chapter) indicates how intricate time sequence is in this novel. As far as I can ascertain, such charts were not a regular feature of his working methods.

# *NOTES*

Volume as well as page number is given in the references, so that page 160 in the first volume, for instance, appears as 1.160.

There has been a previous annotated edition of this novel by Professor Robert Tracy, published in America, by Bobbs Merrill, in 1974. In preparing this edition I took advantage of Professor Tracy's excellently informed chapter on *The Way We Live Now* in his book on Trollope's later novels, cited earlier; I also had the benefit of the introductory matter to his edition, a xerox of which was kindly sent me by Professor N. John Hall (the British Library, the University of London Library and the London Library do not possess Professor Tracy's edition). I did not, however, consult his notes until my own were despatched to OUP. Comparing the sets of notes later has been an interesting exercise since we often make the same annotations in similar form. In some cases Professor Tracy has picked up things I missed or known things I did not. I have therefore made later additions or corrections, following him. Where this has happened, the note is indicated by the mark '(RT)'.

## Introduction

vii. *The Way We Live Now*: Ruth apRoberts finds an echo of Cicero's 'sed quid agas? Sic vivitur'—'what would you have me do? This is the way we live now.' She also points to the influence of Cicero's *De Officiis* and its main distinction between *honestum* and *turpe*. Trollope's *Life of Cicero* was published in 1880.

*An Autobiography*, pp. 354–5 (London, OUP, 1950).

viii. Michael Sadleir, *Trollope: A Commentary*, p. 312 (London, OUP, 1961). The first edition of Sadleir's classic study was published in 1927.

xi. James R. Kincaid, *The Novels of Anthony Trollope*, P. 169 (London, OUP, 1977).

Ruth apRoberts, *Trollope: Artist and Moralist* (London, Chatto and Windus, 1971).

xii. Sadleir, ibid, p. 401.

John Delane (1817–79), editor of *The Times*, 1841–77. He was presumably the author of the magnificent diatribes on current immorality which appeared in the paper after the inquiry into foreign loans, about the same time as *The Way We Live Now* was completed. They culminated in a famously pungent editorial on 11 August 1875. It is plausibly suggested that editor and novelist put their heads together somewhat.

xiii. A. O. J. Cockshut, *Anthony Trollope: A Critical Study* (London, Collins, 1955).

xvii. Bradford A. Booth, 'Trollope and "Little Dorrit"', *Trollopian*, 1947–8, pp. 237–40.

Robert Tracy, *Trollope's Later Novels*, Chapter 6 (London, University of California Press, 1978).

xxvii. See Asa Briggs, 'Trollope, Bagehot and the English Constitution', *Cambridge Journal*, 1951–2, pp. 327–38.

*Composition, Publication and Text*

xxxix. The papers relevant to *The Way We Live Now* are kept under the call mark MS Don. c 10. I am grateful to the Library for letting me examine them.

*The Way We Live Now*

1.1 *'Criminal Queens'*: Trollope seems distantly to guy Agnes Strickland (1796–1874) and her *Lives of the Queens of England*, a multi-volume production published 1840–8. Like Lady Carbury, Strickland also published one unsuccessful novel. Both ladies share associations with squirearchical Suffolk. Miss Strickland, on the other hand, was a lifelong spinster. Chapter II of Trollope's *Autobiography* suggests that Trollope partly drew on memories of his own mother for the creation of Lady Carbury.

1.2. *Broadmore*: more familiarly Broadmoor, the hospital for mentally abnormal offenders. It was opened in 1863.

*Caroline*: George IV's queen. The couple were married for state convenience in 1794 and separated in 1796. Bitterness followed, culminating in Caroline's being repulsed from the coronation in 1821. Given their similar marital crises, Lady Carbury feels some sisterhood.

1.3. *'Morning Breakfast Table'*: the *Daily Telegraph*, I take it, which was overtaking *The Times* in the early 1870s. By the later mentioned 'Evening Pulpit' Trollope alludes to the vogue for evening papers at this period. The *Evening Standard* was begun in 1860; the *Pall Mall Gazette*, with which Trollope had connections, began as an afternoon paper in 1865. It combined high class reviewing with news. By the 'Literary Chronicle', I imagine Trollope is thinking of the *Saturday Review*, although it is clearly an academic trend in reviewing rather than a particular paper which he had in mind. Trollope had a prejudice against literary reviewing and did relatively little of it. (See the *Autobiography*, Chapter XIV.)

1.6. *royalty*: not a very common method of paying authors until the Society of Authors began to push for it in the 1880s. Trollope himself, an inveterate 'free trader', disliked it, thinking royalties tied the author too closely to his publisher.

1.7. *few words over an entire page*: the habit of bulking out books by the means Trollope describes was the result of the practice by which new novels came out commonly in three and non-fiction in two volumes. This in turn was because the circulating libraries were the main purchasers of new books, and they worked on a per-volume lending system.

1.8. *Nullius . . . magistri*: 'Not pledged to swear by the words of any master', Horace.

1.15. *sold out*: Felix must have done so before 1872, when the purchase of commissions was abolished. In his notes Trollope reminds himself to 'enquire about this'.

1.21. *The Beargarden*: the name of this club recalls the Savage (founded 1857). Robert Tracy proposes the bohemian Marlborough Club as a likely original. It was founded by the Prince of Wales in 1869 because he resented restrictions on smoking at White's. The Beargarden has 'smoke all over the house'. The term 'bear' has stockmarket connotations and links with the world of Melmotte. According to the OED it means, among City men, 'to produce a fall in the price of stocks, shares or commodities'.

1.22. *good enough for me*: Felix flippantly quotes the revivalist hymn, 'Give me that old fashioned religion, it's good enough for me.' As Trollope sarcastically notes, his limited education would not permit him to quote Horace's 'Carpe Diem'.

1.30. *the blood royal*: later identified as 'Prince George'. Victoria had no such son. Trollope is being careful.

1.36. *The Peripatetics*: presumably the Travellers' Club. Ironically chosen since the qualification for membership was to have taken a journey of at least 500 miles. Melmotte the wanderer would certainly qualify.

1.56. *Sam Slick's*: a reference to the popular collections of 'shrewd sayings' by Thomas Chandler Haliburton's Yankee clockmaker, Sam Slick. The first volumes came out 1837–40.

1.79. *up even to 110*: i.e. yielding a 10% profit on each £100 share. Trollope makes it clearer in Chapter XXII.

1.90. *Heathen Chinee*: a reference to Bret Harte's humorous poem 'Plain Language from Truthful James' (1870): 'That for ways that are dark, and for tricks that are vain, the Heathen Chinee is peculiar.' The poem's narrative deals with a Chinese who cheats at euchre (an American card game).

1.112. *in the funds*: government sponsored Consolidated Funds ('Consols'). Famously safe, they paid an annual interest of 3%.

1.114. *the proper Medea . . . new and unembarrassed*: in the mythology associated with the golden fleece Medea is a magician with the power to restore men to youth by boiling them in a cauldron with magic herbs. She performs her trick for Jason's father, and spitefully doesn't perform it for the daughters of Pelias.

1.146. *boodying*: sulking. The word is rare; the only two examples the OED can cite are both from other Trollope novels.

1.148. *a model bishop*: there was an ancient Bishopric of Elmham, covering the Suffolk–Norfolk border area, by the fictional Carbury Manor. In his notes, however, Trollope indicated that he was modelling Bishop Yeld on Charles Thomas Longley, the recently deceased (1868) Archbishop of Canterbury. He was headmaster at Harrow during the young Anthony's attendance at the school. The DNB records him as sweet-natured, but in fact rather harsh on Romanism. Trollope also indicated in a letter of 26 January 1875 that Father John Barham was based on a priest he had known at Waltham, 'a convert, and a perfect gentleman,—so poor that he had not bread to eat'. Ritualism was a live issue at this period. There had been riots in the 1860s on the subject, deviation from orthodox Anglican ceremony and defection to Rome. In 1874 Archbishop Tait of Canterbury introduced what became the 'Public Worship Regulation Act'. All this, of course, would have had to do with the largely unwritten part of the novel concerning Roger's 'doubts'.

1.152. *Silly Suffolk!*: still current as an Essex insult for their county neighbours. The *Oxford Dictionary of Proverbs* dates its first usage as 1867.

1.160. *most-favoured-nation clause*: the sense of the term had recently been formulated by the Anglo-French treaty of 1860. 'Most-favoured' status guarantees privileges no less than those currently enjoyed by the most favoured trading partner.

1.178. *leader . . . House of Commons*: in the Anglican church, bishops are an appointment of the crown nominally, actually of the government. In *Barchester Towers* Trollope creates a tense opening by synchronising the old bishop's death with the fall of a ministry.

1.205. *to San Francisco*: in 1869 the Union Pacific met the Central Pacific, completing the continental link to San Francisco. (Note the name of Fisker's and Melmotte's venture.) South American railway construction did not get properly underway until the 1850s, giving European financial expertise and North American technology a vast export opportunity. The Panama railway—a 'small affair' at 47.5 miles long—was completed in February 1855 at an expense of $7.5m.

1.220. *the Marquis of Westminster's*: the second Marquis of Westminster died in 1869 leaving a huge estate, especially in London property.

1.229. *loo*: a simple three-card game. A player who fails to take a trick is 'looed', and has to pay into the pool. Miles later takes advantage of the fact that since not all the pack is distributed in hands (like whist) high cards can be secreted to win tricks.

1.241. *horsehair*: Trollope disliked the chignon which came back into fashion around 1870. It consisted in a large coil, or hump of false hair to make a more impressive coiffure.

1.245. *above honesty*: Robert Tracy points out the similarity of Mrs. Hurtle's enthusiasm and the despotic ideology contained in Napoleon III's life of Julius Caesar, published 1865–66. In his *Autobiography* Trollope calls it 'that most futile book'. Trollope's *The Commentaries of Caesar* was published in 1870.

1.261. *Creusa*: the princess for whom Jason left Medea. Medea did not repine but took a horrible revenge.

1.268. *scrip*: OED: 'a provisional document entitling the holder to a share or number of shares in a joint-stock undertaking, and exchangeable for a more formal certificate when the necessary payments have been completed'.

1.270. *is done with now*: in 1856 the instant marriages solemnised by the blacksmith in Gretna Green were made illegal unless one of the parties had lived in Scotland for at least 21 days.

1.272. *beastliness*: i.e. *bêtise*, stupidity. It is not clear whether Mme. Melmotte is intermittently speaking French.

1.277. *in utrumque paratus*: prepared for either eventuality.
*Paides Pallados*: children of wisdom.

1.279. *or spoil a horn*: either achieve success or be a failure. The first usage is recorded as being in Scott's *Rob Roy*.

1.296. *Lares*: Roman term for deities of the home.

1.311. *merry-thought*: wish-bone.

1.322. *loitering about the Post-office*: in 1868 the private and largely unprofitable telegraph companies were bought out by the government, and their services transferred over the next few years to post-offices. Like many details in the narrative this incidental observation places the events described as after 1870.

1.323. *two counties*: Sheep's Acre farm is on the Waveney, dividing Norfolk and Suffolk.

1.326. *rival the duke's*: Goodwood is in Sussex, like the fictional Pickering Park. It is the seat of the Dukes of Richmond and Gordon. At the spectacular racetrack, Goodwood week is held in July.

1.326. *thus a seat was vacated*: unhistorical. Trollope's interest in Westminster may have been aroused by its passing from the Liberals to the Conservatives when W. H. Smith won it in 1868.

1.327. *since the ballot was introduced among us*: in 1872. For Trollope's dislike of the reform see his *Autobiography*, Chapter XVI.

*the Opposition*: in 1873 the Conservatives were out. Disraeli came back (helped by the ballot) in 1874.

1.329. *The poet laureate*: Tennyson, since 1850. Trollope always avoids names.

*the Prime Minister's translation of Catullus*: Gladstone was PM in 1873, and also a classical scholar. His *Studies on Homer* came out in 1858; *Translations* by him and Lord Lyttleton in 1863.

1.337. *teres atque rotundus*: polished and round.  Horace.

1.338. *printed slip*: i.e. galley proof.

1.347. *gazette your resignation*: have it published in the *London Gazette*, the paper of official record.

1.352. *dated 21st July*: unless Melmotte is playing a very deep game this should surely be June.

1.377. *trussels*: according to the dictionary 'bundles or packages'—but 'tressels' may be intended.

*the Moldavian loan*: vaguely topical.  Moldavia is the northern sector of Roumania.  In the Franco–Prussian war, Roumanian sympathies had been with the French.  As a result the Government was obliged to cover certain railway bonds, normally the responsibility of German firms.  The financial crisis left the Roumanian authorities in debt in 1872, and eager for loans from abroad.

1.385. *a White Star boat*: topical.  In 1869 the Oceanic Steam Company was formed to run a line of steamers between Liverpool and New York.  This White Star line boasted a new fleet of ships (the first was launched in 1870) of unequalled comfort and speed.  All White Star boats, like the Adriatic, had an 'ic' suffix (e.g. Teutonic, Britannic, Majestic).

1.386. *on to fortune*: Shakespeare, *Julius Caesar*, IV, 3, 218.

1.395. *speak daggers*: Shakespeare, *Hamlet*, III, 2, 414.
Trollope was a connoisseur of the Elizabethan and Jacobean drama, and he knew much more of it than his somewhat hackneyed quotations in this novel suggest.

1.396. *the Queen's place*: Queen Victoria's favourite residence, Osborne House was near Cowes.  She bought it in 1846 and eventually died there.

1.400. *Tom-and-Jerry hat*: the allusion is to Pierce Egan's heroes in his low-life best-seller of the early nineteenth century, *Life in London*.  Here it suggests headgear that Felix would think particularly appropriate for a night on the razzle.

1.412. *the Peabodys and the Bairds*: topical.  James Baird was a wealthy industrialist who retired from parliament in 1857 and devoted himself to philanthropic works, mainly in Scotland. In 1873 he bequeathed £500,000 to the Church of Scotland to spread religious teaching via the Baird Trust.  George Peabody was an American philanthropist, long resident in

London, where he died in 1869. He too donated half a million pounds, for the erection of working-class dwellings in London. (It later emerges Melmotte is a slum landlord.)

*the Milesian*: i.e. Irishman. Trollope has in mind the Fenian outrages of the 1860s.

*a submarine wire*: fantastic. But the first submarine cables were laid across the Atlantic in 1865–6. Point de Galle is a port in Ceylon.

*thirty millions sterling*: in 1867 the Turkish Sultan bestowed the title Khedive on Ismail, the notoriously spendthrift ruler of Egypt. The plight of the country's peasantry, the hideously overtaxed fellahin, was desperate. In 1875, the Khedive went bankrupt and was obliged to sell his Suez Canal shares to Britain for £3m—a neat prophecy on Trollope's part.

*lately annexed country . . . great African lakes*: this may refer to General Gordon's attempt to annex Uganda in 1874; or, as Robert Tracy's note suggests, to Ismail's annexations in the same area.

1.421. *the Carlton*: the Conservative club, founded by the Duke of Wellington in 1831. The Pall Mall premises patronised by Longestaffe and his kind were opened in 1855.

1.430. *old hunx*: usually spelled 'hunks', meaning miser.

1.432. *Mettinghams . . . Ilketsals . . . Elmhams*: Trollope knows his Suffolk well, though how he came by his knowledge is not entirely clear. There are a number of villages which confusingly repeat the names John mentions in different compounds; and they are all within a few miles of Bungay.

1.433. *Bury*: Bury St. Edmunds, where the county's executions took place.

1.471. *hanged Mr. Scudamore*: F. I. Scudamore, Trollope's rival at the Post Office, principally responsible for the acquisition of the telegraph system as a government monopoly (RT).

2.12. *The death of Cato*: Roman philosopher, republican and suicide. The first mention of an important motif in the novel.

2.22. *a deputation from the Canadian Government*: topical. Unlike the US, Canada had no transcontinental railway at the period. In 1872 two companies were formed to build it. The government negotiated for amalgamation; there were consequent bribery charges. On its accession in 1873 the new Liberal government made the railway to the Pacific its first priority. It was not, however, achieved until 1886. See the comment on 'the contemplated line from ocean to ocean across British America' in Chapter XLIV.

2.23. *mulled*: a current slang term, meaning to make a bad move in, for instance, football.

*drunk as Cloe*: current slang. Absolutely sloshed.

2.24. *in the town*: one of the nigger minstrel songs which became popular in the 1850s. This composition is often erroneously attributed to Stephen Foster (RT).

2.31. *for a generation*: as a Liberal, Trollope invests this little effusion with partisan scorn. The image of the coach with its Liberal tractive power and Tory brakes was, however, a favourite with him. Although this was written in 1873, he clearly apprehended the Conservative victory of 1874.

2.35. *try the City*: Melmotte is flying high. The member for the City was Lionel Nathan de Rothschild. Rothschild was elected in 1847 but not allowed to sit because as a Jew he could not conscientiously take the oath. He was repeatedly re-elected and finally took his seat in 1858. He was a Whig and Melmotte expects to defeat rather than succeed him.

2.37. *and told he was a god*: Trollope means Disraeli.

2.40. *the Amphytrion of the night*: rather a devious allusion, if I understand it. The Amphytrion myth is centrally concerned with access. He is given an ordeal before he can attain Alcmena, but Zeus forestalls him, by assuming his likeness.

2.46. *and not worse*: compare Trollope's very similar comments in Chapter XX of his *Autobiography*.

2.47. *Hoc . . . militum*: 'this is your member for the knights!' I think the reference is to Cicero and his vigorous attacks in the interests of public probity. The latin is from a poem by Horace attacking the rich, criminal upstart now in public office (RT).

2.62. *Why don't we . . . when they've got one?*: because the Catholic hierarchy was rationally set up in 1850, under the Archbishopric of Westminster. The Church of England's grew irrationally out of the old divisions of the country, resulting in two provinces (York and Canterbury) and 37 bishoprics. Melmotte's claim to be English is made nonsense by such gaffes.

2.82. *his faithful Achates*: Achates, the proverbially loyal friend of Aeneas, another wanderer.

2.93. *admitting the Jews into parliament*: recent enough still to be painful. The first Jewish emancipation bill came forward in 1830, but it was not until 1858–60 that Jews received full parliamentary rights.

2.113. *Non omnis moriar*: Horace. 'I shall not wholly die' (my works will preserve me).

2.128. *Some few years since . . . due to them*: Trollope does not clearly indicate what he is thinking of, though clearly it rankles. Professor N. John Hall suggests to me that what is alluded to here is Disraeli's 'extinct volcanoes' speech, delivered at Manchester in 1872, in which Disraeli savagely attacked members of the Liberal administration.

2.171. *from a political master*: Disraeli again. The frequent references to the leader of the Conservatives in the later parts of the novel suggest that Trollope had premonitions that his party, the Liberals, were on the slide.

2.183. *forehead of the morning sky*: Milton, *Lycidas*, ll. 170–71 (RT).

*Uno . . . alter*: 'On the removal of one, another is not wanting', Virgil.

2.191. *an urban Rosherville*: Rosherville Gardens, opened in 1844. They were in Gravesend, which was a popular resort with Victorian cockneys.

2.213. *He had with his own hand . . . in old Mr. Longestaffe's drawer*: the Pickering sale is a teasing episode. It first figures in Chapter XIII where Dolly is said to block the sale of the family property in Sussex. On page 1.325, however, we are told that 'father and son . . . had been brought to terms', and Pickering Park sold to Melmotte. On page 1.423 Dolly is said to be anxious to get his £25,000 half share. The first mention of title deeds is on 2.61. Only now, are we unequivocally told that Melmotte forged Dolly's signature consenting to the surrender of the property. Dolly fiercely exposes the forgery and opposes the sale in the second volume. And yet, Dolly in the first volume seemed entirely reconciled to the transaction. All in all, it seems a rather clumsy piece of retroactive plotting, made the clumsier by the unlikely business of the shared desk in Bruton Street. I suspect that Trollope, quite late in the novel, had to devise something which would get Melmotte into court for a serious criminal offence. (Simple bankruptcy would not, of course, suffice.)

2.257. *Let not Medea . . . on the stage*: Horace's *Ars Poetica*, l.185. Trollope's translation, apparently.

2.263. *worse than your wife's sister*: for the last twenty years bills to allow marriage with one's deceased wife's sister were brought forward annually. Invariably the reform was approved in the Commons and rejected by the Lords. It eventually got through, long after Lady Pomona's death, in 1906.

*One of the greatest judges . . . is a Jew*: very recent. In 1873 Sir George Jessel was made a judge, the first Jew to achieve the post.

2.267. *after twenty years*: presumably a reference to the celebrated Tichborne case, in which an impostor claimed to be a baronet who had drowned in 1854. The case dragged sensationally on from 1871–74 (RT).

2.357. *manes*: i.e. souls.

2.360. *the one great festival of the year*: when the slaughter of game birds begins.

2.364. *from pen and ink*: Byron, *English Bards and Scotch Reviewers*. The passage quoted from gibes at Cottle's minimal earnings from authorship and his profits from bookselling.

2.365. *It must be in three volumes*: the standard form of new fiction from 1821 to the mid 1890s.

*isn't worth a* ——: a damn. The identical advice was given the young Anthony, trying to sell his early novels. See his *Autobiography*, Chapter IV.

2.366. *Mudie to circulate it*: Mudie's was the 'leviathan' of Victorian circulating libraries. The best advertisement for a new three decker was to be prominently displayed on the library's catalogues.

2.385. *the Marylebone underground railway*: Trollope means the Metropolitan underground railway, which had been operational since 1863. Hetta travels its full length to King's Cross Road.

*the number at which Mrs. Hurtle lived*: how, I wonder, *did* she know?

2.427. *a celibate*: and therefore dabbling with Romanism, to the amusement of the broadly tolerant Bishop Yeld.

*sell the presentation*: since the church is on their land, the Longestaffes have the benefice in their power to bestow. Dolly, however, would sell it rather than enjoy his patronage.

2.429. *uncanonical*: not in accordance with strict ecclesiastical law, since the service presumably takes place after 3.00 p.m. (RT).

*Where 'the wild asses quench their thirst'*: Psalms 104:11: 'They give drink to every beast of the field; the wild asses quench their thirst' (RT).

2.430. *Bismarck*: after 1871 Bismarck totally dominated German political life. Trollope detested such despots.

2.432. *the 12th August*: when the grouse are shot, and the clubs empty anyway.

*court plaster*: sticking plaster. The name comes from its having been used at court to create artificial beauty spots.

2.434. *with half the town*: I can't identify the old song.

2.437. *blue books*: the name for reports and other documents printed by order of Parliament.

2.443. *Wenham ice*: Wenham in northern Massachussets. There are several ponds nearby which produced famously pure ice.

2.454. *especially California*: there were reforms to women's property laws in England in 1870 and 1874, long anticipated as Fisker urges in certain American states.

2.462. *leather or prunello*: a favourite phrase of Trollope's indicating something worthless. It originates in Pope's *Essay on Man*:

> Worth makes the man, and want of it the fellow
> The rest is all but leather and prunella

2.470. *thy golden one away*: Shakespeare, *King Lear*, I, 4, 179.

# THE WORLD'S CLASSICS

ARISTOTLE: The Nicomachean Ethics
*Translated and with an introduction by David Ross*

JANE AUSTEN: Emma
*Edited by James Kinsley and David Lodge*

Mansfield Park
*Edited by James Kinsley and John Lucas*

Northanger Abbey, Lady Susan, The Watsons,
and Sanditon
*Edited by John Davie*

Persuasion
*Edited by John Davie*

Pride and Prejudice
*Edited by James Kinsley and Frank Bradbrook*

Sense and Sensibility
*Edited by James Kinsley and Claire Lamont*

MAX BEERBOHM: Seven Men and Two Others
*With an introduction by Lord David Cecil*

JAMES BOSWELL: Life of Johnson
*The Hill/Powell edition, revised by David Fleeman*
*With a new introduction by Pat Rogers*

CHARLOTTE BRONTË: Jane Eyre
*Edited by Margaret Smith*

EMILY BRONTË: Wuthering Heights
*Edited by Ian Jack*

ANTON CHEKHOV: Five Plays
*Translated and with an introduction by Ronald Hingley*

WILKIE COLLINS: The Woman in White
*Edited by H. P. Sucksmith*

DANIEL DEFOE: Roxana
*Edited by Jane Jack*

# THE WORLD'S CLASSICS

# THE WORLD'S CLASSICS

# THE WORLD'S CLASSICS